Divine Sparks

COLLECTED WISDOM
OF THE HEART

KAREN SPEERSTRA

Morning Light Press
323 North First, Suite 203
Sandpoint, ID   83864

morninglightpress.com

Published by Morning Light Press 2005
Copyright ©2005 by Karen Speerstra

Library of Congress Cataloging-in-Publication Data

Divine sparks : collected wisdom of the heart / [compiled by] Karen
Speerstra.-- 1st ed.
     p. cm.
  Includes index.
  ISBN-13: 978-1-59675-006-7 (alk. paper)
  ISBN-10: 1-59675-006-5
  1. Religion--Quotations, maxims, etc. 2. Spirituality--Quotations,
maxims, etc. I. Speerstra, Karen.
  BL48.D575 2005
  204--dc22
                                                              2005021253

Printed in Canada

MORNING IGHT
P R S S

Divine Sparks

COLLECTED WISDOM
OF THE HEART

First paperback edition 2005

KAREN SPEERSTRA
Editor

MORNING LIGHT
PRESS

323 North First, Suite 203
Sandpoint, ID 83864

To Sophia

Contents

INTRODUCTION

Like a bower bird, I've spent years hoarding shiny word-spangles, burying them deep inside my journals. And then indexing them! After I read that Annie Dillard indexed her journals, I felt less obsessive. Besides providing compost for writing, my journals become safe repositories for ideas I find too numerous and far too precious to trust to my faulty memory.

I was in second grade at the Halle School, near Chippewa Falls, Wisconsin, when I was thrilled to win the prize for reading the most books that year—I believe it was 40, but I can't verify that number because I wasn't keeping indexed journals back then. My teacher, Mrs. Hill, gave me an oversized red hardcover book of C. Collodi's *Pinnochio* and on the flyleaf wrote in that perfect Palmer penmanship of hers: "January 27, 1948. Dear Karen, I certainly hope your acquaintance with Pinocchio is a pleasant one! I am sure his escapades will surprise and thrill you! Congratulations on having given the greatest number of book reports in our room this year!" She was as fond of exclamation points as she was of books, and I credit her with turning me into an early bibliophile. As an author, I subsequently created a few books of my own, as well as one with my older son. And as an editor and publisher, I midwifed numerous authors as they birthed their own books.

"I read books," Sven Birkerts says in *The Guttenburg Elegies*, "to read myself." And I take notes in my journals about the books I've read in order to remember how it is I read myself—and others. In looking over my journals, I began to notice that the writers I most treasure are the ones who speak to my heart as well as to my mind. Furthermore, consistent topic areas began to take shape, like shards in a kaleidoscope. Colorful flashes. Repeated patterns. Echoed voices.

Paula Underwood once assured me, "Wisdom is wisdom, the source cannot matter." So, over the years, I collected bits of wisdom from a variety of authors. But, you may ask, are all these words "Divine Sparks?" I truly believe so. Rudolf Steiner assured me there is no disharmony between "higher experiences" and the events and demands of everyday life.

While I wanted to include quotations like, "Fear is a darkroom for developing negatives," I have no idea who said it, and I had decided "Anonymous" was not one of the authors I wished to include here. Nor did I include any lines from poetry, except, I confess, for a few by Rumi. I thank Coleman Barks, whose own words are also embroidered here, together with the other Rumi-translators, who introduced us to this early thirteenth-century Afghani mystic. I decided to include no lines from songs. No Shakespeare—he's so easy to find everywhere. I also excluded Biblical quotations for the same reason. Rather enjoying the egalitarian nature of this collection, I decided to use no personal titles, but then I made a few exceptions: Mother Teresa, Meister Eckhart and Brother Laurence. To me, they seem like their first names. Others may find my lack of Rabbis and Sris and Saints bothersome. So be it.

In an effort to save pages, I also omitted subtitles in the references. And dates. You all know how to Google. You'll find no entries from the Internet except for Richard Thieme's. When Richard and I last spoke, he was not interested in putting his exceptionally clear wisdom between book covers, or I would have excerpted from his books instead of his website. I include no journal, magazine or newspaper references, except for what Amos Bronson Alcott once wrote in *The Dial*. A clear eye may find other exceptions to my self-imposed rules, but mostly I am consistent. I borrowed nothing from other quotation book collections, and instead, relied on those armfuls of books I dragged home from numerous libraries over the years. And, of course, from the old faithful friends tightly snuggled on my own shelves.

Whenever possible (and believe me, many authors don't tell you where they got their quotations) I include the original book from which each came. And I have made every attempt to play within the rules of fairness set out by copyright law.

"How did you decide what to choose?" many of my friends—as well as my publisher—asked. That's a very good question, since about 175,000 books are published just in the United States each year and I've been reading since—well at least since those first 40 books in second grade. That's a mountain of material to draw from. "It was pretty intuitive," is my usual response. By that I mean when I read something that made my heart thump, or caused me to say, "Ohhh I like that!" in it went. If I ran across a line or two that made me pause and think, "I'd like to read that again," I added it. I don't apologize for the fact that my own spiritual path is Christian, so there may be more quotations weighted in that direction, but you will hear very strong voices from every spiritual path, including some from paths people might not call "spiritual" in the least. Some might even be labeled "New Age" or "Gnostic-lite." I go back to Paula's comment: "Wisdom is wisdom and the source cannot matter." And in a syncretistic collection of this sort, I welcome them all.

I admit many of these quotations were chosen for very personal reasons. Both of my grandmothers and my mother appear here. But why, for instance, the selection on yew trees? I'll tell you. When the idea of putting these quotations together first occurred to me, I was sitting in an infusion chair at Dartmouth Hitchcock Hospital in New Hampshire being IV-injected with pure poison, derived, my oncologist said, from yew trees. It killed many of my cancerous cells but allowed me to continue living and eventually, when the hair came back, so did my energy.

About 1,800 different voices are collected here. Some are from people I know, some from authors I once published. Michael Munn and I, for instance, actually had e-mail conversations about what words of his might be included. Others will just have to take my word for the fact I was "in touch" with them, mentally. As I typed what they had said, I could see their faces and sometimes I could hear again their telephone voices, such as Dee Hock's and Parker Palmer's. I thank them all. I also ask their forgiveness for clipping their wisdom into such foreshortened snippets. In return, I ask you, the reader, to look up (and buy!) their actual books to read more of their wisdom.

Some people whom I invited into these topical conversations are people removed from me by only one or two "degrees of separation." For instance, Heinrich Zimmer was our young friend, Jacob's, grandfather. Jacob drowned off the coast of France when he was only 22. Up until then, he had rarely spoken of his family, so it was not until Jacob was gone that I found myself learning about his grandfather and his great-grandfather who was a Celtic expert and gave lectures on the symbolism behind Tarot cards. Mythology and symbols were ingrained, then, in

Heinrich's thinking as he became an East Indian expert, although he never visited India. After Heinrich's death, his wife, Jacob's grandmother, asked Joseph Campbell to edit Heinrich's work. Joseph was pleased to do so. He estimated it would take him three years. It took him twelve. Campbell once remarked, "If I have a guru, it would be Zimmer—the one who really gave me the courage to interpret myths out of what I knew of their common symbols." Heinrich, he said, could talk of the symbolism of onion soup! I like to think Jacob inherited his own playful, lovable nature from that grandfather. So I welcome both Zimmer and Campbell into this collection and silently thanked Jacob each time I typed one of their thoughts.

Others, such as Matthew Fox, William Sloane Coffin and Krister Stendahl have brought so much spiritual vitality into my life that they appear often, as, of course, does my Rhineland mentor, Hildegard of Bingen. *Divine Sparks* comes from her belief that "we are all sparks of the Divine flame."

I make no apologies for the fact that contained here are more references to Jung than to Freud and to women than to men. Furthermore, I believe spirituality to be intricately linked to all forms of creativity, so I included multiple entries under such topics as art and artists, beauty, color, dance, icons, imagination, music, painting, poetry, sculpture, storytelling, and of course, writing.

In assembling this collection, I invite you into my journals, into my library, into my very soul, to see who has influenced me over the years. You may come to various conclusions, but what will be immediately obvious are the numbers of feminist writers included here, and the topic areas women find relevant. Sophia entered my life sometime in the late '80s when I was checking out hundreds of books in women's studies areas from the Harvard Divinity School Library. That was also when I met, quite literally, Maria Gimbutas. Then I read everything Alice O. Howell wrote, followed by the headier stuff of some Russian Sophiologists, and I claimed Sophia as a living, breathing part of my life forever. On a trip to Turkey, I was thrilled to see "Her" statue holding up part of the porch roof on the Library at Ephesus. You can look under "Sophia" if you want to know more about why I dedicate this work to her.

Some people practice *Lectio divina*. You read a text, memorize it, meditate on it, pray over it and eventually a dialogue takes place between the reader and the various writers. Early manuscript writers often glossed their own ideas into the margins of the text so conversations could take place between several writers as well as the reader.

Every morning, for about four months, I watched our Vermont dawn sky drizzle greys and pinks across my southern office window as I organized and entered three hours' worth of these quotations before breakfast. This book became my *Lectio divina*, my spiritual practice. I glossed, and I began to hear dialogues between the various speakers. I invited them to sit down around an imaginary "topic table"—Blaise Pascal next to Dolly Parton, Reinhold Niebuhr next to Daniel Quinn, Charles Dickens next to John of the Cross—and I heard them responding to various ideas juxtaposed against their own, across time and space. I immersed myself in an expanding wisdom circle of conversations with people I had once met on the pages of books and was now falling in love with all over again: C. S. Lewis. Flannery O'Connor. Walker Percy. W. H. Auden. Denise Levertov. I mentally invited each author to participate, to speak from their hearts, and to listen with intent to what all the others had to say. As so often happens in wisdom circles, the wisdom of the collective became much more than the wisdom of the individuals. It takes courage to speak from your heart. In wisdom circles you learn about deep listening. It is my wish that each person who picks up *Divine Sparks*, feels invited into and warmed by this larger wisdom circle.

I am grateful to Dennis Pence, Darcy Sinclair, Melissa Hammack and most especially to Steve Jadick for recognizing the potential of *Divine Sparks* and bringing it to life in such a compassionate and professional manner.

Karen Speerstra,
Central Vermont, 2005

ABUNDANCE

When you realize there is nothing
lacking, the whole world belongs
to you.

—Lao Tzu

If you yourself have an abundance, do
not say, "The others do not concern me,
I need not bother about them!" If you
were lucky in hunting, let others share it.
Moreover, show them the favorable spots
where there are many sea lions which can
be easily slain.

—Yamana Eskimo
Initiation

The extravagant gesture is the very stuff
of creation. After the one extravagant
gesture of creation in the first place, the
universe has continued to deal exclusively
in extravagances, flinging intricacies and
colossi down aeons of emptiness, heaping
profusions on profligacies with ever fresh
vigor. The whole show has been on fire
from the word go!

—Annie Dillard
Pilgrim at Tinker Creek

You never know what is enough unless
you know what is more than enough.

—William Blake

Expect your every need to be met, expect the answer to every problem, expect abundance on every level, expect to grow spiritually.

—Eileen Caddy

A machine cosmology gives rise to unemployment and scarcity, where a cosmology of connection would encourage economics of abundance.

—Matthew Fox

You do not create abundance. You do not go out and get abundance. Abundance simply is.

—Martia Nelson
Coming Home

ABUSE

Virginia Woolf was protected from sex both by her sister, Vanessa, and her husband, Leonard Woolf.... She'd had plenty of childhood sexual abuse, and a history of mental instability. No wonder she fell in love with Vita Sackville-West, wrote passionately of women's history, insisting on a radical rewriting of the history of men! No wonder, too, she was envious of her sister for having children.

—Sophy Burnham
For Writers Only

Among women, incest is so common as to be epidemic.... Three universal rules: never touch an incest survivor without her permission; never surprise her from behind; never impede her movement.

—E. Sue Blume
Secret Survivors

Monica, mother of St. Augustine, was abused by her husband, Patricius, and is the patron saint of the abused.

—John Matthews
Drinking from the Sacred Well

In societies around the world between 17 and 75% of women say they have been physically assaulted by a partner.

—Alison Jolly
Lucy's Legacy

Why does an abused child become an abusive parent? Why does one woman divorce an alcoholic only to marry another? Why does a person get fired from three successive jobs for insubordination? It's as if our unconscious is saying, "I'm going to make you keep repeating this unhappy scenario until you wake up and pay attention to where it is coming from in yourself."

—Elio Frattanoli
Healing the Soul in the Age of the Brain

Mary Wollstonecraft expressed a need to "save her soul alive" after her father's abuse of her as a child.

—Lois Banner
Intertwined Lives: Margaret Mead, Ruth Benedict and Their Circle

Ruth Benedict: Something within me was murdered. [the author] suspects Ruth Benedict was abused as a child.... Signs: vomiting, doesn't want to be touched, rage against her sister, broken dolls, a sexual fantasy world... displays a frozen watchfulness.

—Lois Banner
Intertwined Lives: Margaret Mead, Ruth Benedict and Their Circle

ACCEPTANCE

The Rule of Acceptance: Everything has its purpose and its own time.

—Michael Garrett
Walking on the Wind

It's strange that Spartacus forgot to tell his brothers in rebellion that they would all be crucified. When there are too many crosses there are none. A drop of blood is ghastly. A sea of blood accepted.

—Calvin Miller
The Song

ACHIEVEMENT

If we are to achieve results never-before accomplished, we must expect to employ methods never before attempted.

—Francis Bacon
Essays

Never measure the height of a mountain, until you have reached the top. Then you will see how low it was.

—Dag Hammarskjöld
Markings

In time even a bear can be taught to dance.

—Yiddish proverb

ACTION

All our acts have sacramental possibilities.

—Freya Stark
Time and Tide

Do not wait for leaders; do it alone, person to person.

—Mother Teresa

Never do a thing for which there is no real need.... Let your deeds combine harmoniously with your environment.

—Rudolf Steiner
An Outline of Occult Science

If we are completely open, not watching ourselves at all, but being completely open and communicating with situations as they are, then action is pure, absolute, superior.

—Chögyam Trungpa

The things you do today, the things you do tomorrow, the things you do next week, have far greater significance than you suspect.... Through your actions today, vast worlds will be created and destroyed. Just as a telescope aimed at a distant star has only to move one tiny millimeter at the fulcrum in order to move many light years at the other end, so you too are at a place of beginning, with many effects on future worlds yet unborn.

—Ken Carey
The Sarseed Transmissions

God appears to you not in person but in action.

—Mohandas (Mahatma) Gandhi &
Erik Erikson
Gandhi's Truth

Thought is action in rehearsal.

—Sigmund Freud

Spirituality is the point where faith and action intersect.

—Giles Constable
The Reformation of the Twelfth Century

Negative actions always bring about suffering, and positive actions always bring happiness.

—Dalai Lama
The Way to Freedom

I think faith exists only in action. There can't be a passive awareness of God.

—Berton Roueché
The River World & Other Explorations

Because questions are intrinsically related to action, they spark and direct attention, perception, energy, and effort, and so are at the heart of the evolving forms that our lives assume.

—Marilee Goldberg
The Art of Asking Questions

Not everyone catches a wild ass, but only a person who is actually running can hope to catch one.

—Sharafuddin Maneri

If we try to quick, quick, we end up going slow, slow.

—Tibetan proverb

You'll never plough a field by turning it over in your mind.

—Irish proverb

ADDICTION

Whenever we develop an addiction, whether it is alcohol or depression, it has only one effect and that is the effect of spirit sleep…. You die a little with every addiction. It is the opposite end of the arrow from enlightenment.

—Lynn V. Andrews
Crystal Woman

The cause of alcoholism and drug addiction is intense emotional pain … only you can extinguish the source of your emotional pain.

—Gary Zukav & Linda Francis
*The Heart of the Soul:
Emotional Awareness*

Meditation is a technique to break addiction to thought.

—Andrew Wei
Spontaneous Healing

Addiction is something that arises as a result of a system that almost works. If you've got something that provides intermittent, unpredictable, positive feedback, it has a high addictive potential, because then you try to engineer the system so that it will be predictable and non-intermittent.

—Jeff Zaleski
The Soul of Cyberspace

But suicide, quick or slow, a sudden spill or a gradual oozing away through the years is the price John Barleycorn exacts. No friend of his ever escapes making the just, due payment.

—Jack London

The result of all this [addiction to perfection] is that we are no longer born. We begin as surgical extractions and we end as surgical extinctions. Between the beginning and the end we are a chemically operated machine subject to more and more refined technology.

—Marion Woodman
Addiction to Perfection

Addiction is the compulsive pursuit of quick fixes.

—Elio Frattaroli
Healing the Soul in the Age of the Brain

Wealth is addictive…. Anorexics must continue to get thinner to feel slim…. Teach children to choose their addictions carefully.

—Mary Catherine Bateson
Peripheral Visions

Drunkards die, not from the liquid alcohol they take so much of, but from their refusal to eat solid food…. Solid food is to the drunkard, a symbolic reminder of the loss of his mother's breast and his ejection from Eden.

—W. H. Auden
The Dyer's Hand

Habit is habit, and not to be flung out of the window by any man, but coaxed downstairs a step at a time.

Mark Twain

Alcohol is a crash diet.

—Bumper sticker

ADVENTURE

Life is either a daring adventure or nothing.

—Helen Keller

Instincts provide biological security, but it takes awareness, free will, and purpose to achieve a life of adventure and creativity. The god within mankind is the spirit of purposeful and creative adventure.

—René Dubos
A God Within

An adventure (Gandolf) says is a "there and back again" affair. A quest is a calling—never one's own desire. No guarantees.

—Ralph C. Westminster
The Gospel According to Tolkien

Without adventure all civilization is full of decay.... Adventure rarely reaches its predetermined end. Columbus never reached China.

—Alfred North Whitehead

It's when you're safe at home that you wish you were having an adventure. When you're having an adventure, you wish you were safe at home.

—Thornton Wilder

AFFIRMATIONS

Rather than focusing our attention on what we do not want, a higher choice is found in identifying that which we choose to bring into our lives, and living from that perspective.... Affirmations have become very popular with followers of some spiritual and esoteric teachings ... it is suggested that by affirming the things that we choose to experience in our lives, often many times each day, they will come to pass.... For some people, their affirmations have worked. For many, however, they have not.... For our thought to become empowered, we must give it energy.

—Gregg Braden
The Isaiah Effect

Celebrate your humanness. Celebrate your craziness. Celebrate your inadequacies. Celebrate your loneliness. But celebrate you.

—Leo Buscaglia
Living, Loving and Learning

Man wishes to be confirmed in his being by man, and wishes to have a presence in the being of the other ... secretly and bashfully he watches for a Yes which allows him to be and which can come to him only from one human person to another.

—Martin Buber

AGING

The Taoist master Nü-yü was once asked, "Sir, you are advanced in years, and yet you still have the face of a child. What can be the secret? Said Nü-yü, "I have been instructed in the Tao."

—Chuang Tzu

I wonder if anyone of us ever becomes an adult, for I have noticed that as people get older, when they "mature," as it is said, they either become wonderfully childlike, or else despicably infantile.

—Frederick Franck
The Awakened Eye

In real life, signs of old womanhood are not supposed to be seen.... Instead of aging normally through their full life cycle, women are constrained to create an illusion that their growth process stops in the first decade or two of adulthood.

—Barbara Walker
The Crone of Age, Wisdom and Power

Above all, now that I feel my life to be brief in time, do I seek to extend it in weight I try to delay the velocity of its flight by the velocity with which I grasp it and to compensate for the speed of its collapse by the zest which I throw into it.

The shorter my hold on life, the deeper
and fuller do I seek to render it.

—Harold Nicholson
Journey to Java

Do not deprive me of my age. I have
earned it.

—May Sarton
The Poet and the Donkey

To grow old is to pass from passion
to compassion.

—Albert Camus

As we age we are more alive than seems
likely, convenient, or even bearable.

—Florida Scott-Maxwell
The Measure of My Days

Old age is ready to undertake tasks that
youth shirked because they would take
too long.

—W. Somerset Maugham
A Writer's Notebook

Time and trouble will tame an advanced
young woman, but an advanced old
woman is uncontrollable by any
earthly force.

—Dorothy L. Sayers

As we grow old… the beauty
steals inwards.

—Ralph Waldo Emerson

The trouble is, old age is not interesting
until one gets there. It's a foreign country

with an unknown language to the young
and even to the middle aged.

—May Sarton
As We Are Now

In the end, your hungers are rewarded:
you are going home. Look, your ship
is ready.

—Patrick (Succat, Patricus) Thomas Cahill
How the Irish Saved Civilization

In Ireland, the older ones move into "the
Western Chamber" of the house.

—Mary Pipher
Another Country

The years do not weigh with the same
burden on all shoulders.

—Simone de Beauvoir

As you got older, and felt yourself to be
at the center of your time and not at a
point in its circumference as you felt
when you were little, you were seized
with a sort of shuddering.

—Thomas Hardy
Jude the Obscure

Volunteerism among seniors has doubled
over the last 25 years.

—Robert D. Putnam
Bowling Alone

Beautiful young people are accidents
of nature, but beautiful old people are
works of art.

—Eleanor Roosevelt

People who, in one life have been habitually selfish, will age quickly in their next life. They seem to shrivel up. On the other hand, if in one life you have been ready to make sacrifices and have loved others, you will remain young and hale.

—Rudolf Steiner
At the Gates of Spiritual Science

Aging helps us to sense that our biography is an inner journey through the outer world.

—William Jennings Bryant
The Veiled Pulse of Time

Older people were expected to be smarter; they are closer to the gods.

—Maxine Hong Kingston
The Woman Warrior

Old people and children should be everywhere. No one stage in life cycle is self-sufficient.

—Christopher Alexander
A Pattern Language

To become mature is to recover that sense of seriousness which one had as a child at play.

—Friedrich Nietzsche

Clearly the trick in life is to die young as late as possible.

—William Sloane Coffin
Credo

An old person doesn't spit without reason.

—Kikuyu proverb

AGNOSTIC

Agnosticism has many faces, all of them based on the conviction that the world is not "word-natures," but word-less, without ideas, "non-speaking"—that concepts and words are entities added by man to reality which exists without him.

—Georg Kühlewind
Becoming Aware of the Logos

O God, if there is a God, save my soul, if I have a soul.

—Ernest Renan

Don't be agnostic—be something.

—Robert Frost

AIR

The breath of the air makes the earth fruitful. Thus the air is the soul for the earth, moistening it, greening it.

—Hildegard of Bingen

… leaves moving in the wind left "tracks" in the air; but since conditions were not right for us, we didn't perceive these.

—Jane Roberts
The World View of Paul Cézanne

Lung-gom, a Tantric discipline which permits the adept to glide along with uncanny swiftness and certainty, even at night, is translated "Wind-Concentration." Wind or Air in Sanskrit is *prana*—the vital energy or breath that permeates all matter.

—Peter Matthiessen
The Snow Leopard

Kalu Rinpoche writes: "The internal experience for the dying individual is of a great wind sweeping away the whole world, including the dying person, an incredible maelstrom of wind, consuming the entire universe." What is happening is that the air element is dissolving into consciousness.

—Sogyal Rinpoche
The Tibetan Book of Living and Dying

AKASHIC RECORD

The clairvoyant eye first of all sees an image representing a fact... from the vast abundance of images that present themselves ... people no longer understand the way spiritual powers are active in the universe, power connected with the powers in the human soul.... It is easy to get the sequence of events wrong when reading the Akashic Record.

—Rudolf Steiner
The Fifth Gospel

There is a psi bank, a planetary information system.... It's a creatively evolving data base: a Planet Brain—a non-linear interpretation of our relationships.

—Jose Argüelles
Earth Ascending

The akashic records are in archetypal space. Poets, mystics, lovers can access this internal continuum.

—Jean Houston

The Christ event is recorded there [in the akashic records]. It truly changed the world.

—Richard Leviton
The Imagination of Pentecost

Memoria: vast storehouse of memory images, the Akashic archives of Mnemosyne, Great Memory, mother of the muses.

—Noel Cobb
Archetypal Imagination

ALCHEMY

Alchemy was not only the mother of chemistry, but also the forerunner of our modern psychology of the unconscious.

—Carl G. Jung
Alchemical Studies

All the intuitive images or thought models that are still used in modern physics and chemistry already existed in alchemy.

—Marie-Louise von Franz
Archetypal Patterns in Fairy Tales

The alchemists had the idea that the alchemical work in the retort and the making of the philosopher's stone is a repetition of the creation, and at the same time a fabrication of the glorified body.

—Marie-Louise von France
Patterns of Creativity Mirrored in Creation Myths

Egypt or Khem, the country of dark soil, the Hebrew "Land of Man," has often been pictured as the motherland of chemistry; so that later this "art of the dark country" became known to Islam as al Kehm, and through Islam to the Western world as alchemy.

—John Read
Prelude to Chemistry

We now find [in the writings of Zosimos] a bewildering confusion of Egyptian magic, Greek philosophy, Gnosticism, Neo-platonism, Babylonian astrology, Christian theology, and pagan mythology, together with the enigmatical allusive language that makes the interpretation of alchemical literature so difficult and so uncertain

—E. J. Homyard
Alchemy

... the alchemists envisioned a universe that was sentient and filled with life, reflecting the permeation of the spirit of God throughout its vastness. In the Emerald Tablet, Hermes had declared that "That which is above is like to that which is below, and that which is below is like to that which is above."

—Stanton J. Lindon
The Alchemy Reader

Nothing is done in the world without the pleasure of God and Nature. Every Element is in its own sphere; but one cannot be without the other; one lives by virtue of the other, and yet being joined together they do not agree; but Water is of more worth then all the elements because it is the mother of all things.

—Michael Sendivogius
A New Light of Alchymie

[We see] Hermes as a cosmic power, creator of heaven and earth and almighty world-ruler. Presiding over fate and justice, he is also lord of the night, and of death and its mysterious aftermath.... He knows "all that is hidden under the heavenly vault, and beneath the earth" and is accordingly much revered as a sender of oracles.

—Garth Fowden
The Egyptian Hermes

Chinese alchemy had a strong mystical character—under the influence of Taoism—which was in strong accordance with the alchemical mysticism from the West ... the Chinese emphasized the point of preparing the medicine of immortality, the elixir of a long life, the theory about the contrasts and not so much the preparation of the gold itself.

—H. M. E. De Jong
"Introduction," Michael Maier
Atalanta Fugiens

Ordinary chemistry does not take into consideration all the properties of a substance, namely, it does not take into consideration "cosmic properties.... The whole of alchemy is nothing but an allegorical description of the human factory and its work of transforming base metals (coarse substances) into precious ones (fine substances.)

—G. I. Gurdjieff & P. D. Ouspensky
In Search of the Miraculous

... the proper art of the spiritual alchemist ... was the production of the spiritual and only valid tincture or philosopher's stone, the mystic seed of transcendental life which should invade, tinge, and wholly transmute the imperfect self into spiritual gold.

—Evelyn Underhill
Mysticism

The purpose of alchemy is the reconstitution of nature into its primal and holy state.... The production of gross gold is merely a by-product of what is really a spiritual process.

—Caitlin Matthews
Sophia: Goddess of Wisdom

Alchemists were profoundly spiritual people whose aim was the transformation of themselves. They were, in effect, the Yogins of Europe.

—F. Lanier Graham
The Rainbow Book

The science of alchemy as evolved under Islamic influence, incorporated a system of seven colours.

—Simon Trethewey
The Alchemy of Light

The alchemists referred to their work as the opus which eventually would produce the Great White Stone, sometimes called the philosopher's stone.

—J. Everett Irion
*Interpreting the Revelation
with Edgar Cayce*

The goal of alchemy is to transmute whatever is heavy and leaden into

something light, alive and liberating, which is why its practitioners referred to it as the "redemption of matter."

—Sharon Seivert
The Balancing Act

Alchemical texts are full of allegory, paradox and a symbolic tension that impels the soul to seek a solution.

—Ignacio L. Götz
On Technology and the Spirit

Basilius Valentiunus ... compares the fires of the last day to the fire of the alchemist, and the world to the alchemist's furnace, and would have us know that all must be dissolved before the divine substance, material gold or immaterial ecstasy, awake.

—William Butler Yeats
Early Poems and Stories

To live life at the center—to incarnate at the center, so that one's limbs move with that fire; to project ourselves into space: this is theatre, flight, daily deed ... we practice an alchemy which draws its fire at that center.

—Mary Caroline (M. C.) Richards
Centering

Spirit and Soul should be united and be carried back to their body.

—Michael Maier
Atalanta Fugiens

Alchemy is one way of imagining the release of spirit from the thick of matter.

—Thomas Moore
The Soul's Religion

The whole process of alchemy is dissolving and making hard again … dissolving the body and making hard the spirit.

—Zecharia Sitchin
The Cosmic Code

The alchemists maintained that mankind suffered a fall; but this lapse from grace was not seen merely as a matter of original sin … In every human body, they (alchemists) say there remains a spark of the Divine Principle which once irradiated its entire being. Cased in the base metal of our fallen state, this star-fire yearns to return whence it came.

—Lindsay Clarke
The Chymical Wedding

ALIVENESS

Human beings fully alive! Such is the glory of God.

—Irenaeus

Don't ask yourself what the world needs — ask yourself what makes you come alive, and then go do it. Because what the world needs is people who have come alive.

—Harold Thurman Whitman

If you are fully alive, alert and responsive to the challenge of every moment, then you are living a spiritual life.

—David Steindl-Rast

We're so engaged in doing things to achieve purposes of outer value that we forget that the inner value, the rapture that is associated with being alive, is what it's all about.… Myth helps you to put your mind in touch with this experience of being alive.

—Joseph Campbell
The Power of Myth

ALPHABET

Man was a reader before he became a writer; a reader of what Coleridge once called the mighty alphabet of the universe.

—Loren Eiseley
The Star Thrower

The alphabet demystifies the world.

—Thomas Cahill
Sailing on the Wine Dark Sea

Lucius Apuleius, a writer and Platonic philosopher of the second century who became a priest of Isis in his later years, writes in his satirical fable The Golden Ass that the sacred books of Isis were: "Partly written with unknown characters, and partly painted with figures of beasts declaring briefly every sentence … strange and impossible to be read of the profane people."

—Donald Tyson
New Millennium Magic

In the Talmud, writing is mentioned as one of ten things created in the Sabbath Eve. Twilight. The 22 square Hebrew letters are sometimes called, Writing of Heaven.

—Richard A. Firmage
The Alphabet Abecedarium

Melchizedek gave Abraham the 22 letters of the Old Hebrew alphabet.

—Edgar Cayce
The Story of the Soul

Cherokee script was invented by Sequoya in 1821: 85 symbols, 6 vowels, 22 consonants and some 200 phoneme clusters and syllables. The type was designed in Boston and 90% of the Cherokee were literate in the script. He didn't speak English but he wanted to create a Cherokee equivalent of the white man's "talking leaves."

—Andrew Robinson
The Story of Writing

When a critical mass of people within a culture acquire literacy, especially alphabet literacy, left hemispheric modes of thought are reinforced at the expense of right hemispheric ones, which manifests in a decline of images.

—Leonard Shlain
The Alphabet Versus the Goddess

The occultist sees in all beings the letters of an alphabet which, united in man form the complete and conscious Word of life.

—Paracelsus

The many letters of the alphabet are in the world around us and the human being is the word.

—Rudolf Steiner
The Christian Mystery

The language of God seems mostly metaphor. His love is like a red, red rose. His love is like the old waiter with shingles, the guitar-playing Buddhist

tramp, the raped child and the one who raped her. There is no image too far-fetched, no combination of sounds too harsh, no spelling too irregular, no allusion too obscure or outrageous. The alphabet of grace is full of gutturals.

—Frederick Buechner
The Alphabet of Grace

The alphabet is a source. A is the roof with its rafters and traverse-beam ... or it is like two friends who embrace and shake hands.

—Victor Hugo

The alphabet is an example of an arbitrary meaning that becomes satisfying. One day I tried to make a sentence with no prepositions or articles—"Anybody can die, evidently." ABCDE. And once you've gone that far, you want to see—"Anybody can die, evidently. Few go happily."... Of course you know as an experienced abecedarian that around X it's going to get very tricky.

—Robert Pinsky & Bill Moyers
Fooling with Words

AMBIGUITY

Delphic ambiguity laid the groundwork for inquirers' confrontations with themselves and their illusions.

—Roger Lipsey
Have You Ever Been to Delphi?

Ambiguity is the warp of life, not something to be eliminated.

—Mary Catherine Bateson
Peripheral Visions

Embrace ambiguity.

—Leonardo da Vinci

God has placed the deepest and most fundamental contradictions in human life not to be resolved but to be lived in the full consciousness of their contradictoriness.

—Jacob Needleman

AMBITION

Healthy ambition should not be confused with neurotic competition.

—Karen Horney & Matthew Fox
A Spirituality Named Compassion

The goose of ambition stirs its wings.

—Maxine Hong Kingston
China Men

My fingers emit sparks of fire with expectation of my future labors.

—William Blake

AMBIVALENCE

The essence of truth is the negation of ambivalence.

—Mary Catherine Bateson
Peripheral Visions

Sacred ambivalence: inside contradictory feelings are held possibilities, potentials, mysteries and open–ended questions.

—John Briggs
Fire in the Crucible

AMEN

"Amen" comes from the Egyptian god, Amun, meaning "The Hidden One."

—John Matthews
Drinking from the Sacred Well

The word ameyn sealed agreements in the Middle East; it was a solemn oath.... From its older roots, ameyn presents the image of the ground from which a particular future growth will occur. One can trace the same sound-meaning back to the ancient Egyptian sacred word Ament … the mysterious ground of being.

—Neil Douglas-Klotz
Prayers of the Cosmos

And now all our minds are one.

—Ending of traditional Mohawk prayer

AMULET

Middle Eastern cultures reek of envy. Babies are protected by charms.

—Mary Catherine Bateson
Peripheral Visions

The word "amulet" derives from an Arabic root meaning "to bear" or "to carry".... An amulet is usually a small object said to possess properties that can ward off evil, prevent accidents, attract good health.... A genuine talisman is the work of a magician, priest, occultist or shaman who understands the subtle energies of the universe and knows how to encapsulate them into an object, picture, or collection of signs and symbols, according to the needs of the applicant.

—Murry Hope
Ancient Egypt

ANGELS

Angels are the formed powers of God's word ... God's instruments ... compacted spirit of nature ... a thousand times ten thousand, unequal in rank, in three realms and seven dominions, according to the seven properties of nature ... The angelical kingdoms are throughout formed according to the divine being, and they have no other form or condition than the divine being has in its Trinity.

—Jacob Boehme
Aurora

... walking and talking with an angel is really fundamentally no different from walking and talking with an ordinary human being. Both the angel and the person are expressions of the ultimate mystery; both are emanations of the Beloved.... There is only one sacredness and we all have it.

—David Spangler
A Pilgrim in Aquarius

"I still don't understand kything. Is it like mental telepathy?"
Proginoskes hesitated. "You might say that mental telepathy is the very beginning of learning to kythe. But the cherubic language is entirely kything—with

you, with stars, with galaxies, with the salt in the ocean, the leaves of the trees."

—Madeleine L'Engle
A Wind in the Door

I saw the light many times before I knew that it was Saint Michael. Afterward he taught me and showed me such things that I knew that it was he. He was not alone, but duly attended by heavenly angels. I saw them with the eyes of my body as well as I see you ...

—Joan of Arc
Joan of Arc, a Self-Portrait

Michael is the most eminent, the most significant Being in the Hierarchy of the Archangels. The ancients called him the "Countenance of God." ... in ancient mythology Jehovah was understood to reveal himself through Michael.

—Rudolf Steiner
The Archangel Michael

The angels are immortal unless, perchance, they become involved in sin as did some of them with the deceptions of Lucifer. The angels are the spirit servants in heaven, and they are neither all-wise nor all-powerful. But all of the loyal angels are truly pure and holy.... Angels are the sure and heavenly guides of the soul of man during that uncharted and indefinite period of time which intervenes between the death of the flesh and the new life in the spirit abodes.

—*The Urantia Book*

We do the works that are of God, along with the holy angels.

—Thomas Aquinas & Matthew Fox
Sheer Joy

Angels are forms, images and expressions through which the essences and energy forces of God can be transmitted and that, since there are an infinite number of these forms, the greatest service anyone can pay the angelic host is never consciously to limit the ways angels might appear to us.

—Don Gilmore
Angels, Angels, Everywhere

We are born to be the companions of the angels. Let us go there again, friend, for that is our country.

—Jalal Al-din Rumi

Every angel is terrible.

—Rainer Maria Rilke

Angels add immensely to the opulence of existence.

—Robert Sardello
The Angels

There is a medieval belief that angels want to sing to us. It makes them happy to do so. All we have to do is listen.

—F. David Peat
Lighting the Seventh Fire

To evoke angels ... we need only to live in quiet expectation of their presence and attune ourselves to their heedings.... From time to time, angels conceive and bring about serendipitous experiences and events in our lives to remind us that we are continually in

God's care and that we are part of a divinely ordered universe.

—Harvey Humann
The Many Faces of Angels

Angels are powerful spirits whom God sends into the world to wish us well. Since we don't expect to see them, we don't.

—Frederick Buechner
Wishful Thinking: A Theological ABC

ANGER

Anyone can become angry—that is easy. But to be angry with the right person, to the right degree, at the right time, for the right purpose, and in the right way—this is not easy.

—Aristotle
The Nicomachean Ethics

Anger is loaded with information and energy.... We cannot allow our fear of anger to deflect us nor seduce us into settling for anything less than the hard work of excavating honesty.

—Audre Lorde
Sister Outsider

Anger comes from the personal level, rage from an archetypal core.... The rage in both sexes comes out of centuries of abuse. If it is taken into relationships, it destroys.

—Marion Woodman
The Ravaged Bridegroom

Underneath anger is usually a feeling of helplessness.... As you develop the ability to receive the pure, vital energy in anger, you open to a powerful new healing source.

—Martia Nelson
Coming Home

All anger is nothing more than an attempt to make someone feel guilty ... and guilt, whose only purpose is to disrupt communication, has no function here.... When you are angry, is it not because someone has failed to fill the function you allotted him?

—*A Course in Miracles*

Anger is fear... Every angry person is a frightened one, dreading some loss.

Richard Bach
One

It is a fact that anger cannot be expressed in a kind way. And if anger is felt, it is always expressed in some way.

Hugh Prather
There Is a Place Where You Are Not Alone

If I lose my temper and retaliate in response to some small experience of suffering that I am not able to bear, I will accumulate negative actions that will have a far-reaching impact in the future.

—Dalai Lama
The Way to Freedom

Can I be angry with the wood
when it is the arm that wields it?
Can I be angry with the arm
when it is the mind that wields it?
Can I be angry with the mind
when it is seeds of past actions or

thoughts, now come to fruition,
which wields it?
I now see with a clarity unknown before.

—Michael Munn
Compassion beyond Fear

The trouble with anger is that it makes us overstate our case and prevents us from reaching awareness. We often damage our case by anger. It is like resorting to war.

—Anaïs Nin

Anger thrives on intimacy.

—Willard Gaylin
Feelings

Anger or hatred is like a fisherman's hook. It's very important for us to ensure that we are not caught by this hook.

—Dalai Lama
The Art of Happiness

ANIMA/ANIMUS

Jung said a man is basically 60% male and 40% female. The female, or recessive, part of the male he called anima. A woman is 60% female and 40% male, and her recessive male part is called the animus.

—Betty Lundsted
Astrological Insights into Personality

The male personification of the unconscious in woman—the animus—exhibits both good and bad aspects, as does the anima in man. But the animus does not so often appear in the form of an erotic fantasy or mood; it is more apt to take the form of a hidden "sacred" conviction.... Just as the character of a man's anima is shaped by his mother, so the animus is basically influenced by a woman's father.

—Marie-Louise von Franz
Man and His Symbols

Anima and animus not only have the same root, but are part of the same tree. They complement and compensate for each other within each individual.

—Lionel Corbett
Betwixt & Between

ANIMALS

When mankind was exiled from Eden, we lost our ability to communicate with the animals.

—Josephus

For the animal shall not be measured by man. In a world older and more complete than ours, they move finished and complete, gifted with extensions of the senses we have lost or never attained, living by voices we shall never hear. They are not brethren, they are not underlings; they are other nations ...

—Henry Beston
Outermost House

Practice love first on animals, they are more sensitive.

—G. I. Gurdjieff
Views from the Real World

Fablers have always known that every animal is a moral waiting to be identified.

—John Ciardi
An Alphabestiary

... the sexton said at length ... "Every one, as you ought to know, has a beast-self—and a bird-self, and stupid fish-self, ay, and a creeping serpent-self too— which it takes a great deal of crushing to kill. In truth, he also has a tree-self and a crystal-self and I don't know how many selves more, all to get into harmony. You can tell what sort a man is by his creature that comes most often to the front."

—George MacDonald
Phantastes and Lilith

Heavy bulls over sixteen feet long jostle for space with tiny deer.... In general, prehistoric man painted what he saw—perfectly proportioned animals.

—Douglas Mazonowicz
Voices from the Stone Age

The truth is, I like dogs better than cats, but I don't know how to draw a dog.

—Theodor S. Geisel (Dr. Seuss)

ANXIETY

Anxiety is the rust of life.

—Og Mandino
The Gift of Acabar

Worry comes from an Old English word meaning literally, "to strangle."

—E. B. McNeil
The Psychology of Being Human

Anxiety is love's greatest killer, because it is like the stranglehold of the drowning.

—Anäis Nin
5th Diary

It's disturbing enough that we go to great lengths in order not to experience it [anxiety], but ambiguous enough that we often have trouble recognizing it when we are experiencing it.... Anxiety makes room for the development of consciousness.

—Elio Frattaroli
Healing the Soul in the Age of the Brain

Be empty of worrying,
Think of who created thought!

—Jalal Al-din Rumi

Anxiety is a directive to action ... it's a product of and a tribute to our imagination, our intelligence, our memory, our individuality, our courage, our variability, our power, our uniqueness. It alerts us, buoys us, motivates us.

—Willard Gaylin
Feelings

If there is a solution to the problem, there is no need to worry. If there is no solution, there is no sense in worrying either.

—Dalai Lama
The Art of Happiness

APPRECIATION

If the only prayer you say in your whole life is "thank you," that would suffice.

—Meister Eckhart

To appreciate a single phenomenon ... you must camp down beside it as for life ... and give yourself utterly to it. It must stand for the whole world to you and (be) symbolical of all things.

—Henry David Thoreau
Journals

ARCHETYPES

... collective unconscious does not develop individually but is inherited. It consists of pre-existent forms, the archetypes, which can only become conscious secondarily and which give definite form to certain psychic contents.... Archetypes manifest themselves through their ability to organize images and ideas.

—Carl G. Jung
The Archetypes and the Collective Unconscious

An archetype is the potential for a particular theme or image which lies dormant until triggered by some situation in the environment or in the conscious or unconscious mental life of the individual. Then it resonates like a bell, its chords heard and felt throughout the personality.

—Allan Combs & Mark Holland
Synchronicity

... archetypes provide structure for experience, just as a river bed gives form to a river ... archetypes help define different paradigms for interpreting what is happening to us.

—Carol S. Pearson
Magic at Work

Archetypal images are alchemical verbs that can hide among everyday things.

—Alice O. Howell
The Dove in the Stone

Jung's method, which bestows universal validity on archetypes and the collective unconscious, is linked to the idea of imagination as participation in the truth of the world.

—Italo Calvino
Six Memos for the Next Millennium

Mythical archetypes assist us to understand who we are and what we should live up to.

—William Strauss & Neil Howe
The Fourth Turning

Archetypal stories, like that of Eve, Lilith and Inanna are like phone lines that connect us to the living presence of ancient beings who can help us in the spiritual journey.

—Joan Borysenko
A Woman's Journey to God

Archetypes are inherited patterns in the human psyche that predispose us to react to certain life events in a somewhat predictable manner. Jung said we project them onto our religions.

—David N. Elkins
Beyond Religion

Civilizations mutate or die through their wounded archetype.

—Bernard Lietaer

A symbol's power is charged by the archetype behind it.

—John R. Van Eenwyk
Archetypes and Strange Attractors

Archetypes shouldn't be thought of as nouns, but adjectives.

—Ira Progoff
Jung, Synchronicity and Human Destiny

Archetypes are about relationships: primary forms and constellations of energy that govern the psyche or that inner self we call the soul.

—Jean Houston
The Passion of Isis and Osiris

Archetypes are vital and can be recognized only from the effects they produce. They are magnetic fields that transform psychic processes into images.

—Marie-Louise von Franz
On Divination and Synchronicity

Jung called them eternal presences.... The life of archetypes is timeless and unlimited. Each has positive and negative, upward and downward, bright and dark sides.

—Jolande Jacobi
Complex Archetype Symbol

Jung said archetypes—patterns—arise in people's dreams and also correspond to myths, art, religions, often from beyond our "real" experiences.

—Robert A. Johnson
Inner Work

ARCHITECTURE

A noble philosopher described architecture as frozen music ... we believe
this beautiful idea cannot be more aptly
resurrected than by calling architecture
music that has merged into silence.

—Johann Wolfgang von Goethe

The new standard of space consists in the
space measurement in time.

—Frank Lloyd Wright
When Democracy Builds

When you build a thing, you cannot
build it in isolation, but must also repair
the world around it and within it so the
larger world becomes more coherent,
more whole; and the thing which you
make takes its place in the web of nature,
as you make it.

—Christopher Alexander
A Pattern Language

Water is the wine of architecture.

—Ada Louise Huxtable

Architecture: frozen symbols which
can be thawed into a palatable language
where measures and motifs are words
and sentences.

—Robert Stacy Judd

ART/ARTISTS

God is an artist and the universe is God's
work of art.

– Thomas Aquinas

All forms of art are different ways of
trying to appreciate the Beautiful, which
is also an aspect of the eternal.

—Anthony Damiani
Looking into Mind

What churches need to do now to renew
self and society is to take spirituality
seriously; this means taking art seriously.

—Matthew Fox
Original Blessing

All works of art ... are religious, sacred
or nothing.

—Arthur Versluis
Egyptian Mysteries

Art can express eternal truth; it is not
limited to the expression of form and
appearance. So wonderfully has God
made the world that a man using a simple
combination of lines, an unpretentious
harmony of colours, can raise this
apparently insignificant medium to
suggest absolute and profound truths
with a perfection which language labours
with difficulty to reach.

—Aurobindo, in Kisher Gandhi
Lights on Life Problems

Art attunes the soul to God.

—Gregg Levoy
Callings

To evoke in oneself a feeling one has
experienced, and having evoked it in
oneself, then by means of movement,
line, color, sounds or forms expressed
in words, so to transmit that feeling that

others experience the same feeling—this is the activity of art.

—Leo (Lev) Tolstoy

The artist is no more and no less than a contemplative who has learned to express himself, and who tells his love in colour, speech or sound. The mystic, upon one side of his nature, is an artist of a special and exalted kind.

—Evelyn Underhill
Practical Mysticism

Truth in art is not imitation, but reincarnation.

—Ursula K. LeGuin
The Wave in the Mind

Among the language of American Indians there is no word for "art." For Indians, everything is art ... therefore it needs no name.

—Jamake Highwater

Works of art are of an infinite loneliness and nothing to be so little reached as with criticism. Only love can grasp and hold and fairly judge them.

—Rainer Maria Rilke
Letter to a Young Poet

To all appearances, the artist acts like a mediumistic being, who, from the labyrinth beyond time and space, seeks his way out to a clearing.

—Marcel Duchamp

The goal of life is rapture; art is the way we experience it.

—Joseph Campbell
A Joseph Campbell Companion

Art is the attention we pay to the wholeness of the world.

—Peter Balin
The Flight of the Feathered Serpent

Art is a collaboration between God and the artist, and the less the artist does, the better.

—André Gide

The artist's task is awakening awe and providing vehicles of expression so that we can express our awe and wonder at existence.... The artist is, by definition, a maker of connections and therefore a mystic.

—Matthew Fox
The Coming of the Cosmic Christ

The artist's function is to animate what we remember, what the senses have let in, what the imagination has sorted and stored.

—Meinrad Craighead
The Feminist Mystic

Art is the antidote for violence. It gives the ecstasy, the self-transcendence that could otherwise take the form of drug addiction, terrorism, suicide or warfare.

—Rollo May
My Quest for Beauty

The role of the artist is exactly the same as the role of the lover. If I love you, I have to make you conscious of the things you don't see.

—James Baldwin

A work of art is a WORK: something made, which in the making follows an idea that comes out of human life and leads back into human life.

—Eudora Welty
The Eye of the Story

The stupid believe that to be truthful is easy; only the artist, the great artist, knows how difficult it is.

—Tom Outland
The Song of the Lark

Works of art always spring from those who have faced the danger, gone to the very end of an experience, to the point beyond which no human being can go.

—Rainer Maria Rilke

The artist is congenitally equipped to see all the time.

—Aldus Huxley

Art is continually working … to take the crust of familiarity off everyday objects …

—Rudolf Arnheim

Each artist must be The Artist to himself, for the world that he creates must be his private vision, as the physical world is God's private vision.

—Jane Roberts
The World View of Paul Cézanne

Art work is not the paint on the canvas or the print on the page; it is the moment of creation by the artist and the moment of understanding by the viewer.

—Walker Percy
Message in the Bottle

By artist I mean of course everyone who has tried to create that which was not here before him, with no other tools and materials than the uncommerciable one of the human spirit …

—William Faulkner

Art does not reproduce the visible. Rather, it makes visible.

—Paul Klee

Paul Klee's work mirrors the spiritual origin of things. He states that the task of the artist is "to lend duration to Genesis."

—Jean Gebser
The Ever-Present Origin

Art is the knowledge of what to leave out.

—Robert Lewis Stevenson

Art is action that deals with the materials and energies outside the body, assembling, refining, combining, manipulating them, until the new state yields a satisfaction not afforded by their crude condition.

—John Dewey
Experience and Nature

Depth survives, condensed and enfolded, in authentic works of art.

—Sven Birkerts
The Guttenburg Elegies

To be an artist, you need a teacher, and it is for this reason above all, that I began collecting carpets.

—Christopher Alexander
A Foreshadowing of 21st Century Art

Inside you there is an artist you don't know about…. Say yes, quickly, if you know, if you've known it from before the beginning of the universe.

—Jalal al-din Rumi

ASTROLOGY

Around 500 B.C., after many years of observation and painstaking analysis of the motions of the heavenly bodies, the stargazers of Babylon discovered that these motions occur in fixed paths, are interconnected, and are tied to time.

—Bruno Borchert
Mysticism

No action of any planet or phase of the Sun, Moon or heavenly body surpasses the rulership of man's individual will power.

—Edgar Cayce
Edgar Cayce's Story of Jesus

Astrology was (and still is) part of a whole ancient language of mythic thought and imagery, an interconnecting symbolic system that was overcome and eventually superseded by the written word and the institutions of the People of the Book, i.e. Judaism, Christianity and Islam.

—Shelia Farrant
Symbols for Women

The Arabs call the seven planets "lords of nativities"…. Astrology was thought to have eight parts: judicial astrology, medicine, physics, agriculture, navigation, alchemy, science of images and the science of mirrors.

—Lynn Thorndike
History of Magic and Experimental Science

Every horoscope has many archetypes…. If we explore the archetypes and observe their instinctual behavior patterns, we will come to understand ourselves and others better.

—Kathleen Burt
Archetypes of the Zodiac

ATTACHMENT

Attachment is suffering. Let everything go as quickly as it comes. All of our ideas, identities, thoughts, opinions, grudges, unresolved expressions, motives, wounds, angers, fears, hopes, dreams, loyalties—create the individual self, which is the barrier to experiencing the essential self.

—Robert Rabbin
Invisible Leadership

Attachment is the great fabricator of illusions; reality can be attained only by someone who is detached.

—Simon Weil

Wake up! At least now, wake up, o foolish one. Consider this whole creation as a mere dream. This world is like a flower in bloom; as you watch it, it wilts right before your eyes. So, why are you attached to it?

—Brahmananda

Only that which cannot be lost in a shipwreck is yours.

—Llewellyn Vaughan-Lee
In the Company of Friends

When mercury is dropped on the ground, its very nature is to remain intact; it never mixes with the dust. As we try to follow the masters' advice and are slowly released from attachment, a great compassion is released in us.

—Sogyal Rinpoche
The Tibetan Book of Living and Dying

ATTENTION

In the very moment a child is born the mother's joy is greatest, because her pain is over. When because of her joy she is less watchful—so says superstition—the hostile powers come and put a changeling in the child's place ... it is very important ... that attention be undividedly concentrated entirely on essential and important things.

—Søren Kierkegaard
Works of Love

The moment one gives close attention to anything, even a blade of grass, it becomes a mysterious, awesome, indescribably magnificent world in itself.

—Henry Miller

With an acetylene torch you can cut steel, and with attention—concentration—you can penetrate into the most difficult problems and come up with an understanding.

—Anthony Damiani
Looking into Mind

If you pay attention at every moment, you form a new relationship to time.... Not only do you become immersed in the moment, you become that moment.

—Michael Ray

What we pay attention to helps define us.

—Diane Ackerman
An Alchemy of Mind

It's fairly predictable that the less attention a small child receives the more he'll require as an adult.

—Terry Hekker
Ever Since Adam and Eve

To observe without distortion is only possible if there is complete attention with your body, your nerves, your mind, your heart, your ears. Then you will see, if you so attend, that there is no entity or being called the observer. Then there is only attention.

—Jiddu Krishnamurti

Attention is living; inattention is dying. The attentive never stop; the inattentive are dead already.

—Dhammapada

I am where my attention is.

—G. I. Gurdjieff

"The Nagual told us to show you that with our attention we can hold the images of the world," La Gorda said. "the art of the dreamer is the art of attention."

—Carlos Castaneda
  The Second Ring of Power

Life is denied by lack of attention, whether it be to cleaning windows or trying to write a masterpiece.

—Nadia Boulanger

The writer should never be afraid of staring. There is nothing that doesn't require his attention.

—Flannery O'Connor
  On Writing

God alone has this power of creative attention, the power to really think into being that which does not exist.

—Simone Weil

Learn to abide with attention in long waiting upon God in the state of quiet; give no heed to your imagination, nor to its operation, for now, as I have said, the powers of the soul are at rest, and are not exercised, except in the sweet and pure waiting of love.

—John of the Cross
  The Ascent of Mount Carmel

The ancients used the word notitia—attention to the quality of things, attentive noticing.

—Shierry Weber Nicholsen
  The Love of Nature and the End of the World

Divided attention can lead to physical exhaustion.

—Eknath Easwaran
  Meditation

When a visitor asked the fifteenth-century master Ikkyu to write down a maxim of "the highest wisdom," Ikkyu wrote one word: Attention. The visitor asked, "Is that all?" Ikkyu then wrote down two words: Attention. Attention.

—A Zen legend

ATTITUDE

Spirituality does not depend upon the environment; it depends upon one's attitude towards life.

—Annie Besant
  The Spiritual Life in the World

It is not what happens to us but how we respond to these circumstances—that is, our attitude toward them—that determines whether they become a thorn or a spur in life.

—Philip Kapleau
The Wheel of Life and Death

H. Jackson Brown said the optimist gets up, goes to the window and says, "Good morning, God." The pessimist goes to the window and says, "Good God! Morning!"

—David G. Myers
Intuition

True spirituality is a mental attitude that you can practice at any time.

—Dalai Lama
The Art of Happiness

AUTHENTICITY

Be yourself. The world worships the original.

—Jean Cocteau

It is easier to live through someone else than to become complete yourself.

—Betty Friedan

If you do not express your own original ideas, if you do not listen to your own being, you will have betrayed yourself.

—Rollo May
The Courage to Create

To become an authentic, spiritual person means to open to our intuition, the part of us that knows… Intuitive decisions make us feel good, even if others think we're crazy. But, as we become

authentic, we no longer worry about what others think.

—Bernie Siegel
Love, Medicine and Miracles

The times I have been most fully me are when I have been wholly involved in someone or something else.

—Madeleine L'Engle
The Summer of the Great Grandmother

A person is alive when he is wholehearted, true to himself, true to his own inner forces, and able to act freely according to the nature of the situation he is in.

—Christopher Alexander
The Timeless Way of Building

Something in ourselves can never be deceived.

—Jane Heap Notes

To be nobody-but-yourself—in a world which is doing its best, night and day, to make you everybody else—means to fight the hardest battle which any human being can fight; and never stop fighting.

—e. e. cummings

AUTHORITY

Authority without wisdom is like a heavy axe without an edge: fitter to bruise than polish.

—Anne Bradstreet
Meditations Divine and Moral

A love-hate relationship with authority is characteristic of an adolescent—wanting authority figures, participating in creating certain authority figures, worshiping authority figures (hero worship) ... while at the same time rebelling, separating and declaring independence.

—L. Robert Keck
Sacred Quest

When we speak with authority, we are authors and we speak the Living Speech of the Elohim. We write and speak worlds into being.

—Rudolf Steiner
Christianity as Mystical Fact

AWAKE/AWAKENING

We are asleep and don't even know it and we may die without awakening, without building the soul.

—G. I. Gurdjieff

In order to awaken, first of all one must realize that one is in a state of sleep. And, in order to realize that one is, indeed, in a state of sleep, one must recognize and fully understand the nature of the forces which operate to keep one in the state of sleep, or hypnosis. It is absurd to think that this can be done by seeking information from the very source which induces the hypnosis.

—P. D. Ouspensky
In Search of the Miraculous

Satori is an awakening from a dream. Awakening and self-realization and

seeing into one's own being—these are synonymous.

—D. T. Suzuki
Zen and Japanese Culture

Complete health and awakening are really the same.

—Tarthang Tulku

The millions are awake enough for physical labor; but only one in a million for effective intellectual exertion; only one in a hundred millions to a poetic or divine life. I have never yet met a man who was quite awake. How could I have looked him in the face?

—Henry David Thoreau

Your vision will become clear only when you look into your heart. Who looks outside, dreams. Who looks inside, awakens.

—Carl G. Jung

Man may be asleep, but he must awake in the right way. One necessity is that when he is awake, he will also have the means to profit by his wakefulness.

—Idries Shah

Each morning, as we wake from sleep, we repeat the creation of the universe.

—F. David Peat
The Philosopher's Stone

Affairs are now soul size. The enterprise is exploration into God.... So will you wake for pity's sake?

—Christopher Frye

AWARENESS

An image that occurs in writing is closer to the mystery of awareness than an image you actually see with your eyes.

—David Plante
Conversations before the End of Time

The Meta-universe does not subject beings to great suffering to become self-aware only to have them dissolve into the great All. Instead we are learning the skills needed to function as ethical, self-referencing beings in the infinite ecologies beyond our material cosmos.

—Duane Elgin
Awakening Earth

Through application comes awareness.

—Edgar Cayce

The question is not what you look at, but what you see.

—Henry David Thoreau
Journals

I learned what view means. People can see view (sic) trees and flowers and grass and hills and sky is view.

—Helen Keller & Joseph P. Lash
Helen and Teacher

You are the universe pressing into an awareness of itself.... We are the space where the Earth dreams. We are the imagination of the Earth, that precious realm where visions and organizing hopes can be spoken with a discriminating awareness not otherwise present in the Earth System.

—Brian Swimme
The Universe Is a Green Dragon

It is in the doing with awareness that the learning comes.

—William Horwood
Duncton Quest

One is always surprised by awareness, for everything is always new.

—Peter Balin
The Flight of the Feathered Serpent

I think it pisses God off if you walk by the color purple in a field somewhere and don't notice it.

—Alice Walker
The Color Purple

AWE

First a shudder runs through you, and then the old awe steals over you.

—Plato (Aristocles)

How could the soul perceive its own beauty and not be overcome by the splendor of the one who is reflected from within us?

—William of Thierry

There cannot be wisdom without an encounter with the body, with that which creates awe, and shakes the ordinary way of life and thought. Without the experience of awe in the face of the mystery of life, there is no wisdom.

—Paul Tillich
The Eternal Now

We doused the burning bush and cannot rekindle it; we are lighting matches in vain under every green tree.

—Annie Dillard
Teaching a Stone to Talk

... awe and wonder—that is the first step in the spiritual journey. Awe is the beginning of wisdom. There can be no compromise on this truth.

—Matthew Fox
Only Connect

Awe is what moves us forward.

—Joseph Conrad

Awe is an intuition for the dignity of all things, a realization that things not only are what they are but also stand, however, remotely, for something supreme.

—Abraham Joshua Heschel
Who Is Man?

Awe is the sense of encounter with some presence larger than ourselves, mysterious, frightening and wonderful, numinous, sacred. We cannot contain it.

—Shierry Weber Nicholsen
The Love of Nature and the End of the World

When I walk in the fields, I am oppressed now and then with an innate feeling that everything I see has a meaning, if I

could but understand it. And this feeling of being surrounded with truth, which I cannot grasp, amounts to indescribable awe sometimes.

—Charles Kingsley

Be struck by awe! It is the beginning of wisdom.

—Matthew Fox

BABIES

God has plans which mortals don't
understand. He rests in the womb
when the new baby forms, whispers
the life dream to infinitesimal cells. He
is cartilage. Memory. It is God in the
house when the curtains lift gently at the
windows and a young child sucks his
itching gums.

—Ellease Southerland
Let the Lion Eat Straw

Out of the union of soul and spirit a child
is conceived—the Jewel in the Lotus,
the new consciousness dedicated to the
possibility of Being. The child is the new
energy that steps out of the past and
turns its face to the future with hope, but
lives in the now.

—Marion Woodman
The Pregnant Virgin

Babies filter nothing, censor
nothing, and care nothing about the
meaning of their actions. They feel what
they feel—and respond accordingly,
unconcerned about the acquired perceptions that later form their psyches.

—Laura Cerwinske
Writing as a Healing Art

The gentle warmth of enclosed regions is the first indication of intimacy. The warm intimacy is the root of all images.

—Gaston Bachelard
The Poetics of Space

The human embryo is created by 50 doublings of the cells; after that the embryo has the opportunity to adapt itself and correct. If it were designed rather than generated, it would have the capability of making a thousand trillion possible mistakes.

—Christopher Alexander
The Process of Creating Life

BALANCE

One must choose in all things a mean, just and good…. Error and confusion dwell in the extremes.

—Pythagoras

Balance means responding to criticism and to applause in the same ways—not to be controlled by either.

—The Baal Shem Tov

The Machine World is so out of balance, it functions without soul or conscience, blindly willing to destroy the planetary ecosystem on which it depends.

—Christina Baldwin
Calling the Circle

Practicing the art of balance in an ever-changing world requires continuous learning.

—Joel Levey & Michelle Levey
Living In Balance

Balance means that things are basically equal. In natural systems dynamic and static balance exists. In one, balancing is maintained by everything changing. In the other, virtually nothing changes.

—Bob Samples
The Metaphoric Mind

Living in balance is living in a state of grace, of delicacy, of gentleness. Love is that which endures. That which is out of balance will not endure. Only by being balanced within ourselves can we hope to balance the world.

—Anodea Judith
Wheels of Life

Imagine life is a game in which you are juggling five balls. The balls are called: work, family, health, friends and integrity. You're keeping all of them in the air. One day you come to understand work is a rubber ball. If you drop it, it will bounce back. The other four are made of glass.

—James Patterson
Suzanne's Diary for Nicholas

Mt. Rushmore teaches a society is best served by a quaternity of temperaments kept in proper balance.

—William Strauss & Neil Howe
The Fourth Turning

Misfit: Jesus was the only One that ever
raised the dead ... and He shouldn't
have done it. He thown(sic) everything
off balance.

—Flannery O'Connor
A Good Man Is Hard to Find

All sunshine makes a desert.

—Arab proverb

BARDO

Dream yoga ... supposedly helps you
stay calm during the bardo, the terrifying aftermath of death, so that you can
safely navigate to nirvana, or into another
incarnation if you prefer.

—John Horgan
Rational Mysticism

From the Tibetan Buddhist point of view,
we can divide our entire existence into
four continuously interlinked realities:
(1) life, (2) dying and death, (3) after
death, and (4) rebirth. These are known
as the four bardos.... The bardo teachings
show us precisely what will happen if we
prepare for death and what will happen if
we do not.

—Sogyal Rinpoche
The Tibetan Book of Living and Dying

BEAUTY

All that is beautiful is difficult.

—Plato (Aristocles)
Greater Hippias

But of beauty, I repeat again that we saw
her there shining in company with the
celestial forms; and coming to earth, we
find her here, too, shining in clearness
through the clearest aperture of sense.

—Plato (Aristocles)
Phaedrus

God is beautiful, and He loves beauty; all
that is beautiful comes from the beauty
of God.

—(Abu al-Qasim) Muhammad

Who can afford to live without beauty? ...
If we get lost in dark despair, beauty takes
us back to Center.

—Piero Ferrucci

The beauty of the world has two edges,
one of laughter, one of anguish, cutting
the heart asunder.

—Virginia Woolf
A Room of One's Own

Never lose an opportunity of seeing
anything that is beautiful, for beauty is
God's handwriting. The beauty of the
stone, the beauty of the light, the beauty
of an opening are a message for you.

—Ralph Waldo Emerson

The beautiful can exist at the edge
precisely because it has nothing to lose
and everything to give away.

—Frederick Turner

Mother's beauty made her powerful and her power made her unflinchingly honest.

—Maya Angelou
I Know Why The Caged Bird Sings

Beauty is not the mistress of nostalgia or avoidance; she is not flimsy.

—John O'Donohue
Beauty

The surfaces of the world are aesthetically uneven. You come around a bend in the road and the world suddenly falls open. When we come upon beautiful things … they act like small tears in the surface of the world that pull us through to some vaster space.

—Elaine Scarry
On Beauty and Being Just

Evil finds a ready home where beauty is despised and ugliness enthroned.

—Calvin Miller
The Finale

Beauty awakens the soul to act.

—Dante Alighieri

Beauty is reality seen with the eyes of love.

—Evelyn Underhill

The more beauty we see, the more we evolve. The more we evolve, the higher we vibrate.

—James Redfield
The Celestine Prophecy

Beauty will save the world.

—Feodor Dostoevski in
Leonard Shlain
The Alphabet Versus the Goddess

Let the beauty we love be what we do. There are hundreds of ways to kneel and kiss the ground.

—Jalal Al-din Rumi

BECOMING

As long as you do not practice it, this dying and becoming, you are only a dreary guest on the dark earth.

—Johann Wolfgang von Goethe

A self is not something static, tied up in a pretty parcel and handed to the child, finished and complete. A self is always becoming. Being does not mean becoming, but we run so fast that it is only when we seem to stop—as sitting on the rock at the brook—that we are aware of our isness, of being.

—Madeleine L'Engle
A Circle of Quiet

If seeds in the black earth can turn into such beautiful roses, what might not the heart of man become in its long journey to the stars?

—G. K. Chesterton

BEES

We will understand, when beginning to pray, that the bees are approaching and entering the beehive to make honey …

—Teresa of Avila
The Way of Perfection

Bees surrender themselves entirely to Venus, unfolding a life of love throughout the whole hive. This life will be filled with wisdom…. Bees receive many influences from the starry worlds.

—Rudolf Steiner
Nine Lectures on Bees

The labour of seaweed as it concentrates in its tissues the substances dispersed, in infinitesimal quantities, throughout the vast layers of the ocean; the industry of bees as they make honey from the juices scattered in so many flowers—these are but pale images of the continuous process of elaboration which all the forces of the universe undergo in us in order to become spirit.

—Pierre Teilhard de Chardin
The Divine Milieu

To all the gods, honey … to the mistress of the labyrinth, honey.

—Inscription on a clay tablet, Knossos

Bees were from the otherworld…. This Celtic expression means may you have the strength to be able to accept one's place in the scheme of things and participate.

—Steve Blamires
Celtic Tree Mysteries

Life in a beehive is established with extraordinary wisdom behind it…. Life in the beehive, much more so than with ants and wasps, is based on successfully cooperating and working with the other bees in the hive… The whole beehive is permeated with life based on love.

—Rudolf Steiner
Bees

The queen, for her part, is the unifying force of the community; if she is removed from the hive, the workers very quickly sense her absence. After a few hours, or even less, they show unmistakable signs of queenlessness.

—Sue Monk Kidd
The Secret Life of Bees

Just as the bee forms honey in its comb, we do our work as if it were honey. And we do so through the powerful knowledge in our soul.

—Hildegard of Bingen

We collect the honey of the visible and store it upon the golden hive of the invisible.

—Rainer Maria Rilke
Letter to Hulewicz

The queen bee, deep in the hive, lays up to 2,000 eggs a day, but only a few male drones mate with the queen—and just once, since the sexual act ends in his death…. In the Hindu cosmology, the Maha Devi, "The Great Goddess," manifests as a queen bee or a divine being surrounded by bees…, Melissa taught mortals how to ferment honey into mead.

—Layne Redmond
When the Drummers Were Women

Bees' waggle dance starts a once in a lifetime swarm. Protect the queen!

—Jim Nollman
Spiritual Ecology

Walt Disney: Sometimes I think of myself as a little bee. I go from one area of the studio to another and gather pollen and sort of stimulate everybody.

—Sonia Cole
Leakey's Luck

The writer, like the bee, gathers honey from whatever circumstances he happens to be in. And had I done that, it would not have mattered what I had written about.

—Antoine de Saint-Exupéry &
Anne Morrow Lindbergh
War Without and War Within

As a bee seeks nectar from all kinds of flowers,
Seek teachings everywhere.

—Dzogchen Tantra

Sit down, sit down bee, St. Mary commanded thee; Sit very still, wait God's will.

—Beekeeper's Prayer

May you have the strength of bees.

—Celtic proverb

BEGINNINGS

I had voyaged to the World's Beginning.... The mind is darkened by what it learns there and cannot understand; the lips are folded, and cannot speak. But I will try to embody for you some semblance of what I saw. I saw Yin, the Female Energy; in its motionless grandeur; I saw Yang, the Male Energy, rampant in its fiery vigor. The motionless grandeur came up out of the earth; the fiery vigor burst out from heaven. The two penetrated one another, were inextricably blended and from their union the things of the world were born.

—Lao Tzu
Chuang Tzu

The beginning signifies an instant in time.

—The Book of Motzu

God is not only the beginning from which we came, He is also the end to which we go. He is the creator of the new as well as the ancient of days.

—Paul Tillich

One of the most difficult things is the first paragraph. I have spent many months on a first paragraph, and once I get it, the rest just comes out very easily.

—Gabriel Garcia Márquez

The beginnings of all things are small.

—Marcus Tullius Cicero

In my end is my beginning.

—T. S. Eliot

We were loved from before
the beginning.

—Julian of Norwich

In spiritual matters we remain beginners.

—Morton T. Kelsey
The Other Side of Silence

For it matters not how small the beginning may seem to be: What is once well
done is done forever. Enter upon your
inheritance, accept your responsibilities,

—Winston Churchill
While England Slept

All great deeds and all great thoughts
have ridiculous beginnings.

—Albert Camus

The beginning is the half of all. Well
begun, half done.

—Greek proverb

BELIEFS

What is important, then, is not the
cultivation of belief or disbelief, but to
understand the process of the mind.

—Jiddu Krishnamurti
On God

Concepts which have proved to be
useful in ordering things easily acquire
such an authority over us that we forget

their human origin and accept them
as invariable.

—Albert Einstein & Victor Mansfield
Synchronicity, Science and Soulmaking

Man is made by his own belief. As he
believes, so he is.

—Bhagavad Gita in
Elio Frattaroli
Healing the Soul in the Age of the Brain

People tend to under value that which
they believe to be impossible or
unattainable.... Beliefs that do not fit
well into the existing ecology of the mind
are more likely to be altered, rejected,
suppressed, or forgotten.

— J. M. Balkin
Cultural Software

Beliefs themselves act as grids,
programming inner experience.

—Jane Roberts
Psychic Politics

Stimulate the belief and see where it leads.

—John Lilly

Some beliefs are like blinders, shutting off
the power to choose one's own direction.
Other beliefs are like gateways opening
wide vistas for exploration.

—Sophia Fahs
It Matters What You Believe

Is this an age of belief, a great
renaissance of faith after a period of
crass materialism? Or is it an age of

madness in which everyone believes
everything? Which?

—Walker Percy
The Second Coming

There are two ways to be fooled: one is to
believe what isn't so, and the other is to
refuse to believe what is so.

—Søren Kierkegaard

Any belief system will make a person
"set" to notice those events and facts that
support their belief and miss those that
do not.

—Peter Russell

"I can't believe that!" said Alice.
"Can't you? the queen said in a pitying
tone. "Try again: draw a long breath, and
shut your eyes."
—Alice laughed. "There's no use trying,"
she said. "One can't believe impossible
things."
—"I daresay you haven't had much
practice," said the queen.

—Lewis Carroll
Through the Looking Glass

Belief in healers, miracle shrines, and
drugs is clearly the basis of placebo
responses, which I regard as classic
examples of spontaneous healing. Belief
also strongly influences perception,
determining what we see and what we do
not see as we move through the world.

—Andrew Weil
Spontaneous Healing

Nothing is more wondrous about
the fifteen billion neurons in the human
brain than their ability to convert

thoughts, hopes, ideas, and attitudes into
chemical substances. Everything begins,
therefore, with belief. What we believe is
the most powerful option of all.... Belief
becomes biology.

—Norman Cousins

I believe that imagination is stronger
than knowledge. That myth is more
potent than history. That dreams are
more powerful than facts. That hope
always triumphs over experience. That
laughter is the very cure for grief. And I
believe that love is stronger than death.

—Robert Fulghum
*All I Really Need to Know
I Learned in Kindergarten*

Those who believe they believe in God,
but without passion in the heart, without
anguish of mind, without uncertainty,
without doubt, and even at times without
despair, believe only in the idea of God,
and not in God himself.

—Unamuno

Beliefs are just bets on the future.

—Louis Menard
The Metaphysical Club

A Bedouin was once asked how he could
believe so strongly in a God he could
not see. The man replied, "If you see the
tracks of a camel in the desert, do you
have to wait to see the camel itself before
believing it exists?"

—James Fadiman & Robert Frager
Essential Sufism

I believe in order that I may know. I do not know in order to believe.

—Anselm

We are born with the seed of belief buried deep inside us.... Belief is a word of love, not thought ... an endearment.... Belief not only points to the mysterious, but arises from the depths and therefore can't be fully understood or controlled.

—Thomas Moore
The Soul's Religion

Belief is limiting and binding, faith is expanding and releasing. Belief fixates; faith liberates.

—*The Urantia Book*

Beliefs too quickly gained can be as quickly lost, while those arrived at over a period of time are more likely to be retained.

—O. Carl Simonton
Getting Well Again

I believe in the sun even when it is not shining. I believe in love even when not feeling it. I believe in God even when He is silent.

—An inscription in a Cologne cellar where Jews hid

BIBLE

The Bible is true, and some things happened.... It is a mistake to look to the Bible to close a discussion; the Bible seeks to open one.

—William Sloane Coffin
Credo

The God of the Bible will not lend himself to our decoration. He is naked God!

—Paul Scherer
Love Is a Spendthrift

I say only what I have seen with my own eyes and you keep quoting the Scriptures!... Experience, O seeker, is the essence of all things.

—Kabir

The Hebrew Bible and the Gospel of Jesus are not Allegory but Eternal Vision or Imagination of All that Exists.

—William Blake

To read the Bible as literature is like reading *Moby Dick* as a whaling manual or *The Brothers Karamozov* for its punctuation.

—Frederich Buechner
Wishful Thinking

BIRDS

It's probable that in the artistic hierarchy birds are the greatest musicians existing on our planet.

—Olivier Messiaen
Conversations with Olivier Messiaen

A bird is a machine working according to mathematical laws. It lies within the power of man to reproduce this machine with all its motions, but not with as much power.... Such a machine constructed by man lacks only the spirit of the bird, and this spirit must be counterfeited by the spirit of man.

—Leonardo da Vinci
Codex Atlanticus

Birds in flight are symbolic of the spirit released from the bondage of earth.

—Joseph Campbell
Thou Art That

I have been searching all my lifetime for only one thing: the essence of flight.... Flight, what happiness!

—Constantin Brancusi

Some birds can somehow distinguish numbers up to seven. But whether this is done by counting or by pattern recognition is not known.

—Gregory Bateson
Mind and Nature

Aldo Leopold wrote of the passenger pigeon's extinction: "For one species to mourn the death of another is a new thing under the sun."

—Alan Atkisson
Believing Cassandra

In Nepal ravens are the constant commentators on village life.... Birds show climate changes.... Birds create a cursive script on the wind.

—David Abram
The Spell of the Sensuous

Birds carry earthly substance out into the cosmos. Songs of birds ascend spiritually into the far distance of space and nourish the highest of spiritual hierarchies—the Seraphims, who pour the song back as a blessing to humans.

—Rudolf Steiner
An Outline of Occult Science

BIRTH

What does god do all day long? She lies on a maternity bed giving birth.

—Meister Eckhart

The body is frozen in the pain.... They put the mask on.... I enter that whirling eternity of rhythms, pressures, sounds, and visions ... no fear. One is past fear. But one is still walking perilously through fire or as through the bottom of the ocean, with leagues of water on top, and only a thin eggshell insulation protecting you.

—Anne Morrow Lindbergh
War Without and War Within

We are midwives to each other. Someday we will bring each other into paradise. Our truest world waits like a phantom limb. Each body, burning like a flame as 2 1/2 million red cells come into being each second, is far less solid than we think. The earth is tinder for spirit. All of it is ready to burst into new flame.

—Michael Murphy
Jacob Atabet

The whole journey is a hidden one. It is the longest human journey from the invisible to the visible. From every inner pathway,

the labyrinth of her body brings a flow of
life to form and free this inner pilgrim.

—John O'Donohue
Beauty

Birth is not one act; it is a process. The
aim of life is to be fully born, though its
tragedy is that most of us die before we
are thus born. To live is to be born every
minute. Death occurs when birth stops.
Physiologically our cellular system is
in a process of continual birth; psychologically, however, most of us cease to be
born at a certain point.

—Erich Fromm

The Japanese have a word for it: saku-
taku-no-ki. Saku—the special sound a
mother hen makes tapping on an egg
with her beak. Taku—the sound a chick
makes tapping from within. No-ki—the
moment the tappings come together.
Saku-taku-no-ki—the instant a chick
pecking on the inside and the mother
pecking on the outside reach the spot.
The egg cracks open. New life emerges.

—Jane Yolen
Take Joy

We are all Mary, virgin and undelivered,
to whom the announcement has been
made, in whom the infant grows.... Let
no one think that the birth of man is to
be felt without terror. The transformations that await us cost everything in the
way of courage and sacrifice.

—Mary Caroline (M. C.) Richards
Centering

No man is sterile. Every soul is pregnant
with the seed of insight. It is vague and
hidden. In some people the seed grows,
in others it decays. Some give birth to
life. Others miscarry it. Some know how
to bear, to nurse, to rear an insight that
comes into being. Others do not ...

—Abraham Joshua Heschel

In the birthchart we balance order and
chaos, becoming and entropy, cause-
effect and synchronicity, potential and
certainty, multi-variable networking and
linear action. No wonder the analysis
of birthcharts has often been called a
meditative art, requiring a "still tuning"
of our brain.

—Shelia Farrant
Symbols for Women

Every time a child is born is a holy time.

—Sydney Amara Morris
*Sacred Dimensions
of Women's Experience*

At the moment of birth ... when the soul
comes to earth, the angel extinguishes the
light of knowledge burning above it, and
the soul, enclosed in its earthly envelope,
enters this world, having forgotten its
lofty wisdom, but always seeking to
regain it.

—Qabbalah

A man that is born falls into a dream like
a man falls into the sea.

—Joseph Conrad

The Goddess presides at the birth of
consciousness, bestowing the gift of
renewal on all seekers.

—Buffie Johnson
Lady of the Beasts

Each of us is born clothed in full
spiritual regalia.

—Chris Griscom
Time Is an Illusion

God's ultimate purpose is birth. He is
not content until he brings his Son to
birth in us.

—Meister Eckhart

What was your original face before you
were born?

—Zen koan

Go under Mercy; Sleep under
the Protection.

—C. S. Lewis
Lewis and His Friends

May you live forever,
Yet never grow old.
May your children have children whose
children you hold.

—Sharon Seivert
The Balancing Act

Baraka

—A Sufi word meaning blessing, spiritual
power, breath of life.

BLESSING

Blessing is an attitude toward all of life,
transcending and moving beyond words.
When family and friends gather around
a table to break bread together, this is
a blessing. When we harden our hearts
against anyone, this is a cursing.

—Madeleine L'Engle
The Irrational Season

First become a blessing to yourself that
you may be a blessing to others.

—Samson Raphael Hirsch

Bless a thing and it will bless you. Curse
it and it will curse you. If you bless a
situation, it has no power to hurt you,
and even if it is troublesome for a time,
it will gradually fade out, if you sincerely
bless it.

—Emmett Fox

BLISS

I say, follow your bliss and don't be afraid,
and doors will open where you didn't
know they were going to be.

—Joseph Campbell
The Power of Myth

Bliss is the natural state of being in all
Life, and all Life Forms return to it.
Highly evolved Life Forms move in and
out of this state at will.

—Duane Elgin
Awakening Earth

Blissful human beings are drawn to all
that is earthly.

—Hildegard of Bingen

BLOOD

Blood and seawater are identical
except we contain iron, ocean water
contains magnesium.

—Theodor Schwenk &
   Wolfram Schwenk
   Water: The Element of Life

No bloodless myth will hold.

—Geoffrey Heil

Affirm your body and your beauty. Know
blood is a blessing, not a curse.

—Maria Harris
   Dance of the Spirit

A woman sheds blood from her body and
from her spirit.

—Meinrad Craighead
   Immanent Mother

Blood is a very special juice!

—Johann Wolfgang von Goethe
   Faust

BODY

The soul loves the body.

—Meister Eckhart

There is only one temple in the world and
that is the human body. Nothing is more
sacred than that noble form.

—Novalis
   (Friedrich von Leopold)

The body is the first proselyte the
soul makes.

—Henry David Thoreau
   Journal

The soul is not really united, unless all
bodily energies, all the limbs of the body,
are united.

—Martin Buber

Whether we are weaving tissue in the
womb or pictures in the imagination, we
create out of our bodies.

—Meinrad Craighead

Man has no Body distinct from his Soul;
for that called Body is a portion of Soul
discerned by the five Senses, the chief
inlets of Soul.

—William Blake

The body is just a particular form of the
universal life energy, whereas the mind is
a more subtle form, which has a greater
capacity for universal attunement and
harmony. Thus the body needs to adapt
itself to the mind. This is why the consideration of belief systems is so important
in healing.

—Jack Schwarz
   Healers on Healing

The Word is made flesh; one must write
with one's body.

—Anne Morrow Lindbergh
   War Without and War Within

The next time you look into the mirror,
just look at the way the ears rest next to

the head; look at the way the hairline grows; think of all the little bones in your wrist. It is a miracle.

—Martha Graham
Blood Memory

Some people regard the body as a place of pleasure, like a club or a hotel or a cinema, and thus destroy its purity and lose their Shakti ... the truth is that your body is without fault.

—Swami Muktananda
Play of Consciousness.

If you think your body and mind are two, that is wrong; if you think that they are one, that is also wrong. Our body and mind are both two and one.

—Shunryu Suzuki
Zen Mind, Beginner's Mind

Years later I would come to know that the body has a vegetable mind, like a plant. It has its own agenda and intent, separate from the mind, the heart, the Will, and if you want to go your own way in spite of the body some negotiation is necessary.

—Diane di Prima
Recollections of My Life as a Woman

The body has been made so problematic for women that it has often seemed easier to shrug it off and travel as a disembodied spirit.

—Adrienne Rich
Of Woman Born

But then, if the body is one with all other bodies, it means that all the other bodies are right there inside it, along with all the falsehoods of the world! There is no lon-

ger only one person's battle; it becomes the whole world's battle.... There is only one body.

—Satprem
Sri Aurobindo or The Adventure of Consciousness

Your body is the journey, and it is where you begin. It is your connection to the physical world—your foundation—the home of your dance.... You are the testing ground of truth.

—Anodea Judith
Wheels of Life

The body is the discipline, the pattern, the law; the spirit is inner devotion, spontaneity, freedom. A body without a spirit is a corpse and a spirit without a body is a ghost.

—Abraham Joshua Heschel
God in Search of Man

Your body's agenda is to survive, to be fed, to be kept safe and to feel pleasure. The soul's agenda is quite different.... Your body lives within the force field you call your soul.

—Neale Donald Walsch
The New Revelations

When you are able to differentiate from your mother (Ceres/Demeter) you'll be able to eat wheat.... What do our bodies reject at the level of the immune system?

—Marian Woodman, Connie Zweig
& Steve Wolf
Romancing the Shadow

These were the lovely bones that had grown around my absence: the connections—sometimes tenuous, sometimes made at great cost, but often magnificent.... And I began to see things in a way that let me hold the world without me in it.

—Alice Sebold
The Lovely Bones

To be in a body is to hear the heartbeat of death at every moment.

—Andrew Harvey

If life and the soul are sacred, the human body is sacred.

—Walt Whitman

Books don't happen in my mind. They happen somewhere in my belly.

—Isabel Allende

The body can feel strange when it inhabits the world in a lighter way, when it encounters a form of happiness or fulfillment for which it has had no apprenticeship.

—David Whyte
Crossing the Unknown Sea

BOOKS

The sufi's book is not composed with ink and alphabet.

—Jalal Al-din Rumi

The magic of books and words may bypass the mind altogether and affect the soul, whose interests focus more around eros and mystery.... Once we get away from the idea that the purpose of reading and writing is to exchange information, then we may discover the enchantment power of letters and books.

—Thomas Moore
The Re-Enchantment of Everyday Life

All that mankind has done, thought, gained or been: it is lying as in magic preservation in the pages of books.

—Thomas Carlyle

And what is the use of a book without pictures or conversation?

—Lewis Carroll
Alice's Adventures in Wonderland

The only books that influence us are those for which we are ready, and which have gone a little farther down our particular path than we have yet got ourselves.

—E. M. Forster

Let them burn the library at Alexandria. It is good that our excessive facilities be no longer available, that forms fall into oblivion: a culture without space or time, limited only by the capacity of our own nerves, will reappear with all the more energy. It is right that from time to time cataclysms occur which compel us to return to nature ... to rediscover life.

—Antonin Artaud

Books break the shackles of time, proof that humans can work magic.

—Carl Sagan
Cosmos

To ignore the sacred books, the best repository of ideas, is an act of childish conceit.

—Mihaly Csikszentmihalyi
Finding Flow

What is a book if not an artifact unfixed in time and space? A mobile receptacle for memories that would otherwise be lost?

—Kanan Makiya
The Rock

Burning libraries is a profound form of murder, or if self-inflicted, suicide. It does to cultural continuity—and hence safety—what destroying species and habitats does to nature's continuity, and hence safety. Burning the Amazon rain forest burns the world's richest library of species.

—Stewart Brand
The Clock of the Long Now

I read books to read myself.

—Sven Birkerts
The Guttenburg Elegies

The largest and heaviest book in the world is inscribed on 14,300 large stone tablets concealed in the caves near the Yunju monastery in Beijing Province, China. In a time of book burnings, 00605 C.E., a monk set about preserving the Buddhist scriptures on stone.

—Stewart Brand
The Clock of the Long Now

A 68-foot-long roll was found in the necropolis of Thebes. It may well be the oldest book in the world.

—Katherine Neville
The Magic Circle

[In the Middle Ages] Monks possessed all the books. Literacy was theirs to give.

—Leonard Shlain
The Alphabet Versus the Goddess

The Book of Kells was the work of an angel, not of man.

—Geraldus Cambrensis

Book truly spoke to book.... Writer to scribe, and scribe to reader, from one generation to the next. These books were open, interfacing and intertextual. No one would see this again until James Joyce wrote *Ulysses*.... Like the Jews before them, the Irish enshrined literacy as their central religious act.

—Thomas Cahill
How the Irish Saved Civilization

No book can ever be finished.

—Karl Popper
The Open Society and Its Enemies

If a book has been a very true book for you, you will always need it again.

—Gertrude Stein

Books are to be attended to as new sounds merely.... They are but a new note in the forest.

—Henry David Thoreau

Books are but piles of stones set up to show coming travelers where other minds have been or at least smoke signals to call attention.

—John Muir

Some books are to be tasted, others are to be swallowed, still others are to be chewed and digested.

—Francis Bacon

The man who will read no good books has no advantage over the man who can't read them.

—Mark Twain

First copyright law: To every cow her calf, to every book, its copy.

—Columcille (Columba) &
Thomas Cahill
How the Irish Saved Civilization

BOREDOM

Boredom is simply a lack of attention.

—Christopher Fremantle

The great enemy of the modern world, "Public Enemy No. 1" is boredom.... Mankind is bored.

—Pierre Teilhard de Chardin
The Future of Man

Boredom is what happens when we lose contact with the universe.

—John Ciardi

In order to live free and happily you must sacrifice boredom. It is not always an easy sacrifice.

—Richard Bach
Illusions

Being bored is an insult to one's self.

—Jules Reynard

When we live with a solitude of heart, we will not experience boredom. It has been suggested that much of what we do is driven by the fear of boredom.

—Herbert Anderson & Freda A. Gardner
Living Alone

Boredom is your fuller life calling to you and your fear of hearing the call.

—Gary Zukov & Linda Francis
The Heart of the Soul

Please remember that no one real is boring.

—Gertrude Stein

BOUNDARIES

We first design structures, then they design our lives.

—Winston Churchill

… a spirituality of boundaries will focus on what happens at the boundary when two different elements meet, for it is there that the soul may manifest, love may act, a creative space may be opened, co-creativity may occur, and the sacred may be revealed.

—David Spangler
A Pilgrim in Aquarius

Every man takes the limits of his own field of vision for the limits of the world.

—Arthur Schopenhauer
Parerga & Paralipomena

BRAIN

The human brain ... a three pound lump of protoplasm... approaches the adult size, weight and number of cells by age two.

—Richard M. Restak
The Brain

Your senses pass on 11 million bits of information to your brain per second. From this glut you process a mere 16 bits of data per second.

—Sharon Seivert
The Balancing Act

This may be what is happening in the experience of deep meditation: neurons become super-conductive flow systems, phase-coherent with other neurons by virtue of quantum tunneling. Resistance is overcome, the usual kinds of perceptual and psychological lenses are no longer operative, and the brain becomes a very different instrument, one that is available to receive messages from the primary reality.

—Jean Houston
The Possible Human

The brain can hold an idea in its stockroom for years, occasionally checking to see if it has changed at all, revising it a little, and then putting it back on the shelf, taking it down again when it seems to have evolved like a lemur from its original form.

—Diane Ackerman
An Alchemy of Mind

If the human brain were so simple that we could understand it, we would be so simple that we couldn't.

—Lyall Watson

Human brains have no fixed program for structuring and selecting what can and should be known.

—Walter Burkert
Creation of the Sacred

Grammar and laws are unique to the left brain.... The human face is perceived by the right brain. Obscuring the faces of women so that even they could not see each other's visages, diminished their collective power because their collective right hemispheres were, in effect, also veiled.

—Leonard Shlain
The Alphabet Versus the Goddess

When one is reading a story, both hemispheres of the brain are engaged.

—Shaun McNiff
Art as Medicine

From the brain and from the brain only, arises our pleasures, joys, laughter, jests, as well as our sorrows, pains, griefs and tears.

—Robin Cook
Brain

The Human Brain contains the fossil memories of its past just as this stratified landscape contains earth's past in the shape of ... stalking dirk-toothed cats.

—Loren Eiseley

BREATH

There is one common flow, one common breathing; all things are in sympathy.

—Hippocrates

Breathing is an act of prayer.

—Frank Waters

Breath is audible. It is a word in itself, for what we call a word is only a more pronounced utterance of breath fashioned by the mouth and tongue. If we said, "First was the breath," it would be the same as saying, "In the beginning was the word."

—Joachim Berendt
Nada Brahma: The World Is Sound

Through your breath you plug your own electro-magnetic field—the subtle energy body that surrounds and penetrates your physical body—into the Universe's electromagnetic field.

—Pir Vilayat Inayat Khan
Awakening: A Sufi Experience

Breathing in I calm my body and mind. Breathing out I smile.

—Thich Nhat Hanh

With every breath we take, God is again pumping into our lungs his exhalation of the breath of life, just as he did for Adam. If he withdrew his breath from the bubble of our world, it would instantly collapse.

—Virginia Stern Owens
On Praising God with Our Senses

Thomas Mann in *The Magic Mountain* says problems of the spirit are often expressed in diseases of the lungs, such as pneumonia.... Learning how to open our lungs is one way of opening to spirit. Breathing is the natural way to the heart.

—Morton T. Kelsey
The Other Side of Silence

In Hawaii, healers are Kahuna Ha, "Masters of the Breath." Some Kahunas learn to store healing energy in the heart, then project it through laying of hands. "Aloha" means love—meeting face to face—alo, of the breath of life—ha.

—Kenneth S. Cohen
Qigong

I picture the earth with its vapor mantle as a huge living organism involved in an increasing in and out-breathing.

—Johann Wolfgang von Goethe in Rudolf Steiner
Chance, Providence and Necessity

The breath that does not repeat the name of God is a wasted breath.

—Kabir

There is boundless breath outside the heavens and it is inhaled by the world.

—Pythagoras

Inspiration follows respiration.

—Michelle Levey

I add my breath to your breath that our days may be long on the Earth.

—Native American song

Here's the new rule: Break the wineglass, and fall towards the Glassblower's breath.

—Jalal Al-din Rumi

BRICOLAGE

Bricolage means making due with the material at hand. Children bricolage well—anything's fair game for play.

—Stephen Nachmanovitch
Free Play

In a world in which humans write thousands of books and one million scientific papers a year, the mythic bricoleur is the person who plays with all that information and hears a music inside the noise.

—William Irwin Thompson

Much of our human activity is like the bricoleur, the odd man who takes whatever is at hand for unintended purposes.

—Levi Strauss

The products of earlier bricolage become the new forms and methods of later bricolage.

—J. M. *Balkin*
Cultural Software

BRIDGE

The whole world is a very narrow bridge, and the main thing is not to fear at all.

—Nachman of Braslow

This world is only a bridge; you may pass over it, but you should not think to build a dwelling place upon it.

—*The Urantia Book*

BUDDHA/BUDDHISM

The root-word buddh means to wake up, to know, to understand. The Chinese and Vietnamese say: "I go back and rely on the Buddha in me."... In Buddhism, knowledge is regarded as an obstacle to understanding, like a block of ice that obstructs the water from flowing.

—Thich Nhat Hanh
Being Peace

Once a father approached a Buddhist master and asked how he could possibly bear to live in a world where he could not protect his children from annihilation. The master picked up a crystal goblet. "I like this glass," he said. "It makes a lovely sound when you flick it, and everything tastes more delicious when poured from its delicate shape. But when a wind comes along and shatters it into a thou-

sand pieces, I won't be surprised. You see,
I know the glass is already broken."

—Common Boundary

The Buddha taught 84,000 methods of
spiritual practice.

—Lucinda Vardey
God in All Worlds

Zen Buddhists define their task as
infinite gratitude for the past. Infinite
service to the present. Infinite
responsibility to the future.

—Stewart Brand
The Clock of the Long Now

Buddha said, "I am enlightened because
I have realized enlightenment is
knowing there is nothing you have to do
to be enlightened.

—Neale Donald Walsch
Tomorrow's God

Christian contemplative discipline
tries to correct the egoistic volition
by an emphasis upon surrender to
God, Buddhism by doctrines of
nonattainment, Taoism by encouraging
reliance on the Tao.

—Michael Murphy
The Future of the Body

The Buddhists assert that the sapphire
produces peace of mind, equanimity, and
chases all evil thoughts by establishing a
healthy circulation … it produces a desire
for prayer, and rings with it more peace

than any other gem; but he who would
wear it must lead a pure and holy life.

—Helena Petrovna Blavatsky
Isis Unveiled

When you sit for a day in meditation you
are a buddha for a day; when you sit in
meditation all your life, you are a buddha
all your life.

—Thomas Cleary
The Original Face

Buddhists present the tradition of Mai-
treya Buddha, the bodhisattva or messenger who has agreed to forego personal
salvation and enlightenment until all
other beings have attained them… That
part of ourselves that feels as though it
will be the last to wake up to the presence
of the divine also serves a purpose in
God's universe.

—Neil Douglas-Klotz
Prayers of the Cosmos

Wonder of wonders! Intrinsically all
living beings are Buddhas, endowed
with wisdom and virtue, but because
men's minds have become inverted
through delusive thinking, they fail to
perceive this.

—Siddhartha Gautama (Buddha)

To practice Buddhism is to wage a
struggle between the negative and positive forces in your mind.

—Dalai Lama
The Way to Freedom

Buddha's mother went to a delightful
grove to give birth. Buddha said, "For

enlightenment I was born, for the good
of all that lives ..."

—Philip Novak
The World's Wisdom

When a Buddhist ascetic has reached
the "fourth degree" he is considered a
rahat ... one who has acquired the power
of lying in the air, becoming invisible,
commanding the elements, and working
all manner of wonders, commonly, and
as erroneously, called *meipo* (miracles).

—Helena Petrovna Blavatsky
Isis Unveiled

The Radio Station WOB—Wisdom of
Buddha—is broadcasting all the time.
But you've got to have a receiving set.

—Heinrich Zimmer

Buddha died, transfigured, saying,
"Nothing is permanent."

—Rudolf Steiner
The Mysteries

CALL/CALLING

God does not call the qualified, God
qualifies the called.

—Neale Donald Walsch
*Tomorrow's God: Our Greatest
Spiritual Challenge*

Artists share the calling, according to
their discipline and crafts, to cast the new
images of mythology.

—Joseph Campbell
Thou Art That

Samuel, Moses and Paul were on the
verge of a very steep learning curve. The
invitation to begin a journey is a labor
of love. God never calls people to rest,
but to work for the rest. And the calls
are in service to the larger good, to be in
stewardship to the growth of others.

—John Dicus

The call comes from the person standing
in front of you who asks, "Will you honor
me? Be kind to me?" ... Honor the little
calls. They prepare you for the big ones.

—David Spangler
The Call

Here's a test to find whether your mission on earth is finished: If you're alive, it isn't.

—Richard Bach

Our highest business is our daily life.

—John Cage

When we are given a big idea to carry forward, I believe we are also given the help we need to carry it. Our major learning is how to perceive help when it comes in so many unanticipated guises, at unacknowledged moments, in different forms than we were expecting, while we are looking the other way.

—Christina Baldwin
Calling the Circle

A call is a process. It can't be controlled by institutions or organizations. People who are called tend to violate the rules in annoying ways.

—Kathleen Norris
The Cloistered Walk

Aslan: You would not have called to me unless I had been calling to you.

—C. S. Lewis
The Silver Chair

I am called back.

—Emily Dickinson's last words

CARETAKING

Am I my brother's keeper? No, I am my brother's brother or sister.

—William Sloane Coffin
Credo

As little as we know of illness, we know even less of care. As much as the ill person's experience is denied, the caretaker's experience is denied even more completely.

—Arthur Frank
At the Will of the Body

Most skeletons of older Neanderthals show signs of severe impairment, such as withered arms, healed but incapacitating broken bones, tooth loss, and severe osteoarthritis. Only care by young Neanderthals could have enabled such older Neanderthals to stay alive to the point of such incapacitation.

—Jared Diamond
The Third Chimpanzee

To care is to be truly present to the moment and discover right there the presence of God. Caregiving is giving eyes to see and ears to hear the movements of God's Spirit right where we are."

—Henri J. M. Nouwen

Tending begins in the womb.

—Shelley E. Taylor
The Tending Instinct

CELEBRATE

Celebrate yourself, and you will see that self is everywhere.

—Starhawk
Dreaming the Dark

Letting go is the basic lesson of life and a necessity if we are to learn how to celebrate the temporary. We must let go of our family, or friends, even our life.

—Clyde Reid
Celebrate the Temporary

CELLS

There is no cell in our bodies that has not been transmitted to us by our ancestors, and the very blood group to which we belong may predispose us to the disease that finally kills. We are all of us chemical particles, inherited not only from our parents, but from a million ancestors.

—Daphne du Maurier
The Rebecca Notebook

The cell membrane discriminates between the system—the "self," as it were—and its environment ... membranes are always active, opening and closing continually, keeping certain substances out and letting others in.

—Fritjof Capra
The Hidden Connections

CELTIC/DRUIDS

Celtic tribes reached Ireland around 350 B.C. ... the Great Barrows and tumuli were already there.

—Thomas Cahill
How the Irish Saved Civilization

The bards believed all things were tending to perfection.... Wise women traced their fingers through labyrinths while humming and produced an altered state.... Rocks which held water are called "bullauns"—healing water.

—Nigel Pennick
Celtic Sacred Landscapes

For the Celts, the mundane was the edge of glory.

—Esther de Waal

The Celtic seer would wrap up in an ox hide and sit beside a waterfall or pool of water and have a prophetic dream.

—Paul Devereux
Re-Visioning the Earth

Druids knew ancient temples were oriented to the Pleiades.... Ogham were notches and lines known as flesc or twig and were often carved on standing stones.... Poets had to learn at least 150 different oghams.

—Steve Blamires
Celtic Tree Mysteries

Mistletoe: healer of all things.

—Paul R. Lonigan
The Druids

Druwid means oak knowledge ... *dru* means oak and *wid* means to know or to see.... Celt comes from the Greek "keltoi" meaning hidden or secret.... Everything that grows on the oak has been sent from heaven.... Mistletoe is gathered on the sixth day of the moon.... The Priest in a white robe cuts the mistletoe with a golden sythe.

—John Matthews,
   The Druid Source Book

The whole nation of Gauls is very much given to religious observances.

—Julius Caesar

Celtic Prayer: Bright angels, walk with me ... favorable company, they come with me. I rise today in heaven's might, in sun's brightness, in moon's radiance, in fire's glory, in lightning's quietness, in wind's swiftness, in sea's depth, in earth's stability, in rock's fixity.

—Patrick

The Sacred Three, my fortress be, encircling me, come and be round my hearth and my home.

—Celtic invocation

Once upon a time when there was no time.

—Celtic storytelling formula

CENTER

When you have found the center within yourself that is the counterpart of the sacred space, you do not have to go into the forest.... You can live from that center, even while you remain in relation to the world.

—Joseph Campbell

Centering is a verb. It is an ongoing process.... Centering as an archetype comes through the potter's wheel and the spinning clay taking shape. But archetypes are Beings of special subtlety and paradox.... The imagery of centering is archetypal. To feel the whole in every part.

—Mary Caroline (M. C.) Richards
   Centering

In my understanding I saw God in a point. In seeing this I saw that God is in all things. God works in creatures because God is in the mid-point of everything.

—Julian of Norwich

As a mountain (a whole structure) moves forward in time, old centers are preserved and new centers are generated; centers will always tend to form in such a way as to preserve and enhance previous structure. Beauty will occur without effort in any world where the wholeness is allowed to unfold smoothly and truthfully, without disturbing previously existing centers. Everything becomes a single system and a single way of understanding.

—Christopher Alexander
   The Process of Creating Life

Every microcosm, every inhabited region, has what may be called a "Center"—that is a place that is sacred above all.

—Mircea Eliade

The center of the cyclone is that rising quiet central low-pressure place in which one can learn to live eternally.... As one leaves center, the roar of the rotating wind deafens one.

—John C. Lilly
The Center of the Cyclone

Center-dwellers need edge-dwellers as pathfinders.

—Richard Thieme

CEREMONY

We must never abandon ceremony but use it as a guide, and later as a friend. Ceremony provides structure for the conscious mind and body to enter a state of spiritual consciousness. Without ceremony we would never transcend the barriers of self.... We fail to see that ceremony is but a teacher, a direction, and we must transcend this to find the absolute and pure consciousness.

—Tom Brown, Jr.
The Vision

The point is to integrate ideas about love and healing, about balance and connection, about beauty and growing, into our everyday ways of being. We have to believe in the value of our own experiences and in the value of our ways of knowing, our ways of doing things. We have to wrap ourselves in these ways of knowing, to enact daily ceremonies of life.

—Bettina Aptheker
Tapestries of Life

CHAKRAS

Since ancient times, spiritual science has understood that human beings have seven energy centers located throughout the body. These "wheels of energy" are called *chakras* in Sanskrit. The understanding of *chakras* can be traced from the earliest teachings in India, to the cultures of Babylon and Assyria, then to the culture of Egypt. From there, it entered the traditions of Hebrews.... The Hebrew menorah reflects this numerical and spiritual connection; the six candles reach up to the seventh, central light of the spirit.

—Jacob Needleman
Foreword, Jean-Yves LeLoup
The Gospel of Mary Magdalene

At the core of each of us spin seven wheel-like centers called *chakras.* Swirling intersections of vital forces, each *chakra* reflects an aspect of consciousness essential to our lives.

—Anodea Judith
Wheels of Life

The "Veil" that separates a man-in-ignorance from God Who Is All Knowledge, is so subtle that even the highest and finest thought cannot pierce through it. This veil consists of seven folds of seven different, deep colours. Each fold is tied with a separate knot ...

—Meher Baba
God Speaks

In an undeveloped person, the *chakra* centers appear immobile and dark in color, inert. In the clairvoyant, they are luminous and in motion.

—Rudolf Steiner
Initiation and Its Results

CHANCE

Chance furnishes me what I need. I am like a man who stumbles along; my foot strikes something, I bend over and it is exactly what I want.

—James Joyce

You write a book and it's like putting a message in a bottle and throwing it in the ocean. You don't know if it will ever reach any shores. And there, you see, sometimes it falls in the hands of the right person.

—Isabelle Allende

Bach might have been forgotten forever had not Mendelssohn discovered some monks wrapping paper parcels in music manuscripts—and gave the St. Matthew Passion back to the world.

—Madeleine L'Engle
Walking on Water

Chance is the pseudonym God uses when he doesn't want to sign his own name.

—Anatole France

Our lives are often touched by chance, are they not? I call it magic, the crossing of our paths with the paths of others. How quickly, how completely, these magic meetings can turn us into directions we never dreamed.

—Dee Brown
Creek Mary's Blood

Life is a juggling act on a tight rope.

—René Dubos
A God Within

All life is a series of chance points, connecting in curves.... [The father watches], not even realizing that at that very moment, his chances still rolled with the clatter of infinite dice. There was only one chance left out of all his chances at play at that moment—only one, which would be irreversible ...

—Marianne Wiggins
Evidence of Things Unseen

Chance opened up perceptions to me, immediate spiritual insights. Intuition led me to revere the law of chance as the highest and deepest of laws.... An insignificant word might become a deadly thunderbolt. One little sound might destroy the earth.

—Hans Arp & Jackson Lears
Something for Nothing

Something that appears to you suddenly, that is meant for you, a thing that you reach for and pick up and hide at your breast, a shiny thing that reminds you of something alive and leaping.

—Eudora Welty
Collected Stories of Eudora Welty

There was nothing accidental, nothing left to chance in the Creator's grand design.

—Edgar Cayce & Jess Stern
The Sleeping Prophet

CHANGE

You cannot step twice into the same
rivers, for fresh waters are ever flowing
in upon you.

—Heraclitus of Ephesus

Some things will never change. Some
things will always be the same. Lean
down your ear upon the earth, and listen.

—Thomas Wolfe
  A Stone, A Leaf, A Door

Throughout history, the really
fundamental changes in societies
have come about not from dictates of
governments and the results of battles but
through vast numbers of people changing
their minds— sometimes only a little bit.

—Willis Harman
  Global Mind Change

Change is anything but predictable.

—Debra M. Amidon
  The Ken Awakening

You cannot make the Revolution. You
can only be the Revolution.

—Ursula Le Guin
  The Dispossessed

In a world moving at hyperspeed, where
so many of us are anxious because of the
rate of change, the soulful move is the
move toward contemplating the source
of things deeply rooted in eternity, the
things that always are.

—Phil Cousineau
  Handbook for the Soul

To live in an evolutionary spirit means
to engage with full ambition and without
any reserve in the structure of the
present, and yet to let go and flow into a
new structure when the right time
has come.

—Erich Jantsch

What's old collapses, times change, and
new life blossoms in the ruins.

—Johann von Schiller

You must be the change you wish to see
in the world.

—Mohandas (Mahatma) Gandhi

Changes occur frame by frame, and,
speeded up, they seem to flow like a
single film

—Diane Ackerman
  An Alchemy of Mind

We must create an environment in
which change enlivens and enriches the
individual, but does not overwhelm him.

—Alvin Toffler
  Future Shock

Mind changing occurs all the time,
especially among the young, and until
death we cannot stop the process.

—Howard Gardner
  Changing Minds

The more organic, less structured the
community is, the more powerful the
pace of change.

—David T. Kyle
  Human Robots and Holy Mechanics

There is no beginning, there is no end. There is only change. There is no teacher, there is no student, there is only remembering.

—Robert Monroe
The Ultimate Journey

When you have a life that is based on who you truly are, no amount of change can shake you, no amount of uncertainty can bring instability.

—Martia Nelson
Coming Home

Change is a fundamental element of consciousness. It is what calls our attention, awakens it, stimulates our questions. We see the red coat in contrast to the white snow.... Without change, our minds become dull and unaware.

—Anodea Judith
Wheels of Life

All aspects of the universe are subject to constant change, continually moving in a direction of enlightenment. Change but provides the doorways through which all must travel to find true peace.

—Meredith Lady Young
Agatha

When one is changing, how does he know that a change is taking place? When one is not changing, how does one know that a change hasn't already occurred?

—Chuang Tsu
Chuang Tsu: Inner Chapters

It is precisely the despair of our times that convinces me that a renaissance is right around the corner.... It is either renaissance or planetary extinction. There is no middle ground.

—Matthew Fox
The Coming of the Cosmic Christ

There is no such thing as loss, really, only change.

—Dorothy Gilman
A New Kind of Country.

You can't dismantle the master's house with the master's tools.

—Audre Lord

Things can not disappear; they can only change.

—Johann Wolfgang von Goethe

All things new must change and only that which changes remains true.

—Carl G. Jung

Let nothing upset you; let nothing frighten you. Everything is changing; God alone is changeless.

—Teresa of Avila

Things are in a constant state of flux, so you can't ever "truly" observe anything.

—Werner Karl Heisenberg

You never change things by fighting the existing reality. To change something, build a new model that makes the existing model obsolete.

—R. Buckminster Fuller

Every new change forces all the companies in an industry to adapt their strategies to that change.

—Bill Gates

Life is a series of natural and spontaneous changes. Don't resist them—that only creates sorrow.... Let things flow naturally forward in whatever way they like.

—Lao Tse

Deep in the chaotic regime, slight changes in structure almost always cause vast changes in behavior.

—Peter Marshall
Nature's Web

Never doubt that a small group of thoughtful, committed citizens can change the world; indeed, it is the only thing that ever has.

—Margaret Mead

CHAOS

First, indeed, of all was Chaos; but next in order, Earth with her spacious bosom. Then Love, who is preeminent amongst all the Immortals.

—Hesiod

Before anything is brought back into order, it is quite normal for it to be brought first into a kind of confusion, a virtual chaos. In this way, things that fit together badly are severed from each other; and when they have been severed, then the Lord arranges them in order.

—Emanuel Swedenborg

Newness is the energy of the edge of chaos, the place where the familiar and the unexpected and unpredictable meet, the place of life and emergence.

—David Spangler
A Pilgrim in Aquarius

In the Marduk epic, the name of Marduk's enemy, Tiamat, suggests in the Babylonian language the chaotic forces of the sea. Mythologically, chaos and evil are related. The chaos of Tiamat has a female tone, and the chaos of Humbaba, the Babylonian giant, has a male tone. Christian texts call all chaotic forces Satan.

—Robert Bly
Iron John

The spiritual gift on the inner journey is to know that creation comes out of chaos, and that even what has been created needs to be returned to chaos every now and then to get recreated in a more vital form.

—Parker Palmer

Wisdom is about living harmoniously in the universe, which is itself a place of order and justice that triumphs over chaos and employs chance for its ultimate purpose.

—Matthew Fox

I think it's impossible not to get some sort of form if you don't think about it. If you do think about it, you can get chaos. But if you don't think about it, you get form ...

—Justin Spring
Fairfield Porter: A Life in Art

The hope lies in the unknown.... The world is up for reinvention in so many ways. Creativity was born in chaos.

—Charles Handy
The Age of Paradox

Chaos theory tells us that when a system is driven beyond equilibrium, the subtle interconnectedness that lies latent beneath its surface can sometimes emerge to reshape the system itself.

—Christopher M. Bache
Dark Night, Early Dawn

Chaos is the result of the human Soul going through a major transformation— the dying of one deep-value system while, at the same time, the emergence of an entirely new deep-value system.

—L. Robert Keck
Sacred Quest

A hidden order in chaos is revealed by a new way of looking.... One thing that's clear is that chaos is feminine, and creation out of chaos is the creation out of the womb, an all-containing potentiality emerging out of darkness.

—Rupert Sheldrake
*Chaos, Creativity and
Cosmic Consciousness*

From out of that primal chaos something true can self-organize.

—John Briggs & F. David Peat
Seven Life Lessons of Chaos

Chaos theory is postulated on the premise that everything we see and engage with is living in one capacity or another; in an alive universe, life abounds

and the more strange and mysterious its manifestations, the more authentic and real it is likely to be. Open systems are amorphous ... a strange attractor is a basis of attraction—pulling the system into visible shape ... spaces that were not visible in two dimensions now become apparent.

—Diarmuid Ó Murchú
Reclaiming Spirituality

The attractor is called a strange attractor if there is a non-repetitive patterns— non-linear, complex, chaotic. Non-linear or chaotic systems are profoundly influenced by the conditions that initiate them.

—David Spangler
Everyday Miracles

Attempts to impose order, to freeze relationships into complex formal structures are counterproductive.

—Ralph Stacey
The Chaos Frontier

Even Chaos has a shape and a place into which that shape fits.

—Edward S. Casey
Getting Back into Place

Deep in the chaotic regime, slight changes in structure almost always cause vast changes in behavior.

—Stuart Kauffman & Michael Crichton
The Lost World

We have a collective nervous breakdown of the old systems giving birth to a renewed search for consolation, meaning and deliverance.

—Mick Brown
The Spiritual Tourist

One must have chaos in one, to give birth to a dancing star.

—Friedrich Nietzche

You think you see chaos? It's really a rich, rolling, swelling, lilting, singing, laughing, shouting, crying, sleeping order.

—Christopher Alexander

With chaos theory came wonder. Its breathtaking insights showed that there was structure to the world and its myriad events even if it was something hard to pull free.

—Mark Ward
Beyond Chaos

Chaos gives Nature the freedom to exercise her creativity.

—Triah Xuan Thuan
Chaos and Harmony

We know simply that nothing is static, nothing is absolutely predictable, and nothing is certain.

—L. Robert Keck
Sacred Quest

Ride the whirlwind. That's the most we can do.

—Arthur C. Clarke

There is no chaos, only as yet unrecognized patterns.

—Paula Underwood Spencer

I now know that in the beginning, Chaos was ignited by an immense burst of laughter.

—René Daumal

CHARITY

… remember that charity is beyond reason, and that God can be known through charity.

—Flannery O'Connor
The Habit of Being

The word for almsgiving … comes from the root ... meaning to purify. It is a means of purifying what bounties God has given by sharing some of it with the poor and the needy.… Muslims agree completely with the dictum of the Gospel's "It is more blessed to give than to receive."

—Seyyed Hossein Nasr
The Heart of Islam

If you have much, give of your wealth; if you have little, give of your heart.

—Arab proverb

CHILDREN

I understand no higher state in this life than childhood.… God joyfully calls saying: "Let all your love be, my child, turn to me. I am everything you need."

—Julian of Norwich

Childhood is the nearest thing to true life.

—André Breton

Whatever else a child may suffer from, it does not suffer from remoteness of life, normally ... it is fully alive, and that is why people, thinking back to their own childhood, long to have that naïve vitality which they have lost in becoming a grown-up. The child is an inner possibility, the possibility of renewal.

—Marie Louise von Franz
The Problem of the Puer Aeternus

My father went on talking to me in a low voice. This is how our people always talk to their children, so low and quiet, the child thinks he is dreaming. But he never forgets.

—Maria Chona
The Autobiography of a Papago Woman

Small children are the most powerful learning engines in the known universe. They effortlessly learn as many languages as are spoken in their households ... they do no homework, have no tests, no grades.

—Daniel Quinn
My Ishmael

A kid can understand anything.

—Theodor S. Geisel (Dr. Seuss)

It takes a long time to become young.... It took me four years to paint like Raphael, but a lifetime to paint like a child.

—Pablo Picasso

A childlike sense of wonder is the key to understanding the mysteries of the esoteric universe.

—Robert Ellwood
The Cross and the Grail

I can imagine that someday we will regard our children not as creatures to manipulate or to change but rather as messengers from a world we once deeply knew, but which we have long since forgotten, who can reveal to us more about the true secrets of life, than our parents were ever able to.

—Alice Miller
For Your Own Good

When you discern a person, ask yourself the question, does this person honor the child within—for then he honors the child in the world.

—Lynn V. Andrews
Flight of the 7th Moon

Children can be told anything—anything. I've always been struck by seeing how little grown-up people understand children, how little parents even understand their own children. Nothing should be concealed from children on the pretext that they are little and that it is too early for them to understand.

—Feodor Dostoevski
The Idiot

Grownups never understand anything by themselves and it is tiresome for children to be always and forever explaining things to them.

—Antoine de Saint-Exupéry
The Little Prince

I, God, am your playmate! I will lead the child in you in wonderful ways for I have chosen you.

—Mechtild of Magdeburg

We are not children once we have pasts.

—Eudora Welty
The Eye of the Story

Kids are bent. They think around corners.

—Stephen King
Notes on Horror

A man may have all the prescribed adult virtues and, if he lacks the childhood virtues, will still be a dunce, a bore, and a liar.

—Wendell Berry
The Hidden Wound

Children grow up, not in a smooth, ascending curve, but jaggedly, their needs inconstant as weather.

—Adrienne Rich
Of Woman Born

Childhood is full of mystery and promise, and perhaps the life fear comes when all the mysteries are laid open, when what we thought we wanted is attained.... Confronted by the uncouth specter of old age, disease, and death,

we are thrown back upon the present, on this moment, here, right now, for all there is. And surely this is the paradise of children, that they are at rest in the present, like frogs or rabbits.

—Peter Matthiessen
The Snow Leopard

Children are basically psychic. Their ability to imagine is so real and so advanced that it can safely be regarded as a well-functioning sense. Their closeness to creation keeps their channels of communication wide open, and their intuitive power is so great that they can often see things with their spiritual eyes that may take adults years.

—Rene Noorbergen
You Are Psychic

100 million children under 18 and sometimes as young as three, live and work the streets in Asia, Africa and Latin America. They often take to the streets to avoid sexual and substance abuse.... They show remarkable resilience and survival techniques.... There is always one moment in childhood when the door opens and lets the future in.

—Patrick Bateson
Paul Martin, Design for a Life

Why should we consider it a serious pathology for one person to abandon one child, but not a serious pathology for a government to abandon millions of children?

—Marianne Williamson
The Healing of America

At about twelve a child begins to understand cause and effect.... From seven to nine, children take everything in with their soul. From nine to eleven, children perceive the difference between the soul quality they see in themselves and what is merely "living."

—Rudolf Steiner
The Kingdom of Childhood

The brutes and bigots, the batterers and the bastards are also children of God.

—Maya Angelou

Our children are us in the tomorrow of life.

—Thomas E. Mails
Fools Crow: Wisdom and Power

We must not trap our children in the merely human.

—Rainer Maria Rilke

Children are the anchors that hold a mother to life.

—Socrates

The future of the world hangs on the breath of schoolchildren

—Hebrew proverb

CHOICE

The slave, in the spiritual order, is the [one] whose choices have delivered him over, bound hand and foot to his own compulsions, idiosyncrasies and illusions, so that he never does what he really wants ... but only what he has to do.

—Thomas Merton
The New Man

One's philosophy is not best expressed in words. It is expressed in the choices one makes.... The process never ends until we die. And the choices we make are ultimately our responsibility.

—Eleanor Roosevelt

We have a spiritual self, a physical self and a consciousness. Therefore we can make choices and are responsible for the choices we make. We may choose order and peace or confusion and chaos.

—Rosa Parks
Diane Mariechild in Open Mind

We must cross the river. We seek a raft to carry us across. Many rafts present themselves. We will know we have chosen the right raft when, upon reaching the other shore, we look back, and we realize that there was neither raft nor river.

—Judy Brown
retelling an old Zen story in *The Choice*

We are at our human finest, dancing with our minds, when there are more choices than two. Sometimes there are ten, even twenty different ways to God, all but one bound to be wrong, and the richness of selection in such situations can lift us onto totally new ground.

—Lewis Thomas
The Medusa and the Snail

Destiny is not a matter of chance, it is a matter of choice; it is not a thing to be waited for, it is a thing to be achieved.

—William Jennings Bryant

"Milton was right," said my Teacher. "The choice of every lost soul can be expressed in the words 'Better to reign in Hell than serve in Heaven.' There is always something they insist on keeping, even at the price of misery. There is always something they prefer to joy—that is, to reality."

—C. S. Lewis
The Great Divorce

A choice to change a diaper, praise a sunset, admit a mistake, or give up a subway seat is a choice for God.

—Peter J. Kreeft
Love is Stronger Than Death

Freedom is a terrible gift, and the theory behind all dictatorships is that "the people" do not want freedom. They want bread and circuses. They want workman's compensation and fringe benefits and TV. Give up your free will, give up your freedom to make choices, listen to the expert and you will have three cars in your garage, steak on the table, and you will no longer have to suffer the agony of choice.

—Madeleine L'Engle
Walking on Water

We can have excuses or we can have health, love, longevity, understanding, adventure, money, happiness. We design our lives through the power of our choices. We feel most helpless when we've made choices by default, when we haven't designed our lives on our own.

—Richard Bach
One

She doesn't write fiction with a cartoon morality. Harry makes choices. Rowling's message is "do the hard right thing."

Dumbledore's advice: choose what is right over what is easy.

—John Granger
The Hidden Key to Harry Potter

Man of Holiness: I will not rob man of his agency to choose for himself, as I have chosen in eternities past. What he will do and who he will become. Wickedness can never be joy. Even I cannot make it so.

—Anne Perry
Tathea

By virtue of being human, all of us have the capacity to choose, to change, to grow.

—Eknath Easwaran
Meditation

Who will prefer the jungle of jade pendants if he once has heard stone growing in a cliff?

—Witter Bynner
Tao Te Ching

CHRISTIAN/ CHRISTIANITY

A church works as an engine of prayer.... The cloister is a "garden" but also a complex machine for memory work.

—Mary Carruthers
The Craft of Thought

It is often said that the Church is a crutch. Of course it's a crutch. What makes you think you don't limp?

—William Sloane Coffin
Credo

Many people go to church to make their last stand against God.

—Karl Barth

A central message of Christian life is this: ask Jesus for but a thimbleful of help and you get an oceanful in return.

—William Sloane Coffin
Credo

I believe in Christianity as I believe that the sun has risen, not only because I see it, but because I see everything in it.

—C. S. Lewis

If Christianity is only a mythology, then I find the mythology I believe in is not the one I like best. I like Greek mythology much better, Irish better still, Norse best of all.

—C. S. Lewis
The Weight of Glory

A true Christian is a true Hindu, and a true Hindu is a true Christian.

—Vivekananda

Silences are the only scrap of Christianity we still have left.

—Søren Kierkegaard

… when Christians say the Christ-life is in them, they do not mean simply something mental or moral. When they speak of being "in Christ" or of Christ being "in them," this is not simply a way of saying that they are thinking about Christ or copying Him. They mean that Christ is actually operating through them.

—C. S. Lewis
Mere Christianity

Never is Christianity lopsided and pathetic, with a long and sallow face, and pinched little morals: always it is the lack of it that is! Christ tied nobody's hands. He set men free to be the selves God meant.

—Paul Scherer
Love Is a Spendthrift

Art is for me the great integrator, and I understand Christianity as I understand art. I understand Christmas as I understand Bach's "Sleepers Awake" or "Jesu, Joy of Man's Desiring;" as I understand Braque's clowns, Blake's poetry.

—Madeleine L'Engle
The Irrational Season

Christians, like any other group of people, are very ordinary and imperfect…. On this Path, the man in splendid archbishop's vestments may actually be well behind the woman in rags. Both roles have their place, and all are God in disguise.

—Robert Ellwood
The Cross and the Grail

Christian impulses are at work even where they are denied.

—Rudolf Steiner
The Fifth Gospel

Michael is essentially a Sun-Spirit. He is therefore the Spirit whose task in our epoch is to bring about a deeper, more esoteric understanding of the truths of Christianity.... Christianity is to be guided into a realm of deeper truths.

—Rudolf Steiner
The Archangel Michael

My own feeling is that writers who see by the light of their Christian faith will have in these times (of prosperity and strength and classlessness) the sharpest eyes for the grotesque, for the perverse, and for the unacceptable.

—Flannery O'Connor
On Writing

Christianity is a myth, too. Only God is the poet and the images he used were real men and actual history. The myth becomes fact.

—Humphrey Carpenter
The Inklings

The Potter books are meant to baptize the imagination in Christian imagery and doctrine.... Initially Rowling was afraid if people knew C.S. Lewis was one of her favorites, and if they were aware of her Christian faith, she'd give away too much of what's coming in the series.

—John Granger
The Hidden Key to Harry Potter

He who would lead a Christlike life is he who is perfectly and absolutely himself.

—Oscar Wilde
The Soul of Man under Socialism

Must then, a Christ perish in every age to save those that have no imagination?

—George Bernard Shaw

Ireland is the only country where Christianity was introduced without bloodshed.

—Thomas Cahill
How the Irish Saved Civilization

Indian yogis ... do not exhibit stigmata resembling Christ's crucifixion wounds, nor for that matter do Eastern Orthodox monks. Only in Western Christendom, and most particularly in Roman Catholicism, have there been numerous ecstatics whose hands and feet bleed on Good Friday

—Michael Murphy
The Future of the Body

Christ is not a model to be imitated, but the Way to be followed.

—W. H. Auden
The Dyer's Hand

A Christian is one who is on the way, though not necessarily very far along it, and who has at least some dim and half-baked idea of whom to thank.

—Frederich Buechner
Wishful Thinking

We'll be delivered of our false idols and Christianity will once more be despicable.

—Walker Percy

CIRCLES

What is eternal is circular and what is circular is eternal.

—Aristotle

At the still point in the center of the circle
one can see the infinite in all things.

—Chuang Tsu

I live my life in widening circles
That reach out across the world.

—Rainer Maria Rilke
The Book of Hours

Come out from the circle of time and
into the circle of love.

—Jalal Al-din Rumi

Imagine a circle where the entire group
has committed itself to problem solving
and accomplishment, rather than
positioning for power.

—Christina Baldwin
Calling the Circle

Gathering in a wisdom circle enables us
to move deeply into ourselves, into that
core which continues to survive, hope,
dream and carry on.

—Charles Garfield, *et al*
Wisdom Circles

Everything the Power of the World does
is done in a circle. The sky is round, and
I have heard that the earth is round like
a ball, and so are all the stars. The wind,
in its greatest power, whirls. Birds make
their nests in circles, for theirs is the
same religion as ours…. Even the seasons
form a great circle in their changing, and
always come back again to where they
were. The life of a (person) is a circle

from childhood to childhood, and so it is
in everything where power moves.

—Black Elk
Black Elk Speaks

The circle is a principle as well as a
shape. It goes counter to the social order,
pecking order, superior/inferior, ranking
order that compares each individual
woman to others. Sitting in a circle, each
woman has a physical position that is
equal to every other woman in the circle.

—Jean Shinoda Bolen
The Millionth Circle

You will be teachers for each other. You
will come together in circles and speak
your truth to each other. The time has
come for women to accept their spiritual
responsibility for our planet.

—Sherry Ruth Anderson &
Patricia Hopkins
The Feminine Face of God

When entering a hogan, one walks
clock-wise around the periphery before
sitting down.

—Thomas W. Cooper
A Time before Deception

The more one knows, the more one
comprehends, the more one realizes that
everything turns in a circle.

—Johann Wolfgang von Goethe

Salisbury Cathedral came to encircle me
as I walked around and around it.

—Susan Howatch

To the Lakota people the year is a circle around the border of the world.

—David Abram
The Spell of the Sensuous

In the sacred hoop, the circle is always left open so that the new may enter. Nothing is permanent, no situation is ever fixed and no category is ever closed.

—F. David Peat
Lighting the Seventh Fire

All human things are in a circle.

—Inscription on Athena's temple, Athens

CLUTCH

Affluence tends to bring with it a stupor, a flatulence of spirit. It is difficult to laugh freely as long as we are clutching all that we have accumulated and are afraid to lose.

—Madeleine L'Engle
The Irrational Season

The history of scientific thought, if it teaches us anything at all, teaches us the folly of clutching ideas too closely. To this extent it is an echo of eastern wisdom which teaches us the folly of clutching anything.

—Gary Zukav
The Dancing Wu Li Masters

"To clutch" in ancient Egyptian and "to clutch the mountain" in Assyrian were euphemisms that signified "to die."

—Peter Matthiessen
The Snow Leopard

COLLECTIVE UNCONSCIOUS/ CONSCIOUSNESS

When something happens here at point A which touches upon or affects the collective unconscious, then it has happened everywhere.

—Carl G. Jung
Letters

Only here, in life on earth, where the opposites clash together, can the general level of consciousness be raised.... True, the unconscious knows more than consciousness does; but it is knowledge of a special sort, knowledge in eternity, usually without reference to the here and now, not couched in language of the intellect.... The collective unconscious is common to all; it is the foundation of what the ancients called the "sympathy of all things."

—Carl G. Jung
Memories, Dreams and Reflections

... our minds are part of an extended web or field of consciousness composed of all the beings who are simultaneously sharing this present moment.

—Christopher M. Bache,
Dark Night, Early Dawn

COLOR

Colors are the wounds of light.

—William Blake

Color possesses me. I don't have to pursue it. It will possess me always, I know it. That is the meaning of this happy hour. Color and I are one. I am a painter.

—Paul Klee

A soprano can break a wine glass if her note happens to hit the natural vibrational note of the glass and, in a sense, this is the way that color too is released. When a ray of light hits the natural vibrational note of an object, it alters the vibration; it becomes absorbed itself in this alteration and what is reflected outwards is the object's color. The Impressionist movement, for instance, was totally immersed in the attempt to capture these vibrations of color.

—John O'Donohue
Beauty

Color must be thought, filtered through the imagination. Without imagination, beautiful colors are hard to construct.

—Gail Sher
The Intuitive Writer

Our spectrum of consciousness is not separate from the spectrum of light.

—Denise Linn
Sacred Space

Generally speaking, colour is a power which directly influences the soul. Colour is the keyboard, the eyes are the hammers, and the soul is the piano with many strings. The artist is the hand which plays, touching one key or another to cause vibrations in the soul.

—Wassily Kandinsky
The Art of Spiritual Harmony

Without color or its equivalent, life to me would be dark, barren, a vast blackness.

—Helen Keller

Bower birds of Australia compose attractive patterns with colored pebbles in front of their nests ... if a pebble is removed, it will replace it with one of the same color.

—René Dubos
A God Within

A light was upon it for which his language had no name.... He [Frodo] saw no colour but those he knew, gold and white and blue and green, but they were fresh and poignant, as if he had at that moment first perceived them and made for them names new and wonderful.

—J. R. R. Tolkien
Lord of the Rings

Man, Sub-Creator, the refracted light through whom is splintered from a single White to many hues, is endlessly combined in living shapes that move from mind to mind.

—C. S. Lewis
Humphrey Carpenter, The Inklings

Light has valleys and peaks; not only do these change constantly along with the relationship between the peaks, but the colors and intensities are never the same. Sometimes light seems to cling to an object, hugging it. Sometimes it scurries around the edges of an object like a tiny insect, glowing, moving so swiftly that you can't really follow it with your eyes.

—Jane Roberts
The World View of Paul Cézanne

An abiding melody of color and sound
echoes through the soul of each person.
For some it is a haunting, lingering
refrain experienced as the clarity of
purpose. For others, it is almost totally
forgotten in the deafening noise of
earth life. Nonetheless, there is an
ancient melody of peace retained within
the recesses of your God-mind and
soul experience.

—Ann Valentin & Virginia Essene
Descent of the Dove

For it is not strange that music, color,
vibration are all a part of the planets,
just as the planets are a part—and a
pattern—of the whole universe.

—Edgar Cayce
Color and the Edgar Cayce Readings

Let us try to sink ourselves completely
into what we receive through colour from
the rich and varied world around us. We
must feel what is in colour if we wish to
penetrate into its true nature, bringing
insight into our feelings.

—Rudolf Steiner
Colour

In the great period of carpet weaving,
the apprenticeship of a dyer lasted fifteen
years. At the end of fifteen years, the
apprentice dyer was required to make a
color which no one had ever seen before.

—Christopher Alexander
A Foreshadowing of 21st Century Art

Like acrobats on a high trapeze
The colors pose and bend their knees
Twist and turn and leap and blend
Into shapes and feelings without end.

—Mary O'Neill
Hailstones and Halibut Bones

Japanese *awo* can mean green, blue or
dark depending on the context.

—Philip Ball
Bright Earth

"Grey" is English, and one very definite
bird-wing, ocean-wave color to me; and
"gray" which is American, and a flatter,
more metallic color.

—Madeleine L'Engle
Circle of Quiet

Tiny spots on a crab's body enlarge
during daytime hours, giving him the
same color as the mudbank he
explores, thus protecting him from his
enemies. At night, the spots shrink, the
color fades and he is almost invisible
in moonlight. These changes are
synchronized with the tides, so that each
day they occur at a different hour ... they
even mark the passage of time in their
laboratory prisons, faithful to the tides in
their fashion.

—E. B. White
The Points of My Compass

COMMITMENT

Socrates had it wrong; it is not the unexamined but finally the uncommitted life that is not worth living.

—William Sloane Coffin
Credo

Until one is committed there is hesitancy, the chance to draw back, always ineffectiveness, concerning all acts and initiative (and creation.) The moment one definitely commits oneself, then Providence moves too. A whole stream of events issues from the decision. Whatever you can do or dream you can, begin it. Boldness has genius, power and magic in it.

—Johann Wolfgang von Goethe

Genuine commitment is a journey into the unknown.

—Madonna Kolbenschlag
Lost in the Land of Oz

Albert Camus said sometimes life beckons us to make 100% commitment to something about which we are 51% sure.

—David G. Myers
Intuition

Concerning all acts of initiative (and creation) there is one elementary truth, the ignorance of which kills countless ideas and splendid plans: the moment one definitely commits oneself, then Providence moves too.

—W. N. Murray
The Scottish Himalayan Expedition

COMMUNICATION

Consider any attempt to communicate as being appropriate.

—Bob Samples
The Metaphoric Mind

Communication is a struggling love with other people.

—Karl Jaspers

COMMUNITY

There is a Providence that brought us here and gave us to each other at this time. In and through us, a greater tapestry of creativity is being woven.

—John O'Donohue
Eternal Echoes

If we speak of a healthy community, we cannot be speaking of a community that is merely human. We are talking about a neighborhood of humans in a place, plus the place itself: its soil, its water, its air, and all the families and tribes of the nonhuman creatures that belong to it.

—Wendell Berry
Sex, Economy, Freedom, and Community

On the most basic level, a sense of deep community restrains us from doing harm to those with whom we feel connected, whether we like them personally or not.

—Carol Frenier
Business and the Feminine Principle

Communities have sometimes been referred to as leaderless groups. It is more accurate to say that a community is a group of leaders.

—Scott Peck
The Different Drum

We have come to the place where we must decide either to live as one people, or perish as fragments.

—Wendell Berry
The Hidden Wound

Community is a necessary part of the Sun Dance. The dancers need the presence of the community to sustain them in their sacrifice and their brave prayer.... The Sun Dance awakens the collective right brain, the mystical energy of the community.

—Matthew Fox
The Coming of the Cosmic Christ

We need to amend the famous slogan of René Dubos: "Think globally and act locally." We need to think both locally and globally and act both locally and globally.... Being rooted in love for our real communities of life and for our common mother, Gaia, can teach us patient passion, a passion that is not burnt out in a season.... What we can do is to plant a seed, nurture a seed-bearing plant here and there, and hope for a harvest that goes beyond the limits of our powers and the span of our lives.

—Rosemary Radford Ruether
Gaia and God

The community stagnates without the impulse of the individual. The impulse dies away without the sympathy of the community.

—William James

Somewhere, there are people to whom we can speak with passion without having the words catch in our throats.

—Starhawk
Dreaming the Dark

There is something magical about any intense, tightly knit group of people working together and playing together, feeling of being in the world while at the same time being apart from it.

—George Leonard & Michael Murphy
The Life We Are Given

It is difficult to accept that all my beloved communities are going to die, and that even while they exist there are incredible spaces between human beings, even the closest.

—Madeleine L'Engle
The Irrational Season

... letting pain be pain links us with others. All social movements and organization were born of pain. Not privatized pain or pain kept to oneself or the wallowing in one's own pain, but pain shared. Unemployment shared. Unjust taxes shared. The evil, bitter taste and experiences of racism, of sexism, of ageism—all shared.

—Matthew Fox
Original Blessing

There is a tendency for living things to join up, establish linkages, live inside each other, return to earlier arrangements, get along, whenever possible. This is a way of the world.

—Lewis Thomas
The Lives of a Cell

Community is oriented toward justice, not to what satisfies my personal need for warmth and kindness. The latter is friendship.

—Matthew Fox
  On Becoming a Musical Mystical Bear

Community is a terrible place. It is the place where our limitations and our egoism are revealed to us.... While we were alone, we believed we loved everyone. Now that we are with others, we realize how incapable we are of loving, how much we deny life to others ...

—Wayne Muller
  How, Then, Shall We Live?

What I saw now was the community imperfect and irresolute, but held together by the frayed and always fraying, incomplete and yet ever-holding bonds of the various sorts of affection.

—Wendell Berry
  Jayber Crow

Community is gathering around a fire and listening to someone tell a story.

—Bill Moyers

Margaret Mead defined an ideal community as one that has a place for every human gift.

—Mary Pipher
  Another Country

We all draw our life, our safety, our intellect, our information, our organiz-

ing ability from the common fund of the community.

—Walter Rauschenbusch
  Christianity and the Social Crisis

You can't call the community together and say, "Now you folks talk to each other for awhile," because then nobody would think of anything important to say. The important subjects come up accidentally.

—Wendell Berry

Call it a clan, call it a network, call it a tribe, call it a family. Whatever you call it, whoever you are, you need one.

—Jane Howard

COMPASSION

The first outburst of everything God does is compassion.

—Meister Eckhart

If we want a genuine smile, then first we must produce the basis for a smile to come. On every level of human life, compassion is the key thing.

—Dalai Lama
  A Policy of Kindness

To show compassion for an individual without showing concern for the structures of society that make him an object of compassion is to be sentimental rather than loving.

—William Sloane Coffin
  Credo

Compassion is a kind of fire—it disturbs, it surprises, it ignites, it burns, it sears, and it warms. Compassion incinerates denial; it especially warms lifestyles. Those who are touched by compassion have their lives turned upside down. That is not necessarily a bad thing.

—Matthew Fox
Creation Spirituality

Healing arises out of compassion. Compassion is a genuine concern for the pain of another. It is distinct from empathy, which requires identification with another and cannot be linked to one's own search for enlightenment. Compassion reflects a desire for the surcease of someone's sorrow, no matter the differences or similarities between healer and patient.

—Rosalyn Bruyere
Healers on Healing

Compassion is a spirituality of meat, not milk; of adults, not children; of love, not masochism; of justice, not philanthropy. It requires maturity, a big heart, a willingness to risk and imagination.

—Matthew Fox
A Spirituality Named Compassion

Our task must be to free ourselves from this prison by widening our circle of compassion to embrace all living creatures and the whole of nature in its beauty.

—Albert Einstein

It is through compassion that a person achieves the highest peak and deepest reach in his or her search for self-fulfillment.

—Arthur T. Jersild
The Psychology of Adolescence

Compassion is daring to acknowledge our mutual destiny so that we might move forward all together into the land which God is showing us.

—Henri J. M. Nouwen
With Open Hands

It happens [the birth of spiritual man out of the animal man] when you awaken at the level of the heart to compassion, com-passion, shared suffering: experienced participation in the suffering of another person. That's the beginning of humanity. And the meditations of religion properly are on that level, the heart level.

—Joseph Campbell
The Power of Myth

Compassion is not pity but celebration. Celebration is a forgetting in order to remember—a forgetting of ego, of problems, of difficulties.... Compassion seeks to understand the relatedness of all things.

—Matthew Fox
A Spirituality Named Compassion

The whole idea of compassion is based on a keen awareness of the interdependence of all these living beings, which are all part of one another and all involved in one another.

—Thomas Merton

Herr Muëller: The greatest tool for good, the most powerful way to change the world is to secretly commit little acts of compassion. You must behave as if your every act, even the smallest, impacted a thousand people for a hundred generations. Because it does.

—Thom Hartmann
The Prophet's Way

Compassion is the fire which the Lord has come to send on the earth.

—Thomas Aquinas

COMPLEXITY

There is a bright future for complexity, what with one thing always leading to another.

—E. G. White

In some manner not yet grasped, the universe came pre-wired to favor complex systems over entropy.... Complex systems seem to locate themselves at the edge of chaos, a zone of conflict and upheaval where the old and new are constantly at war.

—Gregg Easterbrook
A Moment on the Earth

Atoms arrange themselves into complicated structures from stars to snowflakes almost as if the particles were obeying a hidden yearning for organization and order.

—Mitchell Waldrop
Complexity

We aren't machines!

—Henri Poincare

CONFLICT

All life, animal and vegetable, seems in its essence like an effort to accumulate energy and then to let it flow into flexible channels, changeable in shape, at the end of which it will accomplish infinitely varied kinds of world.... But the impetus is finite, and it has been given once for all. It cannot overcome all obstacles. The movement it starts is sometimes turned aside, sometimes divided, always opposed; and the evolution of the organized world is the unrolling of this conflict.

—Henri Bergson
Creative Evolution

We must love them both, those whose opinions we share and those whose opinions we reject. For both have labored in the search for truth and both have helped us in the finding of it.

—Thomas Aquinas

Community is not opposed to conflict. On the contrary, community is precisely that place where an arena for creative conflict is protected by the compassionate fabric of human caring itself.

—Parker J. Palmer
Community, Conflict, and Ways of Knowing

Conflict is the habit of the ages.

—Calvin Miller
The Finale

Perceive all conflict as patterns of energy seeking harmonious balance as elements in a whole.

—Dhyani Ywahoo

Me and my cousin against the stranger; me and my brother against my cousin.

—Saudi proverb

An eye for an eye only makes the whole world blind.

—Mohandas (Mahatma) Gandhi

CONNECTION

All things are penetrated with connectedness.

—Hildegard of Bingen

All things are connected like the blood which unites one family. Man did not weave the web of life; he is merely a strand in it. Whatever he does to the web he does to himself.

—Seattle/Seatlh

All things are connected like blood which unites one family. All things are connected. Whatever befalls the earth befalls the children of the earth. We do not weave the web of life, we are merely a strand in it. Whatever we do to the web, we do to ourselves.

—Seattle/Seatlh

When we seek for connection, we restore the world to wholeness. Our seemingly separate lives become meaningful as we discover how truly necessary we are to each other.

—Margaret Wheatley

Only connect.

—E. M Forster

CONSCIENCE

Our conscience is not yet wholly conscience. It is a twilight. The transition from the non-intentional to the intentional is noticeable. We are not awake enough.

—Emmanual Levinas
Beyond the Verse: Talmudic Readings and Lectures

Every man has a conscience—it is a property of normal human beings. But owing to civilization this function has become crusted over and has ceased to work, except in special circumstances where the associations are very strong. Then, it functions for a little time and disappears again. Such moments are due to strong shock, great sorrow, or insult. At these times conscience unites with personality and essence, which otherwise are altogether separate.

—G. I. Gurdjieff
Views from the Real World

The voice of conscience is so delicate that it is easy to stifle it; but it is also so clear that it is impossible to mistake it.

—Anne Louise Germaine
(Madame de Staël)
Oeuvres Complètes

Conscience is a little three-cornered thing in the heart that stands still when we are good, but when we are bad it turns around a lot. If we keep on going wrong, soon the corners wear off and it does not hurt any more.

—Arizona Indian saying

CONSCIOUSNESS

We are living in a very early period of the Michael Age and what we now possess as intelligence is only just beginning to unfold in general human consciousness.

—Rudolf Steiner
  The Archangel Michael

Consciousness is a sign that we haven't yet learned to live from the soul.

—Thomas Moore
  Original Self

The crisis is in our consciousness, not in the world.

—Jiddu Krishnamurti

When a man learns that just as he broods over himself so does God yearn for him and look for him, he is at the beginning of a higher level of consciousness.

—Adin Steinsaltz
  The Thirteen-Petalled Rose

To be conscious means to be aware, to know, to perceive, to observe. The content of consciousness is your belief, your pleasure, your experience, the particle of knowledge that you have gathered, either through external experience or through

your fears, attachments, pain, the agony of loneliness, sorrow, the search for something more than mere physical existence; all that is one's consciousness with its content.

—Jiddu Krishnamurti
  On Nature and the Environment

Our lives are like islands in the sea, or like trees in the forest, which co-mingle their roots in the darkness underground. Just so, there is a continuum of cosmic consciousness, against which our individuality builds but accidental fences, and into which our several minds plunge as into a mother sea or reservoir.

—William James

It is no longer possible to deny that our thoughts and desires might influence our environment. The most recent cosmologies all include consciousness as an active participating factor in reality. The new explanations of how the world works are strangely like the old beliefs of non-literate people everywhere.

—Lyall Watson
  Lightning Bird

Through becoming conscious we have been driven out of paradise; through consciousness we can come back to paradise.

—Heinrich Jacob
  Explorations in Human Potentialities

The prime characteristic of cosmic consciousness is, as its name implies, a consciousness of the cosmos, that is, of the life and order of the universe … a state of moral exaltation, an indescribable feeling of elevation, elation, and joyousness and a quickening of the moral

sense.... With these come ... a consciousness of eternal life, not conviction that he
shall have this, but the consciousness that
he has it already.

—R. M. Bucke
Cosmic Consciousness

It is the polarity and the integration of
these two modes of consciousness, the
complementary workings of the intellect
and the intuitive, which underlies our
highest achievement.

—Robert Ornstein
The Psychology of Consciousness

If things are evolving, and if human
consciousness is evolving along with
everything else, where do we find a
standpoint from which to understand the
whole process?

—Philip Sherrard
Human Image: World Image

When I picture this vulnerable little ball
turning in the universe and I study the
thrust of the dreams people bring me, I'm
convinced that consciousness is trying
to move from power to love. If we're
going to be a global village, members
of that large community, receiving each
other with all our differences, we need
to accept ourselves as imperfect human
beings. That involves a whole new
understanding of what love is.

—Marion Woodman
Conscious Femininity

I believed, and still believe, that consciousness comes both through spirit and
through matter.

—Marion Woodman
Bone

The human kingdom, beneath the floor
of the comparatively neat little dwelling
that we call our consciousness, goes
down into unsuspected Aladdin caves.
There not only jewels but also dangerous
jinn abide.

—Joseph Campbell
The Hero with a Thousand Faces

What is not brought to consciousness
comes to us as Fate.

—Carl G. Jung

Somewhere in consciousness there
lies a land undiscovered, a land not
yet revealed by religion, philosophy or
science.... I know that it exists for it continually pushes itself into my awareness.
I know that when it discloses itself, it will
change the nature of mankind: wars will
be no more, and the lamb will lie down
with the lion.

—Joel Goldsmith
A Parenthesis in Eternity

It seems that we have made a dreadful
mistake by identifying ourselves
exclusively with our consciousness, by
imagining that we are only what we know
about ourselves. There is much more to
us, parts that speak in tongues that take
some getting used to.

—Lyall Watson
Lifetide

There is nothing in the shiny forest of
space and time that is not rooted in the
center of all consciousness and does not
draw its life from there.

—Moyra Caldecott
The Lily and the Bull

Entropy is the normal state of consciousness—a condition that is neither useful nor enjoyable.

—Mihaly Csikszentmihalyi
Flow

George Miller, cognitive psychologist, describes conscious cognition this way: Two passengers at the ship's rail: "There sure is a lot of water in the ocean," says one. "Yes!—and we've seen only the top of it."

—David G. Myers
Intuition

CONTEMPLATION

To contemplate is to see, to minister is to make visible.

—Henri J. M. Nouwen

Contemplation is the goal of all life. It is knowledge by love.

—Bede Griffiths

We become contemplatives when God discovers Himself in us. At that moment, the point of our contact with Him opens out and we pass through the center of our souls and enter eternity.

—Thomas Merton

Contemplation is simply a different way of seeing … contemplating refuses to live on the surface of things. It is going down and lifting up; it is the act of seeing death where there seems only to be life; seeing life where there seems only to be death.

—James Carroll

The act of contemplation is for the mystic a psychic gateway: a method of going from one level of consciousness to another. In technical language it is the conditions under which he shifts his "field of perception" and obtains his characteristic outlook on he universe.

—Evelyn Underhill
Mysticism

CONTENTMENT

As long as I am content to know that He is infinitely greater than I am, that I cannot know Him unless He shows himself to me, I will have peace and He will be near me and in me and I will rest in Him.

—Thomas Merton

Be content with what you have; rejoice in the way things are. When you realize there is nothing lacking, the whole world belongs to you.

—Lao Tzu

True contentment is the power of getting out of any situation all that there is in it.

—G. K. Chesterton

CONTEXT

We always live in a context. We apprehend a thing in its surroundings, sensory or mental, physical or cultural. To move with our remembered experiences from a familiar context to an unfamiliar one jolts us into awareness, compels us to focus on the particulars of our surroundings, both old and new. It forces us, that is, to take things apart, but also invites us to put them together again with new meanings.

—Loren Eiseley
The Unexpected Universe

The form, then, is that part of the world which we decide to shape, while leaving the rest of the world where it is. The context is that part of the world which puts demands on this form.... The form is the solution to the problem; the context defines the problem.

—Christopher Alexander

No word in context can have more meaning than the writer thinks into it. When a writer does not care about the meaning of a word, we know it.

— Guy Davenport
The Geography of the Imagination

Without context, words and actions have no meaning at all.

—Gregory Bateson
Mind and Nature

CONTROL

Those who control what young people are taught, and what they experience—what they see, hear, think, and believe—will determine the future course for the nation.

—James Dobson
Children at Risk

The opposite of control is celebration... celebration is about energies dancing.

—Matthew Fox
The Coming of the Cosmic Christ

Psychologists have done elegant experiments showing that in rats a lack of control leads to ulcers and the inability to reject cancer, and in humans to anxiety, depression, and defects in the immune system. But what is control?... In the spiritual sense, control refers to the feeling that we are the center of the universe—the fear that the sun might not rise without our intervention.

—Joan Borysenko
Healers on Healing

The British learned the technique of fingerprinting from the Bengalis and then used it to control, them and other Indians.

—Wendy Doniger
The Implied Spider

Our age and that age of the first century have more in common than we think... Both times can be characterized as cosmically scared, frightened ages, caught under principalities and powers where tiny little human beings just know that they cannot do much, that they are not in control, that they are just caught.

—Krister Stendahl
Paul among Jews and Gentiles

CONVERSATION

"What is more edifying than light?"— "Conversation." Comes the answer in Goethe's fairy tale. But this is true only of certain special conversations which, aiming beyond words at wordless understanding, rest on such an understanding or "harmony" in the sphere beyond words.

—Georg Kühlewind
Becoming Aware of the Logos

Conversation is the medium through which collective action emerged. It is the primary vehicle through which we as individuals conceive our world and embrace relationships with others.

—Juanita Brown & David Isaacs
"Building Corporations as Communities," *Community Building*

If you're talking, you are being creative. You're taking concepts and changing them into words so that you can communicate with me. You're more creative than you think you are.

—David Paladin
Painting the Dream

What truly matters in our lives is measured through conversation.

—Peter Block
Stewardship

COSMOS/ COSMOLOGY

Harmony of the Spheres: The Pythagorean concept of the cosmos as consisting of separate spheres, one each for the planets, moon and sun, which move around the earth at different velocities, producing different sounds.

—*Harvard Dictionary of Music*

Our world: cosmos; everything outside it: chaos.

—Mircea Eliade
The Sacred and the Profane

The whole story, which now spans some 14 billion years, tells of how the first-few-minutes mix of hydrogen and helium gases formed into spinning patterns of movements that became the galaxies, within which atoms collided and generated huge amounts of energy. The first stars were born …

—Walter Truett Anderson
The Next Enlightenment

When Krishna's mother looked inside his mouth, she saw in his throat the night sky filled with all the stars in the cosmos.

—Annie Dillard
For the Time Being

On a grand scale, we might envision the entire cosmos as a vast light-pond with ripples spreading, interpenetrating, and creating complex patterns of interactions throughout.

—Allan Combs & Mark Holland
Synchronicity

The term cosmos refers to the totality of the sidereal scheme, including all galaxies, all nebulae, all stars, all planets, all beings, and the divine intelligence associated with them.

—Geoffrey Hodson
Hidden Wisdom

You have to infer the whole dragon from the parts you can see and touch.

—Maxine Hong Kingston
The Woman Warrior

The only hope of people today is probably a renewal of our certainty that we are rooted in the Earth and, at the same time, in the cosmos. This awareness endows us with the capacity for self-transcendence.

—Václav Havel

If the idea of the universe would be presented to the child in the right way, it will create in him admiration and wonder... The stars, earth, stones, life of all kinds form a whole in relation with each other ...

—Maria Montessori

Water occupies a median position between earth and universe and it is the port of entry through which cosmic peripheral forces pass into the earth's realm.... Without a new awareness of water's spiritual nature, we will be unable to save this planet that has been given us as our habitation.

—Theodor Schwenk &
Wolfram Schwenk
Water: The Element of Life

COURAGE

To see what is right and not to do it is to lack courage or principle.

—Confucius

Courage is not simply one of the virtues, but the form of every virtue at the testing point.

—C. S. Lewis
The Screwtape Letters

Life shrinks or expands in proportion to one's courage.

—Anaïs Nin

"The bamboo for prosperity," a Japanese friend explained to me, "the pine for long life, the plum for courage.... the plum for courage because the plum puts forth blossoms while the snow is still on the ground.

—Anne Morrow Lindbergh
Gift from the Sea

I believe that for anyone to create one's world in any of the arts takes courage.

—Georgia O'Keefe

It takes courage to open oneself vulnerably to the depths of a book. The moment I set words down on a page I become responsible for those words.

—Madeleine L'Engle
The Irrational Season

Our word "courage" comes from the French word coeur, "heart." Courage is a willingness to act from the heart, to let your heart lead the way, not knowing what will be required of you next, and if you can do it.

—Jean Shinoda Bolen
Gods in Everyman

Intimacy requires courage because risk is inescapable … it is easier in our society to be naked physically than to be naked psychologically or spiritually—easier to share our body than to share our hopes, fears, aspirations, which are felt to be more personal.

—Rollo May

To dare to be aware of the facts of the universe in which we are existing calls for courage.

—Wilfred Bion
 Attention and Interpretation

We live in a time when the greatest form of courage is to act as if our lives made a difference.

—William Sullivan
 The Secret of the Incas

Dare you have the courage to be who you really are?

—Pir Vilayat Inayat Khan
 Awakening

If you don't dare say "no," how will you ever dare say "yes?"

—Paul Tournier
 The Adventure of Living

To reveal myself openly and honesty takes the rawest kind of courage.

—e. e. cummings

CREATION

Now when Chaos had begun to condense, but force and form were not yet manifest, and there was nought named, nought done, who could know its shape? Nevertheless Heaven and Earth first parted, and the three Deities performed the commencement of Creation; the Passive and Active Essences then developed, and the Two Spirits become the ancestors of all things.

—The Kojiki

Creation myths are collective stories of parenting.

—David Leeming
 Myth: A Biography of Belief

The Holy One created the world like an embryo. As the embryo proceeds from the navel outwards, so God began to create the world from the navel onwards and from there it was spread out in different directions.

—Mircea Eliade

Cuzco means navel.… Cuzco was founded at the location of an uncovered navel stone that emerged from a sweetwater marsh.

—William Sullivan
 The Secret of the Incas

If the particles that we now are came originally from an explosion in or near the sun, an the sun itself came from yet another explosion in a kindred universe, then there is no limit either to the past or to the future, life of some sort is continuous, it has no beginning and no end. Our world may burn, disintegrate: there will be others. New explosions will form new particles, which will unite. Life will go on. Creation is at work, has always been at work, will always be at work.

—Daphne du Maurier
The Rebecca Notebook

The act of creation itself remains a mystery to the creature… the fundamental mark of the created world is becoming, emergence, development, fulfillment.

—Sergei Bulgakov
Sophia

The Creation is continuing and we are a part of it. We are the womb of the future, the co-authors of Creation. Our destiny is to share with the Creative Intention, to take more responsibility for this Intention. As our awareness of it grows, we are becoming co-creators.

—Barbara Marx Hubbard
The Evolutionary Journey

There is no magic, there is only The Creation. There is no supernatural, but there are an infinite number of possible natures.

—Joseph Chilton Pearce
The Crack in the Cosmic Egg

Creation stories are not stories, they're sacred mysteries. You don't talk about sacred mysteries.

—Paula Gunn Allen
Winged Words

Longing: the first ground of creation.

—Phoenician proverb

CREATIVE/ CREATIVITY

God creates the world from moment to moment. Should He desist for an instant the world would perish.

—Rob Swigart
The Book of Revelations

Humankind, full of creative possibilities is God's work. Humankind is called to co-create.

—Hildegard of Bingen

Live creatively, breathing existence.

—Rudolf Steiner

God is creatively present in everyone in every moment whether we are aware of it or not. But when we are in the state of silent gratefulness, we are aware of His Presence.

—Paul Tillich
The Eternal Now

When you are completely caught up in something, you become oblivious to things around you, or to the passage of time. It is this absorption in what you are doing that frees your unconscious and releases your creative imagination.

—Rollo May
The Courage to Create

The creative process is generation and birth as well as transformation and rebirth. The perpetual self-renewal and the dependence on grace of the person

who opens to create are a human parallel
to the eternal rebirth of all that is created.

—Erich Neumann
 Art and the Creative Unconsciousness

The union of feminine and masculine
energies within the individual is the basis
of all creation. Female intuition plus male
action equals creativity.

—Shakti Gawain
 Living in the Light

The truly creative mind in any field is no
more than this: a human creature born
abnormally, inhumanely sensitive.... They
must create, must pour out creation. By
some strange, unknown urgency they are
not really alive unless they are creating.

—Pearl Buck

In the Cave of 200 Hands there are 300
hand images painted in red, brown,
pink.... In the caves, humans first
experienced themselves as co-creators
with the Divine.

—Robert Ryan
 The Strong Eye of Shamanism

We need to remember that we are all
created creative and can invent new sce-
narios as frequently as they are needed.

—Maya Angelou

It doesn't matter if you've never picked
up a pen or can't draw a straight line
or flunked out of music class, you have
a creative self waiting to be awakened
or amplified… You are an original;

therefore, your inspirations are original
as well.

—Gail McMeekin
 *The 12 Secrets of Highly
 Creative Women*

We are not victims. We are not guests.
You and I are colleagues and co-creators
with Him—living in the midst of ongoing
creation and called upon to celebrate
everything that is.

—Martin Bell
 Return of the Wolf

Unless we are creators, we are not fully
alive… Remember, the root word of
humble and human is the same: humus:
earth. We are dust. We are created; it is
God who made us and not we ourselves.
But we were made to be co-creators with
our maker.

—Madeleine L'Engle
 Walking on Water

A first-rate soup is more creative than a
second-rate painting.

—Abraham Maslow

We have to realize that a creative being
lives within ourselves, whether we like it
or not, and that we must get out of its way,
for it will give us no peace until we do.

—Mary Caroline (M. C.) Richards
 Centering

Each person has an inbuilt impetus
toward originality, the urge to perform
in some new manner; to excel in a

completely new way; to do something no one else can do or has done.

—Jane Roberts
The World View of Paul Cézanne

It takes awareness, free will, and purpose to achieve a life of adventure and creativity. The god within mankind is the spirit of purposeful and creative adventure.

—René Dubos
A God Within

The compulsion to take ourselves seriously is in inverse proportion to our creative capacity. When the creative flow dries up, all we have left is our importance.

—Eric Hoffer

When Alexander the Great visited Diogenes and asked whether he could do anything for the famed teacher, Diogenes replied, "Only stand out of my light." Perhaps some day we shall know how to heighten creativity. Until then, one of the best things we can do for creative men and women is to stand out of their light.

—John Gardner
Self-Renewal

[Creativity is] the river beneath the river, which flows and flows into our lives.... The creative force flows over the terrain of our psyches looking for the natural hollows, the arroyos, the channels that exist in us.

—Clarissa Pinkola Estés
Women Who Run with the Wolves

Creative people are especially good at ordering their lives so that what they do,

when, and with whom will enable them to do their best work.

—Mihaly Csikszentmihalyi
Finding Flow

In the future, creativity will be meaningful only if it is relevant to all humanity.

—David Bohm

In order to create there must be a dynamic force, and what force is greater than love?

—Igor Stravinsky

With the word creative we stand under a mystery. And from time to time that mystery, as if it were a sun, sends down upon one head or another a sudden shaft of light—by grace one feels, rather than deserving, for it always is something given, free, unsought, unexpected. It is useless, possibly even profane, to ask for an explanation.

—Pamela Travers
Creators on Creating

Creativity is a continual surprise.

—Ray Bradbury

Our mantra used to be: Grow or die. Now it's: Get creative or collapse.

—Alan Atkisson
Believing Cassandra

CRITIC/CRITICISM

Don't waste your force in criticism. Seek to transform misfortune into good.

—Rudolf Steiner
Initiation and Its Results

One must handle an encounter with an "other" who cares about logic, consistency, directness, and verbal argument very differently from an encounter with an "other" who is concerned about emotion, respect, subtlety, and nonverbal forms of communication. Encounters where these concerns are in synch are far more likely to go well than encounters where the mismatch is pronounced.

—Howard Gardner
Changing Minds

An artist who theorizes about his work is no longer artist but critic.

—H. G. Wells

When I criticize someone, I overlook the possibility that God may be using his faults to correct mine.

—H. A. Hartwick

People ask for criticism, but they only want praise.

—Somerset Maugham

He has the right to criticize who has the heart to help.

—Abraham Lincoln

CULTURE

All culture originates in the spiritual world.... Here, on earth, we merely witness the way in which one event follows the other according to physical laws, while the great spiritual causes remain hidden from us.

—Rudolf Steiner
The Archangel Michael

Suppose that we were able to share meanings freely without a compulsive urge to impose our own view or to conform to those of others and without distortion and self-deception. Would not this constitute a real revolution in culture and therefore eventually in society?

—David Bohm
Changing Consciousness

We have drifted into a culture that fragments our thoughts, that detaches the word from the self and the self from a community ... we are losing the spaces to dance with the every-changing patterns of life. We need to invent a new learning model for business, education, health care, government and family. This invention will come from the patient, concerted efforts of communities of people invoking aspiration and wonder. As these communities manage to produce fundamental changes, we will regain our memory ... the memory of the whole.

—Peter Senge
"Creating Quality Communities"
Community Building

Culture evolves out of the experience of living with a land.

—Linda Hogan
Department of the Interior

The word culture is like a chameleon, Julie. It has no color of its own but rather takes color from its setting. It means one thing when you talk about the culture of chimpanzees, another when you talk about the culture of General Motors .... You'll know you're among people of your culture if the food is all owned, if it's all under lock and key.

—Daniel Quinn
My Ishmael

Culture has always been created by taking new social risks. It has always been scary to step out of our isolated journeys into the circle of firelight, to show up in the company of strangers, to stand there and ask for entrance, or to offer it.

—Christina Baldwin
Calling the Circle

The sudden appearance of an entirely new subculture of individuals who are attempting to construct a whole new approach to the world is what anthropologists call a cultural revitalization movement. It's what a culture does when it is willing to face the fact that the old story doesn't work anymore and that we need to write a new story in which we explore a whole new set of ways of seeing ourselves, our problems and their solutions.... Paul Ray calls it "a lurch toward the new."

—Hank Wesselman
Medicinemaker

Some theorists argue that culture is more than a set of rules, habits and artifacts; it's a structure of feelings, an historically patterned collective identity that is

ritualized and celebrated through its religions and its rhetorics.

—Lynn Schofield Clark
From Angels to Aliens

A culture implies a shared meaning.

—David Bohm
On Dialogue

A mind is not a mind without a culture around it.

—Alison Jolly
Lucy's Legacy

When civilizations truly crash, no one at the time can imagine the depth of the fall.... After Rome fell, Europe went unwashed for a thousand years. Cities emptied, literacy vanished ... the skein of culture was reduced to fragile wisps.

—Stewart Brand
The Clock of the Long Now

Culture is the shape a place takes when it's inside the head of its peoples—all the habits, attitudes and values they take for granted.

—Mary Pipher
Another Country

For Man was a culture-bearer as well as a soul-bearer, but his cultures were not immortal and they could die with a race or an age, and then human reflections of meaning and human portrayals of truth receded, and truth and meaning resided, useless, only in the objective logos of Nature and the ineffable Logos of God.

—Walter Miller, Jr.
A Canticle for Leibowitz

The city is to culture what wilderness is to nature: the epicenter of diversity; the hotbed of evolution, the font from which energy and information flow to the ends of the earth. A great city is a cultural rain forest, endlessly diverse, every inch stuffed to the gills.

—Evan Eisenberg
The Ecology of Eden

Without environment there is no sustainable culture; without sustainable culture there is no sustainable community; without sustainable community there is no sustainable globalization.

—Thomas L. Friedman
The Lexus and the Olive Tree

CYCLES

Time permeates the universe and through its cycles governs all events. For the Maya, the norm of life was to attune what were and would be the burdens of time. Since the cycles were gods, knowledge of time was the root of theological thought.

—René Dubos
A God within So Human an Animal

We enter a "new turning" every 20 years or so. At each turning, people change how they feel about themselves, the culture, the nation and the future.

—William Strauss & Neil Howe
The Fourth Turning

The seventh year always transforms man. It brings about a new life, a new character and a different state.

—Martin Luther

When the Atlantic meets the Pacific, the waters are turbulent. When one major historical epoch meets another, the psychic and emotional waters are likewise turbulent. Navigating those waters is difficult, but mastering the waves brings an exhilaration that those living in less exciting times will never know.

—Marianne Williamson
The Healing of America

Perhaps this is the most important thing for me to take back from beach-living: simply the memory that each cycle of the tide is valid; each cycle of the wave is valid; each cycle of a relationship is valid.

—Anne Morrow Lindbergh
Gift from the Sea

To live, to survive on earth, to care for the soil and to worship, all are bound at the root to the idea of a cycle.

—Wendell Berry
The Unsettling of America

DANCE

Learn to dance, or the angels won't know
what to do with you.

—Augustine

In the summer of 1883, at Carberry,
Manitoba, I had some fifteen baby prairie
chickens hatched under a hen. When
they were two weeks old, we were visited
by a cold driving storm.... I put the
chilled and cowering little things under
the stove.... One of the tiny things, no
bigger than a sparrow ... ran across
the tin, crowing a little bubbling crow,
beating his wings, and stamping with his
two pink feet so rapidly that it sounded
like a small kettledrum.... At once the
rest of them leaped up.... Every one took
the same position—head low, wings out,
beating, tail-stump raised and violently
vibrated, the feet pounding hard ...
these chickens danced exactly as their
parents do, without ever having seen
those parents .... It was evidently and
unquestionably nothing more nor less
than a true dance—a vigorous, rhythmic,
athletic expression of health and joy.

—Ernest Thompson Seton
   The Worlds of Ernest Thompson Seton

I believe that we learn by practice.
Whether it means to learn to dance by
practicing dancing or to learn to live by
practicing living, the principles are the
same. In each it is the performance of

a dedicated precise set of acts, physical or intellectual, from which comes shape of achievement, a sense of one's being, a satisfaction of spirit. One becomes in some area an athlete of God.

—Martha Graham
Blood Memory

There is only the dance.

—T. S. Eliot

Sound and gesture are contemporary, identical and indistinguishable.... Linked to its own past, the gesture fills up with music and becomes rounded, like the universe.... The beauty of gesture renders time visible.

—Catherine David
The Beauty of Gesture

I was born by the sea ... my first idea of movement of the dance, certainly came from the rhythm of the waves ... now I would like to no longer dance to anything but the rhythm of my soul.

—Isadora Duncan

Just as all dances have resting points, so too does all spirituality.

—Maria Harris
Dance of the Spirit

We insist on permanency, on duration, on continuity; when the only continuity possible, in life as in love, is in growth, in fluidity—in freedom, in the sense that the dancers are free, barely touching as they pass, but partners in the same pattern.

—Anne Morrow Lindbergh
Gift from the Sea

The Wu Li Masters know that "science" and "religion" are only dances, and that those who follow them are dancers. The dancers may claim to follow "truth" or claim to seek "reality", but the Wu Li Masters know better. They know the true love of all dancers is dancing.

—Gary Zukav
The Dancing Wu Li Masters

Through dance we experience reality as immediate to us ... we are identified with the universe.... Dance, for us, is a religious expression.

—Dona Marimba Richards
Let the Circle Be Unbroken

At every age ... we are called to join in a dance whose steps must be learned along the way, so it is important to attend and to respond.

—Mary Catherine Bateson
Peripheral Visions

The danse macabre is a waltz with death. This is truth we cannot afford to shy away from.

—Stephen King
Danse Macabre

I have trained myself always to be able to dance in the service of thought.

—Søren Kierkegaard

Music begins to atrophy when it departs too far from the dance; poetry begins to atrophy when it gets too far from music.

—Ezra Pound

Snoopy: To dance is to live.

—Charles Schulz

DARKNESS

The Light that is God flows out and darkens every light.

—Meister Eckhart

Light and darkness dancing together, born together, born of each other, neither preceding, neither following, both fully being, in joyful rhythm. The morning stars sang together and the ancient harmonies were new and it was good. It was very good. And then a dazzling star turned its back on the dark, and it swallowed the dark, and in swallowing the dark it became the dark, and there was something wrong with the dark, as there was something wrong with the light. And it was not good. The glory of the harmony was broken by screeching, by hissing, by laughter which held no merriment but was hideous, horrendous cacophony.

—Madeleine L'Engle
A Swiftly Tilting Planet

This sacred presence ... energizes the substance of the soul from which the new will be crafted However, it also acts as a powerful purgative, bringing to the surface dark and hidden impulses and uninte- grated material within the human psyche which, by being brought up into the light, may be dealt with and transformed.

—David Spangler
A Pilgrim in Aquarius

There are no dark times. There are only people with sawdust in their eyes.

—Nancy Woods
Many Woods

Black is probably the most ancient color, the primal birth-source whence everything emerged. Darkness is the great canvas against which beauty becomes visible.... Black is also the color of ink. Books are printed in black ink ... characters and adventures live inside lines of black narrative.

—John O'Donohue
Beauty

One does not become enlightened by imagining figures of light, but by making the darkness conscious.

—Carl G. Jung

Each of us has a Kali side. Bring her into the light.

—May Sarton

The wonderful working mysteries that are our bodies are filled with darkness. Our heart works just fine—in the dark. Our livers, our intestines, our brain, all the beautiful and harmonious and working parts of our blessed bodies go about their everyday business—at night and during the day—completely in the dark.

—Matthew Fox
Original Blessing

We can know the dark, and dream it into a new image.

—Starhawk
Dreaming the Dark

Turn up the lights. I don't want to go home in the dark.

—O. Henry (William Sydney Porter)

DEATH

Death is the temporary end of a temporary phenomenon.

—Siddhartha Gautama (Buddha)

Do not seek death. Death will find you. But seek the road which makes death a fulfillment.

—Dag Hammarskjöld
Markings

On every level death is the forerunner of life renewed.... The acorn dies for the emergence of the oak. At the birth of the baby the maiden dies to become a mother. In regions of the mind every new idea rings the death knell of ideas worn-out. In the life of the spirit, only through death can there be immortality.

—Irene Claremont de Castillejo
Knowing Woman

… instead of men being, as it were, patches of life scattered through an infinite sea of non-living substance, they are in reality specks of relative death in an infinite ocean of life.

—R. M. Bucke
Cosmic Consciousness

Death is a confirmation of the believer's creed. For the skeptic it is discovery, immense and late.

—Calvin Miller
The Finale

Death cannot be understood without compassion. Compassion teaches me that when my brother dies, I too die. Compassion teaches me that my brother and I are one.

—Thomas Merton
No Man Is an Island

If you are mindful of death, it will not come as a surprise—you will not be anxious. You will feel that death is merely like changing your clothes.

—Dalai Lama
A Policy of Kindness

Nothing is more creative than death, since it is the whole secret of life. It means that the past must be abandoned, that the unknown cannot be avoided, that "I" cannot continue, and that nothing can be ultimately fixed. When a man knows this, he lives for the first time in his life. By holding his breath, he loses it. By letting it go he finds it.

—Alan Watts
The Wisdom of Insecurity

I see too many men delay their exits with a sickly, slow reluctance to leave the stage. It's bad theater as well as bad living.

—John Steinbeck
Travels with Charlie

You don't get to choose how you're going to die or when. You can only decide how you're going to live.

—Joan Baez

We die containing a richness of lovers and tribes, tastes we have swallowed, bodies we have plunged into and swum up as if rivers of wisdom, characters we have climbed into as if trees, fears we have hidden in as if caves. I wish for all this to be marked on my body when I am dead.

—Michael Ondaatze
The English Patient

The act of dying is a huge personal event. Nothing else that you do in your life will bring such change.

—John O'Donohue
Beauty

Without death there would scarcely have been poets on earth.

—Thomas Mann

No thought exists in me which death has not carved with his chisel.

—Michelangelo
(di Lodovico Buonarroti Simoni)

Death does not have to be a catastrophic, destructive thing; indeed, it can be viewed as one of the most constructive, positive, and creative elements of culture and life.... Dying is an integral part of life, as natural and predictable as being born.... If we really want to live we must have the courage to recognize that life is ultimately very short, and that everything we do counts.

—Elisabeth Kübler-Ross
Death, the Final Stage of Growth

Death is contagious ... it is contracted the moment we are conceived.... Death may be an ordinary, everyday affair, but it is not a statistic. It is something that happens to people.

—Madeleine L'Engle
The Summer of the Great Grandmother

The denial of death is one reason for our tolerance of violence. What we watch is not ourselves. We are spectators not participants. Death becomes tolerable when it happens to others.

—Peter J. Kreeft
Love is Stronger Than Death

To die is not to close our eyes when we come to the end of our lives, but to choose to live in too few dimensions.

—J. B. Priestly
Man and Time

A dying man needs to die, as a sleepy man needs to sleep, and there comes a time when it is wrong as well as useless to resist.

—Steward Alsop
Stay of Execution

Death ends a life, but it does not end a relationship, which struggles on in the survivor's mind toward some resolution, which it may never find.

—Robert Anderson
I Never Sang for My Father

There is not death. How can there be death if everything is part of the God-head? The soul never dies and the body is never really alive.

—Isaac Bashevis Singer
A Friend of Kafka and Other Stories

The loss of a parent catapults you into the next generation.

—Richard Adams
The Girl in a Swing

Death is not final, it only interrupts.

—Tom Brown, Jr.
The Search

Your creativity needs your awareness of death for its energy, just as your muscles need long and painful workouts. Cherish your awareness of death as a gift to you from the universe.

—Brian Swimme
The Universe Is a Green Dragon

Every man's death diminishes me.

—John Donne

You have to learn to do everything, even to die.

—Gertrude Stein

Kübler-Ross claimed that many of the people who underwent these experiences [Near-Death-Experiences] resented our desperate attempt to bring them back to life. Death is the feeling of peace and hope. Not one of them has ever been afraid to die again.

—Philip Kapleau
The Wheel of Life and Death

Dying is letting go, shedding, freeing. Sometimes death is a struggle if you have forgotten that you are the creator and you want to cling to your creation. Dying is like an exhalation. You exhale and the body drops off. You just step out of it and walk away.

—Diane Mariechild
Mother Wit

No one dies before he chooses. No one begins a life without knowing how he will end it.… The last blessing we will confer through this body will be given during the act of dying. It is our departing gift, but not the end of our giving.

—Hugh Prather
There Is a Place Where You Are Not Alone

I hold that it is our death and more especially, our consciousness of death, that allows us to be fully human, forces us to define ourselves and allows the possibility of meaning.

—Carol Ochs
Beyond the Sex of God

If physical death is the price that I must pay to free my white brother and sisters from a permanent death of the spirit, then nothing can be more redemptive.

—Martin Luther King, Jr.

When I thought I was learning to live I was also learning to die.

—Leonardo da Vinci
Codex Atlanticus

Death is no more than passing from one room into another. But there's a difference for me, you know. Because in that other room I shall be able to see.

—Helen Keller

A well-spent day brings happy sleep; so life well used brings happy death.

—Leonardo da Vinci

I personally like the certainty of death. It is amazingly relaxing to realize that one can't do everything. If I knew I were going to live forever, I would feel obliged to fix all my imperfections. I would have to learn many more languages; I would worry about my teeth not holding out; I would have to make amends for all the mistakes I have made.

—Esther Dyson

Each of us will die, naked and alone, on some battlefield not of our own choosing.

—Mary Pipher
Another Country

Death is the side of life which is turned away from us and upon which we shed no light.

—Rainer Maria Rilke

Do not fear your death. For when that moment arrives, I will draw my breath

and your soul will come to Me like a needle to a magnet.

—Mechtild of Magdeburg

Death is not the ultimate tragedy in life. The ultimate tragedy is to die without discovering the possibilities of full growth.

—Norman Cousins
Head First: The Biology of Hope

It is said in Celtic countries that a death appears first in the sky, then little by little its darkness descends until at last it touches the earth and becomes a reality in this world.

—Kathleen Raine
The Lion's Mouth

Christians NEVER say goodbye. Go under the Mercy was a phrase these Oxford friends parted with.... Sleep under the Protection.... Heaven is coming home.

—C. S. Lewis & Sheldon Vanauken
A Severe Mercy

To die gracefully is to live fully; to cling too tightly to life is to kill it prematurely.

—Clyde Reid
Celebrate the Temporary

Stars, dinosaurs and spermatozoa must die for us to be born … as worlds had to die for us to be born, so we must die to worlds after worlds once we are born.

—Daphne du Maurier

The day we die, the wind comes down to take away our footprints.

—Southern Bushman proverb

The reason I don't regret dying is that I have had a really good time.

—Studs Terkel's last words

Indians.

—Henry David Thoreau's last word

One of us has got to go.

—Oscar Wilde's last words, turning his face to the ugly wallpaper in his rented room

Jesus, I see you. I'm coming.

—Julia Werner Anderson's last words (author's grandmother)

DEMONS

Slander is a turbulent demon … keep far away from him. Presumptuousness and complacency. Anger is a very malicious spirit. Covetousness is a savage one, and very difficult to tame. Doubt is an earthly spirit that is of the devil. And sadness is the most harmful of all the spirits.

—The Shepherd of Hermas

The madness of demons is rage; the madness of angels, hope.

—A. A. Attanasio
The Dragon and the Unicorn

DEPRESSION

When we go to a medicine person or healer because we are feeling disheartened, dispirited, or depressed, he or she might ask questions like, "When did you stop singing? When did you stop dancing? When did you stop being enchanted by stories? When did you begin finding discomfort in the sweet territory of silence?"

—Angeles Arrien
"Gateway to the Soul,"
Handbook for the Soul

Some say that women aren't more vulnerable to depression, only more comfortable asking for help.

—Diane Ackerman
An Alchemy of Mind

… it was the persistence of Churchill's recurrent fits of depression that seemed to follow him everywhere that caused Churchill to rename his recurrent emotional state his "black dog." … he felt this awareness of his inner shadow was a key component of his ability to sense, understand and deal with the dark energies that swirled from the hearts such as Hitler's and the other murderers of World War II.

—Paul Pearsall
The Heart's Code

I experience depression as a state of high potential energy, wound up and turned inward on itself. If that energy can be accessed and moved, it can be a catalyst for spontaneous healing.

—Andrew Weil
Spontaneous Healing

C. G. Jung made a significant contribution to our understanding of the psychology of depression … feelings of inadequacy, inertia, heaviness, sadness, blackness, lack of interest in life and the pull towards death—are apt descriptions of the lower depths of the psyche. It is no wonder that consciousness, normally activated by the opposite principles—spirit, light, energy, joy, curiosity, life—fights vigorously not to fall into the hands of the unconscious.... Jung discovered two other startling facts: that the unconscious deplores its depressed condition and longs to be made free of it, and that within its blackness it contains a germ of consciousness capable of unifying the conscious and unconscious parts of the psyche, thereby healing the split soul of man.

—V. Walter Odajnyk
Betwixt & Between

Depression comes from a sense of being deprived of something you want and do not have. Remember that you are deprived of nothing except by your own decision, and then decide otherwise.

—*A Course in Miracles*

Depression is a slowing down—the first step for deepening in soul work.

—James Hillman

Depression is a reaction to loss, real or imagined … it's a numbing state, a survival alternative … anger turned against self.

—E. Sue Blume
Secret Survivors

We must make a descent to become familiar with his [Hades] realm. Only

then is it possible to discover that there are riches to be found in the dimness, coldness, and darkness of what mystics refer to as the dark night of the soul and what more psychologically minded people know as a profound depression in which one is cut off from ordinary reality, unable to feel or to bear being in the "sunlight" of everyday.

—Jean Shinoda Bolen
Gods in Everyman

Depression occurs when we lose confidence in our own coping mechanisms.

—Willard Gaylin
Feelings

Sartre felt depressed and threatened by the isness of an oak tree. I suppose the perfect isness of anything would be frightening without the hope of God.

—Madeleine L'Engle
A Circle of Quiet

DESPAIR

It is precisely the despair of our times that convinces me that a renaissance is right around the corner.

—Matthew Fox

It is better to find God on the threshold of despair than to risk our lives in a complacency that has never felt the need of forgiveness. A life that is without problems may literally be more hopeless than one that always verges on despair.

—Thomas Merton
No Man Is an Island

Because our culture is besotted with commodity and entertainment, we are a culture in despair.... It is the shame we feel when we think that our community itself behaves badly.

—Curtis White
The Middle Mind

Descending into the depths of my own nothingness, I was then so raised up that I attained my goal.

—John of the Cross

Despair is never ultimately over the external object, but always over ourselves.... The deepest form of despair is to choose to be someone other than one's self; but the opposite of despair is to will to be that self which one truly is.

—Søren Kierkegaard

Despair is the awkwardest pride of all.

—Wendell Berry
What Are People For?

Despair is hidden arrogance: I have seen the future and it doesn't work. Hope is rooted in trust in the unknown. Work, wait, and hope. That is enough.

—Sam Keen

DESIRE

The fear of our desires keeps them suspect and indiscriminately powerful, for to suppress any truth is to give it strength beyond endurance.

—Audre Lorde
Sister Outsider

Muhammed's son-in-law: Almighty God created sexual desire in ten parts, then he gave nine parts to women and one to men.

—Geraldine Brooks
Nine Parts of Desire

If I find in myself a desire which no experience in the world can satisfy, the most probable explanation is that I was made for another world.

—C. S. Lewis
Mere Christianity

At some point desires can become unreasonable. That usually leads to trouble.... The true antidote of greed is contentment.

—Dalai Lama
The Art of Happiness

DESTINY

Somebody placed the shuttle in your hand: somebody who had already arranged the threads.

—Dag Hammarskjöld
Markings

Remember that you are at an exceptional hour in a unique epoch, that you have this great happiness, this invaluable privilege, of being present at the birth of a new world.

—The Mother
Sri Aurobindo Ashram

We no more know our own destiny than a tea leaf knows the destiny of the East India Company.

—Douglas Adams
The Hitchhiker's Guide to the Galaxy

Our destiny is to go on beyond everything, to leave everything, to press forward to the End and find in the End our Beginning, the ever-new Beginning that has no End.

—Thomas Merton
Conjectures of a Guilty Bystander

History is turning up the fire under the soup in which we float.

—Christopher M. Bache
Dark Night, Early Dawn

Every human person is an aristocrat. Every human person is noble and of royal blood, born from the intimate depths of the divine nature and the divine wilderness.

—Meister Eckhart

It's never too late to go to Ninevah! Never too late to be coughed up onto the shores of one's destiny.

—David N. Elkins
Beyond Religion

A destiny is a range of possibilities that should be brought to fruition but which a person can choose not to cultivate.

—Caroline J. Simon
The Disciplined Heart

Every kind of work may serve the whole of humanity. Don't think you're "destined" for something else.

—Rudolf Steiner
The Way of Initiation

Maktūb. It is written.

—Arabic saying

DESTRUCTION

I have heard from my Indian friends that Shiva has a musical instrument, a drum, in one hand and a flame in another. The flame is destruction and the drum is creation.

—Ilya Prigogine

Breakage, whatever its cause, is the dark complement to the act of making; the one implies the other. The thing that is broken has particular authority over the act of change.

—Louise Gluck
Proofs and Theories

Animals kill to devour, not to destroy.

—Arthur Koestler
Janus

A collective nervous breakdown of the old systems is giving birth to a renewed search for consolation, meaning and deliverance.

—Mick Brown
The Spiritual Tourist

Our systems are breaking down today—all of them. And we feel it. All our professions, all our religions, all our politics and economic and educational establishments need reinventing. They all lack feminine energy, wisdom energy. They lack cosmology and creativity. This gives hope.

—Matthew Fox
Creativity

Every act of creativity is first an act of destruction.

—Pablo Picasso

All poets adore explosions, thunderstorms, tornadoes, conflagrations, ruins, scenes of spectacular carnage.

—W. H. Auden
The Dyer's Hand

DETACHMENT

Here you should know that true detachment is nothing other than this: the spirit stands as immovable in all the assaults of joy or sorrow, honor, disgrace or shame, as a mountain of lead stands immovable against a small wind. This immovable detachment brings about in man the greatest similarity with God.

—Meister Eckhart
Selected Treatises and Sermons

If the detachment is really genuine, you'll find greater freedom and success. If it isn't real, you'll find depression, despair and danger.

—Lazaris

Anyone with a sense of detachment from himself also gains a detachment from the world, including a sense of tolerance.

—Jean Gebser
The Ever-Present Origin

DIALOGUE

Dialogue literally means "thought logos." In ancient Greek, logos means "word" but also "reason."... Dialogue possesses a remarkable power to effect personal and spiritual growth and can offer our world perhaps the greatest means for the healing and further evolution of society.

—Robert Apatow
The Spiritual Art of Dialogue

Thickening occurs in middle domains.... Thickening occurs when each party to the interaction gains in concert with the other.... Thinning, on the other hand, occurs in the failure of working-through.

—Edward S. Casey
Getting Back into Place

Dialogue explores how thought is generated and sustained at the collective level ... our "pool of knowledge" acts like a virus.... It may turn out that such a form of free exchange of ideas and information is of fundamental relevance for transforming culture so that creativity can be liberated.

—David Bohm
On Dialogue

Dialogue must be practiced on the basis of "non-self." We have to allow what is good, beautiful and meaningful in the other's transition to transform us.

—Thich Nhat Hanh
Living Buddha, Living Christ

DISCIPLINE

In Tibetan, the term for discipline is *tsul trim*. *Tsul* means "appropriate or just," and *trim* means "rule" or "way." So discipline is to do what is appropriate or just; that is, in an excessively complicated age, to simplify our lives.

—Sogyal Rinpoche
The Tibetan Book of Living and Dying

Through a spiritual discipline we prevent the world from filling our lives to such an extent that there is no place left to listen.

—Henri J. M. Nouwen

The qualities that make a true artist [are] nearly the same qualities that make a true athlete.

—John Gardner

Discipline is the basic set of tools we require to solve life's problems. Without discipline we can solve nothing.... With total discipline we can solve all problems.

—M. Scott Peck
The Road Less Traveled

A discipline is a learning, and a disciple is a learner, one who follows a teaching … it requires an unflinching attention and a faithful care.

—Mary Caroline (M. C.) Richards
Centering

Discipline is cutting away what we don't need. The only thing left, once we cut away everything we don't need, is God.

—Kevin Ryerson
Spirit Communication

Discipline is a dedication to your truth. Discipline makes something come from something.

—Nancy Slonim Aronie
Writing from the Heart

Do you have the discipline to be a free spirit?

—Gabrièlle Roth
Sweat Your Prayers

DISCOVERY

To know how to wonder and question is the first step of the mind toward discovery.

— Louis Pasteur

The real voyage of discovery consists not in seeking new landscapes, but in having new eyes.

—Marcel Proust

It takes at least fifty years before a major scientific discovery penetrates the public consciousness.

—Erwin Schrödinger

Thus, the task is not so much to see what no one yet has seen, but to think what nobody yet has thought about that which everybody sees.

—Arthur Schopenhauer

Whenever a new discovery is reported to the world, they say first, "It is probably not true." Then after, when the truth of the new proposition has been demonstrated beyond question, they say, "Yes, it may be true, but it is not important." Finally, when sufficient time has elapsed to fully evidence its importance, they say, "Yes, surely it is important, but it is no longer new."

—Michel de Montaigne

The exhilarating quest for discovery, the search to find what magic lies beyond the stars and inside the atom, is at once wonderfully insatiable and wonderfully satisfying. We cannot find happiness in contemplating ourselves; but we can find it in contemplating infinity. Reaching out, with our imaginations, toward its majesty, it will in turn embrace us and inspire us.

—Jacques Cousteau
The Cousteau Almanac

The tools of human thought are both helpful or hurtful depending on when and how they're used.

—J. M. Balkin
Cultural Software

The seeds of great discoveries are constantly floating around us, but they only take root in minds well prepared to receive them.

—Joseph Henry

The ancients knew that the deepest spiritual truths come out of mystery … they danced their way into discovery.

—Bonnie Friedman
Writing Past Dark

It only took two of James Lind's sailors sucking on limes to produce the break-through which cured scurvy.

—Adam Smith
Powers of the Mind

DIVERSITY

Where differences meet, there hostility, fear, and conflict can arise or exploration, discovery, growth, creativity and love can emerge.

—David Spangler
A Pilgrim in Aquarius

Diversity may be both the hardest thing to live with and the most dangerous thing to be without.

—William Sloane Coffin
Credo

If we are to achieve a richer culture, rich in contrasting values, we must recognize the whole gamut of human potentialities, and so weave a less arbitrary social fabric, one in which each diverse human gift will find a fitting place.

—Margaret Mead

If we cannot now end our differences, at least we can make the world safe for diversity.

—John F. Kennedy

New patterns of diversity come into being constantly, like ripple patterns in a pond. The gradual acquisition of new cultural traits, often from another group, always create a gradient of difference within a society, like high and low pressure areas moving across a weather map ...

—Mary Catherine Bateson
Full Circles, Overlapping Lives

God loves "otherness," but hell hates it.

—Clyde S. Kilby
The Christian World of C. S. Lewis

This idea of unity-in-diversity can be followed all the way back to the Pythagorean "Harmony of the Spheres," and the Hippocratics' "sympathy of all things: there is one common flow, one common breathing, all things are in sympathy."

—Arthur Koestler
Janus

Respect for differences was written into the rule books of Irish monasteries.... "Different is the condition of everyone," cautions the rule of St. Carthage, "and different the nature of each place."

—Thomas Cahill
How the Irish Saved Civilization

We need the arts of xenophilia, constructive and habitual ways of welcoming the unfamiliar.

—Thomas Moore
Original Self

DIVINE

Being spellbound within me and Being spellbound within the world can join hands anytime, anywhere and in any way: when I look into the crown of a tree or into someone's eyes ... when I help someone or when someone helps me, when something important happens, or when nothing in particular happens at all. But whenever and however it happens such moments tend to be rare and fleeting. Given the contradictory nature of separated Being, it can't be any other way and it is right that it should be so.

—Václav Havel
Letters to Olga

Divinity is the enfolding and unfolding of everything that is. Divinity is in all things in such a way that all things are in divinity.

—Nicholas Krebs of Cusa &
James Francis Yockey
Meditations with Nicholas of Cusa

The seed of divine nature is the Son of God, the word of God... the seed of God is in us. Now the seed of a pear tree grows into a pear tree, a hazel seed into a hazel tree, the seed of God into God.

—Meister Eckhart

DOLPHINS

The dolphins are the angels of the animal kingdom.

—Barbara Hand Clow
Eye of the Centaur

Terror gave us the dragon, the chimera, and all the other monsters. The dolphin came from the other side, from gratitude and from gladness at the warm sun and smooth caressing water.

—Robert McNally
So Remorseless a Havoc

Dolphins have large brains. Possibly they will some day be able to teach us what brains are for.

—Ashley Montagu

Maybe we all believe that in that moment of final peril a dolphin will save us.

—Eleanore Devine & Martha Clark
The Dolphin Smile

The mysteries surrounding the behavior of the bottle-nosed porpoise, and even man himself, are not things to be probed simply by the dissector's scalpel. They lie deeper. They involve the whole nature of the mind and its role in the universe.

—Loren Eiseley
The American Scholar

One might conclude that the language of the dolphins is composed of 2,000 "words" ... the active vocabulary of the dolphin would be somewhat greater than of many humans.

—Jacques Yves Cousteau
Dolphins

DOUBT

My hosanna has come forth from the crucible of doubt.

—Feodor Dostoevski

To come to doubt, and to a debatement of any religious duty, is the voice of God in our conscience: Would you know the truth? Doubt, and then you will inquire.

—John Donne

Doubt comes in the window when inquiry is denied at the door.

—Benjamin Jowert

Doubt isn't the opposite of faith; it is an element of faith.

—Paul Tillich

To live with creative doubt means to enter into chaos so as to discover there the truth that cannot be measured by words.

—John Briggs & F. David Peat
Seven Life Lessons of Chaos

Learning starts when we are forced with what American philosopher Charles Pierce called an "irritant of doubt"— something that doesn't fit our ideas about the world.

—Sharon Seivert
The Balancing Act

Doubt is a pain too lonely to know that faith is his twin brother.

—Kahil Gibran

When in doubt, eat.

—Andrew Weil
Spontaneous Healing

Doubt may be an uncomfortable condition, but certainty is a ridiculous one.

—François-Marie Arouet (Voltaire)

Doubts are the ants in the pants of faith. They keep it awake and moving.

Frederich Duechner
Wishful Thinking

DRAGON

Michael overcoming the Dragon is an important imagination.... We serve Michael by overcoming the Dragon that is trying to grow to its full height and strength in ideas, which during the past epoch produced materialism.... To defeat this dragon means to stand in the service of Michael.

—Rudolf Steiner
The Archangel Michael

Dragons are mystical, powerful, emerging out of mystery, fierce, benign, known to teach humans the deepest reaches of wisdom. And dragons are filled with fire. Though there are no dragons, we are dragon fire. We are the creative, scintillating, searing, healing flame of the awesome and enchanting universe.

—Brian Swimme
The Universe Is a Green Dragon

We are as ignorant of the meaning of the dragon as we are of the meaning of the universe.

—Jorge Luis Borge

Sid Lonegren speaks of the "energy ley" which, he says, is "usually a six to eight-foot-wide beam of yang energy," whose width varies with time of day, year, and lunar phase, but shoe length is always straight. Wherever energy leys begin, cross each other, or terminate, there is a body of "primary water" underneath.... The Chinese called their ley lines *lung mei*, the paths of the dragon current, which flowed as a white yang tiger in the high mountains and as a yin blue dragon in the low hills and valleys. Where the two *lung mei* met, where the two breaths became one, was a node or power point, full of *chi*.

—Richard Leviton
The Power of Place

You have to infer the whole dragon from the parts you can touch, the old people would say.... I could listen to its voice in the thunder and feel its breathing in the winds.... In spring, when the dragon awakes, I watched its turnings in the rivers.

—Maxine Hong Kingston
The Woman Warrior

There is only one Dragon. It lives inside the earth and is as huge as the whole planet. Its mind thrives within the magnetic field thrown from the core.... Slowly molting within the sliding of tectonic plates, the Dragon renews itself over aeons.

—A. A. Attanasio
The Dragon and the Unicorn

Every dark side has a shadow and when you slay the dragon, the dragon is curled around the treasure.

—Richard Idemon
The Magic Thread

Dragons are our unnamed, unloved parts.

—Carol S. Pearson
The Hero Within

Bilbo Baggins: Never laugh at live dragons.

—J. R. R. Tolkien
The Hobbit

DRAMA

In drama, all the people who see it know it's only a play.... "Well, this is an illusion, it is not for real." ... But the mastery of the actors is going to almost convince us that it's real.... Suppose that God is the one playing all the parts, that God is the child being burned to death with napalm.

—Alan Watts
The Essential Alan Watts

Only the soul knows why it has chosen its drama.

—Shirley MacLaine
Dancing in the Light

Acting is just trying to be as natural as possible in an enlarged way.

—Will Geer

DREAMS

What if in your dream you went to heaven and there plucked a strange and beautiful flower? And what if, when you woke, you had the flower in your hand? Ah! What then?

—Samuel Taylor Coleridge

Dreams are the best evidence that we are not as firmly shut in our skins as we believe.

—Friedrich Hebbel

Dreams can be cultivated, requested, and experienced in ways that are difficult to anticipate.

—Sandra Weintraub
The Hidden Intelligence

The Sng'oi (Senoi) believe the world we live in is a shadow world, and that the real world is behind it. At night, they believe, we visit that real world, and in the morning we share what we saw and learned there.

—Robert Wolff
Original Wisdom

The meaning of a dream will not be found in a theory, but in the dream itself.

—Edgar Cayce
Dreams Your Magic Mirror

Without our dreams we would not be able to step outside ourselves and transcend our limitations.

—Diane Mariechild
Mother Wit

Our truest life is when we are in our dreams awake! Dreams are the touchstones of our characters.

—Henry David Thoreau

One theory about dreaming is that it evolved as both a roadside rest and a memory vat ... a grab bag of old and new, abstract and concrete, visual puns and symbols ... all wadded together.

—Diane Ackerman
An Alchemy of Mind

Dreams are ... illustrations from the book your soul is writing about you.

—Marsha Norman
Fortune Teller

I dream of sensations, colors, odors, ideas, and things I cannot remember ... and what a flash of glory it is! In sleep I never grope but walk freely.

—Helen Keller
The Story of My Life

Every understood dream is like a slight electric shock into higher consciousness.

—Marie-Louise von Franz
Alchemical Active Imagination

The dream image planted in the body acts as a magnet attracting the energy, transforming it and releasing it as healing power.

—Marion Woodman
The Pregnant Virgin

The dream, then, instead of being something apart from reality, a private world of fantasy or imagination, is actually an essential part of our reality which can be shared and communicated by means of imagery.... In our dreams lie the memories and metaphors of our search for sanity.

—Anäis Nin
The Novel of the Future

Dreams are a very tissue of symbols.

—Walker Percy
The Message in the Bottle

Proceed from the dream outward.

—Carl G. Jung

Dealing with dreams is not simple, because right away it involves the individual in a realm of experience beyond himself. Symbols from mythology and from the history of religion continually appear so often that it is difficult to ignore the presence of deeper, universal meanings.... Symbols can never be studied from a book to give an easy shorthand method of understanding dreams. Like any living language they must be read in context and in communication with the personal associations they hold for the dreamer.

—Morton T. Kelsey
Dreams, the Dark Speech of the Spirit

The dream is its own interpretation.... A dream which is not understood is like a letter which is not opened.

—The Talmud

Your dreams are the other side of your waking life, as your waking life is the other side of your dream life.... If you remember that when you are dreaming, you will become awake and alive; and if you remember that when you are awake, you will become dreaming and alive!

—Susan M. Watkins
Conversations with Seth

We sleep to dream. We're amphibians. We live in two elements and we need both.

—Lindsay Clarke
The Chymical Wedding

Our truest life is when we are in dreams awake.

—Henry David Thoreau

Dreams are the individual's folktales and folktales are collective dreams.

—Richard Adams
The Unbroken Web

Dreams are always urging us toward greater wholeness.

—Jack Maguire
Night and Day

Hieronymous Bosch and William Blake did it visually; Samuel Taylor Coleridge and James Joyce managed it with words. They succeeded in diverting the stream of consciousness in ways that allowed dream imagery to survive in the harsh light of day.... We do it every time we daydream.

—Lyall Watson
Lifetide

Our attitude toward [dreams] may be modeled upon Hades, receiving, hospi-table, yet relentlessly deepening, attuned to the nocturne, dusky, and with a fearful cold intelligence that gives permanent shelter in his house to the incurable conditions of human being.

—James Hillman
The Dream and the Underworld

Jung said, "A dream never says 'You ought' or 'this is the truth.'" It presents an image in much the same way as nature allows a plant to grow, and we must draw our own conclusions.... To grasp its meaning, we must allow it to shape us ... then we understand the nature of the experience.

—Jolande Jacobi
Complex Archetype Symbol

Dreams are dynamic mosaics, composed of symbols that express the movements, conflicts, interactions and developments of the great energy systems within the unconscious.

—Robert A. Johnson
Inner Work

Dreams say things we don't know already—that's why they're worthwhile.... Dreams are the royal road to knowing your shadow.

—Karen A. Signell
Wisdom of the Heart

Both dreams and myths are important communications from ourselves to ourselves.

—Erich Fromm

Let us learn how to dream ... and then perhaps we will discover the truth.

—Friedrich von Kekule

Respect your brother's dreams.

—Native American proverb

DUALITY

It was the best of times, it was the worst of times, it was the age of wisdom, it was the age of foolishness, it was the epoch of belief, it was the epoch of incredulity, it was the season of Light, it was the season of Darkness, it was the spring of hope, it was the winter of despair, we had everything before us, we had nothing before us ...

—Charles Dickens
A Tale of Two Cities

Two souls, alas, are housed within my breast.

—Johann Wolfgang von Goethe
Faust

Life leads us at a certain moment to step beyond the dualisms to which we have been educated: primitive and civilized, chaos and order, abnormal and normal, private and public, verbal and non-verbal, conventional and far-out, good and bad.... By an act of centering, we resolve the oppositions in a single experience.... Centering is an act of bringing in, not of leaving out.

—Mary Caroline (M. C.) Richards
Centering

Dualism creates a consciousness, and with it institutions and structures of either/or. One is either good or bad, male or female, strong or weak, spiritual or sensual, for example. Dialectical consciousness is about both/and thinking, both/and relationships. One can be good and bad, male and female, strong and weak, spiritual and sensual.

—Matthew Fox
Original Blessing

Everything begins with a circle of motion. Without positive and negative poles there would be no movement, no creation ... without the dark side, your beauty would not exist. Don't be afraid to look at both sides. You need them both. You must honor all existence as part of the Great Spirit.

—Lynn V. Andrews
Jaguar Woman

To know one thing, you must know the opposite ... just as much, else you don't know that one thing.

—Henry Moore

Jung teaches us that any time we identify too exclusively with one member of a pair of opposites we inevitably constellate the other.

—Victor Mansfield
Synchronicity, Science and Soulmaking

From this point of view of universal creativity and freedom, chaos and evil is no surprise. They are to be expected given the multiplicity of centers of creative power.

—David Ray Griffen
The Post-Modern Reader

Each of us has two natures: the lion and
the lamb … we must simply place the
lion in service to the lamb.

—Alan Arkin
Halfway through the Door

Creation and destruction are poised on
the same point. The center is the center
of withdrawal as well as renewal. In
opening a channel to Beings beyond our
planet, we may not be joined by a free
Spirit of Light, but by one of the lower
tied spirits, the shadowy misshapen
forms that have not progressed beyond
their own lowest potential.

—Moyra Caldecott
The Lily and the Bull

I have put duality away; I have seen the
two worlds are one …

—Jalal Al-din Rumi

EARTH

Once a photograph of the Earth, taken
from the outside, is available ... a new
idea as powerful as any in history will
let loose.

—Fred Hoyle *(1948)*

Suddenly from behind the rim of the
moon, in long, slow-motion moments
of immense majesty, there emerges a
sparkling blue and white jewel, a light,
delicate sky-blue sphere laced with slowly
swirling veils of white, rising gradually
like a small pearl in a thick sea of black
mystery. It takes more than a moment to
fully realize this is Earth ... home.

—Edgar Mitchell
The Home Planet

Once above our blanket of air, we have
turned our telescopes into the depths
of space and back on our small planet
to see it as one interconnected and
interdependent whole.

—Carl Sagan

The earth is the source and being of the
people, and we are equally the being of
the earth. The land is not really a place,
separate from ourselves, where we act out
the drama of our isolate destinies.

—Paula Gunn Allen
The Sacred Hoop

We were once enwombed in the earth
and the silence of the body remembers
that dark, inner longing. Fashioned from
clay, we carry the memory of the earth.

—John O'Donohue
  Beauty

Everywhere on Earth, at this moment,
in the new spiritual atmosphere created
by the idea of evolution, there float, in a
state of extreme mutual sensitivity, love
of God and faith in the world.... Sooner
or later there will be a chain-reaction.

—Pierre Teilhard de Chardin

Once in his life a man (or woman)
ought to concentrate his mind upon the
remembered earth. He ought to give
himself up to a particular landscape in
his experience; to look at it from as many
angles as he can, to wonder upon it, to
dwell upon it. He ought to imagine that
he touches it with his hands at every
season and listens to the sounds that are
made upon it.

—N. Scott Momaday & Barry Lopez
  Arctic Dreams

The earth would be converted into
something less than air were it not
constantly thought, dreamed, sung,
written, sculpted and painted. The world
dissolves when someone ceases to dream,
to remember, to write.

—Carlos Fuentes
  Terra Nuestra

Altogether Earth has about 51 million
square miles of land. Of that about 2%
or about 1 million square miles are
urban and semi-urban; 4 million square

miles are for cultivation and habitation
together. That's it.

—Christopher Alexander
  The Process of Creating Life

Earth and heaven are in us.

—Mohandas (Mahatma) Gandhi &
  Raghavan Iyer
  *The Moral and Political Thought of
  Mahatma Gandhi*

This earth is my sister; I love her daily
grace, her silent daring, and how loved
I am, how we admire this strength in
each other, all that we have lost, all that
we have suffered, all that we know: we
are stunned by this beauty, and I do not
forget: what she is to me, what I am to her.

—Susan Griffin
  Woman and Nature

You must teach your children that the
ground beneath their feet is the ashes of
our grandparents.... This we know, the
earth does not belong to us; we belong
to the earth. This we know. All things are
connected like the blood which unites
one family. All things are connected.

—Seattle/Seatlh

Through the death of Christ Jesus, the
Earth received the Christ impulse. The
greatest event that ever happened on
Earth can only be described in such
simple, halting words.

—Rudolf Steiner
  The Fifth Gospel

The earth isn't solid. It is made of
molecules and atoms, tiny universes filled

with space. It is a place of light, and of magic, if you only open your eyes.

—Dan Millman
Way of the Peaceful Warrior

It suddenly struck me that that tiny pea, pretty and blue, was the earth. I put up my thumb and shut one eye, and my thumb blotted out the planet Earth. I didn't feel like a giant. I felt very, very small.

—Neil Armstrong

Listen with your feelings, see with your heart. Read the earth, listen to the wind as it speaks to you. Gather in its fragrances and touch its differences. Taste it, and see that it is good. This earth is a garden, this life a banquet. And it's time we realized that it was given to all life, animal and man, to enjoy.

—Tom Brown, Jr.
The Search

What is the use of a house if you haven't a tolerable planet to put it on?

—Henry David Thoreau

Gaia is, and Gaia works. But does Gaia know? I am beginning to suspect so.

—Lyall Watson
Beyond Supernature

When we recognize that our planet itself is a living organism co-evolving with humankind we shall become worthy of stewardship.

—Danaan Parry & Lila Forest
The Earthsteward's Handbook

The earth should not be injured, the earth should not be destroyed. As often as the elements of the world are violated by ill-treatment, so God will cleanse them.

—Hildegard of Bingen

In the Gaia hypothesis, earth is defined as a living, breathing, and co-responding body, creating its own atmosphere, filling its own needs, relieving its own stresses.

—Monica Sjoo & Barbara Mor
The Great Cosmic Mother

We are only now beginning to appreciate how strange and splendid it [Earth] is, how it catches the breath, the loveliest object afloat around the sun, enclosed in its own oxygen, fixing its own nitrogen from the air into its own soil, generating its own weather at the surface of its rain forests, constructing its own carapace from living parts; chalk cliffs, coral reefs, old fossils from earlier forms of life now covered by layers of new life meshed together around the globe, Troy upon Troy.

—Lewis Thomas
Late Night Thoughts on Listening to Mahler's Ninth Symphony.

Everywhere in the world there are "power places." They all have their own unique energy and function to enhance and balance Mother Earth. They lie along certain meridians of this planet. Just as there are acupuncture points and meridians in our body, there is also a similar system for Earth.

—Chris Griscom
Time Is an Illusion

We are at odds with our planet.

—Thomas Berry
The Great Work

The Earth is peopling, as apple trees "apple." People are produced from the Earth as apples from apple trees.

—Alan Watts

We are partaking of the planet—to plunder it would be absurd.

—Thomas Aquinas

A short time before the close of the Age of Reptiles, flowers appeared (over a million year span) and changed the face of the planet.

—Loren Eiseley
The Star Thrower

Gaia is not our mother. She could be our daughter.

—Alison Jolly
Lucy's Legacy

Each living being is a swirl in the flow, a formal turbulence, a "song." The land, the planet itself, is also a living being—at another pace.

—Gary Snyder
Turtle Island

Paolo Lugari: The only deserts are deserts of imagination.... The savannas of the tropics are the only big open spaces left today. We have to learn to live in them again.

—Alan Weisman
Gaviotas: A Village to Reinvent the World

Like our cochlea with sensitive membranes, earth has "sensitive membrane," places which serve as entry ports for the forces of the sun and planets.

—Theodor Schwenk &
Wolfram Schwenk
Water: The Element of Life

Whatever happens on earth—man must share the responsibility. But the earth is not just something here and now.... It is also a star among stars ... it hastens through the changing landscapes of "heaven," transforming its own countenance and man's.

—Jean Gebser
The Ever-Present Origin

We don't make spiritual progress in the spiritual world; only on earth. It is here that we learn.

—Rudolf Steiner
An Outline of Occult Science

Earth—the home we treat like dirt.

—Walter Breen
Cynics Dictionary

Mozel tov literally means, "May your planet be favorable."

—Leonard Shlain
The Alphabet Versus the Goddess

We loved the earth, but could not stay.

—Loren Eiseley

ECOLOGY

This is the home, the "ecos" in which we live, it is the divine home.... The proper theology for our era is not about a God out there somewhere, it is about a God who is around us.... It is a very maternal image of God and as Hildegard of Bingen said, "You are hugged by the arms of the mystery of God."

—Matthew Fox
Only Connect

The impact of climatic change may be greater and more drastic than any other challenges that mankind has faced with the exception of the threat of nuclear war.

—Gro Harlem Brundtland
Prime Minister of Norway

The word ecology is like the word ocean. It is the fluid within which our spirit swims. Spiritual ecology does not place the human race first. It does not place the earth first. In fact, it doesn't place the 7th generation first either.... There are no seconds, no thirds, no any other level. The categories drift together.

—Jim Nollman
Spiritual Ecology

The Mediterranean goats were probably responsible for more deforestation and erosion than all the bulldozers of the Judeo-Christian world.

—René Dubois
A God Within

Quick are the mouths of earth and quick the teeth that feed upon this loveliness.

—Thomas Wolfe

The round globe is a vast head, a brain; instinct with intelligence! Or, shall we say, it is itself a thought, nothing but thought ...

—Nathaniel Hawthorne
The House of Seven Gables

The earth will be like a crystalline sea, where all the wonder of the world will be seen, all entirely transparent, and the radiance of God will be the light within it.

—Jacob Boehme & David Walsh
The Mysticism of Innerworldly Fulfillment

The environment tells our bodies how much our lives are valued. When the air we breathe is full of poisons, our lungs get the message that we aren't worth much.

—Starhawk
Truth or Dare

The more species that inhabit an ecosystem, such as forests and lakes, the more productive and stable the ecosystem.... People are the serial killers of the biosphere.

—Edward O. Wilson
The Future of Life

ECONOMICS/ ECONOMY

Balance requires that we recognize when we are taking too much, and when we are taking too little; when we are giving too much, and when we need to take more. Mutuality reminds us that while each individual is unique and each of us needs to affirm our inner wholeness, we also need to build relationships that honor the wholeness of other people and of the natural world around us. These two principles of balance and mutuality are shaping what I call a new economics of empowerment.

—Barbara Brandt
Whole Life Economics

It isn't products that make the tribal economy go round but rather human energy ... and it takes place so unobtrusively that people often mistakenly suppose that they have no economy at all.... Tribal people manage to govern themselves quite effectively without making and selling anything.... There's no way to accumulate their wealth ... no way for it to be concentrated in anyone's hands.

—Daniel Quinn
My Ishmael

From the point of view of Buddhist economics ... production from local resources for local needs is the most rational way of economic life, while dependence on imports from afar and the consequent need to produce for export to unknown and distant peoples is highly uneconomic and justifiable only in exceptional cases and on a small scale.... It is a question of finding the right path of development, the Middle Way between materialist heedlessness and traditionalist immobility, in short, of finding "Right Livelihood."

—E. F. Schumacher
Small is Beautiful

You begin to realize that our economy is based not just on the satisfaction of desire; it's based on the creation of desire.

—Jacob Needleman

... the arrangement of economic matters is believed to be the wellspring of contentment or discontent in all other areas of life. Economic expansion, through industrialism and computerization, is the Holy Grail of materialism, the unquestioned source from whence follows abundance, well-being, and the evolution of society.

—Charlene Spretnak
The Resurgence of the Real

Economy is a distributive virtue, and consists not in saving, but in selection.

—Edmund Burke
Letters to a Noble Lord

Profit exists only if you draw a circle between "me" and "not me" and then measure how much goes out of your circle and how much comes in.

—Thom Hartmann
The Prophet's Way

ECSTASY

The soul really does seem to have left the body.... There, an unearthly light is revealed which she could never have imagined had she spent her entire life trying to dream it up. In an instant her mind is alert to so much at once, that the intellect and imagination could never list a tiny part of it all.

—Teresa of Avila
The Interior Castle

It is through the cracks in our brains that ecstasy creeps in.

—Logan P. Smith
Afterthoughts

Only the united bent of sex and heart together can create ecstasy.

—Anäis Nin

Ecstasy is derived from the Greek word which means to make stand out; the mind makes sensible things stand out because it is concentrated on particular emotions, and on the ideas associated with and springing from these emotions.

—Albert Mordell
The Literature of Ecstasy

During religious excitement a real and pleasant odor is present in the atmosphere.

—Havelock Ellis
Studies in the Psychology of Sex

The average ecstasy state lasts 30-40 minutes. It has a trigger point, a realization point, a peak, a power point, and finally an inspired integration of knowledge to be utilized personally.

—Bernyce Barlow
Sacred Sites of the West

Our thank-you for creation, our fundamental prayer … is our enjoyment

and delight in it. The delight is called ecstasy when it reaches a certain height and it is also prayer. Like all prayer, it touches the creator and we are touched by the creator in that act of ecstasy and thank you.

—Matthew Fox
Whee! We, Wee All the Way Home

EDUCATION

Every education is a kind of inward journey.

—Václav Havel

The primary problems of the planet arise not from the poor, for whom education is the answer; they arise from the well-educated, for whom self-interest is the problem.

—William Sloane Coffin
Credo

What we must remember above all in the education of our children is that their love of life should never weaken.

—Natalia Ginzburg
The Little Virtues

Maria Montessori said only when a child is able to identify its own center of the universe does education really begin.

—Thomas Berry
The Great Work

When will we teach our children in school what they are? We should say to each of them: …You are a marvel. You are unique. In all the world there is no other child exactly like you.... You may become a Shakespeare, a Michelangelo, a Beethoven.... And when you grow up, can you then harm another who is, like you, a marvel?

—Pablo Casals
Joys and Sorrows

C. S. Lewis calls education "irrigating the desert."

—John Granger
The Hidden Key to Harry Potter

Education is the ability to perceive the hidden connections between phenomenon.

—Václav Havel

Education is a narrow, linear, stagnant system that has no regard for the individual. We need "vocational" school learning without the stigma.

—Mary E. Carreiro
The Psychology of Spiritual Growth

Every man must educate himself. His books and teachers are but helps. The work is his.

—Daniel Webster

Education is much more than a matter of imparting the knowledge and skills by which narrow goals are achieved. It is also about opening the child's eyes to the needs and rights of others.

—Dalai Lama
Ethics for the New Millennium

EGO

The word ego, as you may know, comes from the Latin for "I." Sanskrit too has a precise term for self-will: *ahamkara*, from *aham*, "I," and *kara*, "maker." *Ahamkara* is the force that continuously creates our sense of I-ness and its close companions, "me," "my," and "mine."

—Eknath Easwaran
Meditation

The ego is smarter than all of us here put together. It will outwit you at every turn.

—Anthony Damiani
Looking into Mind

If you would swim on the bosom of the ocean of Truth, you must reduce yourself to a zero.

—Mohandas (Mahatma) Gandhi

Art involves a very definite leaving behind of the niggardly part of the ego.

—Flannery O'Connor

Remember that you came here realizing the necessity of struggling only with yourself and thank anyone who helps you engage in this struggle.

—Inscription over the door to G. I. Gurdjieff's Paris home.

Whereas the ego weaves together the world, the shadow unravels the world. Whereas the ego acts as a catalyst of creation in the world, the shadow acts as a catalyst of destruction. Whereas the ego supports the status quo, the shadow is an agent of transformation.

—Connie Zweig & Steve Wolf
Romancing the Shadow

Try to forget yourself and rely on your true voice, your voiceless voice, your nonverbal voice.

—Shunryu Suzuki
Zen Mind

The identification of the "I" is always an illusion, but so powerful an illusion that people will kill and die for it.

—Peter Balin
The Flight of the Feathered Serpent

The Life I am trying to grasp is the me that is trying to grasp it.

—R. D. Laing

The pebble in the brook secretly thinks itself a precious stone.

—Chinese proverb

ELDER

Let your old age be childlike, and your childhood like old age; that is, so that neither may your wisdom be with pride, nor your humility without wisdom.

—Augustine
"Enarrationes in Psalmos"
An Augustine Synthesis

There is no good ritual to initiate a man into old age because life after fifty has not been seen as a stage of development.

—Terry Jones
The Elder Within

Elders often possess the power of the moose.... They know when to be friendly and when to express anger. The moose shows how important it is to give yourself a pat on the back and respect what you have achieved. Likewise, you should give praise and encouragement to everybody else involved.

—Heike Owusu
Symbols of North America

The elder goal is not to retire, but to replenish, to reflect, to pray.

—William Strauss & Neil Howe
The Fourth Turning

EMOTIONS

It is with the heart that one sees rightly; what is essential is invisible to the eye.

—Antoine de Saint-Exupéry,
The Little Prince

Anyone who tells me that my emotions or desires don't exist is in effect telling me that I don't exist.

—Abraham Maslow

You begin to realize that our economy is based not just on the satisfaction of desire; it's based on the creation of desire.

—Jacob Needleman

Emotions can be described as mental states accompanied by intense feelings and associated with bodily changes … in breathing, pulse, muscle tone, glandular secretion of hormones such as adrenalin.… One of the difficulties inherent in the subject is that we rarely experience a pure emotion … (and) imagined satisfaction may lead to a pleasurable experience.

—Arthur Koestler
Janus

Every emotion is a message.

—Gary Zukov & Linda Francis
The Heart of the Soul

Music is the shorthand of emotion.

—Leo (Lev) Tolstoy

EMPATHY

Empathy is the experience of understanding that takes place between two human beings. If you go into a music shop and pluck one string of a violin, each of the other instruments in the store will resonate with sound. Similarly, human beings can resonate with each other to such an extent that they can exchange understanding at a subtle level.… It is the way in which one person can intuitively and directly understand or "reach into" another person without using words.

—Rollo May
Healers on Healing

Empathy builds on self-awareness; the more open we are to our own

emotions, the more skilled we will be in reading feelings.

—Daniel Goleman
Emotional Intelligence

Man has the capacity to love, not just his own species, but life in all its shapes and forms. This empathy with the interknit web of life is the highest spiritual expression I know of.

—Loren Eiseley

Writers don't write from experience, though many are resistant to admit that they don't.… If you wrote from experience, you'd get maybe one book, maybe three poems. Writers write from empathy.

—Nikki Giovanni

Empathy turns the world around until we meet again where first our spirits met. Or perhaps it moves the world forward until we meet where we must meet at last.

—Marcus Bach
The Power of Perception

ENEMY

If you know your enemy, you will win most of the time. If you know yourself, there is no enemy.

—Sun Ysu

Gorbachov said to Reagan: "I am going to do something terrible to you. I am going to take away your enemy."

—Robert Bly & Marion Woodman
The Maiden King

He has no enemies but is intensely
disliked by all his friends.

—Oscar Wilde

ENERGY

Energy is eternal delight.... Energy is the
only life.

—William Blake

Energy is within and without. Exterior
and interior, all the dualities we function
under lose their meaning when you
go deep enough. But we are not all
conscious of the Goddess within us.

—Mountainspirit
WomanSpirit

All things are swirls of energy, vortexes
of moving forces, currents in an ever-
changing sea.

—Starhawk
Spiral Dance

The pulse of life demands an unending
stream of vital energy to keep it going.

—Marija Gimbutas
The Language of the Goddess

Strong impulses are but another name
for energy. Energy may be turned to bad
uses; but more good may always be made
of energetic nature, than of an indolent
and impassive one.

—John Stuart Mill
On Liberty

There are indications that physical energy
and psychic energy may be but two
aspects of one and the same underlying
reality. If this turns out to be the case,
then the world of matter will appear as,
so to speak, a mirror-image of the world
of spirit or of the psyche, and vice versa.

—Carl G. Jung & Marie-Louise von Franz
C. G. Jung

Energy medicine attempts to re-concep-
tualize patterns of information flow in
the body in ways that differ from those of
biochemistry and molecular biology.

—Brendan O'Regan

Since Universe is Energy, part of the
process of understanding ... is to learn
to "see" flows of energy.... As a child I
was asked to "see" the "dancing points
of light" and then to apprehend the shift
from location to flow.

—Paula Underwood Spencer

The conclusion is always the same: love
is the most powerful and still the most
unknown energy of the world.

—Pierre Teilhard de Chardin

Information is our source of energy; we
are driven by it.

—Lewis Thomas
Lives of a Cell

I realize that all questions lead to the
creation of energy.

—Charles Lindbergh

We have reached a point in our evolution that requires us to learn to speak "energy" fluently. Our search to understand the essence of health as well as our newfound passion to form a more mature relationship with the spiritual dimensions of our lives has led us to this crossroads.

—Caroline Myss

This earthwalk is a teaching about the dance of energies. All energies speak to one another in some way. Energy follows thought.

—Lynn V. Andrews
Crystal Woman

There is a vitality, a life force, an energy, a quickening that is translated through you into action and because there is only one of you in all of time, this expression is unique. And if you block it, it will never exist through any other medium and be lost.

—Martha Graham

It [energy] is God's cosmic essence; it is the source of life.

—Ann Valentin & Virginia Essene
Descent of the Dove

... the basic self, immortal and non-physical ... communicates on an energy level with other entities, and has an almost inexhaustible supply of energy at its command.

—Jane Roberts
The Seth Material

Prayer ... the very highest energy of which the mind is capable.

—Samuel Taylor Coleridge

Praying causes energy, celestial and physical, to be directed to a specific area of one's life, and repetition of the same prayer is very effective in drawing in appropriate telepathic vibrations.

—Meredith Lady Young
Agartha

Leadership requires the capacity to absorb the conflicting energies of group members. This shock-absorbing mechanism makes it possible for the leader to be a confluence of diverse energies.

—Debashis Chatterjee
Leading Consciously

People grow toward the giver of energy.

—Richard Daft & Robert Lengel
Fusion Leadership

In Aboriginal philosophy, existence consists of energy. All things are animate, imbued with spirit and in constant motion ... [this] leads to a holistic and cyclical view of the world.

—Marie Battiste
Reclaiming Indigenous Voice and Vision

Vortexes are powerful energy patterns bubbling up from the earth—geophysical anomalies ... holy places to ancient people.

—Bernyce Barlow
Sacred Sites of the West

Energy which is essential for handling intent is continually dispelled from the vital centers located around the liver, pancreas, kidneys ... it settles at the bottom of the luminous sphere that we are. This energy needs to be constantly stirred and rerouted.... Don Juan said, of energy fields, the womb is in a constant state of turmoil and chaos. The tomb moves from a tool of reproduction to a tool of evolution.

—Carlos Castaneda
Magical Passes

Whenever you "die" to something, you release energy and as energy flows, entropy decreases. Something goes down; something goes up.

—Beryl Pogson
The Work Life

When your intention is to transfer loving energy there is no way you can fail ... because in the subtle realms intention is action.

—Leonard Laskow
Healing with Love

A great current of creative energy gushes forth through matter, to obtain from it what it can. At most points it is stopped; these stops are transmuted, in our eyes, into the appearances of many living species.

—Henri Bergson

Air ions are charged molecules of common gaseous elements in the air which form when uncharged.... Negative air ions each have an extra electron, giving them a negative electrical charge, while positive air ions each have one less electron than normal and a positive

charge. In nature, the causative agents of negative air ions include crashing ocean breakers, waterfalls, pine forests, exposed surfaces of rock rich in uranium, and the summits of mountain peaks where electrical charges are highest. An abundance of negative ions ... reduces the level of serotonin in the blood ... reduces fatigue, invigorates us, and improves the protective powers of the mucous membranes of the respiratory system, making us less susceptible to colds and infection.

—James. A. Swan
Sacred Places

ENLIGHTENMENT

Enlightenment is always "sudden" in the sense that during mediation or reverie or relaxation the preliminary thought-concentrating gustatory period usually moves through consciousness quite slowly until, at some unexpected moment, there is an abrupt deepening, followed by a slipping into another dimension, a finding oneself alive in a new atmosphere.

—Paul Brunton
The Notebooks of Paul Brunton

Enlightenment is simply sanity—the sanity in which I see my real situation in the living fabric of all that exits.

—Frederick Franck
The Awakened Eye

Imagine that all of us are icebergs floating on the sea of enlightenment. As an iceberg, you look down into the sea ... and know that you want to be a part of it. Then you discover that you too are made of water, except that you are frozen.

You're just like the sea. The only difference is the temperature.

—Lynn Andrews
Healers on Healing

The enlightened person remains what he is, and is never more than his own limited ego before the One who dwells within him, whose form has no knowable boundaries, who encompasses him on all sides, fathomless as the abysms of the earth and vast as the sky.

—Carl G. Jung
Answer to Job

Enlightenment often occurs for an individual in the courts of conscious contact with one's loving and compassionate God.

—Barbara Metz
The Enneagram and Prayer

The word enlightenment conjures up the idea of some super-human accomplishment, and the ego likes to keep it that way, but it is simply your natural state of felt oneness with Being.

—Eckhart Tolle
The Power of Now

He who knows others is wise. He who knows himself is enlightened.

—Lao Tzu

Enlightenment is not a magical transcendence of the human condition but the full flowering of humanity,

disclosing unity and equilibrium at the heart of the love and suffering we call life.

—Lex Hixon
Coming Home

To be enlightened is to snap out of the movie of life.

—Ken Wilber

We do not become enlightened by imagining figures of light, but by making the darkness conscious.

—Carl G. Jung

Before enlightenment—chopping wood and drawing water. After enlightenment—chopping wood and drawing water.

—Chinese proverb

ENTRAINMENT

The ability of one rhythm to draw another into harmonic resonance is called entrainment.

—Layne Redmond
When the Drummers Were Women

Place one throbbing heart cell in a laboratory dish next to another heart cell and they will beat in their solitary rhythms. Place several heart cells together in a dish without any physical contact between one another and with no synapse connecting them and they suddenly fall into a rhythmic unison, a rhythm that is distinct from the rhythm of each individual cell.

—Paul Pearsall
The Heart's Code

One of the great organizing principles of the world, as inescapable as gravity.

—Stephan Rechtschaffen

ENTROPY

Entropy, the force behind the famous Second Law of Thermodynamics, applies not only to physical systems but to the functioning of the mind as well. When there is nothing specific to do, our thoughts soon return to the most predictable state, which is randomness or confusion ... we turn on the TV set, read listlessly ... have pointless conversations—anything to keep our thoughts on an even keel and avoid becoming frightened by what is happening in the mind.... Entropy is a more primal urge than the urge to create.

—Mihaly Csikszentmihalyi
Creativity

Entropy indicates the degree of disorder existing in a physical system. Where orderly patterns are built up, entropy decreases.... Negentropy is the opposite of entropy.... Negentropy enters the picture whenever order is created out of chaos, as in creative thinking ... the sun is a source of negative entropy.

—Theodor Schwenk &
Wolfram Schwenk
Water: The Element of Life

Living things can reverse entropy.

—Erwin Schrödinger

Every process is subject to a kind of entropic degradation that occurs inexorably unless energy is added at certain vulnerable moments.

—Kathleen Riorden Speeth
Gurdjieff's Work

The usual entropy is a measure of ignorance ... when new data is obtained and registered, ignorance is reduced ... by a certain amount.

—Murray Gell-Mann
Quark and the Jaguar

ENVY/JEALOUSY

Jealousy is a natural, creative human emotion that can get out of hand.

—Thomas Moore
Original Self

The antidote to envy ... that corrosive, itchy emotion ... is one's own work. Always one's own work.

—Bonnie Friedman
Writing Past Dark

Don Juan: What makes us unhappy is to want.

—Carlos Castenada

To be envious in Chinese is "to guzzle vinegar."

—Maxine Hong Kingston
China Men

When yellow wants to be blue, it becomes green.

—Russian proverb

EQUALITY

Christianity became the greatest moral and political revolution in the history of the human race. It ... preached the equality of human souls—the true basis for all other equalities, political, social and economic.

—Otto Rank
Beyond Psychology

ETERNITY

Everything has its origin in the eternal.

—Rudolf Steiner
Cosmic Memory

Remember, you're a child of eternity.

—Rudolf Steiner
The Christian Mystery

A door opens in the center of our being and we seem to fall through it into immense depths which, although they are infinite, are accessible to us; all

eternity seems to have become ours in this one placid and breathless contact.

—Thomas Merton
New Seeds of Contemplation

Almost certainly God is not in Time.... He has all eternity in which to listen to the split second of prayer put up by a pilot as his plane crashes in flames.

—C. S. Lewis
Mere Christianity

There is no separation—no past; eternity, the Now, is continuous. When all the stars have revolved they only produce Now again. The continuity of Now is for ever.... How infinitely deeper is thought than the million miles of the firmament! The wonder is here, not there; now, not to be, now always.

—Richard Jefferies
The Story of My Heart

Love is at work in the circles of eternity, without reference to time, like heat within a fire.

—Hildegard of Bingen

Eternity is not a straight line to infinity, but rather an endless series of coils of the same size compressed into a great spring, known as time, and with the impetus of happening.

—Robert K. G. Temple
The Sirius Mystery

If we take eternity to mean not infinite temporal duration, but timelessness, the eternal life belongs to those who live in the present.

—Ludwig Josef Johan Wittgenstein

How do you suppose we shall spend eternity, when so many of us seem unable to spend time?

—Paul Scherer
Love Is a Spendthrift

Eternity is an act of here and now.

—Joseph Campbell

ETHICS

A man is ethical only when life, as such, is sacred to him, that of plants and animals as well as that of his fellowman, and when he devotes himself helpfully to all life that is in need of help ... to the truly ethical man, all life is sacred.

—Albert Schweitzer

Life swings on an ethical hinge. If you loosen that hinge, all history, and even nature, will feel the shock.

—William Sloane Coffin
Credo

Today we know that time is a construction and therefore carries an ethical responsibility.

—Ilya Prigogine & Isabelle Stengers

In the end, it will all come down to a decision of ethics, how we value the natural world in which we have evolved

and now—increasingly—how we regard our status as individuals.

—E. O. Wilson

Thank God, our time is now, when wrong comes up to meet us everywhere, never to leave us till we take the longest stride of soul men ever took.

—Christopher Frye

Jesus and Buddha have this in common, that their form of ethics ... is not an ethic of action, but an ethic of inner perfection.

—Albert Schweitzer
Indian Thought

EVIL

What is considered as evil is, in reality, the wrong utilization of divine forces. That is why I consider the word "evil" inappropriate. When we speak of evil I prefer to imply the expression of oneself in an ignorant manner. In the course of time one learns through the law of cause and effect.

—Daskalos, quoted by
Kyriacos C. Markides
The Magus of Strovolos

The three poisons: craving, hatred, ignorance.

—Thomas Merton
The Asian Journals of Thomas Merton

The reality of evil is a well-kept secret, guarded by the dark forces themselves; for they thrive on concealment. In contrast, the forces of Light wish always to be known. The power of Light increases as it is brought to consciousness. Darkness loses its power when revealed, for we are then able to see it in action, recognize its purpose, and employ it so that it no longer employs us.

—Patricia Joudry & Maurie D. Pressman
Twin Souls

Understanding evil as the absence of Light automatically requires that we reach for this thing called Light.

—Gary Zukav
The Seat of the Soul

Suddenly there was a great burst of light through the Darkness. The light spread out and where it touched the Darkness the Darkness disappeared. The light spread until the patch of Dark Think had vanished, and there was only a gentle shining and through the shining came the stars, clear and pure. Then slowly, the shining dwindled until it, too, was gone, and there was nothing but stars and starlight. No shadows. No fear.

—Madeleine L'Engle
A Wrinkle in Time

The malevolent energies and destructive forces which have been abroad in our time tell us how strong is the evil that lies mixed with the good in humanity's heart.

—Paul Brunton
Notebooks

Yet it is exactly this world of unprecedented evil—of extermination ovens and concentration camps, of terrorist attacks and ethnic cleansings, of epidemic disease and mass starvation and deadly material self-indulgence— that *The Lord of the Rings* addresses. Far

from encouraging us to turn away from such evils, Tolkien's book forces us to confront them.

—Ralph C. Wood
The Gospel According to Tolkien

[Orcs] are cruel, wicked and bad-hearted. They make no beautiful things, but they make many clever ones.... It is not unlikely that they invented some of the machines that have since troubled the world, especially the ingenious devices for killing large numbers of people at once.

—J. R. R. Tolkien
The Hobbit

Bisha does mean "evil" or "error" but in the Hebraic and Aramaic sense of "unripeness" or inappropriate action.

—Neil Douglas-Klotz
Prayers of the Cosmos

Imaginary evil is romantic and varied; real evil is gloomy, monotonous, barren, boring. Imaginary good is boring; real good is always new, marvelous, intoxicating.

—Simone Weil

Most of the evil in this world is done by people who do it for good purposes. Real evil in this world happens when Satan disguises himself as an angel of light.

—Krister Stendahl & Matthew Fox
A Spirituality Named Compassion

We have plenty of examples in this world of poor things being used for good purposes. God can make any indifferent thing, as well as evil itself, an instrument for good; but I submit that to do this is the business of God and not of any human being.

—Flannery O'Connor
On Writing

Consider hydrogen weapons. Consider biological weapons. Consider the warming of the planet ... torture instruments ... sweatshops ... sex trade .... It is as if human imagination has no bounds.... In short, the capacity for evil in our species is so profound because our creativity is so deep.

—Matthew Fox
Creativity

Any creative encounters with evil requires that we not distance ourselves from it by simply demonizing those who commit evil acts.

—Kathleen Norris

Good and evil will be curiously mingled in any meaningful life process. If we are to become whole, life will send us, not what we want, but what we need in order to grow.

—John A. Sanford
Healing and Wholeness

Since the Middle Ages we have repressed the problem of evil—we pretend it doesn't exist.

—Marie-Louise von Franz
Archetypal Patterns in Fairy Tales

People who always seek evil in others find it.

—Motilal Nehru

EVOLUTION

Evolution is an ascent towards consciousness.

—Pierre Teilhard de Chardin

The brontosaurus became extinct, but it wasn't its fault, so to speak. If we become extinct, it will be our fault.... In order to survive, man has to evolve.

—Jonas Salk

If we can be courageous one more time than we are fearful, trusting one more time than we are anxious, cooperative one more time than we are competitive, forgiving one more time that we are vindictive, loving one more time than we are hateful, we will have moved closer to the next breakthrough in our evolution.

—Arianna Stassinopoulos

We know simply that nothing is static, nothing is absolutely predictable, and nothing is certain. Even our understanding of evolution is, well, evolving.

—L. Robert Keck
Sacred Quest

No person, essence or entity is "ahead" or "behind" any other, but is simply occupying another place in the continuous circle leading to and from the Tao.

—Joya Pope
The World According to Michael

Human evolution is now at a crossroads. Stripped to its essentials, the central human task is how to organize society to promote the survival of our species and the development of our unique potentials.

—Riane Eisler
The Chalice and the Blade

Evolution takes place in environments that are peaceful and with people who support spiritual growth.

—Mary E. Carreiro
The Psychology of Spiritual Growth

From time to time in the past, civilizations from different reality streams crossed over and met with yours. Each time this happened, it became a stimulus for further evolution.

—Olga Kharitidi
Entering the Circle

The universe is evolving toward an even greater destiny and we are the means of this global transformation.

—Pir Vilayat Inayat Khan
Awakening

The fall of man is not a sheer drop. It's more like a scrambling outward and downward.

—Evan Eisenberg
The Ecology of Eden

The lazy word "evolution" has blinded us to the real complexities of the past.

—Giorgio de Santillana &
Hertha von Dechend
Hamlet's Mill

The word "evolving" comes from ... "volare", ascending up, and "evolvere" unfolding like petals of a lotus.

—Richard Idemon
The Magic Thread

Is the universe experiencing heat death? Or is it being carried to higher organizational states?

—Mary Catherine Bateson
Composing a Life

EXCELLENCE

Whatever you do, it is not for fun or study ... you must treat it as the best thing you will ever do.

—Constantin Brancusi

We cannot then sum up human excellence for these reasons: the world is aimless, chancy and huge, and we are blinded by self.

—Iris Murdoch
The Sovereignty of Good

EXCUSES

There are no excuses for anything.... You change things or you don't. Excuses rob you of power and introduce apathy.

—Lynne V. Andrews
Jaguar Woman

The man who cannot dance will say the drum is bad.

—African proverb

EXPECTATION

God expects but one thing of you: that
you should come out of yourself insofar
as you are a created being and let God be
God in you.

—Meister Eckhart

If we do not expect the unexpected, we
will never find it.

—Heracleitus of Ephesus

We are never prepared for what we expect.

—James H. Michener
Caravans

To free us from the expectation of others,
to give us back to ourselves—there lies
the great, singular power of self-respect.

—Joan Didion

When you write, you lay out a line of
words … a miner's pick, a woodcarver's
gouge, a surgeon's probe. You wield it,
and it digs a path you follow. Soon you
find yourself deep in new territory. Is it
a dead end, or have you located the real
subject? You will know this time tomorrow, or this time next year.

—Annie Dillard

As you dream, as you imagine, as you
desire, as you expect, solutions can come
to you.

—Lazaris
Lazaris Interviews

We expect the wrong things from the
right people and the right things from
the wrong people.

—Karl Menninger

Expectation is a matter of feeling, feeling
is a servant to will, the will is the result
of a wish, and a wish is spun from the
power of spirit.

—Marcus Bach
The Power of Perception

Waiting patiently in expectation is the
foundation of the spiritual life.

—Simone Weil

Expect your every need to be met,
expect the answer to every problem,
expect abundance on every level, expect
to grow spiritually.

—Eileen Caddy

Don't pray for the rain to stop. Pray for
good luck fishing when the river floods.

—Wendell Berry

EXPERIENCE

Experience, O seeker, is the essence of
all things.

—Kabir

I go to encounter for the millionth time
the reality of experience and to forge
in the smithy of my soul the uncreated
conscience of my race.

—James Joyce

You can't say "Teach me to paint, but don't ask me to handle a brush."

—Rudolf Steiner

When experience is viewed in a certain way, it presents nothing but doorways into the domain of the soul, and they are all found in the present moment.

—Jon Kabat-Zinn
Handbook for the Soul

For Rumi, the bread of every experience offers nourishment.

—Coleman Barks
The Essential Rumi

The only true injury in life occurs by going into an experience and not being able to find the love in it.

—Martia Nelson
Coming Home

My experience is what I agree to attend to.… Experience is never limited and it is never complete.

—Henry James

The ability to extract wisdom from experience is a skill honed in the crucible.

—Warren G. Bennis & Robert J. Thomas
Geeks and Geezers

When the soul wishes to experience something, she throws an image of the experience out before her and enters into her own image.

—Meister Eckhart

We may "misunderstand," but we do not "misexperience."

—Marie Battiste
Reclaiming Indigenous Voice and Vision

All experience is subjective.

—Gregory Bateson
Mind and Nature

To deny one's experiences is to put a lie into the lips of one's own life. It is no less than a denial of the soul.

—Oscar Wilde

The soul is a series of momentary experiences.

—Alfred North Whitehead

Whatever is in the highest good. I am open to experience.

—Australian Aborigine proverb

F

FAILURE

Really, nothing was easier than to step
from one rope ladder to the other—over
the chasm. But, in your dream, you
failed, because the thought occurred to
you that you might possibly fail.

—Dag Hammarskjöld
Markings

Where you stumble, there your
treasure lies.

—Joseph Campbell

As psychologist Dean Keith Simonton
has demonstrated, the most acclaimed
creators not only create more works
than their peers, they also generate more
failures; the notion that every work by
a master is equally meritorious is
dead wrong.

—Howard Gardner
Changing Minds

I have learned in recent years that my
faults, the defects that keep me from
creating the work I want to do, are not
flaws or failures. They are wounds....
Embrace the wounds, wash them,
bandage them with loving care.

—Sophy Burnham
For Writers Only

Failure means not reaching the goal you have set for a specific time period.

—Cheryl Anne Gilman
Doing the Work You Love

Think like a queen. A queen is not afraid to fail. Failure is another stepping stone to greatness.

—Oprah Winfrey

I want to do it because I want to do it. Women must try to do things as men have tried. When they fail, their failure must be but a challenge to others.

—Amelia Earhart

In Greenland there is no such thing as a poor, or a bad hunter. There are only good hunters. Some are great hunters … those unable to bring home a good catch are simply unfortunate hunters.

—Peter Freuchen
The Peter Freuchen Reader

You must once and for all give up being worried about successes and failures. Don't let that concern you. It's your duty to go on working steadily day by day, quite steadily, to be prepared for mistakes, which are inevitable, and for failures.

—Anton Chekhov

If you want to be successful faster, you must double your rate of failure.

—Thomas Watson

Ever tried? Ever failed? No matter. Try again. Fail again. Fail better.

—Samuel Beckett

What you actually do within 24 hours of having a creative idea will spell the difference between success and failure.

—R. Buckminster Fuller

It isn't easy for an author to remain a pleasant human being; both success and failures are usually of a crippling kind.

—Graham Greene

Failure is the true test of greatness.

—Herman Melville

When you fall, there your God pushed you down.

—Nigerian Proverb

Only he who does nothing makes a mistake.

—French proverb

FAITH

Faith is the union of God and the soul.

—John of the Cross

Faith is some truth that you heartfully merge with. It's like compassion, the merging. Belief is a system of the mind, and the mind is part of ego.... Grasping means you are lacking faith. If you have faith, then grace will stay and it's real.

—Ram Dass
Fierce Grace

You don't demand a thing from God, therefore you receive nothing. You have no faith, therefore you do not receive God's help. You are downright addicted to your worries, therefore the very worst always strikes you. But I call loudly to God, and receive God's help.

—Hildegard of Bingen
Hildegard's Medicine

If faith puts us on the road, hope keeps us there.

—William Sloane Coffin
Credo

Faith teaches us to use our talents to the fullest extent, however slight they may be.... Through faith I create the world I gaze upon; I make my own day and night, tint the clouds with iridescent fires, and behold! A midnight is strewn with other stars. It is faith which lights us into sustaining realities beyond those perceived by the physical senses.

—Helen Keller
All Believers Are Brothers

Real faith is rooted in a basic ignorance about ultimate things, and religion helps us to be in relation to that mystery.... Often people fill in this emptiness by insisting that they possess the truth.

—Thomas Moore
The Soul's Religion

Every work of art is an "act of faith" in the vernacular sense of being a venture into the unknown.

—Denise Levertov
Work That Enfaiths

Even in the life of a Christian, faith rises and falls like the tides of an invisible sea. It's there, even when he can't see it or feel it, if he wants it to be there.... Learn what you can, but cultivate Christian skepticism. It will keep you free—not free to do anything you please, but free to be formed by something larger than your own intellect or the intellects of those around you.

—Flannery O'Connor
The Habit of Being

We act in faith—and miracles occur.... Faith is, faith creates, faith carries. It is not derived from, nor created, nor carried by anything except its own reality.

—Dag Hammarskjöld
Markings

Faith in the eternal arises like the phoenix out of the ashes of all the soul's previous illusions.

—Søren Kierkegaard

Faith is the opening of all sides and every level of one's life to the Divine in-flow.

—Martin Luther King Jr.

Faith is not merely a way of knowing; it is also a way of participating.

—Robert Ellwood
The Cross and the Grail

My faith in a loving Creator of the galaxies, so loving that the very hairs of my head are counted, is stronger in my work than in my life, and often it is the work that pulls me back from the precipice of faithlessness.

—Madeleine L'Engle
Walking on Water

Faith has no other language than symbols.... Faith is the courage to say yes to one's life."

—Paul Tillich

Belief is limiting and binding; faith is expanding and releasing. Belief fixates, faith liberates.

—*The Urantia Book*

A journal is a leap of faith. You write without knowing what the next day's entry will be—or when the last.

—Violet Weingarten
Intimations of Mortality

Faith is to believe, on the word of God, what we do not see, and its reward is to see and enjoy what we believe.

—Augustine

A perfect faith would lift us absolutely above fear.

—George MacDonald
Sir Gibbie

FAMILY

We live with strangers. Those we love most, with whom we share a shelter, a table, a bed, remain mysterious.

Wherever lives overlap and flow together, there are depths of unknowing.

—Mary Catherine Bateson
Full Circles, Overlapping Lives

Everyone on earth belongs to a spirit clan. The problem is you have to find it.

—Lynn V. Andrews
Flight of the 7th Moon

The family you came from isn't as important as the family you're going to have.

—Ring Lardner

We need only realize our parents, remember our grandparents and know ourselves and our history is complete.

—Gertrude Stein

A troubled family does not or cannot notice change, and does not or cannot take steps to grieve losses and celebrate new gains.

—Herbert Anderson
Leaving Home

We may wonder: whom can I love and serve? Where is the face of God to whom I can pray? The answer is simple: that hungry one, that naked one, that lonely one, that unwanted one, is my brother and my sister. If we have no peace, it is because we have forgotten that we belong to each other.

—Mother Teresa

The cold truth is that family dinners are more often than not an ordeal of nervous indigestion, preceded by hidden resentment and ennui and accompanied by psychosomatic jitters.

—M. F. K. Fisher
The Art of Eating

It's difficult to have true dialogue in a family because it's generally a hierarchy organized on a principle of authority.

—David Bohm
On Dialogue

All happy families are like one another; each unhappy family is unhappy in its own way.

—Leo (Lev) Tolstoy
Anna Karenina

Victorians lived in their gingerbread prisons.

—Theodore Roszak
Person/Planet

If the first generation does well, the second one marries well and the third one breeds well, then the others can take care of themselves.

—Old Quaker proverb

FANTASY

Every creative individual whatsoever owes all that is greatest in his life to fantasy. The dynamic principle of fantasy is play, a characteristic also of the child.... Without this playing with fantasy no creative work has ever yet come to birth.... The creative mind plays with the object it loves.

—Carl G. Jung

Fantasy is the richest source of human creativity.... In fantasy no holds are barred.... In fantasy we become not only our ideal selves, but totally different people. We abolish the limits of our powers and perceptions. We soar.

—Harvey Cox
The Feast of Fools

A fantasy is generally like a well, narrow but deep. At its deepest it exhibits ideas that are too old to express in any way but through a story that merely casts a shadow of what the truth itself is. Fantasy creates a world apart in order that it may touch more fittingly and more richly on the great unknown of spirit, soul and universal mechanics that lie all around us.

—Henry Fairlie
The Spoiled Child of the Western World

We make up horrors to help us cope with the real ones.

—Stephen King
Danse Macabre

FATHER

The habit of living together gave rise to the sweetest sentiments known to men: conjugal love and paternal love."

—Jean-Jacques Rousseau

The word patriarchy comes from the Greek *pater* (father) and *arche* (ruling power).... the art of writing emerged on the human scene at about the same time that patriarchy was being firmly established in the human soul. Virtually all of "recorded history," therefore, is written from a patriarchal bias.

—L. Robert Keck
Sacred Quest

FEAR

Fear condemns and love forgives.... Fear is not justified in any form. Only your mind can produce fears.... All healing involves replacing fear with love.... Those you do not forgive you fear.

—*A Course in Miracles*

Where there is fear, there is no religion.

—Mohandas (Mahatma) Gandhi

The process of transforming fear isn't pretending that we have no fear, but embracing fear as a tool for learning and growth.

—Kay Gilley
The Alchemy of Fear

Fear destroys intimacy. It distances us from each other; or makes us cling to each other, which is the death of freedom.

—William Sloane Coffin
Credo

Fear is the direct result of error.

—Rudolf Steiner
An Outline of Occult Science

Ultimately we know deeply that the other side of every fear is a freedom.

—Marilyn Ferguson

I will not die an unlived life. I will not live in fear of falling or catching fire. I choose to inhabit my days, to allow my living to open me, to make me less afraid, more accessible, to loosen my heart until it becomes a wing, a torch, a promise.

—Dawna Markova

It is as if God planted a great big kiss in the middle of our spirit and all the wounds, doubts, and guilt feelings were all healed at the same moment. The experience of being loved by the Ultimate Mystery banishes every fear.

—Thomas Keating

To fear is one thing. To let fear grab you by the tail and swing you around is another.

—Katherine Paterson

Fear gives us red to brighten the world.

—Maxine Hong Kingston
Chinamen

What gives real value to travel is fear.... It is a fact that at a certain moment, when we are so far from our own country ... we are seized by a vague fear, and an instinctive desire to go back to the protection of old habits.... At that moment, we are feverish but also porous, so that the slightest touch makes us quiver to the depths of our being. We come across a cascade of light, and there is eternity.

—Albert Camus
Notebooks

Fear is often an indication I am avoiding myself.

—Hugh Prather
Notes to Myself

We fear the sunrise in us.

—Michael Murphy
Jacob Atabet

If one is afraid of looking into a face, one hits the face.

—William Butler Yeats

Do not fear your enemies: the worse they can do is kill you. Do not fear your friends: at worst they may betray you. Fear those who do not care: they neither kill nor betray you, but betrayal and murder exist because of their silent consent.

—Bruno Yasensky

We become fearful of one another when our loving nature is blocked. Ignorance is at the root of all bigotry and injustice.

—Kevin Ryerson
Spirit Communication

As it takes only one speck of dirt to destroy the purity of clear water, it takes but one speck of fear to hide the presence of love.

—Gerald B. Jampolsky
Out of Darkness into the Light

Fear is the cause of all suffering, all limitations, all negative emotions.

Without fear we can truly learn to give and receive the love we are living for.

—Diane Mariechild
Mother Wit

To live a creative life, we must lose the fear of being wrong.

—Joseph Chilton Pearce

Those who channel fearful energies find that as time passes, the fear vibration grows heavy, depressing. Eventually it brings sleep, gloominess, discouragement, despair. The love vibration brings enthusiasm, energy, interest, perception.

—Ken Carey
Return of the Bird Tribes

Considering how dangerous everything is, nothing is really very frightening.

—Gertrude Stein

Nothing in life is to be feared. It is only to be understood.

—Marie Curie

Once we break through fear, there is nothing but space, sheer possibility. Then we can fly.

—Richard Thieme

Fear means you are Forgetting Every Available Resource.

—Bo Gyllenpalm

FEELINGS

Feelings are for the soul what food is for the body.

—Rudolf Steiner
The Way of Initiation

Our thoughts and feelings are energies that we project out into the environment.... These are the elementals every human being incessantly creates.... Elementals are thought-forms that can assume a variety of shapes and colors; an advanced mystic and clairvoyant can perceive them coming out of the subconscious of a person.

—Kyriacos C. Markides
Fire in the Heart

Feeling may exist only in the presence of thought and emotion, for it represents the union of the two.

—Gregg Braden
The Isaiah Effect

Feeling good and feeling bad are not necessarily opposites. Both at least involve feelings. Any feeling is a reminder of life. The worst "feeling" evidently is non-feeling.

—Willard Gaylin
Feelings

Your feelings are as natural a part of the environment as trees.

—Jane Roberts
Seth Material

It is the dazzling beauty of darkness and light, color and silence, warmth and material and vegetation which makes us

gasp. ... That is what we stand for... Deep feeling is the guiding principle.

—Christopher Alexander
The Process of Creating Life

Resilience is to maintain high levels of positive feelings and well-being in the face of adversity.

—Jerome Groopman
The Anatomy of Hope

The best way to get rid of a feeling you don't want is to let yourself have it.

—Elio Frattaroli
Healing the Soul in the Age of the Brain

FEMININE ENERGY/ WISDOM

... I am the beauty running through the world, to make it associate in ordered groups: the ideal held up before the world to make it ascend. I am the essential Feminine.

—Pierre Teilhard de Chardin
Hymn to the Eternal Feminine

The Eternal Feminine draws us ever upwards.

—Johann Wolfgang von Goethe
Faust

Too much soul is reserved for God, too little for man. But God himself cannot flourish if man's soul is starved. The feminine psyche responds to this hunger, for it is the function of Eros to unite what Logos has sundered. The woman of today is faced with a tremendous cultural task—perhaps it will be the dawn of a new era.

—Carl G. Jung
Aspects of the Feminine

Where the feminine resides, God stoops to humanity and humanity aspires to God.

—Hildegard of Bingen

Feminine wisdom is a continual affirmation of life, through its eternal readiness to respond to the quick of the moment; it is not communicated by the word or rite, but through presence and being.

—Robert Stein
Incest and Human Love

The magical, mythological and feminine ways of dealing with existence left behind thousands of years ago must now be reclaimed by consciousness.

—Edward Whitmont
Return of the Goddess

The Celts do a great deal of work in distinguishing two forms of the feminine energy, or "yin" energy, an earthly form and a starry, moonlike, or sunlike form.

—Robert Bly
Iron John

Feminism catches fire when it draws upon its inherent spirituality. When it does not, it is just one more form of politics and politics never fed our deepest hungers.

—Carol Lee Flinders
At the Root of This Longing

Our feminine wisdom values truth more than information, permanence more than change. It is she in us who desires to see things whole, to see into things, to be able to anticipate and then to wait. When we are in touch with her, we take the long view and are not seduced by expediency.

—June Singer
A Gnostic Book of Hours

It seems as if the female spirit of the world were mourning everlasting over blessings, not lost, but which she has never had, and which, in her discouragement she feels that she never will have, they are so far off.

—Florence Nightingale
The Saviour of Her Race

Today there opens for us
A door once closed,
Which a serpent barred in a woman:
And so there gleams the flower of
our Lady,
Brilliant in the dawn.

—Hildegard of Bingen
Antiphon for the Virgin 1

Femininity is Being that knows its bone truth.

—Marion Woodman
Bone

... it is that feminine energy that is the creative energy, that is the nurturing energy, that is the energy that brings balance, and the energy that brings perception.

—Lazaris
Lazaris Interviews

The serpents are universal symbols for the creative powers of the feminine. In esoteric psychology and physiology they represent the *kundalini*—the serpent power.... It is essentially a feminine force, and thus is not easily comprehended or come to terms with by the masculine dominated intellect. Hence in the paternally oriented Jewish tradition the serpent appears in the Garden of Eden as a bringer of evil, or at least of temptation.

—Gareth Knight
The Rose Cross and the Goddess

Women's spirituality is wild and free, matured, earthy, relational, mystical, embodied, intuitive, sensuous, compassionate.

—Joan Borysenko
A Woman's Journey to God

We are volcanoes. When we women offer our experiences, our truth, all the maps change.

—Ursula K. Le Guin

An evolved feminine will shift the balance of archetypal qualities toward more relatedness, emotional connection, and tolerance for the beauty and darkness of the natural world.

—Del McNeely

The return of God is one of the most ancient expectations of the human race. Every world religion has presented itself as preparing for his return. Every religion still awaits it... The return is the emergence of the feminine side of God, which has been gradually taking shape for centuries in what we call the unconscious. We long to see God, face to androgynous face.

—Marion Woodman
The Pregnant Virgin

Space is the mystery of the feminine from which life is born and reborn.

—Llewellyn Vaughan-Lee
In the Company of Friends

To ancient and modern astrologers, the Earth is a female planet—hinting that all humanity has come to learn more about the Divine Feminine.

—Ted Andrews
The Occult Christ

Only she who attempts the absurd can achieve the impossible.

—Feminist proverb

FIELDS

A morphic field is a kind of habit of nature. Each time a particular form occurs, it is more likely to occur again, whether nonorganic, such as an atom, a molecule, or a snowflake, or living, such as a flower, a bird or a human.

—Allan Combs & Mark Holland
Synchronicity

Every man takes the limits of his own field of vision for the limits of the world.

—Arthur Schopenhauer

There is no place where your energy field stops and another energy field begins.

This means there is no place where your soul ends and another's begins.... You can smell "kitchen air" when bread is baking and it melds into "living room air" ... yet air is one.

—Neale Donald Walsch
The New Revelations

Fields are like a superfine net. The knots appear to float on thin air. When the knots move, the threads move. When one knot moves, when another knot moves, we assume a net connects them.... Nature's memory is in a holofield.

—Ervin Laszlo
The Whispering Pond

Energy can take on any form.... Fields are patterns that organize energy into forms.... The interplay between energy and fields creates systems, patterns of interconnectedness, interaction and behavior.

—David Spangler
Everyday Miracles

Our phenomenal field contains many other bodies and we can move around them. There are multiple subjectivities.

—David Abram
The Spell of the Sensuous

The field of vision is something open, but its openness is not due to our looking.

—Martin Heidegger

The Force is an energy field created by all living things. It surrounds us, it penetrates us, it binds the galaxy together.

– *Star Wars*

FIRE

Fire transforms all things it touches into its own nature.... In the same way we are transformed into God so that we may know him as he is.

—Meister Eckhart

Some day, after we have mastered the winds, the waves, the tides, and gravity, we shall harness the energies of love. Then, for a second time in the history of the world man will have discovered fire.

—Pierre Teilhard de Chardin

The Hindus give an especially powerful divinity, the epithets *prakhar*, "very hot," *jajval*, "burning," or *jvalit*, "possessing fire." The Mohammedans of India believe that a man in communication with God becomes "burning." A man who performs miracles is called *sahib-josh*, *josh* meaning "boiling."

—Mircea Eliade
The Forge and the Crucible

If you are a friend of God, fire is your water. You should wish to have a hundred thousand sets of mothwings, so you could burn them away, one set a night.

—Jalal Al-din Rumi

The idea that time consists of dynamics and rhythmically structured patterns can be illustrated by the symbol of the old Chinese fire clock. This type of clock was constructed by spreading a combustible powder over a labyrinth and igniting it at one end, so that its burning head crept slowly forward like a fuse. Time was marked off according to the progress of the fire.

—Marie-Louise von Franz
Number and Time

Jung said, "the starfish generates so much heat that it not only sets fire to everything it touches but also cooks its own food. Hence it signifies the inextinguishable power of true love.... This fish glows forever in the midst of the waters and whatsoever it touches grows hot and burns into flames. This glow is a fire—the fire of the Holy Ghost."

—Victor Mansfield
Synchronicity, Science and Soulmaking

Jesus, Buddha, and even Moses, had fire in them, but they were equally sanguine and thoughtful.

—Thomas Moore
The Soul's Religion

We cannot not tell of God's presence in our souls.... The Creator Spirit seeks out our own creativity; fire begets fire.

—Meinrad Craighead
Sacred Stories

We want our lives to catch fire and burn blue, not smolder.

—Gregg Levoy
Callings

FOOD

Help yourself to the food and welcome, and then afterward, when you have tasted dinner, we shall ask you who among men you are.

—Homer
Odyssey

There are two desires natural in man, one of food for the sake of the body, and one of wisdom for the sake of the diviner part of us.

—Plato (Aristocles)
Timaeus

Respect the food as though it were for the emperor.

—Dogen Zenji
Moon in a Dewdrop

My food is the will of Him who made me and who made all things in order to give Himself to me through them.

—Thomas Merton
New Seeds of Contemplation

Ought we not when we are digging and ploughing and eating to sing this hymn to God? "Great is God, who has given us such implements with which we shall cultivate the earth: great is God who has given us hands, the power of swallowing, a stomach, imperceptible growth, and the power of breathing while we sleep."

—Epictetus
Discourses

Everything that the senses receive is nourishment ... try always to remain the master of what you absorb.

—Ananda Moyi
Aux Sources de la Joie

There is no death that is not somebody's
food, no life that is not somebody's
death.... The shimmering food-web is the
scary, beautiful condition of the biosphere.

—Gary Snyder
Wake Up and Cook

People wandered into Herakleitus'
kitchen and found him cooking ... he
said, "Here too there be gods!"

—Ignacio L. Götz
On Technology and the Spirit

A good book about food informs us
of matters with which we are to be
concerned all our lives. Sight and hearing
lose their edge, the muscles soften, even
the most gallant of our glands at last
surrenders. But the palate may persist in
glory almost to the very end.

—M. F. K. Fisher
The Art of Eating

Pray for peace and grace and
spiritual food, For wisdom and
guidance, for all these are good, But
don't forget the potatoes.

—J. T. Pettee
Prayer and Potatoes

We lose 25 billion tons on earth of topsoil
every year. It's our future generation's food!

—Thomas Berry
The Great Work

A picture of food does not nourish us.

—Augustine

Food is a cultural product; it cannot
be produced by technology alone
... a healthy culture is a communal
order of memory, insight, value, work,
conviviality, reverence, aspiration.... It
clarifies our inescapable bonds to the
earth and to each other.

—Wendell Berry
The Unsettling of America

What is eaten is sunlight. What is
excreted is the dark night. The breath of
life is in the clouds, and the blood is the
rain that falls on the world.

—Ogotemmeli & Marcel Griaule
Conversations with Ogotemmeli

The whole distinction between art and
trash, food and garbage, depends on the
presence or absence of the loving eye.

—Robert Farrar Capon
The Supper of the Lamb

Remember Verna's honey-glazed donuts?
Weren't they something!

—Tip O'Neil's last words.

FORGIVENESS

When you forgive, some deeper, divine
generosity takes you over.... When you
cannot forgive, you are a prisoner of the
hurt done to you.

—John O'Donohue
Eternal Echoes

Four stages of forgiveness: 1. to forego—
to leave it alone; 2. to forebear—to
abstain from punishing; 3. to forget—to

aver from memory, to refuse to dwell; 4. to forgive—to abandon the debt.

—Clarissa Pinkola Estés
Women Who Run with the Wolves

In Russian, "good-bye" and "forgive me" are practically interchangeable.

—Anne Morrow Lindbergh
War Without and War Within

Forgiveness is really just correcting our own misperceptions.

—Wayne W. Dyer
You'll See It When You Believe It

Angry feelings must be experienced and expressed before genuine forgiveness can be offered and accepted.

—Robert Chernin Canto
And a Time to Live

Life is an adventure in forgiveness.

—Norman Cousins

Forgiveness does not mean ignoring what has been done or putting a false label on an evil act. It means, rather, that the evil act no longer remains as a barrier to the relationship.

—Bernie Siegel
Love, Medicine and Miracles

If you forgive people enough you belong to them, and they to you, whether either person likes it or not—squatter's rights of the heart.

—James Hilton
Time and Time Again

Become aware of the person toward whom you feel resentment and picture good things happening to him or her.

—Emmett Fox
Sermon on the Mount

When you are truly patient and tolerant, then forgiveness comes naturally.

—Dalai Lama
The Art of Happiness

FORTUNE

A man is never so in trial as in the moment of excessive good fortune.

—Lew Wallace
Ben Hur

Fortune and misfortune are like the twisted strands of a rope.

—Japanese proverb

If a man is destined to drown, he will drown even in a spoonful of water.

—Yiddish proverb

FRACTAL

Fractals provide a glimpse of infinity that is well-bounded, of simplicity feeding back on itself to create beautiful complexity…. Because of the fractal nature of ferns, it is possible to generate them on computers, using a few numeric values that describe the basic dimensions of the fern. This is the chaos game, where simple rules combine with chaos to form predictable order.

—Margaret J. Wheatley
Leadership and the New Science

Fractals describe the way things cluster in space and time ... things wear their irregularity in an unexpectedly orderly fashion.

—James Gleick

Composers didn't set out to create music with a fractal structure. It just happened that way.

—Mark Ward
Beyond Chaos

The Mandlebrot set is a whole universe in miniature.

—F. David Peat
The Philosopher's Stone

Edges can only be described with fractal geometry. Edges are unmeasurable except in terms of infinite possibilities.... What happens at edges is too complex to control.

—Thom Hartmann
The Prophet's Way

A fractal can't be understood by breaking it down into its parts—every stay replicates the whole. Fractals are self-similar and self-generated.... Nature is never spent, but infinite.

—F. David Peat
Sacred Stories

FREEDOM

Freedom is perhaps the ultimate spiritual longing of an individual human being, but freedom is only really appreciated when it falls within the parameters of a larger sense of belonging. In freedom is the wish to belong to structure in our own particular way.

—David Whyte
Crossing the Unknown Sea

Freedom is necessary for choice, and choice is necessary for wisdom and growth ... the sacred world of love and wisdom, fiery intelligence and passionate will, imagination and delight—is a world of freedom. It is liberating. But it is also binding and connecting.

—David Spangler
A Pilgrim in Aquarius

Freedom is the way human beings put their past out of play by secreting their own nothingness.

—Jean-Paul Sartre
Being and Nothingness

God therefore gives to human beings the power to utter yes or no—to perceive the whole range of dualities without which there could be no freedom.

—Denise Levertov
Work that Enfaiths

As a writer you are free. You are about the freest person that ever was. Your freedom is what you have bought with your solitude, your loneliness.

—Ursula K. Le Guin

Perhaps the final freedom will be a recognition that every thing in every moment is "essential" and that nothing at all is "important"!

—Helen M. Luke
The Way of Woman

Christian freedom always has its limitations: you are only as free as the servants of God, no less, no more.

—Paul Scherer
Love Is a Spendthrift

Freedom entails freedom to go wrong.... Four-fifths of the world's suffering, says he, grows out of the wickedness of human souls who have misused their freedom of will.

—Clyde S. Kilby
The Christian World of C. S. Lewis

To live in love towards our actions, and to let live in the understanding of the other person's will, is the fundamental maxim of free men.

—Rudolf Steiner
The Philosophy of Freedom

When Merton asked a Buddhist abbot, "What is the knowledge of freedom?" the abbot replied, "One must ascend all the steps, but then when there are no more steps one must make the leap. Knowledge of freedom is the knowledge, the experience, of this leap."

—Marion Woodman
The Pregnant Virgin

To have freedom, give it; to have peace, make it.

—Edgar Cayce
On Reincarnation

There are three sets of mental filters to give up if you want to be truly free: judging, comparing, and needing to know why. The why inevitably becomes clear as you progress in your passage.

—Brugh Joy
Joy's Way

Lives based on having are less free than lives based on doing or on being.

—William James

The capacity to get free is nothing; the capacity to be free—that is the task.

—André Gide

FRIENDSHIP

Let there be no purpose in friendship save the deepening of spirit.

—Kahil Gibran

Friendship needs no words—it is solitude delivered from the anguish of loneliness.

—Dag Hammarskjöld
Markings

Each friend represents a world in us, a world possibility not born until they arrive and it is only by this meeting a new world is born.

—Anäis Nin

Nobody sees a flower—really—it is so small—we haven't time—and to see takes time. Like to have a friend takes time.

—Georgia O'Keefe

With each true friendship, we build more firmly the foundation on which the peace of the whole world rests.

—Mohandas (Mahatma) Gandhi

A soul friend is someone with whom we can share our greatest joys and deepest fears, confess our worst sins and most persistent faults, clarify our highest hopes and perhaps most unarticulated dreams.

—Edward C. Sellner

Friendship is almost always the union of a part of one mind with another; people are friends in spots.

—George Santayana

The most important obligation of friendship is to listen.

—Max Perkins & Scott Berg
Max Perkins: Editor of Genius

Friends exist side by side, absorbed in some common interest or vision for the world. Others may join such a friendship because they share the same vision. Understood this way, friendship is potentially the most inclusive of all relationships.... Friendship is formed out of freedom.

—Herbert Anderson & Freda A. Gardner
Living Alone

"Why did you do all this for me?" Wilbur asked. "I don't deserve it. I've never done anything for you."... "You have been my friend," replied Charlotte ... "I wove my webs for you because I liked you... "

—E. B. White
Charlotte's Web

In the end, all books are written for your friends.

—Gabriel Garcia Márquez

Many people will walk in and out of your life, but only true friends will leave footprints in your heart.

—Eleanor Roosevelt

A friend is someone who abides. Waits.

—Shaun McNiff
Art as Medicine

We have friends in order that we not get killed.

—Martin Marty

I speak a word. My friend speaks back. Then I again, then he, and thus we make a bridge of words so each may fetch across the ditch that lies between what's in his heart.

—Frederick Buechner
Godric

If all men knew what each said of the other, there would not be four friends in the world.

—Blaise Pascal

A friend is another self.

—Aristotle

Friend: One-who-carries-my-sorrows-on-his back.

—Native American expression

Anyone without a soul friend is like a body without a head.

—Irish proverb

FULFILLMENT

We already have everything we need. There is no need for self-improvement.

—Pema Chödrön
Start Where You Are

We shall hear the angels, we shall see the whole sky all diamonds. We shall see how all earthly evil, all our sufferings are drowned in the mercy that will fill the whole world. And our life will grow peaceful, tender, sweet as a caress.

—Anton Chekov

Women fulfill themselves in having babies and men fulfill themselves in destroying them.

—Pearl Buck

FUNDAMENTALISM

There is undoubtedly a strong relationship between fundamentalism and violence. And there are those who will stop at nothing to reign terror and destruction on whomever they perceive as their enemies ... there is a strong relationship between fundamentalism and prejudice.

—Kimberly Blaker
The Fundamentals of Extremism

It is the fundamentalists' belief in the rapture, of being protected from the end-time disasters, that leads some to cling to their separatist world and to avoid social responsibility.

—Charles B. Strozier
Apocalypse

Our goal is not to make the schools better ... the goal is to hamper them so they cannot grow.... Our goal as God-fearing, uncompromised ... Christians is to shut down the public schools ... step by step, school by school, district by district.

—Robert Thoburne
The Children Trap

Fundamentalism does not converse or explore. It presents truth.... This false certainty can only endure through the belief that everyone else is wrong ... it desires power in order to implement its vision and force the others to do as prescribed.

—John O'Donohue
Eternal Echoes

The important thing to remember is that fundamentalist Christian members will go down into any gutter, barroom of filth, or hellish nightmare of shattered family life, and offer a viable alternative with strict rules, "black-and-white" categories of looking at life, and supply a ready-made community of support, friendliness and interaction.... Contrasted with a

155

life of drinking to excess and receiving total wages in a job the breadwinner hates, Fundamentalist Christianity offers an opportunity for that person to have dignity, honor, and blessings.

—David Coffin
Leaving the Fold

Religious training can induce Islamic (or Christian or Jewish) youths to undertake a holy war against infidels or to lead a peaceful life in a pluralistic society.

—Howard Gardner
Changing Minds

... the inquisitor who mistakes his own cruelty and lust of power and fear for the voice of Heaven will torment us infinitely because he torments us with the approval of his own conscience and his better impulses appear to him as temptations. And since Theocracy is the worst, the nearer any government approaches to Theocracy the worse it will be.... Hitler, the Machiavellian Prince, the Inquisition, the Witch Doctor, all claimed to be necessary.

—C. S. Lewis
Of Other Worlds

We are God's people and they are God's (and ours) enemy.... To be crystal clear about one's identity, to know that one's group is superior to all others, to make purity one's motto and purification of the world one's life work—this is a kind of bliss.

—Jessica Stern
Terror in the Name of God

The pitfall of fundamentalism—Jewish, Christian and Islamic—is that when some item is held constant while the context varies, constancy is an illusion

and those who resist change often suffer the reverse.

—Mary Catherine Bateson
Peripheral Visions

FUTURE

Get rid of fear and terror and be serene about the future.

—Rudolf Steiner

The Gospel is first of all a call to leave the past behind and open ourselves to the promise of the future. We have not yet learned how to be full stewards of our gifts.

—Harvey Cox
On Not Leaving It to the Snake

Almost everything that has happened, and its opposite, has been prophesied. The problem has always been to pick and choose among the embarrassing riches of alternative projected futures; and in this, human societies have not demonstrated any large foresight.

—Herbert A. Simon
The Sciences of the Artificial

The future is uncertain ... but this uncertainty is at the very heart of human creativity.

—Ilya Prigogine

People speak about what is in store. But there is nothing in store. The day is made of what has come before. The world itself must be surprised at the shape of that which appears. Perhaps even God.

—Cormac McCarthy
The Crossing

What sort of future is coming up from behind I don't really know. But the past, spread out ahead, dominates everything in sight.

—Robert M. Pirsig
*Zen and the Art of
Motorcycle Maintenance*

We are living in an age when much is in preparation for the immediate future of humanity here on Earth and ... we have to feel ourselves to be people who have some idea that something has to be prepared for the future in human souls.

—Rudolf Steiner
The Fifth Gospel

The future will not be what has happened before; indeed, the only reality that the future has is that it has not happened yet.... For this reason the concept of the future—for the first time—holds out promise, rather than the same old thing. We are not doomed, not bound to some predetermined fate; we are free.

—Thomas Cahill
The Gifts of the Jews

The future is what you dream.

—Morris West

I like the dreams of the future better than the history of the past.

—Thomas Jefferson

The cult of the future has turned us all into prophets.... Our obsession with security is a measure of the power we have granted the future to hold over us.

—Wendell Berry
The Unsettling of America

The future is only the past again, entered through another gate.

—Arthur Wing Pinero

Precisely because the future is essentially unknowable, it forces us to stay broad-minded and fast on our feet.

—Stewart Brand
The Clock of the Long Now

When I pronounce the word Future, the first syllable already belongs to the past.

—Wislawa Szymborska

If one is mentally out of breath all the time from dealing with the present, there is no energy left for imagining the future.

—Elise Boulding

Economic forecasting misses the real future because it has too short a range; fiction misses the future because it has too little imagination.

—Freeman Dyson

There are people who demand room for bold gestures. The future speaks ruthlessly through them.... The future stands firm but we move in infinite space.

—Rainer Maria Rilke

The future is not some fixed entity that awaits us in time.... The question is not what we should do tomorrow, but what should we do today to be ready for tomorrow?

—William Sherden
The Fortune Sellers

We used to think our future was in the stars. Now we know it's in our genes.

—James Watson

Events do not happen; they are just there and we come across them. The "formality of taking place" is merely the indication that the observer has on his voyage of exploration passed into the absolute future of the event in question; and it has no important significance.

—Arthur S. Eddington
Space, Time and Gravitation

The best way to predict the future is to create it.

—Peter Drucker

The future will be a series of overlapping networks in which no group dominates another. The long-term aim would be to create a decentralized society of self-managed communities.... The economy would turn away from maximizing profits to minimizing harm.

—Peter Marshall
Nature's Web

What shape waits in the seed of you to grow and spread its branches against a future sky?

—David Whyte
Crossing the Unknown Sea

The mind of man is capable of anything because everything is in it, all the past as well as all the future.

—Joseph Conrad
Heart of Darkness

Let tomorrow come tomorrow.

—Wendell Berry
What Are People For?

The future speaks ruthlessly through you.

—Jalal Al-din Rumi

GAMBLING

Gambling on a God who has so gambled
on us does not seem so risky in the end.

—Sara Maitland
A Big Enough God

In emotional intensity, game and
gambler coincide.

—Carl. G. Jung

Legalization of gambling: A nation once
built on a work ethic embraces the
belief that it's possible to get something
for nothing.

– Walter Cronkite *&* Jackson Lears
Something for Nothing

Contemporary gambling games recall
ancient rituals—attempts to divine the
decrees of fate and conjure the wayward
force of luck … we keep waiting for that
unearned blessing to shower down.…
Dice descended from soothsayers' bones.

—Jackson Lears
Something for Nothing

GARDENS

To know someone here and there who
thinks and feels with us, and, though

distant, is close in spirit … this makes the earth for us an inhabited garden.

—Johann Wolfgang von Goethe

When I talk about working my flower beds by feel, then, I really mean that I am relying on my diffuse awareness. I am allowing all the peripheral information to come in and inform my decision even if I cannot tell you how I know what I know.

—Carol Frenier
Business and the Feminine Principle

In search of my mother's garden, I found my own.

—Alice Walker
In Search of My Mother's Garden

Entering a garden is like passing through a mystical gate. Things are not the same on the other side, in the interior where nature has been arranged, whether formally or casually, to suggest to our senses and our subliminal imagination a mid-realm somewhere between the conscious, known world of ordinary life and the less conscious, mystery world of the garden.

—Thomas Moore
The Re-Enchantment of Everyday Life

We know that the European walled garden of the Middle Ages drew many inspired traits from gardens that flourished in Persia, Arabia, and other Near Eastern countries…. A stone fountain, for example, three or four feet high, built over a well, had sills or tunnels that carried water out to the four directions.

The alchemists call such a fountain … the well of Hermes.

—Robert Bly
Iron John

When a building works, when the world enters the blissful state that makes us fully comfortable, the space itself awakens. We awaken. The garden awakens.

—Christopher Alexander
The Phenomenon of Life

Gardening is an active participation in the deepest mysteries of the universe.

—Thomas Berry

When we garden, we instinctively act to preserve existing wholeness.

—Christopher Alexander
The Process of Creating Life

Carl Jung studied the human psyche and called the garden a metaphor for the soul—a place of multi-foliate imagery.

—Pamela Woods
Gardens for the Soul

GENDERS

The Cosmic Christ can be both female and male, heterosexual and homosexual.

—Matthew Fox
The Coming of the Cosmic Christ

Gender is infinitely more subtle than biological difference and is never static…. Gender is a state of mind, a product of the imagination. One man experiences masculinity in a way entirely different from another. The femininity of a particular woman is unique, an aspect of her personality, or, even deeper, a manifestation of her soul.

—Thomas Moore
Original Self

The masculine and feminine elements, exactly equal and balancing each other, are as essential to the maintenance of the equilibrium of the universe as positive and negative electricity, the centripetal and centrifugal forces, the laws of attraction which bind together all we know of this planet, whereon we dwell and of the system in which we revolve.

—Elizabeth Cady Stanton
The Woman's Bible

Our deep human sexuality will be fulfilled only when we discover that the lover we seek is divine and beyond finding.

— Thomas Moore
Original Self

Man, alone in his manliness,
is incomplete.
Woman, alone in her womanliness,
is incomplete.
… each searches to find the other so there is both.
So it is that there is man and woman and the fulfillment of each other.

—Ray Grigg
Tao of Relationships

The woman most in need of liberation is the woman in every man.

—William Sloane Coffin
Credo

The world of humanity is possessed of two wings: the male and the female. So long as these wings are not equivalent in strength, the bird will not fly. Until womankind reaches the same degree as man, until she enjoys the same arena of activity, extraordinary attainment for humanity will not be realized; humanity cannot wing its way to heights of real attainment.

—Abudu'l-Bahá

Men and women need each other; we need to learn from each other… men teach women how to organize their consciousness, especially in the everyday world. Women teach men about the Sacred Dream, how to receive and implement the wisdom of their consciousness. Women teach men how to live. Men teach women how to express their dreams and bring an exchange of energy back from the world.

—Lynn V. Andrews
Jaguar Woman

Men are more apt to attribute their success to skill; women to luck.

—Susan Estrich
Sex and Power

The differences between men and women are our most important resource in learning new ways of thinking about difference.

—Mary Catherine Bateson
Composing a Life

The Chipewyans, in northwest Canada, believe that to be female is to be power, whereas men must acquire power.

—Robert Briffault
The Mothers

Terrible things happen to men who are
deprived of the presence of women, for
apparently it is the presence of women
that reminds each man of the best that is
in him.

—Robert A. Johnson
She

If man and woman were the same, that
would be stalemate. The earth would
be sterile. Where the land is flat there is
no flow of water; it has nowhere to go;
it stagnates. In order to produce energy,
you must have opposites—an above and a
below. There must be a difference in level,
and the greater it is the swifter and more
forcefully does the water flow.

—Carl G. Jung
C. G. Jung Speaking

One who has a man's wings, and a woman's
also, is in himself a womb of the world.

—Lao Tzu

GENTLENESS

If human beings can be trained for cruelty
and greed and a belief in power which
comes through hate and fear and force,
certainly we can train equally well for
gentleness and mercy and the power of
love which comes because of the strength
of the good qualities to be found in the
soul of every individual human being.

—Eleanor Roosevelt
The Moral Basis of Democracy

In a gentle way, you can shake the world.

—Mohandas (Mahatma) Gandhi

There is in all things an inexhaustible
sweetness and purity, a silence that is a
fountain of action and joy. It rises up in
wordless gentleness and flows out to me
from unseen roots of all creating being.

—Thomas Merton

It is the weak who are cruel; gentleness is
to be expected only from the strong.

—Leo Rosten

GIFTS/GIVING

God has gifted creation with everything
that is necessary.

—Hildegard of Bingen

The Ground of our being is generosity.
The ultimate source of All That Is, the
support and well of being, is Ultimate
Generosity… We are Generosity-of-
Being evolved into human form.

—Brian Swimme
The Universe is a Green Dragon

To give the respect of recognition is a
form of love; it is one level, one expression of what Martin Buber termed confirmation of being and said was the best gift
one human being could give another.

—Denise Levertov
Light Up the Cave

The many have dispensed with generosity
in order to practice charity.

—Albert Camus

Anticipate charity by preventing poverty.

—Maimonides

Give what you have. To someone, it may be better than you dare to think.

—Henry Wadsworth Longfellow

There is only one real deprivation, I decided this morning, and that is not to be able to give one's gift to those one loves most. The gift turned inward, unable to be given, becomes a heavy burden, even sometimes a kind of poison. It is as though the flow of life were backed up.

—May Sarton

A gift of any kind is a considerable responsibility. It is a mystery in itself, something gratuitous and wholly undeserved, something whose real uses will probably always be hidden from us.

—Flannery O'Connor
   The Nature and Aim of Fiction

All you are unable to give, possesses you.

—André Gide

One must be poor to know the luxury of giving.

—George Eliot

Gifts, by their very nature, must come from a source beyond our control. Otherwise they are not gifts but things taken under duress.

—Shierry Weber Nicholsen
   The Love of Nature and the End of the World

What gifts are you afraid of receiving?

—David Whyte
   Crossing the Unknown Sea

The fragrance always remains in the hand that gives the rose.

—Mohandas (Mahatma) Gandhi

God is not likely to force upon us any gift we don't truly want.

—Sara Maitland
   A Big Enough God

GNOSIS/GNOSTIC

What Muhammad 'Ali discovered at Nag Hammadi is, apparently, a library of writings, almost all of them Gnostic... these divine texts buried... for nearly 2000 years... were denounced as heresy by orthodox Christians in the middle of the second century.

—Dan Burstein
   Secrets of the Code

The existence of the ideal Gnostic disciple is characterized by the term solitary one, which describes the one who has left behind everything that binds human beings to the world. Even women can obtain this goal, if they achieve the "maleness" of the solitary existence.

—Helmut Koester & Dan Burstein
   Secrets of the Code

Much of the trismegistic literature is taken from the original Greek texts.... The Jewish influence was Essenic ... the Trismegistus then came under the influence of the early Christian Gnostics, many of whom adopted large chunks of it in defense of their beliefs which were subsequently labeled "heresies." The most notable of these was Basildes whom Carl Jung believed to be either a fragment of his own group soul ... or himself in a former life.

—Murry Hope
Ancient Egypt

In the beginning, there was not one Christianity, but many. And among them was a well-established tradition of Gnosticism.... Early Christian history proceeds to an untidy story punctuated by loose ends, unknowns, intrigues both political and personal, ironies, and considerable doses of what in today's political vernacular might be called "spin."

—Dan Burstein
Secrets of the Code

The Gnostics truly were "psychonauts" who boldly explored the final frontiers of inner space, searching for the origins and meaning of life. These people were mystics and creative free-thinkers.

—Timothy Freke & Peter Gandy
The Jesus Mysteries

Gnosis is based not in the understanding of the mind but in the sensibility of the heart.... Gnosis speaks through individuals, to each according to his or her own nature.

—June Singer
A Gnostic Book of Hours

Gnosis is privileged knowledge vouchsafed to the courageous.

—Terrence McKenna

Amidst the often very strange cosmology of the Gnostic sects, there can be found what has come to be known as Gnosticism, the belief that spiritual development and salvation are achieved through inner knowing.

—Jacob Needleman, Foreword
Jean-Yves LeLoup
The Gospel of Mary Magdalene

Women are drawn to Gnostics with its stress on personal revelation.

—Mary E. Giles
The Feminist Mystic

The Greek language distinguishes between scientific or reflective knowledge (He knows mathematics) and knowing through observation or experience (He knows me) which is gnosis. As the gnostics use the term, we could translate it as "insight".... As Mary stands up to Peter, so the Gnostics who take her as their prototype, challenge the authority of those priests and bishops who claim to be Peter's successors.

—Elaine Pagels
The Gnostic Gospels

GOALS

The goal is the same; the starting points are different.

—Rudolf Steiner
An Outline of Occult Science

I want to remake the world; anything less is not worth the trouble.

—Karen Cushman

My feeling is if you need a reward to tempt yourself to reach a personal goal, the goal may not be worth reaching. What you do instead of your real work is your real work.

—Robert Ebert

It is good to have an end to journey towards, but it is the journey that matters, in the end.

—Ursula K. LeGuin
The Left Hand of Darkness

There are two tragedies in a man's life. The first is to have failed to have reached your goal; the second is to have reached it.

—Friedrich Nietzche

To undertake a voluntary aim, and to achieve it, gives magnetism and the ability to do.

—Kathleen Riorden Speeth
Gurdjieff's Work

Kierkegaard said "Purity is to will one thing." But blindness is apt to affect anyone who pursues a single goal.

—Mary Catherine Bateson
Peripheral Visions

Your goal is to find out who you are.

—*A Course in Miracles*

If you do not change direction, you end up where you are headed.

—Chinese proverb

GOD

Oh friends, I beg you to come. Come to the living room of God!

—Ramakrishna (Gadadhar Chatterji)

Fundamentally, there is only one Great Ultimate, yet each of the myriad things has been endowed with it and each in itself possesses the Great Ultimate in its entirety. This is similar to the fact that there is only one moon in the sky, but when its light is scattered upon rivers and lakes, it can be seen everywhere. It cannot be said that the moon has been split.

—Chu Hsi
The Philosophy of Human Nature

God is a circle whose center is everywhere, and its circumference nowhere.

—Empedocles

God cannot be shaken out nor strained through a sieve by human argument.

—Hildegard of Bingen

God is a symbol for God.

—Paul Tillich

And thus I saw that God rejoiceth that he is our Brother, and God rejoiceth that he is our Mother, and God rejoiceth that he is our very spouse and our soul is his loved wife.

—Julian of Norwich
Revelations of Divine Love

Dieties change with the times, taking ever new forms, even as the essential archetype remains constant, veiled in its eternal mystery.

—David Leeming
Myth: A Biography of Belief

Oh, God, I did not know you were so big.

—Sojourner Truth
Narrative of Sojourner Truth

On the bookshelf of life, God is a useful work of reference, always at hand but seldom consulted.

—Dag Hammarskjöld
Markings

God is the partner of our most intimate soliloquies.

—Viktor E. Frankl
The Unheard Cry for Meaning

The best way to know God is to love many things.

—Vincent van Gogh

These eyes through which I hoped to see God, are the eyes through which God sees me.

—Meister Eckhart

In all faces is shown the Face of Faces, veiled and as if in a riddle.

—Nicholas Krebs of Cusa

A person is not a thing or a process, but an opening through which the absolute manifests.

—Martin Heidegger

Another name for God is surprise.

—David Steindl-Rast

God is at home.... It is we who have gone for a walk.

—Meister Eckhart

If I spent enough time with the tiniest creature—even a caterpillar—I would never have to prepare a sermon. So full of God is every creature.

—Meister Eckhart

Yah of Yahweh means "God." It also means "word." A daughter of God is also a daughter of the word.

—Gail Sher
The Intuitive Writer

Ain't no way to read the bible and not think God white, she say. Then she sigh. When I found out God was white, and a man, I lost interest... God ain't he or she, but a it... don't look like anything else, including you. I believe God is everything.

—Alice Walker
The Color Purple

God, to me, it seems, is a verb not a noun, proper or improper.

—R. Buckminster Fuller
No More Secondhand God

I am a little pencil in the hand of a writing God who is sending a love letter to the world.

—Mother Teresa

God is subtle, but not malicious.

—Albert Einstein

God is an angel in an angel, a stone in a stone and a straw in a straw.

—John Donne

Once you accept the existence of God—however you define him, however you explain your relationship to him—then you are caught forever with his presence in the center of all things.

Morris West
The Clowns of God

God is the I of the universe.

—A. R. Orage

Every bush is a Burning Bush and the world is crowded with God.

—C. S. Lewis

Every intelligent creature gives the name of God to the best and highest thing he knows.

—*The Urantia Book*

Man cannot meet God—in life or in death—but God can meet man... With God, the passing grade is zero and to pass is a sheer gift.

—Peter J. Kreeft
Love is Stronger Than Death

Open your eyes and the whole world is full of God.

—Jacob Boehme

God is creatively present in everyone in every moment whether we are aware of it or not. But when we are in the state of silent gratefulness we are aware of his presence.

—Paul Tillich

We and God have business with each other; and in opening ourselves to his influence our deepest destiny is fulfilled.

—William James
Varieties of Religious Experience

We are all little particles of something we cannot name, fiercely intelligent and full of overwhelming passion that emerges from the mystery that made us and lives within us—and IS us. I will not call it soul or God or Paraclete or essence or Christ-consciousness. It is old, I know that, but I will not diminish its potential by naming it before it consumes me into itself.

—Whitley Strieber
Transformation

The weight of history is unbearable without the idea of God.

—Carl G. Jung

All That Is is composed of each and every pigeon and wren and cardinal and bird and dog and leaf. And All That Is speaks to Itself constantly through growing worlds and realities and those whispers and those murmurs are lonely only in that they yearn for further creativity.

—Jane Roberts
Adventures in Consciousness

If you could understand this peanut, you would know God.

—George Washington Carver

We need the foolishness of God.

—Madeleine L'Engle
The Summer of the Great Grandmother

God writes straight with crooked lines.

—Charles Peguy

There is a fine old story about a student who came to a rabbi and said, "in the olden days, there were men who saw the face of God. Why don't they any more?" The rabbi replied, "Because nowadays no one can stoop so low."

—Carl G. Jung
Memories, Dreams, Reflections

As you know, any plain person you chance to meet can prove to be a powerful immortal in disguise come to test you.

—Maxine Hong Kingston
China Men

As you know, God can dress up as anybody. Is there anybody He is not dressed up as?

—Hugh Prather
*There Is a Place Where
You Are Not Alone*

It is necessary to name Him whose silence I share and worship, for in His silence He also speaks my own name.... For in the instant in which He calls me "my Son" I am aware of Him as "my Father."

—Thomas Merton
Thoughts in Solitude

Tell me what God you don't believe in and I'm sure we will find that I do not believe in that god either.

—Karl Barth

My me is God!

—Catherine of Genoa

God is not body ... is not soul, intelligence, imagination, opinion, thought, word, number, order, size.... Try to understand, Baudolino: God is a lamp without a flame, a flame without a fire, a fire without heat, a dark light, a silent rumble, a blind flash, a luminous soot, a ray of his own darkness, a circle that expands concentrating on its own center, a solitary multiplicity.... God in his fullness, is also the place, or non-place, where the opposites are confounded.

—Umberto Eco
Baudolino

God has revealed, through the prophet Muhammad, "There are seventy thousand veils between you and Me, and there are no veils between Me and you."

—James Fadiman & Robert Frager
Sufism

Let your "being you" sink into God's "being God."

—Meister Eckhart
Sinking Eternally Into God

God is the perfect, unique mirror without boundaries, containing all faces, all images, and joining all opposites.

—Sabine Melchior-Bonnet
The Mirror

Whatever you imagine, God is the opposite of that.

—Llewellyn Vaughan-Lee
In the Company of Friends

How terrible the need for God.

Theodore Roethke
Notebook

If God were living on earth, people would break his windows.

—Yiddish proverb

If you wish to know God, first know yourself.

—Desert Fathers proverb

The further you go into the desert, the closer you come to God.

—Arabic proverb

God tempers the wind to the shorn lamb.

—Old English proverb

GODDESS

At the very dawn of religion, God was a woman. Do you remember?...

She is slowly finding us and we are quietly everywhere.

—Merlin Stone
When God Was a Woman

The Divine Mother is always sportive and playful. The universe is Her play. She is self-willed and must always have her own way. She is full of bliss.... She wants to continue playing with Her created beings in a game of hide and seek. It's as if she said, go and enjoy the world.

—Ramakrishna
(Gadadhar Chatterji)

"She" is many goddesses from the settings in which her likenesses are found we know that she was worshipped variously as the guardian of childbirth, the source of wisdom, the dispenser of healing, the Lady of the Beasts, the founder of prophecy, the spirit who presided over death.... But despite her various names and her different purposes, she is a single goddess.

—Carl Olson
The Book of the Goddess

The Eternal Feminine is our guide.

—Johann Wolfgang von Goethe

In our long isolation from the Goddess, under the tutelage of our many Father-Gods, there has been gestating within us a strength of form that will allow humanity to withstand the assault of such unitive splendor as few can imagine. Ahead lies a degree of incarnation of the Divine impulses that would have shattered us at an earlier stage in our evolutionary development.

—Christopher M. Bache
Dark Night, Early Dawn

Until women can visualize the sacred
female they cannot be whole.

—Elinor Gadon

I found God in myself and I loved
her fiercely.

—Ntosake Shange
  for colored girls who have considered
  suicide when the rainbow is enuf

Today the goddess is no longer worshipped. Her shrines are lost in the dust
of ages while her statues line the walls of
museums. But the law or power of which
she was but the personification is unabated
in its strength and life-giving potency.

—Esther Harding
  Women's Mysteries

Mother Goddess is reawakening, and
we can begin to recover our primal
birthright, the sheer, intoxicating joy of
being alive.

—Starhawk
  The Spiral Dance

The Goddess can be seen as the symbol,
the normative image of immanence.
She represents the divine embodied in
nature, in human beings, in the flesh. The
Goddess is not one image, but many."

—Starhawk
  Dreaming the Dark

Goddess figurines were sculpted over the
span of about thirty-thousand years.

—L. Robert Keck
  Sacred Quest

What we await in the Second Coming
is what we lack: God's inner dynamic or
process. This—God in his creativeness
rather than in his creation—is the essence
of the feminine, traditionally enacted
in the ancient Mysteries. The return is
therefore the emergence of the feminine
side of God, which has been gradually
taking shape for centuries in what we call
the unconscious. The time has now come
when we can deal creatively with the
concept of God as the union of opposites,
and therefore see the feminine no longer
darkly through a masculine glass, but
face to androgynous face.

—Marion Woodman
  Addiction to Perfection

And no one will listen to us until we listen
to ourselves. The Goddess awakens in our
hearts before she awakens in the world.

—Marianne Williamson

We must find a way to mainstream the
goddess into the universe within which
women are actually living their lives. Or
perhaps it is simply a question of recognizing that she has been there all along.

—Susan Cady, *et al*
  Wisdom's Feast

Let it be known: today the Eternal
Feminine in an incorruptible body is
descending to Earth. In the unfading
light of the new goddess Heaven has
become one with the deeps.

—Vladimir Solovyov

The symbolism of the Goddess is not a
parallel structure to the symbolism of

God the Father. The Goddess does not rule the world; She is the world.

—Starhawk
The Spiral Dance

A return to Goddess worship means a reaffirmation of creativity and birth, the female principle in men and women, and the interconnectedness in life. The goddess is both the earth and the heavens. She is all that lives, and all that lives is part of her. To pollute the earth by nuclear leakage, therefore, is to pollute the Goddess and oneself. To deal in the oppression of any gender or minority is to disrespect the Goddess. To cause harm brings harm in return.

—Diane Stein
The Kwan Yin: Book of Changes

Myths of the Great Goddess teach compassion for all living beings. There you come to appreciate the real sanctity of the earth itself, because it is the body of the Goddess.

—Joseph Campbell
The Power of Myth

Every woman is psychic by birthright/wombright, and every women holds the Python Goddess within her.

—Diane Stein
Stroking the Python

Surely the "womb theology" of the Great Mother, in labor and agony until creation is reborn, is a timely God myth for us today.... This Mother God shatters our illusions of omnipotence and separateness which are fed by cultural ethos of individualism and ego. She dissolves the false god myths and reveals the hidden face of the one true God, the God of

mercy, that mercy which the ancients called "womb-love." In the new myth, God is not "up there," "out there," or "in me." We are in God.

—Madonna Kolbenschlag
Lost in the Land of Oz

… power as linking has from time immemorial been symbolized by the circle or oval—the Goddess's cosmic egg or Great Round—rather than by the jagged lines of a pyramid where, as gods or as the heads of nations or families, men rule from the top.

—Riane Eisler
The Chalice and the Blade

Denied and suppressed for thousands of years, the goddess archetype returns at a time when the breakdown of the old story leaves us desperate for love, for security, for protection, for meaning. It leaves us yearning for a nurturing and cultivation of our whole being, that we might be adequate servants of the planetary culture.

—Jean Houston
The Search for the Beloved

The Goddess is defined with such words as light, love, isness, allness and All That Is … the key principles that come the closest to defining the Goddess … simply put: Imagining, Feeling, Conceiving and Perceiving…. The Goddess energy is the initiating energy or creation…. Her power is immense. All you have to do is open your heart and imagine Her, and She's there.

—Lazaris
Lazaris Interviews

The Goddess is celebrated in the triple aspect of youth, maturity and age or maiden, mother, and crone.... Thus women learn to value youth, creativity and wisdom in themselves and other women.

—Carol P. Christ
Laughter of Aphrodite

The powers of the Goddess are fully released from the underworld in order to create balance with the powers of the gods, the patriarchy. Slowly, women within will awaken just in time to prevent ecocide, the suicide of Planet Earth.

—Barbara Hand Clow
Heart of the Christos

Om is the Goddess herself as sound.

—Heinrich Zimmer
Philosophies of India

The Goddess has infinite aspects and thousands of names—She is the reality behind many metaphors.

—Starhawk
The Spiral Dance

What can be named is small. That whose magnitude can't be imagined is ineffable.

—Nicholas Krebs of Cusa
Dialogue on the Hidden God

There is a spirit that pervades everything, that is capable of powerful song and radiant movement, and that moves in and out of the mind. The colors of this spirit are multitudinous, a glowing, pulsing rainbow.... She is also the spirit that informs right balance, right harmony, and these in turn order all relationships in conformity with her law.

—Paula Gunn Allen
Weaving the Visions

The God who lets us live in the world without the working hypothesis of God is the God before whom we stand continually.

—Dietrich Bonhoeffer
Letters and Papers from Prison

"Both/and" takes us to ... the Creative Matrix. She burns us in her hottest flames to purify us of all that is not us.... She is death in the service of life.

—Robert Bly & Marion Woodman
The Maiden King

The etheric is the realm of Persephone. She sleeps within us and must be awakened.

—Rudolf Steiner

It is among the outcasts and outsiders that the Black Goddess has lingered through recorded history.... There are 200 plus Western European shrines to the Black Virgin.... Black, like the Ka'aba, is the color of the unknown, the unconscious.

—Peter Redgrove
The Black Goddess and the Sixth Sense

Because female history has been so shattered, women are reaching back to prehistory to find elements of the woman's mythology that existed before the Greek division of power into multiple gods.

—Maureen Murdock
The Heroine's Journey

Mary is the Goddess of Christendom,
let in through the back door, nervously
denied actual divinity by the hierarchy
but effectively acknowledged as such by
the ordinary worshipper.

—Penelope Shuttle & Peter Redgrove
The Wise Wound

The Hopi call the beginning goddess "Hard
Beings Woman." While she lives in the
heavenly world, where she owns the moon
and the stars, she is of the Earth, and her
son is the god of crops. She gives the Earth
its solidity, its shape and its inhabitants.

—David Suzuki & Peter Knudtson
Wisdom of the Elders

Our search for a God who looks like us
begins in our own lives. She will be
found there.

—Patricia Lynn Reilly
A God Who Looks Like Me

Goddess is alive and magic is afoot.

—Z Budapest

GOOD/GOODNESS

I know well that heaven and earth and all
creation are great, generous and beautiful
and good … God's goodness fills all
his creatures …

—Julian of Norwich

Not everything is immediately good to
those who love God; but everything is
capable of becoming good.

—Pierre Teilhard de Chardin

Good is the magnetic center towards
which love naturally moves. False love
moves to false good…. When true good
is loved, even impurely or by accident,
the quality of the love is automatically
refined, and when the soul is turned
towards Good the highest part of the soul
is enlivened…. Goodness is connected
with the acceptance of real death and
real chance and real transience and
only against the background of this
acceptance, which is psychologically
so difficult, can we understand the full
extent of what virtue is like.

—Iris Murdoch
The Sovereignty of Good

There are still stars which move in ordered
and beautiful rhythm. There are still
people in this world who keep promises.

—Madeleine L'Engle
A Wind in the Door

What sort of God would it be, who only
pushed from without?

—Johann Wolfgang von Goethe

Am I going to do a good deed? Then, of
all times, Father, into thy hands, lest the
enemy should have me now.

—George MacDonald

Goodness is something so simple;
always to live for others, never to seek
one's own advantage.

—Dag Hammarskjöld

Sometimes what is good is the enemy of what is perfect.

—Laurel Lee
Signs of Spring

Cuthbert hears Godric's confession, forgives his sins and blesses him ... "Go now. Do good, for there's no good a man does in this world, however small, but bears sweet fruit though he may never taste of it himself."

—Frederick Buechner
Godric

Every good and excellent thing in the world stands moment by moment on the razor-edge of danger and must be fought for.

—Thornton Wilder
The Skin of Our Teeth

We're all comrades in the stuff of dust. In our world, pity implies a degrading act of condescension, a patronizing good deed performed by someone in a superior position for the sake of someone presumably inferior.

—Ralph C. Wood
The Gospel According to Tolkien

As a tree torn from the soil, as a river separated from its source, the human soul wanes when detached from what is greater than itself. Without the holy, the good turns chaotic; without the good, beauty becomes accidental.

—Abraham Joshua Heschel

God is good. God will accomplish all good things in me.

—Hildegard of Bingen

Goodness alone is joyous; God's will alone is our best good.

—George MacDonald & Roland Hein
The Harmony Within

Guilt is the guardian of our goodness.

—Willard Gaylin
Feelings

You can't just go on being a good egg. You must either hatch or go bad.

—C. S. Lewis

GOSPEL

The gospel didn't get up out of a feather-bed to yawn its way sleepily through the earth; it got down off a cross, came stalking up out of fire, with the smell of the flames on it.

—Paul Scherer
Love Is a Spendthrift

God does not die on the day when we cease to believe in a personal deity, but we die on the day when our lives cease to be illuminated by the steady radiance, renewed daily of a wonder and the source of which is beyond all reason.

—Wilton Barnhardt
Gospel

Gospel means nothing but a preaching and proclaiming of the grace and mercy of God through Jesus Christ, merited and won by his death … .all that the apostles wrote is in reality one Gospel.

—Martin Luther

Harold Bloom calls the Thomas Jesus unsponsored and free.… Nothing is commonplace in this Jesus.… Everything we seek is already open to you—you need but knock and enter.

—Marvin Meyer
The Gospel of Thomas: The Hidden Sayings of Jesus

Tolkien believed the sacramental and missional life of the Catholic church is enough to convey the Gospel to the world without his help.… Christ has imbued the entire cosmos with his Spirit. There is nothing that does not bear his creative imprint.

—Ralph C. Wood
The Gospel According to Tolkien

The Gospel is first of all a call to leave the past behind and open ourselves to the promise of the future.

—Harvey Cox
On Not Leaving It to the Snake

GRACE

Grace is not a strange, magic substance which is subtly filtered into our souls to act as a kind of spiritual penicillin. Grace is unity, oneness within ourselves, oneness with God.

—Thomas Merton

All the natural movements of the soul are controlled by laws analogous to those of physical gravity. Grace is the only exception.

—Simone Weil

Grace strikes us when we are in great pain and restlessness. It strikes us when we feel that our separation is deeper than usual, because we have violated another life, a life which we loved, or from which we were estranged.

—Paul Tillich & Thomas Moore
Education of the Heart

Experiencing grace involves the expansion of consciousness of self to all of one's surroundings as an unbroken whole, a consciousness of awe from which negative mindstates are absent, from which healing and groundedness result. For these reasons grace has long been deemed "amazing."

—Charlene Spretnak
States of Grace

The winds of grace are always blowing; it is for us to raise our sails.

—Ramakrishna
(Gadadhar Chatterji)

God's grace is the beginning, the middle, and the end. When you pray for God's grace, you are like someone standing neck-deep in water and yet crying for water.

—Ramana Maharishi

Grace is found in both intense peace and activity.… Something inside of us releases, lets go, and says yes in its belonging to the Mystery.

—Joel Levey & Michelle Levey
Living in Balance

… the function of grace, namely to condition men's homecoming to the center from start to finish … grace is the welcoming hand into the center when man finds himself standing at long last on the brink of the great divide where all familiar landmarks have disappeared.

—Marco Pallis
Sword of Gnosis

Grace is something good that comes into our lives unexpectedly and we know that we do not deserve it. When grace comes, even in little things, all life suddenly becomes better … to be in the presence of someone with grace is to become more gracious yourself.

—John Coburn
A Life to Live, A Way to Pray

Sin may flourish and grace abound where they have not yet been suspected.

—Judith Plaskow
Sex, Sin and Grace

Grace is something you can never get but only be given. There's no way to earn it or deserve it or bring it about any more than you can deserve the taste of raspberries and cream or earn good looks or bring about your own birth.

—Frederick Buechner
Wishful Thinking: A Theological ABC

Grace descends from God upon all beings; what becomes of it depends on what they are.

—Simone Weil
The Need for Roots

The existence of grace is prima facie evidence not only of the reality of God but also of the reality that God's will is devoted to the growth of the individual human spirit. What once seemed to be a fairy tale turns out to be the reality. We live our lives in the eye of God, and not at the periphery but at the center of His Vision, His concern.

—M. Scott Peck
The Road Less Traveled

The state of grace is a condition in which all growth is effortless, a transparent, joyful acquiescence that is a ground requirement of all existence. Your own body grows naturally and easily from its time of birth, not expecting resistance but taking its miraculous unfolding for granted; using all of itself with great, gracious, creatively aggressive abandon. You were born into a state of grace; it is impossible for you to leave it. You will die in a state of grace whether or not special words are spoken for you, or water or oil is poured upon your head. You cannot "fall out of" grace, nor can it be taken from you.

—Jane Roberts
The Nature of Personal Reality

In all praying, remember that sonship is a gift … the child of God comes into grace and the new life of the spirit by the will of the Father in heaven. Therefore must the kingdom of heaven—divine sonship—be received as a little child.

—*The Urantia Book*

We have all of us been told that grace is to be found in the universe. But in our human foolishness and short-sightedness we imagine divine grace to be finite. For this reason we tremble.... But the moment comes when our eyes are opened, and we see and realize that grace is infinite. Grace, my friends, demands nothing from us but that we shall await it with confidence and acknowledge it in gratitude. Grace, brothers, makes no conditions and singles out none of us in particular; grace takes us all to its bosom and proclaims general amnesty.

—Isak Dinesen
Babette's Feast and Other Anecdotes of Destiny

Grace is what happens when openness to chance yields a deeper awareness of the cosmos or one's place in it—when luck leads to spiritual insight.... Proust called chance experiences "earthly experiences of grace."

—Jackson Lears
Something for Nothing

Heaven isn't 70 and hell, 69.9. With God, the passing grade is zero and to pass is a sheer gift.

—Peter Kreeft
Love is Stronger Than Death

Grace is remembering, in the moment, that you are alive.

—Barbara Shipka
Leadership in a Challenging World

GRAIL

If we understand the true, inner call resounding in human hearts, we still are and should be seekers for the Holy Grail.

—Rudolf Steiner
Materialism and the Task of Anthroposophy

There are as many possible paths to the Grail as there are roads to Rome, and every one of them is valid.... There is a common language, a mode of consciousness, almost a secret sign which can be read and recognized by all who are similarly engaged.... Yet much as these views differ, they are one in their belief in the Grail as guide, counselor, helper, and as gateway to the interior life.... The Grail is a point of direct contact with a spiritual and supernatural realm.

—John Matthews
At the Table of the Grail

When Parsifal raised the question, "Whom does the Grail serve?" or in simpler terms, "What is the larger purpose in life?" the answer came back clearly that the ultimate aim of life is not the pursuit of personal happiness, but to serve the Grail, or God, or the greater Self through service to the whole.

—Charles Garfield, *et al*
Wisdom Circles

A grail question is a question whose primary purpose is not to elicit data or information but to open up a situation to a new perspective ... reveal the sacred in a situation or can bring to light creative possibilities that we otherwise might have missed seeing.

—David Spangler
A Pilgrim in Aquarius

In practice we cannot separate the word "grail" from the word "cauldron." In early Celtic times it was in the Cauldron (caldron) of Lug that 'universal medicines' were cooked over a special fire.... Under whatever name, it invariably designates a vessel whose contents are taking their part of divinity; are penetrated with it; are in the process of transmutation.

—Louis Charpentier
The Mysteries of Chartres Cathedral

The Grail Legend is a planetary story.... It's always a woman, the Grail Maiden, who holds this chalice, symbol of the sacred feminine, a womb filled with blood that disappeared from the world.... If the patriarchy is to be healed and the planet restored, might women's wisdom be needed?

—Jean Shinoda Bolen
The Millionth Circle

Such was the nature of the Grail that she who had the care of it was required to be of perfect chastity and to have renounced all things false.

—Wolfram von Eschenbach
Parzival

A great sorrow has recently been brought on the land by a young knight who was welcomed as a guest by the rich Fisher King. To him appeared the Holy Grail and the lance with angry blood welling from its point. He did not ask whom it served or whence it came, and because he did not ask this, all the lands are stirred up to war and no knight meets another in the forest without striking him down and killing him if he can.

—Perlesvaus

If the Grail represents the esoteric side of Christianity, its significance lies not only in its being found by just the few, but also in that it is found not by having the right answers, but by asking the right question. The reason Sir Galahad was able to see the Grail was because he correctly asked, "Whom does the Grail serve?"

—Robert Ellwood
The Cross and the Grail

To open the casket that contains the Grail means to enter into direct contact with Christ himself.

—Julius Evola
The Mystery of the Grail

In Welsh, a grail is a collection of stories such as the Bible or Koran.

—Adrian G. Gilbert
The Holy Kingdom

Hitler despised Freemasonry as a Jewish invention, but used Masonry as the model for his inner circle of the Nazi Party. In 1934 Hitler declared "We shall form an Order, the Brotherhood of the Templars, around the Holy Grail, of the pure blood."

—Michael Howard
The Occult Conspiracy

Students of the Grail literature cannot fail to have been impressed by a certain atmosphere of awe and mystery which surrounds that enigmatic Vessel. There is a secret connected with it, the revelation of which will entail dire misfortune on the betrayer.

—Jessie L. Weston
From Ritual to Romance

The Grail Castle is a symbol for wholeness and mystical unity with all things. Then we long to "have" it again…. You can't enter the Otherworld without "the Call."

—Kenneth Johnson & Marguerite Elsbeth
The Grail Castle

"The greatest cover-up in human history," explains Teabing. "Not only was Jesus Christ married, but he was a father. My dear, Mary Magdalene was the Holy Vessel. She was the chalice that bore the royal bloodline of Jesus Christ."

—Dan Brown
The Da Vinci Code

The Parsifal Exercise: What's the greatest danger facing us today? Is it getting more or less? Do you talk about this? With whom? What do they say? What can you/I do about it? What gives you hope?

—Joanna Rogers Macy

GRATITUDE

A thankful heart is not only the greatest virtue, but the parent of all other virtues.

—Marcus Tullius Cicero

If the only prayer you say in your whole life is "Thank you," that would suffice.

—Meister Eckhart

Were there no God, we would be in this glorious world with grateful hearts: and no one to thank!

—Christina Georgina Rossetti

To give thanks is to have the courage to get up in the morning.

—Martin Bell
Return of the Wolf

The ancients sometimes said that the worst sin is ingratitude, which is a forgetting of the greatness, beauty, truth, and goodness of the Source that is constantly creating us—in other terms, a forsaking of Being and of the Good.

—Jean-Yves LeLoup
The Gospel of Mary Magdalene

Gratitude: A labor undertaken by the soul to effect the transformation after a gift has been received…. Passing the gift along is the act of gratitude that finished the labor.

—Lewis Hyde
The Gift

Gratitude is the heart's memory.

—French proverb

GRIEF

Haldir the elf: "The world is indeed full of peril, and in it there are many dark places; but still there is much that is fair, and though in all lands, love is now mingled with grief, it grows perhaps the greater."

—J. R. R. Tolkien
The Fellowship of the Ring

Through mourning we let the dead go and take them in.

—Judith Viorst
Necessary Losses

We are free to grieve precisely because our faith is grounded in the promise of a Presence from whom we cannot be separated.

—Kenneth Mitchell & Herbert Anderson
All Our Losses, All Our Griefs

The great mystery of death and the grief and sorrow that attend it require rituals of storytelling and remembering.

—Herbert Anderson & Edward Foley
Mighty Stories, Dangerous Rituals

Certain hurts and harms and shames can never be done being grieved.... Although there will be scars and plenty of them, it is good to remember that in tensile strength and ability to absorb pressure, a scar is stronger than skin.... Tears are a river that takes you somewhere.

—Clarissa Pinkola Estés
Women Who Run with the Wolves

A woman's crying has been considered quite dangerous, for it loosens the locks and bolts in the secrets she bears. For most women these secret stories are embedded, not like jewels in a crown, but like black gravel under the skin of the soul.

—Nancy Slonim Aronic
Writing from Your Heart

Happiness is good for the body, but it is grief which develops strength of mind.

—Marcel Proust

No one ever told me that grief felt so like fear. The same fluttering in the stomach, the same restlessness, the yawning. I keep on swallowing.

—C. S. Lewis
Journal

When someone you love dies, it is like when your house burns down; it isn't for years that you realize the full extent of your loss.

—Mark Twain

GROUND

Poetry, of course, is the best that human life can offer. But there is also the life of the spirit, and the life of spirit is the analogue, on a higher turn of the spiral, of the animal's life. The progression is from animal eternity into time, into the strictly human world of memory and anticipation; and from time, if one chooses to go on, into the world of spiritual eternity, into the divine Ground.

—Aldous Huxley
Time Must Have a Stop

Deep ground is not the same as the dark earth.

—James Hillman

Ground, then, is the aspect of earth that seeps into the sensuous surface of wild places while also extending that surface downward. It is thus the earth-basis of the world's body, its very flesh.

—Edward S. Casey
Getting Back into Place

GROWTH

In giving birth to a sustainable species-civilization, humanity will probably move back and forth through cycles of contraction and relaxation until we utterly exhaust ourselves and burn through the barriers that separate us from our wholeness as a human family.... Numerous times we may go to the very edge of ruin as a species, hopefully to pull back in time with new levels of maturity and insight.

—Duane Elgin
Awakening Earth

At whatever stage you are, there are always higher stages.

—Rudolf Steiner
An Outline of Occult Science

You grow, not before what you gain of outer fruit, but by the inner unfolding necessary for your success in the struggle.

—Annie Besant
The Spiritual Life in the World

A new domain of psychical expansion, that is what we lack. And it is staring us in the face if we would only raise our heads to look at it …

—Pierre Teilhard de Chardin
The Phenomenon of Man

Growth has not only rewards and pleasures but also many intrinsic pains, and always will.

—Abraham Maslow

The soul is constantly sending out new combinations of itself, reaching out to

become more than it was, challenging itself in new ways, and sometimes suffering the fragmentation that accompanies experimentation.

—Christopher M. Bache
Dark Night, Early Dawn

Don't strain after more light than you've got yet; just wait quietly. God holds you when you cannot hold Him, and when the time comes to jump, He will see to it that you do jump—and you will find you are not frightened then.... So just be supple in His hands and let Him mould you (as He is doing) for His own purposes, responding with very simple acts of trust and love.

—Evelyn Underhill
Letters

What is important is to realize that whether we understand fully who we are or what will happen when we die, it's our purpose to grow as human beings, to look within ourselves, to find and build upon that source of peace and understanding and strength that is our individual self. And then to reach out to others with love and acceptance and patient guidance in the hope of what we may become together.

—Elisabeth Kübler-Ross
Death: The Final Stage of Growth

Curiosity is the doorway that stimulates growth, joy and expansion and allows you to begin to remember who you are.

—Emmanuel
The Choice for Love

Spiritual growth is the process of becoming your Higher Self.... You can grow with joy rather than struggle. You can grow instantaneously.

—Sanaya Roman
Spiritual Growth

Genuinely loving people are, by definition, growing people.

—M. Scott Peck
The Road Less Traveled

Life is sustained by movement, not by foundation.

—Antoine de Saint Exupéry

For every one step that you take in the pursuit of Spiritual growth, take three in personal growth.

—Rudolf Steiner
Knowledge of the Higher Worlds and Its Attainment

We should live like the lotus blossom. It grows out of the water, but its petals are not wet.

—Siddhartha Gautama (Buddha)

The quickest way for a tadpole to become a frog is to live loyally each moment as a tadpole.

—*The Urantia Book*

GUIDE/GURU

It is necessary to have a guide for the spiritual journey. Choose a master, for without one this journey is full of trials, fears, and dangers. With no escort, you would be lost on a road you have already taken. Do not travel alone on the Path.... Whoever travels without a guide needs two hundred years for a two-day journey.

—Jalal Al-din Rumi

I sympathize with experiments in communes, but any time we try to go back to the Garden it can mean being led by a Manson.

—Madeleine L'Engle
The Irrational Season

Some bad gurus may be sociopaths without a mystical bone in their bodies, but mystical experiences may exacerbate or instigate sociopathic behavior.

—John Horgan
Rational Mysticism

Robert Bly calls people who are always seeking gurus perpetual adolescents.

—Mary Pipher
Another Country

A spiritual teacher must call forth whatever is necessary to meet and satisfy the longing and hunger of the student who approaches with sincerity.

—Regina Sara Ryan
The Woman Awake

The true teacher defends his pupils against his own personal influence. He inspires self-trust. He guides their eyes from himself to the spirit that quickens him. He will have no disciple.

—Amos Bronson Alcott
"Orphic Sayings," *The Dial,* July 1840

Disciples do owe unto masters only a
temporary belief and a suspension of
their own judgment till they be fully
instructed, and not an absolute resignation or perpetual captivity.

—Francis Bacon
Advancement of Learning

The role of a spiritual teacher is to help us
distinguish the real from the illusory.

—Thomas Moore
The Soul's Religion

The highest truth cannot be put into
words. Therefore, the greatest teacher has
nothing to say. He simply gives himself in
service and never worries.

—Philip Novak
The World's Wisdom

When you realize Buddha nature, you are
the teacher. You are the teacher of your
master too.

—Shunryu Suzuki

If you think a teacher must levitate, go
work with a vulture.

—Rinpoche

A donkey with a load of holy books is
still a donkey.

—Sufi proverb

HANDICAPPED

The handicapped have a special role to play in the inspiration of community. They teach us to be concrete, to be particular. They have no gift for abstraction. It is now. It is here.

—Mary Caroline (M. C.) Richards
Centering

I gave this mite a fig I denied to all of you—eternal innocence. To you she looks imperfect—but to me she is flawless, like the bud that dies unopened or the fledgling that falls from the nest to be devoured by the ants.... She is necessary to you. She will evoke the kindness that will keep you human. Her infirmity will prompt you to gratitude for your own good fortune.... She will remind you every day that I am who I am, that my ways are not yours and that the smallest dust mote whirled in darkest space does not fall out of my hand ... treasure her!

—Morris West,
The Clowns of God

When the (handicapped) child falls asleep, he is "normal"—far more "perfect" than the adults around him.

—Rudolf Steiner *&* Robert McDermott
The Essential Steiner

Children in need of special care of the soul.

—Rudolf Steiner's name for
developmentally disabled children

HAPPINESS

May all beings never be separated
from happiness.

—Siddhartha Gautama (Buddha)

Happiness consists in finding out
precisely what the "one thing necessary" may be, in our lives, and in gladly
relinquishing all the rest. For then, by a
divine paradox, we find that everything
else is given us together with the one
thing we needed.

—Thomas Merton
No Man Is an Island

It is a good exercise, in empty or ugly
hours of the day, to look at anything, the
coal-scuttle or the bookcase, and think
how happy one could be to have brought
it out of the sinking ship onto the
solitary island.

—G. K. Chesterton
Orthodoxy

One cannot pursue happiness; if he does
he obscures it. If he will proceed with
the human task of life, the relocation of
the center of gravity of the personality
to something greater outside itself,
happiness will be the outcome.

—Robert A. Johnson
He

True happiness, we are told, consists in
getting out of one's self; but the point is
not only to get out—you must stay out;
and to stay out, you must have some
absorbing errand.

—Henry James
Roderick Hudson

"Happiness, my dear Dick," said the
Ghost placidly, "happiness, as you will
come to see when you are older, lies in
the path of duty … "

—C. S. Lewis
The Great Divorce

Happy dreams come true, not because
they are dreams, but only because they
are happy. And so they must be loving.

—*A Course in Miracles*

Happiness comes only when we push our
brains and hearts to the farthest reaches
of which we are capable.

—Leo Rosten

It was a fancy of Tolstoi's that somewhere,
buried underground, if you could but
find it, was a Green Stick with the secret
of everlasting happiness carved upon it.

—Malcolm Muggeridge
Chronicles of Wasted Time

Happiness is not a passing emotion,
but a life of activity of Unfolding
spiritual, intellectual, sensory, physical,
emotional potency.

—Mary Daly
Beyond God the Father

We become happy in the presence of wholeness.

—Christopher Alexander
The Phenomenon of Life

To be happy you must have taken the measure of your powers, tasted the fruits of your passion, and learned your place in the world.

—George Santayana

Flow: happiness, satisfaction, intrinsic motivation … optimal experience … exhilaration, deep enjoyment.… Flow and religion have been connected from earliest times.

—Mihaly Csikszentmihalyi
Flow

More than anything, we seek happiness.

—Aristotle

If you keep a green bough in your heart, surely the singing bird will come.

—Chinese proverb

That is happiness: to be dissolved into something complete and great.

—Tombstone of Willa Cather

"I am so happy."

—Gerard Manley Hopkins' last words.

HARDSHIP

Bad times have a scientific value…
We learn geology the morning after the earthquake.

—Ralph Waldo Emerson

Crisis is meant to be identified, not identified with.

—Martia Nelson
Coming Home

Hardship is the only thing that brings out the good in most people.

—Willa Cather

HARMONY

A magnificent, wonderful harmony exists throughout creation both in the sphere of the senses and beyond, in ideas and in objects, in the realm of nature and that of grace.… The greatest harmony is God, and he has impressed inner harmony on all souls as his image.

—Johannes Kepler
Kepler und di Theologie

Our Teachers tell us that all things within this Universe wheel know of their Harmony with every other thing, and know how to Give-Away one to the other, except man. Of all the Universe's creatures, it is we alone who do not begin our lives with Knowledge of this great Harmony.

—Hyemeyohsts Storm
Seven Arrows

Heraclitus invented the word harmony—harmonia—to mean the balance of conflicting opposites brought about by Logos. He's been called a Christian before Christ.

—Gordon Strachen
Christ and the Cosmos

The voices of individuals are hidden in a chorus while the voices of all are heard, and thus a harmony emerges.

—Macrobius

The harmony of the universe invites us into its community. This means that the human community does not have to invent harmony. It is already present, not only in sound, but in the flow of energy, the give and take, the life and death of the universe.

—Cynthia Serjak
Music and the Cosmic Dance

Truth is above harmony. Those who fear disorder more than injustice invariably produce more of both.

—William Sloane Coffin
Credo

We see that harmony does not mean a balance-at-rest, but a vibrant, bi-polar energy force that urges on all other things.

—Matthew Fox

With an eye made quiet by the power of harmony and the deep power of joy, we see into the heart of things.

—William Wordsworth

Harmony is being on the right path, being one with it.... Harmony happens when behavior and belief come together,

when inner archetypal life and outer life are expressions of each other, and we are being true to who we are.

—Jean Shinoda Bolen
Gods in Everyman

When I, on a certain occasion, asked Professor Einstein how he found his theory of relativity, he answered that he found it because he was so strongly convinced of the harmony of the universe.

—Hans Reichenbach & Lawrence Leshan
The Medium, the Mystic and the Physicist

In the fallen state of consciousness, each human being functions in disregard of the Song of Life that is going on in others. There is no harmony, no direction, no arrangement. You are like the random notes of an orchestra before the conductor unifies the instruments in symphony. The Grand Conductor is calling everyone to attention …

—Ken Carey
The Starseed Transmissions

To be in harmony is to be in a conscious and loving relationship with what is.

—Jean-Yves LeLoup
The Gospel of Mary Magdalene

HATRED

For in truth, in this world, hatred is not appeased by hatred. Hatred is appeased by love alone. This is the eternal law.

—Dhammapada

Love binds; hate separates.

—Empedocles

Hatred we can manage. The tension of human nerves during noise, danger, and fatigue makes them prone to any violent emotion, and it is only a question of guiding this susceptibility into the right channels. If conscience resists, muddle him. Let him say that he feels hatred not only on his own behalf but on that of the women and children and that a Christian is told to forgive his own, not other people's enemies.... But Hatred is best combined with Fear.... The more he fears, the more he will hate.

—C. S. Lewis
The Screwtape Letters

Losing your natural ability to love both yourself and the person who hurt you is the greatest loss possible.

—Martia Nelson
Coming Home

It is the nature of love to create. It is the nature of hate to destroy.

—Madeleine L'Engle
A Wind in the Door

There are no hatreds so great or so deep as those fostered by religion.

—Alice Bailey
Externalization of the Hierarchy

Hate is just a failure of imagination.

—Graham Greene
The Power and the Glory

HEALING

One may heal with holiness, one may heal with the law, one may heal with the knife, one may heal with herbs, one may heal with the Holy Word: amongst all remedies this one it is that will best drive away sickness from the body of the faithful: for this one is the best-healing of all remedies.

—The Zendavesta
The Bible of the World

Thy name is my healing, O my God, and remembrance of Thee is my remedy. Nearness to Thee is my hope, and love for Thee is my companion. Thy mercy to me is my healing and my succor in both this world and the world to come. Thou, verily art the All-Bountiful, the All-Knowing, the All-Wise.

—Baha'u'llah
Prayers and Meditations

The natural healing force within each one of us is the greatest force in getting well.

—Hippocrates

Healing does not necessarily mean to become physically well or to be able to get up and walk around again. Rather, it means achieving a balance between the physical, emotional, intellectual, and spiritual dimensions.... At the end of their lives [five-year-old children with leukemia] they have little or no pain. They are emotionally sound, and on an intellectual level they can share things it is almost impossible to believe could come from a child. To me this is a healing, although they are not well from our earthly point of view.

—Elizabeth Kübler-Ross
Healers on Healing

Healing is a journey deep within oneself—a search for soul, the essence of the self. It seeks to balance the inner and outer worlds, to connect and to integrate. Healing is the reuniting of the body, mind and spirit.

—Diane Mariechild
Mother Wit

People heal with their minds ... that's where the power is. Once you tap into it, you have joined up with a universal energy force. And with that power, nothing is impossible.

—Gerald Jampolsky
The Complete Guide to Your Emotions & Your Health

Healing is embracing what is most feared; healing is opening what has been closed, softening what has hardened into obstruction, healing is learning to trust life.

—Jeanne Achterberg

The healing process is a creative process; you must be sensitive and able to improvise and draw on your knowledge as the situation unfolds ... the attitude of the healer is almost as important as the attitude of the person being healed.

—O. Carl Simonton
Healers on Healing

A healer does not really heal; a healer can only present a mirror.

—Lynn V. Andrews
Healers on Healing

Healing is impossible in loneliness. The body cannot be whole alone.

—Wendell Berry
The Unsettling of America

Bear in mind that "to heal" does not necessarily imply "to cure." It can mean simply helping a patient to achieve a way of life compatible with his own aspirations, even though his disease continues.

—René Dubos

Sometimes healing means learning to care for others, finding new wholeness as a family—being reconciled. Or it can mean easing the pain of dying or allowing someone to die when the time comes. There is a difference between prolonging life and prolonging the act of dying until the patient lives a travesty of life.... We hold fast, but with open hands, because sometimes the most important part of loving can be knowing how and when to let go.

—Cicely Saunders & Sandol Stoddard
The Hospice Movement

Healing is a process, a movement, a transition toward balance, connectedness, meaning and wholeness. Healing is a movement, not an outcome.

—Richard Katz
Sacred Stories

HEALTH

Health is the natural state of humanity. It means being in harmony with ourselves and our universe. When we are in harmony, we feel better, feel more joy, and feel healthier.... The more I can love everything—the trees, the land, the water, my fellow men, women and children, and myself—the more health I am going to experience and the more of my real self I am going to be.

—O. Carl Simonton
Healers on Healing

The essence of health is an inner kind of balance.

—Andrew Weil

To be creative is only to have health: to keep oneself fully alive in the creation, to keep the creation fully alive in oneself, to see the creation anew, to welcome one's part in it anew.

—Wendell Berry
What Are People For?

Internet joke: Health is merely the slowest possible rate at which one can die.

—Alan Atkisson
Believing Cassandra

HEART

The Eye of my heart sees everything.... The heart is a sanctuary at the center of which there is a little space, wherein the Great spirit dwells, and this is the Eye ... of the Great Spirit by which He sees all things, and through which we see Him. If the heart is not pure, the Great Spirit cannot be seen.

—Black Elk *&* Frithjof Schuon
L'Oeil du Coeur

The heart is the king of the body.

—Tikuney Zohar
Tikuney Zohar

Call it by any name, God, Self, the Heart or the Seat of Consciousness, it is all the same. The point to be grasped is this, that Heart means the very core of one's being, the Center, without which there is nothing whatever.

—Ramana Maharshi
The Spiritual Teaching of Ramana Maharshi

The heart actually beats differently in response to the beautiful than in response to the ugly or pernicious ... thinking with the heart will evolve together with the transformation of man's soul in times to come.

—Rudolf Steiner
Mystery Knowledge and Mystery Centres

The heart beats approximately one hundred thousand times a day and forty million times a year. For more than seventy years, it supplies the pumping capacity for nearly three billion cardiac pulsations and propels more than two gallons of blood per minute through the body.

—Paul Pearsall
The Heart's Code

It is only with the heart that one can see clearly, for what is essential is hidden from the eyes.

—Antoine de Saint Exupéry
The Little Prince

The Heart of a wise man should resemble
a mirror, which reflects every object
without being sullied by any.

—Confucius

If metal can be polished to a mirror-like
finish—what polishing does the mirror of
the heart require?

—Jalal al-din Rumi

The heart has its reasons, which reason
does not know.

—Blaise Pascal

When you're not trying to make the heart
into something you think is proper, it
showers you with its magic, and even in
the midst of pain it can offer moments
of rapture.

—Thomas Moore

How could you describe this heart in
words without filling a whole book?

—Leonardo da Vinci
Notebooks

God and devil are fighting there, and the
battlefield is the heart of man.

—Feodor Dostoevski
The Brothers Karamozov

Look into any man's heart you please,
and you will always find, in everyone, at
least one black spot which he has to
keep concealed.

—Henrik Ibsen
Pillars of Society

How slow a heart is to learn, much slower
than the mind. So stupid, the heart, so
tenacious, so heedless of hurt.

—Anne Morrow Lindbergh
War Without and War Within

The greatest challenge of the day is: how
to bring about a revolution of the heart,
a revolution which has to start with each
one of us.

—Dorothy Day

It is better to have a heart that makes love
than a mind that makes sense!

—L. Robert Keck
Sacred Quest

The head does not hear anything until
the heart has listened.... What the heart
knows today the head will understand
tomorrow.

—James Stephens
The Crock of Gold

We stay so well defended that we hesitate
to pursue things passionately enough to
risk a broken heart.

—Gail Godwin
Heart

Only fools hoard their heart. You are
no fool.

—Lynn Park

Nowhere are there more hiding places
than in the heart.

—German proverb

HEAVEN

The roots of heaven are of great emptiness, for in emptiness there is energy, incalculable, vast and profound.

—Jiddu Krishnamurti
Krishnamurti to Himself

In this life we are to become heaven so that God might find a home here.

—Meister Eckhart

If hell is definable as the place where self is eternally fostered, then heaven is the place where self forever renders itself up and in doing so joins that great celestial plan of things in which even Christ took part through the sacrifice of Himself to God.... All things outside self-giving are Satanic.

— Clyde S. Kilby
The Christian World of C. S. Lewis

To the soul overburdened with all the heaviness of earth, the Christ says, "Arise, for your home is in Heaven!—But in order to believe in Heaven and in order to reach Heaven, prove heaven here on earth in your work and in your love!"

—Edouard Schuré
The Great Initiates

Once I heard that piece (Schubert's "Quintet in C") I knew there was a heaven.

—Anthony Damiani
Looking into Mind

A Chippewayan guide named Saltatha once asked a French priest what lay beyond the present life. "You have told me heaven is very beautiful," he said. "Now tell me one more thing. Is it more beautiful than the country of the musk-oxen in the summer, when sometimes the mist blows over the lakes, and sometimes the water is blue, and the loons cry very often? That is beautiful. If heaven is still more beautiful, I will be glad."

—Barry Lopez
Arctic Dreams

Aim at heaven and you will get earth thrown in. Aim at earth and you get neither.

—C. S. Lewis

You have your brush, you have your colors, you paint paradise, then in you go.

—Nikos Kazantzakis

Heaven is like Rivendell, "the last Homely House" in *Lord of the Rings*. Time doesn't seem to pass here; it just is. A remarkable place altogether!
Eternity is not a million years or a trillion millennia; it is not an unending line but a point.

—Peter J. Kreeft
Heaven, the Heart's Deepest Longing

Heaven is not a place nor a condition. It is merely an awareness of perfect oneness, and the knowledge that there is nothing else; nothing outside this oneness, and nothing else within.

—*A Course in Miracles*

Heaven is spread about the earth but men do not see it.

—*Gospel According to Thomas*

Joy is the serious business of heaven.

—C. S. Lewis
Letters to Malcolm

The word crying does not appear in the lexicon of heaven. It is the only word listed in the lexicon of hell.

—Calvin Miller
The Singer

A child of Earth and starry Heaven am I, but of Heaven is my true race.

—Orphic proverb

HELL

Hell is ignorance of God.... Hell is the experience of God, not as light and eternal Grace but as eternal fire instead. God, however, is not the eternal fire. It is human beings who create the distortions, not God.

—Kyriacos Markides
The Mountain

Hell is truth seen too late.

—William Sloane Coffin
Credo

In hell there is no music—an agonizing night that never ends as songless as a shattered violin.

—Calvin Miller
The Singer

Hell's logic consists in preventing murder by murdering all murderers.

—Calvin Miller
The Finale

"... They lead you to expect red fire and devils and all sorts of interesting people sizzling on grids—Henry VIII and all that—but when you get there it's just like any other town.... Only the Greatest of all can make himself small enough to enter Hell. For the higher a thing is, the lower it can descend—a man can sympathize with a horse but a horse cannot sympathize with a rat."

—C. S. Lewis
The Great Divorce

... hell was an actuality to Lewis.... One of the greatest strategies of hell is to remove all genuine naturalness from a man's life, make him give up whatever he really likes in favor of the "best" people, or the "right" food, or the "important" books. Hell gets one of its greatest satisfactions from hearing a patient say, on its arrival there, "I now see that I spent most of life in doing neither what I ought nor what I liked."

—Clyde S. Kilby
The Christian World of C. S. Lewis

We don't create heaven or hell but we prepare ourselves for both by what we carry within us day after day.

—C. S. Lewis

Hell is life drying up.

—James Campbell

Hell—not fiery and romantic, but gray, greasy, dismal—is just around the corner.

—J. B. Priestly

The heresy of one age becomes the orthodoxy of the next.

—Helen Keller

HERETIC/HERESY

According to Germanic custom, the category of "stranger" was not protected. He had no master. He could be killed and his murder could not be punished and his heirs had no rights of inheritance. The outsider was the heretic.

—James Carroll
Constantine's Sword

The Templars were originally supported by the pope ... the council of Nicea convened by Constantine in the 300s rejected pagan beliefs such as reincarnation.... Heretic means "one who chooses."

—Michael Howard
The Occult Conspiracy

Alexandria's Jewish community was violently wiped out in 414, the first pogrom... "heresy" comes from the Greek word meaning "choice."

—James Carroll
Constantine's Sword

In 1209 the Church launched a crusade against Cathars. "Kill them all! God will know His own."

—Michael Howard
The Occult Conspiracy

HERO/HEROINE

The modern hero-deed must be that of questing to bring to the light again the lost Atlantis of the coordinated soul ... of rendering the modern world spiritually significant.

—Joseph Campbell
The Hero with a Thousand Faces

Being a hero is about being committed to the journey of life in the highest possible sense ... the hero of whom we speak is a peaceful warrior, embodying both the so-called feminine qualities of sensitivity and nurturance on the one hand, the masculine ones of assertiveness and strength on the other.

—Lorna Catford & Michael Ray
The Path of the Everyday Hero

Most heroic journeys involve going through a dark place—through mountain caverns, the underworld or labyrinthine passages to emerge, finally, into the light.

—Jean Shinoda Bolen

Only a few achieve the colossal task of holding together, without being split asunder, the clarity of their vision alongside an ability to take their place in a materialistic world. They are the modern heroes ... the last supreme heroes in a soulless society.

—Irene Claremont de Castillejo
Knowing Woman

Hobbits become heroes unexpectedly, and for this reason are all the more appealing. His [Frodo's] heroism lay in the acceptance of an almost impossible task, the endurance to continue in the face of unexpected obstacles, and the ability to resist the power and temptation of the Ring.

—Ruth S. Noel
The Mythology of Middle-Earth

Heroism for this age requires us to take our journeys, to find the treasure of our true selves, and to share that treasure with the community as a whole— through doing and being fully who we are. To the degree that we do so, our kingdoms are transformed.

—Carol S. Pearson
The Hero Within

Your role on earth's existence is truly that of heroes and heroines because you are doing something that no other spiritual beings have the courage to do. You have gone to earth to co-create with God.

—Dannion Brinkley
At Peace in the Light

... how fine is the line between heroism and delinquency.

—Irene Claremont de Castillejo
Knowing Woman

HIERARCHIES

All complex structures and processes of a relatively stable character display hierarchic organization, regardless whether we consider galactic systems, living organisms and their activities, or social organizations.

—Arthur Koestler
Janus

The hierarchy of relations, from the molecular structure of carbon compounds to the equilibrium of species and ecological wholes, will perhaps be the leading idea of the future. (Written in 1936)

—Joseph Needham
Order and Life

Everybody seemed to have some sort of hierarchy, even those who claimed they didn't.... The ingredients of thee hierarchies are holons. A holon is a whole that is a part of other wholes.... Reality is composed of neither wholes nor parts but of whole/parts or holons.

—Ken Wilber
A Theory of Everything

The real world does contain some natural or normal hierarchies and it definitely contains some pathological or dominator hierarchies.... We live in concentric circles—nests within nests ... Deep Structure.

—Ken Wilber
Sex, Ecology, Spirituality

All life is built of holons, in successive layers of complexity.

—Alison Jolly
Lucy's Legacy

At every level of organization, there is a higher level that includes it, right up to the level of the cosmos.

—Rupert Sheldrake
The Rebirth of Nature

There are as many strata at different levels of life as there are leaves in a book. When on the higher levels we can remember the lower levels, but when on the lower we cannot remember the higher.

—Henry David Thoreau
The Journals of Henry David Thoreau

Life accepts only partners, not bosses.... Systems do not accept direction, only provocation.... Systems create themselves and pursue paths of their own making.

—Margaret J. Wheatley &
Myron Kellner-Rogers

To overthrow the hierarchy is pointless; we just want to leave it behind. Diversity, not uniformity, is what works ... less harmful is not good enough.

—Daniel Quinn
Beyond Civilization

HIGHER SELF

Our world view ... includes the principle of the Higher Self. Each of us has this "utterly trustworthy parental being" to use the Huna phrase, who is part of the super-conscious world and a counterpart to our subconscious mind.... There are really no accidents because our Higher

Self stages situations and experiences which are essential for our inner progress.

—George Trevelyn
A Vision of the Aquarian Age

The Higher Conscious holds the answers to and the love for your spirituality, your enlightenment and your growth.

—Lazaris
Lazaris Interview

HINDU/HINDUISM

The Brahmans considered the Vedas their holy books par excellence. They found in them the science of sciences. The word Veda means knowledge. The scientists of Europe have been justifiably drawn to these texts by a kind of fascination. At first they saw in them only a patriarchal poetry; then they discovered in them not only the origin of the great indo-European myths and our classic gods, but also a wisely organized ... profoundly religious and metaphysical system.

—Edouard Schuré
The Great Initiates

Every morning wake up, each one of you, like a young child. At noon, stand majestically as men and women in full development. In the evening, be conscious beings ripened in strength and serenity, who having drunk deep at the fountain of life, watch the approach of death. In the middle of the night, be the Void itself, the darkness of the sky in which a moon ray still shines.

—Anirvan
Letters from a Baul: Life Within Life

Om is in truth the whole universe.

—Philip Novak
The World's Wisdom

No poetry surpasses certain Vedic hymns in moral loftiness, in eminence and intellectual breadth. In them breathes the feeling of the Divine in nature, the Unseen surrounding it and the great Unity pervading the whole.

—Edouard Schuré
The Great Initiates

Haré is a name for God derived from the Sanskrit har, "to steal." What bold imagery! The Lord may be tagged the Divine Thief because he has stolen our hearts, and we cannot rest until we catch him … and Krishna comes from the root karsh, "to draw"—he who ceaselessly draws us to himself.

—Eknath Easwaran
Meditation

HISTORY

There are two histories of the world running parallel—the one visible, one hidden.

—P. D. Ouspensky

History is the track in the snow left by creativity wandering in the Divine Imagination.

—Terence McKenna
Chaos, Creativity and Cosmic Consciousness

History often resembles myth because they are both ultimately of the same stuff.

—J. R. R. Tolkien

Whenever you see a legend, you can be sure, if you go to the very bottom of things, that you will find history.

—Vallet de Viriville

History is the story of the ego of a civilization, while myth is the story of its soul.

—William Irwin Thompson

The history of every country begins in the heart of a man or woman.

—Willa Cather
O Pioneers

Historical events are empty cocoons discarded by the spirit that moved through them.

—Frank Waters
Pumpkin Seed Point

The past is really almost as much a work of the imagination as the future.

—Jessamyn West

As Rome hid its debt to the Etruscans, we have obscured our inheritance from the Red Man.

—Virgil Vogel
This Country Was Ours

Stephen Dedalus: History ... is a nightmare from which I am trying to wake.

—James Joyce
Ulysses

It is a black art, the writing of a history, is
it not? To resurrect the dead, and animate
their bones, as historians do? I think
historians must be melancholy creatures
rather like poets, perhaps, or doctors ...

—Patrick McGrath
Martha Peake

People care about their place in history
when their own past is valued.

—Rosabeth Moss Kanter
On the Frontiers of Management

Writing history is a way of getting rid of
the past.

—Johann Wolfgang von Goethe

History is the Totenbuch, the book of the
dead, kept by the administrators of the
camps. Memory is the Memorbucher,
the names of those to be mourned, read
aloud in the synagogue.

—Anne Michaels
Fugitive Pieces

History is a fable which has been
agreed upon.

—François-Marie Arouet (Voltaire)

The amount of accumulated past
is accelerating.

—Nathaniel Hawthorne

Man is a history-making creature who can
neither repeat his past nor leave it behind.

—W. H. Auden
The Dyer's Hand

HOLY

In reality the main purpose of life is to
raise everything that is profane to the
level of the holy.... When you walk across
the fields with your mind pure and holy,
then from all the stones, and all growing
things and all animals, the sparks of their
soul come out and cling to you, and then
they are purified and become a holy fire
in you.

—Martin Buber

What we are all more or less lacking at this
moment is a new definition of holiness.

—Pierre Teilhard de Chardin
Human Energy

The holy instant is a time in which
you receive and give perfect
communication.... It is the recognition
that all minds are in communication. It
therefore seeks to change nothing, but
merely to accept everything.

—*A Course in Miracles*

Holy means well-being—healthy to
the core.

—Rudolf Steiner
The Christian Mystery

The kind of work we do does not make us
holy but we may make it holy.

—Meister Eckhart

Places, people and things can all be holy
when they have God's mark on them.

—Frederick Buechner
Wishful Thinking

HOME

If I find in myself a desire which no
experience in this world can satisfy, the
most probable explanation is that I am
made for another world.

—C. S. Lewis
Mere Christianity

… it is a dangerous thing to build a home
in the wrong place, at the wrong time, or
in the wrong way. If we want our homes
to be enchanted rather than haunted, we
have to think deeply about what we're
doing when we build and maintain them.

—Thomas Moore
The Re-Enchantment of Everyday Life

You know nothing about whereness. The
only way to come to know where you are
is to begin to make yourself at home.

—George MacDonald
Lilith

When you clear your home you are
also clearing your life, for your home
is a reflection of you—changing your
home's energy changes your energy.
Your home has consciousness and
everything you do to affect its energy
positively is improving your relationship with a living consciousness.

—Denise Linn
Sacred Space

A fireplace is an archetypal image of
home, comfort, and security. It is so
familiar we hardly pay attention to it.
Experiencing fire, water, earth, or air intimately yet freshly, can add new vitality
and meaning to our places…. In the end,
all that really matters is that we approach
wherever we live with full attention and
an open heart.

—Thomas Bender
The Power of Place

For me, moving and staying at home,
traveling and arriving are all of a piece.
The world is full of homes in which I
have lived for a day, a month, a year, or
much longer…. One night in a room
with a leaping fire may mean more to me
than many months in a room without
a fireplace, a room in which my life has
been paced less excitingly.

—Margaret Mead
Blackberry Winter

The definition of a man's own country
was "the place in which I do not have to
ask." Yet to feel "at home" in that country
depended on being able to leave it.

—Bruce Chatwin
Songlines

Home is a company of people with particular values and a particular history….
It is the particular womb out of which
we are born…. Home is a gift we never
earn…. Everyone leaves home a little
differently.

—Herbert Anderson &
Kenneth R. Mitchell
Leaving Home

There are a thousand ways to go
home again.

—Jalal Al-din Rumi

To be happy at home is the ultimate
result of all ambition, the end to which
every enterprise and labor tends.

—Samuel Johnson

Homes are not physical locations, but
situations for living.

—Edward S. Casey
Getting Back into Place

Being happy and at home is what the
whole thing is about.

—C. S. Lewis

You are never alone. You are always home.

—Walter Truett Anderson
The Next Enlightenment

Where are we really going? Always home!

—Novalis (Friedrich von Leopold)

HOMELESS

Not all homeless live on the streets.

—Herbert Anderson &
Kenneth R. Mitchell
Leaving Home

Home territory embodies the plentitude
that being placeless so painfully lacks.

—Edward S. Casey
Getting Back into Place

In Japan, homeless people are called
johatsu, meaning wandering spirit or one
who has lost his identity.

—Jennifer Toth
The Mole People

It's one of our natural paradoxes of
existence: we're not ready to come to our
true home until we're truly homeless.

—M. Scott Peck
In Heaven as on Earth

There are two ways to make a person feel
homeless—one is to destroy his home
and the other is to make his home look
and feel like everybody else's home.

—Thomas L. Friedman
The Lexus and the Olive Tree

Do what you have to do today. Tomorrow
will come. And if it doesn't, you won't
have to deal with it.

—Homeless Credo
New York City

HONESTY

The great majority of us are required to
live a life of constant, systematic duplic-
ity. Your health is bound to be affected
if, day after day, you say the opposite of
what you feel, if you grovel before what

you dislike and rejoice at what brings you nothing but misfortune.

—Boris Pasternak
Doctor Zhivago

Fear is perhaps the greatest enemy of candor.... How can I be sincere if I am constantly changing my mind to conform with the shadow of what I think others expect of me? Others have no right to demand that I be anything other than what I ought to be in the sight of God.

—Thomas Merton
No Man Is an Island

If you do not tell the truth about yourself, you cannot tell it about other people.

—Virginia Woolf

HOPE

Nothing is hopeless; we must hope for everything.

—Euripides

Hope is a memory of the future.

—Gabriel Marcel

An old astronomer clasped his protégé and said, "If Polaris dies tonight, be assured some greater light will take its place."

—Calvin Miller
The Finale

In the midst of winter, I finally learned that there was in me an invincible summer.

—Albert Camus
Actuelles

We are all in the gutter, but some of us are looking at the stars.

—Oscar Wilde
Lady Windermere's Fan

I refuse to accept the cynical notion that nation after nation must spiral down a militaristic stairway into the hell of nuclear destruction. I believe that unarmed truth and unconditional love will have the final word in reality.

—Martin Luther King, Jr.

Hope ... which whispered from Pandora's box only after all the other plagues and sorrows had escaped, is the best and last of all things. Without it, there is only time. And time pushes at our backs like a centrifuge, forcing us outward and away, until it nudges us into oblivion.

—Ian Caldwell & Dustin Thomason
The Rule of Four

Hope, unlike optimism, is rooted in unalloyed reality.... Hope is the elevating feeling we experience when we see—in the mind's eye—a path to a better future. Hope acknowledges the significant obstacles and deep pitfalls along that path. True hope has no room for delusion.

—Jerome Groopman
The Anatomy of Hope

We know in our bones that hope is everything. In the back of our minds, we suspect that it is nothing at all.

—Maurice Lamm
The Powers of Hope

Because stimulants and depressants are so available, we've fallen far into the realm of false optimism and false control. Drug use is a sad diversion of the natural biology of hope.

—Lionel Tiger

I truly believe that a great story must leave the reader with hope. Though I have to admit, I love a good cry.

—Jane Yolen
Take Joy

He who has health has hope, and he who has hope has everything.

—Arabic proverb

HOSPITALITY

There is one thing in the world that satisfies, and that is a meeting with the Guest.

—Kabir

The classic sign of God's mystery is to entertain, to make room for the other.

—Kathleen Norris
Dakota

The true saints are those who transfer the state of house-holdership to the house of God, becoming father and mother, brother and sister, son and daughter, to all creation, rather than to their own issue.

—Erik Erikson
Gandhi's Truth

The Creator God is a gracious, an abundant, and a generous host/hostess. She has spread out for our delight a banquet that was twenty billion years in the making.… God has declared that this banquet is "very good" and so are we, blessings ourselves, invited to the banquet.

—Matthew Fox
Original Blessing

The signs of a hospitable environment are deceptively simple. It is a context in which affirmation is unconditional and expectations are explicit. It is a holding environment in which there is freedom to have "a room of one's own" and freedom to be together.

—Herbert Anderson &
Robert Cotton Fite
Becoming Married

Let all guests who arrive be received like Christ, for He is going to say, "I came as a guest, and you received Me."

—Benedict,
Rule of St. Benedict

To give our Lord a perfect hospitality, Mary and Martha must combine.

—Teresa of Avila
The Interior Castle

True hospitality can be offered only by those who have found the center of their lives in their own hearts.

—Henri J. M. Nouwen

A good host gives the guest the sense that there is all the time in the world, even when they both know that time is a precious commodity.

—Margaret Guenther
Holy Listening

To Bedouins ... hospitality affirms their relationship to God. When Bedouins accept Islam, they become *djar*, meaning "protected neighbors." They come under God's protection and accept God's hospitality. All earthly hospitality is understood as an extension of this divine hospitality, a reflection of God's goodness.

—Philip Zaleski & Paul Kaufman
Gifts of the Spirit

This being human is a guest house, every morning a new arrival.

—Jalal Al-din Rumi

HUGGING

Hugging can lift depression, enabling the body's immunization system to become tuned up. Hugging breathes fresh life into tired bodies and makes you feel younger and more vibrant. In the home, hugging can strengthen relationships and significantly reduce tensions.

—Harold Falk

Our pores are places for messages of love, and physical contact is very important. Four hugs a day are necessary for survival; eight for maintenance, twelve for growth.

—Virginia Satir

Morrie Schwartz told Mitch Albom things never hug you back.

—Ignacio L. Götz
On Technology and the Spirit

HUMANITY

Know, O beloved, that man was not created in jest or at random, but marvelously made and for some great end. Although he is not from everlasting, yet he lives forever; and though his body is mean and earthly, yet his spirit is lofty and divine.

—Al-Ghazzali
The Alchemy of Happiness

I am the vessel. The draft is God's and God is the thirsty one.

—Dag Hammaskjöld
Markings

You must not lose faith in humanity. Humanity is an ocean; if a few drops of the ocean are dirty, the ocean does not become dirty.

—Mohandas (Mahatma) Gandhi

Man becomes truly human only at the time of decision.

—Paul Tillich

All persons are mortal. I am a person. Therefore I am mortal. But I don't believe it.... I had discovered that I was vulnerable. I had had my nose rubbed in it. Like Job, once "I had heard of thee by the hearing of the ear, but now my eye sees thee." Heavy stuff! What do you do with it, aside from trying not to read obituaries?

—Violet Weingarten
Intimations of Mortality

We are not human beings having a spiritual experience. We are spiritual beings having a human experience.

—Pierre Teilhard de Chardin

I am a frayed and nibbled survivor in a fallen world, and I am getting along. I am aging and eaten and have done my share of eating too. I am not washed and beautiful, in control of a shining world in which everything fits, but instead am wandering awed about on a splintered wreck I've come to care for ...

—Annie Dillard
Pilgrim at Tinker Creek

What interests me most is neither still life nor landscape but the human figure. It is through it that I best succeed in expressing the nearly religious feeling that I have towards life.

—Henri Matisse
Notes of a Painter

There are six billion of us now. The estimated number of humans who have ever lived: 100 billion.

—Stewart Brand
The Clock of the Long Now

If anyone had been around four billion years ago, would they ever have guessed that the volcanic landscape, the primeval oceans, the strange mixture of gases in the atmosphere would steadily evolve into such improbable and complex beings as constitute humanity?... What unimaginable developments lie ahead, not only in thousands of millions of years time, but in just one million years?... Where are we most likely to be headed?

—Peter Russell
The Global Brain Awakens

Humanity exists only so that evolution can be accomplished.

—Mary E. Carreiro
The Psychology of Spiritual Growth

We humans are hardwired to remember how to become more fully human.

—Richard Thieme

We are human only in contact and conviviality with what is not human.

—David Abram
The Spell of the Sensuous

Man is the great mystery of God; the microcosm or the complete abridgement of the whole universe ... a hieroglyphic of eternity and time.

—Jacob Boehme
The Signature of All Things

Humanity was made at the end of the week's work when God was tired.

—Mark Twain

The main thing in life is not to be afraid to be human.

—Pablo Casals

HUMILITY

The heights of the spirit can only be climbed by passing through the portals of humility. You can only acquire right knowledge when you have learnt to esteem it.

—Rudolf Steiner
Knowledge of the Higher Worlds and Its Attainment

In God's economy, nothing is wasted. Through failure, we learn a lesson in humility which is probably needed, painful though it is.

—Bill Wilson

Humility is the art of grasping our own limitations, accepting the fact that we are mere specks in the galaxy of great beings, just as our earth is but a minor star in the firmament.

—Ruth Montgomery
The World Before

Humility in itself is naught else but a true knowing and feeling of man's self as he is.

—*The Cloud of Unknowing*

Humility is the foundation of the whole building and unless you are truly humble, our Lord, for your own sake, will never permit you to rear it very high lest it should fall to the ground.... Humility

is the Queen without whom none can checkmate the divine King.

—Teresa of Avila
The Interior Castle

I will build my home from the lesser trees.

—Maori proverb

HUMOR

Humor is wonderful food for the soul. Too much seriousness violates the laws of nature. Living a humorless life, turning a blind eye to the paradoxes around and within us, or never laughing at ourselves shrinks the soul.

—Matthew Fox
Handbook for the Soul

Humor has a tremendous healing effect ... (it) is the sudden seeing of the opposite of what we expect to see. As soon as we can say, "I see the other side," a tension is released and reconciliation can take place—that is what humor is all about.

—Herbert B. Puryear
Edgar Cayce: Reflections of the Path

The divine perspective on our human efforts at meaning is sheer comedy. There is a kind of laughter that comes from the gods, saving us from our depressive seriousness and opening the way toward the only happiness that counts: a forgiving, far-seeing perspective on our efforts to know what can't be known and to become what we can never be.

—Thomas Moore
The Soul's Religion

Freud relished anecdotes and jokes, particularly Jewish jokes, because they were so pregnant with unconscious meanings. Like metaphors, jokes suggest rather than announce their meaning …

—Bruno Bettelheim
Freud and Man's Soul

A laugh is the shortest distance between two people.

—Victor Borge

The opposite of gravity is levity.

—Nancy Margulies

Mirth cleanses the mind of its crazy cobweb designs, leaving space for nurturing to take place.

—Peter Balin
The Flight of the Feathered Serpent

Comedy, if it's about anything at all, is about something gone wrong.

—Steve Allen

ship founded on righteousness, and a righteousness attained in fellowship.

—Dag Hammarskjöld
Markings

Politics, not droughts or over-population, causes hunger.

—Eugene Winden
The Future in Plain Sight

How many people died on September 11, 2001? The UN Food and Agricultural Organization says 35,615 children died that day of hunger.

—Jack Nelson-Pallmeyer
Is Religion Killing Us?

The sight of someone eating will not appease our hunger. The spiritual experiences of others cannot satisfy your yearning.

—Sufi proverb

HUNGER

Jesus made himself the bread of life and lets himself be eaten up. And after we have been satisfied ourselves, by eating his body and drinking his blood, he makes himself the hungry one, the naked one.

—Mother Teresa

Hunger is my native place in the land of the passions. Hunger for fellowship, hunger for righteousness—for a fellow-

1

ICONS

Icons are nothing more than an aid for
spiritual focus and work ... all icons are
miraculous insofar as they depict one
Person. Miracles happen through the
Grace of the Holy Spirit, the Grace of
the Christ.... But it is not the icon that
generates the miracle.... It is the Person
represented in the icon who is considered
to have caused the miracle through the
Grace of Christ and because of the faith
of the individual healed.

—Kyriacos Markides
The Mountain of Silence

No icon painter ever signs his/her work.
It represents a religious archetype that
can't be changed through a painter's
creativity or imagination.... The art of
icon painting can't be separated from
their liturgical functions—it's a sacred,
consecrated thing.... Icons are not easy
to "see" but in their prayerful presence,
they can speak to the searching heart.

—Kyriacos Markides
Riding with the Lion

Icons bear fragments of reality and must
never look like the person it portrays or it
becomes an image.

—Madeleine L'Engle
A Circle of Quiet

An icon is a window into the invisible where we can see what humanness is capable of ...

—Jean-Yves LeLoup
The Gospel of Mary Magdalene

Once he [Rasputin] spent the night in a room with Mary's icon. She wept and told him, "Grigory, I am weeping for the sins of mankind. So, wander and cleanse the people of their sins."

—Edvard Radzinsky
The Rasputin File

Our culture is iconophobic and iconoclastic. We allow images only when they have been safely de-vitalized.

—Noel Cobb
Archetypal Imagination

The body should be understood as a revelation of the spirit ... an icon of the spirit which dwells in it.

—Sergei Bulgakov
Sophia

The icons of old are the codings of tomorrow. And tomorrow holds the promise for recovery of forgotten wisdom.

—Jean Houston

Icon painting is undertaken in parallel with the art of self-perfection.... Icons exist to convey the highest cosmological, philosophical and theological ideas.... Vibrations are caught in color and form and can still be heard.

—Richard Temple
Icons and the Mystical Origins of Christianity

An icon is a window to God.

—Madeleine L'Engle
Penguins and Golden Calves

IDEAS

There can be no property in ideas, because these are gifts of the Spirit, and not to be confused with talents ... whoever conforms himself to an idea and makes it his own, will be working originally, but not so if he is expressing only his own ideals or opinions.

—Ananda K. Coomaraswamy
Christian and Oriental Philosophy of Art

Our concepts are like a thread made of fibers. The solidity of the thread is not due to the presence of a single fiber running its full length, but to the intertwining of a large number of fibers.

—Ludwig Josef Johan Wittgenstein
Philosophical Investigations

Ideas are like rabbits. You get a couple and learn how to handle them, and pretty soon you have a dozen.

—John Steinbeck

What shorthand is to words, symbology is to ideas. This is especially true of religious concepts.

—Elsie Sechrist
Dreams Your Magic Mirror

When I am, as it were, completely myself, entirely alone, and of good cheer, it is on such occasions that my ideas flow best and most abundantly. Whence and how they come, I know not; nor can I force them.... When I proceed to write down my ideas, I take out of the bag of my memory ... what has been previously collected.... For this reason the committing to paper is done quickly enough, for everything is ... already finished; and it rarely differs on paper from what was in my imagination.

—Wolfgang Amadeus Mozart
Holmes, The Life of Mozart

Ideas do not belong to people, Ideas live in the world as we do. We discover certain ideas at certain times.

—Mary Caroline (M. C.) Richards
Centering

I am suggesting that your best idea for a business will be something that is deep within you, something that can't be stolen because it is uniquely yours, and anyone else trying to execute it without the (perhaps unconscious) thought you have given the subject will fail. It's not basically different from writing a novel. A good business and a good novel are faithful and uncluttered expressions of yourself.

—Paul Hawken
Growing a Business

Any powerful idea is absolutely fascinating and absolutely useless until we choose to use it.

—Richard Bach
One

Like a mutation, an idea may be recorded in the wrong time, to lie latent like a

recessive gene and spring once more to life in an auspicious era.

—Loren Eiseley

Every book is the wreck of a perfect idea.

—Iris Murdoch

Ideas are very difficult to sacrifice.

—Mary E. Carreiro
The Psychology of Spiritual Growth

Great ideas come into the world as gently as doves.

—Albert Camus

IDENTITY

When the time comes to you at which you will be forced at last to utter the speech which has lain at the center of your soul for years, which you have, all that time, idiot-like been saying over and over, you'll not talk about joy of words. I saw well why the gods do not speak to us openly, nor let us answer. Till that word can be dug out of us, why should they hear the babble that we think we mean? How can they meet us face to face till we have faces?

—C. S. Lewis
Till We Have Faces

"Let me think: was I the same when I got up this morning? I almost think I remember feeling a little different. But if I'm not the same, the next question is, who in the world am I? Ah, that's the great puzzle!"

—Lewis Carroll
Alice's Adventures in Wonderland

We are what we pretend to be, so we must be careful about what we pretend to be.

—Kurt Vonnegut, Jr.

Curiosity is the doorway that stimulates growth, joy and expansion and allows you to begin to remember who you are.

—Emmanual
The Choice for Love

Our troubles arise from the fact that we do not know what we are and cannot agree on what we want to be.

—Edward O. Wilson

Who I am does not depend on what I do.

—Parker Palmer

I am sure that I am going to look in the mirror and see nothing. People won't stop calling me a mirror. And if a mirror looks into another mirror, what will it find when it looks?

—Andy Warhol

Tell me what you long for and I'll tell you who you are.

—James Hillman

Do you have a Josef Mengele living inside of you? You betcha! And Iago and Lady Macbeth.

—M. Scott Peck

Every dream is a portrait of the dreamer. Get acquainted with your inner personalities as persons in their own right.

—Robert A. Johnson
Inner Work

Every being, whether it be a star or a rock, a flea or a fish, speaks for itself; its own shape, magnitude, character identify it and concretely symbolize it.

—Lewis Mumford
The Myth of the Machine

Biographies are but the clothes and buttons of the man—the biography of the man himself cannot be written.

—Mark Twain

In order to do something one has to be someone.

—Johann Wolfgang von Goethe

Wood may remain ten years in the water, but it will never become a crocodile.

—African proverb

In every man there is a king. Speak to the king and the king will come forth.

—Scandinavian proverb

IDOLS

Idol worship is venerating an image; idol worship places a screen between you and your experience.

—Gary Zukov & Linda Francis
The Heart of the Soul

Anything that we worship other than God is a form of idolatry.… Whenever we absolutize something, be it an ideology, money, or even scientific knowledge, we are into idolatry.

—Kyriacos Markides
The Mountain

If you make an idol, it may stand in at first for some force which is greater than itself, or for some spiritual energy. But gradually the idol is taken to be it—literally; and therefore you give supreme value to that object.

—Owen Barfield & David Bohm
On Dialogue

Carl Mendelius: All idolatry springs from a desire for order. We want to be neat … what we can't cope with is the untidiness of the universe, the lunatic aspect of a cosmos with no known beginning, no visible end and no apparent meaning to all its bustling dynamics.

—Morris West
The Clowns of God

The true teacher knocks down the idol that the student makes of him.

—Jalal Al-din Rumi

IGNORANCE

The most basic illness that the holy elders tell about is ignorance. In their language, however, ignorance does not mean lack of the right kind of information or the right kind of intellectual knowledge. What they really mean is the heart's ignorance of God.

—Kyriacos Markides
The Mountain of Silence

Knowing ignorance is strength. Ignoring knowledge is sickness.

—Tao Te Ching

One dog barks at nothing; ten thousand others pass it on.

—Japanese proverb

ILLNESS

I have never been anywhere but sick. In a sense sickness is a place, more instructive than a long trip to Europe, and it's always a place where there's no company, where nobody can follow. Sickness before death is a very appropriate thing and I think those who don't have it miss one of God's mercies.

—Flannery O'Connor
The Habit of Being

I believe that illness and disease should be defined as any defect in the structure of our bodies or our personalities that prevents us from fulfilling our potential as human beings.

—M. Scott Peck
People of the Lie

Living with cancer as a "dying into life" remains a way of living that I do not yet fully understand…. Cancer has made me sadder and wiser, and therefore richer. Because death is an essential part of life, to be fully alive is to be prepared for it.

—Marion Woodman
Bone

Consider the prevalence of immune system diseases in our society today. What are we being asked to learn about "differences" and "enemies"?

—Neil Douglas-Klotz
Prayers of the Cosmos

Through sickness and death there arises a greater understanding of the physical structure—and the honoring of them comes about. Such experiences bring forth an attunement of individuals to one another—they bring forth unconditional love.

—Sheila Petersen-Lowary
Channels to a New Reality:
the 5th Dimension

Rachel Carson suffered from breast cancer, quite possibly caused by the "sea of carcinogens" she wrote of, but was denounced by the AMA. She died two years after her book was published.

—Alan Atkisson
Believing Cassandra

Leukemia, or blood cancer, is 30% higher than average near nuclear power plants.

—Theodor Schwenk &
Wolfram Schwenk
Water: The Element of Life

Then one day it's not someone else. The name on the report of malignancy is your own … you clench your teeth and try not to hear the cataract. You had thought it was 20 miles downstream, but it's just around the corner.

—Allen Wheelis
The Seeker

Suicide is extremely rare among cancer patients and studies have shown that nearly 90% of all cancer patients say they want to be told the truth.

—Robert Chernin Cantor
A Time to Live

People get sick when they are dispirited. When we're inspirited, happy, confident, creative, the same viruses find us impervious to attack.

—Sidney Jourard
The Transparent Self

When you have a terminal illness, you either have hope or freedom. I've chosen freedom. I try to live for the day.

—William Bettelyoun

It is a distortion, with something profoundly disloyal about it, to picture the human being as a teetering, fallible contraption, always needing watching and patching, always on the verge of flapping to pieces.

—Lewis Thomas
Lives of a Cell

We are in real life, a reasonably healthy people. Far from being ineptly put together, we are amazingly tough,

durable organisms, full of health, ready
for most contingencies.

—Lewis Thomas
The Medusa and the Snail

When the earth is sick and polluted,
human health is impossible … to heal
ourselves we must heal our planet and to
heal the planet we must heal ourselves.

—Bobby McLeod

ILLUSION

All visible objects, man, are but as
pasteboard masks.

—Herman Melville
Moby Dick

Clarity is the perception of wisdom …
being able to perceive and understand the
illusion, and to let it play. It is being able to
see beyond the activities of the personality
to the force of the immortal soul.

—Gary Zukav

The immense hazard and the immense
blindness of the world are only an illusion.

—Pierre Teilard de Chardin

All appearances are verily one's own
concepts, self-conceived in the mind, like
reflections seen in a mirror.

—Padma-Sambhava

IMAGES

The soul thinks in images.

—Aristotle

When you come to the point when
you are no longer compelled to project
yourself into any image or to entertain
any images in yourself, and you let go
of all that is within you, then you can be
transported into God's naked being.

—Meister Eckhart

We make in our measure and in our
derivative mode, because we are made:
and not only made, but made in the
image and likeness of a Maker.

—J. R. R. Tolkien
On Fairy-Stories

All images have meaning because they
contain a spiritual element.

—Sandra G. Shuman
Source Imagery

Imagery is the universal language of
the unconscious. Thinking in pictures
precedes thinking in words.

—Frances E. Vaughan
Awakening Intuition

We live immediately only in the world
of images.

—Carl G. Jung

If we are all created in the divine image,
then our images of God must be fluid
and multifarious.

Judith Plaskow

John Fowles remarked that his novel *The French Lieutenant's Woman* sprang from a single image he saw for ten seconds in a dream. A woman appeared, her face partially concealed by a scarf, standing at the end of a dock in a storm.

—Robert Bly
Iron John

We Indians live in a world of symbols and images where the spiritual and the commonplace are one. To us [symbols] are part of nature, part of ourselves, even little insects like ants and grasshoppers. We try to understand them not with the head but with the heart, and we need no more than a hint to give us the meaning.

—Lame Deer
Lame Deer Seeker of Visions

You must give birth to your images. They are the future waiting to be born ... fear not the strangeness you feel. The future must enter into you long before it happens.

—Rainer Maria Rilke
Letters to a Young Poet

Images provide messages that are understood by the immune system. They link conscious thoughts with the white blood cells in such a way that the appropriate combinations and numbers come rushing forth to perform in ways that not even the most knowledgeable immunologist could command.

—Jeanne Achterberg
Imagery in Healing

A daydream is a meal at which images are eaten. Some of us are gourmets, some gourmands, and a good many take their images precooked out of a can

and swallow them down whole, absent-mindedly and with little relish.

—Richard M. Restak
The Brain

Imagery is always dancing with the sheer delight of an imagination at play because it originates in instinct.

—Robert Bly & Marion Woodman
The Maiden King

If I had a complete image I would lose interest in it.

—Ben Shahn

IMAGINATION

The imagination can cross thousands of miles and can make an impression thousands of miles away, too.

—Paracelsus

Man's imaginative inventions must originate with God and must in consequence reflect something of eternal truths.

—J. R. R. Tolkien

The enemy of whole vision is reasoning power's divorce from the imagination.

—William Blake

Imagination is real because every perception of the world around us is absolutely colored by the narrative or image-filled lens through which we perceive. We are all poets and artists as we live our daily lives, whether or not we recognize this role and whether or not we believe it.

—Thomas Moore
Original Self

I see this continual assertion of imagination as the basis of all spiritual and material life, and I see also that to Christ imagination was simply a form of Love, and that to him Love was Lord in the fullest meaning of the phrase.

—Oscar Wilde
Complete Works of Oscar Wilde

We are condemned to live out what we cannot imagine.

—Thomas Moore
Care of the Soul

We are what we imagine. Our very existence consists in our imagination of ourselves.... The greatest tragedy that can befall us is to go unimagined.

—N. Scott Momaday

The world is but canvas to our imagination.

—Henry David Thoreau

The quality of the imagination is to flow, and not to freeze.

—Ralph Waldo Emerson
The Portable Emerson

For in the imagination is contained all the positive and the highest good; all the negative and the deepest evil.

—Harold Stone
Introduction, *Sand Play*

The imagination may be compared to Adam's dream—he awoke and found it truth.

—John Keats
a letter to Benjamin Bailey

In reality, Kundalini is the power of imagination, the power of fantasy, which takes the place of a real function. When a man dreams instead of acting, when his dreams take the place of reality, when a man imagines himself to be an eagle, a lion, or a magician, it is the force of Kundalini acting in him . Kundalini can act in all centers and with its help all the centers can be satisfied with the imaginary instead of the real.

—G. I. Gurdjieff & P. D. Ouspensky
In Search of the Miraculous

The imagination is committed to the justice of wholeness. It will not choose one side in an inner conflict and repress or banish the other; it will endeavor to initiate a profound conversation between them in order that something original can be born.

—John O'Donohue
Anam Cara

The imagination is not, as its etymology suggests, the faculty for forming images of reality; it is the faculty for forming images which go beyond reality, which sing reality. It is a superhuman faculty.

—Gaston Bachelard
Water and Dreams

Teaching English to adolescents for twenty years gives me the authority to say, Kill the imagination and you kill the soul. Kill the soul and you're left with a listless, apathetic creature who can become hopeless or brutal or both. Kill the metaphors and you kill desire; the image magnetizes the movement of the energy.

—Marion Woodman
Bones

Merely imagining that we are doing something can bring about brain activation similar to what happens when we are actually doing it. Imagery does exert a measurable physical effect on the brain.

—Richard M. Restak
The Brain

The imagination is an eye, a marvelous third eye that floats free. As children, that eye sees with 20/20 clarity. As we grow older, its vision begins to dim.

—Stephen King
Danse Macabre

Imagination grows by exercise and, contrary to the common belief, is more powerful in the mature than in the young.

—W. Somerset Maugham

Because your imagination transcends time, it is one of your greatest touchstones to your own identity.

—Jane Roberts
The Nature of Personal Reality

Imagination means singing to a wide invisible audience.... It makes erotic philosophers of us, as we imagine the world in images that make whole.

—Mary Caroline (M. C.) Richards
Imagine Inventing Yellow

I think the imagination is the single most powerful tool humankind possesses. It beats the opposable thumb.

—Ursula K. LeGuin
The Wave in the Mind

What if imagination and art are not frosting at all, but the foundation of human experience?

—Rollo May

He who does not imagine in stronger and better lineaments ... than his perishing and mortal eye can see, does not imagine at all.

—William Blake

What is now proved was once only imagined.

—William Blake

Logic can take you from A to B, but imagination encircles the world.

—Keith Critchlow
Time Stands Still

Imagination is the highest kite we can fly.

—Lauren Bacall

Go confidently in the direction of your dreams. Live the life you've imagined.

—Henry David Thoreau

IMPROVISATION

The improvisatory artist cannot be sure whether a given improvisation will stand as a work of art or be rejected as an aberration.

—Mary Catherine Bateson
Peripheral Visions

Even crazy quilts are sewn against a backing; the basic sense of continuity allows improvisation.

—Mary Catherine Bateson
Composing a Life

Bards are always partially improvising. Maybe that was the source of Hermes' genius.

—Stewart Brand
The Clock of the Long Now

INCARNATION

The Incarnation accomplished the following: That God became human and that humans became God and sharers in the divine nature.

—Thomas Aquinas
Commentary on the Gospel of St. John

Those who master the law of karma and achieve realization can choose to return in life after life to help others. In Tibet a tradition of recognizing such incarnations or *tulkus* began in the thirteenth century and continues to the present day.

—Sogyal Rinpoche
The Tibetan Book of Living and Dying

It is common for small children who are reincarnations to remember objects and people from their previous lives. Some can also recite scriptures, although they have not yet been taught them.

—Dalai Lama
My Land and My People

When one incarnates, one first takes on the group consciousness of the species at a particular point in its history, and only within that context does more individualized human experience articulate itself.

—Christopher M. Bache
Dark Night, Early Dawn

As a "rule" we incarnate within each 2,100 year period, once as male and once as female. But much depends on one's development.

—Rudolf Steiner
An Outline of Occult Science

As long as man calls anything his own, he cannot attain knowledge of his preceding incarnation.

—Rudolf Steiner
Macrocosm and Microcosm

The Incarnation means that God has come to live among us as we are.

—James Carroll
Constantine's Sword

What might Christ be like if there really were a world like Narnia and he chose to be incarnate and die and rise again in that world as he actually has done in ours?

—C. S. Lewis & Humphrey Carpenter
The Inklings

When writers die, they become books, which is, after all, not too bad an incarnation.

—Jorge Luis Borges

maybe by trying to put it into form. To find the feeling of infinity on the horizon line or just over the next hill.

—Georgia O'Keeffe
Georgia O'Keeffe

INFINITE/INFINITY

Within its deep infinity I saw gathered, and bound by love in one volume, the scattered leaves of all the universe.

—Dante Alighieri

We are, as the aborigines say, just learning how to survive in infinity.

—Michael Talbot
The Holographic Universe

The finite is the mirror of the infinite, its external revealing image.

—Arthur Young

Infinitude is too wide for man to take in. He is therefore permitted to take in portions and spread his vision over the wide circumference by little and little; and in these portions doth the Infinite shadow forth itself, God in all and all in God.

—Amos Bronson Alcott
Journal

I saw no God, nor heard any, in a finite organical perception; but my senses discovered the infinite in everything.

—William Blake

The unexplainable thing in nature that makes me feel the world is big far beyond my understanding—to understand

INFLUENCE

If we create a trace in someone's mind because of what we say or do, that trace may last for a lifetime.

—Les Kaye
Zen at Work

We are creatures of many different dimensions passing through each other's lives like ghosts through doors.

—Loren Eiseley

INITIATION

When initiation is in place, the old men help the boys to move from the mother's world to the father's world.... Initiation asks the son to move his love energy away from the attractive mother to the relatively unattractive serpent father ... he learns to look at the death side of things.

—Robert Bly
Iron John

All initiations actually fall back on the greatest symbol of all: spiritually dying and coming back to life.

—Robert Ellwood
The Cross and the Grail

Socrates died only as an initiate can die—as one to whom death is merely a moment of life like other moments … the initiate learns: die and become.

—Rudolf Steiner
Christianity as Mystical Fact

Plato was, according to tradition, initiated into the mysteries in Egypt.

—Jean Gebser
The Ever-Present Origin

INNOVATION

Einstein didn't go around wracking his brain, muttering to himself, "How, oh how, can I come up with a Great Idea?" You just do what comes naturally…. Mozart said things should "flow like oil." Trying harder is not the trick. The trick is getting the right concept to begin with and then make variations.

—Douglas R. Hofstadter
Metamagical Themas

At first people refuse to believe that a strange new thing can be done, then they begin to hope it can't be done, then they see it can be done—then it is done and all the world wonders why it was not done centuries before.

—Frances Hodgson Burnett
The Secret Garden

Innovation comes only from readily and seamlessly sharing information rather than hoarding it.

—Tom Peters

INTENTION

Intention is, quite simply, the psychological mechanism with which we create reality. Therefore, if we desire to birth a new reality, we begin with a clear intention of what we desire to create.

—Charlotte Shelton
Quantum Leaps

Where intention goes, energy flows…. Your intention can be likened to a journey. Your overall intention is your destination and your specific intentions can be likened to the signposts along the way.

—Denise Linn
Sacred Space

How we set the arrow of our lives in the bow of intentionality creates the shape of the target.

—Richard Thieme

Intent is infinite.

—Carlos Castaneda
Magical Passes

I knew when I grew up that I wanted to be somebody. Now I realize I needed to be more specific.

—Jane Wagner
A Search for Signs of Intelligent Life in the Universe

INQUIRY

Thirst was made for water; inquiry for truth.

—C. S. Lewis
The Great Divorce

It is only when you are constantly inquiring, constantly observing, constantly learning, that you find truth, God or love; and you cannot inquire, observe, learn, you cannot be deeply aware if you are afraid.

—Jiddu Krishnamurti
Think on These Things

Who, indeed, should be more concerned than the artist with the defense of liberty and free inquiry, which are essential to his very creativity?

—Pablo Casals
Joys and Sorrows

Leonardo was, as Kenneth Clark put it, "the most relentlessly curious man in history." The notebooks log his great quest of interestedness ... when he wanted to try out a new pen-nib, he habitually doodled the word dimmi—"Tell me." It is the sound of Leonardo inquiring, seeking another bit of data. Tell me what, tell me how, tell me why.

—Charles Nicholl
Leonardo da Vinci

There do exist inquiring minds, which long for the truth of the heart, seek it, strive to solve the problems set by life, try to penetrate the essence of things and phenomena and to penetrate into themselves ...

—G. I. Gurdjieff

Reason was invented by man only to help decipher the formulas created by God. In everything there is a code and to each code, a key.

—Katherine Neville
The Eight

INSIGHT

Of all that God has shown me, I can speak just the smallest word, not more than a honey bee takes on her foot from an overspilling jar.

—Mechtild of Magdeburg

For Joyce, linear schemes of progress were based on an illusion. He called meldings of past and present "epiphanies," sudden surges of spiritual insight that occurred in "the most delicate and evanescent of moments."

—Jackson Lears
Something for Nothing

Together the patient and I address ourselves to the two-million-year-old man who is in all of us.

—Carl G. Jung

If you have insight you use your inner eye, your inner ear, to pierce the heart of things, and have no need of intellectual knowledge.

—Chuang-Tsu

Behind our existence lies something else that becomes accessible to us only by our shaking off the world.

—Arthur Schopenhauer

The feeling—I won't call it belief—that I had had a sudden opening, had seen through a window, as it were, distant realities that incomprehensibly belonged with my own life, was so acute that I cannot shake it all today.

—William James
A Suggestion about Mysticism

Give me the madman's sudden insight and the child's spiritual dignity.

—Theodore Roethke
Notebook

Only an instant is needed for insight to break through since it comes always as a single unity, not in some digital breakdown. Insight is always complete and perfect in its single instant's appearance, for it is wholeness.... It appears in an all-or-nothing form.

—Joseph Chilton Pearce
The Bond of Power

From time immemorial artistic insights have been revealed to artists in their sleep and in dreams, so that at all times they ardently desired them.

—Paracelsus

INSPIRATION

Inspiration is the art of breathing in.

—Marcus Bach
The Power of Perception

Inspiration seeks the artist as the artist seeks inspiration.

—Jane Roberts
The World View of Paul Cézanne

Writing everyday as one practices the piano everyday keeps one nimble and then when the great moments of inspiration come, one is in good form, supple and smooth.

—Anäis Nin

INTEGRITY

To have true integrity, poise, and courage is to be attuned to the silent and invisible nature within you. Real maturity is the integrity of inhabiting that "immortal longing" that always calls you to new horizons.

—John O'Donohue
Eternal Echoes

Integrity requires that I discern what is integral to my selfhood, what fits and what does not—and that I choose life-giving ways of relating to the forces that converge within me.... By choosing integrity, I become more whole, but wholeness does not mean perfection. It means becoming more real by acknowledging the whole of who I am.

—Parker J. Palmer
The Courage to Teach

INTELLECT

The intellect has little to do on the road to discovery. There comes a leap in consciousness, call it intuition or what you will, and the solution comes to you and you don't know how or why.

—Albert Einstein

Everyone is born a genius; it just takes some of us longer to forget.

—Martha Graham

Genius when it is at work, is in communion with God.

—Jean August Dominique Ingres

To observe without evaluating is the highest form of intelligence.

—Jiddu Krishnamurti

"Do you really think there are no sins of intellect?
"There are indeed, Dick. There is hidebound prejudice, and intellectual dishonesty and timidity, and stagnation. But honest opinion fearlessly followed—they are not sins."

—C. S. Lewis
  The Great Divorce

The idea that we can have cleverness only for ourselves is foolish. We cannot be clever only for ourselves.

—Rudolf Steiner
  The Archangel Michael

Saturn indicates an intellectual nature and makes people contemplative.

—Pico della Mirandola
  in *Saturn and Melancholy*

We are clearly indebted as a species to the play of our intelligence; we trust our future to it; but we do not know whether intelligence is reason or whether intelligence is this desire to embrace and be embraced in the pattern that both theologians and physicists call God.

—Barry Lopez
  Arctic Dreams

Intelligence emerges as the system connects to itself in diverse and creative ways.

—Margaret Wheatley

The genius of an individual lies in the inhabitation of their peculiar and particular spirit in conversation with the world.

—David Whyte
  Crossing the Unknown Sea

Logic by itself is a trap. The unknown should be dealt with patiently and with humility.

—Paul S. Martin *&* Jeffrey Goodman
  Psychic Archeology

Intelligence is like a four-wheel drive. It just enables you to get stuck in more remote places.

—Garrison Keillor

INTENTION

Intention is a power that sets our trajectory as we initiate a path of action.

—Joel Levey *&* Michelle Levey
  Living in Balance

Intent for Don Juan is something like an energetic wave, a beam of energy which attaches itself to us. Intent is infinite.

—Carlos Castenda
Magical Passes

To transform the world, we must begin with ourselves; and what is important in beginning with ourselves is the intention. The intention must be to understand ourselves and not to leave it to others to transform themselves.

—Jiddu Krishnamurti

When we try to pick out anything by itself, we find that it is hitched to everything else in the universe.

—John Muir

Solitons reflect the fact that nature is profoundly interconnected and that sometimes these hidden connections can be triggered to produce a higher form of integrated order.

—Christopher M. Bache
Dark Night, Early Dawn

INTERCONNECTEDNESS

When we look deep into the heart of a flower, we see clouds, sunshine, minerals, time, the earth, and everything else in the cosmos in it. Without clouds there could be no rain, and there would be no flower.

—Thich Nhat Hanh

I've heard it said there's a window that opens from one mind to another, but if there's no wall, there's no need for fitting the window, or the latch.

—Jalal Al-din Rumi

It's the obligation of the building to help the street; the obligation of the fireplace to help the room; the obligation of the wall to help the roof; the obligation of the building to help the garden.... Every building must help to heal the world.

—Christopher Alexander
The Process of Creating Life

INTERDEPENDENCE

It is the story of all life that is holy and is good to tell, and of us two-legged sharing in it with the four-leggeds and the wings of the air and all green things; for these are children of one mother and their father is one spirit.

—Black Elk

In the heaven of Indra, there is said to be a network of pearls, so arranged that if you look at one you see all the others reflected in it. In the same way each object in the world is not merely itself but involves every other object and in fact is everything else.

—Charles Eliot
Japanese Buddhism

Most people would squash a tiny insect without realizing that it is a vital link in the food chain that allows them to live. We are learning more and more about the interdependency of all life. We see how an insecticide in the fields of Iowa affects the fish in the Gulf of Mexico. We are all related, and nothing is complete without the other.

—Tom Brown, Jr.
The Search

The concept [Sacred Hoop] is one of a singular unity that is dynamic and encompassing, including all that is contained in its most essential aspect, that of life.... All movement is related to all other movement.... All movement must be harmonious and balanced and unified.

—Paula Gunn Allen
The Sacred Hoop

The hawk, the swoop and the hare are one.

—Gary Snyder

We believe that everything is dependent on everything else. The sun does not rise in the sky in loneliness; we are with him. The moon would be lost in isolation if we did not greet her with song. The stars dance together and we dance with them.

—Madeleine L'Engle
Dragons in the Water

The earth does not belong to man, man belongs to the earth. All things are connected, like blood which unites us all.

—Seattle/Seatlh

The experiences inherent in women's sexuality are expressions of the essential holistic nature of life on Earth; they are "body parables" of the profound oneness and interconnectedness of all matter/energy.

—Charlene Spretnak
The Politics of Women's Spirituality

For the secret to full living is interconnectivity and interdependence ... the secret is that if I alter anyone of the holographic memory patterns lying in all my cells in this incarnation, then the holographic memory pattern is altered throughout eternity. That is what freedom is, and when understood, is as easy as blowing a feather off your hand.

—Barbara Hand Clow
Eye of the Centaur

The Earth is an extension of our own living organism and in no way separate from ourselves.

—Chris Griscom
Ecstasy is a New Frequency

Everything that is in the heavens, on the earth, and under the earth, is penetrated with connectedness, penetrated with relatedness.

—Hildegard of Bingen

All religions, arts and sciences are branches of the same tree.

—Albert Einstein

Let all men and all women of all races and nations arise together and dance to the joyous music of life. For there is but one Father Spirit and one Mother Earth. All have a common root and destiny. All are children of clay and sun.

—Ken Casey
The Starseed Transmissions

INTUITION

I know of the way of all things by what is within me.

—Lao Tzu

The intuition appears indirectly in aesthetic ecstasy and intellectual creativity, in the pricking of conscience, in the longing for relief from anxieties, or peace of mind. It appears directly only in mystical realization.

Paul Brunton
Notebooks

Like the wolf, intuition has claws that pry things open and pin things down, it has eyes that can see through the shields of the persona, it has ears that hear beyond the range of mundane human understanding.

—Clarissa Pinkola Estes
Women Who Run with the Wolves

The critical benefit our intuition offers is that it gives us the ability to work smarter, not harder—to be the most efficient and creative we can be.... Try intuitive knowing; it is better than depending on luck, maybe more accurate than market research results, and can be the most important guide to your future.

—Sandra Weintraub
The Hidden Intelligence

Intuition will not mislead you but your conscious mentality, which is its receiving agent, may do so.

—Anthony Damiani
Looking into Mind

Intuition is ... an expression of power. It is not a mystical talent to see the future so that you can keep yourself safe ... how well we respond to what it tells us to do depends largely on how psychologically and emotionally capable we feel.

—Caroline Myss
Invisible Acts of Power

I obey only my own instincts and intuition. I know nothing in advance. Often I put down things which I do not understand myself, secure in the knowledge that later they will become clear and meaningful to me. I have faith in the man who is writing, who is myself, the writer.

—Henry Miller
Wisdom of the Heart

What is intuition? The inner whisperings of self—or would you rather call it the voice of God?—The Angel-In-Man. Seek to live as though the Voice was real.

—Marcus Bach
The Power of Perception

The messages left by inspiration or the intuition are highly personal, intimate; left at our back doorstep and no other, and they have to be read by the part of the mind that is peculiarly suited to their translation. They may deal with symbols, for example, instead of the good clear alphabets we're used to.

—Jane Roberts
The Afterdeath Journal of an American Philosopher

In general, intuition flourishes only when it is valued.... Intuition is potentially available to everyone. Some people choose to develop it, others do not.

—Frances E. Vaughan
Awakening Intuition

An intuitive inner feeling is a thought. It is divine. It is you and you are it. Trust it—it is your basic human/divine early-alert system working.

—Wayne W. Dyer
You'll See It When You Believe It

Memory of the future is usually called instinct in animals, intuition in human beings.

—Robert Graves
The White Goddess

Learning to trust your intuition is an art form, and like other art forms, it takes practice to perfect. You don't learn to do it overnight.... Your intuition is always one-hundred per cent correct, but it takes time to learn to hear it correctly.

—Shakti Gawain
Living in the Light

All our progress is an unfolding like the vegetable bud. You have first an instinct, then an opinion, then a knowledge, as the plant has root, bud, and fruit. Trust the instinct to the end, though you can render no reason.

—Ralph Waldo Emerson

It is by logic that we prove; it is by intuition that we discover.

—Henri Poincaré

ISLAMIC/MUSLIM

I have not brought you a new religion. I have brought you the religion, in an unchanged, untampered-with way.

—Muhammad (Abu al-Qasim)

"Islam" is derived from the Arabic root *s-l-m*, which means "peace" and, secondarily, "surrender." A helpful translation of "Islam" might then be "that peace that comes when one's entire being and life are surrendered to God."

—Andrew Harvey
The Essential Mystic

The goal of Islam has always been to train individuals to be aware of God's Compassion and Mercy, to rely in their spiritual lives upon those Divine Qualities, and to reflect these qualities in their human form in their relations with all other beings in God's creation.

—Seyyed Hossein Nasr
The Heart of Islam

A man once asked the prophet what was the best thing in Islam and the latter replied, "It is to feed the hungry and to give the greeting of peace to those one knows and to those one does not know."

—Hadith of Bukhari

The Ka'ba receives its new black clothing on Yom Kippur. There was a covenant between Jerusalem and Mecca. What happened?... Mohammed's followers were a "People of Sacred Direction."

—Kanan Makiya
The Rock

Uterine blood, like the menstruating woman in Islam, is "sacra," both sacred and accursed simultaneously.

—David D. Gilmore
Misogyny

The five pillars of Islam are bearing witness, daily prayer, fasting during the month of Ramadan, charity and pilgrimage to Mecca.... There is an element in us, the *nafs*, that tends to lead us astray. This Arabic term is sometimes translated "ego" or "self," ... "essence" and "breath" ... that which incites us to wrongdoing.

—James Fadiman & Robert Frager
Essential Sufism

Early Islam priests were called "The Sons of the Old Woman" ... in the Prophet's time men and women prayed together in the mosque. In early years, both men and women were literate; by 750 women were denied education.

—Leonard Shlain
The Alphabet Versus the Goddess

I went to Mecca for the first time....
On the road, we passed huge billboards warning non-Muslims to turn back....
We went ... to the section of the huge courtyard that is reserved for women. We prayed. We walked the seven turns, and drank the waters of the Zamzam, where three millennia ago Abraham's second wife, Hagar, was directed by God to find water for her son Ishmael, father of the Arabs. We touched the Ka'aba, the black stone that God gave Abraham, which so many millions of hands had touched before us... in that Colossal, holy place of tradition, toward which one billion

Muslims turn in prayer every day, even I felt a spiritual charge.

—Carmen Bin Ladin
Inside the Kingdom

In Islam all space is ordered in relation to Mecca and all time in relation to salvation and judgment day.

—Mary Catherine Bateson
Peripheral Visions

The veiling of women is neither an original nor a fundamental practice in Islam. The Koran does not command all women to cover their heads, and the habit of veiling women and secluding them in harems did not become common in the Islamic world until some three generations after the Prophet's death, when Muslims began to copy the Christians of Byzantium and Zoroastrians of Persia, who had long treated their women in this way.

—Karen Armstrong
The Battle for God

J

JESUS/CHRIST

In Jesus myth and history meet.

--Bede Griffiths
Return to the Centre

The death of Jesus of Nazareth was the
birth of all-prevailing cosmic love within
the Earth's sphere.

—Rudolf Steiner
The Fifth Gospel

And since the time when Jesus was born,
when He finished growing and died and
rose again, everything has continued
to move because Christ has not yet
completed His own forming.... The
mystical Christ has not yet attained his
full growth.

—Pierre Teilhard de Chardin
The Future of Man

The Cosmic Christ is the divine pattern
that connects in the person of Jesus
Christ (but by no means is limited to that
person).... The Cosmic Christ might
be living next door or even inside one's
deepest and truest self.

—Matthew Fox
The Coming of the Cosmic Christ

He is like a mirror for us all, showing us who we essentially are.

—Stephen Mitchell
The Gospel According to Jesus

A man doesn't go to Gethsemane lightly. He doesn't put up a cross for collateral when what he says is guesswork!… You think he was a dreamer, who died for his dream? He was an unromantic Son of Fact if ever there was one!

—Paul Scherer
Love Is a Spendthrift

Write my words on your heart and earnestly reflect upon them … what you do not understand through your reading and studying, you will know when I come to you.

—Thomas à Kempis
The Imitation of Christ

Jesus Christ is the living voice of Israelite wisdom.

—Eugene La Verdiere
Luke

For three years a spirit lived in the body of Jesus of Nazareth here on Earth whose soul was free of all earthly karma. This means that all the experiences the Christ had, everything he went through in life, had a totally different significance compared to what a human soul may go through.

—Rudolf Steiner
The Fifth Gospel

The blueprint for your true work here on Earth already exists within you … your primary task is to awaken the living Christ in your heart. This is your true identity. Express god in all that you are, and throw away the crutches that have helped you stumble through history.

—Ken Carey
The Starseed Transmissions

Jesus was a perfect balance of male and female aspects. He was assertive and direct, rational and straight-forward. Yet he was a master of subtlety and metaphor. He taught by example as well as by allegory.

—Joan Borysenko
A Woman's Journey to God

He has never left; he can only reappear.

—Alice Bailey
Externalization of the Hierarchy

Poets saw Jesus as the latest theophany of the same suffering Sacred King whom they had worshipped under various names from time immemorial.

—Robert Graves
The White Goddess

Christ is the still point of light at the center of a turning world.

—Gordon Strachen
Christ and the Cosmos

He (Jesus) threw everything off balance.

—Flannery O'Connor
A Good Man Is Hard to Find

Jesus passed through the midst of them.

—Talisman of medieval English travelers

JOURNEY

The world is made round as a divine
punishment; people must return, weary,
at last to the place of their beginning; and
they said: "All roads are now bent."

—J. R. R. Tolkien
The Simarillion

The old maps are outdated; we require
new navigational aids. And the
inescapable fact is you are your own
cartographer now.

—Ralph Blum
The *Book of Runes*

There is only one journey. Going
inside yourself.

—Rainer Maria Rilke

The longest journey is the journey
inwards.... How long the road is. But
for all the time the journey has already
taken, how you have needed every
second of it.

—Dag Hammarskjöld
Markings

Be not afraid. We only start again an
ancient journey long ago begun that
but seems new. We have begun again
upon a road we traveled on before and
lost our way a little while. And now we
try again.... Look up and see His Word
among the stars, where He has set your
name along with His.

—Helen Schucman & William Thetford
A Course in Miracles

There comes a time in the spiritual
journey when you start making choices
from a very different place.... And if a
choice lines up so that it supports truth,
health, happiness, wisdom, and love, it's
the right choice.

—Angeles Arrien

Realize that the journey and the goal
are the same. You are never going to be
formed. You will never reach an ultimate
goal. Life is transition and growth.

—Wayne W. Dyer
You'll See It When You Believe It

"Where are you from?" doesn't really
matter; if we knew where we were from,
we'd know where we are going and we'd
have solved the riddle of our existence.

—Frederick Franck
The Awakened Eye

As we turn every corner of the Narrow
Road to the Deep North, we sometimes
stand up unawares to applaud and we
sometimes fall flat to resist the agonizing
pains we feel in the depths of our hearts.

—Matsuo Basho
The Narrow Road to the Deep North

We would like only, for once, to get to
where we are already.

—Martin Heidegger

Remembrance makes people desire the
journey; it makes them into travelers.

—Jalal Al-din Rumi

All journeys have secret destinations of which the traveler is unaware.

—Martin Buber
The Life of the Hasidim Said

Midlife crisis is a vivid awareness of the roads not taken.

—Caroline J. Simon
The Disciplined Heart

In each of us is an Odysseus ... with no Telemachus to pursue him, with no Ithaca to long for, with no Penelope to return to—an Odysseus on a journey that has been rendered pointless by becoming limitless.... The globe shrinks. Our options multiply.

—Jane Howard
Families

It is good to have an end to journey towards; but it is the journey that matters, in the end.

—Ursula K. Le Guin
The Left Hand of Darkness

Go—not knowing where; bring—not knowing what; the path is long, the way unknown; the hero knows not how to arrive there by himself.

—Russian fairy tale

All that is gold does not glitter; not all those that wander are lost.

—J. R. R. Tolkien

Unless we change the direction we are headed in, we might end up where we are going.

—Chinese proverb

JOY

Joy is the holy fire that keeps our purpose warm and our intelligence aglow.... Joy shall be reflected in all things.

—Helen Keller
Don't Miss the Miracle

A joyful heart is the inevitable result of a heart burning with love.

—Mother Teresa

Where is the joy which is not sooner or later mingled with sorrow? A happiness which is not mixed at some point or at some time with misery?

—Paul Brunton
The Spiritual Crisis of Man

Overflowing with presence, intuition, and joy is who we are.

—Robert Rabbin
Invisible Leadership

The sharing of joy, whether physical, emotional, psychic, or intellectual, forms a bridge between the sharers which can be the basis for understanding much of what is not shared between them, and lessens the threat of their difference.

—Audre Lorde
Uses of the Erotic

Always be joyful, no matter what you are.
With happiness, you can give a person life.

—Nachman of Bratislav

Being, not doing, is my first joy.

—Theodore Roethke

Pleasures and sensations are like ripples
on our surface; happiness and knowledge
are like the undercurrents in our inner
waters; joy and wisdom are sunken
treasures at the very bottom.

—Peter J. Kreeft
Heaven, the Heart's Deepest Longing

In a state of panic, a man runs round in
circles by himself. In a state of joy, he
links hands with others and they dance
round in a circle together.

—W. H. Auden
The Dyer's Hand

Joy is the serious business of heaven.

—C. S. Lewis

This is the true joy in life. To be used for
a purpose recognized by yourself as a
mighty one.

—George Bernard Shaw

The soul knows the truth which, when
assimilated and interpreted by the mind,
causes the heart to leap with joy to
embrace it.

—George Trevelyan
A Vision of the Aquarian Age

Joy is the human's noblest act.

—Thomas Aquinas

Joy is the game, the playing, between God
and God's creation; it is the movement of
delight and imagination and learning and
power, like any game.

—Sara Maitland
A Big Enough God

Joy that is only ours is not real joy.

—Kyriacos Markides
Riding with the Lion

Grief can take care of itself, but to get
the full value of a joy you must have
somebody to divide it with.

—Mark Twain

JUDAISM/HEBRAIC

These Ibrim, these untiring nomads,
these everlasting exiles were known for
centuries, even for thousands of years.
Brothers of the Arabs, the Hebrews like
all Semites were the result of an ancient
mixture of the white with the black race.
They had been seen traveling back and
forth through northern Africa under
the name of Bodons, those men without
shelter and without bed, who pitched
their tents in the vast deserts between the
Red Sea and the Persian Gulf.

—Edouard Schuré
The Great Initiates

Christians must learn that Judaism is not a religion but a way of life.

—Matthew Fox
A Spirituality Named Compassion

Ancient Hebrew is tense and terse, a desert language of spare muscularity.... The entire library of ancient Hebrew runs to a compact cabinet of 24 scrolls.

—Thomas Cahill
Sailing on the Wine Dark Sea

The rules for keeping Passover properly are many, and to a Gentile are mysterious as well as very confusing.... And thus it was old Moses looked after his children, as well as in his bluntly realistic attempts to protect them from pollution and decay, dietetic as well as spiritual, in their wanderings through the hot, filthy countries of the ancient world: he made them see to it that the vessels for their feasting were sterile, freed from most of their omnipresent bacteria by the ceremony, at once mystical and practical, of kashering.

—M. F. K. Fisher
The Art of Eating

Jews have suffered so long because they bear the burden of God in history.

—Edward Flannery

"Holocaust" is rejected by some Jews as it applies to genocide because it comes from the Greek, meaning "burnt offering." The idea that God would accept such an offering is deeply troubling. Instead, they prefer the Hebrew word "shoah", "catastrophe." The opposite of "Ruach" or breath of God, which in Genesis drew order out of chaos.... Between 1933 and 1945 six million Jews

were killed.... On July 16, 1941 near St. Chapelle [Paris] built to hold the Crown of Thorns, 13,000 Jews were rounded up and hauled to camps—4,000 were children.... Under Pope Innocent III, the Lateran Council of 1215 proscribed a mode of dress and an emblem for the Jews. The yellow wheel has worn for six centuries. A conical, pointed hat was added later.... The Christian conscience—mine—can never be at peace.

—James Carroll
Constantine's Sword

One God, imageless, primordially creative and utterly transcendent.... Life's purpose is to be found in the healing of the world so that the world may then reflect, for the good of all, the radiance of its creative source.

—Philip Novak
The World's Wisdom

JUDGMENT

It is said that the great Saint Anthony used to tell his disciples: "When you die and stand before the Judgment seat of God, you will not be asked whether you had become another Anthony, or Paul, or even the great Mary herself, but whether you had become truly yourself."

—Athanasius
Life of Saint Anthony

It is important to revive and revitalize the biblical meaning of judgment (krisis) as that establishment of justice which by necessity means mercy for the wronged and loss for those who have too much.

—Krister Stendahl
Paul Among Jews and Gentiles

Gandalf: Then do not be too eager to deal out death in judgment. For even the very wise cannot see all ends. I have not much hope that Gollum can be cured before he dies, but there is a chance of it. And he is bound up with the fate of the Ring. My heart tells me that he has some part to play yet, for good or ill, before the end; and when that comes, the pity of Bilbo may rule the fate of many—yours not least.

—J. R. R. Tolkien
The Fellowship of the Ring

Our civilization tends more toward critical judgment and condemnation than toward devotion and selfless veneration.

—Rudolf Steiner
Knowledge of the Higher Worlds and Its Attainment

If we do not judge, how can there be justice?… What is non-judgmental justice?

—Gary Zukav
The Seat of the Soul

Don't wait for the last judgment— it takes place every day.

—Albert Camus
The Fall

Let our gardening hands be gentle ones. Let us not root up one another's ideas before they have time to bloom.

—Julia Cameron
The Artist's Way

Happy are those who find fault with themselves instead of finding fault with others.

—(Abu al-Qasim) Muhammad

We judge ourselves by what we feel capable of doing, but others judge us by what we have already done.

—Leo (Lev) Tolstoy

Judgment is dangerous … we make people into objects. Judgment is sterile and like hate, it creates nothing.

—H. A. Hartwick
The Garden

If you want to have rest here in this life and also in the next, in every conflict with another say, "Who am I" and judge no one.

—A Desert Father

JUSTICE/INJUSTICE

Compassion and justice are companions, not choices.

—William Sloane Coffin
Credo

Let our first act every morning be the following resolve: "I shall not fear anyone on earth. I shall fear only God. I shall bear ill-will towards no one. I shall not submit to injustice from anyone.

—Mohandas (Mahatma) Gandhi

Never defer to another on the basis of his or her race, religion, gender, class, fame, wealth, or position. Whites did not create Blacks. Men did not create women nor Christians Jews. What then gives any human being the presumption to judge, diminish or exclude another or expect deference solely on such bases?

—Marian Wright Edelman
The Measure of Our Success

God's justice works in mysterious ways, beyond the reach of our intellects.... Real justice is for God to help us through His Grace to rectify that which truly wronged us.... Our estrangement from our Divine nature. Real justice means the attainment of Theosis, the reunification with God, who created us in His own image. We are endowed with the potential of becoming gods through Grace.

—Kyriacos Markides
The Mountain of Silence

God is bright justice which has no trace of injustice.

—Hildegard of Bingen
Scivas

... justice and compassion must play a great role: to guide, steer, and bridle our imaginations so that they serve a greater cause.

—Matthew Fox
Creativity

The arc of the universe is long, but it bends toward justice.

—Martin Luther King, Jr.

There is one justice upon earth; each Spirit to its own face gives birth.

—Johann Wolfgang von Goethe

What is justice? It is each part doing what is appropriate to it.

—Plato
Republic

Justice is what happens when the party with the most "power" acted or pretended that this was not the case.

—Sara Maitland
A Big Enough God

We need communities of work, land for the landless, true farming communes, cooperatives and credit unions. There is much that is wild, prophetic and holy about our work—but the heart hungers for that new social order wherein justice dwelleth.

—Dorothy Day

Native American justice is rooted in notions of relationship and dialogue rather than adversarial dispute, harmony and balance rather than proof and guilt; renewal rather than punishment.

—F. David Peat
Lighting the Seventh Fire

If you have a full stomach it is not likely that you will think of those who are hungry.

—Cypriot proverb

KABBALA

Inspired by the idea that not only is God necessary to man, but that man is also necessary to God, that man's actions are vital to all worlds and affect the course of transcendent events, the Kabbalistic preachers and popular writers sought to imbue all people with the consciousness of the supreme importance of all actions.... An architect of hidden worlds, every pious Jew is, partly, the messiah.

—Abraham Joshua Heschel
The Earth is the Lord's

Kabbalah is only one of the many terms used, during a period of more than 1,500 years, to designate the mystical movement, its teaching, or its adherents.

—Gersham Scholem
Kabbalah

The Shekhinah, the female presence of god, was venerated by Kabbalists, but women were denied knowledge of this—it was a closely guarded secret.

—John Rowan
The Horned God

The real practical magic contained in the Zohar and other kabalistic works, is only of use to those who read it within.

—Helena Petrovna Blavatsky
Isis Unveiled

KARMA

Who creates karma? We ourselves. What we think, say, do, desire, and omit creates karma.

—Dalai Lama
Ethics for the New Millennium

A law which really makes life comprehensible for the first time.

—Rudolf Steiner
At the Gates of Spiritual Science

Everything we do, whatever its moral value, brings its compensation, either in this life or a subsequent one.... Love, in short, is the solvent of karma, which, we must remember, is not an inexorable law of punishment. Rather, it is a loving influence working on the souls of men until they can awaken to the spirit.

—George Trevelyan
A Vision of the Aquarian Age

Karma is called the Law of Cause and Effect ... karma does exist as long as you believe in it, and as soon as you're willing to drop it, it's gone.... So, yes, you do have karma because you chose it. God didn't impose it. Some say karma is a law. We say it is a choice.

—Lazaris
Lazaris Interviews

Karma is a complex dynamic involving the molding of the past, present and future. We should never reduce it to a simplistic concept of reward and punishment ... karma is the law of action, of change. We can create, and are creating,

ourselves at every moment. Our power is in the present.

—Diane Mariechild
Mother Wit

Karma is simply cause and effect. It is a sacred spiritual law that holds people responsible for their actions.

—Mary E. Carreiro
The Psychology of Spiritual Growth

Karma can be understood as cause and effect in much the same way that physicists understand that for every action, there is an equal and opposite reaction.

—Dalai Lama
The Way to Freedom

The world is one great wheel—an ellipse one was bound to by karma. Wheels within wheels, plans within plans.

—Eric Van Lustbader
The Ninja

Karma can impose crushing responsibility.

—Stewart Brand,
The Clock of the Long Now

KINDNESS

You cannot do a kindness too soon because you never know how soon it will be too late.

—Ralph Waldo Emerson

I expect to pass through this world but once; any good thing therefore that I can do, any kindness that I can show to any fellow creature, let me do it now; let me not defer to neglect it, for I shall not pass this way again.

—Etienne De Grellet

Kindness in words creates confidence, kindness in thinking creates profoundness, and kindness in giving creates love.

—Lao Tzu

Each smallest act of kindness reverberates across great distances and spaces of time, affecting lives unknown to the one whose generous spirit was the source of the good echo, because kindness is passed on and grows each time it's passed, until a simple courtesy becomes an act of selfless courage years later and far away. Likewise, each small meanness, each expression of hatred, each act of evil.

—H. R. White
This Momentous Day

Be kind, for everyone you meet is fighting a great battle.

—Philo of Alexandria

10,000 people in 37 countries were asked what they looked for in a mate. Males and females listed "kindness" first.

—Alison Jolly
Lucy's Legacy

Kindness is the golden thread that holds society together.

—Johann Wolfgang von Goethe

KNOTS

If I were untied, it would be easy. How to undo this knot, how not to want any more, or to want to be, or else to want to be the water that can be placed in all vases.... Me, I am nothing but knotted knots, I am made of nothing but knots that resist, that want to be knots.

—Eugène Ionesco
Journal en Miettes

When I was a child, a nanny ... taught me how to tie my shoelaces and my tie and to remember the different steps by telling me a story about a fox whose tail was still showing after he entered his hole located beneath a tree that was represented by the loop. Much later, I saw in each knot a possible story and in nature an invisible bond mysteriously uniting traces and forms.

—Patrick Conty
The Genesis and Geometry of the Labyrinth

When a monk or a nun is professed in the Orthodox Church, he or she is given, as part of the investiture, a knotted cord.... It is said if each knot is not correctly made, it is because the maker has not prayed continuously and with due attention, for without prayer nothing can be right, since God alone can perfect the work.

—D. M. Deed
Studies in Comparative Religions

The first system of writing was made out of knots, the structure of language is similar to a knot, and according to Hindu philosophy, the word—Braham—is contained in "a knot of phenomena."

—Patrick Conty
The Genesis and Geometry of the Labyrinth

In Egyptian hieroglyphics the knotted cord signified a person's name and because the knot is a symbol for the individual's existence, the knot or bow appears with some frequency in ancient texts.... The cord, like the chain, is a general symbol for binding and connecting.

—Murry Hope
Ancient Egypt

When all the knots of the heart are unloosened, then even here in this human birth, the mortal becomes immortal.

—Katha Upanishad

In order for the divine wisdom to become manifest within chronological time on earth, it must be woven into a fabric of knots representing the intersection of spirit and matter throughout the universe. Only a true initiate, one indoctrinated by the god, will know how to do this.

—Katherine Neville
The Magic Circle

... the knot is in fact also the fundamental element of the first writing system. In ancient China at the time when the I Ching and the Tao te Ching were compiled, reference is made to a system of knots used to compute the laws of conduct and government.

—Patrick Conty
The Genesis and Geometry of the Labyrinth

Knots, Leonardo said, are symbols of both infinity and unity of the world.

—Michael J. Gelb
How to Think Like Leonardo da Vinci

KNOWLEDGE

Know yourself—and you will know the universe and the gods.

—Inscription in the Temple of Delphi

Knowing others is intelligence; knowing yourself is true wisdom.

—Tao Te Ching

The knower and the known are one.

—Meister Eckhart

The known, just because it is known, is the unknown.

—Georg Wilhelm Friedrich Hegel

The larger the island of knowledge, the greater the shoreline of wonder.

—Huston Smith

We don't need someone to show us the ropes. We are the ones we've been waiting for. Deep inside us we know the feelings we need to guide us. Our task is to learn to trust our inner knowing.

—Sonia Johnson
Going Out of our Minds

Strike that thick cloud of unknowing with the sharp dart of longing love, and on no account whatever think of giving up.

—*The Cloud of Unknowing*

Knowledge is happiness, because to have knowledge—broad, deep knowledge—is to know true ends from false, and lofty things from low.

—Helen Keller

The world is made of forms, and they are as it were the debris of a celestial music that has become frozen; true knowledge, or sanctity, dissolves our frozen state and liberates the inner melody.

—Frithjof Schuon
Echoes of Perennial Wisdom

Knowledge, in no matter what kind, has only speculative interest. If it is to be of use to mankind, it must be translated into action. To bring a work into being there must be workers.... Workmen are indispensable of course, but so is measure. Higher or lower, the pyramid of Cheops is only a fine heap of stones.

—Louis Charpentier
The Mysteries of Chartres Cathedral

Knowledge creates doubt, and doubt makes you ravenous for more knowledge.... I know the way of all things by what is within me.... To know that you do not know is the best. To pretend to know when you do not know is disease.

—Lao Tzu

The essential knowledge must be attained by everyone. What is this essential knowledge? For the individual self to know the mystery of the universal Self.

—Nityananda

Knowledge without love is cold light, a false light which leads into the abyss.

—Abram Poljak

Never mistake knowledge for wisdom. One helps you make a living; the other helps you make a life.

—Sandra Carey

Inquiring minds long for the truth of the heart, seek it, strive to solve the problems set by life, try to penetrate to the essence of things and phenomena, and into themselves.... Socrates' words, "know thyself" remain an imperative for all those who seek true knowledge and being.

—G. I. Gurdjieff
Views from the Real World

Apart from the known and the unknown, what else is there?

—Harold Pinter
The Homecoming

The time is past, if ever there was such a time, when you can just discover knowledge and turn it loose in the world and assume that you have done good.

—Wendell Berry
Life is a Miracle

There are ways of transmitting knowledge that feel like intellectual rape: so much logic and such powerful statistics, so many footnotes, that resistance is beaten down. But oddly, overwhelming logic and data often fail to convince.

—Mary Catherine Bateson
Full Circles, Overlapping Lives

When you fear Not Knowing, your natural defense is to try to know.

—Martia Nelson
Coming Home

If fragmentary knowledge proves such a delight
To you, how blessed will it be to see the whole!
Dare, o soul, to let go of the lesser,
Quickly to gain the eternally great.

—Johannes Kepler
Kepler und die Theologie

No man can reveal to you aught but that which already lies half asleep in the dawning of your knowledge.

—Kahlil Gibran

The web which man has spun with his knowledge extends through the starry reaches of sidereal space, as well as backward into the dark realm of pre-history.... Like the orb spider, man lies at the heart of it, listening. Knowledge has given him the memory of earth's history beyond the time of his emergence.

—Loren Eiseley
The Unexpected Universe

Knowledge not lived becomes sin.

—Edgar Cayce
The Sleeping Prophet

To know in truth is to become betrothed, to engage the known with one's whole self, an engagement one enters with attentiveness, care and good will.

—Parker J. Palmer
To Know We Are Known

How much do we know at any time? Much more, or so I believe, than we know we know!

—Agatha Christie
The Moving Finger

Berlioz said of Saint-Saëns: "He knows everything. All he lacks is inexperience."

—Warren G. Bennis & Robert J. Thomas
Geeks and Geezers

And so it was that out of the knowledge humans had amassed, only a few books and hand-copied texts written from memory survived.... It didn't matter to the monks that the knowledge they saved was useless ... this knowledge was empty of content, its subject matter long since gone ... someday or some century an Integrator would come, and things would be fitted together again. So time mattered not at all.

—Walter Miller, Jr.
A Canticle for Leibowitz

All knowledge pursued merely for the enrichment of personal learning and the accumulation of personal treasure leads you away from the Path; but all knowledge pursued for growth to ripeness within the process of human ennoble-

ment and cosmic development brings
you a step forward.

—Rudolf Steiner
*Knowledge of the Higher Worlds
and Its Attainment*

When a person comes into relationship
with certain knowledge he or she is not
only transformed by it, but must also
assume responsibility for it.... There is so
much to know, that it takes a lifetime
of relationships.

—F. David Peat
Lighting the Seventh Fire

Knowledge is available when the time is
ripe, but which of us will take the trouble
to do what is necessary to have it?

—G. I. Gurdjieff

We're all connected, we have shared
knowledge and that knowledge—for
better or worse—is constantly evolving
and changing.

—Thom Hartmann
The Prophet's Way

All you know is what you know now.

—Richard Idemon
The Magic Thread

When you know a thing, to allow that
you know it, and when you do not know
a thing, to allow that you do not know it,
this is knowledge.

—Confucius

KORAN/QU'RAN

Koran means recitation.... Every Muslim
believes the 6,000 verses in the Koran
constitute God's direct instruction ... but
only about 600 are concerned with law.

—Geraldine Brooks
Nine Parts of Desire

His reciters were called "qurra"—men
and women committed each new
revelation to memory and went out to
amplify Mohammed's voice. Qurras were
venerated as holy persons.... After 632
when The Prophet died, the diverse texts
became the Quran.

—Leonard Shlain
The Alphabet Versus the Goddess

The Qur'an states there is nothing on
earth that does not have its correspondence at the super-celestial level in the
"Divine Treasury."

—Pir Vilayat Inayat Khan
Awakening

Mythology says Gabriel dictated the
Koran to Mohammed.

—Harve Humann
The Many Faces of Angels

The Quran reinforces the view that historical failures are consequences of religious
failures. Military victories are attributed to
faithfulness; military setbacks are linked to
doubts.... Muslims are encouraged by the
Quran to work for justice.

—Jack Nelson-Pallmeyer
Is Religion Killing Us?

Look at the Madrassas ... they strive
to become a "huffaz"—one who has
memorized the Qur'an word for word....
Memorization teaches children to
duplicate the lives of their parents.

—Neal Donald Walsh
   Tomorrow's God

LABYRINTH

Labyrinths are divine imprints …
universal patterns most likely created in
the realm of the collective unconscious,
birthed through the human psyche and
passed down through the ages.

—Lauren Artress
  Walking a Sacred Path

Certain forms, such as the labyrinth,
represent explicitly the experience of
initiation—entry into the abyss of the
mysteries, the pilgrimage of the spirit.

—Joan Halifax

This universality of the labyrinth shows
that there exists something common,
shared by all ancient cultural systems,
and, what is more, there exists
something fundamental and central,
seeing as it is the symbol of our origin
and ultimate destruction.

—Patrick Conty
  *The Genesis and Geometry
  of the Labyrinth*

For this mysterious music you had to
be prepared to sacrifice a lot. And so:
Ariadne, faceless, or faceless in memory,
deep inside the labyrinth, in memory
surrounded by a music inaudible in the
ordinary world. Ariadne, surrounded
by nothing but her music; Ariadne, who

was at once his key and his jailer.... Truly wasn't he a Minotaur, alone in the night, alone at his own birth, forever locked into the labyrinth of this century?

—Lars Gustafsson
Stories of Happy People

The labyrinth functions like a spiral, creating a vortex in its center ... an ancient symbol for the Divine Mother, the God within, the Goddess, the Holy in all of creation.... The Divine Feminine is often the missing piece for which both women and men are searching.... We must keep alive the innate part of ourselves that holds on to the invisible thread.

—Lauren Artress
Walking a Sacred Path

Early Christian Fathers rejected the labyrinth because it was too close to goddess traditions. Yet they began appearing, dedicated to Mary.... The one at Chartres measures exactly 666 feet around—Aphrodite's sacred number.

—Layne Redmond
When the Drummers Were Women

It is the Minotaur who conclusively justifies the existence of the Labyrinth.

—Jorge Luis Borges

The labyrinth is the feminine face of God.

—Helen Curry
The Way of the Labyrinth

The Self pulls us inward to our essence which is hidden in the subconscious. It focuses us upon our inner journey.... The nature of this spinning is that it throws off impurities and only at the center is there any stability.

—Marty Cain

LANGUAGE

The language of the lips is easily taught, but who can teach the language of the heart?

—Mohandas (Mahatma) Gandhi

Man became man by breaking into the daylight of language—whether by good fortune or bad fortune, whether by pure chance, the spark jumping the gap because the gap was narrow enough, or by the touch of God, it is not for me to say here.

—Walker Percy
The Message in the Bottle

We are suspended in language.

—Niels Bohr

Everything becomes a little different as soon as it is spoken out loud.

—Hermann Hesse

It is all too easy and too simple to disdain as "superstition" everything one cannot understand, but the ancients themselves knew very well what they meant when they used symbolic language ... the Spirit can always come back to breathe fresh life into the symbols and rites and give them back their lost meaning and the fullness of their original virtue.

—René Guénon
The Sword of Gnosis

There is an incline from silence to language, to the truth of the word; and the gravitational force of this incline pushes truth on still further from language down into the active life of the world.

—Max Picard
The World of Silence

Nature is a language, and every new fact that we learn is a new word.

—Ralph Waldo Emerson
The Norton Book of Nature Writing

Children learn a language not from a book, or even from a teacher, but from their need to communicate.

—Robert Wolff
Original Wisdom

Language is primitive telepathy.

—Terence McKenna

The world is richer than it is possible to express in any single language.

—Ilya Priogogine

To think that we have at our disposal the biggest thing in the universe, and that is language. What one can do with language is … infinite.

—Hélène Cixous
Rootprints, Memory and Life Writing

Language permits us to see. Without the word, we are all blind.

—Carols Fuentes

Human language is a cracked kettle on which we beat out tunes for bears to dance to when all the while we want to move the stars to pity.

—Gustave Flaubert

Language is the self, reflected and clothed in nouns and verbs and adjectives.

—Gelareh Asayesh
Saffron Sky

The bones of language are what [the writer] seeks—spare, smooth, strong, needing no fleshy padding to elaborate a structure already inherently beautiful.

—Mollie Hunter
Talent is Not Enough

You should clearly understand that because everyday language is the whole universe, the whole universe is everyday language.

—Dogen Zenji

I worry about the tyranny of language which is incapable of containing mystery. I worry about the weakening of our theology.

—Madeleine L'Engle
The Irrational Season

When language is corrupted people lose faith in what they hear and this leads to violence.

—W. H. Auden

Rumi is less interested in language, more attuned to the sources of it. He keeps asking, "Who's making this music?"

—Coleman Barks
The Essential Rumi

I am convinced that the day will come when psychologists, poets and philosophers will speak the same language, and will understand one another.

—Claude Bernard

The Greek authors relate that the priests of Egypt had three ways of expressing their thoughts. The first was clear and simple; the second, symbolic and figurative; the third, sacred and hieroglyphic.... Heraclitus expressed the differences perfectly in designating them as "speaking, signifying and concealing."

—Edouard Schuré
The Great Initiates

Tolkien's unparalleled mastery of ancient tongues convinced him that words are rooted in reality because speech arises out of experience.

—Ralph C. Wood
The Gospel According to Tolkien

All Turtle Island people use verb-based language ... it reflects direct experience.

—F. David Peat
Lighting the Seventh Fire

The invention of languages is the foundation. The "stories" were made rather to provide a world for the languages than

the reverse. To me, a name comes first and the story follows.

—J. R. R. Tolkien

What we love becomes our language.

—Wayne Muller
How, Then, Shall We Live?

LAUGHTER

There is, in fact, no real "spirituality" without the laughter which the sense of humor brings. It is not to be confused with frivolity and it cannot exist in anyone who is not a serious person able to explore the darkness and suffering in life.

—Helen M. Luke
The Way of Woman

Laughter is the outward manifestation of increased heart rate and oxygen intake accompanied by some of the most healthy physiological changes that can happen to our body ... twenty seconds of guffawing gives the heart the same beneficial workout as three minutes of hard rowing.

—Paul Pears
The Heart's Code

There seems no doubt that hearty laughter stimulates practically all the larger organs, and by making them do their work better through the increase of circulations that follow the vibratory massage which accompanies it, heightens resistive vitality against disease.

—James L. Walsh
Laughter and Health

At the height of laughter the universe is flung into a kaleidoscope of new possibilities.

—Jean Houston

You grow up the day you have the first real laugh at yourself.

—Ethel Barrymore

Laughter is wine for the soul ... the hilarious declaration made by man that life is worth living.

— Sean O'Casey
Green Crows

Laughter is cosmic joy juice ... we pretend we are separate from one another. But the contagion of laughter reminds us we are one.

—Annette Goodheart
New Realities

In the end, the changed life for women will be marked, I feel certain, by laughter. It is the unfailing key to a new kind of life.

—Carolyn G. Heilbrun
Writing a Woman's Life

Mirth cleanses the mind of its crazy cobweb designs, leaving space for nurturing to take place.

—Peter Balin
The Flight of the Feathered Serpent

LAW

The Law stands for the commandments we need in order to stay alive, the rule that says which side of the road we drive on, the law of gravity. We need to learn the axiom that we cannot take water into our lungs and keep breathing.

—Robert Bly
Iron John

Highest things seek the depth that thus the lowest may mount the height.

—Alanus ab Insuilis

If you help others, you will be helped, perhaps tomorrow, perhaps in one hundred years, but you will be helped. Nature must pay off the debt ... it is a mathematical law and all life is mathematics.

—G. I. Gurdjieff

The law kills, but the Spirit gives life.

—Carol Gilligan

Out beyond ideas of wrongdoing and rightdoing is a field. I'll meet you there.

—Jalal Al-din Rumi

Self realization here on our planet is difficult owing to the extreme density of our mechanical laws.

—Kathleen Riorden Speeth
Gurdjieff's Work

Do not desire at all until you know the true conditions of any sphere.... Ascertain "the laws" first.

—Rudolf Steiner
The Way of Initiation

LEADERS/ LEADERSHIP

"Lead" comes from the Anglo-Saxon *laed*, "to set out on a quest, to navigate into the distant horizon." Leadership includes, but also extends far beyond position power.

—Barbara Shipka
Leadership in a Challenging World

Leaders create meaning out of events and relationships that devastate non-leaders.... Leaders who succeed again and again are geniuses at grasping context.

—Warren G. Bennis & Robert J. Thomas
Geeks and Geezers

The great leaders are like the best conductors—they reach beyond the notes to reach the magic in the players.

—Blaine Lee
The Power Principle

It looks easy, doesn't it? But a symphony conductor is a mother hen with 100 or more chicks and he earns a degree in psychology the hard way.... Some musicians hate conductors. Some musicians hate music.

—Arthur Fiedler

Leaders set "the tone" in their communities or workplaces. People listen carefully to see if what they say "sounds true."

—Sharon Seivert
The Balancing Act

Specific actions are less important than the leader's clarity or consciousness. That is why there are no exercises or formulas to ensure successful leadership.

—John Heider
The Tao of Leadership

When the U. S. had a population of three million, we fielded six world class leaders: Washington, Jefferson, Hamilton, Madison, Franklin and Adams.

—John Gardner

Leadership is all about the release of human possibilities.

—Joseph Jaworski
Synchronicity

A leader is best known when people barely know that he exists ... when his work is done, his aim fulfilled, the people will say, "we did this ourselves."

—Lao Tse

LEARNING

Learning is finding out what you already know; doing is demonstrating that you know it; teaching is reminding others that they know just as well as you. You are all learners, doers, teachers.

—Richard Bach
Illusions

If milk mixed with water is put in front of them [Royal Swans] the swan will separate out the milk and drink it leaving the water behind. That must be the attitude of students.

—G. I. Gurdjieff

With knowledge doubling every year or so, "expertise" now has a shelf life measured in days; everyone must be both learner and teacher, and the sheer challenge of learning can be managed only through a globe-girdling network that links all minds and all knowledge.

—Lewis J. Perelman
School's Out

It is helpful to keep in mind that this is really all about learning!

—Joel Levey & Michelle Levey
Living in Balance

… learning fields are present whenever the essential conditions are met—collective intention focused in group projects of sustained duration and repeated form.

—Christopher M. Bache
Dark Night, Early Dawn

Break the pattern which connects the items of learning and you necessarily destroy all quality.

—Gregory Bateson
Mind and Nature

Leaders need a deep love of learning and a refusal to be anywhere that didn't let you learn or prevented you from learning.

—Dee Hock

The teachers are everywhere. What is wanted is a learner.

—Wendell Berry
What Are People For?

I learn by going where I have to go.

—Theodore Roethke

Creativity is a type of learning process where the teacher and the pupil are located in the same individual.

—Arthur Koestler

The fundamental learning situation is one in which a person learns by helping someone who really knows what he is doing.

—Christopher Alexander
A Pattern Language

Learning is the fundamental pattern of human adaptation, but mostly it occurs before or after or in the interstices of schooling.

—Mary Catherine Bateson,
Peripheral Visions

Learning is never cumulative; it is a movement of knowing that has no beginning and no end.

—Jiddu Krishnamurti
On Learning and Knowledge

I am a lover, skilled in the arts of madness; I have drunk deeply of culture and learning.

—Jalal al-din Rumi

It is in the doing with awareness that the learning comes.

—William Horwood
Duncton Quest

Never let formal education get in the way of learning.

—Mark Twain

Learn your lessons and move on.

—Eileen Caddy
The Dawn of Change

Don't limit a child to your own learning, for he was born in another time.

—Rabbinic proverb

LIE/LYING

A lie distorts the simple fact of our actions and is composed, in varying measure, of fantasy, denial, belief, rhetoric, dogma, fear, guilt, shame, greed, anger, rationalization and justification.

—Robert Rabbin
Invisible Leadership

The dance of deception needs two people at least—one to send the lie and the other to receive it.

—Patricia Wallace
The Psychology of the Internet

Lying is the chief obstacle to seeing oneself.

—Beryl Pogson
The Work Life

Falsely praising a person is lying.

—Augustine

The novelist is, after all, God's liar and if he does his job well, keeps his head and his courage, he can sometimes find the truth that lives at the center of the lie.

—Stephen King
Danse Macabre

LIFE

I am that supreme and fiery force that sends forth all the sparks of life.... I shine in the water, I burn in the sun and the moon and the stars. Mine is the mysterious force of the invisible wind... I am life.

—Hildegard of Bingen
De Operatione Dei

The origin of life appears ... to be almost a miracle, so many are the conditions which would have had to be satisfied to get it going.

—Francis Crick

There is no gene for a snowflake, whereas biological complexity is instructed complexity.

—Paul Davies
The Fifth Miracle

Life is ruled by three things: functionality, adaptability and sustainability.

—Duane Elgin
Awakening Earth

An organism makes a living by "drinking orderliness."

—Erwin Schrödinger

Biology is the study of complicated things that give the appearance of having been designed for a purpose.

—Richard Dawkins
The Blind Watchmaker

All life is equal.... We forget and we consider ourselves superior, but we are after all a mere part of the Creation.... We must continue to understand where we are.... We stand between the mountain and the ant ... as part and parcel of the Creation. It is our responsibility, since we have been given the minds to take care of these things.

—Oren Lyons
in an address to the U.N.

The ancient bards say if you destroy your life in one small corner of the world, you have destroyed it in every small corner.

—Peter Tremayne
The Spider's Web

Life is difficult.... Once we truly know that life is difficult—once we truly understand and accept it—then life is no longer difficult. Because once it is accepted, the fact that life is difficult no longer matters.

—Scott Peck
The Road Less Traveled

Life is a spell so exquisite that everything conspires to break it.

—Emily Dickinson
in a letter to her cousins

Just to be is a blessing, just to live is holy.

—Abraham Joshua Heschel

To live well is nothing other than to love God with all one's heart, with all one's soul, and with all one's efforts.

—Augustine

This life of yours which you are living is not merely a piece of the entire existence but is in a certain sense the whole; only this whole is not so constituted that it can be surveyed in one single glance.

—Joseph Campbell
The Masks of God

If we really want to live, we must have the courage to recognize that life is ultimately very short, and that everything we do counts.

—Elizabeth Kübler-Ross
Death: the Final Stage of Growth

There is a grandeur in this view of life.

—Charles Darwin
The Origin of Species

Wisdom tells me I am nothing. Love tells me I am everything. And between the two my life flows.

—Nisargadatta Maharaj

Life is creative. It plays itself into existence, seeking out new relationships, new capacities, new traits. Life is an experiment to discover what's possible.

—Margaret J. Wheatley &
Myron Kellner-Rogers
A Simpler Way

To live is so startling it leaves little time
for anything else.

—Emily Dickinson

Life itself is the proper binge.

—Julia Child

… Life is tolerable only by the degrees of
mystification we endow it with.

—E. M. Ciorann
  A Short History of Decay

Life is very short and very uncertain; let
us spend it as well as we can.

—Samuel Johnson

We must be willing to get rid of the life
we have planned, so as to have the life
that is waiting for us.

—Joseph Campbell

To live is the rarest thing in the world.
Most people exist … that is all.

—Oscar Wilde

I would rather be a meteor, every atom of
me in magnificent glow than a sleepy and
permanent planet. The proper function
of man is to live, not to exist. I shall not
waste my days in trying to prolong them.
I shall use my time.

—Jack London

Life is valuable in itself and in what it
points to. It is a commitment to the
process of growth and change, the
thwarting of evil, the acceptance of death.

—Carol Ochs
  Behind the Sex of God

Life, like a dome of many-coloured glass,
stains the white radiance of Eternity.

—Percy Bysshe Shelley

Life can only be understood backwards,
but must be lived forwards.

—Søren Kierkegaard

Life is God's novel. Let him write it.

—Isaac Bashevis Singer
  Voices for Life

A slight sound at evening lifts me
up by the ears, and makes life seem
inexpressibly serene and grand. It may be
Uranus, or it may be in the shutter.

—Henry David Thoreau
  Journal

Samwise Gamgee discovers the necessity
of living according to the right story if
we're to have real hope.

—Ralph C. Wood
  The Gospel According to Tolkien

To live, to err, to fall, to triumph, to
create life out of life.

—James Joyce

Life is what's happening while we're busy
making other plans.

—John Lennon

Everyone's life is a fairy tale written by God's fingers.

—Hans Christian Andersen

There must be more to life than increasing its speed.

Mohandas (Mahatma) Gandhi

Life is short, but wide.

—Spanish proverb

LIGHT

Einstein told us that our universe is shaped and defined by light. We live in a visual cage, and what we call time is simply the ever-moving shadow of the bars which confine us.... But suppose that ... we were able to outrun the waves of light which undulate across the universe. As we leap ... across the galaxy we overtake and leave behind the light which left the surface of the earth ... the image will travel forever in this everlasting night, seeking its home among the stars, reaching ever outward toward some hypothetical destination at the universe's problematic end. Is light, then, the stuff our souls are made of?

—Thomas Bontly
Celestial Chess

You are not the oil, you are not the air—merely the point of combustion, the flash-point where the light is born.

—Dag Hammarskjöld
Markings

... far from light emerging gradually out of the womb of our darkness, it is the Light, existing before all else was made which, patiently, surely, eliminates our darkness. As for creatures, of ourselves, we are but emptiness and obscurity.... Radiant Word, Blazing Power ... reach us simultaneously through all that is most immense and most inward within us and around us.

—Pierre Teilhard de Chardin
Hymn of the Universe

I cannot cause light; the most I can do is try to put myself in the path of its beam.

—Annie Dillard
Pilgrim at Tinker Creek

The longing for light is the longing for consciousness.

—Carl G. Jung

There is a light in this world, a healing spirit more powerful than any darkness we may encounter. We sometimes lose sight of this force when there is suffering, too much pain. Then suddenly, the spirit will emerge through the lives of ordinary people who hear a call and answer in extraordinary ways.

—Mother Teresa

Light is the great priestess of landscape.

—John O'Donohue
Beauty

I am an everlasting lamp and burn without respite; My wick and oil are God, my spirit holds the light.

—Angelus Silesius

Bring light to your weavings, or don't sit at the loom.

—Lynn V. Andrews
Jaguar Woman

The transparent windows which keep out the weather and bring in the light, are the doctors who withstand the hurricane of heresy and pour in the light of church doctrine.

—Honorius of Autun

A comparison with cathedrals has come to many Western minds in searching for a metaphor for icebergs, and I think the reasons for it are deeper than the obvious appropriateness of line and scale. It has to do with our passion for light.

—Barry Lopez
Arctic Dreams

It takes light from the sun eight minutes to reach us.

—Ervin Laszlo
The Whispering Pond

The light you send to others will come back to you multiplied.

—Sanaya Roman
Spiritual Growth

You have only a thin shell to break before emerging from the darkness inside the egg into the light of truth. It is a very ancient image. The egg is this world we see. The bird in it is Love, the Love which is god himself (herself) and which lives in the depths of every person.

—Simone Weil
letter to Joe Bosquet

Bindu Nada Kala—first is a point, then it changes to sounds, sounds change into light.

—Hari Dass

Creation comes into being from Saut (Sound) and from Saut spreads all light.

—Shamas Tabrez

Man, Sub-creator, the refracted Light through whom it splintered from a single White to many hues, and endlessly combined in living shapes that move from mind to mind …

—C. S. Lewis & Humphrey Carpenter
The Inklings

… a vague shimmering curtain, faintly tinged with rose and yellow, wavering across the sky … then in a sudden explosion of color the aurora returned and now there were several drifting curtains, blending and shaking and crossing one another until the entire sky was a confusion of diaphanous veils finally converging until they met in a swirling mass directly overhead.

—Sigurd Olson
Runes of the North

The oldest picture is a prehistoric cave drawing from Australia; here the aura is clearly evident and set in greater relief by the coloring.

—Jean Gebser
The Ever-Present Origin

There they dance, arm in arm with the light ... you can hardly tell at last what in the dance is leaf and what is light.

—Henry David Thoreau
Journals

LISTENING

The more faithfully you listen to the voice within you, the better you will hear what is sounding outside. And only he who listens can speak.

—Dag Hammarskjöld
Markings

It is said of a certain Talmudic master that the paths of Heaven were as bright to him as the streets of his native town. Hasidism inverts the order: It is a greater thing if the streets of a man's native town are as bright to him as the paths of Heaven. For it is here, where we stand, that we should try to make shine the light of the hidden divine life.

—Martin Buber
The Way of Man

The mystery, the essence of all life is not separate from the silent openness of simple listening.

—Toni Packer

The more and more you listen, the more and more you will hear. The more you hear, the more and more deeply you will understand.

—Jamyang Kyentse Rinpoche

A lot depends on my commitment to listening and my intention to stay coherent with this note. It is only when my life is tuned to my note that I can lay life's mysterious and holy music without tainting it with my own discordance, my own bitterness, resentment, agendas, and fears.

—Rachel Naomi Remen
My Grandfather's Blessings

It is said in Java that the tiger's hearing is so acute that hunters must keep their nose hairs cut lest the tiger hear their breath whistle through their nostrils.

—Peter Matthiessen
Tigers in the Snow

Nobody started it, nobody is going to stop it. It will take as long as it wants, the rain. As long as it talks, I am going to listen.

—Thomas Merton

If you listen carefully enough to anything, it will talk to you.

—George Washington Carver

Listening is a magnetic and strange thing, a creative force.... When we are listened to, it creates us, makes us unfold and expand.

—Karl Menninger
Love against Hate

It is impossible to over-emphasize the immense need humans have to be really listened to, to be taken seriously, to be understood.

—Paul Tournier

The first duty of love is to listen.

—Paul Tillich

The problem with listening, of course, is that we don't.

—Philip Glass

Listening is the nicest thing that two people can do for one another.

—Thomas G. Banville
  How to Listen, How to be Heard

The spoken word belongs half to him who speaks and half to him who hears.

—French proverb

Listen, or thy tongue will keep thee deaf.

—Native American proverb

LITERATURE

Literature is the most indispensable explanation of our spiritual nature.

—Anthony Destefano
  A Travel Guide to Heaven

Belief in God and His Providence is the very essence of literature. It tells us that causality is nothing but a mask on the face of destiny. Man is constantly watched by powers that seem to know all his desires and complications. He has free choice, but he is also being led by a mysterious hand.

—Isaac Bashevis Singer
  The Image and Other Stories

Literature is the apparatus through which the world tries to keep intact its important ideas and feelings.

—Mary Oliver
  A Poetry Handbook

LITURGY

Liturgy is like a strong tree whose beauty is derived from the continuous renewal of its leaves, but whose strength comes from the old trunk, with solid roots in the ground.

—Pope Paul VI

All good liturgy and ritual that has power to change is filled with metaphor.

—Nelle Morton
  The Journey is Home

Theology is prose and liturgy is poetry… We immerse people in worship so they, too, become a part of metaphoric exchange.

—Gail Ramshaw

LIVING SYSTEMS

Understanding a system means understanding the people who make up that system. And those people are all different.

—Peter Senge
  in Sandra Seagal & David Horne
  Human Dynamics

The major problems of our time are systemic; they cannot be understood in isolation. They need a systemic, or holistic, approach to be solved.

—Fritjof Capra

Living systems are drawn to the edge of chaos because that is where the capacity for information processing and learning and therefore, growth is maximized.

—Dee Hock

If a living system is suffering from ill health, the remedy is to connect it with more of itself.

—Francisco Varella

Systems can't be known ahead of time. Until the system forms, we have very limited knowledge of what might emerge. The only way to know a system is to play with it.

—Margaret J. Wheatley &
Myron Kellner-Rogers
A Simpler Way

The power of open systems is not a property one can own, but a process one opens to.

—Joanna Rogers Macy
Despair and Personal Power in the Nuclear Age

There is something in the geometry of living systems which contributes order by itself.

—Christopher Alexander
The Process of Creating Life

Living systems are not merely self-organizing, but also self-renewing.

—Peter Marshall
Nature's Web

"Strange Attractor" is a region that attracts the behavior of the system toward it ... the system weaves and dances around its influence.

—F. David Peat
Lighting the Seventh Fire

All living things develop toward a destination contrary to the form in which they first present themselves.

—Greek proverb/Hellenic Doctrine

LOGOS

Men should understand the underlying coherence of things; it is expressed in the Logos, the formula or element of arrangement common to all things.

—Hereclitus of Ephesus

We can say of the Logos that he is the everlasting human being, the human prototype, as well as the Lamb slain "before the foundation of the world"—in other words, predestined to become the representative human being on earth.

—Sergei Bulgakov
Sophia

The word Logos means word and speech, and used figuratively, sense and reason ...

the Logos is the first cause and bearer of the Ideas.

—Thomas Schipflinger
Sophia-Maria

"Logos" is more than "Word." It means the fullest expression of a creative idea in outer manifestation.

—Beryl Pogson
The Work Life

Logos is the fundamental principle of ancient Greek culture, very similar to Tao in Chinese culture. For both Chinese and Greek sages, the Tao, or the logos, is the indefinable power and source of all life.

—Robert Apatow
The Spiritual Art of Dialogue

Logos is the point of coherence, of cos-mic-organizing, self-aware intelligence: the I-Consciousness, the Christ-Con-sciousness. The Cosmos is the garment of the Logos.

—Rudolf Steiner & Richard Leviton
The Imagination of Pentecost

In the beginning was the Logos. The spirit is active in anyone who can see this, who can repeat this gesture in himself.

—Georg Kühlewind
Becoming Aware of the Logos

LONELINESS

Loneliness is what happens with a person when the ordinary and necessary needs for attachment and affection are not

met.... Loneliness is a consequence of being afraid of being alone.

—Herbert Anderson & Freda A. Gardner
Living Alone

When you are alone in an office, a house or an empty waiting room you can suffer from restless loneliness but also enjoy a quiet solitude.

—Henri J. M. Nouwen
Reaching Out

More than any other problem, loneliness, the absence of meaningful connection, drains the joy and sense of purpose from our lives.

—Harold Kushner
Who Needs God

Loneliness comes about when our need for more attachment and friends are greater than what we have.

—Herbert Anderson

Why should I feel lonely? Is not our planet in the Milky Way?

—Henry David Thoreau

LOVE

Know it well, love was his meaning.... Who reveals it to you? Love. What did he reveal to you?
Love. Why does he reveal it to you?
For Love.

—Julian of Norwich
Showings

Love feels no burden, thinks nothing of trouble, attempts what is above its strength, pleads no excuse of impossibility ... though weary, it is not tired ... though alarmed, it is not confounded ...

—Thomas à Kempis

During this mortal life we must choose eternal love or eternal death, there is no middle choice.

—Françoise de Sales
Treatise on the Love of God

Love, the Supreme Musician, is always playing in our souls.

—Jalal Al-din Rumi

Love is our true destiny.... We will never be fully real until we let ourselves fall in love—either with another human person or with God.

—Thomas Merton
Love and Living

We cannot do great things in life; we can only do small things with great love.

—Mother Teresa

Love is infinite in experience and meaning. How could it not be? It is the source, substance and future of all being. So, if you would build anything, build it on a web of love and it will be both ephemeral and timeless, momentary and enduring.

—August T. Jaccaci & Susan B. Gault
CEO Chief Evolutionary Officer

Only love can create intimacy, and freedom too, for when all hearts are

one, nothing else has to be one—neither clothes nor age; neither sex nor sexual preference; race nor mind-set.... Love measures our stature; the more we love, the bigger we are. There is no smaller package in all the world than that of a man all wrapped up in himself!

—William Sloane Coffin
Credo

Life flows in two streams: eros and logos. Logos is the meaning, whether articulate or mysterious, and eros the force that keeps everything connected.... Eros may be found in the search for a partner, the making of a home, or the desire for sex.

—Thomas Moore
The Soul's Religion

Oftentimes Love is so poorly packaged that when we have sold everything to buy it, we cry in finding all our substance gone and nothing in the tinsel and the ribbon.

—Calvin Miller
The Singer

Love is that flame that once kindled burns everything, and only the mystery and the journey remain.

—Angeles Arrien

If "I" give my love to you, what exactly am I giving and who is the "I" making the offering, and who, by the way, are you?

—Stephen Mitchell
Can Love Last?

Where love rules, there is no will to power; and where power predominates, there love is lacking. The one is the shadow of the other.

—Carl G. Jung

To love is not a state; it is a direction.

—Simone Weil

Human love ... consists in this: that two solitudes protect and border and greet one another.

—Rainer Maria Rilke
Letters to a Young Poet

Love is a spendthrift, leaves its arithmetic at home, is always "in the red." And God is love.

—Paul Scherer
Love Is a Spendthrift

To love is always to feel the opening, to hold the wound always open.

—Novalis (Friedrich von Leopold)

Love is the strange bewilderment that overtakes one person on account of another person.

—E. B. White

Love is the attraction exercised on each unit of consciousness by the center of the universe in its course of taking shape.

—Teilhard de Chardin
Let Me Explain

Love lives, if it is living love, always against the self-love out of which it arises.

—Georg Kühlewind
Becoming Aware of the Logos

Love is the absolute affirmation of another's meaning.

—Madonna Kolbenschlag
Lost in the Land of Oz

Love is the only force that can make things one without destroying them.

—Pierre Teilhard de Chardin

The task is not to be caring of others instead of thinking about oneself, but to learn how to love and care for ourselves as well as our neighbors.

—Carol S. Pearson
The Hero Within

To name is to love. To be Named is to be loved.

—Madeleine L'Engle
Walking on Water

Love is not saying nice things to people or smiling or doing good deeds. Love is love. Don't strive for love, be it.

—Hugh Prather
Notes to Myself

Only love is strong because it is undivided. The strong do not attack because they see no need to do so.

—*A Course in Miracles*

The world is too dangerous for anything
but truth and too small for anything
but love.

—William Sloane Coffin

For there is only misfortune in not being
loved; there is misery in not loving.

—Albert Camus

To love is to approach each other center
to center.

—Pierre Teilhard de Chardin

To live without loving is not really to live.

—Jean-Baptiste Moliere

Falling in love is not an extension of one's
limits or boundaries; it is a partial and
temporary collapse of them.

—M. Scott Peck
The Road Less Traveled

Where love rules, there is no will to
power; and where power predominates,
there love is lacking. The one is the
shadow of the other.

—Carl G. Jung

Love doesn't just sit there, like a stone; it
has to be made, like bread, remade all the
time, made new.

—Ursula K. LeGuin
The Lathe of Heaven

We were created to love the Infinite—and
this is why, when we love, that which we
love appears so perfect to us.

—Pere Lacordaire

Perhaps love is the process of my leading
you gently back to yourself.

—Antoine de Saint Exupéry
The Little Prince

All negativity is a cry for more love
Love people for who they are, not for
who you want them to be.

—Sanaya Roman
Spiritual Growth

Love does not consist of gazing at each
other, but in looking outward together in
the same direction.

—Antoine de Saint Exupéry

When a child loves you for a long, long
time, not just to play with, but really
loves you, then you become real.

—Margery Williams
The Velveteen Rabbit

Love is the only thing in the world of
which one cannot give too much.

—Ashley Montagu
The Humanization of Man

There is the same difference in a person
before and after he is in love as there is in
an unlighted lamp and one that is burning. The lamp was there and it was a good

lamp, but now it is shedding light too and that is its real function.

—Vincent van Gogh
The Complete Letters of Vincent van Gogh

To grow in love is the only continuity of which we can be sure.

—Elizabeth Yates
Up the Golden Stair

Love, the magician, knows this little trick whereby two people walk in different directions yet always remain side by side.

—Hugh Prather

Love is the ability and willingness to allow those that you care for to be what they choose for themselves, without any insistence that they satisfy you.

—Wayne Dyer

There is a land of the living and a land of the dead, and the bridge is love.

—Thornton Wilder
The Bridge of San Luis Rey

Many things such as loving, going to sleep or behaving unaffectedly are done worse when we try hardest to do them.

—C. S. Lewis

You know I'm really convinced that if you were to define love, the only word big enough to engulf it all would be life. Love is life in all of its aspects. And if you miss love, you miss life. Please don't.

—Leo Buscaglia
Living, Loving and Learning

We are put on earth for a little space that we may learn to bear the beams of love.

—William Blake

Love begins in the self.... If one finds oneself an absolute delight, how can one fail to find others in their wonderful uniqueness delightful.

—Peter Balin
The Flight of the Feathered Serpent

If I truly love one person, I love all persons, I love the world, I love life. If I can say to somebody else, "I love you," I must be able to say, "I love in you everybody. I love through you the world. I love in you also myself."

—Erich Fromm
The Forgotten Language

To love you is to sing with you, cry with you, pray with you, act with you to re-create the world.

—Carter Heyward, Judith Plaskow &
Carol P. Christ
Weaving the Visions

Love demands privacy. It is guarded, fiercely, by a boundary of silence toward what is outside.

—Shierry Weber Nicholsen
The Love of Nature and the End of the World

Without love we are birds with broken wings.

—Mitch Albom
Tuesdays with Morrie

Love is not, by its own desire, heroic.... It exists by its willingness to be anonymous, humble and unrewarded.

—Wendell Berry
What Are People For?

Love doesn't mean doing extraordinary or heroic things. It means knowing how to do ordinary things with tenderness.

—Jean Vanier

Everything wants to be loved.... You ever notice that trees do everything to get attention we do, except walk?

—Alice Walker
The Color Purple

The opposite of love is not hate, it's indifference.

—Elie Wiesel

Love is always a kind of generous fiction-making.

—Martha Nussbaum

This is to love: bear with a fault and not be astonished.

—Teresa of Avila

The Holy Spirit is our harpist, and all strings which are touched by Love must sound.

—Mechtild of Magdeburg

LOYALTY

Total loyalty is possible only when fidelity is emptied of all concrete content, from which changes of mind might naturally arise.

—Hannah Arendt

Loyalty has to be reciprocal.

—Charles Handy
The Age of Paradox

LUCK

Luck is a basic principle of endless possibility .... Lottery tickets materialize luck, but it's also a dispensable fetish, easily thrown away when it's a loser.

—Jackson Lears
Something for Nothing

Better to lie on the razor's edge of luck than to succumb to the hubris of demanding certain outcomes.

—Sophocles

Luck is a star; money is a plaything; time is a storyteller.

—Carl Sandburg

Lucky is the man who does not secretly believe that every possibility is open to him.

—Walker Percy
The Last Gentleman

It is better to be born lucky than clever.

—Chinese proverb

M

MAGIC/MAGICIANS

Magic is the best theology, for in it true
faith is both grounded and discovered.

—Jacob Boehme

… magic lives in the ordinary world, in
the details of our everyday lives. It is in
those simple moments that we can really
appreciate the magic of this world. When
Buddha realized enlightenment, he
touched the Earth. This gesture connected him to the world, it made him the
world's relation.

—Joan Halifax
The Fruitful Darkness

True magic is not a means of control or
manipulation or evil sorcery. It is about
cooperating with the most positive
energy arising in any situation to create
the best outcome for all concerned.

—Carol S. Pearson
Magic at Work

Any sufficiently advanced technology is
indistinguishable from magic.

—Arthur C. Clarke

Magic isn't the fuzzy, fragile, abstract and
ephemeral quality you think it is. In fact,

magic is distinguished from mysticism by its very concreteness and practicality.

—Tom Robbins
Even Cowgirls Get the Blues

All the power of magic is here, in this one thing, the link. All a magician wants is simply a rod that links the two worlds, and he who wishes to be a magus must possess this little rod within himself.... The function of a magic wand is to close the circuit so that energy can flow from one world to the other.

—Omraam Mikhaël Aïvanhov
Cosmic Moral Law

The highest magic is that which lies within ourselves.

—Anodea Judith
Wheels of Life

Magic works acausally. The magician understands grace.... Magicians understand the courage and audacity involved in asserting themselves and their will.

—Carol S. Pearson
The Hero Within

Magicians have always been masters of the space between-times like sunrise and sunset, when the boundaries between the worlds are not firm, when gods can walk the earth and humans can touch the sky.

—J. E. Cirlot
A Dictionary of Symbols

The Magician creates what has never been before by opening us up to

inspiration and then by manifesting new ideas into concrete reality.

—Sharon Seivert
Working from Your Core

In Western society, we tend to think of a magician as one who performs incredible illusions before amazed audiences. In tribal societies, magic involves accessing the realm of the sacred in order to persuade, control, or influence supernatural power to assist in manifesting something in the ordinary, everyday world.

—Hank Wesselman
Medicinemaker

Ancient magicians believed they gained power by discovering their real names— that is, their Essence, and own personal identities.

—Sharon Seivert
The Balancing Act

Puritans were in the minority. Most other people inhabited an enchanted universe.

—Jackson Lears
Something for Nothing

There is something magical about films. The person you are looking at is also somewhere else at the same time. This is a condition of the gods.

—Joseph Campbell
The Place of Myth

Magic has power to experience and fathom things which are inaccessible to human reason.

—Paracelsus

All that we profess to do is but this—to find out the secrets of the human frame; to know why the parts ossify and the blood stagnates; and to apply continual preventives to the effects of time. This is not magic it is the art of medicine rightly understood.

—Edward Bulwer-Lytton
Zanoni

All magic, even today, occurs in the natural-vital, egoless, spaceless and timeless sphere. This requires … a sacrifice of consciousness.

—Jean Gebser
The Ever-Present Origin

Believe in the simple magic of life, in service in the universe, and the meaning of that waiting, that alertness, that "cran-ing of the neck" in creatures will dawn upon you.

—Martin Buber

God is alive and magic is afoot.

—Leonard Cohen

MANDALA

The Sanskrit word *mandala* means "circle." It is the Indian term for the circles drawn in religious rituals … (it) is known in ritual usage as a *yantra*, an instrument of contemplation. It is meant to aid concentration by narrowing down the psychic field of vision and restricting it to the center.

—C. J. Jung
Mandala Symbolism

Through the perfect composition of the mandala, in which no part is superfluous, one becomes aware of the hidden rela-tionships that link and unify everything in the universe.

—Edwin Bernbaum

There is a numerical field in which individual numbers figure as energetic phenomena or rhythmical configura-tions. This "field" which we take to represent the structural outlines of the collective unconscious, is organized around the central archetype of the Self. For this reason historical mandala structures deserve particular attention. In corresponding "cosmic models" and mathematical representations of God, the first four natural numbers predominate to an exceptional degree, just as they did in the systematic divinatory techniques of the past.

—Marie-Louise von Franz
Number and Time

The center of the mandala also represents the still point of the turning universe, the earth in a geo-centric cosmos, and the surrounding square symbolizes the path of the sun, moon, and planets along the ecliptic.

—Gavin D. Flood
Mapping Invisible Worlds

Sacred consciousness, of which the Man-dala is a structural model, conforms to the Hermetic statement, "God is an intel-ligent sphere whose center is everywhere and whose circumference is nowhere."

—José & Miriam Argüelles
Mandala

Mandalas are like snapshots of motion.... They "rotate."

—John R. Van Eenwyk
Archetypes and Strange Attractors

MANIFESTATION

We live in a cosmos that at its deepest level is made of unfolding relationships ... manifestation is an act of participation. We grow what we wish from within ourselves.... The more I can enter into communion and community with my world, the more manifestation will work for me.

—David Spangler
Everyday Miracles

Dreams are a manifestation of the subconscious. Any (personal) condition before becoming a reality is first dreams.

—Edgar Cayce
Dreams Your Magic Mirror

It is said that you reap what you sow. This is because whatever you emanate you will encounter.... You alter your patterns of outer manifestation by altering your inner experience of self.

—Martia Nelson
Coming Home

The human species has within its soul the ability to arrange everything according to its own wish.

—Hildegard of Bingen

MANTRA

The definition of mantra is "that which protects the mind." That which protects the mind from negativity or that which protects you from your own mind, is called mantra.... The mantra I recommend to my students is OM AH HUM VAJRA GURU PADMA SIDDHI TUM ... the mantra of all the buddhas ...

—Sogyal Rinpoche
The Tibetan Book of Living and Dying

A mantra is a "symbol" in the archaic sense of the term—it is simultaneously the symbolized "reality" and the symbolizing "sign."... By working on the "symbol," one awakens all the forces that correspond to it, on all the levels of being.

—Mircea Eliade
Yoga: Immortality and Freedom

The mantram becomes one's staff of life and carries one through every ordeal. It is not repeated for the sake of repetition, but for the sake of purification ... each repetition has a new meaning carrying you nearer and nearer to God.

—Mohandas (Mahatma) Gandhi

... this frequent service of the lips imperceptibly becomes a genuine appeal of the heart ...

—*The Way of a Pilgrim*

The mantram ... can be repeated anywhere and at any time ... the mantram is, above all, a spiritual tool ... exercise care in your choice of a mantram. After all, it will be with you for a long time.

—Eknath Easwaran
Meditation

A Tibetan Monk: A mantra keeps the mind safe, grips it enchantingly so that it isn't diverted into fearsome or ugly thoughts.

—Marsha Sinetar
Developing a 21st Century Mind

Father Maximos: When you practice the Jesus Prayer systematically, it is as if you move about within a polluted city wearing an oxygen mask over your face. Nothing can touch you ... before starting with the Jesus Prayer it is helpful to "warm up the heart" with a few minutes of regular prayer. After that, one can begin to recite and focus on the Jesus Prayer, chasing all other thoughts away.

—Kyriacos C. Markides
The Mountain of Silence

MAPS

A map says to you, read me carefully, follow me closely, doubt me not... I am the earth in the palm of your hand.

—Beryl Markham
West with the Night

The map is not the territory. But a good enough map will get us where we're going.

—Richard Thieme

There is no single "right" map, but merely maps of space that serve different purposes.

—Alvin Toffler

Columbus was a mapmaker before he explored.

—Edward Bernays

Knowledge becomes merchandise.... The Spanish kept their official charts in a double-locked box ... the pilot major had one key and the cosmographer major had the other.

—Daniel Boorstin
The Creators

Maps map and define the kind of Earth that is perceived.

—Paul Devereux
Re-Visioning the Earth

A map is a kind of representation—not just a concept, but many concepts together.... Many worlds are possible. It all depends on representation.

—David Bohm
On Dialogue

Dream: I am riding a bicycle ... in my left hand I carry a map of these paths ... the map blows out of my hand ... it flutters to the ground and is picked up by an old man who stands there holding it for me. I walk back to get the map and when I arrive at the old man, he hands me, not my map, but a small round tray of earth in which are growing fresh grass seedlings.

—Robert K. Greenleaf
The Private Writings of Robert K. Greenleaf

MARRIAGE

The sum which two married people
owe to one another defies calculation.
It is an infinite debt, which can only be
discharged through all eternity.

—Johann Wolfgang von Goethe

There is nothing nobler and more
admirable than when two people who see
eye to eye keep house as man and wife,
confounding their enemies and delight-
ing their friends.

—Homer

No relationship can continue very long at
its highest emotional pitch. But fidelity prepares us for the return of these
moments: that of union, communion,
at-one-ment…. Homer's *Odyssey* is an
example of the connection between marriage and household and earth.

—Wendell Berry
The Unsettling of America

If the old fairy-tale ending "They lived
happily ever after" is taken to mean
"They felt for the next fifty years exactly
as they felt the day before they were married," then it says what probably never
was nor ever could be true, and would be
highly undesirable if it were. Who could
bear to live in that excitement for even
five years?

—C. S. Lewis
Mere Christianity

I love marriage as a subject because it
has to do with a running conversation
between people. The domestic realm is
so rich in contradictions—you live with

another person and know them so well,
yet you remain separate individuals,

—Deborah Garrison & Bill Moyers
Fooling With Words

If you can't stand to be alone, don't
get married.

—Henrik Johan Ibsen

One of the functions served by the
instinctual phenomenon of falling in love
is to provide the participants with a magic
cloak of omnipotence which blissfully
blinds them to the riskiness of what they
are doing when they undertake marriage.

—M. Scott Peck
The Road Less Traveled

Though you can't see it, a red string
around your ankle ties you to the person
you'll marry. He's already been born, and
he's at the other end of the string.

—Maxine Hong Kingston
The Woman Warrior

Marriage is not a love affair. A love affair
is a totally different thing. A marriage is a
commitment to that which you are. That
person is literally your other half. And
you and the other person are one.

—Joseph Campbell
The Power of Myth

This ritual marriage (*hieros gamos*), in
which the king represents the people of
the earth and the priestess the goddess,
was a magical means of helping the
land and the people flourish, and also
provided the king with his royal authority to rule. It brought rain and sunshine,

fertility and creativity.... Sexuality and sacredness were not divided.

—Asphodel P. Long
In A Chariot Drawn by Lions

Canada geese mate for life, with the male singing one part of their song, the female the other. After a mate dies, the survivor sings both parts to keep the whole song alive.

—Diane Ackerman
An Alchemy of Mind

Nearly all marriages, even happy ones, are mistakes: in the sense that almost certainly (in a more perfect world, or even with a little more care in this imperfect one) both partners might be found more suitable mates. But the real soul-mate is the one you are married to.

—J. R. R. Tolkien

MARTYR

"Martyr" in Hebrew means "to sanctify the name." To die rather than to convert.

—James Carroll
Constantine's Sword

The martyrdom of the God-Man and the redemption of the world through His blood has been an essential tenet of many great religions. Nearly all these stories can be traced to sun worship, for the glorious orb of day is the Savior who dies annually for every creature within his universe, but year after year rises again victorious from the tomb of winter.

—Manly P. Hall
The Secret Teachings of All Ages

It is not the suffering but the cause which makes a martyr.

—English proverb

MASTERY

The process of rhythmic repetition patterns our subconscious so that our reactions become automatic. This is what ageless wisdom and the perennial philosophy call mastery, and it is a goal that can only be attained with practice, patience and persistence.

—David A. Schwerin
Conscious Capitalism

People with high levels of personal mastery do not set out to integrate reason and intuition. Rather, they achieve it naturally—as a bi-product of their commitment to use all resources at their disposal. They cannot afford to choose between reason and intuition, or head and heart, any more than they would choose to walk on one leg or see with one eye.

—Peter Senge
The Fifth Discipline

Great men, like great epochs, are explosive material in whom tremendous energy has been accumulated.

—Frederich Nietzche

Personal mastery is a function of the quality of our seeing.... We are visual ragpickers ... in the ordinary state of consciousness, we passively pick up fragmented visual impressions of objects or events. This is a low-energy activity.... High-energy seeing involves ... a discipline of seeing through events to the invisible processes that shape those events.

—Debasshis Chatterjee
Leading Consciously

Self-mastery is an accumulation of the strengths and preserving powers of justice ... self-mastery nourishes the soul in holiness by gathering up the inner aspect of the soul for its fulfillment ... thus our self-mastery nourishes our whole person—body and soul—in holiness.

—Hildegard of Bingen

MATHEMATICS

Let no one who is not a geometer enter.

—Inscription over the door of Plato's
Academy in Athens

The Grand Master of the Templars carried an abacus, the master-builder's staff.

—Louis Charpentier
The Mysteries of Chartres Cathedral

Fold a sheet of paper on itself 100 times. How thick would it be? It it's one millimeter thick, each fold doubling its thickness, it would be 800 trillion times the distance between the earth and the sun.

—David G. Myers
Intuition

There often does appear to be some profound reality about mathematical concepts, going quite beyond the mental deliberations of any particular mathematician. It is as though human thought is, instead, being guided towards some external truths—a truth which has a reality of its own and which is revealed only partially to any one of us.

—Roger Penrose
The Emperor's New Mind

The world is a mathematical, not material structure.

—Werner Karl Heisenberg

Perhaps we are merely one among a myriad of players—gathering bits, abstracting concepts, building great edifices of theory, these mathematical Towers of Babel, that reach higher and higher above the plains. High enough, perhaps, to make out, just barely, the rhythm of other dancers, the flickering of other fires.

—George Johnson
Fire in the Mind

Math is the relation of relationships.

—John Von Neumann

Mathematics teaches us, in fact, to combine like with like.... Its object is to divine the result of a combination without having to reconstruct that combination element by element,

—Henri Poincaré
Science and Hypothesis

Counting by 20's rather than base 10 was practiced by the Celts, Mayans and Olmec.... The Ojibway people have a 16 compound word for "million,"

—F. David Peat
Lighting the Seventh Fire

Let no one read me who is not
a mathematician.

—Leonardo da Vinci
Forster Codices

If only I had more mathematics.

—Albert Einstein's last words

MATTER/
MATERIALISM

God gave Noah the sketch and specs for
a boat and then later gives Moses three
divine blueprints for constructing the
Ark of the Covenant, the Tabernacle and
the first temple. God spoke to Moses out
of a burning bush—transformed matter.

—Ignacio L. Götz
On Technology and the Spirit

The world is too much with us, late and
soon. Getting and spending, we lay waste
our powers.

—John Milton

From the moment that "the spirit of
God moved upon the face of the waters,"
matter and spirit were locked in close
embrace.

—R. C. Zaehner
Matter and Spirit

Matter is frozen light.

—David Bohm

Materialism leaves us trapped in a world
that won't hold together. It's centrifugal. It

splits at every turn into the Ten Thousand
Things, each neatly labeled with a Ph.D.
thesis. In the meantime, we become more
and more obsessed with what we mistake
for our real needs, hopes, fears … and
more and more estranged from our birthright membership of a coherent universe.

—Lindsay Clarke
The Chymical Wedding

There must be more to life than
having everything.

—Maurice Sendak

MEANING

For the meaning of life differs from man
to man, from day to day and from hour
to hour. What matters therefore, is not
the meaning of life in general but rather
the specific meaning of a person's life at a
given moment.

—Victor E. Frankl
Man's Search for Meaning

A single moment can retroactively flood
an entire life with meaning.

—Victor E. Frankl
The Doctor and the Soul

Everything in this world has a hidden
meaning. Men, animals, trees, stars, they
are all hieroglyphics … when you see
them, you do not understand them. You
think they are really men, animals, trees,
stars. It is only later that you understand.

—Nikos Kazantzakis
Zorba the Greek

When I walk the fields, I am oppressed now and then with an innate feeling that everything I see has a meaning, if I could but understand it. And this feeling of being surrounded with truths which I cannot grasp amounts to indescribable awe sometimes.... Have you not felt that your real soul was imperceptible in your mental vision, except in a few hallowed moments?

—Charles Kingsley
Charles Kingsley's Life

... meaning: it is the meaning of "islands of meaning" in the ocean of our struggling, the meaning of lanterns whose light is cast into the darkness of our life's journey, illuminating all the many meanings of its direction.

—Václav Havel
Letters to Olga

One can become too much preoccupied with meaning. What is the meaning of a rose?

—Richard Adams
The Unbroken Web

If there is no meaning in it, that saves a world of trouble, you know, as we needn't try to find any.

—Lewis Carroll
Alice in Wonderland

MEDICINE WHEELS

This seemingly existential paradigm is a rich, complex and subtle symbol of mystical and philosophical depth. Trained apprentices are taught to use the medicine wheel as a map to their innermost being... The key to using the medicine wheel is movement ... from one direction to another in the process of learning.

—Lynn V. Andrews
Jaguar Woman

Medicine wheels can be circular stones corresponding to patterns of stars and planets; they can also be an expression of a person's dream or vision. It is more than a pattern. It's a relationship between the earth and the cosmos ... a circular moment, a process of healing, a ceremony, a teaching.

—F. David Peat
Lighting the Seventh Fire

... the Bear Medicine Society approach a loosely arranged circle of stones. This rock structure is actually a shrine of surpassing sacredness, which the Tewa call the navel of mother earth. It represents the exact spiritual and geometric center of the Tewa universe ... [and] stands as a sort of umbilical connection between fragile human existence and the mysterious, rhythmic upwellings of nature's bounty.

—David Suzuki & Peter Knudtson
Wisdom of the Elders

The circle is the wheel of life. As each one of us sits at a slightly different point on the Medicine Wheel, so each one of us sees things just a little bit differently.

—Sig Lonegren
Labyrinths

MEDIOCRITY

Only a mediocre person is always at his best.

—Summerset Maugham

Great spirits have always encountered violent opposition from mediocre minds.

—Albert Einstein

Mediocrity is deadly and spiritual mediocrity is endemic of our times.

—Regina Sara Ryan
The Woman Awake

MEDITATION

Although there are many kinds, meditation at its highest is a form of mental and spiritual training that aims at stilling and focusing the normally scattered mind, establishing a measure of physical and mental repose, and then becoming an instrument for Self-discovery ... the heart is calmed and the spirit strengthened.

—Philip Kapleau
The Wheel of Life and Death

Let no one imagine that contact with the Overself is a kind of dreamy reverie or pleasant, fanciful state. It is a vital relationship with a current of peace, power, and goodwill flowing endlessly from the invisible center of the visible self.

—Paul Brunton
The Notebooks of Paul Brunton

Essentially, meditation is the technique of creating a center of quietude and stillness within the self and then allowing this center to be flooded with light from the higher planes.

—George Trevelyan
A Vision of the Aquarian Age

One effect of meditation is to soften the barriers between the conscious and the unconscious.

—Allan Combs & Mark Holland
Synchronicity

Meditation is the interior reading of the book of one's memory ...

—Mary Carruthers
The Craft of Thought

A meditative prayer is beyond words.

—Gregg Braden
The Isaiah Effect

According to Cayce, everyone must one day at some level of his progression learn to meditate, because only through mediation will he eventually generate sufficient power to free himself from his lower self.... If some dreams are signs from heaven (superconscious) which can guide our feet back to the source of all lights, then be assured that meditation is one of the means by which we increase our ability to understand our dreams.

—Elsie Sechrist
Dreams Your Magic Mirror

When someone asked a great Sufi master how he learned to meditate he said, "By watching a cat watch a mouse. Just by watching them I learned how to meditate."

—Anthony Damiani
Looking into Mind

The aim of meditation, when culminating in contemplation, is the stilling of all mental activity so that Mind itself, the source and condition of this activity, may be known in its original state. The practice ultimately leads the artist to find beauty and the mystic to find the godlike within himself.

—Paul Brunton
The Spiritual Crisis of Man

Meditation is an ending of ourselves and an opening into the life-stream which flows invisibly behind the visible world of forms—a flow of beauty, peace and love.

—Robert Rabbin
Invisible Leadership

We meditate so that we may be able to see the world as it is.

—Muktananda

Meditation is not a matter of trying to achieve ecstasy, spiritual bliss or tranquility, nor is it attempting to become a better person. It is simply the creation of a space in which we are able to expose and undo our neurotic games, our self-deceptions, our hidden fears and hopes.

—Ram Dass
Journey of Awakening

Two monks ... aged seventy ... and thirty-four demonstrated their practice.... We asked whether what we had seen was the so-called "levitation medita-

tion" and were told that indeed it was ... but there was no floating or hovering.... I then asked the older man if he knew of anyone who could carry out such a feat. He said it was an ability that was present many hundreds of years ago, but not today. I asked the older monk if he would like to levitate, and with a twinkle in his eyes, he responded, "There is no need. We now have airplanes."

—Herbert Benson
The Relaxation Response

Meditation is an open attitude—open in two directions: toward God and toward material life. It is a trusting and attentive attitude of waiting.

—Paul Tournier
The Adventure of Living

We would suggest that meditation, by whatever definition, is basically "getting out of the way."

—Lazaris
Lazaris Interviews

All of us must indeed some day learn to meditate because all of us must some day come to be one with the One Force. And the practice of meditation is the practice of the movement toward that oneness ... meditation is listening to the still small voice.

—Herbert B. Puryear
Edgar Cayce: Reflections on the Path

The more accelerated our life becomes, the more we have to learn to select only the essential, to create our own repose and meditation islands within an uncluttered mental space.

—Anäis Nin
The Novel of the Future

Meditation has no point and no reality unless it is firmly rooted in life.

—Thomas Merton

The first step in filling a container is to be sure it is empty.

—Mark Link
Take Off Your Shoes

Meditation is not a means to an end. It is both the means and the end.

—Jiddu Krishnamurti

Meditation is … the art of suspending verbal and symbolic thinking for a time, somewhat as a courteous audience will stop talking when a concert is about to begin.

—Alan Watts

Meditation has several phases. It has an active moment of sitting down, visualizing, chanting, whatever means the person has; then stillness of mind; then action, going out and doing something.… Action is what manifests that which you perceive in the meditation.

—Dhyani Ywahoo
Weaving the Visions

Meditation is the key entrance into matriarchal nonlinear realities.

—Diane Stein
Stroking the Python

Meditation or Centering Prayer is in a sense a little vacation. A vacation is time out to practice just letting go and giving oneself over to the refreshing things of life.

—M. Basil Pennington
Centered Living

A regular practice of meditation, prayer, writing, giving or simply reciting a mantra can allow our mind to rest in what we love.

—Wayne Muller
How, Then, Shall We Live?

Our mind is presently scattered; its energies need to be channeled like the way water in a hydroelectric plant is channeled to create great force. We achieve this with the mind through meditation, channeling it such that it becomes very forceful, at which point it can be utilized in the direction of wisdom.

—Dalai Lama
A Policy of Kindness

Meditation has nothing to do with the occult, the paranormal. When people ask me if I can bend a key with my psychic energy, I simply confess, "I can't even bend one with my physical energy."

—Eknath Easwaran
Meditation

By concentration and meditation a person works upon his own soul and develops within it the soul-organs of perception.

—Rudolf Steiner
Initiation and Its Results

When we start to meditate with regularity, something happens inside that absorbs, reshapes, and infuses everything we think and feel and do.

—George Fowler
Dance of a Fallen Monk

When a group meditates together the energy generated is more than the sum of its members.

—Llewellyn Vaughan-Lee
In the Company of Friends

MEMES

When you imitate someone else, something is passed on. This "something" can then be passed on again, and again, and so take on a life of its own. We might call this thing an idea, an instruction, a behavior, a piece of information ... but if we are going to study it we shall need to give it a name. Fortunately, there is a name. It is the "meme."

—Susan Blackmore
The Meme Machine

Examples of memes are tunes, ideas, catch-phrases, clothes fashions, ways of making pots or of building arches.

—Richard Dawkins
The Selfish Gene

The memes one chooses can have long-lasting effects, even life-and-death consequence.

—Howard Gardner, *et al*
Good Work

Memes are the cultural building blocks of the cultural software that forms our apparatus of understanding ... [they] are spread by observation and social learning.... Like genes, memes are self-replicating entities. We have filters (beliefs) that winnow memes out.... Religious groups, academic discipline, and political parties may help spread and preserve memes more efficiently than individual actions.

—J. M. Balkin
Cultural Software

Memes are, indeed, the creation of sentient beings. Memes do not merely mimic design, they are design and purpose.

—Alison Jolly
Lucy's Legacy

We can achieve a vision one meme at a time.

—Daniel Quinn
Beyond Civilization

MEMORY

Memory requires certain arts that cultivate it and tease out its many variations and possibilities. Telling stories from childhood or simply from the past brings memory into play. A certain kind of meditation might activate memory, and what may seem to be distractions through meditation—the insistence of memories—may be just what is needed.

—Thomas Moore
Original Self

Memory is the place where our vanished days secretly gather.... The kingdom of memory is full of the ruins of presence.

It is astonishing how faithful experience actually is; how it never vanishes.

—John O'Donohue
Eternal Echoes

We tend to think of memory as monuments we once forged and may find intact beneath the weedy growth of years. But, in a real sense, memories are tied to and describe the present.... One never steps into the same stream of consciousness twice. All the mischief and mayhem of a life influences how one restyles a memory.

—Diane Ackerman
An Alchemy of Mind

The process of repression is not to be regarded as something which takes place once for all, the results of which are permanent ... on the contrary, repression demands a constant expenditure of energy.

—Sigmund Freud
Repression

When I was young I could remember anything, whether it happened or not.

—Mark Twain

Mind you, memories are kidnappable.

—Diane Ackerman
An Alchemy of Mind

Our mother's heart and all hearts that have gone before ours have left traces of our safer, more restful, paradisal infancy. There are cellular memories within us that can remind us of the importance of "being" and not just "doing," of how to lead a more blissful, heart-felt life, and that, contrary to the powerful protective

evolutional drive toward individuality contained within our brain, we are all one.

—Paul Pearsall
The Heart's Code

Memory is a sifter, a shaper, a giver of form and emphasis. It may suppress, or even falsify facts.... But if one is less concerned with reporting what one saw than with reflecting on the seeing, one can hardly say that such recollections are "untrue." Their peculiar value often comes from the combination of memory and imagination, those twin creative powers.

—Madeleine Doran
Something about Swans

See how widely I have ranged, Lord, searching for you in my memory. I have not found you outside it.

—Augustine
Confessions

In general, the heart seems to have a more reliable memory for what benefits the psyche than does the head, which has a rather unhealthy tendency to lead an "abstract" existence, and easily forgets that its consciousness is snuffed out the moment the heart fails in its duty.

—Carl G. Jung
The Collected Works of C. G. Jung

In New Guinea, the breath is regarded as the "seat of the soul." There is a custom common to so-called primitive people of placing one's mouth over that of a dying person in order that the soul and

the traditions stored in memory can be
transmitted on the last breath.

—Edmund Carpenter
*Oh What a Blow That Phantom
Gave Me*

God gave us memory that we might have
roses in December.

—James M. Barrie

And even one good memory may be the
means of saving us.

—Feodor Dostoevski

This [the Platonic idea of memory]
remembering-what-never-happened
must rightly be called imagining, and
this sort of memory is imagination.
Memoria was the old term for both.
It referred to an activity and a place
that today we call variously, memory,
imagination and the unconscious.

—James Hillman
Healing Fiction

The key to remembering is to remind
the self not to be afraid of anything,
anywhere, anytime—ever.

—Emmanuel
The Choice for Love

We carry the memory of childhood like
a photo in a locket, fierce and possessive
for pain and calm; everybody's past is
inviolate, separate, sacrosanct, our heads
are different countries with no maps or
dictionaries, people walk vast deserts of
grief or inhabit walled gardens of joy.

—Michele Roberts
Tales I Tell My Mother

If in our remembrance we find the
depth of our history, will we opt for
description only or choose to ignite the
fuse of our knowledge?

—Michelle Cliff
*Claiming an Identity They Taught
Me to Despise*

Great is the force of memory, enormously
great, my God, a chamber vast and infinite.

—Augustine
Confessions

Memories are shaped and selected, often
profoundly.... Like souls in heaven, they
are saved, but changed.

—Ursula K. LeGuin
The Wave in the Mind

Human memory is encoded in air currents and river sediments. Eskers of ash
wait to be scooped up, lives reconstituted.

—Anne Michaels
Fugitive Pieces

Knowledge is simple recollection.

—Plato (Aristocles)

Decisive, remembered events rearrange
our normal perceptions and patterns,
enabling newness to break in.

—Maria Harris
Dance of the Spirit

We're all contemporaries. There's only a
difference in our memories.

—W. H. Auden

"I have a great memory for forgetting, David."

—Robert Louis Stevenson
Kidnapped

MEN

Paradox: men who most deplore and distrust women are the same ones who admire, want and need them.

—David D. Gilmore
Misogyny

Whar did your Christ come from? From God and a woman. Men had nothin' to do wid Him!

—Sojourner Truth

Ma Joad: "Women got all her life in her arms. Men got it all in his head"…. Women and children knew deep in themselves that no misfortune was too great to bear if their men were whole.

—John Steinbeck
Grapes of Wrath

METAPHOR

Metaphor in its deep creative sense results in wisdom…. A metaphor opens up new space and ushers in a new reality…. If you could say it, you would not need metaphor. If you could conceptualize it, it would not be metaphor. If you could explain it, you would not use metaphor.

—Nelle Morton
The Journey Is Home

Human beings have, for centuries, used metaphors in thinking about time that also describe objects in space. A journey or an exile. The bridge to a new century. A turning wheel. A tree reaching both roots and branches outward into earth and sky…. Wherever there is pattern there can be framework for meaning.

—Mary Catherine Bateson
Full Circles, Overlapping Lives

Metaphor, with all its multivalent concreteness, may be ultimately the most faithful servant of truth. It masks as it also opens one to life.

—Belden C. Lane
Landscapes of the Sacred

Metaphor, far from being a decoration that is added to language, purifies and restores it to its original nature.

—Claude Levi-Strauss

The ultimate source of metaphor is nature…. As we encounter culture, we raise the ghosts of only the last ten to twenty thousand years of human existence. As we encounter nature, we raise the winds of five billion years of natural existence. There is more of nature.

—Bob Samples
The Metaphoric Mind

I found out the truth could be said in whatever metaphor we need to communicate with one another.

—Ram Dass

When we lift up the eyes of the mind to what is invisible, we should consider metaphors of visible things as if they were steps to understanding.

—Hugh of St. Victor

Metaphor isn't just decorative language. If it were, it wouldn't scare people so much.

—Diane Ackerman
An Alchemy of Mind

The idea that metaphor is important to human thinking is not new. It was old when Aristotle said, "to make metaphors implies an eye for resemblances." And, I suppose, one might add it implies an eye for differences as well.

—Jane Yolen
Take Joy

Metaphors flow readily when we are sensitive to our bodies.

—Laura Cerwinske
Writing as a Healing Art

Any metaphor is double-sided, offering both new insight and new confusion.

—Mary Catherine Bateson
Peripheral Visions

Everything happens involuntarily in the highest degree but as in a gale of a feeling of freedom, of absoluteness, of power, of divinity. The involuntariness of image and metaphor is strangest of all; one no longer has any notion of what is an image or a metaphor; everything offers itself as the nearest, most obvious, simplest expression. It actually seems, to allude to something Zarathustra says, as

if the things themselves approached and offered themselves as metaphors.

—Friedrich Nietzche
Ecce Homo

Dead metaphors make strong idols. Dumb as stone, they stand stubbornly in the way; like boulders jutting up in the desert, they block our view of any oasis that may lie ahead.

—Marcia Falk
Weaving the Visions

If you have a mythology in which the metaphor for the mystery is the father, you are going to have a different set of signals from what you would have if the metaphor for the wisdom and mystery of the world were the mother. And they are two perfectly good metaphors.

—Joseph Campbell
The Power of Myth

What really matters in a metaphor is the psychic depth at which the things of the world, whether actual or fancied, are transmuted by the cool heat of the imagination.

—Philip Wheelwright
Metaphor and Reality

We are all connected. Metaphor knows this and therefore is religious.

—Natalie Goldberg
Writing Down the Bones

All metaphors are sexual; a penis in every convex object and a vagina in every concave one.

—Norman O. Brown
Love's Body

Metaphor, in its extended form as story or myth, continues to be the form which most adequately expresses beliefs and values.... In its simplest form, a successful metaphor gives us a shock, helping us, thereby to adapt to a changed reality.... Like "signals" from "worlds not recognized," they come spontaneously but obliquely.

—John Coulson
Religion and Imagination

The world is a Dancer; it is a Rosary; it is a Torrent; it is a Boat; a Mist, a Spider's Snare; it is what you will; and the metaphor will hold.

—Ralph Waldo Emerson
Journals

Why is the metaphor flesh is grass, which is not only wrong (flesh is not grass) but inappropriate (flesh is not even like grass), better and truer than the sentence flesh is mortal, which is quite accurate and logical?

—Walker Percy
The Message in the Bottle

All things are metaphors.

—Johann Wolfgang von Goethe

You don't see something until you have the right metaphor to let you perceive it.

—Robert Stetson Shaw

MICRO/MACROCOSM

As above, so below.

—Hermes Trismegistus

The human embryo is an image of the cosmos. The whole macrocosm projects its force into the human being in order to make possible the genesis of a new human being. The minutest molecule is acted upon by the whole starry heavens.

—Rudolf Steiner
Man: Hieroglyph of the Universe

The universe is worked and guided from within outward.

—Helena Petrovna Blavatsky

The human is the microcosm of the macrocosm.

—Robert Sardello
Introduction, *Speech of the Grail*

Man has been truly termed a "Microcosm," or little world in himself, and the structure of his body should be studied not only by those who wish to become doctors, but by those who wish to attain a more intimate knowledge of god.

—Al-Ghazâlî

Man is the great mystery of God, the microcosm or the complete abridgement of the whole universe ... a hieroglyphic of eternity and time.

—Jacob Boehme
The Signature of All Things

... the symbols of the outside world and the cosmic symbols ... form the psychological basis for the conception of man as a microcosm whose fate, as we know, is bound up with the macrocosm

through the astrological components of
his character.

—Carl G. Jung
The Mysteries

Platonic cosmology themes are the
divine ideas, eternal in the Mind of God
and bodied forth in creatures, the World
Soul, the deep resonance of macrocosm
with microcosm.

—Linda Lopez McAlister
Hypatia's Daughters

The whole drama of the universe is
repeated in ourselves.

—Giuseppe Tucci
The Theory and Practice of the Mandala

Now God has built the human form into
the world structure, indeed even into
the cosmos.

—Hildegard of Bingen

Hildegard broadens and deepens our
understanding and practice of psychology. For her, psychology is not the mere
coping with ego problems but the relating
of microcosm and macrocosm. She sees
the human body and the human psyche
as creation-in-miniature. We are in the
cosmos and the cosmos is in us.

—Matthew Fox
Illuminations of Hindegard of Bingen

When we fall asleep, we pass from the
Microcosm into the Macrocosm.

—Rudolf Steiner
Macrocosm and Microcosm

The laws of the universe are in me in
miniature. Everything is related and
connected. …the laws increase at each
level and every process goes on in a
certain order.

—Beryl Pogson
The Work Life

Can you, O man, recognize yourself both
as microcosmic and macrocosmic, inhabiting two worlds that are united in your
heart. Discover the three-foldness of your
essential being, the four-foldness of the
life-body that permeates you, the seven-
foldness of the soul force that animates
you, the twelve-foldness reflected in the
eternal nature of Self?

—René Guénon

MIND/MINDFULNESS

When you have walked through all this
rubbish, when you have put aside all
these confusing, traditional imitative
things, then the mind is free, then
the mind is alert, then the mind is
passionate. And it is only such a mind
that can proceed.

—Jiddu Krishnamurti
On God

No mind was so good that it did not
need another mind to counter and
equal it, and to save it from conceit and
blindness and bigotry and folly. Only in
such balance could humility be found,
humility which was a lucid speed to
welcome lucidity whenever and wherever
it presented itself.

—Charles Williams
The Place of the Lion

All matter originates and exists only by virtue of a force which brings the particles of an atom to vibration and holds this most minute solar system of the atom together.... We must assume behind this force the existence of a conscious and intelligent mind. This mind is the matrix of all matter.

—Max Planck

The individual mind is immanent but not only in the body ... there is a larger Mind of which the individual mind is only a sub-system. This larger Mind is comparable to God ... but it is still immanent in the total interconnected social system and planetary ecology.

—Gregory Bateson
Steps to the Ecology of the Mind

Know that the soul is eternal; the mind is both physical and spiritual; the body is only temporal.

—Edgar Cayce

As we learn to be more mindful of the present moment, we become more aware of the feedback that life is constantly providing in response to our choices. We begin to use these messages without judgment, viewing them neither as reward nor punishment but as insight.

—Charlotte Shelton
Quantum Leaps

A mind that ceases to take in new information grows stale, less alert, less conscious. Habit and stereotype are not just a threat to my attitude toward the

other. They are a threat to me, to the vitality of my own mind.

—Danah Zohar & Ian Marshall
The Quantum Society

Mind is the builder. The thoughts you hold create the currents over which the wings of your experience must go.

—Edgar Cayce
The Sleeping Prophet

A mind once stretched by a great idea or new understanding will never fully return to its original dimensions.

—William James

In the mind's eye, that ancient seat of imagining, neurons appear to branch like trees, and angels have taffeta bird wings.

—Diane Ackerman
An Alchemy of Mind

Some people change their minds because they want to, others because they have to.

—Howard Gardner
Changing Minds

The evolution of our minds has not kept pace with what we have created.

—Barbara Shipka
Leadership in a Challenging World

You should love God mindlessly so that your soul is without mind and free from all mental activities, for as long as your soul is operating like a mind, so long does it have images and representations. But as long as it has images, it has intermediaries, and as long as it has intermediaries, it has neither oneness nor simplicity.

—Meister Eckhart

Once there was a time when nothing was. Mind of all minds was asleep. How did Original Consciousness become aware of itself? This is the first great riddle that confounded human consciousness, and it confounds us still.

—June Singer
A Gnostic Book of Hours

The mind is not an instrument of knowledge but an organizer of knowledge.

—Aurobindo
The Adventure of Consciousness

The mind of man is capable of anything because everything is in it, all the past as well as all the future.

—Joseph Conrad
Heart of Darkness

There is no limit to your learning because there is no limit on your mind.

—*A Course in Miracles*

Another way to think of mind may be as St. Augustine thought of God, as an emanation that's not located in one place, or one form, but exists throughout the universe. An essence, not just a substance. And, of course, the mind isn't located only in the brain.

—Diane Ackerman
An Alchemy of Mind

The eye as soon as it opens sees all the stars of the hemisphere. The mind in an instant leaps from east to west.

—Leonardo da Vinci
Codex Atlanticus

If non-local mind is a reality, the world becomes a place of interaction and connection, not one of isolation and disjunction.

—Larry Dossey

Computers are, essentially, unitary beasts. They always have boundaries and limits. But the mind can play and transcend limits in which it is placed.

—F. David Peat
The Philosopher's Stone

Meditation is … a systematic technique for taking hold of and concentrating to the utmost degree our latent mental power. It consists in training the mind, especially attention and the will, so that we can set forth from the surface level of consciousness and journey into the very depths.

—Eknath Easwaran
Meditation

A mind that is fast is sick; a mind that is slow is sound; a mind that is still is divine.

—Meher Baba

The healthy mind is compelled toward newness and the unknown.

—Paul Lehmberg
In the Strong Woods

Some forms of madness are no more than
failed transitions from one vision of life
to the next.

—Sheldon Kopp

The man who never alters his opinion is
like standing water and breeds reptiles of
the mind.

—William Blake
The Marriage of Heaven and Hell

A man's mind stretched by a new idea can
never go back to its original dimension.

—Oliver Wendell Holmes

I want to know the mind of God. The rest
is all details.

—Albert Einstein

The stuff of the world is mind-stuff.

—Arthur Eddington

What is mind? No matter. What is
matter? Never mind.

—Thomas Hewitt Key

MINISTER

To contemplate is to see, to minister is to
make visible.

—Henri J. M. Nouwen

I give (man) earthly powers not to
exercise dominion but to minister to his
fellows and in ministering, to learn those

skills which he does not yet possess, each
in its turn, until he has them all.

—Anne Perry
Tathea

MIRACLES

There are two ways to live your life. One
is as though nothing is a miracle. The
other is as though everything is a miracle.

—Albert Einstein

When I was growing up Roman Catholic,
we were bilingual in English and angels.
Miracles could happen every day.

—Caroline Myss
Invisible Acts of Power

"What is that?" he asked stupefied. "That
miracle over there, that moving blue,
what do you call it? Sea? And what's that
wearing a flowered green apron? Earth?
Who was the artist who did it? It's the
first time I've ever seen that, I swear!"

—Nikos Kazantzakis
Zorba the Greek

Miracles do not happen in contradiction
to nature, but only in contradiction to
that which is known to us about nature.

—Augustine

To me every hour of the light and dark
is a miracle. Every cubic inch of space is
a miracle.

—Walt Whitman

Miracles are natural. When they do not occur, something has gone wrong. Miracles occur naturally as expressions of love.

—*A Course in Miracles*

Most miracles, like everything else, are firmly rooted in WHO we are.

—Iris Sangiuliano
In Her Time

To be looking elsewhere for miracles is to me a sure sign of ignorance that everything is miraculous.

—Abraham Maslow

Miracles to the unbelieving create awe and sometimes obedience for a little space; then they are forgotten.

—Anne Perry
Tathea

MISERY

… Julian of Norwich tells us she learned in one of her "showings" that there is a divine plan, both temporal and transcendent, which will account for the unchecked miseries of the world, a plan which our finite minds are incapable of grasping. God informs her, you remember, to trust this and tells her that "All shall be well, and all manner of things shall be well." The time is not yet ripe for us to comprehend this mystery, she is told. But meanwhile all manner of things is not well …

—Denise Levertov
Work That Enfaiths

No person is so helpless as the man in whom joy and misery sleep comfortably together.

—Calvin Miller
The Singer

I've seen them make the sick eat broth by holding it so close the savor draws them on. Maybe misery has a savor too, so if you're near enough, sick though you be with sin, your heart can't help but sip.

—Frederick Buechner
Godric

MODELS

Frames are mental structures that shape the way we see the world. As a result, they shape the goals we seek, the plans we make, the way we act, and what counts as a good or bad outcome of our actions … all words are defined relative to conceptual frames. When you hear a word, its frame (or collection of frames) is activated in your brain.

—George Lakoff
don't think of an elephant!

Try to develop models which are not arbitrary and man-made but organic and natural. The difference is in the intention. Arbitrary man-made models have as their intention manipulation and control. Natural organic models have as their intention resonance and reverence.

—Margaret Mead

All models are wrong—but some are useful.

—W. Edwards Deming

If you know what causes a phenomenon, what results from it, how to influence, control, initiate or prevent it, how it relates to others' states of affairs or how it resembles them ... then to some extent you understand it.... If you understand inflation, a mathematical proof, the way a computer works, DNA, or a divorce, then you have a mental representation that serves as a model.

—Philip Johnson-Laird
Mental Models

MONEY/WEALTH

The word "money" is derived from the Latin *moneta*, meaning mint ... and was originally the name of the goddess in whose temple in Rome money was coined.... It was certainly not by chance that the ancient Romans set their mint in the temple of a goddess and not of a god—for money is a symbolic means of exchange and therefore belongs to the feminine principle of relatedness.

—Helen M. Luke
The Way of Woman

Money enables people who are miserable on the job to spend evening and weekend in the mindless respite of spending.

—John Whiteside & Sandra Egli
Flight of the Phoenix

Money in the modern era is a purely secular force, reflecting the lower nature of man. Cut off from any relation to spiritual aspiration, it has become the most obvious example of a fire raging out of control ... if money is to be secondary in our lives, it can only mean that money serve the aim of self-knowledge.

—Joseph Needleman
Money and the Meaning of Life

There are two ways to be rich: one is to have a lot of money; the other is to have few needs.

—William Sloane Coffin
Credo

Money addiction alters the criteria for judging actions, both public and private. From the money-addicted perspective, the criterion for making decisions is no longer "Is this right or wrong?" but "Will this make money?"

—Barbara Brandt
Whole Life Economics

The money we give our children should be given for no reason; it should be given indifferently so that they will learn to receive it indifferently; but it should be given not so that they will learn to love it, but so that they learn not to love it, so that they realize its true nature and its inability to satisfy our truest desires, which are those of the spirit.

—Natalia Ginzburg
The Little Virtues

Money, which represents the prose of life, and is hardly spoken of in parlors without an apology, is in its effects and laws, as beautiful as roses.

—Ralph Waldo Emerson

A better analogy for the real nature of wealth is the image of lighting candles, rather than the traditional metaphor of cutting up pies. After all, one candle can be used to light others. In reality, more wealth breeds more wealth.

—Sharon Seivert
The Balancing Act

In 1941 Victor Ganz bought Pablo Picasso's painting *The Dream* for seven thousand dollars. He sold it in 1997 for 48.4 million dollars. The worth of the painting increased unimaginably. Its worth, however, has nothing to do with significance ... money is a means, not an end.

—Robert Rabbin
Invisible Leadership

I have always believed that money costs too much, that the price people are willing to pay to have it is far too steep.

—Gregg Levoy
Callings

The price of anything is the amount of life you pay for it.

—Henry David Thoreau

Ahriman, Mephistopheles, Mammon—these terms mean the same—is to be found in money, in everything connected with our natural egotism on Earth. Because human life must inevitably always have some external material aspect, human beings have to reckon with Ahriman.... Ahriman, material nature, must continue until Earth evolution reaches its end.

—Rudolf Steiner
The Fifth Gospel

If intelligence is the new basis of property and wealth, it is odd that we aren't always more eager to grab more of it.

—Charles Handy
The Age of Paradox

Lives based on having are less free than lives based on doing or on being.

—William James

Money may buy the husk of things, but not the kernel.

—Henrik Johan Ibsen

Money, not sex, is the big secret of our time.

—Mary Pipher
Another Country

Money is not a thing; it is a collective idea.

—Alan Atkisson
Believing Cassandra

We will have a new reason for doing business. It will be to generate wealth, defined as access and availability. We will shift from "possessions and power" to "use and cooperation."

—Neale Donald Walsh
Tomorrow's God

Prosperity is relating, not acquiring.

—Tom Brown
The Search

Everything thrust in, everything thrusts after Gold ...

—Johann Wolfgang von Goethe
Faust

MOON

When you've cooked the marrow of the sun and moon,
The pearl is so bright you don't worry about poverty.

—Sun Bu-er

The patriarchal cultures equate male and female with the sun and moon, light and dark, and life and death, while the Tantrics and Tibetans take the opposite tack, woman with sun and man with moon.

— Robert Thurman
Circling the Sacred Mountain

According to the Indian scholar Sir John Woodruffe, the root of the words man, mind, and month all go back to the same Sanskrit root *man*, one meaning of which is "moon."

—Alice O. Howell
The Dove in the Stone

When the moon is full, our brain is also full. We are then in full possession of our senses.

—Hildegard of Bingen

The moon keeps people asleep ... for emotional people, the easiest thing is to go on having the same emotions.

—Beryl Pogson
The Work Life

As Blake saw, the moon is the mirror or key to the door between this world and the next.... Thus Jacob's ladder (Genesis 28: 10-22) spirals through the moon to heaven.

—Jill Purce,
The Mystic Spiral

An eclipse in Chinese is "Frog Swallowing the Moon"—if you bang pot lids together, you'll scare the frog from swallowing the moon.

—Maxine Hong Kingston
The Woman Warrior

MORAL/MORALITY

Everything's got a moral, if only you can find it.

—Lewis Carroll

Science cannot teach men to be moral.

—Albert Einstein

Everything depends on the use to which it is put.

—Reinhold Niebuhr

What is moral is what you feel good after; what is immoral is what you feel bad after.

—Ernest Hemingway

MORNING/DAWN

Morning is precious; morning is essentially private. Morning is when we come to know ourselves in the world again.

—David Whyte
Crossing the Unknown Sea

Grant me to make an unflawed beginning today, for I have done nothing yet.

—C. S. Lewis
The Weight of Glory

Those who have had occasion to keep a vigil through the night know that dawn is a game of subtle shifts.

—Christopher M. Bache
Dark Night, Early Dawn

MOTHER

Coming to know the hidden and forgotten Mother and the marvelous wisdom of the sacred feminine as revealed from every side and angle by the different mystical traditions is not a luxury; it is, I believe, a necessity for our survival as a species.... What knowing the Mother means above all is daring to put love into action. The Mother herself is love-in-action, love acting everywhere and in everything to make creation possible.

—Andrew Harvey
The Essential Mystics

This fair, lovely word "mother" is so sweet and so kind in itself that it cannot truly be said of anyone or to anyone

except of him (Christ) and to him who is the true Mother of life and of all things.

—Julian of Norwich

Alma mater literally means "nourishing mother." We might say that, when we separated humanity from nature, we separated from our nourishing mother.

—L. Robert Keck
Sacred Quest

Our daughters are our younger selves; our mothers are our older selves.

—Naomi Ruth Lowinsky
Stories from the Motherline

We must be willing to suffer our mothers within us, to see to the roots of their behavior within us, and to forgive and transform it in ourselves.

—Marion Woodman & Connie Zweig
To Be a Woman

Having a child is a fast road into the heart of the world.

—Regina Sara Ryan
The Woman Awake

The mother's battle for her child—with sickness, with poverty, with war, with all the forces of exploitation and callousness that cheapen human life—needs to become a common human battle, waged in love and in the passion for survival.

—Adrienne Rich
Of Woman Born

Like a mother who protects her child, her only child, with her own life, one should cultivate a heart of unlimited love and compassion towards all living beings.

—Siddhartha Gautama (Buddha)

The llama is the mother of all ancestors.

—William Sullivan
The Secret of the Incas

Our mother of the growing fields, our mother of the streams, will you have pity upon us? For to whom do we belong? Whose seeds are we? To our mother alone do we belong.

—From a Kagaba myth

MOTIVATION

We must have a pure, honest and warm-hearted motivation, and on top of that, determination, optimism, hope and the ability not to be discouraged. The whole of humanity depends on this motivation.

—Dalai Lama

To the degree to which we are motivated by feelings of enthusiasm and pleasure in what we do—or even by an optimal degree of anxiety—they propel us to accomplishment.... Optimism is the great motivator.

—Daniel Goleman
Emotional Intelligence

MOUNTAIN

Keep your eye fixed on the way to the top, but don't forget to look right in front of you. The last step depends on the first. Don't think you are there just because

you see the summit. Watch your footing, be sure of the next step, but don't let that distract you from the highest goal. The first step depends on the last.

—René Daumal
Mount Analogue

The full beauty of the mountain is not seen until you too consent to the impossible paradox: it is and is not. When nothing more needs to be said, the smoke of idea clears, the mountain is SEEN.

—Thomas Merton
The Other Side of the Mountain

Here on the mountain I have spoken to you clearly.... Here on the Mountain, the air is clear and your mind is clear; as you drop down into Narnia, the air will thicken. Take great care that it does not confuse your mind.... Remember the signs and believe the signs. Nothing else matters.

—C. S. Lewis
The Silver Chair

In most mythological traditions, mountains are seen as the home of the gods. This can be understood symbolically, of course, but it is also a reality: the peaks of high mountains are antennae which put the earth in contact with Heaven.... When you climb a mountain, the higher you go the deeper the silence, and in this silence you discover the origin of all things ...

—Omraam Michaël Aïvanhov
The Path of Silence

Because Japan is a mountainous country, mountains play a vital role in shaping people's living environments. The word *oyama* sometimes means "shrine." The word was derived from *yama*, meaning "mountain." Mountains themselves were considered to be shrines which connect the earth and the sky.

—Kazuo Matsuayashi
The Power of Place

Long before men thought of conquering the mountains, the mountains had conquered man.

—Daniel L. Boorstin
The Discoverers

The Sherpas believe the Goddess doesn't tolerate anything "jiggy-jiggy" (unclean) on her mountain.... They call prayer flags *lung ta* or wind horse.

—Jon Krakauer
Into Thin Air

Thousands of tired, nerve-shaken, over-civilized people are beginning to find out that going to the mountains is going home: that wildness is a necessity; and that mountain parks and reservations are useful not only as fountains of timber and irrigating rivers, but as fountains of life.

—John Muir
National Parks of the West

The snow sprinkled over every rock and gleaming in the sun, was of a radiant beauty that touched me to the heart. I had never seen such transparency, and I was living in a world of crystal.... We were braving an interdict, overstepping a boundary, and yet we had no fears, we continued upward. I thought of the famous ladder of Saint Teresa of Avila; something clutched at my heart.

—Maurice Herzog
Annapurna

To see the greatness of a mountain, one must keep one's distance.

—Angarika Govinda

The mountains, I become part of it....
The morning mists, the clouds, the gathering waters, I become part of it ...

—Navajo chant

MUHAMMAD

Some go first and others come long afterward. God blesses both and all in the line, and replaces what has been consumed, and provides for those who work the soil of helpfulness, and blesses Muhammad and Jesus and every other messenger and prophet.

—Jalal Al-din Rumi
Mathnawi, Book IV

It was from the rock at the Temple Mount, site of the Temple of Solomon, that Muhammad had ascended into heaven. Some Muslim traditions made Jerusalem, and not Mecca, the center and the Navel of the Earth.

—Daniel J. Boorstin
The Discoverers

Muhammed said "the Angels will not enter a house in which there is a picture or a dog.

—Daniel Boorstin
The Creators

One night in 610, the Angel Gabriel came to him and said, "Read. Thou art a Messenger of Allah, and I am Gabriel."...

Mohammed wrote nothing, but his followers wrote 114 sacred recitations or *suras* on scraps of parchment, leather, palm leaves, and on the flat shoulder blades of dead camels. Who knew what order they should be in? So, they decided to put them in order from longest to shortest.... In the Prophet's time, men and women prayed together in the mosque.... In early years both men and women were literate; by 750 women were denied education.

—Leonard Shlain
The Alphabet Versus the Goddess

Muhammed was an illiterate business man who ritually retired to a cave outside Mecca for prayer and fasting.... The Q'uran was revealed to Muhammad verse by verse over the next 21 years.... Muhammad's first biography was written 100 years after the events they portray.

—Jack Nelson-Pallmeyer
Is Religion Killing Us?

Mohammed's followers were called a "People of Sacred Direction."

—Kanan Makiya
The Rock

MUSIC

The Ancient wrapped the whole world in a web of song.

—Bruce Chatwin
Songlines

Necessity holds on her knees the spindle around which the circles of the world turn: a siren is seated on each of these circles; each sings a note and these notes form the most perfect harmonies. This is the music of the world heard by souls before they descend into bodies.... Musical instruments and voices are only a distant echo of the sublime music of creation.

—Plato (Aristocles)
Republic

... through musical sounds we can waken what is dormant, through sweet harmonies calm what is turbulent, and through the blending of various elements quell the discord and temper the different parts of the soul.

—Marsilio Ficino & Thomas Moore
The Planets Within

Though people today no longer know why, the mysteries refer to the existence of two kinds of cognition, ordinary bodily, intellectual cognition and spiritual cognition, which is in fact, a musical cognition, a cognition living in the musical element.

—Rudolf Steiner
The Inner Nature of Music and the Experience of Tone

Before we make music, music makes us.... Music's deep structure is identical with the deep structure of all things.

—George Leonard
The Silent Pulse

... and they sang before him and he was glad. But for a long while they sang only each alone, or but few together, while the rest harkened; for each comprehended only that part of the mind of Ilúvatar from which he came.... And as they looked and wondered this world began to unfold its history, and it seemed to them that I lived and grew … "Behold your music! This is your minstrelsy…"

—J. R. R. Tolkien
Silmarillion

Next I saw the most lucid air, in which I heard … in a marvelous way many kinds of musicians praising the joys of the heavenly citizens.… And their sound was like the voice of a multitude, making music in harmony.

—Hildegard of Bingen
Scivias

All that takes place in nature is permeated with a mysterious music which is the earthly projection of the music of the spheres. In every plant and in every animal there is really incorporated a tone of the music of the spheres.

—Rudolf Steiner

Music is a moral law. It gives a soul to the universe, wings to the mind, flight to the imagination, a charm to sadness, gaiety and life to everything. It is the essence of order, and leads to all that is good and just and beautiful.

—Plato (Aristocles)

Without music life would be a mistake.

—Friedrich Nietzsche

Music is a memory bank for finding one's way about the world.

—Bruce Chatwin
Songlines

All one's life is music, if one touches the notes rightly and in time.

—John Ruskin

Music and rhythm find their way into the secret places of the soul.… Musical innovation is full of danger to the state, for when modes of music change, the laws of the state always change with them.

—Plato (Aristocles)

The Division and Quavering, which please us so much in Musick, have an agreement with the Glittering of Light; As the Moonbeames playing upon a Wave.

—Francis Bacon

For Einstein, music was an expression of religious feeling. He got his theory of relativity by playing the piano and making notes—then secluding himself upstairs for two weeks. His aim was "to obtain a formula that will account in one breath for Newton's falling apple, the transmission of light and radio waves, the stars and the composition of matter."

—Max Jammer
Einstein and Religion

The diminished 5th was outlawed in the Middle Ages. It was called *diabolus musicus*.

—Noel Cobb
Archetypal Imagination

Pythagoras used music to purge the soul … he observed the harmonic intervals in a smithy.

—John Burnett
Early Greek Philosophy

Music attracts the angels in the universe.

—Bob Dylan

The music of this opera
(*Madame Butterfly*) was dictated to me
by God. I was merely instrumental in
getting it on paper and communicating
it to the public.

—Giacomo Puccini

Music is a higher revelation than all
wisdom and philosophy, it is the wine
of a new procreation, and I am Bacchus
who presses out this glorious wine for
men and makes them drunk with delight.

—Ludwig van Beethoven

My idea is that there is music in the air,
music all around us, the world is full
of it and you simply take as much as
you require.

—Edward Elgar

I've listened with intense emotion to the
waves of the sea, to the mountain torrents
and waterfalls, and to all the sound made
by water and wind. And I would add that
I make no distinction between noise and
sound, for me, all this represents music.

—Olivier Messiaen
Conversations with Olivier Messiaen

I play the notes in order, as they are
written. It is God who makes the music.

—Johan Sebastian Bach

Music is the stuff between the notes.

—Claude Debussy

Whence and how these come I know not
nor can I force them.... Nor do I hear in
my imagination the parts successively,
but I hear them *"gleich alles zusammen"*
(at the same time all together.)

—Wolfgang Amadeus Mozart

The Church knew what the psalmist
knew: Music praises God. Music is well
or better able to praise him than the
building of the church and all its decoration; it is the Church's greatest ornament.

—Igor Stravinsky
Conversations with Igor Stravinsky

Straightaway the ideas flow in upon me,
directly from God.

—Johannes Brahms

Music is the outflow of the human mind.

—Robert Schumann

The aim and final reason of all music
should be nothing else but the Glory of
God and the refreshment of the spirit.

—Johan Sebastian Bach

The blues is an impulse to keep the
painful details and episodes of a brutal
experience alive in one's aching consciousness, to finger its jagged grain, and
to transcend it, not by the consolation
of philosophy but by squeezing from it a
near tragic, near comic lyricism.

—Ralph Ellison
Shadow and Art

Playing the blues was a way of exorcising the specter of random force, turning cosmic uncertainty into a song.

—Jackson Lears
Something for Nothing

A symphony is both richly structured and ever fresh. At every instant there is an interplay between the order of the piece and its unfoldment to the listener.

—F. David Peat
The Philosopher's Stone

He was a harp; all life that he had known and that was his consciousness was the strings; and the flood of music was a wind that poured against those strings and set them vibrating with memories and dreams.

—Morgan Llywelyn
Bard

You play Bach your way, and I'll play him his way.

—Wanda Landowska

Hitler saw *Die Meistersinger* over 100 times.

—Christopher Nugent
Masks of Satan

Music helps you feel your feelings, and words help you think your thoughts, but a song helps you feel a thought.

—"The Lemon-drop Kid"

We have fallen into the place where everything is music.

—Jalal Al-din Rumi
Where Everything Is Music

MYSTERY

Mystery is not a vague unknown; it is a specific unknowable.

—Thomas Moore
The Re-Enchantment of Everyday Life

I was suddenly made aware of another world of beauty and mystery such as I had never imagined to exist, except in poetry. It was as though I had begun to see and smell and hear for the first time.... I experienced an overwhelming emotion in the presence of nature, especially at evening. It began to have a kind of sacramental character for me.... I felt again the presence of an almost unfathomable mystery. The song of the birds, the shape of the trees, the colors of the sunset, were so many signs of this presence, which seemed to be drawing me to itself.

—Bede Griffiths
Return to the Center

The root meaning of the word "mystery" is to shut one's eyes and ears. Mystery is silence, darkness. Rilke speaks in his *Book of Hours* of turning inward, of looking deep into himself, and he reports what he finds: "My God is dark." He sees a thousand theologians plunging like divers into the night of God's name.

—David Steindl-Rast
The Music of Silence

Christianity stripped its world of magic and mystery, and of the possibility of spiritual renewal through itself.... It had rendered its people alienated sojourners in a spiritually barren world where the only outlet for the urge of life was the restless drive onward.

—Frederick Turner

The most beautiful experience we can have is the mysterious. It is the fundamental emotion which stands at the cradle of true art and true science.

—Albert Einstein
The World As I See It

Mystery is that which shows itself and at the same time withdraws.

—Martin Heidegger

I think there is nothing in the world but mystery.

—Kenneth Patchen
I Always Return to This Place

One cannot speak about mystery. One must be seized by it.

—René Magritte

We are ourselves paradox, mystery, born and being born out of Mystery Itself.

—Mary E. Giles
The Feminist Mystic

Life comes to me as a series of encounters with Mystery.

—Martin Bell
Return of the Wolf

Those who are willing to be vulnerable move among mysteries.

—Theodore Roethke

I want to be with those who know secret things, or else alone.

—Rainer Maria Rilke

A religious imagination that satisfies intelligence and inspires with honesty can give a person confidence and stability, but only if a degree of mystery is allowed.

—Thomas Moore
The Soul's Religion

Mystery wriggles its way through the intricacies of wonder and confusion.

—Diarmuid Ó Murchú

Mystery is truth's dancing partner.

—Johann Wolfgang von Goethe

MYSTICS/MYSTICISM

When we are touched by mystic grace and allow ourselves to enter its field without fear, we see that we are all parts of a whole, elements of an universal harmony, unique, essential and sacred notes in a divine music that everyone and everything is playing together with us in God and for God.

—Andrew Harvey,
The Essential Mystics

Our aim as mystics is to bring about a balance in our thoughts and emotions, to calm the waters and polish the mirrors so that they will reflect our true self more clearly. The ultimate goal is to break the mirrors that distort it and balance the triangle … each side represents one of the three attributes of the Absolute, total wisdom, total power, and total goodness.

—Kyriacos C. Markides
Homage to the Sun

The mystic in every one of us trusts his or her experience of the divine in nature, which opens our hearts. And when our hearts are open, the divine comes through. This trust of our experience is the basis of all mysticism.

—Matthew Fox
"Creation Spirituality," *Only Connect*

Mysticism is frequently undermined by the dominant forces within established religions. Exclusivity, hierarchy, competition, the conquering hero, and especially fundamentalism do not mix well with the inner path. Mystics have always maintained that all religions and their myths are only partial visions of the truth … when mystics of various traditions are placed in a room together, there is little or no disagreement.

—David Leeming
Myth: A Biography of Belief

Mystical vision is seeing how extraordinary the ordinary is.

—James P. Carse
Breakfast at the Victory: The Mysticism of Ordinary Experience

Mystics and saints maintain a consciousness about the presence of God within themselves and others. They aim to practice this mindfulness at every moment—at prayer, at work, when dealing with each other.

—Caroline Myss
Invisible Acts of Power

A mystic knows without knowledge, without intuition or information, without contemplation or description or revelation.

—Attar

The mystic's words appear in a hundred different forms, but if God is one and the Way is one, how can their words be other than one? They do appear in different guises, but in substance they are one. Variety occurs in form; in substance all is unified.

—Jalal Al-din Rumi

What we call mystical experience occurs when there is a sense of oneness or harmony between the energy or power of our bodies, minds, and spirits and the energy of other beings and the universe itself.

—John E. Mack

A mystical experience is not a satisfying one. It is burning. It is a ride on the tail of a comet, freezing, searing…. In this rare, almost unbreathable atmosphere, sunside and nightside are resolved in paradox, and the incomprehensible is yet in some measure comprehended in contradiction.

—Madeleine L'Engle
The Irrational Season

Rather than asking who is mystical, it might be better to ask who is anti-mystical. You are anti-mystical, I propose, to the extent that you think reality has been or can be explained … by Hinduism or theosophy or Gnosticism lite or superstring theory or any other theory or theology.... Anything that helps you see—really see—the wondrousness of the world serves a mystical purpose.

—John Horgan
Rational Mysticism

Mystical experience is the mirror image of negative paranoia. It sees "the universe is a conspiracy organized for my benefit."

—Andrew Weil
The Natural Mind

Mysticism must rest on crystal clear honesty and can only come after things have been stripped down to their naked reality.

—Etty Hillesum
An Interrupted Life

Mysticism is all about interconnectivity.

—Matthew Fox
The Coming of the Cosmic Christ

We pass into mystical states out of ordinary consciousness as from a lesser into a more, as from a smallness into a vastness, and at the same time as from an unrest to a rest. We feel them as reconciling, unifying states.

—William James
Varieties of Religious Experience

We may not realize it; we may not even like it. But whether we know it or not, whether we accept it or not, mystical experience is always there, inviting us on a journey of ultimate discovery. We have been given this gift of life in this perplexing world to become who we ultimately are: creatures of boundless love, caring, compassion and wisdom. Existence is a summons to the eternal journey of the sage—the sage we all are, if only we could see.

—Wayne Teasdale

Mysticism is to our electronic society what romanticism was to the industrial society. Mysticism provides maps of consciousness for a cybernetic society in which information is more basic than objects or material things.

—William Irwin Thompson

Jean Houston warned ... mysticism begins in mist, has an I in the middle and ends with schism.

—John Horgan
Rational Mysticism

Mysticism is quite different from and far more real than your assumptions about it.

—Olga Kharitidi
Entering the Circle

I believe we become mystics by following that deep, nostalgic longing that stirs at the core of our souls. Tillich called it the reunion with the Ground of our Being.

—David N. Elkins
Beyond Religion

The heart of the mystic could encompass the divine throne and everything the throne contains a hundred million times without the mystic knower being aware of it.

—Ibn 'Arabi

Through the myths our basic psychic needs—our deepest fears and sorrows, our joys and aspirations, our drives and desires—are evoked, confronted and directed. They awaken and maintain a sense of awe and gratitude in relationship to the mystery of the universe and our human existence within it.

—Meinrad Craighead
Immanent Mother

If the cask is to hold the wine, its water must first be poured out.

—Meister Eckhart

MYTH/MYTHOLOGY

There was a myth before the myth began.

—Wallace Stevens

The first function of a mythology is to waken and maintain in the individual a sense of wonder and participation in the mystery of this finally inscrutable universe, whether understood in Michelangelo's way as an effect of the will of an anthropomorphic creator, or in the way of our modern physical scientists—and of many of the leading Oriental religious and philosophical systems—as the continuously created dynamic display of an absolutely transcendent, yet universally immanent, *mysterium tremendum et fascinans*, which is the ground at once of the whole spectacle and of oneself.

—Joseph Campbell
The Way of the Animal Powers, Vol. 1

We can only understand myths and legends when we grasp them as images of a real knowledge of the spiritual world.

—Rudolf Steiner
Paths of Experience

Each of us has a well of images within, which are the saving reality and from which may be born the individual myth carrying the meaning of a life.... But any truly valid "new myth" cannot be rationally invented. It must be born out of the crucible of our own struggles and suffering ...

—Helen M. Luke
The Way of Woman

... it is the artist who brings the images of a mythology to manifestation, and without images (whether mental or visual) there is no mythology.

—Joseph Campbell

Myth is not exactly the same as mythology. Mythology is a collection of stories that range far beyond the limitations of nature and the personal details of human life.

—Thomas Moore
The Re-Enchantment of Everyday Life

Myths are the instruments by which we continually struggle to make our experience intelligible to ourselves.

—Mark Schorer & William C. Doty
The Study of Myths and Rituals

Myths are not only mirrors, but corridors of mirrors. When we enter them, they become systems of thought branching towards the outer world and tunnels of enlightenment rooting towards the unconscious soul. We have constructed them to lead us back and forth from dream to vigil and from sensation to experience, and if we willfully abandon them, we will be left, in the full meaning of the word, senseless.

—Alberto Manguel
God in All Worlds, ed. Lucinda Vardey

The relegation of myth and fairy tale to childhood is a recent phenomenon. Before the twentieth century, myths and fairy tales were the repository of the wisdom of a whole culture.

—Robert A. Johnson
Ecstasy

How should we be able to forget those ancient myths that are at the beginning of all peoples, the myths about dragons that at the last moment turn into princesses.... Perhaps everything terrible is in its deepest being something helpless that wants help from us.

—Rainer Maria Rilke
Letters to a Young Poet

I believe that any event from a person's past immediately becomes a myth, a personal story.

—David Chethlahe Paladin

Myth is not history. It is not truth. And yet it points to truths far beyond historical "fact."

—Sig Lonegren
Labyrinths

Myth ... in its living primitive form, is not merely a story told but a reality lived. It is not of the nature of fiction ... but it is a living reality, believed to have once happened in primaeval times, and continuing ever since to influence the world and human destinies.

—Bronislaw Kasper Malinowski
Myth in Primitive Psychology

Truth happens in myths.

—Madeleine L'Engle
The Summer of the Great Grandmother

Gaps that cannot be closed by perception and reason are closed by magic and myth.

—Walker Percy
The Message in the Bottle

When a myth is shared by large numbers of people, it becomes reality.

—Lawrence Blair
Rhythms of Vision

Myth is the secret opening through which the inexhaustible energies of the cosmos pour into human cultural manifestation.

—James Campbell
The Hero with a Thousand Faces

Myths are the most powerful forces in the universe. We can be imprisoned by them, crippled by them; we can also be liberated and empowered by them. Myths tell us truths about our own experience; they mirror our personal story.

—Madonna Kolbenschlag
Lost in the Land of Oz

Myths are myths only because people into whose hands they pass fail to understand them.

—James Churchward

Myth comes in the same zone as dream, and this is the zone of what I could call the Wisdom Body.

—Joseph Campbell
Transformations of Myth through Time

Myths of the heroes speak most eloquently of men's quest to choose life over death.

—Dorothy Norman
The Hero

Any myth performance takes place in a context that shapes what is being conveyed. ... Myths open toward the future rather than a fossilized fable.

—William G. Doty
Mythography

Our myths may be misguided, but they steer however shakily towards the true harbour.... Myth is the isthmus which connects the peninsular world of thought with the vast continent we really belong to.

—C. S. Lewis

Myth is nothing but the reflection of higher truth.

—Plutarch

Humans without myths are not human.

—Kurt Hoffman
The Reality of Myth

That which never happened is eternally true.

—Julian the Apostate

Tolkien believed that he had not devised his magnificent mythical world so much as he had found it—indeed, that it had been revealed to him by God.

—Ralph C. Wood
The Gospel According to Tolkien

A seven-book format creates a magical setting. Like Dickens, she publishes work while writing Love and Death themes.... The Inklings and Rowling understand and embrace the fact that their "sub-creation" worlds serve a mythological function in a profane culture ... alchemical work is essentially spiritual.

—John Granger
The Hidden Key to Harry Potter

One cannot predict the next mythology any more than one can predict tonight's dream.

—Joseph Campbell

We have lost our immediate feeling for the great realities of the spirit and to this world all true mythology belongs.

—Carl Kerényi

Orpheus is myth looking at itself.... Orpheus is that which deepens imagination by imagining always greater depths to be ensouled.

—Noel Cobb
Archetypal Imagination

The oldest Orpheus tale was probably the
narrative of a shaman's ecstatic journey to
the land of the dead to fetch the soul of a
seriously ill person.

—Robert Ryan
The Strong Eye of Shamanism

Myth vibrates in the middle of a string
pulled taut between the personal and
the abstract.

—Wendy Doniger
The Implied Spider

Myths, like words and sentences, exist as
ends in themselves and it makes no more
sense to ask for the purpose of a language
and mythology than it makes to ask for
the purpose of trees.

—Peter Munz
When the Golden Bough Breaks

Myth is always about soul making.

—Jean Houston
The Passion of Isis and Osiris

Unfold your own myth.

—Jalal al-din Rumi

NAME

Before there were the heavens and the
earth, there was the unnameable.
Naming was the mother of the ten
thousand things.

—Lao Tsu

Each of us has a divine name. Each time
we "wrestle with God" our divine name is
up for reconsideration.

—Gail Sher
The Intuitive Writer

In Wales ... there are five hundred place
names that begin with the preface "llan"
meaning enclosure, holy place, or church,
and ending with a storied description
of the site. The longest of these is the
village of Llanfairpwllgwyngyllgogery-
chwyrndrobwllllantysiliogogogoch on
the island of Anglesei in Northern Wales.
Commonly referred to as "Llanfair P. G.,"
the fifty-eight-letter name refers to "The
Church of St. Mary's by the Pool near the
White Hazel Trees beside the Whirlpool
Rapids and the Church of St.Tysilio near
the Red Caves."

—Belden C. Lane
Landscapes of the Sacred

The Zulus gave Helen Keller the name Homvuselelo, "You have aroused the consciences of many."

—Joseph P. Lash
Helen and Teacher

The ancient Egyptians went to great lengths to safeguard a person's name, for it was a widespread belief that unless the name was preserved, one would cease to exist.

—Murry Hope
Ancient Egypt

It is said a child cries at birth because he is demanding a name. A name is tried out as the baby is being delivered. If the child comes quickly, that name may be the final choice.

—Jean Malaurie
The Last Kings of Thule

A man's life proceeds from his name in the way that a river proceeds from its source.

—N. Scott Momaday
The Names

NATURE

Nature never makes haste; her systems revolve at an even pace. The buds swell imperceptibly, without hurry or confusion, as though the short spring days were an eternity. Why, then, should man hasten as if anything less than eternity were allotted for the least deed.

—Henry David Thoreau &
Arthur G. Volkman
Thoreau on Man and Nature

The Lakota was a true naturalist—a lover of nature. He loved the earth and all things of the earth, the attachment growing with age. The old people came literally to love the soil and they sat or reclined on the ground with a feeling of being close to a mothering power. It was good for the skin to touch the earth and the old people liked to remove their moccasins and walk with bare feet on the sacred earth.

—Luther Standing Bear
quoted by T. C. McLuhan
Touch the Earth

Nature doesn't move in a straight line, and as part of nature, neither do we.

—Gloria Steinem
Revolution from Within

Handle even a single leaf of a green in such a way that it manifests the body of the Buddha.

—Dogen
From the Zen Kitchen to Enlightenment

Because we all share this small planet Earth, we have to learn to live in harmony and peace with each other and with nature. That is not just a dream, but a necessity.

—Dalai Lama in his acceptance speech
for the Nobel Peace Prize

To the dull mind nature is leaden. To the illumined mind the whole world burns and sparkles with light.

—Ralph Waldo Emerson

Yeast cannot be found on the grapes during winter, spring and early summer, but it's extremely abundant on the grapes at the time when they ripen, ready to initiate fermentation as soon as grape juice has been loaded into the vats.

—René Dubos
A God Within

As mind slowly empties itself, nature undresses herself.

—Christopher M. Bache
Dark Night, Early Dawn

Nature is but one, true, plain, perfect, and entire in its own being, which God made from the beginning, placing his spirit in it.

—Michael Sendivogius
New Light of Alchymy

Those who take for their standard anything but Nature, the mistress of all masters, weary themselves in vain.

—Leonardo da Vinci
Notebooks

In the fire of creation, gold does not vanish; the fire brightens. Each creature God made must live in its own true nature; how could I resist my nature, that lives for oneness with God?

—Mechtild of Magdeburg

The mystic chords of memory, stretching from every battlefield and patriot grave to every living heart and hearthstone all over this broad land, will yet swell the chorus of the Union when again touched, as surely they will be, by the better angels of our nature.

—Abraham Lincoln
First Inaugural Address

Nature is part of our humanity, and without some awareness and experience of that divine mystery man ceases to be man. When Pleiades and the wind in the grass are no longer a part of the human spirit, a part of the very flesh and bone, man becomes, as it were, a kind of cosmic outlaw, having neither the completeness and integrity of the animal nor the birthright of a true humanity.

—Henry Beston
The Outermost House

Nature is a theatre for the interrelations of activities. All things change, the activities and their interrelations ... in the modern concept ... there is no possibility of a detached, self-contained existence.

—Alfred North Whitehead
Nature and Life

The strange and paradoxical rule of nature is that we are fullest in our being by forgetting our being. To love nothing is to be nothing, to give is to have.

—Peter J. Kreeft
Heaven, the Heart's Deepest Longing

A river meanders with a certain characteristic kind of bend, a wide curve, and the curves are spaced at about ten times the width of the river. A tree branches in such a manner that the flow of sap does the least work.

—Christopher Alexander
The Process of Creating Life

All nature has meaning, all movement has purpose, even if we are not wise enough to comprehend it.

—Victor Mansfield
Synchronicity, Science and Soulmaking

Nature be your guide; follow her with your art willingly.... Literature be your lamp, shining in the darkness.

—Michael Maier
Atalanta Fugiens

Nature loves to hide.

—Heraclitus of Ephesus

The smallest thing in nature is an entire world.

—Joan Miró

The Mikmaq on the Atlantic coast have no sound for Nature. They have "space" or "place of creation" ... they have cultural literacy with the ecosystem ... every aspect of nature to Mikmaqs is Mintu. They live in harmony with these intelligible essences.... The Mikmaq can perceive the web.

—Marie Battiste
Reclaiming Indigenous Voice and Vision

To understand that humanity is on a collision course with the Laws of nature, is to be stuck in what I call Cassandra's Dilemma.... Growth must end; development must be re-invented.... Earth is a closed system. There are limits to growth, but there are no limits to development.

—Alan Atkisson
Believing Cassandra

The major problems in the world are the result of the difference between the way nature works and the way people think.

—Gregory Bateson

Human beings have a hard time getting nature's messages because of a force field called "Somebody Else's Problem."

—Alan Atkisson
Believing Cassandra

Nature seems to be running a fever. We are the flu.

—William Ruckleshaus

Blue-green algae off the Australian coast is believed to be one of the oldest organisms on earth: 3.56 billion years old.

—George Johnson
Fire in the Mind

Opossums have existed for 60 million years; whales for 12 million... The monarch butterfly with a brain the size of a few grains of sand can navigate 2500 miles.

—Gregg Easterbrook
A Moment on the Earth

If you kill the crows, you'd have to take care of the roadkill yourselves. Let crows be crows.

—Daniel Quinn
My Ishmael

If you kill off the prairie dogs, there will be no one to cry for rain.

—Navajo warning

She is casting rain.

—Welsh proverb

NEGATIVITY

Negative connotations are: anything secret, hidden, dark; the abyss, the world of the dead, anything that devours, seduces, and poisons, that is terrifying and inescapable like fate.

—Carl G. Jung

No one is helpless against the negative intentions of others. Methods of protection are real, powerful, and freely available.

—Larry Dossey
Be Careful of What You Pray for, You Just Might Get It

Negative emotions are contagious.

—Beryl Pogson
The Work Life

NEIGHBOR

Who is my neighbor? To whom am I bound? Who must I love? These are not intelligent questions, and they do not have clear answers. On the contrary, any attempt to answer them involves us in endless subtleties, and vagueness, and ultimate confusion. Love is not limited by classifications.

—Thomas Merton
A Thomas Merton Reader

Your neighbor is your other self dwelling behind a wall. In understanding, all walls shall fall down. Who knows but that your neighbor is your better self wearing another body?

—Kahlil Gibran

If your neighbor says or does something that bothers you, that person should be the first to know. Then he or she can explain or apologize.... Jesus says, give your neighbor a second chance.... If your neighbor won't listen to you after you've spoken to him privately and then come with witnesses, there is no alternative but to make it public—not by noising the wrong all over the neighborhood, but by speaking to the authorities.

—James A. Nestingen &
Gerhard O. Forde
Free to Be

NIRVANA

According to Buddha, nirvana cannot be explained, but has to be experienced. He described it in negative terms, such as being not-born, not-made, not-conditioned ... coolness after fever and escape to a refuge.... Nirvana is antithetical to *atman*, it is a not-self.

—Bruno Borchert
Mysticism

To him [Schopenhauer] Nirvana represented the subjugation of will. Life—the manifestation of the blind will to live—he viewed as a misfortune, claiming that the true philosopher was one who, recognizing the wisdom of death, resisted the inherent urge to reproduce its kind.

—Manly P. Hall
The Secret Teachings of All Ages

Nirvana, the Kingdom of Heaven, is
available here and now.

—Thich Nhat Hanh
Living Buddha, Living Christ

NUMBERS

The world is built upon the power
of numbers.

—Pythagoras

Undoubtedly the names given by the
Pythagoreans to the different numbers
were themselves enigmatical and
symbolic—and there is little doubt that in
the time of Plutarch the meanings these
names concealed were lost. Pythagoras
had succeeded too well in concealing his
symbols with a veil that was from the first
impenetrable, without his oral explanation.

—Albert Pike
*Symbolism for the 32nd
and 33rd Degrees*

For nearly 2500 years philosophers of all
nations have attempted to unravel the
Pythagorean skein.

—Manly P. Hall
The Secret Teachings of All Ages

Everything in the universe is in
numerical harmony.

—Rudolf Steiner
Man: Hieroglyph of the Universe

Numbers do not win arguments. To work
effectively with people you must listen
and speak to their underlying concerns.

—John Whiteside & Sandra Egli
Flight of the Phoenix

... the task of future mathematicians will
be to collect their characteristics and
analyze, when possible, every number in
its logical relationship to all others.

—Marie-Louise von Franz
Number and Time

Innumeracy is as appalling as illiteracy ...
people's minds go blank when they hear
"illions." All big numbers are the same
to them ... such an inability to relate to
large numbers is clearly bad for society. It
leads people to ignore big issues.

—Douglas R. Hofstadter
Metamagical Themas

[For the people in 10th century Basra]
numerology was a way to understand
the principle of unity that underlies
everything. It is a science that is above
nature and yet is the root of all other
sciences. The Pure Being (One) is related
to all other numbers.

—Anne Marie Schimmel,
The Mystery of Numbers

The philosophers perceived that number,
being perfectly abstract, can therefore
be shared by all three worlds: Physical,
spiritual and mystical. Beautiful patterns
of spiritual thought are elaborated by the
adepts in symbolic numerical studies—
patterns which give pure joy because they
are entirely uncontaminated by mundane
or temporal things. The philosophers con-

sidered that the beauty, order and stability of the universe depended on number.

—Kenneth John Conant
*Carolingian and
Romanesque Architecture*

Numbers are the manifestations of beings.

—F. David Peat
Lighting the Seventh Fire

in balance and the spiritual dimension of life seems to predominate consciousness, which results in magic and beauty everywhere. A Jungian analyst might use the term "numinous" to describe the same state of mind.

—James A. Swan
The Power of Place

NUMINOSITY

In Jung's thinking, the activation or awakening of an archetype releases a great deal of power, analogous to splitting the atom.... The power that is released is felt as numinosity—literally a sense of the divine or cosmic.

—Allan Combs & Mark Holland
Synchronicity

Numinosity comes from a profound meeting between a person's subjective feeling response to an image and the cumulative historical energy adhering to that image.

—Patricia Reis
Through the Goddess

The concept of the numinous is an attempt to grasp and define a primordial experience ... the feeling of religious awe, the "pious shiver."

—Jean Gebser
The Ever-Present Origin

The Salish tribe of the Pacific Northwest has a term *skalalitude*, which refers to a sacred state of mind when all things are

ONENESS

There is one common flow, one common
breathing, all things are in sympathy.

—Hippocrates

When will we once again be one? Perhaps
galaxy by galaxy, solar system by solar
system, planet by planet, all creation
must be redeemed. Where were we when
the morning stars sang together, and all
the sons of God shouted for joy?

—Madeleine L'Engle
The Irrational Season

I am neither Christian, Jew, Zoroastrian,
nor Muslim; I am neither of the East nor
of the West, nor of the land nor of the
sea.... Putting aside duality, I have seen
that this world and the next are one. I seek
the One, I know the One, I see the One, I
invoke the One. Allah is the First and the
Last, the Outward and the Inward.

—Jalal Al-din Rumi

I don't divide things into categories.
I don't believe that if you write about
religion you can't write political poems,
or that you can write love poems but you
can't write God poems.

—Marge Piercy *&* Bill Moyers
Fooling With Words

We have come to the place where we must decide either to live as one people, or perish as fragments.

—Wendell Berry
The Hidden Wound

It was a morning in early summer. A silver haze shimmered and trembled over the lime trees. The air was laden with their fragrance. The temperature was like a caress. I remember—I need not recall—that I climbed up a tree stump and felt suddenly immersed in Itness. I did not call it by that name. I had no need for words. It and I were one.

—Bernard Berenson
Sketch for a Self-Portrait

Namaste: I honor the place in you where the entire universe resides. I honor the place in you where, if you are at that place in you and I am at that place in me, there is only one of us. When we experience our Oneness, our total connectedness with all beings, we shall be at peace within our own hearts.

—Danaan Parry & Lisa Forest
The Earth Steward's Handbook

Virtually everything we see and touch and feel is made up of collections of particles that have been involved in interactions with other particles right back through time, to the Big Bang in which the universe as we know it came into being.... Indeed the particles that make up my body once jostled in close proximity and interacted with the particles that make up your body. We are ... parts of the same system.

—John Gribbin
In Search of Schrodinger's Cat

There was once a nun who came to visit Abba Anthony, one of the most celebrated of desert fathers. When a young monk noticed her among the assembled brothers, he was deeply shocked, and demanded to know why a woman was allowed in their remote desert monastery. Abba Anthony answered: Look well among all us monks assembled here, and you will see only one human being—her.

—Jean-Yves LeLoup
The Gospel of Mary Magdalene

In the mystical oneness of everything, even the dissonances are absorbed and heard as something else.

—John Killinger
God, the Devil and Harry Potter

We live in the currents of universal reciprocity.

—Martin Buber

An entire ecosystem can exist in the plumage of a bird.

—Edward. O. Wilson

It's all one seal.

—Eskimo proverb

The sky is the same color wherever you go.

—Arab proverb

ORDER/DISORDER

Every living being, from the smallest bacterium to a blue whale, is a highly ordered collection of energy and matter.

Over time, individual living systems not only retain a high degree of internal organization, they build up this order as they grow and develop. Life appears to move toward increasing order rather than disorder.

—Peter Russell
The Global Brain Awakens

All things, among themselves, possess an order; and this order is the form that makes the universe like God.

—Dante Alighieri

Most of our experience is in the implicate order, but we've been taught not to value it. We value outward order—the explicate.

—David Bohm
On Dialogue

Because the whole is enfolded in each part, so are all other parts, in some way and to some degree.... The more fundamental truth is the truth of internal relatedness—the implicate order ... in this order the whole and hence all the other parts are enfolded in each part.

—David Bohm
Postmodern Science and a Postmodern World

David Bohm: the implicate order is in the first instance a language. It's not a description of reality but ... an inner language. It's more like music.... It's like a painting, but when you step back to see the picture, there is no correspondence between the spots of paint and what you see in the picture. Similarly, the implicate order and its mathematics does not directly come to describe a sort of correspondence with reality. It is simply a language. This language is referring to something that cannot be stated.

—Joseph Jaworski
Synchronicity

The Timeless Way is a process which brings order out of nothing but ourselves; it cannot be attained, but it will happen of its own accord, if we will only let it.

—Christopher Alexander
The Timeless Way of Building

Since there are more ways for disorder to occur than order, the tendency is to move toward disorder.

—Murray Gell-Mann
Quark and the Jaguar

The world is not to be put in order; the world is order incarnate. It is for us to harmonize with this order.

—Henry Miller

To restore order means to liberate oneself from the spell of what seems, and to come back to what is.

—Henri Tracol

Everything that is beautiful is orderly, and there can be no order unless things are in their right relation to each other. Of this right relation throughout the world beauty is born.

—Robert Henri

ORDINARY

The ordinary is the extraordinary.

—Wang Ziang-Zhai

The miracle is not to walk on water, but to walk on land.

—Thich Nhat Hanh

Writers like Wendell Berry, Annie Dillard, and Lewis Thomas all speak of the most ordinary things, yet find in a weasel's stare, a swollen river, a snail's strange life something far more than ordinary.... Whence comes that double magic of recognizing the ordinary as extraordinary and the extraordinary as ordinary?

—Belden C. Lane
Landscapes of the Sacred

It is the everyday things that give life its stability and its framework.

—Sue Bender
Plain and Simple

Jars, apples, hillsides and rocks are quite as much a part of God's creation as angels; and since physical objects are right in front of us, God must have wanted us to take notice.

—Jane Roberts
The World View of Paul Cézanne

Mircea Eliade notes that the most primitive of all sacred places known in the history of religions is the archetypal, simple landscape of stones, water and trees.

—Belden C. Lane
Landscapes of the Sacred

If we had taken a keen vision of all ordinary human life, it would be like hearing the grass grow or the squirrel's heart beat, and we should die of the roar which lies on the other side of silence. As it is, the quickest of us walk about well-wadded with stupidity.

—George Eliot

I long to accomplish a great and noble task, but it is my chief duty to accomplish small tasks as if they were great and noble.

—Helen Keller

Raise the stone and thou shalt find me. Cleave the wood and I am there.

—Oxyrhynchus Papyri

PAIN

When we experience pain our first
instinct is to flee. But pain is real and
demands our deepest compassion and
understanding. Therefore, we should
not respond by fleeing to another world,
but by exploring our own world more
deeply and discovering what the pain
may signal.

—Carol Ochs
Women and Spirituality

I learned that the best way to manage
some kinds of painful thoughts, is to dare
them to do their worse, to let them lie
and gnaw at your heart till they are tired,
and you find you still have a residue of
life they cannot kill.

—George MacDonald
Phantastes

Pain is inevitable. Suffering is optional.

—Susun Weed
Healing Wise

God whispers to us in our pleasures,
speaks in our conscience, but shouts in
our pains: it is His megaphone to rouse a
deaf world.

—C. S. Lewis
The Problem of Pain

Pain and suffering can sometimes be so great in us that the only name for them is no name—thus, nothingness. Pain and suffering can be so great that they are, like God, ineffable. Pain can be so deep, so dark, so silent, so untouchable, and so unresolvable that it can appropriately be called nothing.

—Matthew Fox
Original Blessing

We cause pain for others by our apathetic response to life.

—Barbara Hand Clow
Eye of the Centaur

The avoidance of pain—psychic or physical—is a dangerous mechanism which can cause us to lose touch … with ourselves.

—Adrienne Rich
Of Woman Born

We Japanese have a different philosophy about pain than you Americans. You Americans are accustomed to taking a pill to make the slightest pain go away. We believe that life itself is full of pain, and unless you learn to accept a certain amount of it and cope with it, you exist only at the edge of life.

—Philip Kapleau
The Wheel of Life and Death

Go with the pain, let it take you … it comes in waves like a tide and you must be open as a vessel lying on the beach letting it fill you up and then, retreating, leaving you empty and clear.

—Anne Morrow Lindbergh
War Without and War Within

Only at quite rare moments have I felt really glad to be alive. I could not but feel with a sympathy full of regret all the pain that I saw around me, not only that of men but of the whole creation.

—Albert Schweitzer

Pain signals can be turned on or off … certain drugs like morphine can block pain … our own chemicals called endorphins can mimic morphine. The person's beliefs and expectations can release them. Belief, expectation and desire activate brain circuits.

—Jerome Groopman
The Anatomy of Hope

Even in our sleep, pain that we cannot forget fades drop by drop upon the heart, and in our own despair, against our will, comes wisdom to us by the awful grace of God.

—Aeschylus
Oresteia

Pain gives of its healing power where we least expect it.

—Martin Heidegger

There is no coming to life without pain.

—Carl G. Jung

PAINTING

Something sacred, that's it. We ought to be able to say that word … with its capacity for power, because it is "touched by God." But people would put a wrong interpretation on it. And yet it's the nearest we can get to the truth.... Painting is stronger than I am. It makes me do what it wants. At the start of my work there is someone who works with me.

—Pablo Picasso

All paintings are religious paintings, created out of the mystery of existence, giving evidence for the unseen Creator of the world, just as the painting gives evidence for the artist even when he is not physically present ... the artist's painting is his religion.

—Jane Roberts
The World View of Paul Cézanne

Approach a great painting as you would a great prince. In order to understand a masterpiece, you must lay yourself low before it and await with bated breath its least utterance.

—Kakuzo Okakura
The Book of Tea

In one domain Monet's *Waterlilies* is an assemblage of brushstrokes of oil paint on canvas. In another it is a magnificent painting. Neither domain is more real than the other. Counting the brushstrokes is a perfectly useful activity for certain purposes; so is enjoying the painting for others.

—Lawrence Leshan & Henry Margenau
Einstein's Space & Van Gogh's Sky

What the painter inquires into is not the nature of the physical world, but the nature of our reactions to it.

—E. H. Gombrich
Art and Illusion

J. M. W. Turner would strap himself to the mast of a boat and be transported into the heat of a storm at sea, which he would later paint in tumultuous heavings and sobbings of color.

—Diane Ackerman
Deep Play

You can't say Cézanne painted apples and a tablecloth and have said what Cézanne painted.

—Jean Peal Bishop

Why do you place a sofa in the middle of the jungle?
One has a right to paint one's dreams.

—Jean-Jacques Rousseau

PARADIGM

The reception of a new paradigm often necessitates a redefinition of the corresponding science. Some old problems may be relegated to another science or declared entirely "unscientific." Others that were previously non-existent or trivial may, with a new paradigm, become the very archetypes of significant scientific achievement.

—Thomas Kuhn
The Structure of Scientific Revolutions

Paradigm is the basic way of perceiving, thinking, valuing and doing associated with a particular vision of reality.

—Willis Harman

There are at least 41 different definitions of "paradigm." Not only does a paradigm have many meanings, but it may mean different things to different people. Even Thomas Kuhn, who first popularized the term in 1962, used the concept of paradigm in no less than 21 different ways ... succeeding paradigms exist as alternative realities ... a view of reality always subject to change.

—Gerald Nadler, *et al*
Creative Solution Finding

A new paradigm comes along because it solves problems ... that couldn't be solved under the old paradigm.... Create your own vision of what we might become as old paradigms slip away and new ones coalesce.

—Michael W. Munn
Beyond Business as Usual

You can't embrace the new paradigm until you let go of the old.

—Marilyn Ferguson

Paradigms and models are mummies stored in the tomb of the mind.

—Robert Rabbin
Invisible Leadership

A paradigm is a map, not the land; a menu, not the meal—a mere representation of something which it is not.

—Robert Rabbin
Invisible Leadership

Consider a new paradigm to be a new wineskin. One does not harvest a new crop of grapes, crush them, and pour them into old, dried-up wineskins. Rather, one seeks a new wineskin that is supple and soft, giving and forgiving,

flexible and eager to be made wet, one that welcomes newness and creativity.

—Matthew Fox
The Coming of the Cosmic Christ

The creative process is the paradigm for the full emotional acceptance of the reality of death, and it opens us to the concept of rebirth.

—Patricia Reis
Through the Goddess

Trying to understand what's happening using old words, old images, old paradigms is like telling time by broken clocks.

—Richard Thieme

New paradigms need new techniques, new methodologies, new examples, new injunctions and new data.

—Ken Wilber
Sex, Ecology, Spirituality

PARADISE

"Paradise" comes from ancient Iran—the "pairidaeze" or walled garden.

—Paul Devereux
Re-Visioning the Earth

Paradise, for Zen, is accessible now and here, for it is our everyday world, but perceived with the awakened eye.

—Frederick Franck
The Awakened Eye

Paradise is an image of the higher nature of the human being with nothing evil attached to it. Knowledge could be acquired only at the expense of life.

—Rudolf Steiner
The Christian Mystery

Every beloved object is the focus of a paradise.

—Novalis (Friedrich von Leopold)

What if man could re-enter paradise, so to speak, and live there both as man and spirit, whole and intact man spirit, as solid flesh as a speckled trout, a dappled thing, yet aware of itself as a self!

—Walker Percy
Love in the Ruins

We are midwives to each other. Someday we will bring each other into paradise.

—Michael Murphy
Jacob Atabet

PARADOX

A paradox refers to two statements that apparently contradict each other but are ultimately true.

—Herbert Anderson

A paradox are things stretched so far apart they don't seem to have anything to do with each other—but they have everything to do with each other. It's a teeter-totter.

—Herbert Brokering

A paradox is a truth standing on its head waving its legs to attract attention.

—G. K. Chesterton

We travel toward our destiny, like Jonah, in the belly of paradox.

—Thomas Merton
The Sign of Jonah

The more turbulent the times, the more complex the world, the more paradoxes there are.... Living with paradox is not comfortable or easy.... Paradox confuses us because things don't behave the way we expect them to behave. Paradox ... asks us to live with simultaneous opposites.

—Charles Handy
The Age of Paradox

I learned to make my mind large, as the universe is large, so that there is room for paradoxes.

—Maxine Hong Kingston
The Woman Warrior

A paradox has no discernible solution. Pay attention to it, don't try to eradicate it.

—David Bohm
On Dialogue

The cross speaks of the greatest paradox of all: That to live we have to die. To walk the way of the cross, to allow one's life to be torn by contradiction and swallowed up in paradox, is to live in the reality of resurrection, in the sign of Jonah. For the cross overcomes all contradictions. In symbol and in reality, the crossing point is the point of transformation.

—Parker Palmer
The Promise of Paradox

Paradox only exists in language. In reality, there is no paradox. When we start talking about things, paradox begins to merge. The only way to see a Koan is to be in it, and the only way to be in it, is to forget the self.

—John Daido Loori
Sacred Stories

We are ourselves paradox, mystery, born and being born out of Mystery Itself.

—Mary E. Giles
The Feminist Mystic

Myths attempt to explain paradoxes, including why properness sometimes leads to tragedy and why smartness sometimes leads to losses.

—William G. Doty
Mythography

Quantum thinking is the ability to think paradoxically. This skill enables us to transcend the bounds of binary logic and create highly innovative responses to all of life's challenges.

—Charlotte Shelton
Quantum Leaps

The paradoxical vision allows no total victories within the confines of human existence.

—Robert Benne
The Paradoxical Vision

Paradox is in the order of things. Life involves continuity and discontinuity at the same time; the way to stay together successfully demands separation.

—Herbert Anderson &
Kenneth R. Mitchell
Leaving Home

Time is everything and nothing; we are all connected and we are all alone.

—Bill Kloefkorn

The willingness to carry the paradox of well-being within distress is the ability to hold power.

—Martia Nelson
Coming Home

Nothing vast enters the life of mortals without a curse.

—Sophocles

Good and ill are one.

—Heraclitus of Ephesus

Arabic invites subtlety.... One of the words for "woman" is *hormah*, it comes from the root word for "holy, sacrosanct," and "sinful, "forbidden."

—Geraldine Brooks
Nine Parts of Desire

The strongest person is the one who is capable of great humility.

—Beryl Pogson
The Work Life

I have nothing to say, and I am saying it.

—John Cage

I am lying.

—Epimenides

Be will-less with a will.

—Friedrich Schiller

PARENTING

When a dialogue between parents and their children has become possible—possible though always difficult, always complicated by mutual prejudices, bashfulness, inhibitions—it is necessary that in this dialogue we show ourselves for what we are, imperfect, in the hope that our children will not resemble us but be stronger and better than us.

—Natalia Ginzburg
The Little Virtues

The hardest of a parent's task is to know when the task is done.

—Diana L. Paxson
White Mare, Red Stallion

As long as any adult thinks he can invoke his own youth to understand the youth before him, he is lost.

—Margaret Mead

What the mother sings to the cradle goes all the way down to the coffin

—Henry Ward Beecher

PARTICLES/WAVES

If I ask it a particle question, it will give me a particle answer; if I ask it a wave question, it will give me a wave answer. The electron does not have objective properties independent of my mind.

—Fritjof Capra
The Turning Point

Because electrons are both waves and particles (both at the same time), their wave aspects will interfere with each other; they will overlap and merge, drawing the electrons into an existential relationship where their actual inner qualities—their masses, charges, and spins as well as their positions and momenta—become indistinguishable from the relationship among them... they cease to be separate things and become parts-of-a-whole.

—Danah Zohar
The Quantum Self

Everything that has already happened is particles. Everything in the future is waves.... The advancing sieve of time coagulates waves into particles at the moment now.

—Lawrence Bragg

A particle is a collapsed wave with the quantum taken out of it; the past is the collapsed future with the possibility taken out of it.

—Elio Frattaroli
Healing the Soul in the Age of the Brain

Like particles and waves, the energy of the universe is forever taking different forms.

—Joan Borysenko
A Woman's Journey to God

When we test for particles, we get particles; when we test for waves, we get waves.

—George Johnson
Fire in the Mind

What is it to praise? Be particles.

—Coleman Barks
The Essential Rumi

PASSION

Derived from the Latin *passio*, passion meaning suffering ... the word applies to any emotion which goes beyond the bounds of reason, consuming and possessing... When suffering breaks through the small personal context and exposes a man to the pain and darkness of life itself, the way is opened to that ultimate state of passion beyond all passions of desire.

—Helen M. Luke
The Way of Woman

Soul is where the fires of our passions burn. It is where our love is most alive. The soul longs for this deeper love, for a connection between form and formlessness, for a continuum between the earth and the divine.

—Benjamin Shield
Handbook for the Soul

We may affirm absolutely that nothing great in the world has been accomplished without passion.

—Georg Wilhem Friedrich Hegel

One thing is sure: man today must be obsessed; if he is, there is still hope. If he is passionate, meaning com-passionate ... there is hope.

—Elie Wiesel
Messengers of God

Be still when you have nothing to say; when genuine passion moves you, say what you've got to say, and say it hot.

—D. H. Lawrence

... there might be something of magic in every person. There is; once it burned brightly in the species, making many things possible. Now, it grows duller with each successive generation, as if passion were being slowly leached away.

—Morgan Llywelyn
Red Branch

Passions are vices or virtues in their highest powers.

—Johann Wolfgang von Goethe

Everything can become a passion, even serving God.

—Isaac Bashevis Singer

PAST

There is no present or future—only
the past happening over and over
again—now.

—Eugene O'Neill
A Moon for the Misbegotten

The past is both a comfort and a warning.

—Stewart Brand
The Clock of the Long Now

What calls up the past like rich
pumpkin pie?

—John Greenleaf Whittier

The past is almost as much a work of the
imagination as the future.

—Jessamyn West

The past is the root upon which we
grow. Destroy the root and the whole
plant withers.

—Morgan Llywelyn
Bard

I tell you, the past is a bucket of ashes.

—Carl Sandburg

PATHS

There is a divine path, and once we put
our feet upon that path, we no longer
find ourselves floundering, restless and
pleading for someone to pull us from the
mire. Find that path through meditation
and prayer.

—Ruth Montgomery
The World Before

I have always known that at last I would
take this road, but yesterday I did not
know that it would be today.

—Narihara

When earthquakes, floods, hailstorms,
drought, and famine will be the life of
every day, the time will have then come
for the return to the true path.

—Robert Boissiere
Meditations With the Hopi

Turn aside from highways and walk
by footpaths.

—Pythagoras

There is no such thing as an incorrect
path—for on this journey you cannot
"not get" where you are going. It is simply
a matter of speed—merely a question of
when you will get there.

—Neale Donald Walsch
Conversations with God

God is squarely across the road, no
matter what road!

—Paul Scherer
Love Is a Spendthrift

Each path is only one of a million paths.
Therefore, you must keep in mind that
a path is only a path ... your decision to
keep on the path or to leave it must be
free of fear and ambition.... Ask yourself

and yourself alone one question: does this path have a heart?

—Carlos Casteneda
Teachings According to Don Juan

There are many bridges. Some of these are marked under the name of religion. Yoga is a bridge. Sufism is a bridge. In the end, there is only one bridge to follow, and that is the bridge of love.

—Lynn V. Andrews
Star Woman

Agnes Whistling Elk: There are other ways of seeing. All of life is a trail that leads to the Great Tree or Great Spirit. Everyone is on this path. Some are, for the moment, lost. Some are resting. Some realize the truth but can go no further.

—Lynn V. Andrews
Jaguar Woman

There are many goals and many paths to these goals. In the course of many life-times, all available paths will be trod.... Each life, each lesson, is appropriate to the process of evolution and learning, and there is no shortcut to transcending.

—Chelsea Quinn Yarbro
Michael's People

We are all striving to climb the same mountain. All ways lead to the summit, but not all ways suit everyone. Each must choose a way or be thrown into some confusion.

—George Trevelyn
A Vision of the Aquarian Age

We cannot travel the path to higher knowledge if we are constantly losing

ourselves in either pleasure or pain as a result of the ever-changing impressions that confront us.

—Rudolf Steiner
Theosophy

Follow Him through the Land of Unlike-liness; You will see rare beasts and have unique adventures.

—W. H. Auden
For the Time Being

All paths lead to the same goal: to convey to others what we are. And we must pass through solitude and difficulty, isolation and silence, in order to reach forth to the enhanced place where we can dance our clumsy dance and sing our sorrowful song.

—Pablo Neruda

The "answer" is not in technique, but in taking a path with heart.

—Michael Ray

Only the backward path will lead us forward.

—Martin Heidegger

You may follow one stream. Know that it leads to the Ocean, but do not mistake the stream for the Ocean.

—Jan-Fishan

The straight and crooked path is one and the same.

—Heraclitus of Ephesus

The Path I walk Christ walks it. May the
land in which I am be without sorrow....
Bright angels walk with me—dear presence—in every dealing.

—Columcille's Prayer

Everything you meet along the path
is yourself.

—Zen proverb

May you find the path that leads
you toward the purpose of your
life, illumination.

—Sufi proverb

Seek the way by retreating within; seek
the way by advancing boldly without.

—Egyptian proverb

Pilgrims, there is no path, there is
only wandering.

—Inscription in a basilica along the way
   to Compostella, Spain

PATIENCE/
IMPATIENCE

The greatest prayer is patience.

—Siddhartha Gautama (Buddha)

Be patient with everyone, but above all
with yourself.... All profitable correction
comes from a calm, peaceful mind.

—Francoise de Sales

Patience is the art of the possible. When
we expect more than we are capable of
assimilating, we are pushing too fast in
our soul's upward climb. Better to reach
for a lamp than a star, if we are groping
in the dark.

—Ruth Montgomery
   The World Before

Be patient. God's delays are never
God's denials.

—Og Mandino
   The Gift of Acabar

We must not wish to become everything
at once, nor to become saints in four days.

—Margaret T. Applegarth
   Twelve Baskets Full

I have no more patience than anyone
else. It's just that I use mine.

—Ignace Jan Paderewski

Only with winter-patience can we bring
the deep-desired, long awaited spring.

—Anne Morrow Lindburgh

Patience is a state of mind that forbears
in the face of harms inflicted by others.

—Dalai Lama
   The Way to Freedom

You can always improve things if you are
prepared to wait.

—Freeman Dyson

When you are patient, an unkind word or
thoughtless act will not agitate you. You

will not want to run away or retaliate. Your support will hold steady, based as it is on deep respect and the knowledge that the Lord lives in the other person.

—Eknath Easwaran
Meditation

Patience attracts the treasures of higher knowledge; impatience repels them ... valuable as all higher knowledge is, we must not crave for it to come to us.

—Rudolf Steiner

All spiritual growth requires walking the quiet path of patience.

—Rainer Maria Rilke

Just be patient! Have patience, patience! And endure. And finally all the blessings of womanhood will be yours.

—Heinrich Zimmer
The Percival Lesson

Intolerance is the densest barrier to spiritual growth.

—Helen M. Luke
Dark Woods to White Rose

Her father ground his ink blacker and blacker. The blacker the ink, the more patient the man.

—Maxine Hong Kingston
China Men

Have patience and the mulberry leaf will become silk.

—Spanish proverb

PATTERN

What pattern connects the crab to the lobster and the orchid to the primrose and all four of them to me? And me to you?... The pattern which connects is a metapattern. It is a pattern of patterns.

—Gregory Bateson
Mind and Nature

It is as plausible to align our identity with the larger pattern, interexistent with all beings, as to break off one segment of the process and build our borders there.

—Joanna Rogers Macy

Pattern pleases us, rewards a mind seduced and yet exhausted by complexity.

—Diane Ackerman
An Alchemy of Mind

The distinction between animate and inanimate begins to dissolve, for everything is in a pattern of continuous rebirth and everything is the manifestation of one underlying creative potential.

—F. David Peat
The Philosopher's Stone

To Gurdjieff, every event had a meaning and was part of a pattern.

—Beryl Pogson
The Work Life

The ear for the story and the eye for the pattern were [the people's]; the feeling was theirs; we came out of this land and we are hers.

—Leslie Marmon Silko
Ceremony

A pattern of events cannot be separated from the space where it occurs.

—Christopher Alexander
The Timeless Way of Building

PEACE

Peace on the outside comes from peace on the inside. Peace on the inside comes from understanding that we are all God.

—Shirley MacLaine
Dancing in the Light

There will be no peace in the Americas until there is justice for the earth and her children.

—Leslie Marmon Silko
Yellow Woman and a Beauty of Spirit

Peace, in the sense of the absence of war, is of little value to someone who is dying of hunger or cold.... Peace can only last where human rights are respected, where the people are fed, and where individuals and nations are free.

—Dalai Lama
A Policy of Kindness

Competition is a great disturber of inner peace.

—Theodore Isaac Rubin
Reconciliations

Mankind must remember that peace is not God's gift to his creatures; peace is our gift to each other.

—Elie Wiesel

Nothing can bring you peace but yourself.

—Ralph Waldo Emerson

In finding peace and recognizing the light in yourself, we say there's a hearth in your heart where the Creator has given you something very sacred, a special gift, a special duty, an understanding. And now is the time for us to clean out those hearths, to let that inner light glow.

—Dhyani Ywahoo
Weaving the Visions

What is the use of postmarking our mail with exhortations to "pray for peace" and then spending billions of dollars on atomic submarines, thermo-nuclear weapons, and ballistic missiles?

—Thomas Merton
New Seeds of Contemplation

The greatest danger to peace is a military band.

—Christopher Morley

The key to peace lies close to the earth.

—Peter Marshall
Nature's Web

When many agree that peace is possible, heaven will grow from a weak and help-less concept to a manifested experience involving an entire planetary family.

—Ann Valentin & Virginia Essene
Descent of the Dove

The stillness and the peace of now enfold you in perfect gentleness.

—*A Course in Miracles*

PERCEPTION

Man has closed himself up till he sees all things through the narrow chinks of his cavern.

—William Blake
The Marriage of Heaven and Hell

We are a people of prejudiced perception. We unknowingly screen our view of reality.

—Michael W. Munn
Beyond Business as Usual

If the doors of perception were cleansed, everything would appear to man as it is, infinite.

—William Blake

We see through the prism of our categories.

—Joseph Chilton Pearce
The Crack in the Cosmic Egg

If the only tool you have is a hammer, you tend to see every problem as a nail.

—Abraham Maslow

Travelers to Germany before the last war reported that the Germans were the nicest people in Europe.

—Walker Percy
The Message in the Bottle

The accuracy of our perceptions depends on our ability to behaviorally explore the world.

—Richard M. Restak
The Brain

The world is not a fixed, solid array of objects, out there, for it cannot be fully separated from our perception of it. It shifts under our gaze, it interacts with us, and the knowledge that it yields has to be interpreted by us.

—J. Bronowski
The Ascent of Man

You cannot see the Milky Way in New York City any more ... we risk the loss of our sensual perception. And if you lose those, naturally, you try to compensate by other stimulations, by very loud noise, or by bright lights or drugs.

—René Dubos

Perception is ongoing interchange—a silent conversation I carry on with things. By perceiving (really seeing) I enter into a sympathetic relation with the perceived.... The act of perception is always open-ended and unfinished.

—David Abram
The Spell of the Sensuous

Perception is a mirror, not a fact.

—*A Course in Miracles*

PERFECTION

Dear God, It is great the way you always get the stars in the right places.

—Jeff
Children's Letters to God

Perfection is neither more nor less than the faithful cooperation of the soul with this work of God, and is begun, grows, and is consummated in the soul unperceived and in secret.

—Jean-Pierre de Caussade
Abandonment to Divine Providence

Picasso created over 20,000 works of art, most of which were considered worthless. But he learned and sharpened his technique from each try.

—Ray Anthony & Malcom Kushner
High Octane Selling

The horse that will bear us quickest to perfection is suffering.

—Meister Eckhart

For every one step that you take in the pursuit of higher knowledge, take three steps in the perfection of your own character.

—Rudolf Steiner
Knowledge of the Higher Worlds and Its Attainment

Having high standards and sense of duty that transcends personal self-interest is laudable. However, when our standards are so high that we deem ourselves unacceptable unless we meet them, we are in trouble.... Medusa wants everything permanent, perfect, engraved in stone.

—Marion Woodman & Jill Mellick
Coming Home to Myself

An incest survivor tries to be perfect and invisible.

—E. Sue Blume
Secret Survivors

Perfection rapes the soul.

—Marion Woodman & Jill Mellick
Coming Home to Myself

Being perfect means viewing yourself with new eyes—letting yourself arrive fully into life.

—Wayne Dyer
The Sky's the Limit

Perfection is the utilizing of all the modes of mind, finding that the Trees of Life and Knowledge are twins from the same taproot. Perfection is daring to embrace the universe itself as our true dimension, daring to steal the fire of the gods, to walk on water or fire unafraid, to heal, to claim plenty in time of dearth, to behold boldly that which is desired and become what we have need to be.

—Joseph Chilton Pearce
The Crack in the Cosmic Egg

George Bernard Shaw once wrote to Jascha Heifetz after a concert "My dear Mr. Heifetz: My wife and I were overwhelmed by your concert. If you continue to play with such beauty, you will certainly die young. No one can play with such perfection without provoking the jealousy of the gods. I earnestly implore you to play something badly every night before going to bed ..."

—Ignacio L. Götz
On Technology and the Spirit

Perfectionism is the assumption that the world is not perfect. It assumes one choice is better than another. What if all choices create perfect circumstances?

—Gary Zukov & Linda Francis
The Heart of the Soul

Man of Holiness: To be perfect is to do your best, without shadow of deceit or cowardice, without self-justification or dissembling. It is to strive with an honest mind and a pure heart and an eye single to the love of good.... I give no commandments except I make a way that they may be accomplished.

—Anne Perry
Tathea

PERSEVERANCE

The best way out is always through.

—Robert Frost

There's a tree that grows in Brooklyn. Some people call it the Tree of Heaven. No matter where its seed falls, it makes a tree which struggles to reach the sky. It grows in boarded-up plots and out of neglected rubbish heaps. It grows up out of cellar gratings. It is the only tree that grows out of cement.

—Betty Smith
A Tree Grows in Brooklyn

We can do anything we want if we stick to it long enough.

—Helen Keller

Diamonds are only chunks of coal that stuck to their jobs, you see.

—Minnie Richard

The person who removes a mountain begins by carrying away small stones.

—Chinese proverb

One may go a long way after one is tired.

—French proverb

PERSPECTIVE

Every constellation is but a gathering of distant suns. It is mere perspective that makes Betelgeuse a star. Seen close enough she is a raging fire.

—Calvin Miller
The Singer

To a frog that's never left his pond the ocean seems like a gamble.

—Coleman Barks
The Essential Rumi

PHILOSOPHY

Like the meridians as they approach the poles, science, philosophy and religion are bound to converge as they draw nearer to the whole.

—Pierre Teilhard de Chardin

When philosophy comes into its own, it is not without a long prehistory. Without Homer's poetry, the Dionysian festivals, and the Solonic laws, and above all, without the genius of the Greek language, no Western philosophy as we have it now would have developed. And everyone who participates in the language and art and the cult and social life of a culture is a collaborator in the creation of its philosophy.

—Paul Tillich
Biblical Religion and the Search for Ultimate Reality

There is no need for temples; no need for complicated philosophy. Our own brain, our own heart is our temple; my philosophy is kindness.

—Dalai Lama

Imagine a philosophic fish trying to describe water.

—Victor Mansfield
Synchronicity, Science and Soulmaking

Philosophy is written in this grand book the universe, which stands continually open to our gaze. But the book cannot be understood unless one first learns to comprehend the language and to read the alphabet in which it is composed. It is written in the language of mathematics, and its characters are triangles, circles, and other geometric figures, without which it is humanly impossible to understand a single word of it; without these, one wanders about in a dark labyrinth.

—Galileo Galilei
The Assayer

European philosophy is a series of footnotes to Plato.

—Alfred North Whitehead

In philosophy, you go horizontally; in mysticism, you go vertically.

—Elie Wiesel

The whole of philosophy is like a tree, the roots of which are metaphysics, the trunk is the science of physics and the branches … all the sciences.

—René Descartres

The old growth forests of philosophy have been logged and the owl of Minerva has fled.

—Sven Birkerts
The Guttenburg Elegies

PHYSICS

In the twentieth century, physicists faced, for the first time, a serious challenge to their ability to understand the universe. Every time they asked nature a question in an atomic experiment, nature answered with a paradox.

—Fritjof Capra
The Turning Point

Physics is, as the academic jargon has it, a "hard-nosed" science, completely down to earth, whereas parapsychologists float somewhere in nebulous Cloud-cuckoo-land.... the Principle of Complementarity … turns the so-called "elementary building blocks" of classical physics into Janus-faced entities that behave under certain circumstances like hard little lumps of matter, but in other circumstances as waves or vibrations propagated in a vacuum.

—Arthur Koestler
Janus

The fundamental symbol for the classical scientific world view was the billiard table with the billiard balls glancing off one another. The fundamental symbol for the world view that has emerged from the twentieth century theoretical physics is that of the musical symphony.

—Brian Swimme & Mathew Fox
Manifesto for a Global Civilization

When searching for harmony in life one must never forget that in the drama of existence we are ourselves both actors and spectators.

—Niels Bohr & P. A. Schlipp
Albert Einstein

In classical physics change is nothing but a denial of becoming and time is only a parameter, unaffected by the transformation that it describes.

—Ilya Prigogine

In modern physics the "essential stuff" of the universe can't be reduced to billiard balls and atoms; it's relationships.... In quantum physics there is a kind of vibrant silence. It is called the vacuum state.... In this state of nothingness is, in fact, an infinite ocean of energy ...

—F. David Peat
Lighting the Seventh Fire

PILGRIMS/ PILGRIMAGE

St. Columba of Iona, in the Celtic tradition, spoke of three kinds of authentic pilgrims: those who were able to plan and sustain an actual pilgrimage, those who had intended to do so but were prevented by injury or death, and those whose situation never allowed them to leave home but whose longing for the place brought them to it as surely as those who had made the trip.

—Belden C. Lane
Landscapes of the Sacred

The religious pilgrimage is a ritual journey. The pilgrim knows exactly where he is going, exactly what he will find there, and exactly what he is supposed to do once he gets there.... The effect on the pilgrim can be analogous to that on the mythic hero who discovers the ultimate lost object or comes face to face with Ultimate Reality.

—David Leeming
Myth: A Biography of Belief

Pilgrims are persons in motion passing through territories not their own—seeking something we might call completion or perhaps the word clarity will do as well, a goal to which only the spirit's compass points the way.

—Richard R. Niebuhr

Wherever I go, I go to Jerusalem.

—Nachman of Bratislav

The tradition of pilgrimage is as old as religion itself.... The pilgrim participates; the tourist observes.

—Lauren Artress
Walking a Sacred Path

Two million people are chosen to go to Mecca each year by lottery.

—Geraldine Brooks
Nine Parts of Desire

The word *hajj*, the journey to Mecca that every Muslim must make at least once in his or her life, comes from an old Semitic word meaning "to go around, to go in a circle." Whether it be around a person, a shrine, a temple, a lake, a mountain, a country, or even as some have done, around the world … by drawing the circle, we define the center.

—Gregg Levoy
Callings

Pilgrimage … like many other acts of piety, may be reasonable or superstitious, according to the principles upon which is it performed. Long journeys in search of truth are not commanded.… Truth, such as is necessary to the regulation of life, is always found where it is honestly sought.

—Samuel Johnson
History of Rasellas, Prince of Abissinia

The Crusades replicated the women's experience of going to the tomb and asking, "Where is he?"

—Rudolf Steiner

For a moment of night we have a glimpse of ourselves and of our world islanded in its stream of stars—pilgrims of mortality, voyaging between horizons across eternal seas of space and time.

— Henry Beston
Outermost House

Whether we go to the Ganges or Graceland, maintaining a spirit of observance and self-reflection is key.

—Gregg Levoy
Callings

PLACE

Whither shall I look when I praise Thee? Upward or downward, inward or outward? For Thou art the place in which all things are contained; there is no other place beside Thee: all things are in Thee.

—Hermes
Hermetca

God Himself is called Place, for He encompasses all things, but is not encompassed by anything.

— Philo of Alexandria

There are … places where one breathes in spirit, places where a man can steep himself in it, or if you prefer, where he quickens the sense of the divine in himself. This is the greatest gift of Earth and Heaven to man.

—Louis Charpentier
The Mysteries of Chartres Cathedral

Odysseus never did sail "beyond the sunset." He eventually made his way back to Ithaca, his old home and kingdom, which he found to be in a dreadful mess, usurped by rogues. He set to, and sorted it out. It was there, where he had come from, that he made his "newer world." There is no escaping. The future for us, too, is in our own place, if we can learn to see it differently, and are "strong in will" to change it.

—Charles Handy
The Relevance of a Decade

Place is something the soul makes for storing images.

—Albert Magnus

It's not down on any map; true places never are.

—Herman Melville

Tell me the landscape in which you live and I will tell you who you are.

—José Ortega y Gasset

France is a land, England is a people, and America is a willingness of heart.

—F. Scott Fitzgerald

My wound is geography. It is also my anchorage, my port of call.

—Pat Conroy
The Prince of Tides

An individual is not distinct from his place; he is that place.

—Gabriel Marcel

To be rooted is perhaps the most important and least recognized need of the human soul.

—Simone Weil
The Need for Roots

The human's persistent effort to anchor meaning in place expresses itself in endless variations.... That's why Luther happened to remember that it was on the privy in the monastery at Wittenberg where he was struck in 1512 by the freeing words of justification by faith in Romans 1:17.

—Belden C. Lane
Landscape of the Sacred

Geomancy is commonly known as the "art of harmonious placement," for it has been used to find the right time and place for all human activities.

—Richard feather Anderson
The Power of Place

The words "Feng Shui" translate literally as "wind and water," a name which conveys the spirit of this centuries-old paradigm for ordering human affairs to increase health, prosperity, and good fortune.

—James Swan
The Power of Place

The question of questions for mankind— the problem which underlies all others, and which is more deeply interesting than any other—is the ascertainment of the place which Man occupies in nature and of his relations to the universe of things.

—Thomas Huxley

Is there a spiritual geography, are there certain places upon the earth which are more, or less, attuned to certain modes of consciousness? And if so, do such qualities belong to the earth itself, to certain qualities of light, or sound, or scent or rock formation?

—Kathleen Raine
The Lion's Mouth

The most gifted travel writers—from Lawrence Durrell to Peter Matthiessen—have all performed the impossible task of affording entry to the landscape and consciousness of another world.

—Belden C. Lane
Landscapes of the Sacred

Each blade of grass has its spot on earth
whence it draws its life, its strength; and
so is man rooted to the land from which
he draws his faith together with his life.

—Joseph Conrad

When a man leaves home, he leaves
behind some scrap of his heart … it's the
same with a place a man is going to. Only
then he sends a scrap of his heart ahead.

—Frederick Buechner
Godric

The place God calls you to is the place
where your deep gladness and the world's
deep hunger meet.

—E. B. McNeil
The Psychology of Being Human

God uses special times and places
to heighten and intensify experiences
and acts which are always at least
potentially present.

—Martin Marty

The memories in things speak recipro-
cally with people, where the very earth
remembers the imprints of history.… The
specific place-names should be spoken
aloud upon arriving at each one. This
way you bring alive what happened and
still happens there.

—Kenneth Lincoln
Native America Renaissance

The idea of a sacred place … is apparently
as old as life itself.

—Joseph Campbell
The Mythic Image

They [Lummi Tribal Council] say that
logging these trees will destroy sacred
places which collectively contribute
to the most precious thing of all—that
which in the Salish language is called
skalalitude or "a sacred state of mind
where magic and beauty are everywhere."

—James A. Swan
Sacred Places

People of the Goddess Danu believe
there are a few extraordinary places on
this earth which predispose people to
hope, or especially challenge that hope.
Men tend to be ambivalent about such
places precisely because their otherness is
frightening and fascinating.… Ireland is
one of those places, a sacred center above
the heart of the goddess, Ierne.

—Morgan Llywellyn
Bard

The holes and tunnels of an old warren become smooth, reassuring and
comfortable with use. There are no snags
or rough corners.… All the faults have
been put right and everything in use is of
proved value.

—Richard Adams
Watership Down

Most of us have to be transplanted before
we blossom.

—Louise Nevelson

There is always in life a place to leave and
a new place to find, and in between a
zone of hesitation and uncertainty tinged
with more or less intense anxiety.

—Paul Tournier
A Place for You

We continue to displace ourselves—no longer with unity of direction, like a migrant flock, but more like the refugees from a broken ant hill.

—Wendell Berry
The Unsettling of America

People give pain, are callous and insensitive, empty and cruel … but place heals the hurt, soothes the outrage, fills the terrible vacuum that these human beings make.

—Eudora Welty

Everything is somewhere and in place.

—Aristotle

Places remember events.

—James Joyce
Notebook

The soul of a landscape, the spirits of the elements, the genius of every place will be revealed to a loving view of nature.

—Karl Jaspers
Philosophy

We all have three essential places: the place we live, the place we work, the place we gather for conviviality.

—Ray Oldenburg
The Great Good Place

Every place is given its character by certain patterns of events that keep on happening there. These patterns are always interlocked with certain geometric patterns … they may be dead or alive …

when they are dead, they keep us locked in inner conflict.

—Christopher Alexander
The Timeless Way of Building

The sorghum-sweet serenity of the place skewered me squarely for an instant on a knifeblade of nostalgia for the rural South.

—William Styron
Sophie's Choice

Let the site tell you its secrets.

—Christopher Alexander
A Pattern Language

Panther Canyon was like a thousand others—one of those abrupt fissures with which the earth in the Southwest is riddled—so abrupt that you might walk over the edge of any one of them on a dark night and never know what had happened to you.

—Willa Cather
Song of the Lark

Oakland: There is no there, there.

—Gertrude Stein

Wisdom sits in places.

—Apache proverb

PLAY/PLAYING

Play is at its best when performed for its own sake, not for any purpose or achievement other than itself. Play is self-discovery in the here and now. It is spontaneous, yet has its own discipline.

It is light, yet potentially passionate. It is discovery, and it is enjoyment of one's own and others' possibilities, capacities, and limitations. Most, if not all, great discoveries, even in science, have been the result of intense effort along with playful curiosity and joy of exploration on the part of the discoverer.

—Edward Whitmont
The Return of the Goddess

The Spiritual Path can be one of immense play and deep inner joy.

—Sanaya Roman
Spiritual Growth

We are making hay when we should be making whoopee; we are raising tomatoes when we should be raising Cain or Lazarus.

—Annie Dillard
Pilgrim at Tinker Creek

Learning to have fun will eventually mean reaching and touching God/Goddess/All That Is.

—Lazaris
Lazaris Interviews

Man is completely human only when he is at play.

—Friedrich Schiller

In play the mind is prepared to accept the unimagined and incredible, to enter a world where different laws apply, to be relieved of all the weights that bear it down, to be free, kingly, unfettered and divine.

—Hugo Rahner
Men at Play

Play, fantasy, the imagination and free exploration of possibilities: these are the central powers of the human person.

—Brian Swimme
The Universe Is a Green Dragon

Allowing the imagination to play means to lighten up from time to time, to let our fantasies run free.... Opening the mind to a lighthearted, playful attitude, we may avail ourselves of intuition, which is a particular kind of gnosis or knowledge, that seems to come through the now permeable borders of the conscious mind.

—Allan Combs & Mark Holland
Synchronicity

Play is finite creativity in the magic dimension of illusion.

—Eugen Fink & Jacques Ehermann eds.
Game, Play, Literature

The aesthetic of accident sanctioned irony rather than morality, play rather than work, acceptance of the phenomenal world rather than commitment to transform it.

—Werner Karl Heisenberg
Uncertainty Principle

All we had to do was to construct a set of molecular models [for DNA] and begin to play—with luck, the structure would be a helix.

—James Watson

Play extends to pure thought. It involves doing novel things without regard to whether they may be justified by a specific payoff.

—Patrick Bateson & Paul Marti
Design for a Life

Deep play is ecstatic play. It involved the sacred and the holy.... Sacred places catapult people into deep play.

—Diane Ackerman
Deep Play

It [the monastic life] is ... a good sort of playing which is ridiculous to men, a very beautiful sight to the angels ... it is a joyous game.

—Bernard of Clairvaux

When I'm playful, I use the meridians of longitude and parallels of latitude for a seine, and drag the Atlantic Ocean for whales!

—Mark Twain
Life on the Mississippi

Art, play and life in general have lost their supernatural moorings.

—Mihaly Csikszentmihalyi
Flow

No wonder kids grow up crazy. A Cat's Cradle is nothing but a bunch of x's between somebody's hands and little kids look and look at those x's... no cat and no cradle.

—Newt Hoenikker
Cat's Cradle

Play is the only way the highest intelligence of humankind can unfold.... And what does every child believe every adult is capable of doing? Of actually being able to bend the world to an inner desire, exactly what the child is busily practicing in his passionate play. And what does every child dream? Of possessing his own powers over the world when he grows up.

—Joseph Chilton Pearce
The Magical Child

We don't stop playing because we grow old, we grow old because we stop playing.

—Satchel Paige

The creative mind plays with the object it loves.

—Carl G. Jung

PLEASURE

I was learning the far more secret doctrine that pleasures are shafts of the glory as it strikes our sensibility. As it impinges on our will or our understanding, we give it different names—goodness or truth or the like. But its flash upon our senses and mood is pleasure.

—C. S. Lewis
Letters to Malcolm: Chiefly on Prayer

Every perfect action is accompanied by pleasure. By that you can tell that you ought to do it.

—André Gide

When wolves perceive pleasure or danger, they first become utterly still ...

statues, utterly focused so they can see, so they can hear, so they can sense what is there, sense what is there in its most elemental form.

—Clarissa Pinkola Estés
Women Who Run with the Wolves

You change people by delight, by pleasure.

—Thomas Aquinas

POETRY

Poetry is not a luxury. It is a vital necessity of our existence. It forms the quality of the light within which we predicate our hopes and dreams toward survival and change, first made into language, then into idea, then into more tangible action. Poetry is the way we help give name to the nameless so it can be thought.... Poetry is not only dream and vision; it is the skeleton architecture of our lives. It lays the foundations for a future of change, a bridge across our fears of what has never been before.

—Audre Lorde
Sister Outsider

You can learn about the pine only from the pine, or about bamboo only from bamboo.... The object and yourself must become one, and from that feeling of oneness issues your poetry.

—Matsuo Basho

Poetry and mysticism both derive from a common source, the ground or depth of the soul where the Mystery of Being is experienced. But the poet is always driven to "symbolize" his experience, to express it in words or in paint or in music. The mystic seeks the experience in itself, beyond words or sounds or images.

—Bede Griffiths
Return to the Center

All language is poetry.

—Diane Ackerman
An Alchemy of Mind

Poetry does not move us to be just or unjust, in itself. It moves us to thoughts in whose light justice and injustice are seen with a fearful sharpness of outline.

—J. Bronowski
The Common Sense of Science

For most people, poetry is a solitary affair, like meditation or prayer.

—Bill Moyers
Fooling with Words

Poetry in the larger sense of the word—poems, stories, myths, paintings, dances, dreams—is the most exhilarating and transporting vehicle for travel there is.

—Thomas Moore
Original Self

Anything can be poetry that is felt as poetry.

—Mary Caroline (M. C.) Richards
Centering

Poetry takes something that we know already and turns it into something new.

—T. S. Eliot

Poets are the antennae of the race.

—Ezra Pound

Poetry is the alchemy which teaches us to convert ordinary materials into gold.

—Anäis Nin
The Novel of the Future

A poem is a momentary stay against confusion.... Like a piece of ice on a hot stove the poem must ride on its own melting.... Poetry is a way of taking life by the throat.

—Robert Frost

A good poet is someone who manages, in a lifetime of standing out in thunderstorms, to be struck by lightning five or six times; a dozen or two dozen times and he is great.

—Randall Jarrell
Poetry and the Age

Poets, like small children and magicians, cannot help believing that words may affect reality.

—Robin Skelton
The Poet's Calling

Poetry, like the moon, does not advertise anything.... The success of the poem is determined, not by how much the poet felt in writing it, but by how much the reader feels in reading it.

—John Ciardi

Poetry is the impish attempt to paint the color of the wind.

—Maxwell Bodenheim

Poems of great energy are usually distillations of words and sentiments outside themselves. Poems are by nature a compression.

—Peter J. Kreeft
Heaven, the Heart's Deepest Longing

Poetry is the journal of a sea animal living on land, wanting to fly in the air. Poetry is a search for syllables to shoot at the barriers of the unknown and the unknowable.

—Carl Sandburg

Poetry is nothing but health speech.

—Henry David Thoreau

The acid test of poetic sensibility is whether one can derive joy from a recital of the names of Paris underground railway stations.

—W. H. Auden
Making, Knowing and Judging

Poets are simply those who have made a profession and a lifestyle of being in touch with their bliss.

—Joseph Campbell
The Power of Myth

He would be a poet ... who nailed words to their primitive senses, as farmers drive stakes in the spring, which the frost has heaved; who derived his words as often as he used them—transplanted them to his page with earth adhering to their roots.

—Henry David Thoreau
Walking

The Mahabharata is the longest epic poem—an Indian classic. Ganesh was scribe for it.

—Victor Mansfield
Synchronicity, Science and Soulmaking

Poetry is the language in which man explores his own amazement.

—Christopher Fry

Poetry is the art of overhearing ourselves say things from which it is impossible to retreat.

—David Whyte
The Heart Aroused

A poem is never a put-up job, so to speak. It begins as a lump in the throat, a sense of wrong, a homesickness, a lovesickness. It is never a thought to begin with.

—Robert Frost & Elaine Berry
Robert Frost on Writing

You always run up against poetry in England.

—Virginia Woolf in a letter to Vita Sackville-West

POLITICS/POLITICAL

We all become political when we realize that our lives are not bounded by the perimeters of self, family, and home, and when we feel and act from that realization. A person is more than an individual, more than a self.

—Thomas Moore
The Re-Enchantment of Everyday Life

The dichotomy between the spiritual and the political is false, resulting from an incomplete attention to our erotic knowledge. For the bridge which connects them is formed by the erotic ... the passions of love in its deepest meanings.

—Audre Lorde
Take Back the Night

Politics will itself become the art of the people, the act of preserving and celebrating Mother Earth, the art of doing justice and keeping balance and harmony.

—Matthew Fox
The Coming of the Cosmic Christ

Those who think religion and politics are not connected don't know much about politics, nor about religion.

—Mohandas (Mahatma) Gandhi

Politics is not the art of the possible. It consists of choosing between the disastrous and the unpalatable.

—John Kenneth Galbraith

Nothing in politics ever happens by accident; if it happens, you can bet it was planned!

—Franklin Delano Roosevelt

Political power grows out of the barrel of a gun.

—Mao Tse-tung

Politics are almost as exciting as war, and quite as dangerous. In war, you can only be killed once, but in politics, many times.

—Winston Churchill

All politics is applesauce.

—Will Rogers

The trouble with socialism is that it would take too many evenings.

—Oscar Wilde

POSSIBILITIES

To love life and men as God loves them—for the sake of their infinite possibilities.

—Dag Hammarskjöld
Markings

People do walk fire. We are an open possibility.

—Joseph Chilton Pearce
The Crack in the Cosmic Egg

I realized that if what we call human nature can be changed, then absolutely anything is possible. And from that moment, my life changed.

—Shirley MacLaine
You Can Get There from Here

All things are possible once enough human beings realize that everything is at stake.

—Norman Cousins

I see people as possibilities they may grow into.

—Beryl Pogson
The Work Life

POTENTIAL

In every block of marble I see a statue, see it as plainly as though it stood before me, shaped and perfect in attitude and action. I have only to hew away the rough walls which imprison the lovely apparition to reveal it to other eyes, as mine already see it.

—Michelangelo
(di Lodovico Buonarroti Simoni)

We are living in what the Greeks called the *kairos*—the right moment—for a "metamorphosis of the gods," of the fundamental principles and symbols … so much is at stake and so much depends on the psychological constitution of modern man…. Does the individual know that he (and she) is the makeweight that tips the scales?

—Carl G. Jung
Collected Works of Carl Gustav Jung, Vol. 10

If seeds in the black earth turn into such beautiful roses, what might not the heart of man become in the long journey to the stars?

—G. K. Chesterton

If you don't live up to your greatest potential, then you are cheating God.

—Louise Nevelson

Our fires are damped, our drafts are checked, we are living on only a small percentage of our abilities.

—William James

To live creatively is to die each day to the old and make way for the new in oneself, for the potential self that is waiting to be born. It is to be willing to constantly release assumptions about what we should be doing, or where our lives should be going, and to live in a state of wonder as a young child asking: Who will I be today?

—Julie Redstone
Teaching the Heart to Sing

Limestone is on its way to becoming marble.… It's not a person's depth you must discover, but their ascent.

—Anne Michaels
Fugitive Pieces

You can count the apples on a tree but you cannot count the trees in an apple.

—African proverb

POVERTY/POOR

Poverty has many faces. People can, for example, be poor in space alone. Last month I talked to a man who lives in a four-room apartment with a wife, four children, and relatives besides. He has a regular job and can feed his family, but he is poor in light and air and space.

—Dorothy Day
Loaves and Fishes

The poor man is not he who is without a cent, but he who is without a dream.

—Harry Kemp

It's not that I'm poor, it's just that I don't have any money.

—Laurel Lee
Signs of Spring

The best reason for listening to and learning from the poor is that this is one way God is revealed to us.

—Doris Janzen Longacre
Living More with Less

The Greek word for "poor" literally means "beggarly." The "poor in spirit" are those who recognize that they must beg for their spirit from a source beyond themselves. Such people find the kingdom, while those who regard themselves as self-sufficient do not receive the highest gift.

—John A. Sanford
The Kingdom Within

"Blessed are the poor in spirit …" "Poor in spirit" is a traditional Aramaic idiom meaning "humble."

—Neil Douglas-Klotz
Prayers of the Cosmos

Jesus made himself the bread of life and lets himself be eaten up … this is why poor people are such great people; they are Jesus in full reality.

—Mother Teresa

There are three billion people living in poverty; of them, 1.3 billion live in absolute poverty… The wealthy must redefine wealth, not the poverty-stricken.

—Neale Donald Walsch
Tomorrow's God

The spiritual poverty of the western world is much greater than the physical poverty of our people. You in the West have millions of people who suffer such terrible loneliness and emptiness. They feel unloved and unwanted ... what they are missing really is a living relationship with God.

—Mother Teresa

Remember that those who attack are poor.

—*A Course in Miracles*

Rags make paper; paper makes money; money makes banks; banks make loans; loans make poverty, and poverty makes rags.

—English proverb

POWER

On the whole, I do not find Christians, outside of the catacombs, sufficiently sensible of conditions. Does anyone have the foggiest idea what sort of power we so blithely invoke?... it is madness to wear ladies' straw hats and velvet hats to church; we should all be wearing crash helmets. Ushers should issue life preservers and signal flares; they should lash us to our pews.... The waking god may draw us out to where we can never return.

—Annie Dillard
Teaching a Stone to Talk

We sometimes fall into the delusion that power is elsewhere, that it belongs to a different group, that we are unable to find access to it. Nothing could be farther from the truth. The universe oozes with power, waiting for anyone who wishes to embrace it.

—Brian Swimme
The Universe Is a Green Dragon

"Strength" must be redefined not as power-over, but as power-with.

—Matthew Fox
The Coming of the Cosmic Christ

Speaking first to be heard is power over. Hearing to bring forth speech is empowering.

—Nelle Morton
The Journey is Home

We seek power to brace ourselves against helplessness.

—Karen Horney

Power is not only a matter of coercive forces. It operates through exclusions from access to those institutions and practices through which dominance is exercised. One of these is language.

—Simone de Beauvoir
The Second Sex

God is the power of relationships.

—Carter Heyward
The Redemption of God

To make people feel worthless, society robs them of their pride; this has happened to women. All the institutions of our culture tells us—through words, deeds and even worse, silence—that we are insignificant. But our heritage is our power.

—Judy Chicago
The Dinner Party

The exercise of power, the submission of some to the will of others, is inevitable in modern society; nothing whatever is accomplished without it.... Power can be socially malign; it is also socially essential.

—John Kenneth Galbraith &
Fritjof Capra
The Hidden Connections

Power actually resides in the house.... The oldest houses are the dance houses in which the power of motion is fixed.

—Gerardus van der Leeuw
Sacred and Profane Beauty

In the so-called "primitive" societies there are two words for power, *mana* and *taboo*: the power which creates and the power which destroys; the power which is benign, and the power which is malign. Odd that we have retained in our vocabulary the word for dangerous power, *taboo*, and have lost the *mana*.

—Madeleine L'Engle
Walking on Water

Power is the ability to take one's place in whatever discourse is essential to action and the right to have one's part matter.

—Carolyn G. Heilbrun
Writing a Woman's Life

No power may be exercised with greater precision than the power of suggestion.

—Eudora Welty
The Eye of the Story

The way we exert power is the entry point for violence in our world.

—Madonna Kolbenschlag
Lost in the Land of Oz

When a man is deprived of the power of expression, he will express himself in a drive for power.

—José Arguelles

The problem comes when we do not recognize power within ourselves as well as within others and when we do not recognize our connection to all beings within the circle of life.

—Carol P. Christ
Laughter of Aphrodite

Do you not see that all your misery comes from the strange belief that you are powerless?

—*A Course in Miracles*

Abilities are innate, but the power to use them requires intercourse with the world.

—Carol Ochs
Behind the Sex of God

All empowerment of others is self-empowerment.

—Sanaya Roman
Spiritual Growth

The suppression of female symbolism and female power by the canonical traditions of the West is being reversed as modern women lay claim to their own forms of spirituality and power … the challenge facing those who have deeply experienced exclusion as part of their own history is to create new traditions that do not exclude others.

—Carol P. Christ
Laughter of Aphrodite

Power consists to a large extent in deciding what stories will be told.

—Carolyn G. Heilbrun
Writing a Woman's Life

Power is the strength and the ability to see yourself through your own eyes and not through the eyes of another. It is being able to place a circle of power at your own feet and not take power from someone else's circle.

—Lynn V. Andrews
Flight of the Seventh Moon

Mastering others is strength. Mastering yourself is true power.

—Tao Te Ching

Everything we do for someone else, or he for us, is ultimately empowering or disempowering.… Every action is an exchange of power between two people, no matter if that action is altruistic or acquisitive.

—Caroline Myss
Invisible Acts of Power

At the moment when they are at their own point of power, most people have no idea of the magnificent choice they face.

—Martia Nelson
Coming Home

Natural events are potent because they act in accordance with how things work. They simply are. Study natural processes: the light in the sky, the gravity of earth, the unfolding of your own ideas and insights, the emptiness of space, the fullness of life, and the behavior of saints.

—John Heider
The Tao of Leadership

I give [men] earthly power not to exercise dominion but to minister to his fellows, and in ministering to learn those skills which he does not yet possess, each in its turn, until he has them all.

—Anne Perry
Tathea

Craft … comes from the German word *kraft*, meaning power or strength. As Emerson said, the law is: "Do the thing and you shall have the power. But they who do not the thing, have not the powers." We can't fake craft.

—Mary Caroline (M. C.) Richards
Centering

Power is of two kinds. One is dominated by the fear of punishment, and the other by the arts of love. Power based on love is a thousand times more effective and permanent than the one derived from fear of punishment.

—Jack Nelson-Pallmeyer
Is Religion Killing Us?

Power is the greatest aphrodisiac.

—Henry Kissinger

Love and power are not opponents.

—James Hillman
Kinds of Power

True power is the power to be connected to, the power to be in harmonious relationship with.

—Diane Mariechild
Open Mind

Power is made for service.

—Mechtild of Magdeburg

PRACTICE

Be soft in your practice. Think of the method as a fine silvery stream, not a raging waterfall. Follow the stream, have faith in its course. It will go its own way, meandering here, trickling there. It will find the grooves, the cracks, the crevices. Just follow it. Never let it out of your sight. It will take you.

—Sheng-yen

Munindra-ji, one of my first Dharma teachers, used to say that in spiritual practice, time is not a factor. Practice cannot be measured in time, so let go of the whole notion of when and how long.

—Joseph Goldstein
Insight Meditation

Mindfulness practice means that we commit fully in each moment to being present. There is no "performance." There is just this moment.

—Jon Kabat-Zinn
Wherever You Go There You Are

PRAISE

Lewis confesses that when he first became a Christian he was disturbed by the continuous command in the Psalms to praise God. It sounded as if God were saying, "What I most want is to be told that I am good and great."… Then he discovered the principle that praise is simply the sign of healthy understanding.

—Clyde S. Kilby
The Christian World of C .S. Lewis

I think we delight to praise what we enjoy because the praise not merely expresses but completes the enjoyment! It is not out of compliment, lovers keep telling one another how beautiful they are; the delight is incomplete till it is expressed.

—C. S. Lewis
The Joyful Christian

God love everything you love and a mess of stuff you don't. But more than anything else, God love admirations.

—Alice Walker
The Color Purple

We participate, in a sense, in noble deeds when we praise them sincerely.

—John Milton

Praise is the word we speak when we are in love…. With praise, the human is doing what we were birthed by the universe to do: to tell the truth of the wonders and the goodness of what is.... Let us learn to praise our ability to see what is.

—Matthew Fox
Creativity

Praise is the recognized form of making noise in the presence of superiors ... it tends to become music ... ascends like incense ... it lifts the heart.

—Walter Burkert
Creation of the Sacred

Each thing prays according to the rank it occupies in nature, and sings the praise of the leader of the divine series to which it belongs, a spiritual or rational or physical or sensuous praise; for the heliotrope moves to the extent that it is free to move, and in its rotation, if we could hear the sound of the air buffeted by its movements, we should be aware that it is a hymn to its kind, such as it is within the power of a plant to sing.

—Henry Corbin
Creative Imagination in the Sufism of Ibn' Arabi

Praise is the natural expression of our being.

—Llewellyn Vaughan-Lee
In the Company of Friends

Falsely praising a person is lying.

—Augustine

PRAYER

When you utter a word before God, then enter into that word with every one of your limbs.

—Martin Buber
Tales of the Hasidim

We need to pray in such a way that a longing should be aroused in all our members and powers, and all our senses, eyes, ears, mouth and heart, that they should all be directed towards this same end.

—Meister Eckhart
Sermons and Discourses

When I marched with Martin Luther King in Selma, I felt my legs were praying.

—Abraham Joshua Heschel

Prayer is the art of presence. Where there is no wonder there is little depth of presence.

—John O'Donohue
Eternal Echoes

What is the use of praying if at the very moment of prayer, we have so little confidence in God that we are busy planning our own kind of answer to our prayer?

—Thomas Merton
Thoughts in Solitude

As my prayer became more attentive and inward I had less and less to say. I finally became completely silent.

—Søren Kierkegaard

Prayer is a concrete, measurable, and directive force in creation. Prayer is real. To pray is to do "something!"

—Gregg Braden
The Isaiah Effect

Prayer is not sending in an order and expecting it to be fulfilled. Prayer is attuning yourself to the life of the world, to love, the force that moves the sun and the moon and the stars.

—David Steindl-Rast
The Music of Silence

Prayer, crystallized in words, assigns a permanent wave length on which the dialogue has to be continued, even then our mind is occupied with other matters.

—Dag Hammarskjöld
Markings

To pray means to bring God back into the world, to establish His kingship for a second at least. To pray means to expand His presence.

—Abraham Joshua Heschel
The Insecurity of Freedom

Lord Jesus Christ, have mercy on me. When you practice the Jesus Prayer systematically, it is as if you move about within a polluted city wearing an oxygen mask over your face. Nothing can touch you.

—Kyriacos Markides
The Mountain of Silence

Contemplative prayer is a process of interior transformation, a relationship initiated by God and leading, if we consent, to divine union.

—Thomas Keating

There is a way of beholding which is a form of prayer.

—Diane Ackerman
An Alchemy of Mind

I went and leaned my forehead against the ancient stones and felt waves of energy coming out of the Wall. Men in black garb were rolling out torahs on tables from the caves at the north end. Prayer groups were gathering around every table with its torah, and I heard the sounds of each prayer service starting up one after the other. They came together in a fugue, funneling all the prayers out of the stones and up to Heaven.

—Alan Lew
One God Clapping

Prayer is a practice in choice. Every day I must choose to follow this ritual or ignore it.

—Christina Baldwin
Calling the Circle

Prayer is either a sheer illusion or a personal contact between embryonic, incomplete persons (ourselves) and the utterly concrete Person.

—C. S. Lewis

And so one must isolate himself from the world prior to spoken prayer, separating from the noise of the world with the intent that he now draw near to speak with the Eternal. Once he has isolated himself from the world and its uproar, then ... the "garments" that separate Divinity from him ... pass away. Then the Divinity within them reveals itself.

—Merkaz Chasidei Piesetznah
Derekh Ha-Melekh

Alice Kaholusuna: Before the missionaries came, my people used to sit outside their temples for a long time meditating and preparing themselves before entering. Then they would virtually creep to the altar to offer their petition and afterwards would again sit a long time outside, this time to "breathe life" into their prayers. The Christians, when they came, just got up, uttered a few sentences, said Amen and were done. For that reason my people called them *haoles*, "without breath," or those who failed to breathe life into their prayers.

—Madeleine L'Engle
Walking on Water

The discipline of prayer is to keep oneself open to God and be ready to respond. The answer comes when there is an inner quickening.

—Howard Thurmant
Meditations of the Heart

What's prayer? It's shooting shafts into the dark. What mark they strike, if any, who's to say.

—Frederick Buechner
Godric

He prayed as he breathed, forming no words and making no specific requests, only holding in his heart, like broken birds in cupped hands, all those people who were in stress or grief.

—Ellis Peters
A Morbid Taste for Bones

To pray means to open our hands before God. In prayer, you encounter God in the soft breeze, in the distress and joy of your neighbor and in the loneliness of your own heart.

—Henri J. M. Nouwen
With Open Hands

I believe that God prays in us and through us, whether we are praying or not (and whether we believe in God or not). So, any prayer on my part is a conscious response to what God is already doing in my life.

—Malcolm Boyd

Prayer is a means of perfect protection, perfect ordering of your lives in every moment.

—John D. Rea
Patterns of the Whole

Red Weasel: Dreamer-of-the-Sun told me that I may pray with my mouth and the prayer will be heard, but if I sing the prayer it will be heard sooner by Wakan' Tanka.

—Kenneth Lincoln
Native American Renaissance

Prayer makes the soul one with God.

—Julian of Norwich
Revelations of Divine Love

What seems our worse prayers may really be, in God's eyes, our best.... God sometimes seems to speak to us most intimately when he catches us, as it were, off our guard.

—C. S. Lewis
Letters to Malcolm

To pray is to be in touch with oneself in a new way: to listen to the melody, not made by ourselves, that sounds at the core of our being and, from beyond the sickness that deafens us, summons us to be alive.

—Gregory Baum
Man Becoming

Teach your mouth to say that which you have in your heart.

—Poeman
The Sayings

The Prayer of the heart has no interest in being right.... It does not try to unlock God's heart or to put a part of God to good use. It embraces God.... Now the heart is singing with the heart of God, and all the earth is a chorus.

—Hugh Prather
There Is a Place Where You Are Not Alone

The soul may ask God for anything and never fail. You may ask God for his presence, or for wisdom, and receive each at his hands. Or, like the Israelites in the Sinai wilderness, we ask God to go away.

—Annie Dillard
Teaching a Stone to Talk

He offered a prayer so deeply devout that he seemed kneeling and praying at the bottom of the sea.

—Herman Melville
Moby Dick

To pray does not mean to listen to oneself speaking. Prayer involves becoming silent and being silent and waiting until God is heard.

—Søren Kierkegaard

For Pueblo people, pottery is a prayer realized in physical form. Pottery holds life because pottery is the vessel created from the sacred earth.

—Marie Battiste
Reclaiming Indigenous Voice and Vision

Prayer is like lying awake at night, afraid, with your head under the cover, hearing only the beating of your own heart. It is like a bird that has blundered down the flue and is caught indoors and flutters at the window panes.... But sometimes a prayer comes that you have not thought to pray, yet suddenly there it is and you pray it.... Sometimes the bird finds that what looks like an opening is an opening, and it flies away.

—Wendell Berry
Jayber Crow

Know that through prayer remembering comes, then recognition, then acceptance, then at-oneness, then final liberation.

—*Tibetan Book of the Dead*

"Amen" comes from the Egyptian god, Amun, meaning "The Hidden One."

—John Matthews
Drinking from the Sacred Well

Man of Holiness: No prayers are unanswered, but many answers are unheard because Man's Spirit listens only to its own voice and has not yet learned to hear Mine. And sometimes the answer is "no" or "not yet" because what is asked for will not bring the happiness he imagines. I know him better than he knows himself.

—Anne Perry
Tathea

Without Laughter and Work, Prayer turns Gnostic, cranky, Pharisaic, while those who try to live by Work alone, without Laughter or Prayer, turn into insane lovers of power, tyrants, who would enslave Nature to their immediate desires.

—W. H. Auden
Introduction, *The Star Throwers*

Agnostic's Prayer: Oh God, if there is a God, save my soul, if I have a soul.

—Ernest Renan

Lord, help me to keep my hands off things that don't belong to me, such as other people's lives.

—Colleen Townsend Evans
Start Loving

May my body be a prayerstick for the world.

—Joan Halifax
The Fruitful Darkness

When it's prayer time, pray; when it's partridge time, partridge!

—Teresa of Avila

Pray to God, but row for the shore.

—Russian proverb

Pray, but row against the rocks.

—Native American proverb

Prayer or no prayer, you can't eat out of an empty bowl.

—Slovak proverb

PRESENCE

Faith was never a matter of believing He existed, but of trusting in the Presence that was experienced and known to exist as a self-validating datum. It seems likely that far more people in our time neither experience the Presence of God, nor the Presence of His Absence, but the absence of His Presence.

—R. D. Laing
Spiritual Emergency

They [archetypes] are an eternal presence, and it is merely a question of whether or not consciousness perceives this presence.

—Carl G. Jung

PRESENT

Confine yourself to the present.

—Marcus Aurelius

Nothing is worth more than this day.

—Johann Wolfgang von Goethe

The flower, the sky, your beloved can only be found in the present moment.

—Thich Nhat Hanh

The present moment is all you ever have. There is never a time when your life is not this moment.

—Eckhart Tolle
The Power of Now

To place ourselves in the present moment is to remember ourselves.

—P. D. Ouspensky
I Am the Fourth Way

Above all, we cannot afford not to live in the present.

—Henry David Thoreau

In rivers, the water that you touch is the last of what has passed and the first of that which comes: so with present time.

—Leonardo da Vinci

Each day is an incarnation … there is no time, only a present in which all things occur.

—Jane Roberts
The Nature of Personal Reality

If you allow the future to remain in the future and simply deal with the present now—it will be simpler … Even five minutes from now is the future, it is not the present.

—Diane Stein,
Stroking the Python

The Now is endlessly mystical and transforming. When we stop and gaze we are astounded to discover at the edges of our fears the jeweled stitchery from God's hand, the embroidery of love sewing our days together in all seasons.

—Robert Merrill Eddy &
Kathy Wonson Eddy
Writing with Light

To attend means to be present, sometimes with companionship, sometimes with patience. It means to take care of.

—Mary Catherine Bateson
Peripheral Visions

The present is a freely given canvas. That it is being constantly ripped apart and washed downstream goes without saying; it is a canvas, nevertheless.

—Annie Dillard

More and more I find I want to be living in a Big Here and a Long Now.

—Brian Eno

Yesterday is but a dream, tomorrow is but a vision. But today well lived makes every yesterday a dream of happiness, and every tomorrow a vision of hope. Look well, therefore, to this day.

—Sanskrit proverb

Only that which is temporary endures.

—French proverb

PRIDE

Pride is spiritual cancer—it eats up the very possibility of love or contentment or even common sense.

—C. S. Lewis

St. Bernard and St. Thomas Aquinas denounced the *libido sciendi*, an unchecked appetite for learning, as the first degree of pride.

—Sabine Melchior Bonet
The Mirror

Despair is the too-little of responsibility, as pride is the too-much.

—Wendell Berry
What Are People For?

PROBLEMS

We cannot solve the problems we have created with the same thinking that created them.

—Albert Einstein

There is no such thing as a problem without a gift for you in its hands.

—Richard Bach
Illusions

You have never given any problem to the Holy Spirit He has not solved for you, nor will you ever do so.

—*A Course in Miracles*

The drowning man is not troubled by rain.

—Sufi proverb

PROCESS

The road is always better than the inn.

—Miguel Cervantes

Scientists often describe ... the exhilaration that comes from the pursuit of truth and of beauty ... the joy of discovery, of solving a problem.... It is the pursuit that counts, not the attainment.

—Mihaly Csikszentmihalyi
Creativity

The Feminine prefers process to product, meandering and enjoying the pleasure of the journey, rather than, like the masculine style, determining the goal and moving directly toward it in a straight line.

—Marion Woodman & Connie Zweig
To Be A Woman

PROPHESY

Our age is filled with prophecies of doom and breakdown, which are obviously alarming. But the greater truth is that there is no death without rebirth, no

renewal without the breaking down of
outdated structures and habit patterns.

—George Trevelyan
A Vision of the Aquarian Age

Prophesy ... allows us to witness the
future consequences of choices that we
make in the present.

—Gregg Braden
The Isaiah Effect

Beware, O earth, the prophet who claims
to know the time but never wears a watch.

—Calvin Miller
The Finale

... the story of Oedipus, or *The Man who
Would be King*, or *The Hobbit*, in most of
them the very steps taken to prevent the
fulfillment of the prophecy actually bring
it about.

—C. S. Lewis
Of Other Worlds

There is the grain of the prophet in the
recesses of every human existence.

—Abraham Joshua Heschel
God in Search of Man

Mayan and Aztec almanacs predicted the
arrival of Cortez to the day! 11 Ahau. The
people were surprised only by their cruelty.

—Leslie Marmon Silko
Yellow Woman and a Beauty of Spirit

The mark of the prophet is to speak
the truth in love with courage—come
what may.

—Cornel West

PSYCHIC

We are all psychic ... the body is
indeed the temple of the living God.
There He has promised to meet thee, to
commune with thee. There is the psychic
development, the psychic phenomena
that ye seek.

—Edgar Cayce

No way of being-in-the-world is higher
than another. One may be more difficult to
attain, but each is valid on its own terms.

—Lawrence Leshan
*The Medium, the Mystic and the
Physicist*

Our solar plexus in the pit of the stomach
is a receiving station for wireless telegra-
phy over which we can receive all sorts of
thought-telegrams.

—Karl Ludwig Schleich

Children are universally psychic. They
know that reality is multi-sided, other
facets existing but not showing....
Children "know things," talk with
invisible playmates, fairies, dream vividly
and fully, astral travel, predict deaths as
everyday happenings, foresee births, see
elementals and spirits. All these are real
and take place in a child's real world,
an alternate world to outside-the-circle
concepts of reality.

—Diane Stein
Stroking the Python

False prophesy is always about self-interest and quest for power.... Ignorance is

the breeding ground for false prophesy and bigotry.

—William Sherden
The Fortune Sellers

The clairvoyant must retain a firm footing on the earth.

—Rudolf Steiner
Knowledge of the Higher Worlds and Its Attainment

PURPOSE

This is the true joy in life, the being used for a purpose recognized by yourself as a mighty one ... the being a force of nature instead of a feverish, selfish little clod of ailments and grievances complaining that the world will not devote itself to making you happy.

—George Bernard Shaw

What do we live for if not to make the world less difficult for each other?

—George Eliot

My own working assumption is that we are here as local Universe information gatherers. We are given access to the divine design principles so that from them we can invent the tools that qualify us as problem solvers in support of the integrity of an eternally regenerative Universe.

—R. Buckminster Fuller

Each man has only one genuine vocation—to find the way to himself.... His task is to discover his own destiny—not an arbitrary one—and live it out wholly

and resolutely within himself. Everything else is only a would-be existence, an attempt at evasion, a flight back to the ideals of the masses, conformity, and fear of one's own inwardness.

—Hermann Hesse

What you love is a sign from your higher self of what you are to do.... There is a higher purpose to your life, a special contribution you came to make. You can know the Higher Will by listening within.

—Sanaya Roman
Spiritual Growth

You and I are on the verge of moving into an age where man is discovering the new spiritual dimensions of himself, and you and I want to be free of those blocks at the mental and physical and emotional levels to bring more balance into our lives that we may represent and fulfill God's purpose in this earth, his purpose for us. For you and I have no other excuse for being.

—Hugh Lynn Cayce & Sally Hammond
We Are All Healers

What is my role, my duty, my goal, amidst this bewildering breath-taking drama in which I find myself involved?

—Heinrich Zimmer
Philosophies of India

Why should I live? Why should I do anything? Is there in life any purpose which the inevitable death that awaits me does not undo and destroy?

—Leo (Lev) Tolstoy
My Confessions

Know, O beloved, that man was not created in jest or at random, but marvelously made and for some great end.

—Al-Ghazzali

Everything depends on the use to which it is put.

—Reinhold Niebuhr

We are a pathway along which God's purpose runs, and its progress through us hurts.

—H. A. Hartwick
The Garden

The purpose of life is to leave one's mark upon the cave. The meaning of life is revealed at the point where all our marks converge.

—Lois Gould

When we align our thoughts, emotions and actions with the highest part of ourselves, we are filled with enthusiasm, purpose and meaning. ... We are joyously and intimately engaged with our world.

—Gary Zukav
The Seat of the Soul

Entelechy, a Greek word meaning the dynamic purpose that drives us toward realizing our essential self ... gives us our higher destiny and the capacities and skills that our destiny needs for its unfolding. It is the *entelechy* of an acorn to be an oak tree.... And it is the *entelechy* of a human being to be ... God knows what!

—Jean Houston
The Mythic Life

He who has a why to live can bear with almost any how.

—Friedrich Nietzche

No one is useless in this world who lightens the burdens of it to anyone else.

—Charles Dickens

Things happen—people come—events stack up.
When you're least aware of it, purpose happens.

—Rainer Maria Rilke

The purpose of life is a life of purpose.

—George Bernard Shaw

Here's a test to find whether your mission on earth is finished: if you're alive, it isn't.

—Richard Bach
Jonathan Livingston Seagull

PYRAMID

Where there were no mountains, people built artificial mountains ... stepped pyramids—the Ziggurats—of Mesopotamia ... meant both the summit of a mountain and a man-made stepped tower.... The earliest Egyptian pyramid was a stepped pyramid.... On the other side of the world simpler, starker pyramids were rising, symbols of the universal awe of mountains.

—Daniel J. Boorstin
The Discoverers

The stones of the Great Pyramid were cut to such precision that to produce such fine work these days, we would need to employ lasers.... The ancient Egyptians moved (without the wheel) over six million tons of stone to build a single structure containing more masonry than all the churches and cathedrals built in England since the time of Christ.

—Jean Houston
  The Passion of Isis & Osiris

Recent scientific experiments appear to confirm the fact that the Great Pyramid is no ordinary structure, as it possesses properties which are at variance with any known scientific phenomena ... [were] they constructed as tombs, places of worship, safe habours during a cataclysm, or time capsules.

—Murry Hope
  Ancient Egypt

QUANTUM THEORY

It was Max Planck who, in 1900,
developed his Quantum Theory. By
mathematical means he assumed that
radiant energy was not emitted in a flowing stream of different wave lengths, but
in definite bundles or quanta.

—Faber Birren
What Is Light? What Is Color?

Nobody understands quantum theory.

—Richard Feynman

If someone says that he can think about
quantum physics without becoming
dizzy, that shows only that he has not
understood anything whatever about it.
Anyone who is not shocked by quantum
theory has not understood it.

—Niels Bohr

Everything that has already happened is
particles, everything in the future is waves.

—Annie Dillard

In one stroke the Victorian battleground
where the laws of God and the laws of
nature clash meaninglessly with each was

swept away. Quantum physics left us with the nature of the text of possibilities.

—Angela Tilby
Soul: God, Self and the New Cosmology

Quantum mechanics, or quantum physics as it is commonly called, differs from classical physics as dramatically as night differs from day.... The laws that govern the classical realm are in direct opposition to how things work at the subatomic level of the universe.... At the subatomic level, particles do not move in a continuous manner. Rather they make unexpected and unexplainable quantum leaps.

—Charlotte Shelton
Quantum Leaps

(The quantum world) is a vast porridge of being where nothing is fixed or measurable ... somewhat ghostly and just beyond our grasp... A wonderful well of potential, filled with indeterminate relationships, sort of ebbing and flowing into each other, creating new realities, coming apart and going back to other realities. And everything is wonderfully interlinked and interrelated.

—Danah Zohar

When the world ceased to be a machine, when we began to recognize its dynamic, living qualities, many familiar aspects of it disappeared.

—Margaret J. Wheatley
Leadership and the New Science

Quantum physics is simply the scientific explanation for how God—"the system" if

you please—looks at its individual parts and watches itself impacting those parts.

—Duane Elgin
Awakening Earth

Quantum particles: the dreams that stuff is made of.

—David Moser

Everything comes from everything. Everything is made out of everything and everything returns into everything.

—Leonardo da Vinci & Michael J. Gelb
How to Think Like Leonardo Da Vinci

QUEST

To quest is to question, and the quality of the sacred quest has more to do with the questions we ask today than with the answers entombed within past dogma.

—L. Robert Keck
Sacred Quest

Women's spiritual quest concerns a woman's awakening to the depths of her soul and her position in the universe.

—Carol P. Christ
Diving Deep and Surfacing

Sophists asked: Could the questing mind, cleansed of pride, at least find a way to knowledge that might be the highest, permanent good? Could the seeking itself be a solace?

—Daniel J. Boorstin
The Seekers

What counts, Sam says, is not whether
the Quest succeeds, but whether we turn
back or slog ahead.

—Ralph C. Wood
The Gospel According to Tolkien

QUESTIONS

It is not the answer that enlightens, but
the question.

—Eugène Ionesco
Découvertes

A world without questions, with the
mystery all gone, would be a world
without God.

—Paul Sherer
Love Is a Spendthrift

Believe that the answer exists within
you—and wants to be found.

—Robert Apatow
The Spiritual Art of Dialogue

What is the ultimate truth about ourselves? Various answers suggest themselves. We are a bit of stellar matter gone
wrong. We are physical machinery—pup-
pets that strut and talk and laugh and
die as the hand of time pulls the strings
beneath. But there is one elementary
inescapable answer: We are that which
asks the question.

—Arthur Eddington

Existential intelligence entails the human
capacity to pose and ponder the biggest
questions: "Who are we? Why are we
here? What is going to happen to us?

Why do we die? What is it all about, in
the end?"

—Howard Gardner
Changing Minds

Learning to ask questions is to follow the
upward stream in human evolution....
We only learn to ask questions when we
are able to develop the inner balance
that allows reverence and devotion to
be retained when it comes to the sacred
spheres of life ... by not judging but
asking questions, not only of people who
may be able to tell us, but above all of the
world of the spirit.

—Rudolf Steiner
The Fifth Gospel

To ask seriously is to be willing to receive
an answer.... Because the Spirit can
always ask, learning can always take place.

—Herbert Brokering
Wholly Holy

The question often arrives a terribly long
time after the answer.

—Oscar Wilde

A vital question, a creative question, riv-
ets our attention. All the creative power
of our mind is focused on the question.

—Verna Allee
The Knowledge Evolution

Discovering strategic questions is like
panning for gold. You have to care about
finding it, you have to be curious, and
you have to create an anticipation of
discovering gold, even though none of us
may know ahead of time where we'll find
it. You head toward the general territory

where you think the gold may be located,
with your best tools, your experience,
and your instincts.

—Juanita Brown, David Isaacs &
Nancy Margulies
The Dance of Change

Live the questions now. Perhaps you will
then gradually, without noticing it, live
along some distant day into the answer.

—Rainer Maria Rilke

If you ask the right questions, it can
unloose a secret jam of thoughts.

—Paul Lehmberg
In the Strong Woods

Asking the proper question is the central
act of transformation.

—Clarissa Pinkola Estes
Women Who Run with the Wolves

Asking good questions is half of learning.

—Muhammad (Abu al-Qasim)

Questions without answers must be
asked very slowly.

—Anne Michaels
Fugitive Pieces

An answer is always a form of death.

—John Fowles
The Magus

You see things; and you say, "Why?"
But I dream things that never were, and
say, "Why not?"

—George Bernard Shaw
Back to Methuselah

Language was invented to ask questions.
Answers may be given by grunts and
gestures, but questions must be spoken.

—Eric Hoffer
Reflections on the Human Condition

Asking a question is the simplest way
of focusing thinking ... asking the right
question may be the most important part
of thinking.

—Edward de Bono

Exploring the question brings more
wisdom than having the answer.

—*A Course in Miracles*

It is said that when author Gertrude Stein
was on her deathbed, she asked over and
over again, apparently puzzled, "What is
the answer?" then, quite suddenly, Stein
sat bolt upright. Her last words were,
"No—what is the question!?"

—Sharon Seivert
The Balancing Act

Remember No is an answer.

—Words over a New England church door

RADIANCE

There is no creature that does not have
a radiance. Be it greenness of seed, blossom or beauty, it could not be creation
without it To be a creature is to be
brilliant, beautiful and on fire.

—Hildegard of Bingen

The Celtic word *glas* refers to the color of
a mountain lake.

—Philip Ball
  Bright Earth

Ascend with great intelligence from earth
to heaven, and again descend to earth,
and unite together the powers of higher
things and lower things. Thus you will
receive the glory of the whole world, and
darkness will fly away from you.

—Hermes Trismegistus
  8th Inscription of the Emerald Tablets

I am a flame of fire, blazing with passionate love; I am a spark of light, illuminating the deepest truth …

—*The Black Book of Carmarthen*

The heart of man has been so made
by God that, like a flint, it contains a
hidden fire which is evolved by music
and harmony, and renders man beside
himself with ecstasy. … they fan into

flame whatever love is already dormant
in the heart.

—Al-Ghazzali

RAINBOW

A Hebrew belief asserted that if Yahweh
lays aside his bow and hangs it in the
clouds, this is a sign that his anger has
subsided.... North American Indians
were among those who thought of the
rainbow as the Pathway of Souls....
Among the Japanese the rainbow is identified as the Floating Bridge of Heaven.

—Carl B. Boyer
The Rainbow: From Myth to Mathematics

As when the rainbow, opposite the sun
A thousand intermingled colors throws.
With saffron wings, then dewy Iris flies
Through heaven's expanse, a thousand
varied dyes.
Extracting from the sun, opposed in place.

—Virgil

Color comes from plucking the rainbow.

—Philip Ball
Bright Earth

What is the rainbow, Lord?
A hoop for the lowly.

—Jack Kerouac
The Dharma Burns

Rainbows exist only when there are eyes
and minds to see them.

—Rutherford Platt
The Rainbow Book

It takes both rain and sunshine to make
a rainbow. If life is to be rounded and
many-colored, like the rainbow, both joy
and sorrow must come to it.

—Jeanine Steuck
Good Morning, Judy

The work will wait while you show your
child the rainbow, but the rainbow won't
wait while you do the work.

—Patricia Clafford

The way I see it, if you want the rainbow,
you gotta put up with the rain.

—Dolly Parton

Rainbow! All music is a rainbow!

—Pablo Casals

READING

Monks have always recognized reading as
a bodily experience, primarily oral. The
ancients spoke of masticating the words
of scripture in order to fully digest them.

—Kathleen Norris

Reading gives God more glory when
we get more out of it, when it is a more
deeply vital act not only of our intelligence but of our whole personality,
absorbed and refreshed in thought, meditation, prayer or even in the contemplation of God.... Books can speak to us like
god, like men or like the noise of the city
we live in.

—Thomas Merton
Thoughts in Solitude

Every book is rewritten by the reader.

—Lynn V. Andrews
Flight of the 7th Moon

The man who will read no good books
has no advantage over the man who can't
read them.

—Mark Twain

John Stuart Mill was pushed to read at a
very early age—by the time he was
eight he'd read Aesop's Fables in the
original Greek, which he began to study
at three ... he read Homer, Greek plays,
Latin classics. At twelve he began studying Aristotelian logic in the original as
well as Scholastic commentaries; at 20 he
said he was a mere reasoning machine;
then he read Wordsworth.

— Ignacio L. Götz
On Technology and the Spirit

If you don't have the time to read, you
don't have the time or the tools to write.

—Stephen King
On Writing

Readability I have been told, is not
everything. Neither is breathing, but it
does come before whatever comes next.

—John, Ciardi, Introduction
The Craft of Writing

Watch a child's body when he is reading
if you want to see the real reader.

—William Sloane
The Craft of Writing

To read is to translate ... a bad reader is a
bad translator.

—W. H. Auden
The Dyer's Hand

A book is a mirror; if an ass peers into it,
you can't expect an apostle to look out.

—C. G. Lichtenberg

REALITY

"What is real?" asked the Rabbit one
day.... "Real isn't how you are made," said
the Skin Horse. "It's a thing that happens
to you. When a child loves you ... then
you become real.

—Margery Williams
The Velveteen Rabbit

Reality is always much bigger than the
data we collect.

—Charlotte Shelton
Quantum Leaps

Great caution must be exercised in using
the word real.

—Max Planck
*Scientific Autobiography and
Other Papers*

The real environment is altogether
too big, too complex, and too fleeting
for direct acquaintance.... Man is no
Aristotelian god contemplating all
existence at one glance.... He is the
creature of an evolution who can just

about span a sufficient portion of reality
to manage his survival.

—Walter Lippmann
Public Opinion

I refuse to be intimidated by reality anymore. After all, what is reality anyway?
Nothin' but a collective hunch. Reality is
the leading cause of stress amongst those
in touch with it.

—Jane Wagner
*The Search for Signs of Intelligent Life in
the Universe*

Speaking creates reality. What you say is
what you get. So say it.

—John Whiteside & Sandra Egli
Flight of the Phoenix

Only through conscious observation
does anything become real.

—John Gribbin
In Search of Schrödinger's Cat

What matters is being spontaneously
open to the reality of God.

—Thomas Merton
The Springs of Contemplation

Reality is the child of two parents: The
inexhaustible environment of information, and the ineffable conscious mind.

—Robert Jahn

What we think depends on what we perceive. What we perceive determines what
we believe. What we believe determines

what we take to be true. What we take to
be true is our reality.

—Gary Zukav
The Dancing Wu Li Masters

I have no doctrine. I only point out
something. I point out reality. I point out
something in reality which has not or too
little been seen.

—Martin Buber

Reality has no inside, outside,
or middle part

—Bodhidharma

A higher order of reality has
smashed through.

—Paul Scherer
Love Is a Spendthrift

Reality is created tiny bit by tiny bit.

—Martia Nelson
Coming Home

Reality is, and is always, both subjective
and objective, inner and outer. This can
only be understood in the total context of
the whole universal environment.

—Robert Ellwood
The Cross and the Grail

In truth, all reality is one.

—Rudolf Steiner
Theosophy

Everything in our lives is there because
we put it there.... Most of the time we are

completely unaware of when and how we do this.

—Sandra J. Stevens
Being Alive Is Being Psychic

I saw that reality might not be a fixture—crudely, inescapable there—but a continuing, spontaneous enterprise of the imagination. It might be shaped, remade, revalued, again and again, through each act of perception, each inventive gesture of relationship.

—Lindsay Clarke
The Chymical Wedding

To cut up reality and make it more real.... This is the intricate music of the art of fiction. It's the music I have always tried to play.

—John Steinbeck

Crazy Horse dreamed and went into the world where there is nothing but the spirits of all things. That is the real world that is behind this one, and everything we see here is something like a shadow from that world.

—Black Elk
Black Elk Speaks

There are some men for whom a tree has no reality until they think about cutting it down.

—Thomas Merton
A Thomas Merton Reader

For most people, it is impossible to believe that anything is possible in our reality.

For then, they would have to take full responsibility for what we have created.

—Barbara Hand Clow
Eye of the Centaur

A newly-created concrete reality has been laid in our arms; we answer for it.

—Martin Buber & Aubrey Hodes
Martin Buber

Sometimes reality is too complex. Fiction gives it form.

—Jean-Luc-Godard

Real things are sharp and knobbly and complicated and different.

—C. S. Lewis
Miracles

In every seed of every weed, in the knee-joint of a dead wasp's leg, the structure of the Whole of Reality is laid bare for those who have eyes to see.

—Frederick Franck
The Awakened Eye

Reality depends partly on how we measure it.

—Ken Wilber
Up from Eden

Look reality in the eye and deny it.

—Garrison Keillor

You can't buy corn with a bag of gold at the end of the rainbow.

—African American proverb

RECEIVING/ RECIPROCITY

A person becomes a person only when he is capable of standing open to all the gifts which are prepared for him … when someone accepts a gift, he admits another into his world and is ready to give him a place in his own being…. Ultimately, a gift becomes a gift only when it is accepted.

—Henri J. M. Nouwen
With Open Hands

Whatever is received is received according to the nature of the recipient.

—Thomas Aquinas

When you "receive" in a relationship, you receive from yourself.

—Neale Donald Walsch
Tomorrow's God

Our new paradigm shift points to reciprocity … intention replaces knowledge.

—Richard Higgs
Hiding in the Light

REINCARNATION

The Soul is older than the body. Souls are continuously born again into this life.

—Plato (Aristocles)

Every soul comes into this world strengthened by the victories or weakened by the defeats of his previous life.

—Origin (Adamantius)

In each life the human spirit appears as a repetition of itself, with the fruits of its experiences in earlier lifetimes.

—Rudolf Steiner
Theosophy

The whole purpose of reincarnation is to facilitate the continuity of a being's work.

—Dalai Lama
Freedom in Exile

When a circle is completed, one simply moves on to other rounds.

—Lynn V. Andrews
Star Woman

Imagine a wide ocean with a golden yoke adrift upon it. In the depths of the ocean swims a single blind turtle, who surfaces for air once every hundred years. How rare would it be for the turtle to surface with its head through the hold in the yoke? The Buddha said that attaining a precious human rebirth is rarer than that.

—Dalai Lama
The Way to Freedom

The concept of reincarnation linked to the stars and the passage of the Sun and Moon through the Zodiac is not confined to Egypt but is found in many other cultures and was indeed current in the Mediterranean until Greek times, for example in the beliefs of Pythagoras…. In India now the making of a birthchart, the casting of a horoscope, is a normal and usual event, and the practice of astrology is intimately related to the wider pattern of beliefs, including that of reincarnation.

—Sheila Farrant
Symbols for Women

Our personal inner geometry of stars and shadows was formed over eons of experience on many worlds and is a legacy we must treasure until we finally arrive Home on the day all hearts share their secrets.

—Robert Ellwood
The Cross and the Grail

We are not trapped by a difficult past life any more than we are by a difficult childhood.

—Diane Mariechild
Mother Wit

There are no accidents. Just because the body is small does not mean the spirit is. For some souls there only needs to be a short time upon the planet. When one has completed one's purpose, even if that purpose is to aid or support another by an early death, then dying is still the choice of the soul—even in an infant body. There are even those who enter the body for a short period of time simply as teachers for those about them.

—Sheila Petersen-Lowary
Channels to a New Reality

The self "mediates" an earthly form (the body) whereby it can pass through the experiences of the three-dimensional world, and by greater awareness takes a further step toward realization.

—Carl G. Jung & Karl Schlotterbeck
Living Your Past Lives

You have all been reincarnated and when you are finished living your series of earthly lives, you will continue to exist in other systems of reality. In each life you experience conditions that you have chosen beforehand, circumstances and challenges tailored to fit your own needs and to develop your own abilities. You live in the Spacious Present.

—Jane Roberts
The Seth Material

Every cell in your body is holding the energy of experience, not only from this lifetime, but every lifetime ... our concept of linear time is too limited. Holographic time is the actual reality.

—Chris Griscom & Shirley MacLaine
Dancing in the Light

Each soul will have to voluntarily return and experience the emotional equivalent, good or bad, of all that he has caused others to experience. Whatever weakness we persecute in others, we shall eventually inherit. Each soul is its own judge and jury. To have freedom, give it. To have peace, make it.

—Edgar Cayce
On Reincarnation

You do not understand your own multi-dimensional reality; therefore, it seems strange or unbelievable when I tell you that you live many existences at one time. It is difficult for you to imagine being in two places at once, much less in two or more times.

—Jane Roberts
Seth Speaks

I always remember the saying of the Cabalists that man's mission is the correction of the mistakes he made both in this world and in former reincarnations.

—Isaac Bashevis Singer
The Image and Other Stories

I am just as certain as you see me here that I have existed a thousand times before and I hope to return a thousand times more.

—Johann Wolfgang von Goethe

It is absolutely necessary that the soul should be healed and purified and if this does not take place during its life on earth, it must be accomplished in future lives.

—Gregory (the Illuminator)

As far back as I can remember I have unconsciously referred to the experiences of a previous state of existence ... as the stars looked to me when I was a shepherd in Assyria, they look to me now a New Englander.... And Hawthorne, too, I remember as one with whom I sauntered in old heroic times along the banks of the Scamander amid the ruins of chariots and heroes.

—Henry David Thoreau
The Writings of Henry David Thoreau

I cannot think of permanent enmity between man and man, and believing as I do in the theory of rebirth, I live in the hope that if not in this birth, in some other birth I shall be able to hug all humanity in friendly embrace... Where is the good of knowing in detail the numberless births we have gone through? Life would be a burden if we carried such a tremendous load of memories. A wise man deliberately forgets many things.

—Mohandas (Mahatma) Gandhi
The Phoenix Mystery

We are given new chances that we may learn, that we may evolve.... Nothing of real value is ever lost, nor our misdeeds, our cruel and treacherous acts, forgotten

until we have atoned for them. It is not that some being is keeping account of our thoughts and deeds, but we ourselves keep a complete record ... and we reap the sum total of these thoughts and deeds in our every embodiment.

—Paramananda
Reincarnation and Immortality

The object of reincarnation is learning, and each soul passes through a myriad of experiences that the cycle of lifetimes is meant to fill.... Every soul lives the gamut of emotions and lifestyles, life experiences, and works on specific learning tasks.

—Diane Stein
Stroking the Python

We live as many physical existences as we feel we must in order to develop our abilities and prepare ourselves to enter other dimensions of reality.

—Jane Roberts
The Seth Material

My doctrine is: Live so that thou mayest desire to live again; that is thy duty. For in any case, thou wilt live again!

—Friedrich Nietzche

After all, it is no more surprising to be born twice than it is to be born once. Everything in Nature is resurrection.

—François-Marie Arouet (Voltaire)

The cat has four legs, one in each corner. He also has nine lives, which he does not use in the West because of Christianity.

—From a Hindu child's essay on The Cat

REJECTION

A writer needs the sensitivity of a
butterfly in touching the outside
world—and the skin of a rhino to
withstand its disregard.

—Sophy Burnham
For Writers Only

We have read your manuscript with
boundless delight. If we were to publish
your (book) it would be impossible for
us to publish any work of lower standard.
And, as it is unthinkable that in the next
thousand years we shall see its equal, we
are, to our regret, compelled to return
your divine composition and to beg you
a thousand times to overlook our short
sight and timidity.

—Rejection letter from a
Chinese publisher

RELATIONSHIP

Relation is the essence of everything that is.

—Meister Eckhart

All real living is meeting.

—Martin Buber

Everything that exists is an expression of
relationships, alliances and balances of
energies, powers and spirits.

—L. David Peat
Lighting the Seventh Fire

It later became clear to me that no matter
what we do in science or any other area,

it will not help if we don't find a way to be
related to each other at a deep level.

—David Bohm

Spiritual practice is really about weaving
a network of good relationships.

—Dhyani Ywahoo

Relationship is a cold word. It has no
vibrancy like, for instance, kinship,
which immediately stirs something in
one's blood, or like love with its infinity
of overtones.

—Irene Claremont de Castillejo
Knowing Woman

It is the corrosive daily frustrations, the
inability to communicate or to establish
meaningful relationships that is so
soul-shrinking.

—Edward T. Hall
Beyond Culture

If we belong to God, God belongs to us;
we are in a relationship. This is mysticism
of course, but any one of us can experience it daily. God is related to us in a
personal way. That's the experiential basis
for the notion that God must have all the
perfection that makes me a person and
none of the limitations.

—David Steindl-Rast
Belonging to the Universe

There is an innate striving in all forms
of matter to organize into relationships.
There is a great seeking for connections,
a desire to organize into more complex
systems that include more relationships,

more variety.... Attraction is an organizing force of the universe.

—Margaret Wheatley &
Myron Kellner-Rogers
a simpler way

In safe relationships, you can trust that
you will not be lied to and will be free of
exploitation, where the other does not
feel superior at your expense, does not
betray your confidences, or intrude upon
your boundaries.

—Jean Shinoda Bolen
Ring of Power

In the best relationships, synergy is
created. You and I become more together
than we are on our own. We help each
other experience the Sacred.

—Sharon Seivert
The Balancing Act

When indeed shall we learn that we are
all related one to the other, that we are all
members of one body?

—Helen Keller

Entering into relation is an act of the
whole being. It is an act by which we
constitute ourselves as human.

—Martin Buber

If we think about it, we find that our life
consists in achieving a pure relationship
between ourselves and the living universe
about us.

—D. H. Lawrence

The meeting of two personalities is like
the contact of two chemical substances. If
there is any reaction, both are transformed.

—Carl G. Jung

Once the realization is accepted that
even between the closest human beings
infinite distances continue to exist, a
wonderful living side by side can grow
up, if they succeed in loving the distance
between them which makes it possible
for each to see the other whole and
against a wide sky!

—Rainer Maria Rilke

To get along with other people, find the
rhythm that harmonizes with their own
and then bring them into harmony. Find
within yourself that which fills their
inner void and addresses that in them.

—Neil Douglas-Klotz
Prayers of the Cosmos

All is relationship. Perhaps the ultimate
ethic of immanence is to choose to make
that relationship one of love.

—Starhawk
Dreaming the Dark

All things are related—related in
different, complicated ways. But all
things are not one.

—C. S. Lewis

As we penetrate into matter, nature does
not show us any isolated building blocks,
but rather appears as a complicated web
of relations between the various parts of
the whole. These relations always include
the observer in an essential way.... In
atomic physics, we can never speak about

nature without at the same time, speaking about ourselves.

—Fritjof Capra
The Tao of Physics

Only in the mirror of relationship do you see the face of what is.

—Jiddu Krishnamurti

The more uncertain I have felt about myself, the more there has grown up in me a feeling of kinship with all things.

—Carl G. Jung
Memories, Dreams, Reflections

Relationship must always be created, then re-created.

—Linda Sussman
The Speech of the Grail

Lascaux suggests a mysterious understanding between men and other living creatures which bespeaks relationships beyond our imagination, infinitely remote from our analytical capacity.

—Giorgio de Santillana &
Hertha Von Dechend
Hamlet's Mill

When mathematicians and anthropologists go back generation after generation, connecting all genealogical lines, they contend that all men now alive are 50th cousins at most.

—Norman Cousins
The Celebration of Life

The function of Aboriginal values and customs is to maintain the relationships that hold creation together.

—Marie Battiste
Reclaiming Indigenous Voice and Vision

While European philosophy tended to find reality in substance, Chinese philosophy tended to find it in relation.

—Joseph Needham
Science and Civilization in China

The fulcrum to Indian life is relatedness.

—Kenneth Lincoln
Native American Renaissance

The worst thing a Navajo can say of someone is "He acts as if he has no relatives."

—Trudy Griffin-Pierce
Earth is My Mother, Sky is My Father

The Mohawks have 120 terms to express family relationship.

—F. David Peat
Lighting the Seventh Fire

We are all Relations. The Household of God is big enough for all.

—Joan Borysenko
A Woman's Journey to God

Death ends a life, but it does not end a relationship, which struggles on in the survivor's mind toward some resolution, which it may never find.

—Robert Anderson
I Never Sang for My Father

RELIGION

Religion means "that which reconnects."

—Denise Levertov
Light Up the Cave

... the Latin word *religare*—meaning to bind back, to re-collect—not only people, but ideas—to make sense of things in the cosmos.

—David Leeming
Myth: A Biography of Belief

Religion: the social place we go to work on our inner life.

—Ira Progoff

I have a terrible need ... shall I say the word? ... of religion. Then I go out at night and paint the stars.

—Vincent van Gogh

Religion is a system of symbols which act to produce powerful, pervasive, and long-lasting moods and motivations.

—Clifford Geertz
The Interpretation of Cultures

It is curious that it should be in America of all places, that a European should really experience religion ... the moment I saw the brilliant, proud morning shine high up over the deserts of Santa Fe, something stood still in my soul, and I started to attend.

—D. H. Lawrence
Phoenix: The Posthumous Papers of D. H. Lawrence

Religion is always serious play and playful seriousness, and so one would expect to feel real joy and vivacity in the precinct of a genuine shrine.

—Thomas Moore
The Re-Enchantment of Everyday Life

All art worthy of the name is religious. Whether it is made of lines or of colors, if this creation is not religious, it is not art. It is nothing more than a document, an anecdote.

—Henri Mattisse

Religion is the vision of something which stands beyond, behind and within the passing flux of immediate things ...

—Alfred North Whitehead

Trust in the religious sphere has been hard to come by.

—Kathleen Norris
Dakota

We must choose our own kneeling places and not have thrust upon us an agenda foreign to our spirits.

—Marilyn Sewell
Cries of the Spirit

Religion is like riding a bicycle: the only safety there is lies in riding! Otherwise you can't even stay on. Momentum is the secret of poise. You'll spend all the days of your pilgrimage being upset, until you learn to fling yourself on such faith as you have, and instead of trying to put

up with the wrongs that people do you,
swing out to see them right!

—Paul Scherer
Love Is a Spendthrift

For many people, religion is a rigid
concept, somewhat like a stone that is
passed from generation to generation.
We don't add to it, change it, or challenge it; we just pass it along. But even
the most cursory study of the history
of religions would undermine such a
view. Religious traditions are far more
like rivers than stones ,,, flowing and
changing.... Sometimes they dry up
in arid land; sometimes they radically
change course and move out to water
new territory. All of us contribute to the
river of our traditions.

—Diana Eck
Encountering God

New names for eternal archetypes
emerge, rise, and fall in the name of a
"religion." We cannot be against religion,
but to be for it, we need to see the
deeper purpose common to all religions.
And by that ... I mean Jung's profound
psychological purpose in appealing to the
divinity within each individual.

—Alice O. Howell
The Dove in the Stone

To be religious is to give your life so
that the world may be more beautiful,
more just, more at peace; it is to prevent
egotistical and self-serving ends from
disrupting this harmony of the whole.

—Arturo Paoli
Meditations on Saint Luke

According to Erik Erikson, it was
Gandhi's mother who first taught him "a

certain basic religiosity—the undogmatic
sense of being carried along by a demanding and yet trustworthy universe."

—Matthew Fox
Original Blessing

A fundamental element of religion is an
intimate relationship with the land on
which the religion is practiced.

—Vine Deloria
God is Red

There is only one religion, though there
are a hundred versions of it.

—George Bernard Shaw

Let us not seek to bring religion to others,
but let us endeavor to live it ourselves.

—Paul Tournier

It is more important to create a safer,
kinder world than to recruit more people
to the religion that happens to satisfy us.

—Dalai Lama

From being an activity mainly concerned
with symbols, religion will be transformed into an activity concerned mainly
with experience and intuition—an everyday mysticism and giving significance to
everyday rationality, everyday tasks and
duties, everyday human relationships.

—Aldous Huxley

From Judaism, Christianity, and Islam
to Hinduism, Buddhism, Taoism and
Native American and Goddess religions,

each offers images of the sacred web into which we are woven.

—Joanna Macy

No religion is completely "new," no religious message completely abolishes the past. Rather, there is a recasting, a renewal, a revalorization, an integration of the elements—the most essential elements—of an immemorial religious tradition.

—Mircea Eliade

Detached from real issues and real evils, the language of religion became abstract, intensely pious, rhetorical, inflated with phony mysticism and joyless passion. The religious institutions became comfort stations for scribes and publicans and Pharisees.

—Wendell Berry
The Hidden Wound

The heart of religion lies in its personal pronouns.

—Martin Luther

Religion is not a museum of cult objects but a living tissue of beliefs, professions, avowals. The central act of myth and religion is the act of belief and worship.

—Walker Percy
The Message in the Bottle

Being religious means asking passionately the question of the meaning of our existence and being willing to receive answers even if the answers hurt.

—Paul Tillich

A man grows religious by means of reflection.

—Albert Schweitzer

You see, religion is really a kind of second womb. It's designed to bring this extremely complicated thing, which is a human being, to maturity, which means to be self-motivating, self-acting.

—Joseph Campbell
The Power of Myth

A man must invent his own religion or be enslaved by another's.

—William Blake

It's a tricky business, studying the unconverted through the eyes of the converted.

—Jackson Lears
Something for Nothing

It is clear that the religious impulse assumes its true significance and meaning only when it takes hold of the being of the human being so deeply that it pervades everything that the person brings forth out of his or her thinking, feeling and will.

—Rudolf Steiner
Reverse Ritual

Because religion is so deep, as profound as it is transcendent, it touches upon those issues that motivate us and yet remain hidden from awareness.

—Thomas Moore
The Soul's Religion

Our religions are training programs that enable us to bootstrap ourselves to the next level once we turn ourselves on.

—Richard Thieme

Religion is about humankind finding relationship to One Higher Source—God within.... Religions become corrupted when leaders/authorities controlled "God's Will."

—James Redfield
The Celestine Prophecy

All religion begins with the cry, "Help!"

—William James

All issues are ultimately religious.

—Arnold Toynbee

All religions have been true for their time.

—Joseph Campbell
The Place of Myth

The lovers of God have no religion but God alone.

—Jalai Al-din Rumi

Judaism says, "The Messiah is going to come, and that's the end of history"; Christianity says, "The Messiah is going to come back, and that's the end of history"; Islam says, "The Messiah came; history is irrelevant".

—Stewart Brand
The Clock of the Long Now

RENEWAL

People have been replacing the all-wood Ise Shrine every 25 years for over 1,000 years.... It's a monument to continuity—an unbroken lineage of structure, records and traditions. Materials are re-distributed to other shrines throughout Japan.... cakes and sake used for the renewal ceremonies are from rice ceremonially transplanted in the same seven-acre rice paddies used for over 2,000 years. Continuity and perpetual renewal go together.

—Stewart Brand
The Clock of the Long Now

Creation is a continuity and therefore must be renewed.

—Marie Battiste
Reclaiming Indigenous Voice and Vision

Renew thyself completely each day; do it again, and again, and forever again.

—Chinese proverb

REPENTANCE

Old paint on canvas, as it ages, sometimes becomes transparent. When that happens it is possible in some pictures, to see the original lines; a tree will show through a woman's dress, a child makes way for a dog, a large boat is no longer on an open sea. This is called pentimento because the painter "repented," changed his mind. Perhaps it would be as well to say that the old conception, replaced by a later choice, is a way of seeing and then seeing again.

—Lillian Hellman
Pentimento

Repentance is begun when we acknowledge our sins and are sincerely sorry for them … the sinner experiences anguish of heart and is filled with a painful longing for the salvation and mercy of God.

—Martin Luther

"Repent," if considered as "rethink," can bring a better understanding, at least mentally, than the usual emotional responses to the word repent. It does not mean "to be sorry for," for this is empty of progress…. Perhaps by rethinking more rationally and gaining a new understanding we might change entirely so as to have a tremendous awakening as to our own responsibility.

—J. Everett Irion
Interpreting the Revelation With Edgar Cayce

For as some people enjoy bad health, so others enjoy a bad conscience. Repentance is *metanoia*, or "change of mind"; and without it there cannot be even a beginning of the spiritual life…. This necessary change of mind is normally accompanied by sorrow and self-loathing. But these emotions are not to be persisted in…. In Middle English "remorse" is rendered as … "again-bite." In this cannibalistic encounter, who bites whom?

—Charles de Condren
The Perennial Philosophy

The Tibetan language doesn't even have an equivalent for the English word "guilt," although it does have words meaning "remorse," or "repentance" or "regret," with a sense of "rectifying things in the future."

—Dalai Lama
The Art of Happiness

RESONANCE

One can feel the resonance between opposites in flamenco dancing. Defender and attacker watch each other … each is a pole with its separate magnetic charge, each is a nation defending its borders, each is a warrior enjoying the heat of extravagant passion, a distinguished passion which is fierce, eagle-like, mysterious.

—Robert Bly
Iron John

Resonance (there is no wisdom without it) is a natural phenomenon, the shadow of import alongside the body of fact, and it cannot flourish except in deep time…. We are destroying deep time. Not by design, perhaps, but inadvertently.

—Sven Birkerts
The Guttenburg Elegies

RESPONSIBILITY

There is no one but us, there is no one to send … there is no one but us. There never has been.

—Annie Dillard
Holy the Firm

You must behave as if your every act, even the smallest, impacted a thousand people for a hundred generations. Because it does.

—Thom Hartmann
The Prophet's Way: Touching the Power of Life

In dreams begins responsibility.

—William Butler Yeats

The major sin of humankind is not pride—not trying to become more than we were created for—but shirking responsibility for full actualization of human potential.

—Harvey Cox
On Not Leaving It to the Snake

Responsibility is the navel-string of creation.

—Martin Buber

The best way to avoid responsibility is to say, "I've got responsibilities."

—Richard Bach
Illusions

To be responsible means to be capable of giving a response ... those of us who write are responsible for the effect of our books.... Like it or not, we either add to the darkness of indifference and out-and-out evil which surround us or we light a candle to see by.

—Madeleine L'Engle
Circle of Quiet

You become responsible, forever, for what you have tamed.

—Antoine de Saint-Exupéry
The Little Prince

You are not responsible for making other people's lives work; they are.

—Sanaya Roman
Spiritual Growth

Every act has meaning ... "accident" is a word born of confusion ... accident is

a way to lay down the responsibility for your action and ask another to pick it up for you.

—Lynn V. Andrews
Medicine Woman

REST

There are red letter days in our lives when we meet people who thrill us like a fine poem, people whose handshake is a brimful of unspoken sympathy and whose sweet, rich natures impart to our eager, impatient spirits a wonderful restfulness.

—Helen Keller

Sleep is that period when the soul takes stock of what it has acted upon, from one rest period to another; drawing comparisons, as it were, that make for harmony, peace, joy, love, long suffering, patience, brotherly love and kindness—all fruits of the spirit.

—Edgar Cayce
Dreams Your Magic Mirror

The more accelerated our life becomes, the more we have to learn to select only the essential, to create our own repose and meditation island within an uncluttered mental space.

—Anäis Nin
The Novel of the Future

We owe most of our great inventions and most of the achievements of genius to idleness—either enforced or voluntary.

—Agatha Christie

The notes I play like every pianist. But the pauses, ahhh, the pauses.

—Arthur Rubinstein

I can tell a good musician by the way he plays the rests.

—Wolfgang Amadeus Mozart

The antidote to exhaustion is not necessarily rest—it is wholeheartedness.

—David Whyte
Crossing the Unknown Sea

All of human unhappiness stems from one thing: not to know how to remain in repose in a room.

—Blaise Pascal

Hurry is contagious…. Happily, the opposite also holds true. When someone at peace and free from hurry enters a room, that person has a calming effect on everyone present.

—Eknath Easwaran
Meditation

There is no buoyancy in sharks; they cannot rest. They must keep swimming till they die.

—Russel Hoban
Turtle Diary

All action begins in rest.

—Lao Tzu

Too much rest itself becomes a pain.

—Homer

It takes a heap of loafing to write a book.

—Gertrude Stein

RESURRECTION

The conviction that a man who died came back to life is, of course, a paradox. But that paradox may contain the secret of its powerful appeal … it speaks the language of human emotions. It addresses itself to that which may be our deepest fear, and expresses our longing to overcome death.

—Elaine Pagels
The Gnostic Gospels

Every parting gives a foretaste of death; every coming together again a foretaste of the resurrection.

—Arthur Schopenhauer
Studies in Pessimism

We look forward to the restitution of all things, not only of the soul but also of the body…. After a man's body has decayed in the earth, it will rise in much greater beauty and glory.

—Martin Luther

Resurrection is an assertion about God before it is a puzzling reported fact about Jesus … the first shines through the second.

—Joseph Sittler
The Ecology of Faith

Be like the fox who makes more tracks than necessary, some in the wrong directions. Practice resurrection.

—Wendell Berry
Manifesto

REVELATION

Revelation is as ancient as conscious humanity. The fruit of inspiration, it arises out of the night of time. ... All powerful initiators have perceived in one moment of their lives the radiance of central truth, but the light which they drew from it was refracted and colored according to their genius, their mission, their particular time and place.

—Edouard Schuré
The Great Initiates

Revelation means getting a peek at the reality that is always there.

—Martin Bell
Return of the Wolf

All true metaphysics begins with *metanoia*, a turning toward the truth of a revelation. Turning toward the Divine Being born again has been corrupted by Protestant literalism ... *metanoia* isn't so much a rejection of the world as an embracing of the divine.

—Arthur Versluis
Theosophia

This Book of Revelation assaults our fear of metaphor head-on. The language of revelation can be dangerous especially if forced back into the literal.

—Kathleen Norris
The Cloistered Walk

The Revelation: a window on the journey of the soul.

—F. Aster Barnwell
Meditations on the Apocalypse

This is a revelation of Jesus Christ. It's revealed in an esoteric sense/form. So read this Apocalypse as a Mystery. The words are only signs.... The mystery of Revelation is that the Mysteries shall no longer be kept hidden. The Unique Mystery is to become the universal mystery.

—Rudolf Steiner

The Revelation of St. John the Divine is perhaps one of the most controversial books ever written ... history seems replete with stories of various gatherings of people to await the Second Coming of Jesus; even from about 200 A.D.... The Book of Revelation is just that—a revelation.

—J. Everett Irion
Interpreting The Revelation with Edgar Cayce

There is no pure revelation. Wherever the divine is manifest, it is manifest in "flesh," that is, in a concrete physical and historical reality.

—Paul Tillich
Biblical Religion and the Search for Ultimate Reality

REVERENCE

It is as impossible to live without reverence as it is without joy.

—Henry Beston
The Outermost House

Reverence is one's response to an awesome experience.

—Lucinda Vardey
God in All Worlds

Reverence is appreciating everyone and everything; you see beyond the shell of appearance and into essence.

—Gary Zukav & Linda Francis
The Heart of the Soul

RHYTHM

The essence of rhythm is the preparation of a new event by the ending of a previous one.... Everything that prepares a future creates rhythm; everything that begets or intensifies expectation ...

—Susanne K. Langer

Combining rhythm and melody together means that as we begin to breathe together we also vibrate together as we share pitch.... We risk being part of something much bigger than we are, something not to be controlled as much as to be with and in. As we are "in" love, so we are "in" music, "in" rhythm, "in" melody.

—Cynthia Serjak
Music and the Cosmic Dance

Clouds, torsos, shells, peppers, trees, rock, smokestacks are but interdependent, interrelated parts of a whole, which is life—Life rhythms felt in no matter what, become symbols of the whole.

—Edward Weston
Edward Weston, Photographer

Hans Jenny, the founder of cymatics, the study of wave forms, lends support to the theory that vibrations give form to the material world. When sound waves are introduced to various material substances—water, alcohol, pastes, oils, etc. they create symmetrical patterns with uniform characteristics. Rhythm shapes matter ... the pulse of life.... Falling in love with someone is falling into the same rhythm.

—Layne Redmond
When the Drummers Were Women

When you lose the rhythm of the drumbeat of God, you are lost from the peace and rhythm of life.

—Cheyenne proverb

RISK

We stand on the brink of a precipice. We peer into the abyss—we grow sick and dizzy. Our first impulse is to shrink from danger. Unaccountably, we remain.

—Edgar Allan Poe
The Imp of the Perverse

The only way to succeed in creating is to know that it's all right to fail. Risk is the only catalyst for innovation. You have to be terrified and use that terror to create.

—Mandy Patinkin

... the love affair with life, is to live as variously as possible, to groom one's curiosity like a high-spirited thoroughbred, climb aboard, and gallop over the thick, sun-struck hills every day. Where there is no risk, the emotional terrain is flat and unyielding, and despite all its dimensions, valleys, pinnacles, and detours, life will seem to have none of its magnificent geography, only a length.

—Diane Ackerman
A Natural History of the Senses

We cannot live without loving others, and each time we love someone we take a risk, the risk of being rejected. We cannot live without trusting others, and each time we trust somebody we take a risk by making ourselves vulnerable ... and all these risks we take, confident in a happy ending.

—G. Peter Fleck
The Blessings of Imperfection

And the day came when the risk to remain tight in a bud was more painful than the risk it took to blossom.

—Anäis Nin

Life is so terribly short, so precious—what we need to do ourselves and help our children to learn is the necessity of risk.

—Eda LeShan

How can you go out on a limb if you don't know your own tree?

—Eudora Welty
The Eye of the Story

It is only by risking our persons from one hour to the next that we live at all.

—William James

Be reckless with your energy and reckless with your being ... the gods are reckless or you would not have a world. The flowers are reckless or you would not have a spring or an autumn.

—Jane Roberts
Psychic Politics

A complete lack of caution is perhaps one of the true signs of a real gourmet; he has no need for it, being filled as he is with a God-given and intelligently self-cultivated sense of gastronomical freedom.

—M. F. K. Fisher
The Art of Eating

The attraction of risk lies in its subtle ambivalence; a man fears it, but he loves it at the same time ... it is the risk of failure which lends adventure its fascination.

—Paul Tournier
The Adventure of Living

Instead of shying away from risks, I attack them, provoke them.

—Pablo Picasso

Failure is a sure sign that you're not playing it safe, that you're still experiencing, still taking creative risks. If you're succeeding too much, you're doing something wrong.

—Woody Allen

The back porch is more secure, but the fun is in jumping the fences.

—Marjorie Holmes

RITUAL

Ritual comes from an Indo-European root which means "to fit together.

—Alan Combs & Mark Holland
Synchronicity

It is through rites that Heaven and earth are harmonious and sun and moon are bright, that the four seasons are ordered and the stars are on their courses, that rivers flow and that things prosper, that love and hatred are tempered and joy and anger are in keeping…. Rites require us to treat both life and death with attentiveness.

—Hsün Tzu

Ritual is the way we carry the presence of the sacred. Ritual is the spark that must not go out…. Rituals were designed to remind us over and over and over again of our true relationship to life: that of a grateful amazed supplicant at the feet of mystery.

—Christina Baldwin
Calling the Circle

The slow-moving ritual, characteristic of all ceremonies, is closely bound up with the rhythm of the astral movements. At the same time, every rite is a meeting, that is, a confluence of forces and patterns; the significance of rites stems from the accumulated power of these forces

when blended harmoniously one with the other.

—J. E. Cirlot
A Dictionary of Symbols

Rituals that are alive and meaningful feed our souls.

—Carol S. Pearson
Magic at Work

In the Eucharistic sacrament, whether Christian, Mexican, or Hindu, bread and wine are "charged with meaning": God is a meaning.

—Ananda K. Coomaraswamy
Coomaraswamy, Selected Papers

As the ritual progresses I often see them in their new … home and perceive the effect of the energies being directed to them. Frequently their loved ones also either see or feel them near during the ceremonies. I have seen long-standing grief eradicated completely after the sorrowing ones attended a memorial service.

—I. M. Kontzevitch
The Acquisition of the Holy Spirit

To the Navajo the artistic or aesthetic value of the sandpainting is found in its creation, not in its preservation. Its ritual value is in its symbolic or representational power and in its use as a vehicle or conception. Once it has served that purpose, it no longer has any ritual value.

—Gary Witherspoon
Language and Art in the Navajo Universe

Rituals not only construct reality and make meaning; they help us fashion the world as a habitable and hospitable place.... The reciprocity of narrative and ritual enhances the possibility of weaving human and divine stories into a single fabric.

—Herbert Anderson & Edward Foley
Mighty Stories, Dangerous Rituals

No other creature we know of relives the legends of his forefathers, blows out candles on a birthday cake or dresses up and pretends he is something else.

—Harvey Cox
The Feast of Fools

Behind every ritual there is a narrative.

—Virginia Beane Rutter
Woman Changing Woman

All original rituals were intended to connect the profane with the sacred.

—John R. Van Eenwyk
Archetypes and Strange Attractors

In ritual one lives through events, or through the alchemy of its framings and symbolings, relives semiogenetic events, the deeds and words of prophets and saints, or if these are absent, myths and sacred epics.

—Victor Turner
From Ritual to Theatre

Ritual is a statement of what we want and a remembrance of the great cycle of things.

—Brooke Medicine Eagle

Ritual is a sort of metaphysical housework intended to sustain some continuity

in the world ... when the ceremonies lapse, the natural order sickens.

—Mary Catherine Bateson
Peripheral Visions

Ritual is the original womb of art; its waters continue to nourish creativity.

—Starhawk
Truth or Dare

Flannery O'Connor conveyed baptism through its exaggeration, in one novel as a violent death by drowning. Once asked why she created such bizarre characters, she replied, "For the near-blind you have to draw very large, simple caricatures."

—Walker Percy
Message in the Bottle

The ritual of crowning England's kings and queens would have little significance if it were held at midnight at a location disclosed only to a few intimate family members.

—William G. Doty
Mythography

ROSICRUCIAN

... the rose female and the cross male, both ... typify the generative processes.

—Manly P. Hall
The Secret Teachings of All Ages

The rose and the cross have individually been given various interpretations, and in Christian symbolism they are sometimes found representing the Virgin Mary and Christ ... C. G. Jung has shown how the rose is a symbol lying deep in the collective unconscious. It represents the maternal womb and also perfection achieved by balance. The cross is linked … with the tendency for man's inner consciousness to seek fourfold patterns.

—Christopher Mcintosh
The Rosicrucians

"The Rosicrucians!" repeated the old gentleman, and in his turn he surveyed me with deliberate surprise. "Who but a Rosicrucian could explain the Rosicrucian mysteries! And can you imagine that any member of that sect, the most jealous of all secret societies, could themselves lift the veil that hides the Isis of their wisdom from the world?"

—Edward Bulwer-Lytton
Zanoni

Rosencreutz (1378-1484) is known to have brought back to Europe the ceremonial invocations of the planetary spirits and of the star spirits in general which he learned in Arabia and from the natives of Morocco.... The Rosicrucians used to have dealings with the beings from higher worlds. Their basic book, the Confessio, refers to "the service of the angels and spirits" …

—Willy Schrödter
A Rosicrucian Notebook

Rudolf Steiner's writings and lectures are full of references to Rosicrucianism and Christian Rosenkreuz whom he saw as an adept who appeared in other incarnations. He believed, for example, that Rosenkreuz had come as the Comte de Saint Germain to warn Marie Antoinette's lady-in-waiting of the impending Revolution.... When we try to reduce Rosicrucianism to its basic elements we are left with little more than a name, a symbol, a legend, certain occult associations, and a Gnostic type of outlook. Yet somehow this strange organism has succeeded in surviving and growing over a period of more than three centuries.

—Christopher Mcintosh
The Rosicrucians

Christian Rosenkreutz was allowed to ask many questions, to inquire concerning deeply significant riddles of existence in a way that was quite new when compared with earlier human experiences.... The Rosicrucians perceived how completely times had changed for the whole of human life, and therewith how completely the relation of the gods to humankind had also changed.... What for others was science, they enhanced into true wisdom.

—Rudolf Steiner
The Archangel Michael

Rosicrucians mingled Hermetic symbols with Christian.... The Rosicrucians continuously help the world, but in invisible and unfathomable ways.

—Julius Evola
The Mystery of the Grail

Communion with adepts takes place "on the other side." One must command one's soul, evening after evening before going to sleep, to visit the adept one longs to see and to inform the body so that it will remember the experience on waking.

—Gustav Meyrink
A Rosicrucian Notebook

Genuine Rosicrucians possessed—on their own admission and according to reports by outside observers—the gift of completely controlled astral projection ... when they talked of "meeting together at the house "Sancti Spiritus" they meant entering the spiritual plane in the spiritual body, the "glorified rose," the "crystallized salt."

—Willy Schrödter
A Rosicrucian Notebook

Rosicrucians regarded the Holy Grail as the feminine symbol for perfection—the "age to come."

—Michael Howard
The Occult Conspiracy

They cut through the crystallizations of dogma, approached the spiritual world directly, returning with a new version of its inexhaustible riches.

—Dennis Richard Danielson
The Book of the Cosmos

The exercises of the oriental Freemasons ... are nothing but a work carried out on themselves for improvement and gaining higher knowledge.... The exercises have persisted in the usage of the three signs of recognition of the modern masons: Sign, Grip and Word, except that originally, these three were not signs of recognition, not merely symbols, but magical operations intended for the assimilation for the subtle radiations of the primal force into the body, thus making it more spiritual.

—Willy Schrödter
A Rosicrucian Notebook

These groups of seekers are like the "league" described in Hermann Hesse's *Journey to the East*.... There remains other layers of veils to be removed. But

that must remain the privilege of the individual seeker.

—Christopher McIntosh
The Rosicrucians

Follow Nature! Follow Nature! As she works so will I work!

—Rosicrucian proverb

RULES

Rules at best are signposts, never hitching posts.

—William Sloane Coffin
Credo

We would like to change the rules of the game. But then we find if we don't play by the rules, we don't play at all.

—Madeleine Kunin

S

SABBATH

The Sabboth was originally Saturn's day—
the day when mysterics were celebrated
that gave self-knowledge.

—Beryl Pogson
The Work Life

Sabbatu is the Babylonian word from
sa-bat meaning "heart-rest," the day
of the Full Moon when the Goddess
was thought to be menstruating. It was
unlucky to work on that day, to eat
cooked food or to travel. The Hebrews
picked up on the four lunar quarters and
declared Shabat every seven days.

—Penelope Shuttle & Peter Redgrove
The Wise Wound

All festivals and holy days begin at
night. The Sabbath begins at sundown.
According to the Jewish tradition, this is
of moral significance. It is not difficult to
have confidence in the day.... The Jewish
day begins at night to symbolize the
faith, even in the darkness, that light will
prevail and that a new morrow will dawn
upon mankind.

—William B. Silverman
Rabbinic Wisdom and Jewish Values

The goal of Shabat/Sabbath is to "rest" in the presence and consciousness of God.

—Thom Hartmann
The Prophet's Way

SACRAMENT

A sacrament is a door from one world to another.

—Peter J. Kreeft
Love Is Stronger Than Death

When sacrament happens around our dinner table with friends or family, I, a woman, have done the sacred work and I preside at that sacred moment.... There is in our feeding the mystery of paradox ... the profound lives within the ordinary.

—Sarah Hall Maney
Sacred Dimensions of Women's Experiences

The Mass is a picture of the highest mysteries of all time ... the human needs sacramental acts and spiritual forms.

—Rudolf Steiner & Alfred Heidenreich
Growing Point

SACRED

The road to the sacred leads through the secular.

—Abraham Heschel
I Asked for Wonder

Whenever and wherever justice replaces injustice, healing replaces suffering, abundance and sharing replace poverty and greed, wisdom replaces ignorance, forgiveness replaces hatred, community replaces separation and isolation, vision and courage replace fear, and love replaces indifference, there the sacred world comes into being. There the soul emerges.

—David Spangler
A Pilgrim in Aquarius

All of the larger-than-life questions about our presence here on earth and what gifts we have to offer are spiritual questions. To seek answers to these questions is to seek a sacred path.

—Lauren Artress
Walking a Sacred Path

The idea of a sacred place where the walls and laws of the temporal world may dissolve to reveal a wonder is apparently as old as the human race.

—Joseph Campbell
The Mythic Image

The sacred cannot be constructed. It makes itself.... Men can never deliberately create sacred precincts.

—Richard Rubenstein &
Rolfe L. Hunt, eds.
Revolution, Place, Symbol

In a world without friendship and love, how could we even begin to understand the meaning of the sacred?

—Stanley Kunitz & Bill Moyers
Fooling with Words

Sacred space always rests upon a foundation of power. What differentiates sacred power from, let us say, electric power or political power is that the experience of power is so moving to the subject that its source is attributed to a supernatural referent.... The idea of the sacred is that it presents a power that is eternal and changeless, and this power manifests itself in the myths, symbols and rituals of any authentic religious tradition.

—Walter L. Brenneman, Jr.
The Power of Place

If Jung is correct and there is an archetype of Sacred Space within us, then when we go to such a place... we accept the possibility that some kind of transformation may occur. This acceptance may not be conscious, but is there, and it makes change, growth, or healing possible.

—David La Chapelle
Sacred Land, Sacred Sex, Rapture of the Deep

The sacred is encountered within the sphere of relations.

—Martin Buber

A truly sacred world allows for a sense of mockery and play that turns the weight of reality around.

—Kenneth Lincoln
Native American Renaissance

Through experience of the sacred, the mind grasps the difference between what is revealed as real, potent, rich and meaningful and that which is deficient in those qualities—in other words, the chaotic and perilous flux of things, their fortuitous and meaningless appearances and disappearances.

—Mircea Eliade
Ordeal by Labyrinth

Occasionally one sees something fleeting in the land, a moment when line, color and movement intensify and something sacred is revealed, leading one to believe that there is another realm of reality corresponding to the physical one but different.

—Barry Lopez
Arctic Dreams

Hold every moment sacred ... give each its true and due fulfillment.

—Thomas Mann

In every, every terrestrial mystery, there is, as it were, a sacred core.

—Joseph Conrad
The Arrow of Gold

There is nothing so secular that it cannot be sacred, and that is one of the deepest messages of the Incarnation.

—Madeleine L'Engle
Walking on Water

SACRED GEOMETRY

There is geometry in the humming of the strings. There is music in the spacings of the spheres.

—Pythagoras

What is God? He is length, width, height and depth.

—Bernard of Clairvaux
On Consideration

The circle symbolizes wholeness, the square indicates stability, the triangle represent goals and dreams, the cross stands for relationship, and the spiral means growth.

—Angeles Arrien
Signs of Life

… geometry is a language and the most appropriate only to signify the mind or the spirit and the world, but it only signifies it; it does not lead us to believe in Something.

—Patrick Conty
The Genesis and Geometry of the Labyrinth

Geometry deals with pure form, and philosophical geometry re-enacts the unfolding of each form out of a preceding one. It is a way by which the essential creative mystery is rendered visible.

—Robert Lawlor
Sacred Geometry

A line is not used haphazard; it serves to draw out the ruling forms, which are a projection of the music of the spheres; a projection in rhythms which unfold in the image of the Great Law.

—Louis Charpentier
The Mysteries of Chartres Cathedral

A line reveals a million things.

—Novalis (Friedrich von Leopold)

A certain mystique surrounds it and yet it can be defined quite simply as the geometry of Euclid, used for symbolic purposes, in the service of traditional and sacred architecture.… Its pedigree goes back a long way, to the pyramids of Egypt, the ziggurats of Mesopotamia,

Hindu temples and Islamic mosques. In the Judaic tradition it began as early as the time of Moses, when he was told to make a holy tent, or tabernacle, according to the measurements which he had been shown by God on Mount Sinai, and to the measurements of the Temple of Solomon, whose proportions were given by Yahweh to King David.

—Gordon Strachan
Chartres: Sacred Geometry, Sacred Space

For the human spirit caught within a spinning universe in an ever confusing flow of events, circumstance and inner turmoil, to seek truth has always been to seek the invariable, whether it is called Ideas, Forms, Archetypes, Numbers of Gods. To enter a temple constructed wholly of invariable geometric proportions is to enter an abode of eternal truth.

—Robert Lawlor
Sacred Geometry

Sacred space is a place where one can go to get help in contacting non-physical realms. Among others, these can be places of emotion, intuition and of the spirit.… A very special kind of geometry called "sacred geometry" was utilized in the construction of these places.

—Sig Lonegren
Labyrinths

The creation of shapes through the use of numbers and geometry as mathematical expressions, recalls the Archetypes reflected through the World of symbols. Mathematics, then, is a language of the intellect, a means of spiritual hermeneutics whereby one can move from the sensible to the intelligible world.

—Laleh Bakhtiar
Sufi: Expression of the Mystic Quest

In Taoism the proportion 7:5:3 is a magic square, an image of the harmony of the universe around which dynastic Chinese buildings and landscape environments were oriented. The asymmetrical triangle is pregnant geometrically, and is considered the idea of transformation of consciousness in physical form by Japanese Rinzai Zen Buddhist

—Norris Brock Johnson
The Power of Place

You will understand everything, if you understand the theory of Geometry.... Make a circle out of a man and a woman, out of this a square, out of this a triangle, make a circle and you will have the Philosopher's Stone.

—Michael Maier
Atalanta Fugiens

The secret of great cathedrals is that their proportions conform to cosmic laws, "shaping" people who spend time in them.

—Theodor Schwenk & Wolfram Schwenk
Water: The Element of Life

Evolution is the law of Life. Number is the law of the Universe. Unity is the law of God.

—Inscription in the Temple of Delphi

SACRIFICE

Sacrifice is not a thing coming to a man from without; it issues from within him, and has its birth in his heart. When the heart is deeply moved, expression is given to it by ceremonies; and hence, only men of ability and virtue can give complete exhibition to the idea of sacrifice.

—Confucius

The sacrifice to Brahman consists of sacred study. ... With sacrifice nourish the gods in return they will nourish you also.

—*The Vedic Experience: Mantramanjan*

It is good to sacrifice the lower for the higher, and evil to sacrifice the higher for the lower.

—Bill Tyson
New Millennium Magic

We can't sacrifice something we don't have already and we can't give up something that is not ours to give.

—M. Scott Peck

The question sacrifice asks is: "What are you willing to give up to ensure your own unfolding, and the unfolding of what is holy in your life?" Unfortunately sacrifice is typically seen as deprivation—belt tightening, inconvenience, the tossing of virgins into volcanoes, the nailing of men onto crosses.

—Gregg Levoy
Callings

You can't be the flower and the bud at the same time. If you're going to be a flower, you must give up your bud-ness;

once your flower goes to seed, you must sacrifice your "flower-ness."

—Richard Idemon
The Magic Thread

SAFETY

When we feel safe, we can be truly creative and productive. When we're not, we are in survival mode and spend our time and energy licking our wounds.

—Cheryl Anne Gilman
Doing the Work You Love

Despite our wish for safety, there is less that resembles a steady career or a straight career path.... We may imagine a place in the hierarchy of our organization where we will find safety and security, from which we will then speak out, but find ourselves just as unsure even as we pace the supposedly safe upper floor of the building.

—David Whyte
Crossing the Unknown Sea

Banishing our innocence in the name of safety and good sense, we find that our capacity for vitality and enthusiasm is lost.

—David Whyte
The Heart Aroused

SAINTS

The perfect mystic is neither an ecstatic devotee lost in contemplation of Oneness nor a saintly recluse shunning all commerce with mankind. The true saint goes in and out among the people, eats and sleeps with them, buys and sells in the market, marries and takes part in social intercourse, and never forgets God for a single moment.

—Abu Sa'id

Father Maximos: Even saints had to face obstacles in their spiritual struggle. We are the beneficiaries of their mistakes and triumphs.

—Kyriacos C. Markides
The Mountain of Silence

In his holy flirtation with the world, God occasionally drops a handkerchief. These handkerchiefs are called saints.

—Frederick Buechner
Wishful Thinking

A saint is one who makes goodness attractive.

—Laurence Housman

God, deliver us from sullen saints.

—Teresa of Avila

Without saintly examples to feed the imagination, we starve.

—Phyllis McGinley
Saint-Watching

Saint: a dead sinner revised and edited.

—Ambrose Bierce
The Devil's Dictionary

SALVATION

Becoming the most we can be is also the definition of salvation. The term literally means healing.

—M. Scott Peck
A World Waiting to Be Born

If being is by nature holy there is no salvation except of everything that exists.

—Pierre Teilhard de Chardin
Human Energy

This, then, is salvation: When we marvel at the beauty of created things and praise their beautiful Creator.

—Meister Eckhart

Events happen under their own steam as random as rain, which means that God is present in them not as their cause but as the one who even in the hardest and the most hair-raising of them offers us the possibility of that new life and healing which I believe is what salvation is.

—Frederick Buechner
Telling Secrets

If that world is saved, it will not be by old minds with new programs but by new minds with no programs at all.

—Daniel Quinn
Beyond Civilization

Nothing worth doing can be achieved in our lifetime, therefore we must be saved by hope. Nothing which is true or beautiful or good makes complete sense in any immediate context of history; therefore we must be saved by faith. Nothing we do, however virtuous, can be accomplished alone; therefore we must be saved by love.

—Reinhold Niebuhr

Each meal we eat today is like a "farewell meal" of Mother Earth since, when we eat, we always eat Mother Earth. Mother Earth, then, is a constantly sacrificed "paschal lamb" whose blood is spilled for our healing, nourishment and salvation.

—Matthew Fox
The Coming of the Cosmic Christ

SANCTUARY

The essential ingredient in a temenos is the perimeter that marks out the space, whether a wall, a fence, a hedge of flowers and bushes, or some rocks that only imply the full perimeter. Having crossed the border, we find ourselves in a special place where certain things happen and other things do not.

—Thomas Moore
The Re-Enchantment of Everyday Life

Catherine Doherty, "The Baroness," was a child in Russia when she visited a forest hermit who went to "the desert" to find God and to pray for humanity.... She founded the Poustinia Movement with tiny sanctuaries.... "Poustinia" is a place where the heart is instructed in a new way of seeing and hearing. In the Russian tradition they literally left everything behind, taking only a loaf of bread, water, the clothes on one's back.

—Regina Sara Ryan
The Woman Awake

The grounds around the Temple of Artemis [Ephesus] were called an asylum. Amazons once took refuge there.... How could Artemis have allowed her temple to be burned? She was away, people said, attending Alexander's birth.

—Margaret George
The Memoirs of Cleopatra

SATAN/DEVIL

The devil is always suggesting that we compromise our high calling by substituting the good in place of the best.

—William Sloane Coffin
Credo

The devil is no fool. He can get people feeling about heaven the way they ought to feel about hell. He can make them fear the means of grace the way they do not fear sin. And he does so not by light but by obscurity, not by realities, but by shadows; not by clarity and substance, but by dreams and the creatures of psychosis.

—Thomas Merton
The Seven Storey Mountain

The best way to drive out the devil, if he will not yield to texts of Scripture, is to jeer and flout him, for he cannot bear scorn.

—Martin Luther

Luckily or unluckily, the Devil is as real as his Brother, and may at any moment tempt us to abandon poetry for power.

—Mary Caroline (M. C.) Richards
Centering

If all the trees were scribes and all branches pens, and if all hills were books and all waters ink, they could not give a sufficient description of the sorrow which Lucifer has brought into this place.

—Jacob Boehme
Aurora

If a man is not rising upwards to be an angel, depend on it, he is sinking downwards to be a devil. He cannot stop at the beast. The most savage of men are not beasts; they are worse, a great deal worse.

—Samuel Taylor Coleridge
Table Talk of Samuel Coleridge

Mammon is the god of hindrances, who places destructive, hindering things in the path of progress ... certain infectious diseases, unknown in earlier times, are brought about by the god Mammon.

—Rudolf Steiner
The Archangel Michael

Satan's greatest ruse is to convince us that he does not exist, but for Rasputin, Satan was not only a reality, but was always nearby.

—Edvard Radzinsky
The Rasputin File

Hurry is not of the devil, it is the devil.

—Carl G. Jung

The Evil One will accept and even sponsor a lesser good in order to prevent a greater good—or to produce a greater evil.

—Christopher Nugent
Masks of Satan

SCAPEGOAT

In Israel the sins of the tribes were ceremonially loaded onto the head of the scapegoat who represented the god Azazel, Messenger of the Lord, who took them away each Day of Atonement. The prefix scape meant "the Azazel-goat" in the original language.

—Barbara Walker
The Woman's Dictionary of Symbols and Sacred Objects

The practice among ancient Jews of choosing a scapegoat upon which to heap the sins of mankind is merely an allegorical depiction of the Sun Man who is the scapegoat of the world and upon whom are cast the sins of the twelve houses (tribes) of the celestial universe.

—Manly P. Hall
The Secret Teachings of All Ages

The ideal scapegoat must itself be free of any traits of guilt.

—John Lash
Twins and the Double

Once any group is successfully scapegoated as a subhuman threat to "normal" values by a propaganda machine, emboldened thugs take over.

—Frank Rich & James Carroll
Constantine's Sword

SCIENCE

Science without religion is lame, religion without science is blind.... The whole

purpose of science and art is to awaken the cosmic religious feeling.

—Albert Einstein

Religion and science are the two conjugated faces or phases of one and the same act of complete knowledge—the only one which can embrace the past and future of evolution so as to contemplate, measure and fulfill them.

—Pierre Teilhard de Chardin
The Phenomenon of Man

With all your science, can you tell me how it is that light comes into the soul?

—Henry David Thoreau

Science can change the compound states of matter easier than it can change its mind.

—Calvin Miller
The Song

Science affects the way we think together.

—Lewis Thomas

When science begins the study of nonphysical phenomena it will make more progress in one decade than in all the previous centuries of its existence.

—Nicola Tesla

For the scientist who has lived by his faith in the power of reason, the story ends like a bad dream. He has scaled the mountains of ignorance; he is about to conquer the highest peak. As he pulls himself over the final rock, he is greeted by a band of theologians who have been sitting there for centuries.

—Robert Jastrow
God and the Astronomers

The wisdom of modern science is working to catch up with the wisdom of the ancient Greeks.

—Jerome Groopman
The Anatomy of Hope

Science is a moving target, always undergoing constant transformation.

—Victor Mansfield
Synchronicity, Science and Soulmaking

Science is a long history of learning how to fool ourselves.

—Richard Feynman

The essential goal of science is to provide a single theory that describes the whole universe.

—Stephen W. Hawking
A Brief History of Time

Genetic engineering is a monstrous idea whose time should not have come.

—Jeremy Rifkin

Only the very simplest questions can be answered in the laboratory.

—Elio Frattaroli
Healing the Soul in the Age of the Brain

Science's established vision is blurring.

—Ilya Prigogine
World Futures

Science: a vulture whose wings are dull realities.

—Edgar Allen Poe

I think the Universe is a message written in Cosmic Code, and the scientist's job is to decipher that code.

—Heinz Pagels

Christianity will not have been properly grasped until it has permeated the earth right down into the physical sciences.

—Rudolf Steiner

What if science were a branching labyrinth of possibilities?

—George Johnson
Fire in the Mind

Postmodern science must therefore overcome the separation between truth and virtue, value and fact, ethics and practical necessity. To call for this … is, of course, to ask for a tremendous revolution in our whole attitude to knowledge. But such a change is now necessary and indeed long overdue. Can humanity meet in time the challenge of what is required?

—David Bohm & Charles Jenks
A Post-Modern Reader

SCULPTURE

Eskimo art reflects the absence of the notion of creation. There is no real equivalent of our words "create" or "make." The closest term means "to work on"; it is a restrained kind of activity, like the aim of the Eskimo carver of ivory to release the characteristic form of the piece in hand.

—Arthur Cotterell
A Dictionary of World Mythology

As the carver holds the unworked ivory lightly in his hand, turning it this way and that, he whispers, "Who are you? Who hides there?" And then he says, "Ah, Seal ... " Then humming and chanting he brings it out. Seal. Hidden energies. It was always there. He did not create it, he released it. He helped it step forth.

—Marcus Bach
The Power of Perception

The beauty of a composed intricacy of form; and how it may be said ... to lead the eye in a kind of chase.

—William Hogarth

A piece of sculpture can render space visible and vocal. It frees the eye and the heart to glimpse the embrace of the invisible.

—John O'Donohue
Beauty

The mason looks at the archetypes, grasps the divine model and makes an impression of it in real material.

—Dionysus the Areopagite
de Ecclesiastica IV 3

Now, I really make the little idea from clay, and I hold it in my hand. I can turn it, look at it from underneath, see it from one view, hold it against the sky, imagine it any size I like, and really be in control almost like God creating something.

—Henry Moore

It is while carving stone that you discover the spirit of your material.... Your hand thinks and follows the thoughts of the material ... a well-made sculpture should have the power to heal the beholder. It must be lovely to touch, friendly to live with.

—Constantin Brancusi

Simple and composed movement. Simple and composed force.

—Leonardo da Vinci
Notebooks, [notes near a sketch of a trotting horse]

The Japanese American sculptor Isamu Noguchi would ponder a rock for ten years before he decided if he'd use it.

—Jackson Lears
Something for Nothing

One perception must immediately and directly lead to a further perception.

—Isamu Noguchi

They conjured the spirits of demons and angels and implanted them in likenesses through holy and divine rites ... statues ensouled and conscious, filled with spirit and doing great things ... statues that could make people ill and heal them.

—Hermes Trismegistus
Asklepius

What garlic is to salad, insanity is to art.

—Augustus St. Gaudens

We are all artists sculpting human souls.

—Thomas Moore

SECRET

Gurdjieff said the ancients encoded their knowledge in "legominisms"—material structures such as temples and pyramids or in songs and dances, or playing cards.... He was allowed in an esoteric society: Sarmoung or Sarmon Brotherhood, which he believed founded Babylon in 2400 B.C. when the Egyptians were building the Great Pyramid.

—Adrian G. Gilbert
Magi

When a man dies, his secrets bond like crystals, like frost on a window. His last breath obscures the glass.

—Anne Michaels
Fugitive Pieces

To love life through our labor is to be intimate with life's inmost secrets.

—Kahlil Gibran

Esoteric divine powers are operative on every level of the cosmos.

—David Walsh
The Mysticism of Innerworldly Fulfillment

There is a secret society of men who feel their mission in life is to alter the course of civilization ... scientists and engineers, but in effect they are mystics.

—Katherine Neville
The Eight

According to the Gnostics, some of the disciples, following his instructions, kept secret Jesus' esoteric teaching; this they taught only in private, to certain persons who had proven themselves to be spiritually mature, and who qualified for "initiation into gnosis"—that is, into secret knowledge.

—Elaine Pagels
The Gnostic Gospels

Recognize what is right before your eyes and what is hidden will be revealed to you.

—The Gospel According to Thomas

Everything in Russia is secret but nothing is hidden.

—Edvard Radzinsky
The Rasputin File

SECURITY

Our obsession with security is a measure of the power we have granted the future to hold over us.

—Wendell Berry
The Unsettling of America

Each moment is a middle zone between the past and the future ... there is a past security to be lost before we find a new security. The person who has had the benefit of a solid support in childhood from which to launch out into life, will have no difficulty in letting go of that support and in finding fresh support somewhere else and living like that, lightly moving from support to support like the trapeze artist flying from trapeze to trapeze.

—Paul Tournier
A Place for You

Security doesn't come from a double-locked, chain-latched steel door. It comes from within.

—Tom Brown
The Search

Security is mostly a superstition, it does not exist in nature, nor do the children of men as a whole experience it. Avoiding danger is no safer in the long run than outright exposure. Life is either a daring adventure or nothing at all!

—Helen Keller

SEEING/SIGHT

The meaning of life is to see.

—Hui Neng

Forgive them for they see not what they look at. Hence, they know not what they do.

—Frederick Franck
The Awakened Eye

The eyes are our most sensitive organ, and when you look and look and look into another person's eyes you are looking at the most beautiful jewels in the universe ... because that's the universe looking at you. We are the eyes of the cosmos.

—Alan Watts
The Essential Alan Watts

The human eye always sees twice in the one look: the thing and the emptiness.

—John O'Donohue
Beauty

The greatest thing a human soul ever does in this world is to see something.... To see clearly is poetry, prophesy and religion, all in one.

—John Ruskin
Modern Painters

All that we see are our visualizations. We see not with the eye, but with the soul.

—Mike Samuels
Seeing with the Mind's Eye

We are like dwarves seated on the shoulders of giants. If we see more and further than they, it is not due to our own clear eyes or tall bodies, but their bigness.

—Bernard of Chartres

We never see only what we see; we always see something else with it and through it! Seeing creates, seeing unites, and above all seeing goes beyond itself.

—Paul Tillich

To see more is to become more.

—Pierre Teilhard de Chardin

All other creatures look down toward the earth, but man was given a face so that he might turn his eyes toward the sun and his gaze upon the sky.

—Ovid (Publius Ovidius Naso)
Metamorphoses

We can choose to see just misery and failure, pain and conflict, anguish and agony, but we can also choose to see, in the midst of all the darkness that surrounds us, the light of God's face.

—Henri J. M. Nouwen
Foreword, *Writing with Light*

The observed is profoundly affected by the observer and the observer by the observed. It's one process. Krishnamurti used to say, "The observer is the observed."

—David Bohm
On Dialogue

The day is coming when a single carrot, freshly observed, will set off a revolution.

—Paul Cézanne

You must learn to look at the world twice.

—Jamake Highwater

Looking is what saves us.

—Simone Weil

What I do not see, I do not know. I see, hear and know simultaneously and learn what I know as if in a moment.

—Hildegard of Bingen

We see all created things because they are; but they are, because God sees them. And because they are, we see them outwardly; because they are perfect, we see them inwardly.

—Augustine

Men have no eyes but for those aspects of things which they have already been taught to discern.

—William James
Principles of Psychology

Rilke was Rodin's secretary for a while, and Rodin one day advised him to go down to the zoo and try to see something. Rilke did, and spent some time watching a panther. Rodin respected seeing, the ability to observe, to use the terrific energy of the eyes, to pay attention to something besides one's own subjectivity.

—Robert Ornstein
The Psychology of Consciousness

The question is not what you look at but what you see.

—Henry David Thoreau
Journal

Why does an eye see a thing more clearly in dreams than the imagination does while awake?

—Leonardo da Vinci
Notebooks

The task is not so much to see what no one has seen, but to think what nobody yet has thought about that which everybody sees.

—Arthur Schopenhauer

To see clearly is poetry, prophecy and religion all in one.

—John Ruskin
Stones of Venice

The imagination is an eye, a marvelous third eye that floats free. In the child, that eye sees with 20/20 clarity; with age, its vision dims.

—Stephen King
Notes on Horror

SEEKING/SEARCH

For thirty years I sought God. But when I looked carefully I found that in reality God was the seeker and I the sought.

—Bayazid Bistami

Searching for the invisible is not for the faint-hearted.

—Stephen Hawking

However hard you may search for it, you will never be able to grasp if. You can only become it.

—Ikkyu

We do not find because our eyes are blinded.

—Annie Besant
The Spiritual Life in the World

When you search for the Beloved, it is the intensity of the longing that does all the work. Look at me and you will see a slave of that intensity.

—Kabir

Were the eye not sun-like in itself, how could we see the Sun?

—Johann Wolfgang von Goethe

The timetable of a seeker's advance depends on several factors, but without doubt the most important of them all is the strength of the longing within his or her heart for the Higher.

—Paul Brunton
Notebooks

Some seek wealth; others health and fitness; yet others crave name and fame; but the wise prepare their destinies, before night-time comes.

—Moses Maimonides

A seeker knocked at the door of the beloved—God—and a voice from inside asked: "Who is it?" The seeker answered: "It is I"; and the voice said, "In this house there is no I and You." The door remained locked. Then the seeker went into solitude, fasted and prayed. A year later he returned and knocked on the door. Again the voice asked: "Who is it?" Now the believer answered: "It is You." Then the door opened.

—Jalal Al-din Rumi

Great seekers never become obsolete. Their answers may be displaced, but the questions they posed remain. We inherit and are enriched by their ways of asking.

—Daniel J. Boorstin
The Seekers

It is looking at things for a long time that ripens you and gives you a deeper understanding.

—Vincent van Gogh

Looking at your soul.

—Ojibwa word for "mirror"

SELF

The Self existed before the birth of this body and will remain after the death of this body. So it is with the series of bodies taken up in succession. The Self is immortal.

—Ramana Maharishi

Know yourself: the temptation of self-deception is very great. It helps to know what you look like, especially when writ large in astral ink.

—Rudolf Steiner
Intuitive Thinking as a Spiritual Path

We shall understand the world when we understand ourselves; for it and we are inseparable halves of one whole. We are children of God, divine seeds.

—Novalis (Friedrich von Leopold)

We argue with ourselves: I should be doing something useful. But the truth is, I can't do anything useful if there's no I to do it.… That is what going into the chrysalis is all about—undergoing a metamorphosis in order one day to stand up and say I am.

—Marion Woodman
The Pregnant Virgin

I find the term "reinventing the self" interesting. Who did the original invention?

—Ursula K. LeGuin
The Wave in the Mind

The serene happiness of the soul can never be broken by the anguish and misery of its shadow the person. No grief or passion, no fear or pain can get into it. That part of his being which always remains in heaven, is the Overself. That part which descends to suffer and struggle on earth, is the personality.

—Paul Brunton
The Spiritual Crisis of Man

We are engaged in a race between self-discovery and self-destruction. The forces that may converge to destroy us are the same forces that may foster societal and self-discovery.

—Duane Elgin

A biography is considered complete if it merely accounts for six or seven selves, whereas a person may have as many as a thousand.

—Virginia Woolf
Orlando

Self intimacy is a virtue by which I grow in awareness and acceptance of this particular human being I am becoming. It is a strength of mature self-love which is the ground for my love and care for the other.

—Evelyn Whitehead & James Whitehead
Seasons of Strength

We do not believe in ourselves until someone reveals that deep inside us is valuable, worth listening to, worthy of our trust, sacred to our touch. Once we believe in ourselves we can risk curiosity, wonder, spontaneous delight or any experience that reveals the human spirit.

—e. e. cummings

The human self is not a finished thing, it is constantly unfolding. Experience is, then, essentially creative.

—John O'Donohue
Beauty

For a self is a thing the world is least apt to inquire about, and the thing of all things the most dangerous for a man to let people notice that he has. The greatest danger, that of losing one's own self, may pass off as quietly as if it were nothing;

every other loss, that of an arm, a leg, five dollars, a wife, etc. is sure to be noticed.

—Søren Kierkegaard

In other living creatures ignorance of self is nature; in man it is vice.

—Boethius (Anicius Manlius Severinus)

A self is not something static, tied up in a pretty parcel and handed to the child, finished and complete. A self is always becoming. Being does mean becoming, but we run so fast that it is only when we seem to stop—as sitting on the rock at the brook—that we are aware of our own isness, of being …

—Madeleine L'Engle
Circle of Quiet

The true feminine is the receptacle of love. The true masculine is the spirit that goes into the external unknown in search of meaning. The great container, the Self, is paradoxically both male and female and contains both.

—Marion Woodman
Addiction to Perfection

What woman essentially lacks today for doing great things is forgetfulness of herself, but to forget oneself it is first of all necessary to be firmly assured that now and for all the future, one has found oneself.

—Simone de Beauvoir
The Second Sex

In art, the self becomes self-forgetful.

—Flannery O'Connor

SENSES

You will at once feel your senses gather themselves. They seem like bees which return to the hive and then shut themselves up to work at the making of honey; and this will take place without effort or care on your part.... At the first call of the will they come back more and more quickly. At last, after many and many exercises of this kind, God disposes them to a state of absolute repose and perfect contemplation.

—Teresa of Avila

This sense for the divine was discovered by the prophets.... Solomon already realized that there are two modes of sense perception, one mortal, transient, and human, and the other immortal, spiritual, and divine.

—Origin
First Principles

Our present senses are but rudiments of what they are destined to become.

—Henry David Thoreau

Smells are surer than sights and sounds to make your heart-strings crack.

—Rudyard Kipling

If you atrophy one sense you also atrophy all the others: a sensuous and physical connection with nature, with art, with food, with other human beings.

—Anaïs Nin

The long *a* of the English alphabet ... has for me the tint of weathered wood, but a French *a* evokes polished ebony ... The

confessions of a synesthete must sound tedious and pretentious to those who are protected from such leaking and drafts by more solid walls than mine are.

—Vladimir Nabokov & Diane Ackerman
A Natural History of the Senses

Beauty and grace are performed whether or not we will or sense them. The least we can do is be there.

—Annie Dillard

SEPARATION

Just as we have learned to separate ourselves from each other and from the environment, we now need to learn how to reunite ourselves with other entities around us without losing our hard-won individuality.

—Mihaly Csikszentmihalyi
Flow

I've heard it said that there's a window that opens from one mind to another, but if there's no wall, there's no need for fitting a window, or the latch.

—Jalal Al-din Rumi

Most people now are living on the far side of a broken connection and that is potentially catastrophic.

—Kent Haruf
Plainsong

If we think of the world as separate from us and constituted of disjointed parts to be manipulated with the aid of calcula-tions, we will tend to try to become separate people, whose main motivation with regard to each other and to nature is also manipulation and calculation.

—David Bohm
Postmodern Science and a Postmodern World

Evil is separation. Theologically, it is separation from God. Psychologically, it is separation within oneself.

—John A. Sanford
The Kingdom Within

Pilgrimage to the place of the wise is to find escape from the flame of separation.

—Jalal Al-din Rumi

SERENDIPITY

Serendipity, first cousin to coincidence and twin brother of synchronicity, coined by Horace Walpole in 1754. [He had] read "The Three Princes of Serendip." They were always making discoveries by accidents and sagacity, of things they were not in quest of.

—Phil Cousineau
Soul Moments

Our lives are often touched by chance, are they not? I call it magic, the crossing of our paths with the paths of others. How quickly, how completely, these magic meetings can turn us into directions we never dreamed of.

—Dee Brown
Creek Mary's Blood

How did it occur to Jules Verne to make the fictional Nautilus the same dimensions as U.S. atomic subs 150 years later? ... He also chose Florida as the place of the first moon shot and the fictional Nautilus took 73 hours and 13 minutes to travel from earth to the moon.... Apollo took 73 hours, 10 minutes.

—Charles Berlitz
Doomsday

SERVICE

Consciously or unconsciously everyone of us does render some service or other. If we cultivate the habit of doing this service deliberately, our desire for service will steadily grow stronger, and will make not only for our own happiness, but for the world at large.

—Mohandas (Mahatma) Gandhi

Service is both taking actions in the world and embodying the attitude of being a servant, one whose task is to be a source of energy for others.... Service is like the muscle of the soul.

—David Spangler
A Pilgrim in Aquarius

The only ones among you who will be truly happy are those who have sought and found how to serve.

—Albert Einstein

Give of your hands to serve and your hearts to love.

—Mother Teresa

... everything we do counts. There is really no such thing as a small act of service or goodness.

—Caroline Myss
Invisible Acts of Power

Service is the rent we pay to be living. It is the very purpose of life and not something you do in your spare time.

—Marian Wright Edelman

To serve others is to give of oneself with no personal gain or reward. The energy of service is the only remedy for problems of darkness and barriers to our evolution. Service is the only energy that can generate enough continued light and fire to combat the darkness.

—Mary E. Carreiro
The Psychology of Spiritual Growth

He profits most who serves best.

—Robert Greenleaf
Servant Leadership

Service is an attitude founded on the recognition that the World has supported you, fed you, taught you, tested you, whether or not you earned it.... Service is both a means and an end, for in giving to others you open yourself to love, abundance and inner peace. You cannot serve others without uplifting yourself.

—Dan Millman
Everyday Enlightenments

People think service is a kind of charity—strong people giving to weak people, healthy people giving to sick people, rich people giving to poor people, together people giving to people who aren't so together. To me, true service is an experience of wholeness, fulfillment, fullness, self-reliance, and self-sufficiency for all parties.

—Lynne Twist & Dan Millman
Everyday Enlightenments

Service is not the complete surrender of personal desire. It is through desire we discover what animates and moves us.

—David Whyte
The Heart Aroused

On February 7, 1837, God spoke to me and called me to His service.

—Florence Nightingale

I am never weary of being useful.

—Leonardo da Vinci

The soil in return for service keeps the tree tied to her, the sky asks nothing and leaves it free.

—Rabindranath Tagor
Fireflies

We are called to help the stranger and the good deed you just received is yours to pass on to another.

—Julia Peterson Berg

I am a bow in your hands; draw me lest I rot.
Do not overdraw me; I shall break.
Overdraw me and who cares if I break!

—Nikos Kazantzakis

There is no way of serving the gods than by spending oneself for man.

—Chinese proverb

The libido is the impulse to life. It comes from the heart … the heart is the organ of opening up to somebody else.

—Joseph Campbell
Power of Myth

SEX/SEXUALITY

Sex is just the beginning, not the end. But if you miss the beginning, you will miss the end also.

—Bhagwan Shree Rajneesh

When religion is anthropocentric and lacks a cosmology, it has very little to tell us that is good news about sexuality, which is so special a gift of the cosmos. When this happens, culture secularizes and misuses it. Pornography substitutes for mysticism.

—Matthew Fox
The Coming of the Cosmic Christ

Sex is a part of life, no more or less important than a star or a flower. It can only provide satisfaction when it's not overloaded with expectations.

—Peter Balin
The Flight of the Feathered Serpent

Our sexuality is our desire to participate in making love, making justice in the world; our drive toward one another; our movement in love; our expression of our sense of being bonded together in life and death.

—Carter Heyward, Judith Plaskow &
Carol P. Christ
Weaving the Visions

Sexuality is both responsibility and joy, while rape and pornography are not sexuality but assault.

—Diane Stein
The Kwan Yin

Tantra sees each human being as an organism that is part of a larger whole— the surrounding environment, the planet Earth, nature itself—in which rhythm and vibration are the unifying factors.

—Margo Anand
The Art of Sexual Ecstasy

Tantra introduces new dimensions of breathing, posture, play and trust to sexuality and re-creates it.

—Matthew Fox
Creativity

When we demean sex we demean our humanity.

—Mona Charen

Sexuality is the energy of our relating as women to everyone and everything … the greater intercourse we enjoy with the world in and through its creator.

—Dorothy H. Donnelly & Mary E. Giles
The Feminist Mystic

Sex and violence became linked in Babylon—Gilgamesh—Marduk and

others dismembered the ancient
Goddess religion.

—Starhawk
Truth or Dare

Sex is like nitroglycerin. It can be used
either to blow up bridges or heal hearts.

—Frederich Buechner

Of the 56 possible positions for sex, only
eight can be achieved without laughing.

—Woody Allen

SHADOWS

The work on the shadow is only a
preparation for a life of service. Having
experienced the depths of our own darkness, we can never judge another person,
nor can we be frightened by the darkness.

—Llewellyn Vaughan-Lee
In the Company of Friends

A good way of learning to detect one's
shadow is to notice what qualities in
others make us angry or irritated.

—Irene Claremont de Castillejo
Knowing Woman

What has no shadow has no strength
of life.

—Czeslaw Milosz

But if we are able to see our own shadow
and can bear knowing about it, then a

small part of the problem has already
been solved.

—Carl G. Jung

… in myths the shadow often appears
as a twin, for he is not just the "hostile
brother," but the companion and friend,
and it is sometimes difficult to tell whether
this twin is the shadow or the self …
upper and lower reflect one another.

—Erich Neumann
*The Origins and History
of Consciousness*

Look for your other half who walks
always next to you and tends to be who
you aren't.

—Antonio Machado

What we project onto others, and what
we often act out in moments of dis-
sension, is psychic material Carl Jung
termed "the human shadow." The shadow
consists of the unexplored, feared, and
unwanted aspects of our personalities—whatever doesn't fit into the ego
ideal of the good self.

—Christina Baldwin
Calling the Circle

I tell you that goodness—what we in our
ordinary daylight selves call goodness: the
ordinary, the decent—these are nothing
without the hidden powers that pour
forth continually from their shadow sides.

—Doris Lessing
*The Marriage Between Zones Three,
Four and Five*

All the good that may be within you in
your shadow lies hidden in the dark. All

the transformative power of the psyche is left untapped if you are afraid to enter the dark. We must relinquish our old selves. We must die on the cross of personality.

—Normandi Ellis
Dreams of Isis

Where the light is brightest the shadows are deepest.

—Johann Wolfgang von Goethe

Whereas the ego weaves together the worlds, the shadow unravels the world. Whereas the ego acts as a catalyst of creation in the world, the shadow acts as a catalyst of destruction. Whereas the ego supports the status quo, the shadow is an agent of transformation.

—Connie Zweig & Steve Wolf
Romancing the Shadow

If you, as a parent, haven't touched your own shadows, it scares you when your kids show you theirs.

—Richard Idemon
The Magic Thread

To image someone's shadow summons their soul.... Photographers are "The Shadow Catchers."

—M. Scott Momaday
House Made of Dawn

It takes courage to go to the "bad" side of one's self—to acknowledge it, embrace it, and learn from it.

—Robert A. Johnson
Inner Work

My continuing passion is to part a curtain, that invisible shadow that falls between people—the veil of indifference to each other's presence, each other's wonder, each other's human plight.

—Eudora Welty

SHAMAN

The shaman is not only a medicine man, accompanier of the dead, the prophet of the Most High; he is also the poet and sage who preserves and explains the narratives of the past and composes new ones concerning the present. Sometimes he is a sorcerer who gives demonstrations of a world in which anything is possible.

—Bruno Borchert
Mysticism

Though no shaman can explain to himself how and why, he can, by the power of his brain, derive from the supernatural, as if it were by thought alone, divest his body of its flesh and blood, so that nothing remains but his bones. And he must then name all the parts of his body, mentioning every single bone by name ... with the special and sacred shaman's language.

—Knud Rasmussen & Mircea Eliade
Shamanism

The process of shamanism is the process of becoming a total being, so that you can become a teacher by example, so that in turn you can evolve into a much higher state of awareness.

—Lynn V. Andrews
Healers on Healing

The shaman moves between realities, a magical athlete of states of consciousness, engaged in mythic feats.... A characteristic phase of more advanced shamanism is having personal certainty and knowledge of one's own spirit helpers.... But shamanic initiation is a never-ending process of struggle and joy ...

—Michael Harner
The Way of the Shaman

The shaman is a master of escaping the mind-body matrix that characterizes ordinary consciousness and entering the shamanic or nonordinary state of consciousness. In this dream-like state, the imaginal realm reshapes itself, creating a placeless, timeless field in which the shaman can participate in the consciousness of other creatures.

—Tom Cowan
Fire in the Head

The shaman's adventures in the other world, the ordeals that he undergoes in his ecstatic descents below and ascents to the sky, suggest the adventures of the figures in popular tales and the heroes of epic literature.

—Mircea Eliade
Shamanism, Archaic Techniques of Ecstasy

Shamans have always been messengers between human dimensions. They are people of action.

—Olga Kharitidi
Entering the Circle

In the Arctic, the shamanic peoples who live according to the rhythms of animals regard the reindeer as a spiritual messenger who travels between heaven and earth, transporting the sham to the spiritual world, where he gathers wisdom to bring back to help heal the community.... .The reindeer also carries the souls of the dead to the spirit world for rebirth.

—Linda Schierse Leonard
Creation's Heartbeat

In this kind of school we learn about fear, anger, hate, confusion. We learn about other worlds and how to travel between both. We learn about our strengths and weaknesses, power, love, reality, healing, and life itself. We learn that there are, indeed, two separate but interrelated worlds of existence, the physical and the spiritual.

—Grizzlybear Lake
Native Healer

The transformation of human consciousness is the shamanization of humanity.

—Kenneth Ring

Dante was a great shaman and the Shamanic journey in many ways parallels his. Journeys start from where we are. Everything starts from where we are.

—Evelyn Eaton
The Shaman and the Medicine Wheel

Elements of peak and shamanic experiences, such as prolonged trance states, spiritual awakenings, sudden healings, meeting with ghosts, and other paranormal events, are often foreshadowed by various types of inner experiences, or "callings," such as serious illness, near-death experiences, periods

of near insanity, or "big" dreams of wise
spirit figures.

—Arnold Mindell
The Shaman's Body

SHINTO

Shinto mythology tells us that Japan is
filled with eight million kami-spirits or
gods. Kami reside in rocks, trees, grasses,
small hills, caves, tiny islands, rivers,
oceans, and mountains; and in every
snake, fox and deer literally everywhere
and anywhere.... To awaken the spirits,
one claps hands twice or rattles a bell
hanging at the entry of the shrine.

—Kazuo Matsuayashi
The Power of Place

Kami, the divine spirits of Shinto, are
everywhere, populating all natural things,
especially those with unusual size or
form, such as mountains or distinctive
trees. They have a profound creative and
harmonizing power which can never be
fully understood, because it transcends
our faculties of cognition.... Mountains
such as Mount Fuji are not simply the
dwellings of mountain deities but, according to some, their physical embodiments.

—Brian Leigh Molyneux
The Sacred Earth

SIGNS

It must be understood that Sign is the
equal of speech, lending itself equally to
the rigorous and the poetic—to philosophical analysis or to making love—

indeed, with an ease that is sometimes
greater than that of speech.

—Oliver Sacks
Seeing Voices

A sign (like thunder before rain) is
something that directs our attention to
something else. A symbol does not direct
at all.

—Walker Percy
Message in the Bottle

Signs come from without, but get their
meaning from the living psyche; they
refer to a reality which they represent
in relation to the recipient.... Note
the "signs" and you will know what to
expect.... Success is achieved when
one is ready to accept the sign at the
appropriate moment, integrate it into
the particular situation and thus create a
meaningful cosmos.

—Walter Burkert
Creation of the Sacred

SILENCE/STILLNESS

Many people confuse silence with
solitude. That is why they are afraid of
silence: they are afraid of loneliness. The
truth is, though, that silence is inhabited.
If you want to ensure that you will never
be poor and lonely, seek silence, for true
silence is inhabited by countless beings.

—Omraam Michaël Aïvanhov
The Path of Silence

Nothing in the Universe is so like God
as Silence.

—Meister Eckhart

Silence is the language God speaks. Everything else is a broad translation.

—Thomas Keating

Everything true and great grows in silence.

—Ladislaus Boros
God Is with Us

The seed of mystery lies in muddy water.... Water becomes still through stillness. How can I become still? By flowing with the stream.

—Lao Tzu

The discipline of silence is a kind of nourishment of the word ... by keeping silence we must learn to speak.... I hear what it is that I speak to you.

—Gregory the Great
[quoted in] *Material for Thought*

Even if there is noise, there is always some silence underneath and in between the sounds. Listening to the silence immediately creates stillness inside you. And what is stillness other than presence, consciousness freed from thought forms?

—Eckhart Tolle
The Power of Now

There is no such thing as silence. Something is always happening that makes a sound.

—John Cage

I feel that art has something to do with the achievement of stillness in the midst of chaos. A stillness which characterizes prayer, too, and the eye of a storm.

—Saul Bellow

In a world where language and naming are power, silence is oppression, is violence.

—Adrienne Rich

Silence moves people. That is why it is so essential to meditation practices, including the art of listening to our images.

—Matthew Fox
The Coming of the Cosmic Christ

Sinking again into silence, the truth of words bears us down into the silence of God.

—Thomas Merton
Thoughts in Solitude

When we dare to stop talking, silence speaks.

—James Carroll

Silences are the only scrap of Christianity we still have left.... Every human being who knows how to keep silent becomes a divine child, for in silence there is concentration upon his divine origin.

—Søren Kierkegaard

To see there must be silence.

—Frederick Franck
The Awakened Eye

Silence is the mother of speech.

—Thomas Merton
A Thomas Merton Reader

In this chatty society, silence has become a very fearful thing. For most people, silence creates itchiness and nervousness.

—Henri J. M. Nouwen
The Way of the Heart

Every human being who knows how to keep silent becomes a divine child, for in silence there is concentration upon his divine origin; he who speaks remains a human being.

—Søren Kierkegaard

What we hear when the thunder crashes is not thunder pure, but thunder-break-ing-upon-silence-and-contrasting-with-it.

—William James

Forever Oneness, who sings to us in silence, who teaches us through each other, guide my steps with strength and wisdom.

—Marlo Morgan
Message from Forever

Silence is man's spontaneous reaction to the experience of numinous presence, to God-in-the-midst.

—Rudolf Otto

Down below, submerged, the words are waiting. And one must descend, go to the bottom, be silent, wait.

—Octavio Paz
The Bow and the Lyre

In silence, she could hear the hum of the universe, the infinite harmony of separate sounds that make the One Ultimate Silence and nothing happens by accident.

—Moyra Caldecott
The Lily and the Bull

Much silence makes a mighty noise.

—African proverb

Don't talk unless you can improve upon the silence.

—Vermont proverb

SIMPLICITY

You can't force simplicity, but you can invite it in by finding as much richness as possible in the few things at hand.

—Thomas Moore
The Re-Enchantment of Everyday Life

I do not think that any civilization can be called complete until it has progressed from sophistication to unsophistication, and made a conscious return to simplic-ity of thinking and living.

—Lin Yutang
The Importance of Living

Entities are not to be multiplied beyond necessity.

—William of Occam

Parsimony, or Occam's razor, is the principle that one should never accept a complex explanation if a simple one suffices.

—Alison Jolly
Lucy's Legacy

Make everything as simple as possible, but not simpler.

—Albert Einstein

The greatest thing a human soul ever does in the world is to see something and tell what it saw in a plain way.

—John Ruskin

Live simple in means, rich in end.

—Bill Devall
Deep Ecology

I would rather ride on a load of hay in the country than the finest hack in the city.

—*McGuffy Reader*

SIN

We cannot return to Eden, for we have never left. We cannot betray God, for we are that God. We can only forget that this is so, and that forgetting is sin and punishment enough.

—Robert Rabbin
Invisible Leadership

The concept of original sin is alien to Jewish tradition.

—Elie Wiesel
Messengers of God

The doctrine of original sin is not found in any of the writings of the Old Testament. It is certainly not in chapters one to three of Genesis.

—Herbert Haag
Is Original Sin in the Scripture?

My soul is like a mirror in which the glory of God is reflected, but sin, however insignificant, covers the mirror with smoke.

—Theresa of Avila

There is only one sin and that is to impose your will on another. Otherwise life is a celebration, a costume ball and at the close of each lifetime we shed our costumes.

—Ruth Montgomery
Aliens Among Us

Definition of sin: today I failed to have fun X number of times.

—Sara Maitland
A Big Enough God

Original sin is lack of energy.

—M. Scott Peck

Some there are who are much more ashamed of confessing a sin than of committing it.

—Marguerite of Navarra
The Heptameron

"Sin" in Greek means "off your mark."

—Kyriacos Markides
Riding with the Lion

To editors, dullness, not dishonesty, is the unforgivable sin.

—Donna Woolfolk Cross
Word Abuse

SINGERS/SINGING/ SONG

Singing is running sound through your body.

—Virginia Beane Rutter
Woman Changing Woman

The singer stands at the center of sound, of motion, of life.

—M. Scott Momaday

The Latin word *canatre* is generally translated as "to sing." Its original meaning, however, was "to work magic."

—Joachim Berendt
Nada Brahma: The World Is Sound

The Gothic church was truly itself when filled with song.

—Rudolf Steiner

SLEEP

Every night in sleep, human beings are in the realm of the Hierarchies in the spiritual world with their I and astral body, which are outside the physical body and ether body.

— Rudolf Steiner
Reverse Ritual

Dreamlessly the true men of earlier times slept.... In sleep the soul engages in intercourse.

—Chuang Tsu

May we not imagine that possibly this earthly life of ours is to the other life what sleep is to waking? May not all our life be a dream and death an awakening? But an awakening to what? And supposing that everything is but the dream of God and that God one day will awake? Will he remember his dream?

—Miguel de Aunamuno
The Tragic Sense of Life

Most of the world is either asleep or dead. The religious people are, for the most part, asleep. The irreligious are dead.

—Thomas Merton
No Man Is an Island

Blessed are those who sleep, for they will go on sleeping.

—Friedrich Nietzche

The waking have one common world, but the sleeping turn aside each into a world of his own.

—Heraclitus of Ephesus

I am morally certain that the genuine Rosicrucians knew of a processus vitae interruptionis (a method of suspended animation), and this is borne out by the wealth of old stories concerning old men dressed in antique costumes or vestments who were found sleeping in the mountain caves.

—Willy Schrödter
A Rosicrucian Notebook

Sleep is the similitude of death and waking of the resurrection.

—Al-Ghazali

Man does not see the real world. The real world is hidden from him by the wall of imagination. He lives in sleep.

—G. I. Gurdjieff

There have been times in my life when I fell asleep with tears in my eyes, but in my dreams the most delightful visions came to me to comfort and cheer me, and the next morning, I would rise again feeling fresh and happy.

—Johann Wolfgang von Goethe

In the newborn, 50 per cent of total sleep is spent in REM sleep.

—Shirley Motter Linde & Louis M. Savary
The Sleep Book

SOLITUDE

Too tired for company, you seek a solitude you are too tired to fill.

—Dag Hammarskjöld
Markings

No one can stand in these solitudes unmoved, and not feel that there is more in man than the mere breath of his body.

—Charles Darwin
The Voyage of the Beagle

Loneliness is the poverty of self; solitude is the richness of self.

—May Sarton

I have a taste for solitude and silence, and for what Plotinus called "the alone to the Alone."

—Annie Dillard
Teaching a Stone to Talk

Our language has wisely sensed the two sides of being alone. It has created the word loneliness to express the pain of being alone. And it has created the word solitude to express the glory of being alone.

—Paul Tillich
Courage to Be

Solitude is loneliness transformed into a space within which God, self, and others can show up.

—M. Basil Pennington
Centered Living

We are not forced to take wings to find Him, but have only to seek solitude and to look within ourselves.

—Teresa of Avila
The Way of Perfection

What is needed is, in the end, simply this: solitude, great inner solitude. Going into yourself and meeting no one for hours on end—that is what you must be able to do.

—Rainer Maria Rilke
Letters to a Young Poet

Solitude is not something you must hope for in the future. Rather, it is a deepening of the present, and unless you look for it in the present you will never find it.

—Thomas Merton
Merton

Solitude enables you to make contact with yourself ... to be the prophet of God within you who speaks a unique language to each man.

—Antonin Sertillanges

"Solitude in a Crowd"—In all our outward activity, remain inwardly free. Learn not to identify yourself with anything whatsoever.

—Llewellyn Vaughan-Lee
In the Company of Friends

Today, I feel centered, and time is a friend instead of an old enemy.... We are one, the house and I, and I am happy to be alone—time to think, time to be.

—May Sarton
Journal of a Solitude

It's not a place to be intellectual. But a place to be quiet. Solitude heightens experience.

—Regina Sara Ryan
The Woman Awake

True solitude is found in wild places, where one is without human

obligation.... One returns from solitude laden with the gifts of circumstance.

—Wendell Berry
What Are People For?

When we find our being in God, we live with a solitude of the heart.

—Herbert Anderson & Freda A. Gardner
Living Alone

I must have a room to myself, which shall be my room. I have in my own mind itched on Mrs. Whipple's room. We can put the stove in it. I have bought a carpet ...

—Harriet Beecher Stowe

Appealing workplaces are to be avoided. One wants a room with no view, so imagination can meet memory in the dark.

—Annie Dillard

... Secret and self-contained, and solitary as an oyster.

—Charles Dickens
A Christmas Carol

My beloved is the mountains, the solitary wooded valleys, strange islands ... silent music.

—John of the Cross

SOPHIA

Let it be known: today the Eternal Feminine in an incorruptible body is descending to Earth. In the unfading light of the new Goddess heaven has become one with the depths.

—Vladimir Soloviev

Those who have visited the church of St. Sophia in Constantinople and have fallen under the spell of what it reveals, will find themselves permanently enriched by a new apprehension of the world in God, that is, of the divine Sophia.

—Sergei Bulgakov
Sophia

When you follow her, you cannot take a wrong turning; when you pray to her you cannot lose hope. When she protects you, you are never afraid. When she leads you forward, you are never tired. When her grace shines on you, you arrive at your goal.

—Bernard of Clairvaux

You're the face of all races
The voice of the ages
The arms of love.
You're the hands of a compass
Guiding us, guiding us, guiding us home.

—Naneki Elliott
Mornings with Mother Mary

Sophia is the feminine, dark, yielding tender counterpart of the power, justice, creative dynamism of the Father.

—Monica Furlong
Merton: A Biography

The mystery of the Virgin Mother lies in her fiat, her acceptance of life's experiences.... It is this experience that links Innana, Kore, Mary and Sophia who descend into life and become of one nature

with it.... Alchemy is the proper craft of Sophia, for she transforms one thing into another, allowing the true gold of creation to shine through the prima material.

—Caitlin Matthews
Sophia: Goddess of Wisdom

Holy Wisdom, the Divine Sophia, appeared in the world as prophesied by the prophet Baruch and this appearance took place in Mary. Theologically expressed, Sophia became human in Mary ... it is a conception that is deeply rooted in the Russian Church's devotion to Mary.

—Thomas Schipflinger
Sophia-Maria

Mary was the bearer of Sophia just as Jesus was the bearer of Christ.

—Robert Powell
The Most Holy Trinosophia

The divine sparks of the Universe are one in Sophia. As Bride, she unites with Bridegroom in the unified God-head.

—Marion Woodman
Bones

Sophia is the One at the heart of creative acts. She was present at the beginning and she is the ongoing process... Her vision will keep us moving.

—Susan Cady, *et al*
Sophia

Sophia is the receptacle in which God's eternal will seeks, sees and finds itself.

—Jacob Boehme
Signature

After the day of rest, Sophia [Wisdom] sent Zoe [Life], her daughter, who is called Eve, as an instructor to raise up Adam.... When he saw her, he said, "You will be called 'The Mother of the Living' because you are the one who gave me life."

—Elaine Pagels
The Gnostic Gospels

Our Mother thou who art in the darkness of the underworld, may the holiness of thy name shine anew in our remembering.

—Robert Powell
The Sophia Teachings

SORROW

Only the passing sorrows curse heaven. The big sorrows just listen.

—De Musset

All sorrows can be borne if we put them in a story or tell a story about them.

—Isak Dinesen

Aragorn: But let us not be overthrown at the final test, who of old renounced the Shadow and the Ring. In sorrow we must go, but not in despair. Behold! We are not bound for ever to the circles of the world, and beyond them is more than memory. Farewell!

—J. R. R. Tolkien
Lord of the Rings

Those who do not know how to weep with their whole heart, don't know how to laugh either.

—Golda Meir

Guilt is the very nerve of sorrow.

—Horace Bushnell
Sermons on Living Subjects

You cannot prevent the birds of sorrow from flying over your head, but you can prevent them from building nests in your hair.

—Chinese proverb

SOUL

The soul passes through the body like sap in a tree; we are watered by a Divine Breath, we blossom, grow strong. The soul sustains the body and the body sustains the soul.

—Hildegard of Bingen

No one can give a definition of soul. But we know what it feels like.... The soul is a burning desire to breathe in this world of light and never to lose it—to remain children of light.

—Albert Schweitzer
Reverence for Life

God is in all things as a state of being, as activity and power. But only in the soul does he give birth, for although all creatures are as it were a footprint of God, only the soul is naturally formed in the image of God.

—Meister Eckhart
Sermons and Resources

The soul doesn't evolve or grow, it cycles and twists, repeats and reprises, echoing

ancient themes common to all human
beings. It is always circling home.

—Thomas Moore
Original Self

Our souls become what we make of
them. So will the soul of cyberspace, for
cyberspace mirrors us in our entirety,
including our souls. ... If, in the strange
days to come, we attend to the sacred,
then the soul of cyberspace, though beset
by human frailty, will be a sacred one.

—Jeff Zaleski
The Soul of Cyberspace

The new meaning of soul is creativity
with mysticism. These will become the
foundation of the new psychological
type and with him or her will come the
new civilization.

—Otto Rank

A soul is forged out of fire and rock crystal. Something rigorous, hard in an Old
Testament sense, but also as gentle as the
gesture with which his tender fingertips
sometimes stroked my eyelids.... One
can be born with a 12-year-old soul. One
can also be born with a thousand-year-
old-soul.... "Soul" is quite different from
what we call "heart." There are plenty of
people who have a lot of "heart" but very
little soul.

—Etty Hillesum
*An Interrupted Life: The Diaries
of Etty Hillesum*

Soul is what connects you to everyone
and everything else. It is the sum of all
the choices you make. It is where your
beliefs and values reside. Soul is at the
center of our relationships to others, and
for me it is at the center of the business

enterprise. They don't tell you this in
business school.

—Tom Chappell
The Soul of a Business

Every moment and every event of every
man's life on earth plants something in
his soul.... Souls are like wax waiting for
a seal. By themselves they have no special
identity. The wax that has melted in God's
will can easily receive the stamp of its
identity, the truth of what it was meant
to be.

—Thomas Merton
New Seeds of Contemplation

Our soul is one to God, Unchangeable
goodness, and therefore between God
and our soul, there is neither wrath nor
forgiveness because there is no between.

—Julian of Norwich

The most important thing happening
in the world right now is the
transformation of humanity's Soul.
Nothing else comes close.

—L. Robert Keck
Sacred Quest

As the keeper of the past, the soul is continually collecting treasures for the spirit.

—Rudolf Steiner
Theosophy

You cannot hide the soul.

—Herman Melville
Moby Dick

Soul is personality, ego, the personal YOU. Spirit is the force from which we draw our spiritual being, and it may be drawn from various sources both more and less advanced than we would consider our own soul, or ego to be.

—Ruth Montgomery
The World Before

The soul is the life force—the only "permanent" part of a person. Evolution is a process of being lifted, by the soul, out of human pain and suffering.... Spiritual will means a person uses her energy on behalf of the soul rather than on behalf of the human personality.

—Mary E. Carreiro
The Psychology of Spiritual Growth

God is not found in the soul by adding anything but by a process of subtraction.

—Meister Eckhart

My soul in its entirety was presented to me in the form of a clear mirror: the back, the top, the bottom, all glowing with light.

—Teresa of Avila

The soul comes alive when it feeds on sacred energy (poignancy, wonder and awe) and one's existence becomes infused with passion, power and depth.... We meet the soul when we are stirred by music, moved by a poem, absorbed in a painting, touched by a ceremony or symbol.... She will slip through the net of every conceptual system and elude every scientific expedition that goes after her.

—David N. Elkins
Beyond Religion

Soul is immeasurably deep and can only be illuminated by insights, flashes in a great cavern of incomprehension.

—James Hillman

You could not discover the limits of soul, even if you traveled every road to do so; such is the depth of its meaning.

—Heraclitus of Ephesus

Soul is a succession of fields of consciousness.

—Normandi Ellis
Dreams of Isis

If the soul could have known God without the world, the world would never have been created.

—Meister Eckhart

God is the sigh of the soul, for he has created in our hearts the longing for love.

—Llewellyn Vaughan-Lee
In the Company of Friends

No encounter with a being or a thing in the course of our life lacks a hidden significance ... the highest culture of the soul remains basically arid and barren unless, day by day, waters of life pour forth into the soul from those little encounters to which we give their due.

—Martin Buber & Aubrey Hodes
Martin Buber

Sometimes I go about pitying myself and all along my soul is being blown by great winds across the sky.

—Ojibway proverb

Waste no more time talking about great souls and how they should be. Become one yourself.

—Marcus Aurelius

SOUND

Somewhere deep inside there is a sound that is mine alone, and I struggle daily to hear it and tune my life to it.

—Rachel Naomi Remen
My Grandfather's Blessings

When a thing ceases to be, its sound disappears from the world.

—Joan Halifax
The Fruitful Darkness

The syllable "aum" represents the music of the soul. This melody is heard only when the divine Power Center in man is roused to activity.... There is no confusion or distortion as happens with drugs and no loss of memory as happens in hypnosis. The intellect remains unaffected, and there is no overlapping or aberration.... From a point of consciousness the soul now seems to stretch from end to end, an ineffable and intangible intelligence present everywhere.

—Gopi Krishna
The Awakening of Kundalini

All things ... are aggregations or atoms that dance and by their movements produce sounds. When the rhythm of the dance changes, the sound it produced also changes... Each atom perpetually sings its song, and the sound, at every moment, creates dense and subtle forms.

—Fritjof Capra
The Tao of Physics

If sound waves carry on to infinity, where are their screams now? I imagine them somewhere in the galaxy, moving forever towards the psalms.

—Anne Michaels
Fugitive Pieces

As geometrical figures are created by drawing a violin bow over the edge of a glass plate, so the forms around us are the crystallized sound-figures of the archetypal forces of the Heaven Worlds.

—Max Heindel
Rosicrucian Cosmo-Conception

The Chinese can't hear Americans at all; the language is too soft and western music unhearable.

—Maxine Hong Kingston
The Woman Warrior

SPACE

Listen to your inner selves and look into the infinity of space and time. There reverberate the song of the stars, the voice of the numbers and the harmony of the spheres... What do the stars do? What do the numbers say? What do the spheres revolve? O souls that are lost and saved, they relate, they sing, they revolve—your destinies!

—Hermes
Hermes

Open space is the acceptance of the unknown, the unpredictable, the unseen, and the mysterious.

—David Spangler
A Pilgrim in Aquarius

Space has a spiritual equivalent and can heal what is divided and burdensome in us.

—Gretel Ehrlich
The Solace of Open Spaces

Human beings are invariably driven to ground their religious experience in the palpable reality of space.

—Belden C. Lane
Landscape of the Sacred

For religious man, space is not homogeneous; he experiences interruptions, breaks in it; some parts of space are qualitatively different from others.... In actual fact, the place is never "chosen" by man. It is merely discovered by him.

—Mircea Eliade
The Sacred and the Profane

Space is not static, but is instead a serene explosion of expanding creativity, filling all the eons of pasts and futures, without exhausting its openness.

—Tarthang Tulku

Dimensionality consists in a reaching out that opens up.

—Martin Heidegger
Time and Being

The purpose is not to create or make something happen, but to allow the space for it to happen.

—Morton T. Kelsey
The Other Side of Silence

The Aivilik Eskimos have at least twelve words for wind.... They integrate time and space as one thing and live in acoustic-olfactory space rather than visual space.

—Peter Redgrove
The Black Goddess and the Sixth Sense

No American can understand the need for time—that is, simply space to breathe. If you have ten minutes to spare, you should jam that full instead of leaving it as space around your next ten minutes. How can anything ripen without those "empty" ten minutes?

—Anne Morrow Lindbergh
War Without and War Within

It is hard to face that open space.

—Neil Armstrong

No one is from this planet. Everyone is from God ... a space being ... we all come from inner space. All that we are are thoughts.

—Björn Örtenheim

SPEECH

In the course of humanity's historical evolution, speech has emerged from a primeval song element. The further we go back into prehistoric times, the more speech resembles recitation and finally singing ... song and speech ... were one.

—Rudolf Steiner
The Inner Nature of Music and the Experience of Tone

The old must often try to be silent, if it is within their power, since silence may be like space, the intensely alive something that contains all. The clear echo of what we refrained from saying, everything, from the first pause of understanding, to the quiet of comprehension.

—Florida Scott-Maxwell
The Measure of My Days

A line runs from the meditations of the heart to the words of the mouth ... the line runs both ways. The words of the mouth become the meditation of the heart, and the habits of loose talk loosen the fastenings of our understanding.

—Richard Mitchell
Less Than Words Can Say

The Indian has effectively been silenced by the intricacies of his own speech.

—N. Scott Momaday

The white man seems to think that speech is some sort of proof of superiority over dumb creation. It is not. It is one of the many gifts the Great Spirit has given to man. To the Indian, silence is the cornerstone of character.

—Tom Brown
The Search

According to a male Dogon elder, spoken language was originally a swirling garment of vapor and breath worn by the encompassing earth itself. Later this undulating garment was stolen by the jackal, an animal whose movements ever since have disclosed the prophetic speech of the world to seers and diviners.

—David Abram
The Spell of the Sensuous

Echo is the soul of the voice exciting itself in hollow places.

—Michael Ondaatje
The English Patient

Laziness in speech leads to foolishness of thought.

—George Orwell

If you change the names of things, you change how people will regard them.

—Neil Postman

The best things can't be told. The second best are misunderstood.

—Heinrich Zimmer

We can know more than we can tell.

—Michael Polanyi

Life be in my speech,
Sense in what I say
Till I come back again.

—Celtic prayer

SPIDER

The metaphor of the spider offers a fine image of the web-spinning, interdisciplinary character of spirituality, as it connects various historical, anthropological, psychological, and myth-and-symbol concerns in exploring the human search for self-transcendence. It also exemplifies how a particular metaphor, especially one drawn from nature, is able to carry over (meta-phora) abstract theological ideas into concrete, lived experience.

—Belden C. Lane
Landscapes of the Sacred

Spider Grandmother continued to walk—the thread of her webbing spinning out behind her.... Many days of darkness passed. And then a glow of orange appeared before her in the distance, telling her that she had reached the land of the Sun People ... quickly so no one saw her, she pinched off a small piece of bright orange flame, popped it into her bowl and walked quietly away. Following the web that she had spun, she began the long walk home ... the fire grew brighter and larger as she walked, until its brightness and its heat became so unbearably intense that she flung the blazing fireball into the air. Tiny and old as she was, she flung the fire so high up in the heavens that it stayed there and became the sun.... Yet Spider Grandmother thought to keep a small piece. This she placed in the bowl and brought back to her people, giving them the second gift of fire ...

—From a Native American myth

Spiders are associated with complex symbolism, representing variously the hub of the web of all creation, the sun and its rays, the Great Mother or moon goddess, the spinners of destiny, and the forces of birth and death.

—John E. Mack
Passport to the Cosmos

Long ago the Spider was in the place where only she was. There was no light or dark ... there was only Spider.... In that place where she was alone and complete with her power, she thought about her power, how it sang to her, how she dreamed from it, how she wished to have someone to share the songdream with her. Not because she was lonely, but because the power's song was so complete, she wished for there to be others who could also know it.

—Paula Gunn Allen
Grandmother of the Light

In the Eastern understanding the spider is the symbol of Mother. My Mother is both within and without this phenomenal world.... Giving birth to the world, she lives within it. She is the Spider and the world is the spider's web she has woven.... The spider brings the web out of herself and then lives in it.

—Andrew Harvey
Dialogues with a Modern Mystic

The common spider's web-making activities are controlled by a fixed inherited canon (which prescribes that the radial threads should always bisect the laterals at equal angles, thus forming a regular polygon); but the spider is free to suspend his web from three, four or more points of attachment—to choose his strategy according to the lie of the land.

—Arthur Koestler
Janus

When she [Spider Woman] awoke to life and received her name, she asked, "Why am I here?"

"Look about you," answered Sotuknaang. "Here is the earth we have created. It has shape and substance, direction and time, a beginning and an end. But there is no life upon it. What is life without sound and movement? So you have been given the power to help us create this life. You have been given the knowledge, wisdom, and love to bless all the beings you create. That is why you are here."

—Frank Waters
  Book of the Hopi

The Spider's web as a spiral net converging is a natural/symbolic re-minder of the importance of positive paranoia, of seeing/making new patterns of perception as preparation for the latter/deeper stages of Journeying.

—Mary Daly
  Gyn/Ecology

Like the orb spider, man lies at the heart of it, listening … fingering the universe against the sky. Knowledge has given him the memory of earth's history beyond the time of his emergence…. The web extends through the starry reaches of sidereal space, as well as backward into the dark realm of pre-history.

—Loren Eiseley
  The Unexpected Universe

Remember, spiders spin their silk out of their own bodies.

—Robert Merrill Eddy &
  Kathy Wonson Eddy
  Writing with Light

SPIRAL

Astronomers and physicists now believe that it is a spiral force which creates the universe itself.

—Frances Hitching
  Earth Magic

Spinning—like singing—is equivalent to bringing forth and fostering life…. Spinsters possess the inner capacity to spin, spiral, dance and sing.

—Mary Daly
  Gyn/Ecology

The serpent is the one land-living vertebrate which naturally and frequently reproduces all the geodetic spiral patterns and so it seems reasonable to assume that both the serpent and the spiral are representations of the geodetic spiral.

—Guy Underwood
  The Pattern of the Past

The spiral form invites both halves of our brains to be involved: the understanding that comes through the left half of the brain comes through our linear mind, which absorbs information through words and logic; the right brain is in touch with images, sensations, memories and feelings that are personal and collective, in time and timeless, and it imposes no order or logic on them. An "aha!" recognition comes when there is a crossover from right to left or left to right … we then know something on multiple levels and are affected or moved by what we know.

—Jean Shinoda Bolen
  Gods in Everyman

Double spiral motifs symbolize unity in duality. An early example is the caduceus, the Greco-Roman herald's staff, on which two spiraling snakes form an image of opposing forces unified.

—Jack Tresidder
1,001 Symbols

SPIRIT

The Spirit shot through me like a bolt of lightning ... ever deeper and clearer from one step to another—it was the real Jacob's ladder.

—Jacob Boehme
Aurora

Everyone who is seriously involved in the pursuit of science becomes convinced that a Spirit is manifest in the Laws of the Universe—a Spirit vastly superior to that of man, and one in the face of which we, with our modest powers, must feel humble.

—Albert Einstein

Our life will not be genuine if we do not follow the dictates of the spirit.

—Martin Buber

Spirit ... is the point of human transcendence.... It is also the point where human beings communicate. At that point of the Spirit we are all open to one another.

—Bede Griffiths

The great need of our time is for people to be connected to spirit; for people to be connected to a core of feeling in themselves that makes their lives vital

and full of meaning, that makes life a mystery evermore to be uncovered.

—Harold Stone
Sandplay

I asked these spirit figures if I was seeing them or if I was seeing what was in my own brain. They answered, "Both."

—Eileen Garrett

In the astral world, every lie is a murder. Every thought and every feeling a reality.... The eyes of the spirit can be opened in every person if he has the necessary energy and patience.

—Rudolf Steiner
At the Gates of Spiritual Science

My hand is entirely the implement of a distant sphere. It is not my head that functions but something else, something higher, something more remote. I must have great friends there, dark as well as bright.... They are all very kind to me.

—Paul Klee

There is but one good illustration of SPIRIT—WIND! Everything else is too visible.

—Calvin Miller
The Song

Spirit is a long, drawn-out breath. Spirituality, on the other hand, may be said to denote the mind grafted onto the wind that is spirit. More concretely, it is the practical way in which we ready ourselves to let Being blow us on or, to use another metaphor, to shine among us.

—Ignacio L. Götz
On Technology and the Spirit

Common talk of sacred history and profane history, religious education and secular education, all these phrases that are so commonly used, hypnotize the public mind into a false view of the Spirit and the world. The right way is to say that the Spirit is the life, the world the form, and the form must be the expression of life.

—Annie Besant
The Spiritual Life in the World

Spirit is like the word whale: so many contradictory behaviors, various metabolic rates, modes of consciousness, so much sheer size differential tangled up in one unassuming term. Our culture has stuck a perfectly good word full of harpoons.

—Jim Nollman
Spiritual Ecology

Every spirit without a body is raw and does not know itself; now, every spirit desires a body both for its food and its joy … there is no understanding without a body.

—Jacob Boehme

The Spirit World isn't a place but a multiplicity of viewpoints. There are as many universes as there are points of view.

—Iris Bethayes
Spirit Guides

Things of the spirit are not parlor games … it's like playing with matches.… Only the strongest dare turn inward.

—Morton T. Kelsey
The Other Side of Silence

SPIRITUALITY

I believe deeply that we must find, all of us together, a new spirituality.

—Dalai Lama

The day of my spiritual Awakening was the day I saw—and knew I saw—all things in God and God in all things.

—Mechtild of Magdeburg

One should not give up, neglect or forget his inner life for a moment, but he must learn to work in it, with it and out of it, so that the unity of his soul may break out into his activities.

—Meister Eckhart

Spiritual development is not an option.

—Robert Rabbin
Invisible Leadership

Spirituality means to me living the ordinary life extraordinarily well.

—William Sloane Coffin
Credo

Above all things, it is needful that there should be no disharmony between higher experiences and the events and demands of everyday life.

—Rudolf Steiner
Initiation and Its Results

Spirituality is our response to the Soul's DNA and our sense of a deep, divine meaning and purpose in life.

—L. Robert Keck
Sacred Quest

Just as we take in substances from our physical surroundings and incorporate them into our bodies, we also take in spiritual substance from our spiritual surroundings and make it our own. This spiritual substance is eternal nourishment for human beings.

—Rudolf Steiner
Theosophy

Religion is a bridge to the spiritual—but the spiritual lies beyond religion. Unfortunately, in seeking the spiritual we may become attached to the bridge rather than crossing over it.

—Rachel Naomi Remen

Spiritual principles are universal.... Treating people the way you want to be treated is a simple yet profound spiritual principle, one which led to the abolition of one of the worst labor practices in history—slavery.

—Laurie Beth Jones
Jesus, CEO

Spirituality is expressed in everything we do. It is a style, unique to itself, that catches up all our attitudes: in communal and personal prayer, in behavior, bodily

expressions, life choices, in what we support and affirm and what we protest and deny.

—Anne Carr
Women's Spirituality

The spiritual life justifies itself to those who live it; but what can we say to those who do not understand? This, at least, we can say, that it is a life whose experiences are proved real to their possessor, because they remain with him when brought closest into contact with the objective realities of life.... These highest experiences that I have had of God's presence have been rare and brief—flashes of consciousness which have compelled me to exclaim with surprise—God is here!

—J. Trevor
My Quest for God

The majority of men live without being thoroughly conscious that they are spiritual beings.

—Søren Kierkegaard

Spirituality is the ability to find peace and happiness in an imperfect world and to feel one's own personality is imperfect but acceptable.

—Bernie Siegel
Love, Medicine and Miracles

The spiritual world lies all about us, and its avenues are open to the unseen feet of the phantoms that come and go, and we perceive them not save by their influence or when at times a most mysterious Providence permits them to manifest themselves to mortal eyes.

—Henry Wadsworth Longfellow

Spirituality isn't an escape from the world, but an expansion of the world. The spiritual dimension enriches and sustains us—it does not limit or deny us. Spirituality is a celebration of love and life.

—Diane Mariechild
Mother Wit

True spirituality is not a way of escaping human suffering—nor does it set up barriers separating individuals from each other.... Spirituality is the process by which a person is ripped apart.

—Martin Bell
Return of the Wolf

Millions of spiritual creatures walk the earth unseen, both when we wake and when we sleep.

—John Milton

When we shall be endowed with our spiritual bodies, I think they will be so constituted that we may send thoughts and feelings any distance in no time at all and transfer them warm and fresh into the consciousness of those we love.

—Nathaniel Hawthorne

Spiritualism is the greatest revelation the world has ever known. I have seen spirits walk around the room and join in the talk of the company. We are continually conscious of protection around us.

—Arthur Conan Doyle

Biology and spirituality—sexuality and spirituality—cannot be separated without destroying the living holism and produc-

ing the dead mechanism: robot sex, robot piety, robot labor, robot existence.

—Monica Sjoo & Barbara Mor
The Great Cosmic Mother

It is by the door of the deep self that we enter into the spiritual knowledge of God.

—Thomas Merton

Spirituality is a metaphysically freighted notion.

—David Carr & John Haldane
Spirituality, Philosophy and Education

Spirituality is basic—it's like breathing. But some of us breathe heavily, some lightly, some deliberately, others unselfconsciously.... Spirituality defines the quality of life of spirit ... it can't be "thingified." Or immobilized.

—Ignacio L. Götz
On Technology and the Spirit

True maturation on the spiritual path requires that we discover the depth of our wounds.

—Jack Kornfield
A Path with Heart

If spirituality is not in and of this world, chances are it is neurotic.

—Thomas Moore
The Soul's Religion

"Rein" is the Sami word for "way"....
Our spiritual trek is like the pregnant reindeer's yearly run to the mountains to

give birth. Jung said the psyche does have a sense of direction.

—Linda Schierse Leonard
Creation's Heartbeat

Spirituality is older, more enduring and more pervasive than all the religions put together. It's the practical living out of deep values.

—Diarmuid Ó Murchú

All one must do, in the shower of spiritual rain that is now descending, is to be alert to the opportunity that is about one.

—Meher Baba *&* D. E. Stevens
Listen, Humanity

What then, could be of consequence if not the spiritual?

—Jean Gebser
The Ever-Present Origin

In the spiritual life, I am always at the beginning.

—Ralph Blum
The Book of Runes

STARS

You see many stars at night in the sky but find them not when the sun rises; can you say that there are no stars in the heaven of day?

—Ramakrishna (Gadadhar Chatterji)

It may come as a shock to learn that nearly all the atoms in your body and in the earth were once part of a star that exploded and disintegrated, and that probably those same atoms were once the debris of still an earlier star.

—Kenneth F. Weaver

The stars, the planets and human and natural life were interlinked symbols for the Egyptians, composing a deep philosophy of life and our place in the universe as well as being approachable on a popular level.

—Shelia Farrant
Symbols for Women

If the stars would appear one night in a thousand years, how men would believe and adore and preserve for many generations the remembrance of the city of god which had been shown.

—Ralph Waldo Emerson

Stars scribble in our eyes the frosty sagas, the gleaming cantos of unvanquished space.

—Hart Crane
The Bridge

STEWARDSHIP

Stewardship is the responsible care of property belong to another. "Usufruct" is, according to the Oxford Dictionary, "the right of temporary possession, use, or enjoyment of the advantages of property belonging to another, so far as may be had without causing damage or prejudice to this."

—Wendell Berry
What Are People For?

Be a steward of your energy.

—Marlo Morgan
Message from Forever

A woman I recently read about described how when she was nine years old she was saved from drowning off the coast of Oregon—by a seal. Later in life she returned the favor by working to save that species.

—Gregg Levoy
Callings

STONES

We need stones around us to echo the substance of our own lives—hard, solid, heavy, timeless, and subtly hued.... Stone, maybe more than any other material, has been known forever to be magical, to have powers to heal, guide, house divinity and mark place of burial.

—Thomas Moore
The Re-Enchantment of Everyday Life

Stones contain memories of the universe.

—Lynn Andrews
Flight of the 7th Moon

Natural stones used for tools are called "eoliths" or dawn-stones.

—René Dubos
A God Within

Supernatural beings are often said to reside in rocks. The Sami of northern Russia believe that certain unusual stones known as *seite* are inhabited by spirits that control the surrounding animals.... in

the south of India, rocks heaped in village shrines are regarded as the *ammas*, local goddesses who guard villages.

—Brian Leigh Molyneaux
The Sacred Earth

Temples in Egypt were often rebuilt on the site of older temples and these new structures were enlivened by the conscious placement of what was called the "seed stone"—a stone that was over part of the former building and now incorporated into the new temple ... impregnating this new temple with its renewed, creative power.

—Jean Houston
The Passion of Isis & Osiris

To make the wind blow, people in New Guinea strike a "wind-stone" lightly with a stick. To strike it hard would bring a hurricane.

—James Frazer
The Golden Bough

This rough stone knows not that it contains noble gold. This holds also of us.

—Jacob Boehme

Abandoned stones which I became interested in invite me to enter into their life's purpose. It is my task to define and make visible the intent of their being.

—Isamu Nobuchi
The Isamu Nobuchi Garden Museum

Megalithic man could have set up his grid of ley lines simply by charging stones ... and placing them in straight lines or circles.

—J. Havelock Fidler
Ley Lines

STORIES

God made man because he loves stories.

—Elie Wiesel

No story sits by itself. Sometimes stories meet at corners and sometimes they cover one another completely, like stones beneath a river.

—Mitch Albom
The 5 People You Meet in Heaven

Draw your chair up close to the edge of the precipice and I'll tell you a story.

—F. Scott Fitzgerald

My story is important not because it is mine ... but because if I tell it anything like right, the chances are you will recognize that in many ways it is yours.

—Frederick Buechner

A story is like something you wind out of yourself. Like a spider, it is a web you weave, and you love your story like a child.

—Katherine Anne Porter

I hope you will go out and let stories happen to you, and that you will work with them, water them with your blood and tears and your laughter till they bloom, till you yourself burst into bloom.... This

is the work. The only work.... Stories set the inner life into motion.

—Clarrisa Pinkola Estes
Women Who Run with the Wolves

A real story touches not only the mind but also the imagination and the unconscious depths in a person, and it may remain with him or her through many years, coming to the surface of consciousness now and then to yield new insights.

—Helen M. Luke
The Way of Woman

What do stories do when they are not being told? Do they live in villages? ... Do they tell each other to each other?

—Howard Norman
The Wishing Bone Cycle

According to Tolkien the appeal of the fairy story lies in the fact that man there most fully exercises his function as a "sub-creator"; not, as they love to say now, making a "comment upon life" but making, so far as possible, a subordinate world of his own.... For Jung, fairy tale liberates Archetypes which dwell in the collective unconscious, and when we read a good fairy tale we are obeying the old precept, "Know thyself."

—C. S. Lewis
Of Other Worlds

The essence of fairy-stories is that they satisfy our heart's deepest desire: to know a world other than our own, a world that has not been flattened and shrunk and emptied of mystery.

—Ralph C. Wood
The Gospel According to Tolkien

If (a child) is going to be frightened, I think it better that he should think of giants and dragons than merely of burglars. And I think St. George or any bright champion in armour, is a better comfort than the idea of the police.

—C. S. Lewis
Of Other Worlds

A story is a little knot or complex of that species of connectedness which we call relevance.

—Gregory Bateson
Mind and Nature

We experience a frisson when we say the words story or soul because we know we are plunging into the liminal space that exists at the edge of the knowable and unknowable, the real and the wondrous.... Story is very simple. A story is "something that happened and ... "

—Deena Metzger
Nourishing the Soul

Some stories leave a train of light behind them, meteor-like, so that much later than they strike our eyes we may see their meaning like an aftereffect.

—Eudora Welty
The Eye of the Story

Stories exist to be exchanged. They are the currency of human growth.

—Jean Houston
The Search for the Beloved

... without a story you have not got a nation, or a culture, or a civilization.

—Laurens Van der Post

A story should be something like the earth, a blazing fire at the core, but cool and green on the outside.

—Madeleine L'Engle
The Summer of the Great Grandmother

We are all part of the old stories; whether we know the stories or not, the old stories know about us. From time immemorial, the old stories encompass all events, past and future.

—Leslie Marmon Silko
Yellow Woman and a Beauty of the Spirit

There are many stories that live in the woods and around the sacred places of the world. Every once in a while they find someone that they like and they come to them.

—Lynn V. Andrews
Crystal Woman

Fairy stories open a door on other time and if we pass through, through only for a moment, we stand outside our own time, outside time itself, perhaps.

—J. R. R. Tolkien

Sara Kendell once read somewhere that the tale of the world is like a tree ... it encompassed the grand stories that caused some change in the world and were remembered in ensuing years as, if not histories, at least folktales and myths. By such reasoning, Winston Churchill could take his place in British folklore alongside the legendary Robin Hood; Merlin Ambrosilus had as much validity as Martin Luther. The scope of their influence might differ, but they were all of the same tale.

—Charles de Lint
Moonheart

Flood stories appear in 217 cultures.

—Bruce Feiler
Walking the Bible

There is a difference between taking a story literally and taking it seriously.

—Robert S. McElvaine
Eve's Seed

Change the name and the story is about you.

—Horace

There are stories the man recites quietly into the room which slip from level to level like a hawk.

—Michael Ondaatje
The English Patient

Life will go on as long as there is someone to sing, to dance, to tell stories and to listen.

—Oren Lyons

No one knows the whole Fable; only parts of it.

—Edwin Muir

Everywhere he looked, he saw a world made up of stories.

—Leslie Marmon Silko

It's all a question of story.... The Old Story—the account of how the world came to be and how we fit into it—is not functioning properly, and we have not learned the New Story ... we are between stories.

—Thomas Berry

STORYTELLING

A great hill marks the place where the Senecas first emerged from the Earth Mother.... There too, it is said, the first stories ever heard were whispered from a crevice in the great, smooth rock ... the Storytelling Stone.

—Belden C. Lane
Landscapes of the Sacred

"To begin at the beginning," was the old story-telling formula, and it was a very sound one, if "the beginning" could only be definitely ascertained!

—Jessie L. Weston
From Ritual to Romance

When one hears a story one takes pleasure in it for different reasons—for the euphony of its phrases, an aspect of the plot, or because one identifies with one of the characters. With certain stories certain individuals may experience a deeper, more profound sense of well-being.... The listener who "takes the story to heart" will feel a pervasive sense of congruence within himself and also with the world.

—Barry Lopez
Crossing Open Ground

Jesus employed his right brain.... Storytellers work out of the right brain and speak to the right brain of others with messages of intellectual depth that strongly challenge left brains.

—Matthew Fox
The Coming of the Cosmic Christ

No such thing as pure fantasy exists. There is only a succession of folk memories filtered through the storyteller's imagination and since all mankind shares in these memories, they are the common store on which the modern storyteller must draw in his attempts to create fantasy.

—Mollie Hunter
Talent Is Not Enough

A story teller in Cree is literally "Someone-Who-Lies-Without-Harming-Anyone."

—Kenneth Lincoln
Native American Renaissance

A good story knows more than its teller.

—John O'Donohue
Beauty

Storytelling is bringing up, hauling up; it is not an idle practice.... There must be a little spilled blood on every story if it is to carry the medicine.

—Clarissa Pinkola Estés
Women Who Run with the Wolves

To tell a story you must travel inward.... Story is the umbilical cord that connects us to the past, present and future.... The Kalahari Bushmen have said, "A story

is like the wind. It comes from a far-off place, and we feel it."

—Terry Tempest Williams
Pieces of White Shells

The stories we tell, whether human or divine, mythic or parabolic, order experience, construct meaning, and build community.... We are our stories.

—Herbert Anderson & Edward Foley
Mighty Stories, Dangerous Rituals

Language is for telling, not for naming. All knowledge is made up of stories we can tell. Where we can tell no story, we can have no knowledge.

—Richard Mitchell
Less Than Words Can Say

Storytelling is passing along gossip—it's good to talk.

—Natalie Goldberg
Writing Down the Bones

... people live in stories that structure their worlds.... Whoever can give his people better stories than the ones they live in is like the priest in whose hands common bread and wine become capable of feeding the very soul ...

—Hugh Kenner
The Pound Era

All of us remembering what we have heard together—that creates the whole story, the long story of the people.

—Leslie Marmon Silko
Storyteller

We're storytellers and what story could be more grand than the story of creation?

—Brian Greene
The Fabric of the Cosmos

Stories sustain us—we need to share them with our friends. Even the act of telling them creates community and invites more stories.

—William G. Doty
Mythography

Narratives have the ability to "make themselves true" through use. Narratives can't change the past, but can change the way people remember the past.

—J. M. Balkin
Cultural Software

We tell ourselves stories in order to live.... We look for the sermon in the suicide, for the social or moral lesson in the murder of five. We interpret what we see, select the most workable of the multiple choices.

—Joan Didion
The White Album

Storytellers always retell.

—Robert Bly & Marion Woodman
The Maiden King

Our personal stories can become the ground of the new myths we need in order to create the world anew.

—Starhawk
Truth or Dare

Aslan, the Great Lion of God, tells you only your story.

—C. S. Lewis

Something from inside me takes lodging inside you.

—Native American storyteller

If the story is beautiful, its beauty belongs to us all. If the story is not, the fault is mine alone who told it.

—Swahili storyteller

STRANGER

In the cherry blossom's shade, there's no such thing as a stranger.

—Issa

Dogs bark at everyone they do not know.

—Heraclitus of Ephesus

Invite the stranger in, knowing you will both be changed.

—Joy Anderson

Offering hospitality to the stranger may originate in a sense of compassion, or the belief that in serving humanity we serve God.

—Daniel S. Wolk

Aboriginal language has no concept of "stranger."

—Marie Battiste
Reclaiming Indigenous Voice and Vision

According to Germanic customs, the category of "stranger" was not protected ... he had no master. He could be killed and his murder could not be punished and his heirs had no rights of inheritance. The outsider was the heretic.

—James Carroll
Constantine's Sword

The mountains never meet, but people can always encounter each other.

—Irish proverb

The tears of a stranger are only water.

—Russian proverb

STRENGTH

You gain strength, courage and confidence by every experience in which you really stop to look fear in the face. You are able to say to yourself, "I lived through this horror. I can take the next thing that comes along." You must do the thing you think you cannot do.

—Eleanor Roosevelt

I have never believed that my limitations were in any sense punishments or accidents. If I had held such a view, I could never have expected the strength to overcome them.

—Helen Keller

The world breaks everyone and afterward many are strong at the broken places.

—Ernest Hemingway

Even in the jungle, force is not called for all the time. In fact, mostly suspension is what is called for, and force only occasionally.

—David Bohm
On Dialogue

I'd rather live a year as a lion than a hundred years as a sheep.

—Friedrich Nietzche

Roots can crack rocks.

—Kenneth Cooper

Never give a sword to a man who can't dance.

—Celtic saying

When spider webs unite, they can tie up a lion.

—Ethiopian proverb

STRESS

I am coming to believe that anything that promotes isolation leads to chronic stress and in time may lead to illnesses like heart disease. Anything that promotes a sense of intimacy, community and connection can be healing.

—Dean Ornish

To relieve stress, mediate and fly …
imagine you're an eagle; feel the wind on
your feathers.

—Grizzlybear Lake

Reframe stress as challenges and oppor-
tunities; generate reality-based hope.

—Howard Clinebell
Well Being

Female rats have such rapid hormonal
changes that you can't get a clear picture
of their stress responses…. Most of the
biological studies of human stress use
only men…. Oxytocin is a stress hor-
mone … it leads to tending and touching…. Under stress at work, men tend to
"pick at" their families…. Under stress at
work, women are more affectionate, hug
more and "tend" to them.

—Shelley E. Taylor
The Tending Instinct

Rule # 1 Don't sweat the small stuff;
Rule # 2 It's all small stuff.

—R. S. Eliot

SUCCESS

The word success is an ambiguous word.
Success with respect to the outside? Or
success with respect to oneself? And if it
is a success with respect to the outside,
then how do you evaluate it? … Success
is not one of my motives, because success
stands in contrast to failure.

—Subrahmanyan Chandrasekhar &
Mihaly Csikszentmihalyi
Creativity

There is nothing stranger than success….
Human beings seem to have the amazing
ability to turn any sudden gift of freedom
or spaciousness into its exact opposite.

—David Whyte
Crossing the Unknown Sea

The paths we take depend on our own
definitions of success.

—Virginia O'Brien
Success on Our Own Terms

Success is nothing more than going
from failure to failure with
undiminished enthusiasm.

—Winston Churchill

All my life I have teetered between wanting to be successful and despising what
constitutes success.

—Malcolm Muggeridge
Chronicles of Wasted Time

Stop. Ask yourself, "What are ten ways I
could succeed at this?

—Ellen Langer
Mindfulness

The dictionary is the only place where
success comes before work.

—Arthur Brisbane

SUFFERING

There is in man a fear of joy as keen as the fear of suffering pain, because true joy precludes all the comforts of self-pity.

—Helen M. Luke
The Way of Woman

Once suffering is completely accepted, it ceases in a sense to be suffering.

—M. Scott Peck

All suffering is separation from Source.

—Martia Nelson
Coming Home

So long as little children are allowed to suffer, there is no true love in the world.

—Isadora Duncan

Suffering is like the seed of that herb when planted in the earth. That seed remembers itself and endures in the darkness so that it can grow up into the sunlight one day as an entirely transformed flower.

—Lynn V. Andrews
Crystal Woman

Suffering is a human condition that is sought for various reasons.... You are alive as the result of your great curiosity for human experience ... you want to participate in human drama.

—Jane Roberts
A Seth Book

Without our suffering, our work would just be social work, very good and help-ful, but it would not be the work of Jesus Christ.... Only by being one with us has he redeemed us. We are allowed to do the same.

—Mother Teresa

To make any progress we must not make speeches and organize mass meetings but be prepared for mountains of suffering.... Suffering is the badge of the human race.

—Mohandas (Mahatma) Gandhi &
Raghavan Iyer
The Moral and Political Thought of Mahatma Gandhi

Call the world "The vale of Soul-making."... Do you not see how necessary a World of Pains and troubles is to school an Intelligence and make it a soul? A Place where the heart must feel and suffer in a thousand diverse ways.

—John Keats
Letter to George and Georgiana Keats

He [Rasputin] was beaten badly at 28 and discovered the "joy of suffering".... Holy Fools in Russia agreed to respect ordinary life and simulate madness, to endure suffering and thus to partake of His suffering.... The most beautiful cathedral in Moscow, next to the Kremlin, was dedicated to the Holy Fool, Basil the Blessed.

—Edvard Radzinsky
The Rasputin File

It is only by living completely in this world that one learns to have faith. One must completely abandon any attempt to make something of oneself.... In so doing we throw ourselves completely into the arms of God, taking seriously, not our own suffering, but those of God in the world.

—Dietrich Bonhoeffer

Every tear ... can be said to express the sadness and suffering of the universe; the mute anguish of all the oceans, compressed into a single consuming droplet.

—Jean Gebser
The Ever-Present Origin

Do not murmur when you suffer in doing what the spirits have commanded, for a cup of water is provided.

—Ute proverb

SUFIS

Love is the religion, the universe its book.

—Jalal Al-din Rumi

Sufism is notoriously difficult to define, but in essence it is a path of the heart, of the sacred heart, a path of direct experience ... to the living presence of Allah the Beloved.

—Andrew Harvey
The Essential Mystics

Every Muslim will meet God eventually, but Sufis want him stage center in this very life.

—Huston Smith
The Essential Rumi

This is the Sufi notion of mystical union: "When the soul lies down in that grass the world is too full to talk about ideas,

language, even the phrase 'each other' doesn't make any sense."

—Bill Moyers
Fooling with Words

Sufism is truth without form.... The first may have been a woman—Fatima—Muhammed's daughter. His descendants are called "People of the House"....
Sufis call "A Moses Basket" any cultural artifact in which a liberating teaching is concealed for preservation until such time as it can be retrieved by those who can perceive its value and apply it to life.

—Thomas Cleary & Sartaz Aziz
Thoughts from the Twilight Goddess

According to the traditional teachers of some Sufi orders, Sufism predates all the established religions in the Middle East and has survived through secrecy and a certain amount of "shape-shifting." In Sufism, an elaborate science of the nafs outlines various stages of evolution in the subconscious self—from animal to barely human to fully human to divine.

—Neil Douglas-Klotz
Prayers of the Cosmos

Sufi mystics in the Middle Ages meditated on flowers in order to experience angelic natures.

—Suzanne Zuercher
Enneagram Spirituality

The Sufi is absent from himself and present with God.

—Hujwiri

A synonym for Sufism in Arabic is "path" (or *tariqah*).... It refers to a path in the desert from one oasis to the next. It is a trackless path; the sands shift constantly. You need a guide who has traveled the spiritual path, who knows the way and its pitfalls and dangers.

—James Faiman & Robert Frager
Essential Sufism

Sufism is a science devoted to the disciplines of cleansing and perfecting the instruments of perception so that they reveal the nature of reality in an understood fashion.

—F. David Peat
Lighting the Seventh Fire

Sufis are known as the "sweepers" or "garbage bins of humanity" for we absorb the darkness in people's hearts so they can come closer to [Him.]

—Llewellyn Vaughan-Lee
In the Company of Friends

The most common practice of Islamic mystics, or Sufis, is the *dhikr*, the recollection of God … simply repeating Allah, it is said, brings the one who prays directly into the divine presence. In some Sufi circles, "Allah," is repeated rapidly and eventually shortened until only the final syllable, pronounced "Hu," remains. Eventually even the "Hu" is dropped and only breathing remains.

—Philip Zaleski & Paul Kaufman
Gifts of the Spirit

From the alone to the Alone.

—Llewellyn Vaughan-Lee
In the Company of Friends

Lord, increase me in knowledge; My Lord, increase me in bewilderment.

—Sufi prayer

SUN

The Sun, the hearth of affection and life, pours burning love on the delighted earth.

—Arthur Rimbaud

Sun symbols, such as the swastika, appear on early Minoan art…. Women dance with the sun.

—Lucy Goodison
Moving Heaven and Earth

The shining light which we generate on earth radiates effects out into the universe…. This radiance goes out for a certain distance only and is then reflected back again … what astronomy sees as a fiery ball of gas is simply the reflection of a spiritual element that makes a physical impression.

—Theodor Schwenk &
Wolfram Schwenk
Water: The Element of Life

A sun is much more than a flaming ball of hydrogen showering heat and light upon its planetary children. It serves primarily as a depository for celestial knowledge. The sun's core is like a gigantic cosmic library whose contents await plucking.

—Patricia Pereira
Songs of the Arcturians

When the sun rises at dawn as Kheperi, the Light manifests as all potentiality. When the sun sets at dusk as Atum, it is all absorption, the Light receding into the hidden realms from which it came. By day, high above earth, the sun god Ra is the visible light power that constantly pulses, generating energy, warmth, strength and light, all the fundamentals of life. Therefore was Light a triune god called Kheperi-Ra-Atum.

—Normandi Ellis
Dreams of Isis

The eye of the great God.... Pouring upon us at each time and season.... Glory be to thee thou Gracious Sun, face of the God of life.

—Celtic sun prayer

SURRENDER

Touching Nirvana, touching the ultimate dimension, is a total and unconditional surrender to God. If the wave knows its ground of being is water, it overcomes all fear and sorrow.

—Thich Nhat Hanh
Living Buddha, Living Christ

Surrender has never been my favorite word. I always thought it had only one meaning, which was to lose and be defeated. There is also a spiritual meaning to the word. To surrender is to accept that there is a waxing and waning rhythm to events and to trust that good things can happen without our needing to control them.

—Peter Block
Stewardship

I want to move into a universe I trust so much that I give up playing God. I want to stop holding things together.... I want to surrender my care of the universe and become a participating member, with everyone I work with, in an organization that moves gracefully with its environment, trusting in the unfolding dance of order.

—Margaret Wheatley
Leadership and the New Science

If you let yourself be absorbed completely, if you surrender completely to the moments as they pass, you live more richly in those moments.

—Anne Morrow Lindbergh

We need a set of rough principles to guide us lest we surrender to something too small, to false gods, gurus, and groups.... The followers of Jim Jones took the full dose of poison. Overbelief can be deadly.

—Sam Keen
Hymns to an Unknown God

Since God has given us many faculties, including free will and intelligence, our surrender must be complete and total, not limited to certain faculties. It must involve the whole of our being, otherwise, hidden thoughts and emotions as well as false ideas can continue with a fallacious sense of external surrender of one's will to God to produce acts in the name of religion that can have calamitous consequences.

—Seyyed Hossein Nasr
The Heart of Islam

SURVIVAL

Every good and excellent thing in the world stands moment by moment on the razor-edge of danger and must be fought for.

—Thornton Wilder
The Skin of Our Teeth

There is no such thing as survival of the fittest, only survival of the fit. This means that there is no one answer that is right, but many answers that might work.

—Margaret J. Wheatley &
Myron Kellner-Rogers
a simpler way

Why does resiliency surprise us? We are born survivors.

—Diane Ackerman
An Alchemy of Mind

Spiritual growth is now replacing survival as the central objective of the human experience.

—Gary Zukov & Linda Francis
The Heart of the Soul

SYMBOLS/SYMBOLISM

Luckily for us, symbols mean very much more than can be known at first glance.

—Carl G. Jung
The Collected Works of C. G. Jung

A symbol must be unlike what it symbolizes in order that it may be transformed and "become" what is symbolized ... a cup cannot be a symbol for a cup.... A symbol does something the sign fails to

do: it sets the object at a distance and in the public zone where it is beheld intersubjectively by the community of symbol users.

—Walker Percy
Message in the Bottle

Symbols ... are merely veils of light rendering visible the "Divine Dark."

—Anna Kingsford
Kore Kosmou

A symbol is never completely in the light. It holds a vital line into the rootage in the dark.... A symbol constantly nudges thought towards new windows of seeing.

—John O'Donohue
Eternal Echoes

Jung believed that a symbol's ability to express more than could be put into words was essential to its meaning.... Tillich also believed that symbols cannot be produced intentionally, but that they grow and die by mysterious, unconscious processes and therefore can never be subject to human control or conscious manipulation.

—Carol P. Christ
Laughter of Aphrodite

Symbol systems cannot simply be rejected, they must be replaced. Where there is no replacement, the mind will revert to familiar structures at times of crisis, bafflement or defeat.

—Carol Christ
Womanspirit Rising

A symbol can never be fully interpreted. It can only be experienced.... Symbols which are transposed into the words of ordinary language become rigid in them, they grow dim and very easily become "their own opposites," confining the meaning within narrow dogmatic frames …

—P. D. Ouspensky
In Search of the Miraculous

… symbols and art objects do not stand for things; they manifest them, in their fullness. You begin by using symbols, and end by contemplating them.

—Annie Dillard
Living by Fiction

The truer the symbol, the deeper it leads you, the more meaning it opens up.

—Flannery O'Connor
On Writing

Symbols hold the mind to truth but are not themselves the truth, hence it is delusory to borrow them. Each civilization, every age, must bring forth its own.

—Henrich Zimmer
Philosophies of India

The Teddy-bear exists in order that the child may endow it with imaginary life and personality and enter into a quasi-social relationship with it … a crucifix exists in order to direct the worshiper's thought and affections to the Passion … hence devout people may prefer the crudest and emptiest icon. The emptier the more permeable.

—C. S. Lewis
An Experiment in Criticism

Symbols point beyond themselves. They make it possible for us to slip

through time and leap over places. They unlock emotions.

—Herb Brokering
Wholly Holy

Symbols awaken individual experience and transmute it into a spiritual act, into metaphysical comprehension of the world.

—Mircea Eliade
The Sacred and the Profane

The symbol of the Goddess was not merely omitted from the Jewish and Christian canons, but forcibly evicted from them.

—Carl Olson
The Book of the Goddess

Words can be tossed off rapidly, but symbols need time to reverberate in the mind.

—Susan Howatch
Mystical Paths

Symbols are not stationery ideas that are pushed about, but concentration of energy endowed with motion.

—Jane Roberts
Psychic Politics

Symbols point beyond themselves, but through a mind-concept.

—Ignacio L. Götz
On Technology and the Spirit

Symbols speak directly to the psyche.

—Joseph Campbell
Thou Art That

The world of symbols is not a tranquil and reconciled world; every symbol is iconoclastic in comparison with some other symbol, just as every symbol, left to itself, tends to thicken, to become solidified in an idolatry.

—Paul Ricoleur
The Symbolism of Evil

Meanings are in people, not in the symbols.

—Dale Spender
Nattering on the Net

A true symbol always encloses two complementary poles, always ambivalent and ambiguous.

—Jean Gebser
The Ever-Present Origin

Symbols unlock dimensions and elements of our soul which correspond to the dimensions and elements of reality.

—Paul Tillich

Symbols first generate chaos, then build symmetry.

—John R. Van Eenwyk
Archetypes and Strange Attractors

Concepts and words are symbols, just as visions, rituals and images are; so too are the manners and customs of daily life. Through all of these a transcendent reality is mirrored.

—Heinrich Zimmer
Philosophies of India

Symbolism is the storehouse of cultural memory. We don't even have a word for symbolism, yet we are all wrapped up in it. You have the word, but that is all.

—Lame Deer
Seeker of Visions

One bloom can suggest summer.

—Jane Roberts
The World View of Paul Cézanne

The universe is but one vast symbol of God.

—Thomas Carlyle

SYNCHRONICITY

Events can, so to speak, bunch together in time and space, not because one is causing the other but because their meanings are linked.

—Carl G. Jung
Memories, Dreams, Reflections

Coincidence is God's way of remaining anonymous.

—Bernie S. Siegel
Peace, Love and Healing

Synchronicity is the measure of our inner balance, our contact with the divine, our wholeness.

—Pierre Lutin

Jung's essay on "synchronicity," published in 1952, was partly based on Paul Kammerer's book *Das Gesetz der Serie*, published in 1919.... Kammerer defined his concept of "seriality" as the concurrence in space or recurrence in time of meaningfully but not causally connected events.... He regarded single coincidences as merely the tips of the iceberg which happened to catch the eye among the ubiquitous manifestations of "seriality."

—Arthur Koestler
Janus

Since synchronicities abound at times of transition, we can also expect to find the Trickster present at such time, giving with one hand while he might take away with the other, but he will certainly play a few tricks in the process.

—Robin Robertson, from the Foreword
Synchronicity

I looked up the [Nuremberg war crimes] trials in the library and was horrified to find that they are published in a form almost useless to the researcher. They are abstracts, and are catalogued under arbitrary headings. After hours of search I went along the line of shelves to an assistant librarian and said, "I can't find it, there's no clue, it may be in any of these volumes." I put my hand on one volume and took it out and carelessly looked at it, and it was not only the right volume, but I had opened it at the right page.

—Dame Rebecca West,
Hardy, Harvie & Koester
The Challenge of Chance

Synchronicity requires a human participant, for it is a subjective experience in which the person gives meaning to the coincidence.... The person links the two events together.... Synchronistic events

are the clues that point to the existence of an underlying connecting principle.

—Jean Shinoda Bolen
The Tao of Psychology

When I pray, coincidences start to happen. When I don't pray, they don't happen.

—William Temple

Synchronicity is an event or series of events when the external and internal worlds affect each other, making meaningful experiences that change our lives.

—Jessika Satori
Synchronicity: The Entrepreneur's Edge

Synchronicity holds the promise that if we will change within, the patterns in our outer life will change also.

—Jean Shinoda Bolen

Arthur Koestler believed that synchronicity springs from the highest integrative potential on the human level.... Synchronistic coincidences are boundary events. They cross margins between psychological reality on the one hand and physical reality on the other.

—Alan Combs & Mark Holland
Synchronicity

Miss Marple: Any coincidence is always worth noting. You can throw it away later if it is only coincidence.

—Agatha Christie

Every time I have become aware of a synchronicity experience, I have had an accompanying feeling that some grace came along with it.

—Jean Shinoda Bolen

If synchronicity is true, is it not always true?

—Carl G. Jung

The work that needs to be done is the work with synchronicity.

—Marie-Louise von Franz

A better word than "coincidence" for synchronicity might be "co-occurrence".... Synchronicity carries a principle of orderedness that occurs in the universe regardless of causal connections and beyond space and time.

—Ira Progoff
Jung, Synchronicity and Human Destiny

Perhaps synchronicities, like dreams and symptoms, are happening all the time and we simply don't notice them until they reach a certain level of explicitness.... Maybe they have to shout and wave flags, splash their perfume around, and put on sequins and dance a hootchy-kootchy. In the Age of Information, a lot competes for our attention.

—Gregg Levoy
Callings

metaphoric mind. In the pulse of the universe, the vision is being born anew.

—Bob Samples
The Metaphoric Mind

When we look at organisms that work ... we find that there is one particular quality that they all share: the many components naturally and spontaneously function together, in harmony with the whole.... This harmonious interaction can be described by the word synergy, derived from the Greek *syn-ergos*, meaning "to work together." Synergy does not imply any coercion or restraint, nor is it brought about by deliberate effort ... elements function in ways that are spontaneously mutually supportive.

—Peter Russell
The Global Brain Awakens

The power of knowledge is such that one idea can be used simultaneously by 50 or 500 or 500 million people. All of these individuals can win, and because of synergy they can win more individually by sharing knowledge than by not sharing it.

—Barry Carter
Infinite Wealth

SYNERGY

Synergy, the positive version of unity, is dawning in the human mind. It has always been with us ... in the quiet mists of the

TALENT

The greatest formal talent is worthless
if it does not serve a creativity which is
capable of shaping the cosmos.

—Albert Einstein

Talent is a question of quantity. Talent does
not write one page; it writes three hundred.

—Jules Reynard

Where your talents and the needs of the
world cross, there lies your wisdom.

— Aristotle

"Father, I was so afraid I would make a
mistake that I didn't do anything. Here's
the paper you gave me," he said with a
blank stare. "Do you mean you wouldn't
even try?" his Father asked. "Wouldn't
that be a mistake not to try? Let's make
a picture now so that you will have
something to show at the Festival of Art."

—Gerard A. Pottebaum
The Festival of Art

Talent is ordinary. Disciplined talent
is rare.

—James Michener

Give me a condor's quill! Give me
Vesuvius' crater for an inkstand!

—Herman Melville

The mountain does not laugh at the
river because it is lowly, nor does the
river speak ill of the mountain because it
cannot move about.

—Japanese proverb

TALMUD

The buzzing of the Talmud escapes from
a hive of silence.

—Emmanuel Levinas

The Talmud says all the world is watered
with the dregs of Eden.

—Evan Eisenberg
   The Ecology of Eden

The Jews invented the Talmud to answer
new questions not readily resolved by the
Torah; so too, with the Q'uran, by
the Hadith.

—Leonard Shlain
   The Alphabet Versus the Goddess

TAO

In many respects, the concept of Tao
resembles the Greek concept of logos....
"In the beginning was the Tao."

—Jean Shinoda Bolen
   The Tao of Psychology

The Tao is an empty vessel, it is used
but never filled ... hidden deep but ever
present.... It is the source of the ten
thousand things.

—*Tao Te Ching*

Out of Tao comes unity; out of unity
comes two; from two comes three; from
three all things come.

—Lao Tzu

Eastern, and especially Chinese mysticism majors on harmony, stillness,
conformity with the Tao (the Way),
resignation, and "absorption."

—Bruno Borchert
   Mysticism

The Tao Te Ching can be read in one half
hour or a lifetime.... It is the action of
non-action.... The Tao never does anything, yet through it all things are done.

—Philip Novak
   The World's Wisdom

The I Ching does not offer itself with
proofs and results; it does not vaunt itself,
nor is it easy to approach. Like a part of
nature, it waits until it is discovered.... To
one person its spirit appears to be as clear
as day; to another shadowy as twilight; to
a third, dark as night.

—Jean Shinoda Bolen
   The Tao of Psychology

The Tao that can be told is not the
Eternal Tao; the name that can be named
is not the Eternal Name.

—Lao Tzu
   Tao Te Ching

Lao Tzu's teaching can be summed up in the phrase: Make no dams. He only wrote 5,000 characters in his Book of Tao.

—Leonard Shlain
The Alphabet Versus the Goddess

TEACHER/TEACHING

Everyone teaches all the time. To teach is to learn.

—*A Course in Miracles*

Learning is finding out what you already know; doing is demonstrating that you know it; teaching is reminding others that they know just as well as you. You are all learners, doers, teachers.

—Richard Bach
Illusions

You will be teachers for each other. You will come together in circles and speak your truth to each other. The time has come for women to accept their spiritual responsibility for the planet.

—Sherry Ruth Anderson &
Patricia Hopkins
The Feminine Face of God

Simple things are almost always the hardest to explain ... showing someone how to tie a shoelace is easy. Explaining it is almost impossible.

—Daniel Quinn
My Ishmael

Mentoring begins when your imagination falls in love with the fantasy of another.

—James Hillman

Good teachers possess a capacity for connectedness. They are able to weave a complex web of connections among themselves, their subjects, and their students so that students can learn to weave a world for themselves.

—Parker J. Palmer
The Courage to Teach

Rumi says that identity must be torn down, completely demolished along with its little tailoring shop, the patch-sewing of eating and drinking consolations. Inner work is not all ecstatic surrender. Don't listen too often, Rumi advises, to the comforting part of the self that gives you what you want. Pray instead for a tough instructor.

—Coleman Barks
The Essential Rumi

"The best thing for being sad," replied Merlyn ... "is to learn something. That is the only thing that never fails you.... Learn why the world wags and what wags it. That is the only thing which the mind can never exhaust, never alienate, never be tortured by, never fear or distrust, and never dream of regretting. Learning is the only thing for you."

—T. H. White
The Once and Future King

The teacher handles the living and growing child with the same sense of immediacy and particularity and beauty that the artist experiences in relation to his materials and vision.... The teacher helps the child to live into art and knowledge as into a single realm.

—Mary Caroline (M. C.) Richards
Centering

Great teachers are the realized ones. They are the noble chiefs and leaders who have conquered all illusion.... They have solved the riddle of paradox and duality. They can speak only truth.

—Lynn V. Andrews
Jaguar Woman

Sometimes the best teacher teaches only once to a single child or to a grownup past hope.

—Loren Eiseley

He who wants to teach us a truth should place us in a position to discover it ourselves.

—José Ortega y Gasset

Teaching is an act of love, a spiritual cohabitation, one of the few sacred relationships left in a crass secular world.

—Theodore Roethke

A teacher affects eternity; he can never tell where his influence stops.

—Henry Adams

Teaching is about finding face, finding heart, finding foundation and doing so in a context of family, community and relationships with a whole environment.

—Marie Battiste
Reclaiming Indigenous Voice and Vision

Our first teacher is our own heart.

—Cheyenne proverb

TECHNOLOGY

The good news is that technology can make us smart. In fact, it already has ... the bad news is that technology can make us stupid. The technology for creating things has far outstripped our understanding of them.

—Donald A. Norman
Things That Make Us Smart

The danger of technology is neither more nor less than the danger of any use we make of ourselves.... Historically, the same minds that produced spears painted the walls of the caves at Lascaux.... If the very technology that enslaves was seen as another instance of the presence of God among us, perhaps its use would become more humanitarian.

—Ignacio L. Götz
On Technology and the Spirit

Fools with tools are still fools.

—Norman O. Brown

Digital files have 1/10th the readable life span of acid-laced newsprint.... Digital storage is easy; digital preservation is hard.

—Stewart Brand
The Clock of the Long Now

The architecture of cyberspace is the ultimate labyrinth. On each integrated circuit, on every microchip, we can discern but cannot decipher the secret key, the complicated emblem of collective intelligence.

—Pierre Lévy
Collective Intelligence

If cyberspace is a digital ocean, then Christianity online is its tidal wave.

—Jeff Zaleski
The Soul of Cyberspace

A new technology always tries to look like an old technology. The first "horse-less carriage" had whip sockets in their dashboards.... The first typeface tried to look like calligraphy.

—Richard Thieme

Nature's "design" and "technologies" are far superior to human science and technology. They were created and have been continually refined over billions of years of evolution, during which the inhabitants of the Earth Household flourished and diversified without ever using up their natural capital—the planet's resources and ecosystem services on which the well-being of all living creatures depend.

—Fritjof Capra
The Hidden Connections

Computers are always right, but life isn't about being right.

—John Cage

TEMPLES/CHURCHES/ MOSQUES

A temple is a landscape of the soul. When you walk into a cathedral, you move into a world of spiritual images. It is the mother womb of your spiritual life—mother church. All the forms around are significant of spiritual value ... the form is secondary. The message is what is important.

—Joseph Campbell
The Power of Myth

Monuments to God are not edifices we build, but moments of encounter—in the wilderness of our own lives.

—Martin Bell
Return of the Wolf

The modern temple suffers from a severe cold. Congregants preserve a respectful distance between the liturgy and themselves. They say the words, "Forgive us for we have sinned," but of course, they are not meant.

—Abraham Joshua Heschel
Man's Quest for God

The American who has been confined in his own country, to the sight of buildings designed after foreign models, is surprised on entering York Minster or St. Peter's at Rome, by the feeling that these structures are imitations also—faint copies of the invisible archetype.

—Ralph Waldo Emerson

Ancient churches and abbeys, in that through time they have channeled the devotions and aspirations of our ancestors—back to the remotest times when the site may have been but a grove on a holy hill—are of particular value and importance for those who can work with them, even if some have been occluded by ancient or modern ignorance. The power of some of these old sites was diverted from spiritual and inner Earth ends by ecclesiastical and political ambitions of some of our forebears. Hence the evidence we see of great splendors in stone falling into decay. Nonetheless, the original pure source of power may be felt and seen shining through as fountainheads are unblocked.

—Gareth Knight
The Rose Cross and the Goddess

The Temple is to space what the Sabboth is to time.

—Abraham Joshua Heschel

I like the silent church before the service begins, better than any preaching.

—Ralph Waldo Emerson

THANKSGIVING

A single Japanese word captures this sense of indebtedness to everyone and everything that makes a meal possible: *itadakimasu* (pronounced EE ta da kee mas). Saying it at the beginning of a meal honors the sun, the rain, the earthworms, the farmers, the merchants, the cook—everyone and everything that collaborate to bring the meal together. In a word—*itadakimasu*—you are honoring the Source of Life behind it all ... there is no English equivalent.

—Charles Garfield, *et al*
Wisdom Circles

Write five things down you are grateful for, and do it every day.

—Oprah Winfrey

In the Kikuyu language there is no phrase for "thank you." Instead they say, "It is good."

—Dan Millman
Everyday Enlightenments

THEOLOGY

[Hermes Trismegistus] is called the first author of theology; he was succeeded by Orpheus, who came second amongst ancient theologians: Aglaophemus, who had been initiated into the sacred teaching of Orpheus, was succeeded in theology by Pythagoras, whose disciple was Philolaus, the teacher of our Divine Plato.

—Marsilio Ficino
Argumentum

Theology is faith in search of reason.

—Anselm

The theology of creativity will necessarily be the theology of the Holy Spirit re-forming us in the likeness of Christ, raising us from death to life with the very same power which raised Christ from the dead. The theology of creativity will also be a theology of the image and the likeness of God in humanity.

—Thomas Merton
The Theology of Creativity

Bad art has a way of becoming bad theology. And bad theology in turn cripples life.

—Daniel Berrigan

The object of theology is not God, but God's manifestation, which is expressed in religious symbols.

—Paul Tillich

Religious experience, being essentially spiritual, can never be fully understood by the material mind; hence the function of theology, the psychology of religion.

—*The Urantia Book*

C. S. Lewis compared the difference between theology and faith to the difference between maps and the sea coast.

—Carol Doran & Thomas H. Troeger
Trouble at the Table

Health is the state about which medicine has nothing to say; sanctity is the state about which theology has nothing to say.

—W. H. Auden

The secret of a good sermon is to have a good beginning and a good ending and have the two as close together as possible.

—George Burns

THEOSOPHY

The Theosophical Society ... was organized at New York in 1875. The object of its founders was to experiment practically in the occult powers of nature, and to collect and disseminate among Christians information about the Oriental religious philosophies.

—Helena Petrovna Blavatsky
Isis Unveiled

Through Theosophy I became aware that art could provide a transition to the finer regions which I will call the spiritual realm.

—Piet Mondrian

Theosophy is that ocean of knowledge which spreads from shore to shore of the evolution of sentient beings; unfathomable in its deepest parts, it gives the greatest minds their fullest scope, yet shallow enough at its shores, it will not overwhelm the understanding of a child.

—*The Ocean of Theosophy*

THINKING/THOUGHT

Thinking is the talking of soul with itself.... All thoughts begin in wonder.

—Plato (Aristocles)

All we are is the result of what we have thought.

—Siddhartha Gautama (Buddha)

Thought has created a lot of good things. It is a very powerful instrument, but if we don't notice how it works, it can also do great harm.

—David Bohm
Changing Consciousness

There can be no progress, however, on the path to higher knowledge unless we guard our thoughts and feelings in just the same way we guard our steps in the physical world.

—Rudolf Steiner
Knowledge of Higher Worlds and Its Attainment

A great many people will think they are thinking when they are merely rearranging their prejudices.

—William James

Thinking begins when we have experienced that reason, glorified through the centuries, is the most obstinate adversary of thinking.

—Martin Heidegger
Holzwege

Thinking your way out of thought is like trying to get out of quicksand by pulling yourself up by the hair.

—Fritjof Capra
The Web of Life

In Buddhist psychology, addiction to thought is seen as a major obstacle to enlightenment, because when our attention is focused on thought, we cannot experience reality.

—Andrew Weil
Spontaneous Healing

To think is to create.

—Alan Cohen
The Dragon Doesn't Live Here Anymore

As we change what we think, we change all human-made systems.

—Barbara Shipka
Leadership in a Challenging World

… the thinking process is rather like listening to what the symbol itself has to say. Then thinking becomes an instrument which lends itself to self-expression of the material. This is what Jung calls symbolic thinking. It is something difficult to learn and the more one has learnt the scholarly way, the more difficult it is to switch to this symbolic thinking. But through it you have an invaluable instrument for understanding the raw material of the psyche and its new and not yet known expressions, which we have to know if we want to deal with the unconscious. I would encourage you to make an effort in this direction, for it can bring out of otherwise unintelligible material a new light and wealth of understanding.

—Marie-Louise von Franz
Redemption Motifs in Fairy Tales

The important thing is not to think much but to love much; and so do that which best stirs you to love.

—Teresa of Avila
Interior Castle

The Pueblo Indians told me that all Americans are crazy, and of course I was somewhat astonished and asked them why. They said, "Well, they say they think in their heads. No sound man thinks in his head. We think in the heart."

—Carl G. Jung
The Collected Works of C. G. Jung

Thoughts transmit themselves, and a powerful thought will always transmit itself whether for good or evil. We are protected, mercifully on the whole, from the knowledge of the power of our thoughts. That is one reason why I never put my darkest thoughts into poetry.

—Kathleen Raine

The need to subject ourselves to the hard work of thinking if we want to develop our capacity for higher knowledge cannot be emphasized enough.

—Rudolf Steiner
Theosophy

While you think thoughts, you do not own them. They do not stay like tamed animals within the cage of your skull … they are not collected like rocks. They are more like butterflies.

—Jane Roberts
The World View of Paul Cézanne

Agnes Whistling Elk: Fears always manifest themselves to the one who creates them…. Take responsibility for your thoughts and the beings they create.

—Lynn V. Andrews
Jaguar Woman

Even as radio waves are picked up wherever a set is tuned-in to their wave length, so the thoughts which each of us think each moment of the day go forth into the world to influence for good or bad each other human mind.

—Christmas Humphreys
Concentration and Meditation

One must, in writing poetry, be dealing always with living thought, the living mind-stuff of the universe.

—Kathleen Raine

A thought created once has power, but a thought created repeatedly has greater power.

—Diane Stein
Stroking the Python

Thinking it through is the last thing an ideologue wants to do.

—Ron Suskind
The Price of Loyalty

When you've finished with a thought, it's not gone. It's folded back into the rest of consciousness. It may unfold again in another form.

—David Bohm
On Dialogue

Every thought is a feat of association; thus, all thinking is metaphoric.

—Robert Frost & Elaine Berry
Robert Frost on Writing

Everything has been thought of before, but the problem is to think of it again.

—Johann Wolfgang von Goethe

Thoughts are the soul's speech with itself…. When we express our thoughts to another in words, we express our minds and reveal who we truly are.

—Robert Apatow
The Spiritual Art of Dialogue

New ways of thinking about familiar
things can release new energies and make
all manner of things possible.

—Charles Handy
The Age of Unreason

I am the thoughts of all people
Who praise my beauty and grace.

—*Black Book of Camarthen*

To think that I am not going to think of
you any more is still thinking of you. Let
me then try not to think that I am not
going to think of you.

—Zen proverb

THRESHOLD

Threshold comes from to thrash/thresh—
a place where grain is beaten out from its
husk, where what has been hidden
is manifested.

—Linda Sussman
The Speech of the Grail

A threshold will be crossed when we
actually begin to understand what we see.

—David Rothenberg

The familiar life horizon has been
outgrown, the old concepts, ideals and
emotional patterns no longer fit, for
the time for the passing of a threshold is
at hand.

—Joseph Campbell
Hero with a Thousand Faces

People could see Artemis standing
in the doorway ... she helped people
across thresholds.

—Buffie Johnson
Lady of the Beasts

TIME

God created time so everything wouldn't
happen at once.

—Jack Smith

God had infinite time to give us; but how
did He give it? In one immense tract of
lazy millennium? No, but He cut it up
into a neat succession of new mornings.

—Ralph Waldo Emerson

Eternity is in love with the productions
of time.

—William Blake

Time is the number of motions with
respect to earlier and later ... in fact the
number of continuous movement.

—Aristotle

Time is not all what it seems. It does not
flow in only one direction, and the future
exists simultaneously with the past.

—Albert Einstein

Without being free of time, you cannot
be free of fear ... if you had no thought

about tomorrow, you would not be afraid of tomorrow.

—Jiddu Krishnamurti
The Collected Works of J. Krishnamurti, Vol. XIV

The universe of power where shamans spend most of their time bears slight resemblance to the mundane world. There time works quite differently. Synchronism and anachronism are the rule, and much chronological time can pass in the ordinary world while only moments or hours pass in the universe of power.

—Paula Gunn Allen
Grandmother of the Light

(The Greeks) had two words for time: Chronos and Kairos.... Chronology, the time which changes things, makes them grow older, wears them out, and manages to dispose of them, chronologically, forever.... Kairos is not measurable. Kairos is ontological. In kairos we are, we are fully in isness, not negatively, as Sartre saw the isness of the oak tree, but fully, wholly, positively. Kairos can sometimes enter, penetrate, break through chronos; the child at play, the painter at his easel, Serkin playing the *Appassionata*, are in kairos. The saint at prayer, friends around a dinner table, the mother reaching out her arms for her newborn baby, are in kairos.

—Madeleine L'Engle
A Circle of Quiet

Time is the substance from which I am made. Time is a river which carries me along, but I am the river; it is a tiger that devours me, but I am the tiger; it is a fire that consumes me, but I am the fire.

—Jorge Luis Borges

No event is unique, nothing is enacted but once ... every event has been enacted, is enacted, and will be enacted perpetually; the same individuals have appeared, appear, and will appear at every turn of the circle.

—Henri-Charles Puech & Thomas Cahill
The Gifts of the Jews

We ourselves stand mesmerized beneath time's looming shadow, afraid to remember space, and thus our fate lies limp along its horizontal wall—not daring to dream the great beyond!

—Chris Griscom
Time Is an Illusion

It is in dreams that historical time is abolished and the mythical time regained—which allows the future shaman to witness the beginning of the world.

—Mircea Eliade and Jean & Wallace Clift
Symbols of Transformation in Dreams

The model we all take for granted—deep time, the time of geology—we only discovered in the nineteenth century.... The message of deep time is: We may not have as much time as we thought; the universe is dynamic, capable of turning sudden corners.

—Terence McKenna
Chaos, Creativity and Cosmic Consciousness

How you slice up your time also reflects how you identify yourself.

—Iris Sangiuliano
In Her Time

Time is one of the great archetypal experiences of man, and has eluded all our attempts towards a completely rational explanation.

—James Frazer
The Voices of Time and the Study of Time

Shortage of time is the greatest shortage of our time.

—Fred Polak

The Hopi language contains no references to "time" either implicit or explicit. At the same time it is capable of accounting for and describing correctly, in a pragmatic or operational sense, all observable phenomena of the universe.

—Benjamin Lee Whorf
The Philosophy of Time

Instead of time or space or past or future, the Hopi metaphysics has: The Manifest, The Manifesting, The Unmanifested.

—George Johnson
Fire in the Mind

Don't waste our time on trifles. You are dealing with that immensity out there.

—Carlos Castaneda

Killing time is a suicidal act.

—Gail Sheehy
Passages

As if you could kill time without injuring eternity.

—Henry David Thoreau
Walden and Other Writings of Henry David Thoreau

Wasting time is wasting yourself.

—Kenneth Atchity
A Writer's Time

There are four ways of wasting one's time: doing nothing, not doing what we ought, doing it badly, doing it at the wrong moment.

—François-Marie Arouet (Voltaire)

In many African languages the same word is used both for "yesterday" and "tomorrow." The present is the center of time, but distance from the present is more important than direction. Past and future are not seen as opposites, merely as more remote forms of the present. This makes the ancestors very real and well capable of exerting a profound influence over everyday activities.

—Lyall Watson
Lightning Bird

Time is not a line but a dimension, like the dimensions of space. If you can bend space you bend time also, and if you knew enough and could move faster than light, you could travel backward in time and exist in two places at once.

—Margaret Atwood
Cat's Eye

Time is our destiny. Time is our hope. Time is our despair. And time is the mirror in which we see eternity.

—Paul Tillich
The Shaking of the Foundations

The angels in Heaven do not know what time is, for in Heaven there are no days and years, but only changes of state.

—Emannuel Swedenborg
Arcana Celestia

Time expands in all directions, and away from any given point. The past is never done and finished, and the future is never concretely formed. You choose to experience certain versions of events. You then organize these, nibbling at them, so to speak, a bit "at a time."

— Jane Roberts
The Unknown Reality

Time permeates the universe and through its cycles governs all events. For the Maya, the norm of life was to attune what were and would be the burdens of time. Since the cycles were gods, knowledge of time was the root of theological thought.

—René Dubos
A God Within So Human an Animal

When you sit with a nice girl for two hours you think it's only a minute. But when you sit on a hot stove for a minute you think it's two hours. That's relativity.

—Albert Einstein

Christmas is an example of timeless time.

—Giorgio de Santillana &
Hertha Von Dechend
Hamlet's Mill

Why do we remember the past, and not the future?

—Stephen W. Hawking
A Brief History of Time

Life can only be understood backward, but it must be lived forward

—Niels Bohr

Earthquakes, war, murder, the burning of libraries … bad things happen fast. Reforestation, the growth of a child, the maturing of an adult, building a library … good things happen slow.

—Stewart Brand
The Clock of the Long Now

All times go on existing side by side for all of eternity. Always all times. Nothing is lost, left behind, only changed.

—Leslie Marmon Silko
Yellow Woman and A Beauty of Spirit

If time is not linear (as Einstein suggested), but is somehow cyclical or telescoped, so that all things happen coevally even though we perceive them as individuated, then there is a far more intimate relationship than we usually imagine between memory and reality. And it is all part of the sheer wonder of existence, the magic of being.

—John Killinger
God, the Devil and Harry Potter

Time is simply the yardstick of our separation. If we are particles in a sea of distance, exploded from an original whole, then there is a science to our solitude. We are lonely in proportion to our years.

—Ian Caldwell & Dustin Thomason
The Rule of Four

"Time" is an energetic process moving within a pattern. The opening in the mandala.

—Marie-Louise von Franz
Number and Time

The new physics requires as many clocks as you like, each set to a different correct time.

—Albert Einstein

They [people saying the Catholic divine offices] are not following time, but sustaining it.

—Michael Serres

The power of the Vietnam Memorial in Washington D.C. lies in the listing of the deceased names in order in which they died, by date, reminding viewers of the impermanence and passing of time.

—Leonard Shlain
The Alphabet Versus the Goddess

The man who writes about himself and his own time is the only man who writes about all people and about all time.

—George Bernard Shaw

Take time by the forelock. Now or never! You must live in the present, launch yourself on every wave, find your eternity in each moment.

—Henry David Thoreau

Agnes Whistling Elk: All of time is but the snap of an arrow in the bow of the Great Spirit.

—Lynn V. Andrews
Medicine Woman

I would rather be a meteor, every atom of me in magnificent glow, than a sleepy and permanent planet. The proper function of man is to live, not to exist. I shall not waste my days in trying to prolong them. I shall use my time.

—Jack London

Prince Myshkin: At that moment I seem somehow to understand that extraordinary saying that there shall be no more time. Probably this is the very second that was not long enough for the water to be spilt out of Mahomet's pitcher, though the epileptic prophet had time to gaze at all the habitations of Allah.

—Feodor Dostoevski
The Idiot

The Balinese don't tell you what time it is—they tell you what kind of time it is. They have a word "ruwat" which means "thick time." Densely textured time.... This is the time of conjunctures between the worlds of humans, spirits and gods.

—John Broomfield

The incalculable eons are but one moment—and this moment is no moment. Men are thought moments of such flashing brevity that for all practical purposes, they could be called timeless.

—Frederick Franck
The Awakened Eye

Time is a ride and you are on it.

—Danny Hillis

Time is a circus, always packing up and moving away.

—Ben Hecht

All my possessions for a moment of time.

—Elizabeth I (last words)

God works in moments.

—French proverb

Life is short, but wide.

—Spanish proverb

For every sin but the killing of Time there is forgiveness.

—Sufi proverb

Once upon a time when there was no time …

—Celtic proverb

TOUCH

The shaman … was licensed to practice, dancing around the bedside making smoke, chanting incomprehensibilities

and touching the patient everywhere. The touching was the real professional secret … the laying on of hands.

—Lewis Thomas
The Youngest Science

Let's stay in touch … for it is the loving physical touch expressing spiritual closeness that can, by God's grace, console the crying, comfort the lonely, and give peace to the dying.

—G. Peter Fleck
The Blessings of Imperfection

The sense of touch in its generic state is infinitely varied and gives a powerful type of mystical experience in the classical sense … every cell of the subtle body undergoes a stimulus that is similar to a rushing wind; it translates as pure love … the body is the only vehicle by which we may attain identity with God.

—Joseph Chilton Pearce
Magical Child Matures

The future of religion lies in the mystery of touch.

—D. H. Lawrence

TRADITIONS

In human affairs, aesthetic form comes into being when traditions exist that, strong and abiding like mountains, are made pleasing by a lucid beauty. By contemplating the forms existing in the heavens, we come to understand time and its changing demands. Through contemplation of the forms existing in human society, it becomes possible to shape the world.

—I Ching
Hexagram #22 Grace

Traditions are group efforts to keep the unexpected from happening.

—Mignon McLaughlin

TRAGEDY

Tragedy occurs when one is blocked from doing what is most beneficial for oneself and one's friends or community... the condition of tragedy is the belief that one thinks one knows, when one really does not know.

—Robert Apatow
The Spiritual Art of Dialogue

Men are not angered by mere misfortune but by misfortune conceived as injury.

—C. S. Lewis
The Screwtape Letters

The soul is born old, but grows young. That is the comedy of life. The body is born young and grows old. That is life's tragedy.

—Oscar Wilde

One man's death is a tragedy; the death of a million is a statistic.

—Joseph Stalin

TRANSITION

First there is an ending, then a beginning, with an important empty or fallow time in between. That is the order of things in nature. Leaf-fall, winter, and then the green emerges again from the dry brown wood. Human affairs would flow along similar channels if we were better able to stay in the current.

—William Bridges
Transitions

One of the most profound results of undertaking this journey is becoming aware of the serendipitous events in your life, as you learn to recognize and trust the natural unfolding of your life's patterns.

—Deborah L. Knox & Sandra S. Butzel
Life Work Transitions

Artemis helps in times of transition.

—Buffie Johnson
Lady of the Beasts

Transition is making sense out of life changes.

—William Bridges
Making Sense of Life's Changes

There are four kinds of transitions: space, time, emotion and viewpoint.

—Sylvia Burack
The Writer's Handbook

Troubles and uncertainties are normal during a period of transition. Sunrise is always preceded by an increase in night's chill.

—Boris Mouravieff

TRANSCENDENCE

The realization of an identity that transcends the constraints of ordinary selfhood has been celebrated ... by Christian and Islamic mystics. "My Me is God, nor do I recognize any other Me except my God himself," wrote Saint Catherine of Genoa.

—Michael Murphy
The Future of the Body

Art is a school of self-transcendence. So is a voodo session or a Nazi rally.

—Arthur Koootlei
Janus

We must find transcendence within ourselves, independent of exterior objects, ideas, people—or rather people as objects.

—Alan Arkin
Halfway through the Door

TRANSFORMATION

The world is a spinning die, and everything turns and changes: man is turned to an angel, and an angel to man; and the head to the foot, and the foot to the head. Thus all things turn and spin and change, this into that, and that into this, the topmost to the undermost, and the undermost to the topmost. For at the root all is one, and salvation inheres in the change and return of things.

—Nahman of Bratzlav

Nothing is created, nothing is lost, everything is transformed.

—Lavoisier

Even a thought, even a possibility, can shatter us and transform us.

—Friedrich Nietzche
Eternal Recurrence

We transform the world by what we discover in the spiritual world—and that is our test.

—Rudolf Steiner
Initiation and Its Results

Transformation comes from looking deeply within, to a state that exists before fear and isolation arise, the state in which we are inviolably whole just as we are.

—Sharon Salzberg

Follow your bliss and what looks like walls will turn into doors.

—Joseph Campbell

Winter makes the wolf of the woods go pale.

—François Villon

When water turns to ice, does it remember one time it was water?

—Carl Sandburg

What the caterpillar calls the end of the world, the master calls the butterfly.

—Richard Bach

As we explore the crisis in the chrysalis, keep in mind that every one of us probably has both the dying caterpillar and the emerging butterfly within us.

—L. Robert Keck
Sacred Quest

The moment of conversion comes for all of us when we are no longer able to maintain the image of ourselves that once contented us.

—Suzanne Zuercher
Enneagram Spirituality

Truly horrendous things happen inside a cocoon. First, there is total disintegration. Everything that was a caterpillar breaks down into chaotic matter, into a primal ooze, an amorphous smear. Only once the caterpillar has consented to that annihilation can the butterfly be constructed. The caterpillar has to risk it all, for the emergence of its own beauty.

—Sara Maitland
A Big Enough God

Transmitted through the Orphic mystery cult, the tradition of sharing the slain god's flesh and blood, entered in a symbolic guise into the rites of Christianity. To the devout, Holy Communion is the supreme experience of self-transcendence.

—Arthur Koestler
Janus

The ego does not choose the process of self-transformation. It is written in the destiny of the soul and activated in response to the call of the Self.

—Llewellyn Vaughan-Lee
In the Company of Friends

We live in an active, open-ended, transformative infinity, a generativeness. Every experience we have is infinitely deep.

—Ken Wilber
Up from Eden

TREES

The tree bears its thousand years as one large majestic moment.

—Rabindranath Tagor

If you come upon a grove of old trees that have lifted their crowns up above the common height and shut out the light of the sky by the darkness of their interlacing boughs, you feel that there is a spirit in the place, so lofty is the wood.

—Seneca (Lucius Annaeus)
Epistles

Ancient trees of Ireland were focal points of tribal meeting and were thought to possess memory and have the power of witness. Trees were central emblems of tribal continuity.

—Caitlin Matthews & John Matthews
The Encyclopedia of Celtic Wisdom

Did you know that trees talk? Well they do. They talk to each other, and they'll talk to you if you listen…. I have learned a lot from trees: sometimes about the weather, sometimes about animals, sometimes about the Great Spirit.

—T. C. McLuhan
Touch the Earth

Trees are the teachers, revealers, containers, companions, and protectors of the sacred, and our relationship to them, whether we meet them gently in a forest or, muscled and equipped, cut them down for the price of lumber, touches on our deepest values, emotions, and sense of meaning.

—Thomas Moore
The Re-Enchantment of Everyday Life

The Two Trees of Valinor recall the Tree of Life and the Tree of the Knowledge of Good and Evil in Genesis. Like the Two Trees, the trees of the Garden of Eden had supernatural powers and grew in a divine land now beyond mortal reach … in the Elder Edda … the gods found two trees on the shore of the newly created world and transformed them into the first man and woman named Ask and Embla, Ash and Elm.

—Ruth S. Noel
The Mythology of Middle-Earth

A stand of aspens in Oregon is reputed to be the largest single organism on Earth, an underground mass from which over a hundred thousand trees tower.… The trees work in unison … telegraph their mood and news. Under attack, they send chemical messages to their neighbors, warning them of danger so they can rally a defense.

—Diane Ackerman
An Alchemy of Mind

The Tree Musketeers: Tara Church, a Girl Scout, was eight when she decided to plant a tree. Then she started the only non-profit in the world run by children … the organization has planted more than a million trees since 1987.… Tara Church

was young enough to change the world and old enough to do it.

—Warren G. Bennis & Robert J. Thomas
Geeks and Geezers

Trees hold their living energy in a vivid visual image of rhythm and balance.… A tree becomes sacred through recognition of the power it expresses.

—Nathaniel Altman
Sacred Trees

Oak stands for the still, unconscious core of the personality.

—Carl G. Jung
Alchemical Studies

The word "tree" has the same etymological roots as "truth".… Truthing will never be complete or finished.

—Linda Sussman
The Speech of the Grail

Imitate the trees. Learn to lose in order to recover and remember that nothing stays the same for long, not even pain.

—May Sarton

Trees carry the memory of rainfall. In their rings we read ancient weather.

—Anne Michaels
Fugitive Pieces

The tree is a tremendous electrical machine connecting earth and sky … an energetic chemical laboratory of psychoactive pheromones.

—Peter Redgrove
The Black Goddess and the Sixth Sense

If trees grew words rather than leaves, I would be a writer. But trees grow leaves which are images and substances, so I am an artist.

—Jane Roberts
The World View of Paul Cézanne

Ludwig II of Bavaria is said to have honored certain particularly impressive trees in his park by having them saluted.

—Carl G. Jung
Alchemical Studies

TRICKSTER

The Trickster enters the human world to make things happen … to break and reestablish relationships, to reawaken consciousness of the presence and the creative power of both the sacred Center and the formless Outside. Then he returns to that hidden threshold which he embodies and makes available as a passage to save people from ruin.

—Robert Pelton
The Trickster in West Africa

Hermes, Coyote, and the other trickster gods are filled with irreverent vitality and creativity…. Like other tricksters, the imagination knows no boundaries and may appear anywhere. As patrons of travelers and guide of souls, Hermes, who personifies the imagination, leads us to the heights or depths of experience, to the light of Olympus or to the shadows of Hades. He also guides us across the boundaries of ordinary reality to experience other states of

consciousness…. The Trickster delights in frolicking with symbols.

—Allan Combs & Mark Holland
Synchronicity

Every generation occupies itself with interpreting the Trickster anew. No generation understands him fully, but no generation can do without him. … And so he became and remained everything to every man—god, animal, human being, hero, buffoon, he who was before good and evil, denyer, affirmer, destroyer and creator. If we laugh at him, he grins at us. What happens to him, happens to us.

—Paul Radin
The Trickster

A truly sacred world allows for a sense of mockery and play that turns the weight of reality around.

—Kenneth Lincoln
Native American Renaissance

A clown in our language is called a *heyoka*. He is upside-down, backward-forward, yes-and-no man, a contrary-wise…. The wise old people know that the clowns are thunder-dreamers, that the thunder-beings commanded them to act in a silly way, each *heyoka* according to his dream.

—Lame Deer
Lame Deer: Seeker of Visions

The diviner and the artist are tricksters with the wit to make music from noise.

—Louis Hyde
Trickster

Tricksters are adept at springing traps.

—Jackson Lears
Something for Nothing

The trickster is about chaos, the unexpected, the "why" of creation and the consequences of unacceptable behavior.

—Marie Battiste
Reclaiming Indigenous Voice and Vision

The trickster courts chaos and takes on sacred cows.

—John R. Van Eenwyk
Archetypes and Strange Attractors

TRINITY

He who creates the worlds without ceasing is threefold. He is Brahma, the Father; he is Maya, the Mother; he is Vishnu, the Son; Essence, Substance and Life, each includes the others, and all three are one in the Ineffable.

—Brahmanic Doctrine
Upanishads

The Trinity is the threefold revelation of the One, of God.

—Georg Kühlewind
Becoming Aware of the Logos

Just at the flame contains three essences in the one fire, so too, there is one God in three persons. How is this so? The flame consists of shining brightness, purple vigor and fiery glow.

—Hildegard of Bingen
Scivias

The deep wisdom of the Trinity is our Mother, in whom we are enclosed ...

—Julian of Norwich

The more I reflect about the three kayas and the threefold process of the bardos, the more fertile and intriguing parallels I find with the innermost vision of other spiritual traditions.... God as represented by the Trinity, of Christ the incarnation being manifested in form out of the ground of the Father through the subtle medium of the Holy Spirit. Could it not be at least illuminating to envision Christ as similar to the Nirmanakaya, the Holy Spirit as akin to the Sambhogakaya, and the absolute ground of both as like the Dharmakaya?

—Sogyal Rinpoche
The Tibetan Book of Living and Dying

TRUST

When we are centered and in touch with reality, we are trustful persons.

—M. Basil Pennington
The Way of Centering Prayer

As soon as you trust yourself you will know how to live.

—Johann Wolfgang von Goethe

Trust is something abused children lack, and children raised with a Monster God inside them have a hard time regaining it.

—Kathleen Norris
Ghosts, A History

Trust cannot be given carelessly, for there is much woundedness about.... And yet there are people of honor and places of refuge. One might well ask, what is the alternative to trust? Have we not had isolation enough?

—Marilyn Sewell
Cries of the Spirit

Patients who are hopeful, largely because of their religious faith and their trust in their physician, have a more rapid return to health and a higher rate of survival.

—Jerome Groopman
The Anatomy of Hope

It is easy to say you believe a rope is strong as long as you are merely using it to cord a box. But, suppose you had to hang by that rope over a precipice? Wouldn't you then first discover how much you really trusted it?

—C. S. Lewis

TRUTH

What is truth?… Truth is the Lord of heaven guiding the earth…. Truth is … great wisdom, many wisdoms. Truth is the word that cannot fail. Mighty power, surpassing all. Everlasting blessing. Speak the truth, tell the facts.

—From the African Ifa Oracle

The Truth does not change according to our ability to stomach it emotionally.

—Flannery O'Connor
The Habit of Being

Go deep enough and there is a bedrock of truth, however hard.

—May Sarton
Journal of Solitude

If you want to write the truth, you must write about yourself. I am the only real truth I know.

—Jean Rhys

Daskalos: It is through confusion that you will enter into Knowledge. Because if you do not get confused you will not focus your attention toward discovering the Truth and you will not find it. You will be content with situations that are not the Truth.

—Kyriacos C. Markides
The Magus of Strovolos

Convictions are more dangerous enemies of the truth than lies.

—Friedrich Nietzshe
Human, All Too Human

Truth is that which does not contaminate you, but empowers you.

—Gary Zukav
The Seat of the Soul

Whoever deeply searches out the truth and will not be deceived by paths untrue, shall turn unto himself his inward gaze, shall bring his wandering thoughts in circle home and teach his heart that what it seeks abroad, it holds in its own treasure chests within.

—Boethius (Anicius Manlius Severinus)

All truth passes through three stages. First, it is ridiculed. Second, it is violently opposed. Third, it is accepted as being self-evident.

—Arthur Schopenhauer

Truth must not be conveyed until the potential recipient is ready ... the real truth resides within all faiths and so is accessible to anyone of any culture.

—Robert Ellwood
The Cross and the Grail

You have noticed that the truth comes into this world with two faces. One is sad with suffering and other laughs; but it is the same face, laughing or weeping.

—Black Elk

The truth cannot come from outside to the inside but must emerge from the inside and pass through an inner form.

—Meister Eckhart

For this is the thing the priests do not know, with their one God and One truth: that there is no such thing as a true tale. Truth has many faces and the truth is like to an old road to Avalon; it depends on your own will, and your own thoughts, whither the road will take you.

—Marion Zimmer Bradley
The Mists of Avalon

Lord, grant me weak eyes for things that are of no account and strong eyes for all the truth.

—Søren Kierkegaard

Fiction is the truth inside the lie—morality is telling the truth as your heart knows it.

—Stephen King
Danse Macabre

The greatest truths are too important to be new.

—W. Somerset Maugham

Truth in art is not imitation, but reincarnation.

—Ursula K. LeGuin
The Wave in the Mind

There are trivial truths and great truths.

—Niels Bohr

The soul is the perceiver and revealer of truth.

—Ralph Waldo Emerson

If our meanings are incoherent, how are we going to participate in truth?

—David Bohm
On Dialogue

Being true to the truth as best one knows it, is a Native trait that could help dissolve distrust, inaccuracy, and animosity.

—Joachim Berendt
Nada Brahma: The World is Sound

What I tell you three times is true.

—Lewis Carroll
The Hunting of the Snark

The truth was not a line from here to there and not ever-widening circles like the rings on a sawn log, but rather trails of oscillating overlapping liquids that poured forth but then assumed a shape and lift of their own, that circled back around in spirals and fluctuations to touch and color all truths that came after that one.

—Jeffrey Lent
In the Fall

Truth has to be lived, not taught. Prepare for battle!

—Hermann Hesse
The Glass Bead Game

Truth is not a fixed point; it is not static; it cannot be measured by words.... Truth is what holds us all together.... A mind that is not empty can never find the truth.

—Jiddu Krishnamurti

[Truth is] the latent feeling of fellow-ship with all creation ... the subtle but invincible conviction of solidarity that knits together the loneliness of innumer-able hearts.

—Joseph Conrad

Truth always survives censorship.

—Lindsay Clarke
The Chymical Wedding

Truth appears differently in different lands and again according to the living materials out of which its symbols are hewn.

—Heinrich Zimmer
Philosophies of India

Truth is a matter of the imagination. The soundest fact may fail or prevail in the style of its telling: like that singular organic jewel of our seas, which grows brighter as one woman wears it and, worn by another, dulls and goes to dust. Facts are no more solid, coherent, round, and real than pearls are. But both are sensitive.

—Ursula K. LeGuin
The Left Hand of Darkness

The truth, life itself, is always startling, strange and unexpected.

—Brenda Ueland
If You Want to Write

He who wants to teach us a truth should place us in a position to discover it ourselves.

—José Ortega y Gasset

A man finds the truth to be true only when he makes it true.

—Martin Buber & Aubrey Hodes
Martin Buber

Truth spoken directly from the heart and skillfully illumined by the mind has an enormous power that cannot be eliminated even in the academic setting.

—Christopher M. Bache
Dark Night, Early Dawn

All great truth begins life as blasphemy.

—George Bernard Shaw

Truth sits upon the lips of dying men.

—Matthew Arnold

Truth is like a lizard; it leaves its tail in your fingers and runs away knowing full well that it will grow a new one in a twinkling.

—Ivan Turgenev

Tell all the Truth, but tell it slant.

—Emily Dickinson

Children say that people are hanged sometimes for speaking the truth.

—Joan of Arc at her trial

If you want the truth, just see what your original face was—before you were born.

—Buddhist proverb

An old error is always more popular than a new truth.

—German proverb

The Double belongs unquestionably to the dark side of world mythology and folklore. It represents duality in its most perplexing and sinister aspect: the Twin as monstrous or metamorphic duplicate of its original.... The twin is a shadow figure or ... the embodiment of whatever we tend to deny or repress.

—John Lash
Twins and the Double

TWINS

My face is a caricature of her, and her soul is a caricature of mine ... we are that perilous pair.

—Rose O'Neil
Garda

The Gnostics spoke a great deal about the twin, whom they imagine to have been separated from us at birth. The twin retains the spiritual knowledge given us before birth. The twin, when he or she reenters the psyche, insists on intensity and seriousness.

—Robert Bly
Iron John

UBIQUITY

Goddess worship, feminine values and women's power depends on the ubiquity of the image.

—Leonard Shlain
The Alphabet Versus the Goddess

If you could understand this peanut, you would know God.

—George Washington Carver

Salamanders, fiddle tunes, you and me and things, the split and burr of it all, the fizz into particulars ... the rocks shape life, and then life shapes life, and the rocks are moving.... The galaxy is a flung thing, loose in the night, and our solar system is one of many dotted campfires ringed with tossed rocks.

—Annie Dillard
Teaching a Stone to Talk

UNCONSCIOUS

Jung maintained that Luther led straight to Freud and the discovery of the personal unconscious because the outer symbolic trappings, beautiful as they were, were removed from the Protestant

Church, forcing each person to confront the mystery within the psyche.

—Alice O. Howell
The Dove in the Stone

The unconscious is a universal ocean in which all of us have roots.

—Anäis Nin

UNDERSTANDING

To understand the flavor of wine, you must drink it. However, to understand its nature and the essence of the wine itself, you must become a winemaker. You must grow the grapes with care and attention and then you must stomp and dance upon them to press out the juice.

—David Spangler
A Pilgrim in Aquarius

There is nothing we may do to arrive at understanding, for understanding is an accident. The most we can do is become accident prone.

—Flannery O'Connor

You can't experience the truth of another person without feeling love. Understanding and love go together. When we nourish the soul, we automatically nourish our capacity to love another person.

—Jacob Needleman
Handbook for the Soul

To be unable to understand the mysteries of faith is by no means to be unable to

believe them.... It is after the initial act of belief that the believer begins to see.

—Thomas Merton
The Ascent to Truth

If you want to be truly understood, you need to say everything three times, in three different ways. Once for each ear ... and once for the heart.

—Paula Underwood Spencer

We do not write in order to be understood, we write in order to understand.

—C. Day-Lewis

Lord, grant that I may seek more to understand than to be understood.

—Francis of Assisi

If we understand it, it is not God,

—Augustine

UNICORN

"I am not real. And yet in a sense I am that which is the only reality.... You called me, and because there is a great need, I am here. As long as there are even a few who belong to the Old Music, you are still our brothers and sisters." The light of the unicorn's horn pulsed. "Before the harmonies were broken, unicorns and winds danced together with joy and no fear."

—Madeleine L'Engle
A Swiftly Tilting Planet

The tapestry *The Lady and the Unicorn* displayed in the Cluny Museum in Paris extols the feminine and the delights of the senses.... She is holding a mirror, a symbol most frequently associated with Venus/Aphrodite, in which the unicorn is reflected. Flanking her in each panel of the tapestry are the lion (of Judah) and the unicorn, both medieval symbols for Christ.

—Margaret Starbird
The Woman with the Alabaster Jar

The unicorn is a wonderful creature—a white horse with gazelle's feet and a shining horn on its brow. The horse traditionally symbolizes intelligence. The white horse, therefore, is purified intelligence, and the horn rising from the brow symbolizes the pineal gland, the third eye, the principle of enlightenment.

—George Trevelyan
A Vision of the Aquarian Age

The nature of this wondrous animal is that he is both fierce and meek, like to a scapegoat. His virtue is no less famous than his strength, inasmuch that the wild beasts do not drink from the deep pools until he has stirred them with his horn and thus he purifies the means of life for those who have no virtue to do it themselves.

—Barbara Jefferis
Time of the Unicorn

The Chinese say their unicorn or Chi-Lin, over four thousand years old, comes from heaven on very rare occasions to herald the birth of someone great and good.

—Bonnie Jones Reynolds
The Truth about Unicorns

The Unicorn ... lodges under an apple tree, the tree of immortality-through-wisdom. It can be captured only by a pure virgin—Wisdom herself. The purity

of the virgin stands for spiritual integrity. The unicorn lays its head on her lap and weeps for joy.

—Robert Graves
The White Goddess

The unicorn comes from a timeless realm and represents the transcendent, ultimate possibilities we have all lost sight of.

—Peter S. Beagle
The Last Unicorn

UNIQUENESS

Individuality rises out of the soul as water rises out of the depth of the earth.

—Thomas Moore

You shall become who you are.

—Friedrich Nietzche

I don't develop. I am.

—Pablo Picasso

UNITY

The part always has a tendency to unite with its whole in order to escape from its imperfections.

—Leonardo da Vinci

Two things alone cannot be satisfactorily united without a third;

for there must be some bond between them drawing them together.

—Plato (Aristocles)
The Collected Dialogues

When the soul knows something, it loses its unity.

—Plotinus

Man came from Unity; Earth led to differentiation. In Christ all become one again.

—Rudolf Steiner
An Outline of Occult Science

All that man has here externally in multiplicity is intrinsically One. Here all blades of grass, wood and stone, all things are One. This is the deepest depth …

—Meister Eckhart

We are a drop in the ocean; whatever happens to the ocean happens to the drop, whatever happens to the drop happens to the ocean.

—Paramahansa Yogonoanda

Firstly there is the unity in things whereby each thing is at one with itself, consists of itself, and coheres with itself. Secondly, there is the unity whereby one creature is united with the others and all parts of the world constitute one world.

—Pico della Mirandola
Opera Omnia

All creation proceeds from unity, and all manifested things must return and be resolved again into unity. Herein is to be

found the involutionary and evolutionary cycles of progression, both spiritual and material.

—Corinne Heline
The Sacred Science of Numbers

Separate yourself from all twoness. Be one in one, one with one, one from one.

—Meister Eckhart

A genuine unified theory enables us to know the world better rather than to know more of it.

—Ervin Laszlo
The Whispering Pond

The concept of shalom is a vision of harmony and wholeness, of nations and tribes gathered as one, of a unity and balance between nature and the environment and the social economy.

—Madonna Kolbenschlag
Lost in the Land of Oz

UNIVERSE

Come, let us gossip about the universe.

—William James

The Universe is a vast net that contains all time and all space. At every nexus point in the net, there is a multi-faceted diamond. Each of the facets of that diamond reflect every other diamond.… They co-originate. When one comes alive, they all come alive.

—John Daido Loori
Sacred Stories

Everything in the universe is animate and alive. All is the product of a common life force and the Producer is never cut off from the product.

—Plotinus

God has eighteen thousand universes and this your world is just one universe from among them.

—Ibn Arabi

The universe is contained in a mosquito's wing.... But if one atom from its place is moved, the universe at once is overturned.

—Mahmun Shabistari
The Secret Garden

The universe is made of stories, not of atoms.

—Muriel Rukeyser
The Speed of Darkness

Constantly regard the universe as one living being, having one substance and one soul; and observe how all things have reference to one perception, the perception of this one living being; and how all things act with one movement; and how all things are the cooperating causes of all things which exist.

—Marcus Aurelius

The universe is a teaching and learning machine. Its purpose is to know itself.

—Itzhak Bentov

A human being is a part of the whole, called by us the "Universe," a part limited in time and space. He experiences himself, his thoughts and feelings as something separated from the rest—a kind of optical delusion of his consciousness. This delusion is a kind of prison for us, restricting us to our personal desires and to affection for a few persons nearest us.

—Albert Einstein

Katagin Roshi: Your little will can't do anything. It takes Great Determination ... it means the whole universe is behind you and with you.

—Natalie Goldberg
Writing Down the Bones

What if the Universe were indeed the mind of God, operating as a holographic entity so that each part of the macrocosm is a perfect, though perhaps less distinct, mirror image of the whole? This would mean that we are all of the same matter.

—Liz Simpson
The Healing Energies of Earth

The whole of the created universe has been breathlessly anticipating your arrival.

—Martin Bell
Return of the Wolf

The universe begins to look more like a great thought than a great machine.

—James Jeans

In knowing yourself you will know the universe.

—Jiddu Krishnamurti
Krishnamurti's Journal

The secret of Aikido is to harmonize ourselves with the movement of the universe and bring ourselves into accord with the universe itself. He who has gained the secret of aikido has the universe in himself and can say, "I am the universe."

—Morihei Ueshiba

The universe holds together and only one way of considering it is really possible, that is, to take it as a whole in one piece.

—Pierre Teilhard de Chardin

He whose soul remains forever turned in the direction of God... finds himself nailed to the very centre of the universe. It is the true centre, it is not in the middle, it is beyond space and time, it is God.

—Simone Weil
Waiting on God

It is the imagination that gives shape to the universe.

—Barry Lopez
Of Wolves and Men

The universe is wild-game-flavored as a hawk's wing. Nature is miracle all.

—William James

Albert Einstein was once asked, "What is the most important question you can ask in life?" He answered, "Is the universe a friendly place or not?"

—Matthew Fox
The Coming of the Cosmic Christ

If the universe were fundamentally separate from the Divine, true partnership or union with God would be impossible. But since the universe is God's life, our own mind, our own dream is an open door to the Divine.

—Lex Hixon
Coming Home

Things are as they are because they were as they were. The universe is an evolving system of habits.

—Rubert Sheldrake
Chaos, Creativity and Cosmic Consciousness

The universe is vast and so is the hierarchy of celestial presences, meaning presences which have evolved to a place of universal love and perfection.

—Meredith Lady Young
Agartha

The question, "Do other universes exist?" is one for scientists—it isn't just metaphysics.... Our universe doesn't seem to be quite as simple as it might have been.

—Martin Rees & Tom Siegfried
Stranger Matters

Quintessence is no other than a quality of which we cannot by our reason find out the cause.

—Michel Montaigne

For the heavenly sphere of stars and planets, Aristotle involved a surreal substance generally known as the ether. Later on ... this "fifth essence" came to be called quinta essential.... If quintessence exists, it fills all of space with some bizarre form of matter-energy ... it isn't constant.

—Tom Siegfried
Strange Matters

It now seems possible that we, the Earth, and indeed, the entire visible universe are stuck on a membrane in a higher-dimensional space, like dust particles that are trapped on a soap bubble.

—Steven Abel & John March-Russell
The Search for Extra Dimensions

Whether we like it or not, our lives will leave a mark on the universe.

—Mihaly Csikszentmihalyi
Finding Flow

I believe that the universe is one being, all its parts are different expressions of the same energy, and they are all in communication with each other.... This whole in all its parts, so beautiful, and is felt by me to be so intensely in earnest, that I am compelled to love it, and to think of it as divine.

—Robinson Jeffers

The great astronomer Tycho Brahe put on his court robes before going to his telescope.

—Madeleine L'Engle
The Circle of Quiet

The universe is no longer distant and alien to us, but intimate and familiar.

—Trinh Xuan Thuan
Chaos and Harmony

The universe is infinite and like God, the center of the universe is everywhere.

—Nicholas Krebs of Cusa

There is no way back into the past. The choice is the Universe—or nothing.

—H. G. Wells

All life is the product of the interplay between the earth and the universe with its spirit-created patternings; water is the mediator, the heart organ that lives out its rhythmical being in-between.

—Theodor Schwenk &
Wolfram Schwenk
Water: The Element of Life

In the archaic universe all things were signs and signatures of each other, inscribed in the hologram, to be divined subtly.

—Giorgio de Santillana &
Hertha Von Dechend
Hamlet's Mill

To take rocks, trees, planets or stars as the primary reality would be like assuming that the vortices in a river exist in their own right and are totally independent of the flowing river itself. Things enfold and are enfolded by the entire universe.

—David Bohm

The clearest way into the Universe is through a forest wilderness.

—John Muir

The universe is but one great city, full
of beloved ones, divine and human by
nature, endeared to each other.

—Epictetus

I and all things in the universe are one.

—Chuang-Tzu

I know there is life on other planets
because someone is using this one as an
insane asylum.

—George Bernard Shaw

The inhabitant or soul of the universe
is never seen; its voice alone is heard ...
a gentle voice, like a woman, a voice so
fine ... that even children cannot become
afraid. And what is says is "*Sila ersinar-
sinivdluge*," Be not afraid of the Universe.

—Inuit teaching

Love everything in the universe,
because the Sun and Moon and Earth are
all one body.

—Chinese proverb

V

VALUES

All values set boundaries. A value is a way of saying yes to certain behaviors and no to others. It allows us to make a judgment, to be discerning, to say that some things are right and others are wrong.

—David Spangler
 A Pilgrim in Aquarius

We cannot suspend our values during the workday and think we will have them back when we get home. We're all interconnected. There is a spiritual dimension to business just as to individuals.

—Ben Cohen & Jerry Greenfield

Every man, says Lewis, is ultimately forced to believe either that values reside simply in himself or else that they have objectivity apart from his or her feeling about them. There is an infinite difference between the two views. If values are objective and one man may be right and another wrong, then there will be an obligation to try to discover the right value and champion it. And then there can be no ought in a world where there is no objective value.... One can only criticize within the Tao or moral order, not outside it.

—Clyde S. Kilby
 The Christian World of C. S. Lewis

The human mind has no more power of inventing a new value than of imagining a new primary colour, or, indeed, of creating a new sun and a new sky for it to move in.

—C. S. Lewis
The Abolition of Man

The habit of art is the habit of enjoying vivid values.

—Alfred North Whitehead
Science and the Modern World

The true value of anything is revealed most clearly by its absence.

—Peter J. Kreeft
Love Is Stronger Than Death

And of what value is the grain of sand at the heart of a pearl?

—Richard Adams
Shardik

VIBRATION

Nothing rests; Everything moves; Everything vibrates.

—Three Initiates
The Kybalion, Hermetic Principles

The vibration of the soul is like electricity—some wiring systems are capable of sustaining only a very low current—others, stronger.... Souls cannot grow without making the connections that will allow the electrical current to flow and the vibration to increase.

—Mary E. Carreiro
The Psychology of Spiritual Growth

Every lake and basin has its own vibratory pulsing pattern, conditioned by size, shape. It is set by the moon moving east to west.

—Theodor Schwenk &
Wolfram Schwenk
Water: The Element of Life

VIOLENCE

Violence against women is the source and paradigm of all other manifestations of violence.

—Mary Daly
Gyn/Ecology

Every fifteen seconds a woman is beaten in the United States—and one-third of all women murdered in the nation are victims of boyfriends, husbands, and former partners.... An alarming number of men still believe violence is an acceptable means to gaining a woman's compliance.

—Kimberly Blaker
The Fundamentals of Extremism

In America at least two million women a year are battered by an intimate partner and 1500 are murdered by the same partner.... Single mothers are 71% more violent toward their children than married ones.

—Michael P. Ghiglieri
The Dark Side of Man

Stonings are called in Iran, lapidations and are done for adultery.... Today in Iran, men are buried up to their waists and women to their chests. The size of the stones are carefully regulated. Pebbles are too small, so death is endlessly prolonged; boulders are too mercifully quick. Part of the Hajj ritual in Mecca is stoning of the pillars, representing Satan. Women become "pillars."

—Geraldine Brooks
Nine Parts of Desire

To what degree do I accept violence as a tool for change?

—David Spangler
A Pilgrim in Aquarius

Veiled violence is violence whose religious or historical justifications still provide it with an aura of respectability and give it a moral and religious monopoly over any "unofficial" violence ... revenge is violence imitating violence.

—Gil Bailie
Violence Unveiled

Between fifteen and twenty million Blacks were enslaved in Africa and exported to the New World.... Evil need not be exotic; it may be banal, but at its center is wanton, destructive violence.

—Christopher Nugent
Masks of Satan

If one is afraid of looking into a face, one hits the face.

—William Butler Yeats

The best response to violence is healing.

—Marie Battiste
Reclaiming Indigenous Voice and Vision

VIRGIN

The woman who is in touch with her inner virgin ... finds herself saying things she has never said before, verbalizing questions she never asked before. She tries to speak from her feminine reality while at the same time aware of the masculine standpoint.

—Marion Woodman
The Pregnant Virgin

Virgin means One in Herself; not maiden inviolate, but maiden alone, in herself. To be virginal does not mean to be chaste, but rather to be true to nature and instinct.

—Nor Hall
The Moon and the Virgin

Virgin strength is required to surrender to Spirit and to bring forth the Divine Child—new consciousness.

—Marion Woodman
Bone

Virgin originally meant a woman whose status was in her own right—one not subject to the rule of any man.

—Penelope Shuttle & Peter Redgrove
The Wise Wound

VIRTUE

By cultivating one's nature one will return to virtue.

—Chuang-Tzu

The man of perfect virtue, wishing to be established himself, seeks also to establish others; wishing to be enlarged himself, he seeks also to enlarge others.

—Confucius

The capacity to engage in virtuous behavior: to show forgiveness, to express gratitude, to be humble, to display compassion and wisdom.

—Richard A. Emmons
The Psychology of Ultimate Concerns

If the hangover preceded the binge, drunkenness would be considered a virtue and not a vice.

—Gregory Bateson

VISION/VISIONS

Vision is the art of seeing things invisible.

—Jonathan Swift
Thoughts on Various Subjects

These are the times when the unknown revels itself to the spirit of man in visions.... Those that depart still remain near us—they are in a world of light.... Though invisible to some they are not absent. Sweet is their presence; holy is their converse with us.

—Victor Hugo
Toilers of the Sea

To know is not to prove, nor to explain. It is to accede to vision. But if we are to have vision, we must learn to participate in the object of vision. The apprenticeship is hard.

—Antoine de Saint Exupéry
Flight to Arras

The greatest insight, thought and art concerning the human condition and its divine aspirations are rooted in the phenomenon of inner vision.

—José Arguelles & Miriam Arguelles
Mandala

We cannot wait for great visions from great people, for they are in short supply at the end of history. It is up to us to light our own small fires in the darkness.

—Charles Handy
The Age of Paradox

A great deal of the cerebral cortex is devoted to vision. Located at the back of the head, this part of the brain mostly occupies itself with processing of information from the retinas of the eyes, but when it disengages from that task and turns inward, one of the most important channels for mind/body communication becomes available.

—Andrew Weil
Spontaneous Healing

All my seven Narnian books, and my three science fiction books, began with seeing pictures in my head.... The Lion all began with a picture of a Faun carrying an umbrella and parcels in a snowy wood. This picture had been in my mind since I was about sixteen. Then one day, when I was about forty, I said to myself: "Let's try to make a story about it."... I don't know where the Lion came from or why He came. But once He was there He pulled the whole story together, and soon He pulled the six other Narnian stories after Him.

—C. S. Lewis
Of Other Worlds

A great flash of light from heaven pierced my brain and made my heart and my whole breast glow without burning them, as the sun warms the object that it envelops with its rays. In that instant my mind was imbued with the meaning of the sacred books, the Psalter, the Gospel, and the other books of the Old and New Testament.... And again, I heard a voice from heaven instructing me thus; and it said: "Write in this way, just as I tell you."

—Hildegard of Bingen
The Book of Divine Works

I simply dream dreams and see visions, and then I paint around those dreams and visions.

—Raphael (Sanzio)

A vision creates a personal responsibility to carry out its directive.

—Marie Battiste
Reclaiming Indigenous Voice and Vision

We need a broader vision to match the world in which we act with an image that includes the forest and the trees, the baby and bathwater.

—Mary Catherine Bateson
Peripheral Visions

The most visionary among us look like miners crawling through a tunnel in a dark mountain, their little lamps illuminating a square foot of dirt.

—Richard Thieme

VOCATION

Vocation: from Latin, "vocare" to call. Who's calling?

—E. B. McNeil
The Psychology of Being Human

The Greek word *diakonia* means the way God has assigned you in life to be of service in a special way. For monks it may be to pray without ceasing, as St. Paul put it. Or it may be any number of vocations.

—Kyriacos Markides
Riding with the Lion

If your vocation isn't meaningful, you have two choices: find a way to make it meaningful or get out of it and into something you know you can make meaningful.

—Wayne Dyer
The Sky's the Limit

VOID

The Great Void cannot but consist of *ch'i*; this *ch'i* cannot but condense to form all things; and these things cannot but become dispersed so as to form (once more) the Great Void.

—Chang Tsai

In spite of using terms like empty and voice, the Eastern sages make it clear that they do not mean ordinary emptiness when they talk about Brahman, Sunyato or Tao, but on the contrary, a Void which has an infinite creative potential.

—Fritjof Capra
The Tao of Physics

The ancient Hindu texts, the Upanishads, claim that the only reality is the formless, infinite eternal void from which all things come and to which they return.

—John Horgan
Rational Mysticism

Nothingness spreads around us. But in this nothing we find what we did not know existed.

—Susan Griffin
Woman and Nature

Outside of God, there is nothing but nothing.

—Meister Eckhart

Everything depends on this: a fathomless sinking into a fathomless nothingness.

—Johannes Tauler

Evil is not something that truly exists, Tolkien profoundly discerns; it is nothing. Therein lies its real terror. If evil had a logical explanation, if it could be entirely explained as a perversion or distortion of the good, then it could be combated with considerable success. But because it is a devastating nothingness, a nameless black void, it possessed an irrationality that does not submit entirely to rational and moral control … evil always has the character of absurdity.

—Ralph C. Wood
The Gospel According to Tolkien

I find myself in the Void, but the Void is totally saturated with love.

—Bede Griffiths

All things are not on all sides jammed together and kept in by body: there is also void in things… If there were not void, things could not move at all; for that which is the property of body, to let and hinder, would be present to all things at all times; nothing therefore could go on, since no other things would be the first to give way.

—Lucretius
On the Nature of Things

God dwells in the nothing-at-all that was prior to nothing.

—Meister Eckhart

Nothing is more real than nothing.

—Samuel Beckett

Arabs adapted a symbol from the Hindu *sunja*—a word meaning empty—which they expressed as a dot. This dot, in Islam, became the zero.

—Michael Ayrton
Fabrications

VULNERABLE

What is this darkness? What is its name? Call it: an aptitude for sensitivity. Call it: a rich sensitivity which will make you whole. Call it: your potential for vulnerability.

—Meister Eckhart

Those who are willing to be vulnerable move among mysteries.

—Theodore Roethke

The bird with the thorn in its breast, it
follows an immutable law: it is driven
by it knows not what to impale itself
and die singing. At the very instant the
thorn enters there is no awareness in it
of the dying to come; it simply sings and
sings until there is not the life left to utter
another note. But we, when we put the
thorns in our hearts, we know. We understand. And still we do it. Still we do it.

—Colleen McCullough
  The Thorn Birds

WAITING

In biblical understanding, to wait does
not guarantee the arrival of what one
waits for, but it is not ... negative or static.
Waiting and hoping belong together   in
Hebrew, they are the same word.

—Joe Sittler
  Essays on Nature and Grace

Was there a tree there yesterday? Will
there be one there tomorrow? Godot does
not come, but in the waiting, we care for
and tend each other. Waiting is caring.

—Tom Wicker
  A Time To Die

The average man finds life very uninter-
esting as it is. And I think that the reason
why is that he is always waiting for
something to happen to him, instead of
setting to work to make things happen.

—A. A. Milne

Waiting is the dead space, the empty
in-between.

—Iris Sanguiliano
  In Her Time

A cube sequestered in space and filled
with time, Pure time, refined, distilled,

denatured time without qualities, without even dust.

—Howard Nemerov
Waiting Rooms

All good things come to those who wait.

—Ellen Anderson

WALKING

Solvitur ambulando.... It is solved by walking ...

—Augustine

Walking is the rhythm in which the human being best relates to its environment.

—Paul Devereux
Re-Visioning the Earth

[Especially among the Sufi] the action or rhythm of walking was used as a technique for dissolving the attachments of the world and allowing one to lose themselves in God.

—Bruce Chatwin

I only went out for a walk and finally concluded to stay out till sundown, for going out, I found out, was really going in.

—John Muir *&* Stephen Trimble
Words from the Land

WAR

Since wars begin in the minds of men, it is in the minds of men that we have to erect the ramparts of peace.

—From the UNESCO Charter

War is always the cause for remorse, never for exhilaration.... Let us recall that wars begin in the mind. We have first to think others to death.... It's not them and us; it's just us.... Humanity has outlived war—but doesn't know it.

—William Sloane Coffin
Credo

Never fight evil as if it were something that arose totally outside of yourself.

—Augustine

War's amputees sire children eager to mature and take their bloody turn at death.

—Calvin Miller
The Finale

Wars and temper tantrums are the makeshifts of ignorance.

—Joseph Campbell
Reflections on the Art of Living

Being at war does not necessarily mean that you attack in an outer way. You may simply carry on a long inner experience of war, hating people for what they have done to you or have taken from you.... Whenever you are at war with someone else, you are always at war with yourself, too.

—Martia Nelson
Coming Home

Instead of hating the people you think are warmakers, hate the appetites and the disorder in your own soul, which are the causes of war.

—Thomas Merton

We must not kill our enemies, but kill their desire to kill.

—Mohandas (Mahatma) Gandhi

Nothing is so apt to challenge consciousness and awareness as being at war with oneself.

—Carl G. Jung
Psychological Reflections

War, like an idea or a belief system, is man's greatest addiction and his greatest vulnerability.

—Lynn V. Andrews
Crystal Woman

Our lot as men is to learn, and one goes to knowledge as one goes to war … with fear, with respect, aware that one is going to war, and with absolute confidence in one's self.

—Carlos Castaneda
A Separate Reality

Contrary to what pacifists and other human persons would like to believe, wars, when they break out, tend to be popular. They offer the illusion of an escape from the boredom which is the lot of, particularly, technological man.

—Malcolm Muggeridge
Chronicles of Wasted Time

The desert's name is Trinity. One day the sun rose twice there in a single mourning and man saw his face reflected in the underside of Heaven.

—Marianne Wiggins
Evidence of Things Unseen

The bomb first was our weapon, then it became our diplomacy. Next it became our economy. Now it's become our culture. We've become the people of the bomb.

—E. L. Doctorow

As hunting was ceasing to be a viable way of life, what men did was pretty scary. They invented war.

—Barbara Ehrenreich

Microbes have killed more people than wars have.

—Tess Gerritsen
Gravity

The atomic bomb has changed everything except our way of thinking. And so we drift helplessly towards unparalleled disaster.

—Albert Einstein

I can't tell you what weapons will be used in World War III, but I can tell you what will be used in World War IV: sticks and stones.

—Albert Einstein

WARRIOR

Wherever we are, we can train as a warrior. The practice of meditation, loving-kindness, compassion, joy, and equanimity are our tools.... We will find that tenderness in sorrow and in gratitude. We will find it behind the hardness of rage and in the shakiness of fear. It is available in loneliness as well as in kindness.

—Pema Chödrön
The Places That Scare You

The female warrior knows that life is an adventure of the spirit.... She knows that this earthwalk is only a dream born of a greater dream beyond our imagination.

—Lynn V. Andrews
Star Woman

We are put here in this life like a battle-field and we must fight the good fight.

—Catherine of Siena
Dialogue with Divine Providence

So this spiritual warfare of ours must be constant and never ceasing, and should be conducted with alertness and courage in the soul.

—*Unseen Warfare*

Tenderness contains an element of sad-ness.... You feel so full and rich, as if you were about to shed tears. Your eyes are full of tears, and the moment you blink, the tears will spill out of your eyes and roll down your cheeks. In order to be a good warrior, one has to feel this sad and tender heart. If a person does not feel alone and sad, he cannot be a warrior at all.

—Chögyam Trungpa
Shambhala

"To renew" applies when we are fighting with the enemy, and an entangled spirit arises where there is no possible resolu-tion. We must abandon our efforts, think of the situation in a fresh spirit, then win in a new rhythm. To renew, when we are deadlocked with the enemy, means that without changing our circumstance we change our spirit and win through a different technique.

—Miyamoto Musashi
A Book of Five Rings

The Native American Yaqui way of knowledge and Don Juan's concepts of the warrior and the double are eternal ideas that appear everywhere—not only in indigenous traditions, but in the dreams of people of all races, religions, and ages.

—Arnold Mindell
The Shaman's Body

From the fury of the Northmen, good Lord, deliver us.

—Old English prayer

WATER

Limitless and immortal, the waters are the beginning and end of all things on earth.

—Heinrich Zimmer

In the whole world there is nothing softer and weaker than water. And yet nothing measures up to it in the way it works upon that which is hard. Nothing can change it. Everyone on earth knows that the weak conquers the strong and the soft conquers the hard.

—*Tao Te Ching*

Truth is one; only it is called by different names. A lake has many *ghats*. From one *ghat* the Hindus take water in jars and call it *jal*. From another *ghat* the Mussulmans take water in leather bags and call it *pani*. From a third the Christians take the same thing and call it water.... Everyone is going toward God. They will all realize Him if they have sincerity and longing of heart.

—Ramakrishna (Gadadhar Chatterji)

A great ocean creates a great soul in a people, and the diminishment of the ocean diminishes the people.

—Thomas Moore
The Re-Enchantment of Everyday Life

You are like Rilke's Swan in his awkward waddling across the ground; the swan doesn't cure his awkwardness by beating himself on the back, by moving faster, or by trying to organize himself better. He does it by moving toward the elemental water, where he belongs. It is the simple contact with the water that gives him grace and presence. You only have to touch the elemental waters in your own life, and it will transform everything.

—David Whyte
Crossing the Unknown Sea

The human body consists mainly of water. So does a cucumber. So does the surface of the Earth ... the balance in a river is especially precarious, especially delicate because the water never stops moving. The pressure never relents. The boundary between life and death

is measured in millimeters. There is no room for error.

—David Quammen
Natural Acts

It was a rumbling, rushing sound, the sound of moving water, waterfall water, white water. And I understood that these two things went together—the depth of a dark infinity and this energy of water. I understood "This is who God is. My Mother is water and she is inside me and I am in the water."

—Meinrad Craighead
The Mother's Songs

If there is magic on this planet, it is contained in water.

—Loren Eiseley
The Immense Journey

Esau was dying of thirst when he sold his birthright ... when you go a long time without water, the throat finally hardens and closes and one can no longer be saved even if at last one finds water. But the people who live in the desert discovered, if you make a paste from beans or similar vegetables and stuff it in the mouth and throat and around the neck of the sufferer, little by little, the moisture seeps into the throat and a tiny thread is opened and water, one drop at a time, can finally pass. The "mess of pottage" was lentils.

—Anne Morrow Lindbergh
War Without and War Within

The Element Water represented the Chaos of Waters in ancient Creation mythologies. This was not the dark, destructive chaos of later thought, but a creative, seeding "chaos" of the generating seas and oceans of the world.... The sea for us is still a symbol of generation, the "mother of mankind" from which we came and to which we shall eventually return.... Our bodies are mostly water (if it were squeezed out what was left would make up something the size of a small marble), and in our feelings, our emotions, our most basic (and sexual) sense of self we respond to the pulse of the tides, the throb of water.

—Shelia Farrant
Symbols for Women

A Maori father places water on the brow of his children to say, "Be careful today."

—Thomas W. Cooper
A Time before Deception

A close-up of a water drop is a beautiful multi-foliate rosette, if the water is living and clean. If it's polluted, an ill-defined and fuzzy, less complicated form appears.

—Theodor Schwenk &
Wolfram Schwenk
Water: The Element of Life

Water is yielding but all-conquering; it conquers by yielding.

—Beryl Pogson
The Work Life

Cora Du Bois: When the Indians all die, then God will let the water come down from the north. Everyone will drown. That is because the White People never cared for land or deer or bear.

—David Suzuki & Peter Knudtson
Wisdom of the Elders

As everyone knows, meditation and water are wedded for ever.

—Herman Melville
Moby Dick

Running water is a holy thing.

—Cornwall/English proverb

Please wash me, but don't make me wet.

—German proverb

WEB/NET

The Diamond Net of Indra is a Buddhist concept. The universe is a vast net that contains all time and all space. At every nexus point in the net, there is a multi-faceted diamond. Each of the facets of that diamond reflects every other diamond; in a sense, each diamond contains every other diamond. If you look at one diamond, you see the entire net throughout space and throughout time, into the past and into the future. If you shake one piece of the net, the entire net reverberates from it. What you do to any one part, you do to the totality. So each diamond represents every single thing in the universe: every particle, every speck of dust, every atom. They are co-dependent and mutually arising. They co-originate. When one comes alive, they all come alive.

—John Daido Loori
Sacred Stories

To Teilhard de Chardin, the total mental activity of humanity may be thought of as a web, or perhaps a membrane, that encircles the entire earth. This noosphere, or sphere of mind, is analogous to the biosphere, the sphere of organic life on Earth.

—Allan Combs & Mark Holland
Synchronicity

According to The Book of the Dead, a dreaded net was believed to exist in the Underworld which was greatly feared by the dead and dying. In fact, the departed was required to know the name for every single part of it, including ropes, weights, cords, hooks and so forth, if he wished to make use of it rather than become ensnared by it after his demise.

—Murry Hope
Ancient Egypt

WEEPING

Tears carry creative power.... In herbal folklore, tears are used as a binder, to secure elements, unite ideas, join souls.... In fairy tales, tears change people, remind them of what is important and save their very souls.... Tears are a river that take you somewhere. Weeping creates a river around the boat that carries your soul-life. Tears lift the boat off the rocks, off dry ground, carrying it downriver to someplace new, someplace better.

—Clarissa Pinkola Estés
Women Who Run with the Wolves

When I arrived in this world, I was crying, and everyone else was laughing; and when I left this world, I was laughing and everyone else was crying!

—Kabir

Tears from sadness contain toxins; tears literally cleanse the body.

—E. Sue Blume
Secret Survivors

You may forget with whom you laughed, but you will never forget with whom you wept.

—Arab proverb

WHALES

The blue whale is the largest animal that ever lived on land or sea, weighing 150 tons at maturity ... 300,000 were harvested in the 20th century.

—Edward O. Wilson
The Future of Life

And enormous mother whales lie dreaming, suckling their whale-tender young and dreaming with strange whale eyes wide open in the waters of the beginning and the end.

—D. H. Lawrence

Whales sing only in winter and only males sing. They all sing the same song, but the song changes as the individual whales make up new phrases, which other whales copy. When the whales leave for the summer feeding grounds, they stop singing, but when they return the following winter, they pick up right where they left off, as if the intermission had lasted 15 minutes instead of six months.... Why is the humpback song so complicated and so long? The mystery remains.

—Robert McNally
So Remorseless a Havoc

Once they [the great whales] too, lived on land in a brutal, savage world, where the only rule was kill or be killed. But they grew into wisdom and moved into the sea … cherishing each other and enjoying every moment of life to the utmost, while improving the reach of their own vast mental powers.

—Morgan Llywelyn
Bard

WHOLENESS

Beneath the broken surface of life there is a hidden wholeness.

—Thomas Merton

The virtue of the universe is wholeness. It regards all things as equal.

—*Tao Te Ching*

The living organism and the body social are not assemblies of elementary bits; they are multi-leveled, hierarchically organized systems of sub-wholes containing sub-wholes of lower order, like Chinese boxes. These sub-wholes— or "holons," as I have proposed to call them—are Janus-faced entities which display both the independent properties of wholes and the dependent properties of parts.

—Arthur Koestler
Janus

All things are connected like the blood that connects us all. Man does not weave the web of life, he is merely a strand in it.

Whatever he does to the web, he does to himself.

—Seattle/Seatlh

When we build relationships with each other based on an unconditional respect for the individual and trust in each other, we move from being individuals to being part of a greater whole without losing our unique identities. We go from I to we without losing me.

—Daniel S. Hanson
Cultivating Common Ground

Once you have seen the larger pattern, you cannot go back to seeing the part as the whole.

—Ursula K. Le Guin
Four Ways to Forgiveness

Wholeness is like a flower with four petals. When it opens, one discovers strength, sharing, honesty and kindness. Together these four petals create balance, harmony and beauty.

—Marie Battiste
Reclaiming Indigenous Voice and Vision

The true state of affairs in the material world is wholeness. If we are fragmented, we must blame it on ourselves.

—David Bohm

Every one of us carries a deforming mirror where he sees himself too small or too large, too fat or too thin.… One discovers that destiny can be directed, that one does not need to remain in bondage to that first imprint made on childhood sensibilities, one need not be branded by the first pattern. Once the

deforming mirror is smashed, there is
the possibility of wholeness, there is the
possibility of joy.

—Anaïs Nin

The "wild" can occur anywhere.

—Edward S. Casey
Getting Back into Place

WILDERNESS

We have transformed wilderness
into scenery.

—Wendell Berry
The Unsettling of America

The intellect is a little garden, walled with
a gate. You are in total control there....
Outside that garden is the Wild Country.... You can choose the path, but you
can't choose when there's going to be a
lightning storm.... The Ultimate territory
beyond Wild Country is the Ocean....
That's where what is true for you is in
some form true for every single live thing
in the Universe.... In the Garden, nothing is true; everything is created. In the
Wild Country things are just true within
that context. But in the Ocean ... things
are true at every level, ultimately true.

—Jeni Couzyn & Randall Jarrell
Poetry and the Age

To become open to multiple layers
of vision is to be both practical and
empathic, to practice the presence of
God or gods and to practice wilderness.
Learning the paths of human culture, we
are attentive as well to the undomesti-
cated outdoors and the essential wildness
spinning on in subatomic spaces, forever
generating new patterns.

—Mary Catherine Bateson
Peripheral Visions

WILL

So soon as man contemplates his free will
he thinks of it as a means of doing the
opposite of God's will, though he finds
that only by doing God's will does he find
happiness. Yet, the notion of serving God
sits ill with him, for he sees it as a sacrifice of his will. Only in disillusion and
suffering, in time, space, and patience,
does he come to the wisdom that his real
will is the will of God, and in its practice
is happiness and heaven.

—Edgar Cayce
Edgar Cayce's Story of Jesus

Our power grows with a sense of
purpose.... If we are unclear about that
purpose, then it's hard to know just what
our will is in a given situation. The task of
consciousness is an accurate assessment
of who we are, for within that mystery
lies the purpose our wills must address.
Once we know our will, its strength
increases through time.

—Anodea Judith
Wheels of Life

An empty spirit is one that is confused
about nothing, attached to nothing, and
has no concern whatever in anything for
its own gain, for it is all sunk deep down
into God's dearest will and has forsaken
its own.

—Meister Eckhart

The highest reality is not thought, but will.

—F. W. J. Schelling
The Deities of Samothrace

Your little will can't do anything. It takes Great Determination … it means the whole universe is behind you and with you.

—Katagiri Roshi

I will to will thy will.

—Scandinavian proverb

WIND

It was the wind (prophet, scientist, talker) who told the story of Chernobyl to other countries and revealed the awful truth.

—Marie Battiste
Reclaiming Indigenous Voice and Vision

Northern European wind-lore teaches the quality of the wind at the moment of the first breath determines the characteristic of that life. The infant's first inspiration is from the virtue of the prevailing wind.

—Nigel Pennick
Celtic Sacred Landscapes

The Aivilik Eskimo has at least 12 words for wind.

—Peter Redgrove
The Black Goddess and the Sixth Sense

The Holy Wind swirled through the human being, then left its marks as lines on finger and toes.

—Navajo proverb

WISDOM

All wisdom is given to us on loan.

—Thomas Aquinas

We each contain an enduring spark of that Wisdom at the heart of all creation. Isolated and unsupported, it is but a small spark. United with others, those sparks grow into a flame of illumination and strength for us all.

—Charles Garfield, *et al*
Wisdom Circles

Holy wisdom is not clear and thin like water, but thick and dark like blood.

—C. S. Lewis
Till We Have Faces

Puzzlement is the beginning of wisdom.

—Erich Fromm

Wisdom consists in doing the next thing you have to do. Doing it with your whole heart and finding delight in doing it.

—Meister Eckhart

When you want to expand, you must first contract; when you want to be strong, you must first be weak; when you want to take you must first give. This is called the subtle wisdom of life.

—Lao Tse
Tao Te Ching

Let us learn from this: Wisdom is wisdom, the source cannot matter.

—Paula Underwood Spencer

We attain wisdom not by creating ideals but by learning to see things clearly, as they are.

—Joseph Goldstein & Jack Kornfield
Seeking the Heart of Wisdom

Be wise enough not to be fooled by your limited perspective, and humble enough to wonder, "What is really going on here that I cannot comprehend?"

—Joel Levey & Michelle Levey
Living in Balance

Knowledge can be communicated, but not wisdom. One can find it, live it, be fortified by it, do wonders through it, but one cannot communicate and teach it.

—Hermann Hesse
Siddhartha

Let us now learn how to be a people who seek the wisdom of ordered council … however many, however few, however old, however young, seek the wisdom of ordered council.

—Paula Underwood Spencer
The Walking People

Wisdom, then, is born of the overlapping of lives, the resonance between stories.

—Mary Catherine Bateson
Full Circles, Overlapping Lives

And once in a great while an *isumatag* becomes apparent, a person who can create the atmosphere in which wisdom shows itself.… It is a nameless wisdom esteemed by all people. It is understanding how to live a decent life, how to behave properly toward people and toward the land.

—Barry Lopez
Arctic Dreams

Fairy tales don't come from old wisdom, they come from old foolishness—just as potent.

—Eudora Welty
The Eye of the Story

This, the stream of esoteric wisdom, has flowed like a clear underground current through every epoch of history, emerging in varying forms to influence minds in each generation able to receive its nourishment.

—George Trevelyan
A Vision of the Aquarian Age

The word "medicine" and the name Medea, the medical herbalist witch, came from the same root—a root meaning knowledge or wisdom.

—Robert Briffault
The Mothers

The wisdom of the heart is all important. For wisdom is unbalanced and distorted when held only at the intellectual level.

The silver wisdom of the head must be changed to the golden wisdom of the heart by the warmth of human love.

—Gareth Knight
The Rose Cross and the Goddess

Wisdom makes us humble, relaxed with our human condition, responsible to self and others, and God.

—Suzanne Zuercher
Enneagram Spirituality

Wisdom is the knowing, not of facts, but of truths—Solomon and Socrates represent wisdom incarnate and Athena or Minerva were wisdom deified—is predicated on the assumption that one person can somehow grasp a total picture of life and its laws, comprehending the whole and the relation of its parts.

—Sven Birkerts
The Guttenburg Elegies

Wisdom is the way that you learn to decipher the unknown; and the unknown is our closest companion. So wisdom is the art of being courageous and generous with the unknown, of being able to decipher and recognize its treasures.

—John O'Donohue
Anam Cara

Wisdom knows that behind the Many is the One. Wisdom sees through the confusion of shifting shapes and passing forms to the groundless Ground of all Being.

—Ken Wilber
Sex, Ecology, Spirituality

Wisdom, according to ancient sages, comes from letting the yin side

predominate when its time comes, and functioning from the yang side when its turn comes.

—Robert A. Johnson
Inner Work

Age 56 is when the great planet Saturn spins back for the second time on your natal chart. This is the age we recognize as the doorway into the age of wisdom.

—Z Budapest
Grandmother of Time

Wisdom is a reliable vessel to bring you across the ocean of old age, sickness, and death. It is a bright lamp that brings light into the darkness of ignorance.

—Dogen Zenji
Enlightenment Unfolds

Wisdom is like the rain. Its source is unlimited, but it comes down according to the season.

—Jalal Al-din Rumi

Wisdom is to be read in the immense book of God, which is the world.

—Tommaso Campanella

There is wisdom in all creative works.

—Hildegard of Bingen

To attain knowledge, add things everyday; To attain wisdom, remove things every day.

—*Tao Te Ching*

Wisdom is common sense in an
uncommon degree.

—Samuel Coleridge

Knowledge is lost, but wisdom is
never forgotten

—Neale Donald Walsch

WISH

You are never given a wish without also
being given the power to make it true.
You may have to work for it, however.

—Richard Bach
Illusions

Wishes are recollections coming from
the future.

—Rainer Maria Rilke

WIT

In old Anglo-Saxon, the word wisdom
is very clear: it is *inwit*. *Inwit* is Sophia
dwelling within us. Besides being wise,
she is oftentimes witty, dancing circles
around the hoary-bearded theologians
and philosophers, and giggling sympa-
thetically at their efforts ...

—Alice O. Howell
The Dove in the Stone

Wit is the salt of conversation, not
the food.

—William Hazlett

Wit is a propensity of thoughts and
words; or, in other terms, thought and
words elegantly adapted to the subject.

—John Dryden

WOMEN

You may not remember, but let me tell
you this, someone in the some future
time will think of us.

—Sappho

The powers of the Goddess are fully
released from the underworld in order
to create balance with the powers of
the gods, the patriarchy. Slowly, woman
within will awaken just in time to prevent
ecocide, the suicide of Planet Earth.

—Barbara Hand Clow
Heart of the Christos

Imagine a woman who believes it is right
and good she is woman,
A woman who honors her experience
and tells her stories,
Who refuses to carry the sins of others
within her body and life.

—Patricia Lynn Reilly
A God Who Looks Like Me

Fathers have been raping their daughters
for countless centuries, and thus the pain
of incest has karmically accumulated not
just in individuals, but in the collective
tissue of the human psyche. This ancient
pain now seems to be pouring into
our collective awareness as part of the

re-emergence of the feminine and the re-empowerment of women.

—Christopher M. Bache
Dark Night, Early Dawn

A woman's heart always has a burned mark.

—Louise Labé

That she bear children is not a woman's significance. But that she bear herself, that is her supreme and risky fate.

—D. H. Lawrence
Women in Love

A woman's shadow is female ... that frozen rage is what I must explore—O secret, self-enclosed and ravaged place! This is the gift I thank Medussa for.

—May Sarton
The Muse as Medussa

Women and children have literally stayed alive ... because women form friend-ships.... Women are heavily involved in stitching up all the little rips and tears in the social fabric—no one tells women how to do this.

—Shelley E. Taylor
The Tending Instinct

Women are very good at giving lip service to the idea that their needs are as important as everyone else's, without really living it.

—Carol Frenier
Business and the Feminine Principle

Her only interests were cooking and the Koran. She prayed five times a day, and she lived in a world that was strictly bound by an invisible cage of tradition. The Arabic word for woman, *hormah*, derives from the word *haram*: sin.... Everything seemed to be *haram*, or sinful; and if it wasn't sinful it was *abe*, shameful.

—Carmen Bin Ladin
Inside the Kingdom

The misogynist works to exclude women; the friendly father figure works to keep them infantile.

—Mary Catherine Bateson
Composing a Life

Women, when they are old enough to have done with the business of being women, and can let loose their strength, must be the most powerful creatures in the world.

—Isak Dinesen
The Monkey

At menopause life can burn into one long pre-menstrual experience. Hormones slap you up against the doors of your unfinished business.

—Maura Kelsea

The most creative force in the world is the menopausal woman with zest.

—Margaret Mead

The Grandmother Lodge is the lodge of white haired wisdom who no longer give the power of their blood away, but hold it for energy to uphold the Law.

—Brooke Medicine Eagle

Women are glorified, elevated and praised so that they can be humiliated, restricted and blocked at every turn. The inevitable reverse image of the madonna is the whore. We are women—not whores or madonnas!

—Dorothee Solle

In the whole mythological tradition, woman is there. All she has to do is realize that she's the place that people are trying to get to. When a woman realizes what her wonderful character is, she's not going to get messed up with the notion of being pseudo-male.

—Joseph Campbell & Maureen Murdock
The Heroine's Journey

WONDER

Wonder is a searching attitude of simultaneously knowing and not-knowing, of finding pattern and breaking apart, [it] goes against the grain of our organizing mind, but is intrinsic to the creativity of introspection, art, and empathy.

—Alfred Margulies
The Empathic Imagination

The fairest thing we can experience is the mysterious. It is the fundamental emotion which stands at the cradle of true art and true science. He who knows it not and can no longer wonder, no longer feel amazement, is as good as dead, a snuffed-out candle.

—Albert Einstein
The World As I See It

People travel to wonder at the height of mountains, at the huge waves of the sea,

at the long courses of rivers, at the vast compass of the ocean, at the circular motion of the stars; and they pass by themselves without wondering.

—Augustine

Wonder is the basis of worship.

—Thomas Carlyle

Every bush is a Burning Bush and the world is crowded with God.

—C. S. Lewis

This, then, is the extravagant landscape of the world, given, given with pizzazz, given in good measure, pressed down, shaken together, and running over.

—Annie Dillard
Pilgrim at Tinker Creek

The world will never starve for wonders; but only for the want of wonder.

—Gilbert K. Chesterton

God does not die on the day when we cease to believe in a personal deity, but we die on the day when our lives cease to be illuminated by the steady radiance, renewed daily, of a wonder, the source of which is beyond all reason.

—Dag Hammarskjöld
Diaries

Wonder kept dazzling me and I recall only wonder, [for] the larger the island of knowledge, the longer the shoreline of wonder.

—Huston Smith

To be surprised, to wonder, is to begin
to understand.

—Jose Ortega y Gasset

I think us here to wonder.

—Alice Walker
The Color Purple

WORDS

Every creature is a word of God.

—Meister Eckhart

The first word "Ahhhhh" blossoms into
all others. Each of them is true.

—Kukei
Singing Images of Fire

By following the trail of Om you
attain Brahman, of which the Word is
the symbol.

—Ramakrishna (Gadadhar Chatterji)
The Gospel of Sri Ramakrishna

God can do nothing but speak the
Eternal Word.... God is the Word which
pronounces itself.

—Meister Eckhart
Meister Eckhart

Words create a vibratory field.... To
ancients, breathy sounds of vowels were
the sacred names of the gods escaping
the lips.

—Jean Houston
The Passion of Isis and Osiris

You should utter words as though heaven
were opened within them and as though
you did not put the word into your
mouth, but as though you had entered
the word.

—Martin Buber

Our speech can build a world of peace
and joy in which trust and love can flourish, or it can create discord and hatred.

—Thich Nhat Hanh

No word spoken is ever lost. It remains
and it vibrates; and it vibrates according
to the spirit put into it.

—Pir Vilayat Inayat Khan
Music

All words are spiritual—nothing is more
spiritual than words—Whence are they?
Along how many thousands and tens
of thousands of years have they come?
Those eluding, fluid, beautiful, fleshless
realities, Mother, Father, Water, Earth,
Me, This, Soul, Tongue, House, Fire.

—Walt Whitman

What is the phrase for the moon? And
the phrase for love? By what name are
we to call death? I do not know. I need a
little language such as lovers use, words
of one syllable.

—Virginia Woolf
The Waves

Short words are best and the old words
when short are best of all.

—Winston Churchill

Sweet words are like honey: a little may refresh, but too much gluts the stomach.

—Anne Bradstreet
Meditations Divine and Moral

You must be very patient…. First you will sit down at a little distance from me—like that—in the grass. I shall look at you out of the corner of my eye, and you will say nothing. Words are the source of misunderstandings. But you will sit a little closer to me, every day …

—Antoine de Saint-Exupéry
The Little Prince

A word's aura signifies a universe, access to which is contained in its aura. We step in gingerly, and the sound spins us to a vortex of an unknown galaxy of other meaningful sounds.

—Gail Sher
The Intuitive Writer

She and Palizot clung to each other for a minute. Neither could say anything. It was an end, and words are for beginnings.

—Ursula Le Guin
The Beginning Place

Words are believed to carry the power to make things happen, ritualized in song, sacred story and prayer.

—Kenneth Lincoln
Native American Renaissance

Wherever we go we are surrounded by words. Words softly whispered, loudly proclaimed, or angrily screamed; words spoken, recited or sung; words on records, in books, on walls, or in the sky…. Words, words, words! They form the floor, the walls and the ceiling of our existence.

—Henri J. M. Nouwen
The Way of the Heart

A word is not a crystal, transparent and unchanged; it is the skin of a living thought and may vary greatly in color and content according to the circumstances and the time in which it is used.

—Oliver Wendell Holmes
The Complete Works of Oliver Wendell Holmes

Fiction writers make a reality of words.

—Ursula K. LeGuin
The Wave in the Mind

On average, a person knows about 80,000 words. We learn about 13 new ones a day, until we graduate from high school.

—David G. Myers

Etymology: The energy of a word unleashed.

—Mary Carruthers
The Craft of Thought

The difference between the right word and the almost right word is the difference between lightning-bug and lightning.

—Mark Twain

Prose is words in the best order; poetry, the best words in the best order.

—Samuel Taylor Coleridge

Don't use words. Who you are stands above you and thunders so loudly all the while I can't ear a word you're saying.

—Thomas W. Cooper
A Time before Deception

A score of words and deeds issue from me daily, of which I am not the master. They are begotten of weakness and born of shame. I cannot assume the elevation I ought ... for want of sufficient bottom in my nature.

—Ralph Waldo Emerson

Where concepts are lacking, a word is found to fill the vacuum.

—Johann Wolfgang von Goethe
Faust

The word is always a mirror of inner silence, and myth a reflector of soul.

—Jean Gebser
The Ever-Present Origin

When words are divorced from experience, they become deceptive.

—Bruno Borchert
Mysticism

Auntie had tried desperately to reconcile the family with the people; the old instincts had always been to gather the feelings and opinions that were scattered through the village, to gather them like willow twigs and tie them into a single prayer bundle that would bring peace to all of them. But now the feelings were twisted, tangled roots, and all the names for the source of this growth were buried under English words, out of reach, and there would be no peace and the people

would have no rest until the entanglement had been unwound to the source.

—Leslie Maron Silko
Ceremony

It is precisely when words are uprooted from their concrete origins and converted into empty abstractions that they can be put to wicked purposes.

—Ralph C. Wood
The Gospel According to Tolkien

A person who wouldn't dream of using someone else's toothbrush will feel not a qualm about using someone else's tired expressions.... Cliché means the metal plate cast from a page of type; you can make copies without having to reset the typeface ... slogans are empty vessels that can be filled with any content.

—Donna Woolfolk Cross
Word Abuse

Words exist because of meaning; once you've got the meaning, you can forget the words. Where can I find a man who has forgotten words so I can have a word with him?

—Chuang Tzu
Chuang Tzu

All words are pegs to hang ideas on.

—Henry Ward Beecher

May your words be sweet and juicy, for people often serve them back to you!

—Patricia Schroeder

In the end was the word and the word was with men.

—John Steinbeck

The Word is for everyone in this world, it must come and go and be interchanged, for it is good to give and receive the forces of life.

—Dogon proverb

In the primal beginning was the Word.

—Inscription above the library in Ephesus

WORK

Your work is to discover your work and then with all your heart to give yourself to it.

—Siddhartha Gautama (Buddha)

One must not always think so much about what one should do, but rather what one should be. Our works do not ennoble us; but we must ennoble our works.

—Meister Eckhart

I think most of us are looking for a calling, not a job. Most of us ... have jobs that are too small for our spirit.

—Studs Terkel
Working

The Amish honor what we would call the process and the product. Both. What I saw among the Amish was the amazing amount of energy available to people who get pleasure from what they are doing and find meaning in the work itself. But they are practical people who want that can of beans at the end of the day and the sixty-six jars of relish. For them it's all connected.

—Sue Bender
Plain and Simple

There is only one joy greater than the joy of a job well done: the joy of a job well done together.

—Daniel S. Hanson
Cultivating Common Ground

Life is a means for work. Harmony is your outcome.

—Rudolf Steiner

I don't like work—no man does—but I like what is in work—the chance to find yourself. Your own reality—for yourself, not for others—what no other man can ever know.

—Joseph Conrad
Heart of Darkness

Allie learned: there is a task and a task teller, a set of directions, instructions, perhaps a map, a carrying out of the task, a finishing of the task, a return to the task teller to report success, a thanking, a getting paid, an assignment of another task.

—Walker Percy
The Second Coming

If you love your work, everyone benefits.

—John Whiteside & Sandra Egli
Flight of the Phoenix

Good work is a way of living … it is unifying and healing. It brings us home from
pride and despair and places us responsi-
bly within the human estate. It defines us
as we are; not too good to work with our
bodies, but too good to work poorly or
joylessly or selfishly or alone.

—Wendell Berry
  The Unsettling of America

Work steadily, even shyly, in the spirit
of those medieval carvers who so fondly
sculpted the undersides of choir seats.

—John Updike

When Matisse was asked whether he
believed in God, his response was, "Yes,
when I'm working."

—Marion Woodman
  Conscious Femininity

It is your work in life that is the ultimate
seduction.… The work one does is a way
of keeping a diary.

—Pablo Picasso

The outward work can never be small if
the inward one is great, and the outward
work can never be great if the inward is
small or of little worth.

—Meister Eckhart

No one else can tell you what your life's
work is, but it's important that you find it.
There is a part of you that knows—affirm
that part.

—Willis W. Harman

An essential portion of any artist's labor
is not creation so much as invocation.

—Lewis Hyde

When you talk about your own work
you're somewhat in the position of a
well digger who tries to describe from
the bottom of a well the mountain range
that was in front of him when he started
digging. You don't really understand it
very well.

—Saul Bellow

The average man finds life very uninter-
esting as it is. And I think that the reason
why is that he is always waiting for
something to happen to him instead of
setting to work to make things happen.

—A. A. Milne

Work is love made visible.

—Kahlil Gibran

The notion that one is too good to do
what it is necessary for somebody to do is
always weakening.

—Wendell Berry
  The Hidden Wound

Nothing is work until one would rather
be doing something else.

—Laurel Lee
  Signs of Spring

Work generally takes up about one third
of your time.… To make the best use of
one's free time, one needs to devote as

much ingenuity and attention to it as one would to one's job.

—Mihaly Csikszentmihalyi
Finding Flow

Seeing the work that is to be done, who can help wanting to be the one to do it?

—Wendell Berry
What Are People For?

It is not necessary to have great things to do. I turn my little omelet in the pan for the love of God

—Brother Laurence

The work is a long stage. We're players doing good ... the Work is for the strong, not the wishy-washy.

—Beryl Pogson
The Work Life

Only the love of work, not of success, leads to progress.

—Rudolf Steiner
Knowledge of the Higher Worlds and Its Attainment

The work is to liberate the oppressed and the oppressor.

—Nelson Mandela

Do your work for the sake of the work as if you were in God's temple serving your Beloved. Every job is just as important as another and the difference is one's attitude.

—Terry Cole-Whittaker *&* Jack Canfield
Heart at Work

If you care to dig for gold you might find it; if not, be content with straw.

—Heraclitus of Ephesus

Let the beauty we love be what we do.

—Jalal Al-din Rumi

I love people who harness themselves, an ox to a heavy cart, who pull like water buffalo, with massive patience.

—Marge Piercy

Närings liv is the Swedish word for business… it literally means "nourishment for life."

—The *Närings Liv* Project

How do I work? I grope.

—Albert Einstein

He who rises late, must trot all day and can scarcely overcome his duties at nightfall.

—*McGuffy Reader*

The work will teach you how to do it.

—Estonian proverb

Praise Allah, but first tie your camel to a post.

—Sufi proverb

WORLD

Know that the world is a mirror from head
to foot,
In every atom are a hundred blazing suns.
If you cleave the heart of one drop of water,
A hundred pure oceans emerge from it.
In the pupil of the eye is a heaven.

—Mahmud Shabistari
The Garden of Mystery

We thus arrive at the image of a world-
mosaic or cosmic kaleidoscope, which, in
spite of constant shufflings and rear-
rangements, also takes care of bringing
like and like together.

—Paul Kammerer
Das Gesetz der Serie

The world is poor because her fortune
is buried in the sky and all her treasure
maps are of the earth.

—Calvin Miller
The Finale

The world is now too dangerous for
anything less than Utopia.

—R. Buckminster Fuller

The present-day global landscape is one of
profound crisis, which could end either in
the death of humankind or in the break-
through to a new civilization.... It is up to
all of us who live today on this planet.

—Mikhail Gorbachev

There is no need for you to leave the
house. Stay at your table and listen. Don't
even listen, just wait. Don't even wait, be
completely alone and quiet. The world
will offer itself to you to be unmasked;

it can't do otherwise; in raptures it will
writhe before you.

—Franz Kafka

The seat of the soul is where the inner
world and the outer world meet.
Where they overlap, it is in every point
of the overlap.

—Novalis (Friedrich von Leopold)

God has arranged all things in the world
in the consideration of everything else.

—Hildegard of Bingen

I'd like to turn people on to the fact
that the world is form, not just function
and money.

—Claes Oldenburg

We are connected with the world through
perception, feeling, will and thinking.

—Rudolf Steiner
Theosophy

The world is a Dancer; it is a Rosary;
it is a Torrent; it is a Boat; a Mist; a
Spider's Snare; it is what you will; and the
metaphor will hold.

—Ralph Waldo Emerson
Journals

We are inventing a new and original
world. Imagination is seizing power.

—Theodore Roszak
The Making of a Counter Culture

We dwarf the world when we demand
that what is deep should appear in the
same way as that which is superficial.

—José Ortega y Gasset

In some ways the world is coming to
resemble a vast work of art, something
fantastic and frantic like Hieronymous
Bosch's *Garden of Earthly Delights*... The
closer you get to the canvas, the more
detail is revealed ... we live our lives
between the tiny and the titanic.... Deep
down we know that the world is not
really chaotic and capricious. We know
that it has a rhythm to it even if it is one
that we cannot hum or write down.

—Mark Ward
Beyond Chaos

Colonization created new world views that
were self-legitimizing.... No matter how
dominant a worldview is, there are always
other ways of interpreting the world.

—Marie Battiste
Reclaiming Indigenous Voice and Vision

If you can't see the world, you can't see
the interactions shaping the world.

—Tom Friedman
The Lexus and the Olive Tree

The modern world is desacrilized, that is
why it is in a crisis. The modern person
must rediscover a deeper source of his
own spiritual life.

—Carl G. Jung

If the world is whole, why do so many
people see it as broken?

—Ken Wilber
A Theory of Everything

If I find in myself a desire which no
experience in this world can satisfy, the
most probable explanation is that I was
made for another world.

—C. S. Lewis
Mere Christianity

Is God fully actualized independent of
the world?

—F. W. J. Schelling

The World-Soul is not in the world;
rather the World is in it, embraced by it
and molded by it.

—Ken Wilber
Sex, Ecology, Spirituality

Whatever we know of the world, there is
always more.

—David Bohm

Almost anything you do will seem
insignificant but it is very important that
you do it.... You must be the change you
wish to see in the world.

—Mohandas (Mahatma) Gandhi

This world is only a bridge; you may pass
over it, but you should not think to build
a dwelling place upon it.

—*The Urantia Book*

WORSHIP

Worship at its best is a social experience with people of all levels of life coming together to realize their oneness and unity under God.

—Martin Luther King, Jr.
All Believers Are Brothers

Whenever beauty overwhelms us, whenever wonder silences our chattering hopes and worries, we are close to worship.

—Richard C. Cabot
What Men Live By

Wonder is the basis of worship.

—Thomas Carlyle

Humanity is being brought to the moment when it will have to choose between suicide or adoration.

—Pierre Teilhard de Chardin

Worship is playing eschatological games to summon the future.

—Marianne Micks

Worship makes wet the heart, ignites the magic of imagination.

—Matthew Fox
The Coming of the Cosmic Christ

Church language is a kind of Yiddish, a language which is heart-warming in the ghetto but totally useless for communicating to the outside world.

—Krister Stendahl

True worship is the manifested demonstration of reverence for The Source in everyday activities.

—Ann Valentin & Virginia Essene
Descent of the Dove

Prayer may enrich the life, but worship illuminates destiny.

—*The Urantia Book*

Worship leads to justice and justice leads to peace.

—Carol Doran & Thomas H. Troeger
Trouble at the Table

Matthew Fox said the agenda of the 3rd Millennium is to strip down religions to their spiritual experience—developing worship that awakens people instead of bores them. That empowers them.

—Mick Brown
The Spiritual Tourist

Before you, in some form, are … a pool, a book, bread, and wine. Around you are people, the primary thing. In this place, at an appointed time, these all will interact. If you let them, they will interact with you.

—Gordon Lathrup
Holy Things; Holy People; Holy Ground

WRITING

Oh, Thou Great One, seen by (his) father, Guardian of the Book of Thot. See, I come as a spirit, a soul, a mighty one, provided with the Scriptures of Thot. Hurry … bring me the water bowl, the palette, the writing tools of Thot, and the mysteries dwelling therein.

—*Egyptian Book of the Dead*

The ancient Chinese said: There are only three Arts: poetry, calligraphy and drawing. These are the arts which, through heart, brain and hand, and with a minimum of materials, achieve the highest level of intensity and clarity.

—Friedrich Neugebauer
The Mystic Art of Written Forms

The invention of writing is attributed to Nisaba, goddess of writing, accounting and scribal knowledge.... In Egypt she was called Sheshat—"she who is foremost in the house of books."

—Layne Redmond
When the Drummers Were Women

Writing is my form of celebration and prayer, but it is also the way in which I organize and inquire about the world.

—Diane Ackerman
An Alchemy of Mind

We do not write in order to be understood, we write in order to understand.

—C. Day-Lewis

The pen is the tongue of the mind.

—Miguel de Cervantes
Don Quixote

To write is to note down the music of the world.

—Hélène Cixous
Rootprints, Memory and Life Writing

As for my next book I am going to hold myself from writing it till I have it impending in me: grown heavy in my mind like a ripe pear; pendent, gravid, asking to be cut or it will fall.

—Virginia Woolf

When you write, you lay out a line of words. The line of words is a miner's pick, a woodcarver's gouge, a surgeon's probe. You wield it, and it digs a path you follow. Soon you find yourself deep in new territory. Is it a dead end, or have you located the real subject? You will know tomorrow, or this time next year.

—Annie Dillard

Writing is the language of the hand, the idiom of the mind, the ambassador of intellect, and the trustee of thoughts, the weapon of knowledge and the companion of brethren in the time of separation.

—An Islamic author

All I can do ... is to write daily, read as much as possible, and keep my vocabulary alive and changing so that I will have an instrument on which to play the book if it does me the honor of coming to me and asking to be written.

—Madeleine L'Engle
The Irrational Season

Good writers are those who keep the language efficient. That is to say, keep it accurate, keep it clear.

—Ezra Pound

Go into yourself. Search for the reason that bids you write; find out if it is spreading out its roots in the deepest places of your heart, acknowledge to yourself whether you would have to die if it were denied you to write.

—Rainer Maria Rilke
Letters to a Young Poet

One writes not to be read but to breathe—one writes to think, to pray, to analyze. One writes to clear one's mind, to dissipate one's fears, to face one's double, to look at one's mistakes—in order to retrieve them…. Like prayer, you go to it in sorrow more than in joy.

—Anne Morrow Lindbergh
War Without and War Within

A poet can't afford to be aloof. The tools of his trade are the people he bumps up against.

—Rod McKuen
On Being a Writer

Writing practice softens the heart and mind, helps to keep us flexible so that rigid distinctions between apples and milk, tigers and celery disappear.

—Natalie Goldberg
Writing Down the Bones

A writer strives to express a universal truth in the way that rings the most bells in the shortest amount of time.

—William Faulkner
On Being a Writer

If everybody became a poet, the world would be so much better. We would all read to each other.

—Nikki Giovanni
On Being a Writer

We write to taste life twice.

—Anaïs Nin

The blank page on which I read my mind.

—Dylan Thomas

Egyptian script was called "Writing of Divine Words." [They] washed off the ink with beer and then "drank the knowledge."

—Richard A. Firmage
The Alphabet Abecedarium

There is nothing in the world that should not be expressed in such a way that an affectionate seven year old boy can see and understand it.

—Leo (Lev) Tolstoy

Only in writing can the cry from the great cross on Golgotha still be heard in the minds of men.

—Loren Eiseley
The American Scholar

YEARNING

Like billowing clouds, like the incessant
gurgle of the brook, the longing of the
soul can never be stilled.

—Hildegard of Bingen

Fiction is the art form of human yearning.

—Robert Olen Butler

We all yearn for meaning, for truth, for
love, for relationship, for God.

—Regina Sara Ryan
The Woman Awake

YEW TREES

Yew, the death-tree in all European
countries, sacred to Hecate in Greece and
Italy.... In Ireland the yew was "the coffin
of the vine".... Yews make the best bows....
It is likely that the Latin *taxus*, Yew, is connected with *toxicon*, Greek for the poison
with which arrows were smeared.

—Robert Graves
The White Goddess

The yew is a flexible force but also hard;
it endures beyond all other things. The
yew is evergreen in the winter—life in the

midst of death—and is used to build fires, thus becoming the "sun within."

—Edred Thorsson
At the Well of Wyrd

Of what wood is the poisonous, handsome tree.... It is no tree but an apparition of the *sidhe*, its nature is not of this world ...

—Caitlin Matthews & John Matthews
The Encyclopedia of Celtic Wisdom

Yew is the popular name for the ten species of *Taxus*.... All parts of the plant ... are highly poisonous.... Yew poisoning is ... sudden death—within five minutes following some sort of convulsion.... The poison is also found in dried parts of the plant, so these should be cleared away and burnt.

—*The Oxford Encyclopedia of Trees of the World*

Yew is the traditional cemetery tree because priests of the Old Celtic religion regarded it as a symbol of immortality and planted it in their sacred groves, where Christian cemeteries were later situated. In this way, the death-and-resurrection connotations of the yew were perpetuated.

—Barbara Walker
The Woman's Dictionary of Symbols and Sacred Objects

YOGA

All life is Yoga.

—Aurobindo

The word Yoga is derived from the Sanskrit root *yuj* meaning to bind, join, attach and yoke, to direct and concentrate one's attention on, to use and apply.... In the practice of Yoga, every cell is consciously made to absorb a copious supply of fresh blood and life-giving energy, thus satiating the embodied soul.

—B. K. S. Iyengar
The Concise Light on Yoga

Yoga is of two main kinds: the purely psychical Raja Yoga and the physiological Hatha Yoga. Raja Yoga has a certain affinity with the instructions of the Orders of Christian knights.

—Willy Schrödter
A Rosicrucian Notebook

Yoga means communion, becoming one with the object in mind.... The traditional Yogic cleansing practice called Bhramari vibrates the entire nervous system, brain and body, by buzzing the vocal cords, imitating the buzzing of bees.

—Layne Redmond
When the Drummers Were Women

The practice of Yoga induces a primary sense of measure and proportion. Reduced to our own body, our first instrument, we learn to play it, drawing from it maximum resonance and harmony.

—Yehudi Menuhin, Foreword
The Concise Light on Yoga

Yoga is a generic name for any discipline by which one attempts to pass out of the limits of one's ordinary

mental consciousness into a greater
spiritual consciousness....
The Yoga we practice is not for ourselves
alone, but for the Divine.

—Aurobindo

Yoga Sutras promote many-sided
development. They outline a practice
with eight steps.... These eight
dimensions of practice include physical,
emotional, ethical, cognitive, and
volitional training and evoke many kinds
of meta-normal capacity.

—Michael Murphy
The Future of the Body

Yoga cannot be organized, must not be
organized. Organizations kill work. Love
is everywhere, in everything, is everything. But if you confine it, enclose it in a
box or in a definite place, it disappears.

—Vanda Scaravelli

In Pondicherry, India, I watched a yogi
in trance being fed by his followers. His
eyeballs were rolled back so that only
the whites of his eyes could be seen. He
sat erect in the lotus position; and his
face shone with ecstasy. According to
the people around him, he had achieved
nirvikalpa samadhi and "would never
return to this world."

—Michael Murphy
The Future of the Body

Yoga ... is India's mature answer to the
universal question: Who am I? ... an
esoteric tradition within the versatile
religious culture of Hinduism. It is one of
the world's oldest and most continuous
branches of spiritual inquiry and, second

only to shamanism, the longest and most
intense experiment of the human spirit.

—Georg Feurerstein
The Shambhala Encyclopedia of Yoga

The practice of Yoga brings us face-to-face
with the extraordinary complexity of
our own being, the stimulating but also
embarrassing multiplicity of our personality, the rich endless confusion of Nature.

—Aurobindo

YOUTH

Youth seems a time when all meat was
juicy and tender, and no game too swift
for a hunter. When I was young, every
day was as a beginning of some new
thing, and every evening ended with the
glow of the next day's dawn.

—Ivaluarjuk, Peggy V. Beck &
A. I. Walters
The Sacred

My grandfather would sing a particular
song and tell me "remember it." I would
try. Sometimes I would ask my grandmother to help me remember. She would
only tell me that that was between my
grandfather and me. She would not
interfere and it was the same with what
my grandmother was teaching—my
grandfather did not interfere. And these
things they were advising me, their
thoughts were the same.

—Soge Track, Peggy V. Beck &
A. I. Walters
The Sacred

ZEN

Bodhidharma, who according to legend brought Ch'an, or Zen from India to China, is said to have defined the fundamental principle of Zen as: "A special transmission outside the scriptures; no dependence upon words and letters; direct pointing to the heart of man; seeing into one's nature and the attainment of Buddhahood."

—Frederick Franck
The Zen of Seeing

May I add that I am interested in yoga and above all in Zen, which I find to be the finest example of a technique leading to the highest natural perfection of man's contemplative liberty. You may argue that the use of a koan to dispose one for satori is not different from the use of a drug. I would like to submit that there is all the difference in the world.

—Thomas Merton
The Hidden Ground of Love

... Zen satori is: It is to be with God before he cried out, "Let there be light." ... When the bridge flows and the water does not, there is satori.... Satori does not perceive eternity as stretching itself over an infinite number of unit-instants but in the instant itself, for every instant is eternity.

—Daisetz Teitaro Suzuki
Living by Zen

Zen pretty much comes down to three things—everything changes; everything is connected; pay attention.

—Jane Hirschfield & Bill Moyers
Fooling with Words

Whosoever speaks of Zen as if it were a Buddhist sect or school of thought is a devil.

—Dogen Zenji

Monk: "What is Zen?
Tosu (Zen Master): "Zen."

—Daisetz Teitaro Suzuki
Zen and Japanese Culture

Zen is that which brings us in direct contact with the inner workings of life—archery, No play, tea ceremonies, calligraphy ... drawing.

—Frederick Franck
The Awakened Eye

Tea drinking is the art of being truly present with each other and the situation, sensitive to the sacred quality of everything. It is the realization of a spirit of absolute poverty, nonattachment or emptiness (*sunyata*) beyond any dichotomies of body and spirit, subject and object, good and evil. Out of this no-whereness and no-timeness the practitioners of the tea ceremony drink their cup of tea together, all the time experiencing *sunyata* or emptiness, the heart of Zen, as the fountain of infinite freedom.

—Elizabeth Dodson Gray &
   Marlane van Hall
   *Sacred Dimensions of
   Women's Experience*

Koans change perceptions.

—Jim Nollman
Spiritual Ecology

Zen Buddhists define their task as "infinite gratitude for the past. Infinite service to the present. Infinite responsibility to the future."

—Stewart Brand
The Clock of the Long Now

Dogen [a principal founder of Japanese Zen] understood effortful Zen practice as taking place in a Cosmos permeated by grace, in an Order, that is, in which surrender, or at least alignment, but not attainment, was the proper attitude.... One of Zen's laments is that we remain blind to the graceful immanence of the Buddha-nature, failing to draw on its powers.

—Philip Novak
Buddhist-Christian Studies

No snowflake ever falls in the wrong place.

—Zen proverb

He who knows does not speak, he who speaks does not know.

—Zen proverb

ZENDO

A zendo is a meditation room, and a dojo is a martial arts training hall ... both refer to specialized environments meant to cultivate awareness, expand consciousness, and teach us to blend with reality: they are places of enlightenment.

—Robert Rabbin
Invisible Leadership

This zendo is not a peaceful haven, but a furnace room for the combustion of our egoistic delusions.

—Eido Roshi

ZODIAC

Our word Zodiac comes from the Greek word meaning, "living creatures" (from which is also derived zoo and zoology), and *diakos* meaning "wheel" (hence the term "Wheel of Life" and its connection with the Hindu "Wheel of Maya"), and it describes the star-clusters that provide the backcloth for the sun's annual journey through our skies.... The names, with the exception of Libra, and the images come to us from the Greeks who in turn derived them from the Babylonians and Egyptians.

Shelia Farrant
Symbols for Women

Twelve individuals grouped as the Zodiacal constellations are grouped around the Sun. Such was the Round Table: King Arthur at the center, surrounded by the Twelve, above each of whom a Zodiacal symbol was displayed, indicating the particular cosmic influence with which he was associated. Civilizing forces went out from this place to Europe.

—Rudolf Steiner
The Archangel Michael

The powers of the zodiac are not to be found in the far reaches of interstellar space.... They are found in the human mind, which encompasses the universe at its center point. The zodiac powers were uncontained and formless until the human mind drew circles around them and gave them names.

—Donald Tyson
New Millennium Magic

ZOROASTRIANISM

After 1200 B.C. they [the non-Aryan Iranian tribes] trekked slowly southwards. The priest Zoroaster arose among them with a new message. In the sixth century B.C., this message became the state religion of the great kingdom in the region of the Euphrates and Tigris. It is one of the most significant roots of Western mysticism.... Zoroaster was a contemporary of Moses.... Zoroaster felt compelled to preach a new message of hope to his people ... fired by his love for the All-Highest.... He was obsessed by purity: pure thought (truth) pure life (environment) and pure action(righteousness).

—Bruno Borchert
Mysticism

In Iraq, Muslims had come into contact with an older and more complex religious world and some were influenced by Christian, Jewish, or Zoroastrian mythology.... All these myths, in a modified form, would become important to the esoteric vision of the Shiah.

—Karen Armstrong
The Battle for God

Mithraism is often regarded as a heretical offshoot of Zoroastrianiam ... a reformed version.

—Adrian G. Gilbert
Magi

Certain medieval authorities, among them the Abbé de Villars, held that Zarathustra (Zoroaster) was the son of Vesta, believed to have been the wife of Noah and ... Oromasis. Hence from that time onward, undying fires have been maintained upon the Persian altars in honor of Zarathustra's flaming father.

—Manly P. Hall
The Secret Teachings of All Ages

Zoroaster taught that from time to time a world teacher will be sent in order to give a new religious impetus.... Zoroastrian priests' vision of history: a prolonged struggle between good and evil ending in destruction by fire and the resurrection of the good. They measured this struggle in terms of episodes: twelve millennia divided into four periods of 3000 years. They said that Zoroaster would appear in each period, returning three times, born of a virgin.

—Bruno Borchert
Mysticism

Author Index